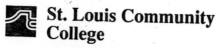

THE MESSENGER

THE MESSENGER

The Rise and Fall of
Elijah Muhammad

Karl Evanzz

Pantheon Books, New York

All rights reserved under International and Pan-American Copyright Conventions.
Published in the United States by Pantheon Books, a division of Random House, Inc., New York,
and simultaneously in Canada by Random House of Canada Limited, Toronto.

Pantheon Books and colophon are registered trademarks of Random House, Inc.

Library of Congress Cataloging-in-Publication Data

Evanzz, Karl.
The messenger : the rise and fall of Elijah Muhammad / Karl Evanzz.
p.   cm.
Includes bibliographical references and index.
ISBN 0-679-44260-X
1. Elijah Muhammad, 1897–1975.   2. Black Muslims—Biography.
3. Afro-Americans—Biography. I. Title.
BP223.Z8E434 1999
297.8'7'092—DC21
[b]   99-11826
CIP

Random House Web Address: www.randomhouse.com

Book design by Chris Welch

Printed in the United States of America

First Edition
2   4   6   8   9   7   5   3   1

In
loving memory
to my mother; and
to Dad; to my immediate
and extended family, expressly
Donald Brown, one of America's most
gifted musicians and prolific composers; and
to Malcolm Shabazz, with faith, love, and prayer.

CONTENTS

PREFACE

America's long and divisive experiment with school integration may be quietly coming to an end. Although both black and white Americans strongly support the ideal of integration, the persistence of de facto residential segregation has made integration difficult to obtain by anything short of extraordinary measures.

—*Book Notes,*
Harvard Law Review *(1996)*[1]

A generation ago, 80 percent of Blacks went to church. Today that figure is 40 percent. . . .

—Christianity Today,
March 4, 1996[2]

At a time when many denominations are seeing a decline in membership, Islam is said to be the fastest-growing religion in the United States. . . .

—Congressional Quarterly Researcher,
April 30, 1993[3]

If the 1993 bombing of the World Trade Center in New York City had occurred on any day other than February 26, there would not have been speculation about it being the work of the black separatist sect known as the Nation of Islam. Nor would some African Americans have wondered whether the bombing was an elaborate government measure to equate Islam with terrorism, and in that way suppress its growing appeal to blacks, as it had done with Marcus Garvey and Pan-Africanism in the early part of this century.[4] However, as it did happen on February 26—the date members of the Nation of Islam believe is literally God's birthday—the attention of some scholars familiar with the sect focused on Chicago, where thousands of Muslim admirers of Minister Louis Farrakhan had gathered.[5]

To most Americans, the Nation of Islam is synonymous with Louis Farrakhan, the controversial minister who, to nearly everyone's amazement, inspired up to one million black men to gather in Washington on October 16, 1995, for a day of "atonement."[6] While the mass media credited Farrakhan with conceiving the idea of the Million Man March, he had said some months before the march that the initial idea came out of a thirty-two-year-old conversation between himself and a man he habitually refers to as "the Honorable Elijah Muhammad."

"I was visiting with the Honorable Elijah Muhammad as we watched the 1963 March on Washington," Farrakhan wrote in an article published on the World Wide Web in the fall of 1995. "He said he saw too much frivolity, joking, and a picnic atmosphere." He promised Farrakhan that one day the Nation of Islam, which he, Muhammad, headed at the time, would call for its own march on Washington. In calling for the Million Man March, Farrakhan maintained that he was fulfilling another of Muhammad's "prophecies."[7]

Farrakhan referred to Elijah Muhammad often during his three-hour address on the first anniversary of his brother Alvan's death, but most young Americans outside the African-American community had no idea whom he was talking about. Foreigners were even more in the dark and were equally nonplussed by Farrakhan's allusions to Sufism and esoterica in this, his first, nationally televised address. But among African Americans, the name Elijah Muhammad had a ring as familiar as Big Ben's to the British and connotations as unique to them as those of the pyramids to the Egyptians. They have always regarded Elijah Muhammad as the primary embodiment of the sect and the single most significant mover in the skyrocketing conversion of African Americans to Islam.[8]

Indeed, most of the estimated four million African Americans who have converted to Islam did so after reading pamphlets and books written by Elijah Muhammad or after visiting one of the hundreds of storefront mosques he opened over a period spanning five decades. That hip-hop artists as dissimilar as Afrika Bambaataa, Brand Nubian, and Public Enemy have recorded rap songs in praise of him is a testament to his enduring influence in Black America. "Get back on the right track," a popular hip-hop group urged listeners some years ago, by listening to "the word from the Honorable Elijah Muhammad."[9] Today, large colorful posters featuring his likeness dominate dormitory rooms on college campuses across the country, while small, framed black-and-white photographs of him are displayed on nightstands and mantels in the homes of many black senior citizens.

Who, exactly, was Elijah Muhammad?

Asking that is tantamount to quizzing college freshmen on the nature of "truth": it will beget answers as varied as the faces in the classroom. To acolytes of Minister Farrakhan of Chicago and Minister Silis Muhammad of Atlanta (the head of a splinter group of the Nation of Islam), Elijah Muhammad was the seal of God's prophets, the Messiah whose coming was foretold in the Holy Bible and the Holy Quran. Muhammad himself fostered this idea and, for years, tried to convince his family (some of whom had studied Islam at prestigious universities in the United States and in the Middle East) that he, Elijah of Gilead, and the seventh-century prophet Muhammad were one and the same.[10]

For Imam Wallace Muhammad of Chicago, his father Elijah was a proud parent of eight children who brought African Americans back to their "old-time religion," as millions of Africans who came here in chains were Muslims.[11] But he was not, Wallace and orthodox Muslims vehemently insist, the prophet portrayed by Farrakhan and Silis Muhammad, and obviously not the same Muhammad who transcribed the Holy Quran. To millions of African Americans, Elijah Muhammad was not so much a prophet as a self-schooled psychoanalyst who advanced unorthodox theories about the nature and role of religion and race in mental dysfunction. When they were publicized in the early 1960s, Muhammad's ideas shocked seminarians and the medical establishment alike. His theories on human behavior, like those of B. F. Skinner, at first stunned behavioral psychologists, but they subsequently used some of them in dealing with their own clients of color. His ideas concerning the nexus between diet and disease were dismissed thirty years ago, but have since been confirmed by federally funded studies and by nutritionists around the world.[12] To many Jewish groups, he was an uneducated antisemite whose philosophy was expressed in the outlandish orations of Khallid Muhammad, a former Farrakhan protégé.[13] To orthodox Muslims, he was a heretic akin to the founders of the Baha'i faith and the Ahmadiyya Movement. All these perceptions, like the tactile experiences of the ten blind men describing the elephant, reflect elements in his persona; any one or group of them fails to capture the complete picture of the man.

Hence, this biography. It is, in some respects, strange that no authoritative and comprehensive biography of Elijah Muhammad appeared before the centennial of his birth. I can recall quite vividly the interview District of Columbia talk-show host Cathy Hughes did some years ago with former heavyweight boxing champion Muhammad Ali in which this very issue was raised. Why, Hughes asked, did Ali suppose there were no biographies of "this great man" whom he, too, called "the Honorable Elijah Muhammad."

"The Champ," as Ali is endearingly referred to by his admirers, couldn't explain why, except to suggest that Americans were still unwilling or uninterested in acknowledging Elijah Muhammad's contributions to African-American history and the growth of Islam in the West. Elijah Muhammad's impact on the social and religious roads that African Americans have taken is undeniable, as Ali pointed out, but the reasons for the absence of an accurate, thorough biography since his death in 1975 have little or nothing to do with denying him his mark on black history.

The real reasons are multifaceted, but foremost among them are, on the one hand, the shroud of secrecy that characterized Elijah Muhammad's relationship with the media and, on the other, the iconoclastic nature of the Nation of Islam, the sect Elijah Muhammad cofounded in the early 1930s and led until his death. Muhammad's disciples—from his own children to Farrakhan to rank-and-filers—were reticent about discussing his life because they were afraid that outsiders would deliberately distort his character and pervert the portrait of his life. Many of those I interviewed expressed the view that a non-Muslim biographer would paint an even darker and grimmer picture of the man and his religious movement than the mainstream media did while he was alive. Several of the Muslims I talked to cited press coverage of the bombing of the World Trade Center and the subsequent skewed depictions of the bombing suspects (all of them Muslims) as an example of the mainstream media's Judeo-Christian bias.

An equally important reason for the lack of an authoritative biography is that for a long time many scholars and Muhammad's critics feared the wrath of his diehard followers, some of whom have a "mujahedin" mentality. The most rational basis for this fear of vengeance was, of course, the assassination of Malcolm X, the first person to publicly criticize Elijah Muhammad, his mentor. On February 21, 1965, Malcolm X was shot sixteen times during the opening minutes of an address to his followers in Harlem. Although the actual assassins were identified only recently, it has since been discovered that there were at least a half-dozen squads assigned to Harlem's Audubon Ballroom that afternoon, all bent on ensuring that the words Malcolm X uttered that day would be his last. Elijah Muhammad's staunchest apologists now claim that Malcolm X's corpse left a figurative path of blood from the Audubon Ballroom to FBI headquarters in Washington and CIA headquarters in

Langley, Virginia, where a joint covert counterintelligence campaign against Black Muslims had begun in 1964. The campaign, which was designed to "neutralize" Malcolm X and Elijah Muhammad and to destroy the Nation of Islam in the process, was generally successful.

Declassified government documents lend credence to this argument, but one truth remains unaltered and inalienable: Whatever role the government played in instigating internecine warfare between Malcolm X and Muhammad, the black men who killed Malcolm X had as much free will as everyone else. There are dozens of other instances of attacks upon Muhammad's alleged detractors, many of which are chronicled in this book. As such, it is little wonder that journalists and scholars have shied away from writing anything that might be regarded as critical of him or injurious to his reputation. A parallel disincentive to scholars and writers interested in interpreting his life bears upon the issue of loyalty. Since the rise of the Black Power movement in the late 1960s, dogma among black nationalists is that one cannot claim to admire Malcolm X and simultaneously write dispassionately about Elijah Muhammad (the same argument has been made, by the way, about Malcolm X and Dr. Martin Luther King Jr.).

To be sure, the Nation of Islam's secretiveness and reputation for violence have not been the only impediments to writing a biography of Elijah Muhammad. The federal government—particularly the FBI—has hindered scholars wanting to write a comprehensive account of his life by violating the letter and the spirit of the Freedom of Information and Privacy Act. As a case in point, on January 4, 1974, a German student working on a doctoral thesis on the Nation of Islam wrote then FBI director, Clarence Kelley, to request the Bureau's files on Wallace D. Fard. At the time the student, Yeseult Cleirens, was a graduate assistant at Union Theological Seminary in New York to Dr. C. Eric Lincoln, author of The Black Muslims in America, the first comprehensive study of the Nation of Islam, which was published in the early 1960s. Ms. Cleiren's request wasn't rejected outright—that would have been a clear violation of the new law—but she was asked to prepay such exorbitant research and photocopying fees that she had to forgo her request.

A testament to bureaucratic bullying, Kelley's letter indicated that the

FBI might charge as much as $12,000 for processing the main file on Fard, and that a $3,000 deposit was required before the Bureau would even consider processing the file. Similar requests to the FBI from various scholars met with much the same response in the five years following Cleirens's request.[14] In September 1978, I filed a lengthy request pursuant to the Freedom of Information and Privacy Act on Elijah Muhammad, Wallace D. Fard, and other prominent members of the Nation of Islam. Although it took nearly a decade for the FBI to release some of the files, the file on Fard was a big disappointment. Contrary to Kelley's suggestion that the file was a massive one, the main file contains fewer than 400 pages, and the field office files released thus far are about the same. Thus, documents that the FBI told Cleirens would cost thousands of dollars can be acquired today for less than $100.[15] When the data from the Fard file were evaluated, along with information from files on some fifty individuals and organizations, I realized that Elijah Muhammad's journey was as incredible and multidimensional as that of his most important and loyal disciple, Malcolm Shabazz, better known as Malcolm X.

I think you'll agree.

THE MESSENGER

UNDERCOVER

If there is any fixed star in our constitutional constellation, it is that no official, high or petty, can prescribe what shall be orthodox in politics, nationalism, religion, or other matters of opinion or force citizens to confess by word or act their faith therein.

> —Minersville School District v. Gobitis
> *(U.S. Supreme Court)*[1]

Laws are silent in the midst of arms.

> —*Cicero*, Pro Milone[2]

On September 20, 1942, under the cover of still slumbering skies, a swarm of Chicago police officers and FBI agents surrounded the South Side home of a fugitive proclaimed by his adherents as the "Prophet."[3] In a moment, they hoped, their extensive counterintelligence operations against the fugitive's group and other black "pro-Japanese" organizations would pay the ultimate dividend: the arrest and apprehension of black nationalist leaders on sedition charges.

They were especially eager, though, to capture the Prophet, an elusive religious zealot who changed names faster than a chameleon changes color. The head of a sect blacklisted by the U.S. attorney general, the Prophet jumped bail in July while awaiting trial in Washington, D.C., and FBI director J. Edgar Hoover was damned angry about it.[4]

The Prophet, known to law enforcement officials in seven states as Ghulam Bogans, Muck Muck, Mohammed Rassoull, or by one of a dozen other aliases, headed a sect called the Allah Temple of Islam. Most of his followers called him the Honorable Elijah Muhammad, and referred to themselves as the Lost-Found Nation of Islam.[5]

At seven o'clock, three FBI agents, armed with warrants and weapons, approached the front entrance to 6026 Vernon Avenue; other agents and police officers covered the side and rear. An agent banged on the door. Awakened by the loud knocking, Nathaniel Muhammad, the fugitive's sixteen-year-old son, went to the door and peered through the pane.

"May we come in?" an agent asked the silhouetted figure on the other side of the door. "We'd like to talk to your father."

"Just a minute," Nathaniel replied as he hurriedly backed away.

The agents waited for several minutes and then one of them knocked again, this time nearly hard enough to break the glass. Again, he saw a male figure peering at him through the curtain. The shadow and the silence angered him.

"This is the FBI, boy! Open this damn door or we'll break it down!" Nathaniel quickly complied.

"Are you Ghulam Bogans's son?" the agent in charge asked gruffly.

The reason Elijah Muhammad used so many aliases was because other Muslim ministers who challenged his heirship of the Nation of Islam had pursued him sporadically since 1934 with the intent of killing him. Another reason was that police officers in several cities had been injured during fracases with Muslims and some were engaged in a vendetta against him. Ghulam Bogans was the alias he had used most recently, and that was the name on his arrest record when he was taken into custody in Washington on May 8, 1942, on charges of draft evasion.[6]

"No one lives here by that name," Nathaniel answered.

"Well," the agent asked angrily, "is Elijah Muhammad here?"

"No, the Honorable Elijah Muhammad is not here right now."

The white agents and several police officers pushed past the youth and began searching the house. As they reached the top of the stairway on the second floor, several women and children peered out of bedroom doorways. One woman walked toward the agents.

"I'm Clara Muhammad," she said. "What right do you have to barge into my home at this hour of the morning?"

"We're looking for Elijah, ma'am, alias Ghulam Bogans," an agent answered contemptuously. "We're the FBI."

"Well, you can just look somewhere else because he's not here."

"Do you know where your husband is at this hour of the morning, ma'am?" the agent asked sardonically.

"No," she answered, "I have no idea where he is right now."

The agents ignored her, and proceeding as though the house belonged to them now, approached a woman standing at a bedroom door. It was Elijah Muhammad's twenty-year-old daughter, Ethel.

"Is Ghulam Bogans or Elijah Muhammad here, ma'am?"

"My mother said he's not here, so he must not be here," she answered irately.

Lottie Muhammad, who was standing in the hallway, was the next occupant questioned. She, too, denied that her father was in the house.

The younger children were quickly asked about their father's where-abouts. First thirteen-year-old Herbert was questioned, then twelve-year-old Elijah Jr., then Wallace, who was nine. They even asked the toddler, Akbar, if he knew where his father was. The answers were all nearly the same. Their father wasn't home, they said. He had left almost a week ago, and, no, they had no idea when he might return.

The agents and officers left the house after completing a cursory search but only pretended to leave the vicinity, hoping that Elijah would try to escape in the car that they recognized as his parked just in front of the Vernon Avenue address. When no one left the premises after a forty-minute stakeout, the agent in charge of the operation ordered the group to conduct another search of the house. This time, they were far more thorough. They carefully searched the first floor, and in an alcove beneath the stairwell to the second floor, they discovered sixteen card-board boxes packed with newspaper clippings, copies of Elijah Muham-mad's sermons, personal correspondence, and organizational material. After a quick scan, the agents realized they had struck an intelligence mother lode.

The boxes were a gold mine of information about the Nation of Islam. The papers documented the history of the sect—its origins, mem-bership, financial records, and operational techniques—dating from 1933, which was the year that Elijah Muhammad took over the sect from the mysterious founder, W. D. Fard Muhammad, also known as Master Fard. Fard, who also used more than a dozen aliases, was wor-shipped by Nation of Islam members as the Lord-King, or in their ver-nacular, as "God in human form." For them, Fard and Allah were one and the same.

While several officers confiscated the boxes, others continued to ferret for the fugitive. Suddenly, an agent searching the upstairs hallway noticed something suspicious: an elderly woman was guarding the entrance to her bedroom. She held the doorknob tightly, and appeared anxious. The old woman was Elijah's seventy-one-year-old mother, Marie. The agent brushed her aside and tried to open the door. Though feeble and partially blind, she struck out, hitting him repeatedly in the face and about the shoulders. Another agent subdued her.

The FBI agent in charge of the operation went into the bedroom. The first thing he noticed was that the floor had an odd look. Part of the floor near a large carpet was free of dust, as though someone had only recently moved a rug. The agent turned on his flashlight, looked under the bed, and saw a rolled-up oriental rug. He tried to pull the rug toward him but it was much too heavy. He knew immediately that the case was all wrapped up, so to speak.

"Come outta there, boy!" the agent demanded. "This is the FBI! You're under arrest."

As the rug rolled slowly out toward the outer edge of the bed, several of the officers drew a bead on it with the weapons they had in their hands. "Please, don't shoot him!" Clara cried. The children rushed toward the the bedroom door, fearing calamity, but the officers blocked the way.[7]

"Stand back so no one gets hurt," one of the officers warned with his weapon drawn. As the rug unrolled, the agents saw a short, frail olive-skinned man. It was, indeed, the long-sought fugitive. He crawled from underneath the bed, stared nervously at his captors, and dusted himself off. Afraid that he might be shot "accidentally," he kept his eyes on the agents' hands and guns. After frisking him, the agents told him to get dressed. A half hour later, as the sun rose on Chicago's South Side, Muhammad emerged from his bedroom wearing a dark blue pinstriped suit and tie.

At seven fifty-five, he was handcuffed and advised that he was under arrest as a fugitive from justice. His family wept as he was led away. After handing temporary custody of the fugitive over to the Chicago police, FBI agents in unmarked cars trailed the cruiser taking Muhammad to the Cook County Jail.

Although Muhammad's family feared his fate, their image of him was not tarnished by his capture. To them, he remained the Prophet Muhammad, the seal of Allah's messengers. But to the Chicago Police Department photographer who took his mug shots that morning, he was just another Negro with a number under his neck.

After being booked and fingerprinted, Muhammad was taken into a darkened interrogation room where police and FBI men bombarded him with questions about his cult and its political activities, particularly in regard to pro-Japanese espionage.[8]

The semiliterate suspect endured an interrogation that lasted all morning and well into the afternoon. By the time it was over, he had been stripped of his mask of divinity, and had given the agents a wealth of information about himself, his family, and the Nation of Islam, information that undoubtedly brought him face to face with reality for the first time in ages. There were no tales of miracles in the oral autobiography, nothing that made the suspect's life any different from the lives of a million other men. His testimony was condensed into a four-page confession, which he was asked to sign.

He refused.

"My word is my bond," Muhammad muttered. "It is as good as my signature."[9]

"Is your name Elijah Poole?" he was asked.

"My name is Elijah Muhammad. In my early life I was known as Elijah Poole. But Poole is not my real name or my father's real name," the suspect said slowly. "It's the name of the slavemaster of my grandfather."

CHAPTER ONE
BROTHER'S KEEPER

The nigger was calm, cool, towering, superb. The men had approached and stood behind him in a body. He overtopped the tallest by half a head. He said: "I belong to the ship."

. . . He held his head up in the glare of the lamp . . . a head powerful and misshapen with a tormented and flattened face—a face pathetic and brutal: the tragic, the mysterious, the repulsive mask of a nigger's soul.

> —*Joseph Conrad,*
> The Nigger of the Narcissus *(1897)*[1]

"Shut the doors, shut the windows, shut everything! the Invisible Man is coming!"

> —*H. G. Wells,*
> The Invisible Man *(1897)*[2]

Yes, I was a slave. And I'll say this to the whole world: Slavery was the worst curse ever visited on the people of the United States.

> —*John Rudd, a former slave*[3]

9

As he lay on his deathbed at the beginning of the bitter-cold winter of 1861, eighty-two-year-old Middleton Pool Jr. had no inkling that the lifestyle he had enjoyed for nearly a century was his invisible, emaciated bedfellow. A former Georgia politician—he had served one term as a justice of the peace in 1820 and was an adjunct member of the Georgia House of Representatives in 1824[4]—the ailing master of nearly fifty slaves faced the same task as his father before him, an obligation that made politics seem as challenging as riding a carousel. In the three decades past, he had purchased, sold, and traded more than a hundred slaves, his plantation and its magnificent mansion reflecting not only his investment acumen but also the productivity of his human chattel. As his final twilight hovered, he struggled with the daunting task of dividing his land and personal property among his feeble wife Nancy, seven daughters, three sons, and the three children of his deceased daughter.[5] He first sold some of his slaves to his close friends John H. Pitman and his brother Nimrod,[6] which allowed him to pay off creditors and so bequeath his human and real property to his heirs without encumbrances.

The smallest share of his holdings went to Elizabeth Hood and Mary Everett, the adult children from his first marriage. Middleton Pool, who had moved from Watson County to DeKalb County before finally settling in Sandersville, still owned a modest piece of land in DeKalb, where Elizabeth and Mary resided, and he willed half of it to each of them. He also gave Elizabeth two adult slaves, a male named Simon and a female named Hannah, who had several young children. Mary received two adult slaves as well, Milly and Warren. In addition to the slaves, both daughters received $1,000 and an equivalent mix of personal property. As a final gesture of gentility, he ordered the executors of his estate to "sell my negro girl Biddy at public outcry to the highest bidder," then to divide the net profit from the auction between his two oldest daughters.[7]

The bulk of his estate, which was in Washington County, was divided among the five children born of his union with Nancy and the children of Winifred Pool Rushing, their daughter who had died in 1858. Upon naming James Rushing, his daughter's widower, trustee for Winifred's children, he bequeathed to Joseph, Catherine, and Elizabeth Rushing two slaves (Silvy and Fanny), two cows and calves, a sow and her piglets, and some furniture. He also wrote that they would inherit additional property after his will was probated.

Pool gave his daughter Catherine H. Bateman 218 acres of farmland valued at $1,500, a male slave named Bill, and two female slaves, Sally and Rachel, along with their children. Like Winifred and his other children, Catherine received various farm animals, furniture, and other small personal items. He bequeathed his home and the surrounding acreage to his son Thomas, with the proviso that "[My] present wife Nancy Pool is to have one room in said residence to live in until her death, or as long as in their mutual discretion this would be proper and desirable."[8] Another son, William B. Pool, was to take Isaac, a twenty-three-year-old slave, as his property. Middleton ordered William to "hire out" Isaac, and to use the money thus earned to take care of eighty-year-old Nancy's financial needs for the rest of her life. After Nancy's death, Pool wrote, William could sell Isaac and keep the proceeds as remuneration for all the bother. He also awarded Thomas two male slaves, Warren and Reuben, along with Harriet and her brood. William Pool inherited a slave named Bob, a young female slave named Dolly, and Sally and her children. His third son, James I. Pool, received the slaves named Ben and Wright and a woman named Eliju and her children. His fifth and last child, Jane Swint, a young widow, inherited a childless slave named Easter and a "boy" named Irwin. She also became the new mistress of Lucky and her children.

Each of Middleton Pool's children by Nancy was to receive more slaves after his will was probated, and in all, nearly fifty slaves were distributed among them. Like most slaveowners, Middleton Pool based his division of slaves on their individual market value instead of on familial ties, which were certainly considered, but only secondarily. After Washington County Probate Court certified the will on June 9, 1862, the rest of Middleton's slaves were apportioned among his children and three grandchildren, each receiving some six slaves apiece.[9]

The Pool children's days as slavemasters were short-lived, however. In September 1862—only four months after the slaves officially became the property of Middleton's heirs—President Abraham Lincoln decreed an end to slavery in Georgia and elsewhere in the Confederacy. The preliminary proclamation became permanent on January 1, 1863, formally freeing Pool's slaves along with three to four million other Africans in America. Two years later, slavery was banned constitutionally with the passage of the Thirteenth Amendment. Despite these legislative and executive measures, and notwithstanding General Robert E. Lee's hoisting of the white flag in April 1865 to end the Civil War, the Confederacy's collapse and surrender to General Ulysses Grant meant little to the first generation of Africans born free in the South. Southern soldiers and businessmen with all or most of their wealth invested in the "peculiar institution" remained embittered by the pummeling they had taken in their own backyard. Many organized and connived in every conceivable way to maintain the courtly lifestyle they had known before the war.

Of all the former slaves who remained on the Pool plantation, perhaps none stood out more than a light-skinned mulatto named Irwin Pool. Unlike many slaves who changed their surnames to commemorate their freedom,[10] Irwin not only kept his master's name, but his firstborn was the namesake of his former master's son. Though little is known about Irwin Pool's parentage, census records indicate that his father was a Caucasian. The records don't reveal his father's name, but circumstances suggest that he may have been the consequence of an illicit interracial affair on the part of William B. Pool, which would explain why Irwin named his first son William. Like his father, William B. Pool served one term as a commissioner in Sandersville, followed by a single term as a justice of the peace. In fact, when Middleton Pool died in early 1861, William was one of several county commissioners who oversaw the final dispensation of the estate.[11]

William Pool (or Willie, as he was nicknamed by his family) was born to Irwin and Peggy Pool in 1866 on the same Sandersville plantation as his parents, who toiled there first as slaves and then as indebted share-croppers. Since Congress passed its first major civil rights bill that year (nullifying the Black Codes)[12] and ratified the Fourteenth Amendment two years later, one would surmise that the times held great promise for Willie's generation. However, being born free in 1866 in Georgia was meager cause for celebration, as white racial antagonism robbed Willie Pool's generation of the quality of life one normally associates with free-dom and democracy. His childhood was not much better than that of his once-enslaved parents. Despite being born during the zenith of Recon-struction, the first generation of Africans born free in America were essen-tially steered into a state of servitude before they reached adulthood. The primary reason for the failure of Reconstruction and its affirmative-action-type programs was the contentious relationship between Con-gress and President Andrew Johnson, who was sworn in upon Lincoln's assassination on April 14, 1865.[13] Johnson issued mandates without conferring with state legislatures, scholar Woodrow Wilson wrote at the denouement of Radical Reconstruction, further embittering Southern politicians and power brokers of the humiliated and defanged Confeder-acy. Consequently, Wilson wrote, legislative houses in the Southern states decided,

> in the very same sessions in which they gave their assent to the emanci-pating amendment, virtually to undo the work of emancipation, sub-stituting a slavery of legal restraints and disabilities for a slavery of private ownership.[14]

The social advancements produced by Reconstruction were pushed so far backward that the period is sometimes called "Deconstruction."

Before Willie Pool reached his first birthday, the Ku Klux Klan (KKK) evolved from a segregated social club in Pulaski, Tennessee, into a full-fledged white terrorist organization headed by former Confederate general Nathan Bedford Forrest of Nashville.[15] Consistent with his grandiose delusion of making the Thirteenth Amendment disappear and returning blacks to slavery, Forrest bestowed upon himself the lofty title of Grand Wizard. By 1867, the Klan and a sister group known as the Knights of the White Camellia were making a mockery of liberties that the Constitution and new civil rights laws had given African Americans. These and similar racially intolerant organizations were quite successful in using extrajudicial means to create a climate of terror, fear, and hatred. By the time Willie Pool was ten years old, a visitor to Georgia would not have known that there had ever been a Reconstruction era. With the creation of the Liberal Republican Party, formed solely to hasten the dismantling of Reconstruction programs, the disfranchisement of African Americans snowballed. When federal troops assigned to the South to aid in Reconstruction were withdrawn, so too were the civil rights of blacks.

"The greatest social problem before the American people today is, as it has been for a hundred years," former Confederate soldier and writer George W. Cable wrote in 1885,[16] "the presence among us of the Negro." The curse of slavery continued, and the Constitution and its new amendments became a parody of the principles of democracy, as "Jim Crow" laws supplanted civil rights legislation. One great irony of the end of the nineteenth century is that Robert Todd Lincoln, the slain president's son, took control of the Pullman Company, a national railway transportation concern that not only resorted to violence and engaged in a Supreme Court fight to block improvements in the working conditions of its white employees, but also clung to the pernicious practice of Jim Crowism.[17] The Supreme Court abetted the process of "Deconstruction" through a series of rulings that catered to political expediency rather than justice. In 1890, for instance, it helped the South strip blacks of suffrage by ruling that federal officials had to defer to their state counterparts in monitoring state and local elections. It also ruled that states could, pursuant to their own laws, segregate public transportation facilities. The severest blow to African Americans came from the Court in 1896 when it handed down *Plessy v. Ferguson*. There, the Court held that the Fourteenth Amendment to the Constitution was not intended to abolish social distinctions based on color. Justice Henry B. Brown read the majority opinion:

The argument also assumes that social prejudices may be overcome by legislation, and that equal rights cannot be secured to the negro except by an enforced commingling of the two races. We cannot accept this proposition. . . . If one race be inferior to the other socially, the constitution of the United States cannot put them upon the same plane.[18]

The quality of life for African Americans had so deteriorated by 1890 that many fled from Dixie in fear; so many left, in fact, that the migration was called the "exodus." Booker T. Washington, the distinguished founder and president of Tuskegee Institute, sought to relieve racial hostilities with his "Atlanta Compromise" speech at the Cotton Exposition of 1894. "To those of my race who depend on bettering their condition in a foreign land or who underestimate the importance of cultivating friendly relations with the Southern white man," Washington said,

Cast down your bucket where you are—cast it down in making friends in every manly way of the people of all races by whom we are surrounded. Cast it down in agriculture, mechanics, in commerce, in domestic service, and in the professions. . . . And in this connection, it is well to bear in mind that whatever other sins the South may be called to bear, when it comes to business, pure and simple, it is in the South that the Negro is given a man's chance in the commercial world, and in nothing is this Exposition more eloquent than in emphasizing this chance.[19]

Irwin Pool and his family seemed to have heeded Washington's advice, for most of them remained in Georgia despite its deteriorating racial climate and the bad luck that had befallen the state. Some did leave to head northward, but others moved only a few miles from the plantation that had been home for as long as they could remember. A few moved from Sandersville to nearby Oconee, Georgia.[20]

For Bishop Henry McNeal Turner, whose prominence as a national spokesman for black people was rivaled only by Washington's, the political views of the latter were inimical to true freedom. A strong voice in the African Methodist Church, Bishop Turner argued that the Atlanta Compromise and the *Plessy* verdict quashed any hopes that blacks would ever be accepted as American citizens. In a manuscript entitled *The Black Man's Doom*, Bishop wrote that *Plessy* precluded any chance of Africans gaining recognition as Americans. For Turner, separation of the races, with blacks returning to Africa, was the only way to prevent a full-scale race war.

> The negro race was brought to this country by the sanction of heaven to be civilized and Christianizied by this giant white race, at present the dominant race of this world; as soon as that was done his business was to return to Africa, and begin the work of civilizing his kindred, and this nation should assist him, and there will be no peace either to the Negro or to the nation until that is consummated. . . . I see no other theater but Africa where the Negro can work out his own destiny and attain to honorable distinction.[21]

Turner, the first black man to serve as an army chaplain (he was appointed by President Lincoln in 1863, but resigned after nine months), was elected to the first Reconstruction legislature of Georgia, but was expelled, along with his fellow black legislators, in 1868.[22] His refusal to beg white legislators to rectify his unconstitutional dismissal made him a hero to African Americans, particularly his fellow Georgians. His ouster from the legislature further buttressed his conviction that black people would never experience real freedom in America. The only solution to the race problem, he told a crowd of thousands in Atlanta on September 27, 1903, was racial separation: "This nation or its aggregated people will either have to open a highway to Africa for the discontented black man or the Negro question will flinder this government."[23]

His views on blacks fighting to defend America were equally controversial and he argued after his ouster:

> We have pioneered civilization here; we have built up your country . . . for two hundred and fifty years. . . . The black man cannot protect a

country if the country doesn't protect him; and if, tomorrow, a war should arise, I would not raise a musket to defend a country where my manhood is denied.[24]

Although he was a mulatto—his mother and maternal grandmother were white[25]—Turner was perhaps the premier black nationalist of the era, and was among the first black clergymen to advocate the portrayal of biblical figures, including Jesus Christ, as blacks. "God is a Negro," Turner proclaimed.[26] As he was chief lord of the African Methodist Episcopal Church schools and chancellor of Morris Brown College, his opinions carried great weight. He was revered by black clergymen, whose number included Irwin and his son Willie, for his outspokenness. Both Irwin and Willie were itinerant Baptist preachers at a time when the church served as a spiritual center and a political base for African Americans.[27]

As blacks sought ways to negotiate life after slavery, and the South withdrew from its dependence upon human chattel, an equally evil type of servitude—American imperialism—replaced it as an important source of revenue. What had begun as a form of nationalism known as "Manifest Destiny" in 1845 had expanded to encompass areas far beyond America's borders, and in 1889, was a leading cause of the Spanish-American War. In the aftermath of Spain's humiliating defeat, the United States took temporary title to the Philippines, and in 1897 annexed Hawaii, which was then under Japanese control. Although the Japanese protested bitterly, they eventually capitulated.[28] When Japanese and Chinese workers refused to work the fields in Hawaii after the Americans took over, African Americans were sent there to replace them, just as they were shipped from Africa to replace recalcitrant Native American slaves.[29] The United States was hardly alone in this new form of human exploitation. The nations of Europe were staking claims all over the world. African kingdoms fell into European hands like overripe apples after a gust of wind. Most of the countries exploited by America and Europe were considered "nondeveloped," and their indigenous populations were primarily nonwhite. Among the fallen in Africa, for instance, was Asantehene Agyeman Prempeh I, the last Muslim ruler and last king of the ancient Ashanti empire in Africa. King Prempeh was taken into captivity in Sierra Leone's Freetown by the British in 1897.[30]

While blacks continued to free themselves from the clutches of racism in America, another expression of racism—antisemitism—was plaguing Europe and Russia. Just as Southern politicians accused blacks of trying to take over the country with the aid of carpetbaggers, a derisive forged document purporting to detail plans of an international Jewish conspiracy to dominate the world appeared on the streets of Paris and elsewhere, causing hysteria. The document, known as the *Protocols of the Learned Elders of Zion*, caused many Europeans to fear the growing presence of Jews in government and commerce, and political parties began to form in Hungary, Austria, Germany, and France to retard the assimilation of Jews. In 1893, when the forged document was circulating in Paris, a Jewish officer in the French army was accused of treason. After a year-long investigation that turned up little by way of incriminating evidence, Captain Alfred Dreyfus was found guilty of passing military secrets on to an attaché of the German embassy in Paris. Following the verdict, Dreyfus was publicly stripped of his medals and sentenced to life imprisonment on Devil's Island.

Just as Turner viewed the *Plessy* verdict as evidence that blacks needed a homeland in Africa, journalist Theodor Herzl viewed the Dreyfus Affair as a refutation of the assumption that Jews could be integrated into European society. The solution to the "Jewish problem," he said, was a Jews-only state, preferably in Palestine. Influenced by the international impact that Harriet Beecher Stowe's novel *Uncle Tom's Cabin* had on the world's view of slavery, Herzl wrote a novel titled *The Ghetto*, which was published during the first phase of Dreyfus's trial. In the novel, Herzl's protagonist, giving voice to the author's own views, concludes that the only solution to antisemitism was a separate state for Jews. If the United States could carve Liberia into the breast of Africa for its former slaves, Herzl reasoned, a new Zion could be created by partitioning Palestine. The book was well received by many European Jews and Herzl became known as a spokesman for Zionism. In February 1896, he crystallized his political views in *The Jewish State*, which articulated his dream of the day when the Jewish diaspora would end, and even described how the society would function.[31]

When Americans expressed outrage over the Dreyfus Affair, noted black journalist Ida B. Wells-Barnett flailed her white countrymen for their glaring hypocrisy, writing in *Arena* magazine:

> A few months ago the conscience of this country was shocked because, after a two-week trial, a French judicial tribunal pronounced Captain Dreyfus guilty. And yet, in our own land and under our own flag, the writer can give day and detail of one thousand men, women, and children who during the last six years were put to death without trial before any tribunal on earth.[32]

In the months after the *Plessy v. Ferguson* decision was handed down in 1896, Herzl visited Constantinople to solicit Sultan Abdul Hamid II's aid in creating a Jewish state (Palestine was under the rule of the Ottoman empire at the time). Although his diplomatic endeavor was unsuccessful, it led to the First Zionist Congress, which met in Basel, Switzerland, in August 1897, at which Herzl was the keynote speaker. In seeking a homeland for Jews, he said, he conceived of a land as holy as "Lourdes and Mecca and Jerusalem."[33]

As the notion of a Jewish state gestated in the minds of European Jewry, Willie and Marie brought forth another child, a boy who, like Herzl, would harbor a lifelong dream of creating a new nation. Born on October 7, 1897,[34] the boy was named Elija, in homage to the biblical prophet who, it is said, will come to warn his people before the Apocalypse. The name and all that it implied seemed fitting, for the evil in men appeared to be winning the war for human nature; Americans from every stratum of the social pyramid feared that a "race war" between blacks and whites was looming. It was also the turn of the century, and many agreed with the Millerites that the Second Coming was imminent. The 1890s, historian Lerone Bennett wrote, was "the worst decade for blacks in the history of America."[35] That may strike some as hyperbole, but the grim statistics support his assessment: one-third of all African Americans lynched since 1882 were victimized between 1890 and 1900.

In 1897 alone, 123 blacks were lynched, the third highest number for a single year in a century.[36] In Georgia and other former Confederate states, racial hatred raged like flames on a cross at a Klan picnic.

Perhaps nothing underscored the depravity of the political discourse more than the most controversial issue of the day: whether the nation should pass uniform antilynching legislation. Three weeks after Elija's birth, Georgia governor W. Y. Atkinson, in his annual address to the state's general assembly, spoke passionately about the rise in the African-American prison population and the skyrocketing rate of lynching as an expedient but extralegal resolution of disputes:

> In a free government like ours, there is no excuse for lynching. If there is evidence to convict, the courts will punish. If there is not, punishment should not be inflicted. The courts of our State can be trusted to punish the guilty and protect our property, our persons, and the honor and virtue of our women.[37]

The governor didn't have to spell out what he meant; everyone understood that he was mainly addressing the issue of black men allegedly forcing themselves on white women. A less diplomatic House member pointed out that Southerners "only lynch people for rape or attempt to rape." He implied that lynching was the best means of preventing future crime. The subtlety of the governor's message was offset by the frankness of J. W. Law, the only African American in the Georgia House of Representatives, who addressed the issue a month later. "The only solution to the lynching question in Georgia that I can see," Law told his colleagues, "is the education of the Negro. Ignorance causes more crime in Georgia than any other thing. Educate the Negro and you will prevent the crime of rape."[38]

William Pool raised Elija and his other children in much the same way that he had been raised. Like his father, Willie was a dirt-poor sharecropper eking out a living on plantations around Sandersville. He was a devoutly religious man whose skin shade told the tale of miscegenation in the South. His caramel-colored complexion placed him among the "privileged" freedmen in the South, meaning he received a Bible-based education, but he was nonetheless only marginally literate. He was imbued with the strong sense of pride shared by many mulattoes by virtue of their mixed blood. But he had other traits that set him apart from both blacks and whites, including charisma and an unyielding faith that he possessed a greater affinity with God than most men. Just as William B. Pool followed his father into politics, Willie Pool emulated the Reverend Irwin Pool by becoming a preacher. He began his career in the pulpit at Zion Hope Baptist Church near Wenona, Georgia. As he matured, he became an itinerant minister, traveling from county to county to proselytize. By his twenty-fifth birthday, he was a much sought-after preacher in black Baptist churches.

A modest beauty, Marie Pool was a quiet woman whose complexion was the rich dark chocolate of a Hershey's Kiss. Born in Georgia in 1871, she married Willie when she was sixteen.[39] Their first child, a boy they named Sam, was born in early 1888. Their first daughter, Annie, was born the following year, followed by Willie Jr. in 1891, and a girl christened Tommie in 1892. Their fifth child, Hattie, was born in 1894, and another daughter, Lula, in 1896.[40] Elija, their seventh child, was born in 1897. The family remained in Sandersville until 1900, then moved roughly seventy miles southwest to Cordele, Georgia. At the time, Marie was pregnant again, this time with another son, Charlie, who was born in the spring.[41]

The need to support his large family competed with Pool's ministerial ambitions. After the birth of Lula, he moved the family to Havana, Arkansas, where promises of better wages and greater preaching opportunities awaited him. He stayed in Havana long enough to make lasting friendships with the Hatchett and Freeman families, but the promised prosperity eluded him. With another child on the way and a static income, Willie left Arkansas and moved back to Cordele. His failure to find his calling in Havana sorely tested his marriage, and shortly after the return to Cordele, there was a rumor that he had sired a son by another woman. True or not, four years passed before Marie gave birth again, this time to another son. From the outset, Elija took a paternal view of his baby brother, Jarmin. As a toddler, Jarmin worshipped Elija and the two became as close as twins. It wasn't long, however, before the cries of another newborn demanded Elija's time. The nine-year-old was called upon to tend his little sister, Emma, who was born in 1906. Emma was followed by Johnnie, a boy born less than a year later. The twelfth child, James, was born in 1909 and the thirteenth and last child, John, in 1912.

At the turn of the century, black children in Cordele attended one of two "colored-only" schools. Children whose parents attended the Colored Methodist Episcopal Church went to the Holsey-Cobb Institute, while Presbyterians sent their children to the Gillespie-Selden Institute.[42] However, it was distance more than religion that dictated the choice for Elija. The Methodist school, overseen by Bishop Turner, was closer to the Pool's home, so Elija attended Holsey-Cobb. "I walked five miles to school every day," Elija recalled.[43] Shortly after he started school at the age of six, Elija's demeanor changed. Once a very active child, he suddenly became quiet and introverted, often parking himself in a corner of the living room with the Holy Bible the minute he finished his homework and after-school chores. He would spend "hours poring through the Bible, with tears shining in his eyes," Marie Pool recalled years later.[44]

There are several possible explanations to account for Elija's preoccupation with the Holy Bible. Primarily, it afforded him an opportunity to mimic as well as to appease his father, a strict disciplinarian and a fire-and-brimstone preacher who focused on apocalyptic themes—and with good reason. War, political assassinations, and universal epidemics had many people wondering if the world was ending. Born on the heels of Lincoln's assassination, the first American president to die at the hands of an assassin, fifteen-year-old Willie Pool stood in shock along with the rest of the nation when President James Garfield was shot and killed in 1881, and again when President William McKinley was assassinated twenty years later. America's declaration of war on Spain after the sinking of the battleship *Maine* in Havana Harbor in 1898 added to the doomsday atmosphere, as did a series of imperialism-driven economic conflicts between the United States and European and Asian nations. On top of all this turmoil was the growing despair over the devastating mortality statistics among Southern blacks during this period. At a briefing with President Theodore Roosevelt about the alarming incidence of consumption, Dr. Seal Harris, a professor of medicine at the University of Alabama, said that "the negro race was likely to become extinct" in America. The death rate among blacks, he said, was higher than the birth rate.[45]

Olive-skinned Elija was perhaps his father's favorite child. As a toddler, he usually sat in a big chair behind the pulpit while the Reverend Pool preached, and afterward sat on his father's lap. The hellish visions his father's words painted gradually overwhelmed him. Whites were demonized in Willie Pool's sermons. In black churches where images of a Caucasian Christ hung on the walls, one supposes that Elija envisioned a netherworld akin to Bosch's *Garden of Earthly Delights*. Indeed, whites were sometimes portrayed as devils incarnate on antilynching posters, and so Elija grew up fearing both the wrath of God and the KKK. "I used to go to church and the preacher would preach that hellfire. It looked so plain to me that I would be afraid to go home," he recollected.[46] The sermons weren't the only aspect of the religious services that disturbed the youngster. The hymns, some of which were popular spirituals from the slave era, also frightened him. Originally a spiritual such as "Steal Away to Jesus" was a song of hope for life after slavery, but to Elija's ears thirty years later, it must have sounded like a death wish. "Steal away, steal away home, I ain't got long to stay here," one verse goes. That was a fairly morbid thought for a youngster. When the choir started singing, Elija recalled years later, "I would cry. They would frighten me. So my grandmother took me out and gave me a spanking a couple of times and I learned to keep my mouth shut."[47]

Already suffering nightmares from the spirituals and the sermons, Elija was further traumatized by five difficult and tragic events between 1903 and 1905. The first, of course, was starting school, as it was the first time that he was separated from his parents. The second was a weekend trip into "town," which was emotionally charged because his safety there was in the hands of whites, any one of whom could have attacked him with impunity. Elija was once approached in the town by a neatly dressed white man who smiled at him as he drew near. When he was only a few feet away, the man opened his hand, and the youngster was momentarily paralyzed as he realized that the man held the severed ear of a black person, an ear being one of several lynching trophies (the most coveted souvenir was a black man's reproductive member).[48]

The third shock did not involve him directly, but was equally horrific. A few days after his sixth birthday, a black man was lynched in the heart of Cordele's downtown district.[49] During this traumatic period Elija became a bed-wetter. His father viewed the problem as abnormal, unclean, and ungodly, and while his mother was generally sympathetic Willie Sr. lost patience when it went on for several years. Although Elija tried desperately to stay dry—he often would lie awake half the night— nothing seemed to help. The enuretic episodes continued until he was twelve years old, which was, coincidentally, the age at which he left school in the fourth grade and began spending nearly the entire day working the land with his family.[50]

The fourth psychic trauma made national headlines. In 1903, federal courts were forced to revisit the issue of the constitutionality of slavery because white landowners in the South were using questionable contracts to keep poor farmhands, primarily African Americans, in peonage. Although the Supreme Court held in the *Slaughterhouse* cases that peonage was equivalent to involuntary servitude, outlawed by the Thirteenth Amendment, state statutes in Georgia and elsewhere in the old Confederacy were couched in language aimed at skirting the amendment. For a time black families lived in fear of being kidnapped by nightriders and winding up in de facto slavery as news accounts of peonage became more frequent. Finally in 1904 Congress sought to put an end to the practice by enacting a statute that specifically abolished peonage.[51]

The fifth and final nightmare, which made peonage seem civil by comparison, centered around the World's Fair in St. Louis in 1904, where the most popular exhibit was the cage in which Pygmies from south central Africa were locked up like wild animals. "The three . . . represent the lowest degree of human development,"[52] the *St. Louis Republic* newspaper reported on March 6, 1904. Some news accounts of the trip to Africa by the white men searching for these "curious specimens" read like an Indiana Jones adventure. On May 5, for example, the *Republic* reported that a leader of the expedition narrowly escaped being eaten alive by cannibals. When the fair opened, Ota Benga and the other Pygmies were the center of attention; fairgoers found them fascinating, primarily because Ota Benga often carried an orangutan around the cage like a father holding a small child, to the endless bemusement of people who had come from around the world. Benga, one newspaper reporter wrote, "was not much taller than the orangutan. . . . Their heads are much alike, and both grin the same way when pleased."[53]

When the fair ended, Ota Benga was not returned to Africa as his captors had promised, and in 1906 he was imprisoned in a monkey cage at New York City's Bronx Zoo. The very idea that black people could be legally treated as zoo animals terrified African Americans, particularly children. After all, if the Bronx Zoo was allowed to encage an African, what was there to prevent another zoo from doing the same to an African American? Black-owned newspapers around the nation editorialized against Benga's treatment, and New York City's black citizens lodged a formal complaint with the zoo and the mayor over the gross indignity and violation of fundamental human rights. "The person responsible for this exhibition degrades himself as much he does the African," said Dr. R. S. MacArthur, the spokesman for a delegation of black churches. "We send our missionaries to Africa to Christianize people, and then we bring one here to brutalize him."[54] At first the mayor ignored the protest, but later agreed to release Benga from the cage and make him a ward at the Howard Colored Orphan Asylum in Brooklyn. Like kidnapped Africans during the Middle Passage who preferred a watery grave in the Atlantic to eternal enslavement in America, Benga could not accept the idea of never going home again. In July 1916, at the age of twenty-eight, he committed suicide.

Geronimo, the Native American hero who had won and lost battles against William T. Sherman, was also among the "anthropological exhibits" at the fair. Although he wasn't caged like the Africans, an armed guard followed him everywhere he went and he was billed as the "Human Tyger." Geronimo's mistreatment was considered justifiable because he was categorized by the U.S. War Department as a prisoner of war.

The plight of Geronimo and Benga represented a new form of prejudice concocted to justify American apartheid. Called "scientific racism"
or "intellectual racism" and based upon false anthropological assumptions, the new racism "spread the propositions that the Negro was
inherently inferior and lacked the moral fiber to appreciate democracy
or participate in it, and that he had no history, civilization or culture
worthy of the name."[55] The immorality of scientific racism was buttressed by a spate of court decisions, state laws, and studies by distinguished academics. In November 1908, the Supreme Court ruled in
Berea College v. Commonwealth of Kentucky that segregated schools
were not a violation of the equal protection clause of the Constitution.
Justice David Josiah Brewer wrote for the majority opinion:

> The Thirteenth, Fourteenth, and Fifteenth Amendments to the Consti-
> tution of the United States were adopted for the protection of the col-
> ored race, and their primary purpose was to establish absolute civil
> equality—that is, to place the colored race, in respect to civil rights,
> upon the same basis as the white race. But the effect of the Fourteenth
> Amendment is not only to secure equal civil rights to the colored race,
> but to protect the white race also in the unmolested enjoyment of all
> its rights of person and property.[56]

Elija lived in a world whose racism was worsening as he grew older.
In 1905, just a few weeks before his eighth birthday, the Georgia legislature passed an ordinance calling for segregation in all public parks.
Although it was the first state to do so, its neighbors soon followed suit.
During the next twelve months, politicians and the press alike urged a
revival of the KKK, and there was talk of disfranchising blacks. With
social insult after social insult being hurled at blacks, it was only a matter of time before the "race war" became a self-fulfilling prophecy in
the state. Ironically, one of the biggest race riots in Georgia's history
occurred in 1906 while Booker T. Washington was in New York
extolling the virtues of life in the South to African Americans. Washington, who was in Harlem on September 20 to address the Committee for

Improving the Industrial Condition of Negroes in New York, told a gathering of about 800 that black people in the North had become too dependent upon whites for even the most basic necessities of life, so that blacks in the South were in many respects better off.

"Begin to be the creators of something and do not be so dependent upon other people," Washington urged them.

America is the best country I have ever seen, and all those who say it isn't are always glad to get back. I have seen a city in the South with a colored mayor and negroes owning and operating factories successfully. Why not do it in the North?[57]

In concluding his argument he said,

If Mayor McClellan issued an order that all colored people were to wear shoes tomorrow made by their own race, the whole lot of you would have to go barefooted. Stand together and begin to create for yourselves and save money and I am sure that there will be a glorious future for you all in the North.

It was true that blacks were more self-sufficient in the South, but it was equally true that the majority were paying an enormous price for failing to join the exodus. The high price became evident only days after Washington's speech in Harlem.

On the very day that Washington delivered his talk, an Atlanta newspaper began running articles encouraging its readers to join the rapidly expanding KKK organization. The endorsement of the Klan by the *Atlanta News* came after six white women were allegedly assaulted by black men during July and August 1906 (in one case, a black man was accused of "assault" after innocently suggesting to two white women that they should get their friend, also a white woman, off the street quickly because she was too drunk to walk). In mid-September, the newspaper editorialized on the need to disfranchise African Americans, whom it deemed genetically incapable of being civilized. The final and greatest insult, however, came on September 21 when the publication offered white Georgians remuneration for what it christened a "lynching bee."[58]

The day after the reward was posted, the *Atlanta News* put out a special evening edition reporting, under screaming headlines, that four white women had been assaulted overnight. Word of the alleged attacks created what one paper called "lynch fever" among young white men. After Sunday church services on September 22, hundreds of lynch mobs formed, and "Kill the niggers" became a rallying cry. Black servants had to use public transportation to get to their employer's homes in high-income neighborhoods, so the mobs lay in wait for any black people—particularly black men—to emerge from mass-transit vehicles. The first fatalities that bloody Sunday night were two black men who had been riding in the rear of a railway car that also carried two white women in the front. The mob shot dozens of rounds into the car, killing the men instantly.[59]

For the next two days, attacks on blacks in Atlanta continued, even though President Theodore Roosevelt sent 3,000 federal troops to Georgia at Governor Joseph M. Terrell's request. The incidence of attacks spread across the state like a California brushfire. By Tuesday, September 24, not one black face was to be seen in Atlanta's white neighborhoods, and many students and faculty at the all-black Clark University had been arrested and jailed for protesting the mob violence, which, according to the newspapers, involved 10,000 to 15,000 young white men. For the first time in their lives, newspapers reported, Georgia's elite had to make their own beds and cook their own meals, take care of their own livestock, and even care for their own babies. Life had, in essence, become a nightmare for both races. By the time calm was restored, more than a dozen black men had been lynched and hundreds had suffered serious injuries.[60]

When he was approached by a *New York Times* reporter to comment on the Atlanta riot, Washington declined. He was so distraught over the news from Georgia, the reporter wrote later, that he had checked out of the Manhattan Hotel and headed home to join an integrated committee formed to restore calm.

But another Southerner, a popular white writer who was also a man of the cloth, was clearly elated by reports of the slaughter of the innocent. The Reverend Thomas Dixon Jr., author of a best-seller titled *The Clansman*, told reporters that whites would continue taking drastic measures against blacks until the nation's former slaves were expelled from America. "The insolence of the negro in Atlanta has grown greatly," Dixon said.

> There will be many outbreaks as long as the negro continues to live in the same community as the white man. . . . Such assaults of negroes on white women as caused the outbreak in Atlanta reduce civilization to an absurdity. When this is done we are face to face with a great issue. We can only meet this issue by removing the cause, which is a ridiculous attempt to assimilate into our race an animal, who as a race is four thousand years behind the Aryan race in development. The way to remove the cause is by colonization. Separate the negro from the white man. Take him out of the country and settle him in the West Indies, South America, or Africa.[61]

Dixon's views reflected those expressed by Francis Hopkinson Smith. The popular white novelist, painter, and lecturer caused an uproar in the North when he wrote in the *New York Herald* that "granting suffrage to the negro was the greatest crime of the century." Smith argued further that "negroes should be where they were before the [Civil] war."[62]

The Atlanta riot was followed by virulent expressions of white rage. Senator Benjamin "Pitchfork" Tillman of South Carolina struck out against African Americans, telling a crowd of 4,000 in Augusta on October 7, 1906 (which happened to be Elija's ninth birthday), "There are some people who say that a race problem settles itself, but I make a prediction that in less than ten years, I fear less than five, there will be an immense number of bloody race riots, North and South, beside which the Atlanta riot will pale into insignificance." He also took a swipe at unskilled black laborers, whom he condemned as a "roving class of negroes who pose at sawmills, on railroads," and elsewhere, and who he said were of the most depraved character. "Worthless scum of a race, these are creatures who are threatening our women and precipitating riots."[63] The attack on the morals of black sawmill and railway workers struck a nerve in the Pool household, as Willie Pool worked at the sawmills and railroads to support his large family.

Dixon's and Tillman's tirades also angered blacks in the North, particularly Bishop C. S. Smith of Detroit. "There are not enough Tillmanites between Cape Cod and hell to hurl the American Negro back into slavery or permanently impair his onward march," Smith told the congregation of the Bethel African Methodist Episcopal Church on November 23. He labeled Reverend Dixon a "degenerate son of perdition who has stolen the livery of Heaven to serve the devil." Dixon, Smith said, "has forfeited his right to live, deserves to die, and to die the death of a cur dog." Shortly after delivering this stinging sermon, Smith left for Liberia to meet with government officials there about the possibility of more African Americans immigrating.[64]

The Day of Doom foretold by Daniel and in the Book of Revelations seemed to have arrived, or at least it appeared so to nine-year-old Elija. As rioting spread from Georgia to neighboring states—in what seemed to be a final showdown between the black and white races—Elija searched the Holy Bible to try to make sense of things. Luckily, his grandfather had taken a special interest in him, perhaps to bridge the gap that was developing between the sullen son and his self-righteous father. Noticing that Elija habitually came inside after finishing his chores, grabbed the Holy Bible, and lay on the floor reading until someone interrupted him, his bemused grandfather began calling the lad "Elijah the Prophet." Although he used the nickname partly in jest and partly to inspire Elija, the title stuck; his parents and siblings started calling him by it. What the youngster didn't know was that his grandfather had taken the idea for the nickname from a nationally known black Baptist minister named William Saunders Crowdy. After receiving a "divine revelation" in 1900 in which a vision of God called him to lead black people to their "true religion," Crowdy established a new faith whose central tenet was that America's former slaves were the "original Jews," and that he, Crowdy, was a reincarnation of Elijah the Prophet. Like Prophet F. S. Cherry, Crowdy preached that God and the first people on

Earth were black. His church, the Church of God and Saints of Christ, used the Old Testament as its holy book, but its theology was based on Judaism, Christianity, and black nationalism. By 1903, Crowdy was among the most successful black preachers in America. There were branches of the Church of God in several states, including Kansas, Virginia, Philadelphia, and New Jersey, and the Prophet traveled across the country to preach at revivals before he was partially paralyzed by a stroke.[65]

Each year, thousands of Crowdy's followers gathered in a selected major city to celebrate his birthday. In 1906, the celebration was held in Plainfield, New Jersey. Dressed in a brown suit and wearing white gloves and a silk mortarboard, Elijah the Prophet reigned over a weekend feast attended by thousands of his acolytes from across the country. All of his key aides had glorious titles as well. His chief assistant, Joseph Crowdy, was known as Father Joseph. Another aide was called Father Abraham, and another, Mother Sarah. He even had his own "twelve apostles."[66] Crowdy's claim aside, Elija Pool slowly began to take his nickname seriously, to imagine there was a hidden link between his destiny and the story of Elijah of Gilead, the last messenger of God, according to the Old Testament. Elijah of Gilead survived in the wilderness only because ravens, carrying food in their beaks, brought him nourishment. For Elija of Cordele, the much feared and maligned bird immortalized by Edgar Allan Poe was a perfect metaphor for black people in America.

CHAPTER TWO

ROOTS

I look inside myself and see my heart is black.
—*Rolling Stones,*
"Paint It Black"[1]

He spreads his knees, awkwardly, until he can feel the leather of her boots. He leans forward to surround the hot turd with his lips, sucking on it tenderly, licking along its lower side . . . he is thinking, he's sorry, he can't help it, thinking of a Negro's penis, yes he knows it abrogates part of the conditions set, but it will not be denied, the image of a brute African who will make him behave. . . . .

—*Thomas Pynchon,*
Gravity's Rainbow[2]

On the morning of my arrival in the town I casually dropped into the store of the general merchant who, I had been informed, had been one of the leaders of the mob. . . . When he told of the manner in which the pregnant woman had been killed he chuckled and slapped his thigh and declared it to be "the best show, Mister, I ever did see. You ought to have heard the wench howl when we strung her up."

—*Walter H. White,*
I Investigate Lynchings[3]

The inaugural address of President William Howard Taft resounded with promise for African Americans. It reflected a keen awareness of the plight of all minorities, and was particularly poignant regarding African contributions to America's rapid economic development. "I look forward with hope to increasing the already good feeling between the South and other sections of the country," Taft told the nation on March 4, 1909.[4]

> The consideration of this question cannot, however, be complete and full without reference to the negro race, its progress and its present condition. . . . The progress which the negro has made in the last fifty years, from slavery, when its statistics are reviewed, is marvelous. . . . The negroes are now Americans. Their ancestors came here years ago against their will, and this is their only country and their only flag. They have shown themselves anxious to live for it and to die for it.[5]

Like Lincoln, Taft recognized that the primary cause of the nation's great racial divide was the xenophobia of white Americans. As commander-in-chief, he tried to show by his words and deeds the necessity for whites to bridge the gap. In May 1909, when he delivered the commencement address at the all-black Howard University (built with federal funds in 1867), Taft reiterated his belief that the nation owed reparations to blacks:

> This institution is the partial repayment of a debt—only partial—to a race which the government and the people of the United States are eternally indebted. . . . Everything I can do as an executive in the way of helping along this university I expect to do.[6]

Despite his lofty aims, the president lacked sufficient support to move the nation forward on the issues of racial tolerance and equal rights.

Taft's first speech at Howard University made front-page headlines. But when he returned to speak at the school on April 18, 1912, few people outside the campus paid much notice. The nation and the world were mourning the worst maritime disaster in history: the sinking of the *Titanic,* which took the lives of over 1,500 people, some of them from among the American elite. But there had been signs even earlier that America's heart was hardening on the "Negro question."

Many in academia embraced and even championed the new racism. The president of the nation's most prestigious postsecondary school delivered several speeches in the months after President Taft's inauguration expressing racial views antithetical to those of the president, who was also a well-respected legal scholar. Although he was a progressive educator (having instituted the idea of a liberal arts education), Harvard University president Charles William Eliot was no pioneer in racial matters; on the contrary, his philosophy was strictly simian in nature. Eliot, from whom one would have logically expected enlightenment, denounced any "racial mixing," or amalgamation, and was a leading supporter of Southern demands for a complete separation of the races.[7]

Although whites were the main carriers of the race virus, most of its casualties were black. Not even Washington, one of the few African Americans invited to the White House in the early 1900s, was immune to the venomous rage it aroused in its host. On a trip in 1911 to the heartland of American liberalism, New York City, he was viciously beaten by a gang of white men for allegedly "approaching" a white woman—the kind of hate crime normally associated with places below the Mason-Dixon line.[8]

Intellectual racism typically bore the imprimatur of scholarship and science. One author wrote in rebuttal to a statement by black scholar William E. B. Du Bois:

> Let us repeat that the "color problem" is not a problem of color but of mentality. The difference between the white man, who has produced all civilizations, and the negro, who has no cultural possessions save

those which he has received from the white man, is not a color difference merely.

If the negro had proved himself the master of things and the Caucasian had proved himself dependent upon the negro's progress, we
should readily concede superiority to the negro. But as the history of
civilization shows the white man to be the master of things and the
colored race merely the beneficiaries of the white man's progress, we
cannot deny superiority to the white man.[9]

Professor Edmund Davison Soper expressed similar views, though
with more subtlety, in his book, *The Religions of Mankind*:

The people of ancient Egypt were in all probability a mixture of
African tribes, called by many Hamitic, and Semites, who at a very
early age, long before the opening of its recorded history came over
from Arabia, fused with the natives, and formed the Egyptian type as
we know it even in our own time.[10]

Soper completely ignored evidence that the coal-black Nubian civilization existed long before Egypt's, and proffered the idea that "fair-
skinned" Egyptians had civilized "cave-dwelling" Africans.

Eight months after Taft's first speech at Howard, a Chicago cattle
breeder held white scientists enthralled at a meeting in Boston with his
solution to the "Negro problem." On January 2, 1910, Q. T. Simpson
proudly announced to members of the American Association for the
Advancement of Science that the black race could be bred out of existence through genetic manipulation:

I think we are on the verge of gaining complete control over these
chromosomes [governing race], and that means the control of
color. . . . By a set process of treatment with baths or injections this
new tide in the affairs of the black man will be brought about and
these new color units in the cells of the creature will be attenuated or
destroyed. Today we can do it by breeding. Tomorrow we can change
the color of the blacks' offspring by treating these color-controlling

cells with a stimulant to war against the chromosomes. . . . I am at work on a process which I think will ultimately give us the results I desire.[11]

Similar views took hold in Europe, particularly in Germany after World War I. In the forefront of this assault on reason were *The Secret Doctrine* by Madame Helena P. Blavatsky, *Foundations of the Nineteenth Century* by Houston Stewart Chamberlain, and the writings of Arthur de Gobineau, who argued that a racially superior Aryan race had been polluted with the inferior genes of Semites and other Africans. Years later, members of Anton Drexler's newly formed Nazi Party used these writings and the pseudoscience of phrenology to justify racist views about blacks and other groups, particularly Jews. A scholar reflecting on this period wrote:

Slowly, a new religion evolved . . . a cult of race, based on the supremacy of the Aryans and the vilification of the Jews. It was called the *Volkisch*—or Pan-German—movement, and it enjoyed great popular appeal. A racial theory of history was developed, and it heralded the coming of a new Messiah.[12]

In relegating African Americans to play the black kettle in the allegory of America's "melting pot," scientific racism cast them out, forcing them to devise their own definitions of themselves. They weren't here, black intellectuals retorted, just to slave over the stove and to burn like Ham's skin, as was written in the Holy Bible and the Talmud. In 1911, author James Morris Webb wrote *The Black Man: The Father of Civilization*, a controversial tome that contended that there was proof in the Bible that the first people on the planet were Africans. The Garden of Eden was in Africa, he argued, and place names in the Bible were nearly all in Africa and Asia. Morris, who later played a prominent role in Marcus Garvey's Universal Negro Improvement Association, helped lay the foundation for what was labeled "Pan-Africanism." Webb wrote a second book in 1919 in which he argued that a black man would be the Messiah that Christians expect to return to Earth in the final days.[13]

Elija Pool came of age in the midst of this maelstrom. Although he was no longer in school, he read as much as he could about race and religion, and he was fascinated by new archaeological findings suggesting African origins of mankind. He occasionally ran across newspaper articles, some of which credited early nonwhite civilizations with being more than a presumed missing link to apes. "Where man originated is not known—very likely in southern Asia, possibly in Africa, certainly not in Europe, anthropologists say," one such article stated. The focus of the story in the *Savannah Tribune* in 1912 was the finding of a British anthropologist who had developed a new theory on the original color of man. "Some turned black, others brown and others yellow, all according to the climate in which they found themselves."[14] Generally, though, the American popular culture and the U.S. judiciary and legislature refused to acknowledge that black people had a history or culture before slavery.

It had taken whites a century to accept the idea that slaves were not chattel or three-fifths of a white man, and at the then current rate of racial enlightenment, it would take at least another century for black assimilation. Influential black philosophers and theologians such as Turner and Webb were not willing to wait that long. America had rejected blacks, they argued, so perhaps it was time for blacks to reject America. The rejection took many forms, and generally led to what is inaccurately thought of as the Harlem Renaissance.

The cultural revolution in Harlem was but a rosebush in a botanical garden; the whole African-American culture was undergoing a radical change. In 1909, for instance, the National Association for the Advancement of Colored People (NAACP) was founded (as an outgrowth of the Niagara Movement), followed two years later by the National Urban League (NUL). In 1913, a new type of black organizations surfaced in major metropolitan areas. While the NAACP and NUL were primarily nonwhite, their aim was assimilation. These new organizations, among them the Moorish Science Temple of America, the Ancient Order of Ethiopian Princes, the African Blood Brotherhood, the Black Hebrews, and the Universal Negro Improvement Association, had at the core of their philosophy tenets that rejected the idea of blacks being integrated into America's melting pot. They argued that blacks were the "pot" in the metaphor, a neccessary utensil as opposed to a vital ingredient. By the third year of Taft's presidency, most blacks felt alienated from the American government and the American Dream. The experience of fourteen-year-old Elija and the black citizens of Cordele in 1912 may offer some insight as to the causes.[15]

Front-page headlines in Georgia on January 30, 1912, illustrated clearly the racial dichotomy of American justice. Some papers led with news about Clarence Darrow, a prominent white labor lawyer who was indicted by a grand jury in Los Angeles for allegedly attempting to bribe jurors on behalf of clients charged with dynamiting the *Los Angeles Times* building. Public reaction to the indictment was minimal, and Darrow posted the $20,000 bond and went home. In stark contrast, other Georgia newspapers led with a story about a young horse-and-carriage driver, or hack. No one will ever know the complete truth of how eighteen-year-old Albert Hamilton spent the evening of January 29 because he never had a chance to tell anyone. Hamilton, a close friend of Elija's and a neighbor of the Pool family, was a popular hack around Cordele. As far as anyone remembers, he had never been in trouble with the law and was in all respects a model citizen. Like many hacks, he worked twelve hours a day, which is why his carriage was seen parked on Eleventh Avenue around seven o'clock that evening.[16]

In 1912, Eleventh Avenue in Cordele was akin to Park Avenue in New York or Rodeo Drive in Los Angeles—home to the locally rich and famous. Mr. A. F. Churchwell was standing on his front porch at approximately seven o'clock on January 29 when he saw a teenage girl lying in the street near his home. Hurrying to her aid, he realized that she was the daughter of one of Cordele's most distinguished families. Her clothes were disheveled, he said later, and she appeared to have been molested. Churchwell helped her to her feet, and then took her to his home. He left her resting on a sofa while he went to get a physician and the sheriff, both of whom returned with him shortly.

Upon being questioned, the teenager told Sheriff John H. Ward that she had been walking down Eleventh Avenue around six-thirty that evening when a "big, burly negro"[17] jumped out from behind a fence, grabbed her, and then dragged her behind the fence and assaulted her.

Upon hearing her account, the sheriff related the story to his deputies. Bloodhounds were quickly put onto the alleged assailant's trail, but a pouring rain had started, washing away any scent the dogs might have picked up. Meanwhile, Churchwell helped the girl's father take her home. A short while later, Ward and his deputies went to the girl's home to question her in detail about the suspect's appearance. After she gave them a description, the officers went to Cordele's "negro town" and arrested Albert Hamilton and three other young black men who were known to have been around Eleventh Avenue that day. They were confined in Crisp County Jail overnight.

"Every effort is being made to catch the negro," one newspaper reported in the center column of its front page early Tuesday morning, "and if he is captured he will probably be lynched."[18]

At roughly the same time that the morning newspapers were hitting the streets, the girl positively identified Hamilton as her assailant. By nine o'clock, almost every white citizen of Cordele had heard that Hamilton was in custody. Sheriff Ward grew worried as a mob formed outside the jail. Forty minutes later, he sent a telegram to Governor Joseph M. Brown urging him to send assistance to Cordele at once. "Send troops to Cordele from Albany or Fitzgerald," Ward's first of four telegrams stated. "Immediate need. Crowd furious. Girl identifies her assailant." By ten minutes after ten, the size of the lynch mob had doubled, and there was no word from the governor. The mob broke down the door and rushed into the jail as Ward sent another telegram. "Crisp [County] jail being broken. Rush troops. Answer."[19] Regrettably, the nearest troops were forty miles away, so even if the governor had answered the first telegram, it would have taken half a day for assistance to arrive. Within seconds of his sending the fourth telegram, the mob stormed the jail, took the keys from Ward, and kidnapped the terrified young man. They dragged him across the street as he screamed and begged for his life. Like everyone else in "negro town," he had heard about the lynching of three young black men and a woman in a nearby town the week before.[20]

"We're going to string you up, nigger!"[21] someone yelled as the crowd kicked and beat Hamilton and dragged him to "negro town." His punishment was meant to serve as another grim and wholly unnecessary warning about what happens when a black man is accused of touching a white woman. The mob continued to beat the boy while two men lassoed a large tree branch. While terrified black residents peeped out of their windows at the goings-on, the badly bruised and now nearly unconscious suspect fell to his knees. The terrorists fixed the noose around Hamilton's neck and tightened it. An anxious group of volunteers pulled the opposite end of the rope upward, and pushed Hamilton's body into the cold wind. After the rope was secured around the trunk of a tree, hundreds in the mob aimed their rifles and shotguns at the dangling, dying youth. By the time the smoke cleared, Hamilton had been shot more than 300 times. As the mob proudly dispersed, an amateur photographer snapped pictures of the mutilated victim, and then ran excitedly to the local camera shop and had the most gruesome photograph made into a postcard.[22]

That evening, the white photographer took hundreds of copies of the postcard to Douglas and other nearby towns to sell them. "I knew that nigger all my life,"[23] the forty-year-old ghoul from Cordele claimed as he hawked his macabre merchandise. Back in Cordele, the Pools and their neighbors were afraid to go near Hamilton's body, even after the lynch mob had been gone for several hours. Coroner J. A. Stephens arrived at the scene late in the afternoon and cut him down. Elija and other residents of the black enclave huddled around the Hamilton family, crying as they tried to console them, for they all knew that it could have been any one of them instead of Albert lying on the muddy ground in a pool of blood.

"I cried all the way home," Elija sadly recalled. "If I ever got to be a man, I told myself, I would find a way to avenge him and my people."[24] Although they wanted to take Albert away for burial, the white coroner told them not to touch the body, saying that he couldn't release it until after he completed his inquest. The inquest took less than half an hour, as there was really nothing left to investigate. A young man had been lynched, the white mob who did it had disappeared, and the citizens of "negro town" who witnessed it were too afraid of retaliation to say anything. As no one came forward with information, the coroner quickly ruled that Albert Hamilton had died of hanging and gunshot wounds.

At the funeral, the church choir sang songs that Elija and Albert once sang during Reverend Willie Pool's services. With each tear that fell from his eyes, Elija said later, his heart filled with a little more rage against white people. Memories of the good times he had shared with Albert ran through his mind, only to be trampled by flashbacks of his friend's bullet-riddled body dangling from a barren tree. For weeks after the funeral, Elija had nightmares. He would wake up, shivering, his bed linen wet from a cold sweat. The image of Albert hanging from the tree became etched in Elija's memory like a scar on a branded steer.

A primal event in shaping his lifelong contempt for whites, Hamilton's murder made Elija decide to leave Cordele as soon as he could afford to. He took a job working alongside his father at the local sawmill, and by the spring of 1913, had saved enough money to be able to move out of his parents' home and rent a room in a boarding house not far from the mill.[25]

Just when it appeared to Elija that his life was settling down into some semblance of normalcy, a single bullet fired in Europe changed everything. On June 28, 1914, a Serb nationalist assassinated Archduke Franz Ferdinand of Austria-Hungary in Sarajevo. At first, the assassination and the European war that broke out in its wake held little or no significance for Elija or anyone else outside Europe, but American perceptions changed over the next year, particularly after the Germans torpedoed the British passenger ship *Lusitania*, in May 1915, killing 128 Americans. Young white American males realized then that it was only a matter of time before they, too, would be called upon to go to war, but nearly two more years went by before the United States officially declared war on Germany. While conscription became a life-and-death issue for white men, it opened up new employment opportunities for blacks, whom the War Department initially equated with India's "untouchables." By the winter of 1917, Elija was promoted to a supervisory position at the sawmill, and while he reported to a white foreman, the twenty-year-old oversaw the work of black men twice his age, including his own father.[26]

At a social gathering around Thanksgiving, Elija strutted around the dance area like a proud peacock. His reputation as a handsome, eligible, employed bachelor circulated among the young single women that evening, among whom was Clara Belle Evans, a slender, cocoa-complexioned beauty. Before the night was over, Elija was smitten; he had discovered Cordele's Cleopatra. Although Clara had lived in Cordele from the age of four, the two of them, while seeing one another around town from time to time, had never been formally introduced.

Clara was born in Wenona, Georgia, on November 2, 1899.[27] Her father, a farmer named Quartus Evans, was born on November 25, 1871 (the same year as Elija's mother), and her mother, Mary Lue Thomas, on May 1, 1872, both in the tiny Georgia town of Perry. In the summer of 1903 the family made the five-mile move from Wenona to Cordele, where Clara attended public school through the eighth grade. After a year-long courtship, Elija asked Clara to marry him, and without waiting for her parents' consent, the couple were wedded in Cordele on March 7, 1919.[28]

While it was the first truly blissful period in Elija's life in a long while, the specter of his being drafted loomed over the newlyweds. Black Americans were not even considered for conscription when the Great War began, for despite their demonstrations of bravery, loyalty, and intelligence in the American Revolutionary War, the War of 1812, the Civil War, and the Spanish-American War, their participation in World War I was initially precluded because the War Department abided by Jim Crow laws, as did the rest of the federal government. The military brass believed that black men lacked the courage and the intellect to help the nation win a war of global dimensions. It wasn't until May 1, 1917, when the Central Committee of Negro College Men issued a public pronouncement at Howard University concerning the willingness of black men to fight for their nation, that the War Department considered blacks capable of combat.[29] The military's change of heart came about, some noted, amidst the worst pandemic since the Black Death. Moreover, the blacks would fight in segregated units led by white officers, as was the historical pattern. Two months later, 700,000 African Americans, including Elija, registered for the draft, but the war ended in November 1918, and the Treaty of Versailles, signed on January 28, 1919, sent soldiers from nearly twenty nations home—only days before Elija was

scheduled to report to his local draft board for preinduction procedures.[30] The war's end proved a mixed blessing for African Americans.
When white veterans returned home, competition for jobs escalated, and
many white employers fired black workers for the most nebulous reasons. By late spring in 1919, working conditions at the sawmill had
become particularly unpleasant; the ratio of black employees to whites
reversed quickly, causing mounting tensions within the mill. Now that
there were enough whites to replace the black supervisors, Elija became
the target of unprovoked and repeated racial epithets from foremen. "I
would ask them to just fire me if they didn't like my work," he said upon
reflection, "but just don't curse me."[31] The sawmill was a microcosm of
racism's new ferocity after the war. While no one individual can be
blamed for kindling the "race war" of 1919, one of the most powerful
industrialists in the world was rightly accused of fueling the fires of "Red
Summer," so called because more blacks were lynched in eight months
of 1919 than in any year of the preceding decade.[32]

Three weeks before the Treaty of Versailles was signed, automobile
manufacturing magnate Henry Ford began publishing the *Dearborn
Independent*, a small newspaper he intended to use as a vehicle for
exposing the national security and cultural threats he believed that
blacks, Catholics, Jews, and other ethnic and religious groups posed to
America. In his view, the mass media, which he argued were controlled
by Jews and Catholics, were covering up many conspiracies, the greatest
among them being the "secret plan" of Jews to dominate the world
"through financial control and war."[33] The Bolshevik revolution, Ford
contended, was but one indicator of what was called an "international
Jewish conspiracy."

The *Dearborn Independent* took great pains to point out that the revolution's rhetoric was provided by two Jewish intellectuals, Karl Marx
and Friedrich Engels. That Marx preached atheism (writing that religion
was the opiate of the people) was one more indication of the Jewish plot
to undermine all religions (Ford ignored the fact that Marx was at odds
with his own father, a respected rabbi). Of the conspiracy, coupled with
demographic trends developing through immigration, Ford warned,
"the United States of fifty or a hundred years hence [will be] inhabited

only by Slavs, Negroes, and Jews, wherein the Jews will naturally occupy the positions of economic leadership."[34]

To help distribute the newspaper around the nation, Ford gave a free subscription to everyone who purchased a Model T between 1919 and 1921. He stopped printing the tabloid after it had libeled a Jewish attorney and in the face of a political backlash. By then, however, the tract known as the *Protocols of the Learned Elders of Zion* was being studied at the highest levels of the U.S. government. Shortly after Ford began running the articles, FBI director J. Edgar Hoover requested a dozen copies of the *Protocols* from the State Department. For Hoover, a rabid racist who saw conspiracies around every corner and under every bed, the fraudulent document "confirmed" his own biased beliefs about Jews, the spread of Communism, and the gullibility of black people.[35]

"Ever since 1917," Hoover wrote in the introduction to his first book,

> I have observed the rise of international Communism with great concern, particularly Communist efforts to infiltrate and infect our American way of life. The Communist Party, USA, started in 1919 as a small, disorganized group of fanatics. Today, it is a dedicated, conspiratorial group operating under modern conditions as an arm of revolution. There is no doubt that America is now the prime target of international Communism.[36]

Hoover's discovery of the Communist threat in 1917 coincided with his nationwide campaign of spying on prominent African-American leaders, among them Asa Philip Randolph of the Brotherhood of Sleeping Car Porters, and the Reverend Martin Luther King Sr., a civil rights activist in Alabama. Randolph, who founded the *Messenger* magazine with Chandler Owen in November 1917, was targeted by Hoover after he published an article in 1918 explaining why many African Americans supported Germany during the Great War. Following a short trial, Randolph and Owen were sentenced to one to two years in jail, and the *Messenger* magazine's second-class mailing privileges were revoked.[37]

Randolph resumed writing for the *Messenger* after he was released, at which time he received a death threat from the KKK. In September 1922, the Klan sent a box containing the severed hand of a Caucasian (presumably one who favored racial integration) along with a letter complaining about Randolph's pro-integrationist articles:

> If you are not in favor with your own race movement [referring to a dispute between Garvey and Randolph], you can't be with ours. There is no place in our race for you and your crowd. We have sent you a sample of our good work, so watch your step. . . . Now be careful how you publish this letter in your magazine or we may have to send your hand to someone else. Don't think we can't get you and your crowd. Although we are in New York City, it is just as easy as if you were in Georgia.[38]

In the meantime, Hoover's war against the spread of Communism was focused elsewhere. With the passage of the Immigration Act of 1918, he initiated a massive campaign that targeted aliens he suspected of being Communists. By the time the Great War ended, thousands of so-called Red Radicals had been deported or charged with espionage. During a one-week period in 1920, some 6,000 alleged Communists were sent to detention centers at Hoover's behest.[39] But the Red Scare paled in comparison with Red Summer, when the blood of nearly eighty black lynching victims stained Northern city streets and Southern country roads.

Ford's antisemitic campaign affected African Americans more than it did American Jews, but that was of little consolation. Antisemitism in Europe was equally strong during the era. As Red Summer ended, a young Austrian corporal in the German army, who had been inspired by Ford's articles, began to plot a pogrom against Jews. The soldier, Adolf Hitler, made an unsuccessful bid in November 1919 to take over the city government in Munich and place the newly formed Nazi Party in control.[40]

The Great Migration of blacks northward had created a housing shortage in Detroit, Chicago, New York City, and other sprawling metropolitan areas. Furthermore, blacks were readily accepting employment under any conditions in order to survive, which angered whites because it undermined the strength of labor unions (which barred blacks). The *Dearborn Independent* gave justification to the mounting antagonism that lower-class whites were harboring, and the racial and cultural conflict boiled over that summer.

The carnage of 1919 actually began in Georgia on April 14 in a church in the town of Millen. Two white policemen interrupted the church service to hunt for a black fugitive. The parishioners protested the intrusion and tried to evict them. A riot resulted, during which both officers and four parishioners died by gunfire. As word of the policemen's deaths traveled across the hillsides, lynch mobs formed to exact vengeance on the town's black community. A black suspect in the Millen jail was kidnapped and lynched. Seven black-owned lodges and five churches were burned to the ground over the next several days. A month later, a seventy-two-year-old black man was lynched in Milan, Georgia, for killing a white man he had caught assaulting a black woman.[41]

In Chicago, where the black population had doubled between 1915 and 1919, racial tensions had been brewing since the 1917 indictment of Representative Oscar S. DePriest, a popular African-American U.S. congressman.[42] Antiunion activities also had escalated racial hostilities. The city erupted in July 1919, following the June 21 lynching of Stanford Harris and Joseph Robinson by two white gangs as they left their jobs in a predominantly white area. Weeks after the lynching, placards were posted all over poor white neighborhoods to the effect that an effort would be made "to get all the niggers" in Chicago on Independence Day, which was also the second anniversary of the worst race riot in the history of East St. Louis (over 200 blacks were killed).

The rioting began on July 27 and lasted for nearly a week. When it was over, thirty-eight people were dead. Of the twenty-three blacks who died, all except two had been lynched; one victim was stoned to death while a white photographer captured the entire episode.[43] A riot in Knoxville in late August resulted in eight deaths, one of them a black woman who was taken from the jail and lynched. In October, lynch mobs formed in Elaine, Arkansas, after black farmers tried to organize a union to protest the low wages white cotton planters were paying them. When the rioting ended, two hundred blacks were dead.

After white mobs burned several black schools and churches in Georgia on the first day of September, Elija and Clara concluded that it might be safer to start a family someplace else where there was a larger black community than in Cordele.[44] Elija had heard that there were plenty of jobs in Macon and Atlanta, so the twenty-one-year-old and his wife set their sights northward. In mid-September, they decided upon Macon, where there was a large and prosperous black community. Macon was also close enough to Cordele so they would be able to return home for special occasions.

From the outset, however, there were ominous signs that life for blacks in Macon wasn't as good as they had been led to believe. On October 7, 1919, Elija's twenty-second birthday, a black prisoner named Eugene Hamilton was kidnapped and shot to death by a lynch mob in Monticello, a small town near Macon. The mob seized Hamilton from the sheriff as he was being transported to Macon for security reasons.[45] The lynching dispelled any notion of security that Elija had taken from the "safety in numbers" axiom that prompted him to leave Cordele. There was no black community in Georgia large enough to insulate them against the likelihood of lynching: The day before Eugene Hamilton was murdered two black men were burned alive in Augusta and on Sunday, October 5, another black man was lynched near Sandersville— four racially motivated murders in the state in three days.

With his resources depleted, Elija had little choice but to remain in Macon for the time being.[46] In November he found a job at the Cherokee Brick Company. After a brief apprenticeship in masonry, he worked as a bricklayer and brick cleaner. The dust from the bricks aggravated an asthmatic condition that he had developed, and so he sought other work as spring approached. In early 1920, he found a job as a gang laborer at the Southern Railway Company's division in Macon with a starting salary of $9 a week. Though he began working for the railroad with the hope of eventually joining the prestigious brigades of sleeping-car porters, his dream was never realized.[47] From the financial end, it didn't matter; he made as much as a laborer as he would have as a porter.

Southern Railway, then the target of intense labor union unrest, had recently agreed to a new contract in which black workers were guaranteed a $1 a year pay increase (though their weekly wage was still considerably lower than that of the company's white workers).

Despite racial segregation, or maybe because of it, black professionals and black-owned businesses thrived in Macon. It must also be noted that the city itself was experiencing a period of healthy economic growth. The first-rate black-owned banks, clothiers, and theaters, as well as the large number of doctors and lawyers, gave the young man from Cordele his first inkling of the economic power African Americans were capable of harnessing when they worked together.[48]

Elija's improving economic situation and job security allowed the young couple to start a family. Emmanuel Pool was born on February 3, 1921,[49] and a daughter they christened Frances Lee Pool (her name was later changed to Ethel) was born in the following year on October 24.

In 1921, Macon and other big cities in Georgia were in the throes of tremendous labor-related upheavals. Trouble between unionized and nonunion workers continued to escalate, and in the spring of 1922 hostilities between black and white railway workers led to increasingly violent confrontations. On May 5, racial strife sparked violence at the Atlanta, Birmingham & Atlantic Railroad after a white worker crossed an integrated picket line in the state's capital. As the scab entered the railway building, someone hiding in bushes across the street fired a handgun in the direction of the building, fatally wounding a black man standing on the picket line. Before long there was a full-fledged riot. While attempting to subdue the crowd, a white policeman shot another black worker, who died the next day. Two months later, trouble spread to Southern Railway, where some black workers refused to join the union (some union members were accused of using intimidation tactics against them). On Friday, July 28, a black railway employee was arrested after allegedly pulling a gun and aiming it at two pro-union white workers who were insisting that he join the picket line. Watson Reed, the black employee, was arrested and taken into custody without incident.[50]

The next day, however, Macon exploded, belying the veneer of racial calm that had prevailed in the city for so long. It was Saturday, and the corner of Broadway and lower Cherry Street was packed with people out shopping or otherwise celebrating the weekend. At around six o'clock, a black man entered the black-owned Hatfield's Poolroom and soon got into a disagreement with a group of customers. As the argument intensified, the intruder, Willie Glover, pulled out a gun and shot two of them. Several minutes later, three sheriff's deputies arrived to arrest him, but he had already left the pool hall. As the deputies were leaving, Deputy Walter G. Byrd saw Glover standing on the sidewalk. Before Byrd, who was black, could reach for his weapon, Glover shot him through the heart and he died by the time the ambulance arrived. Although only one of the three deputies was white, rumors rapidly spread that a white officer had been shot and killed in the black part of town, and that the suspect had eluded capture and had hopped a train bound for Atlanta.[51]

Shortly after ten o'clock that night, Lamar Poole, Macon's chief of detectives, ordered that all trains leaving Macon be searched for Glover, and every conductor was given a detailed description of the suspect. Although several black police informants told the sheriff in Macon that Glover had taken a car to the railroad station in Forsythe (one informant had been in the same car), the sheriff made no attempt to capture him for fear that Glover would be lynched in Macon, where a mob of about 500 whites had already assembled. A conductor recognized Glover on an Atlanta-bound train and alerted the Griffin police, who seized Glover when the train stopped at the Griffin depot.

Afraid he would be lynched, Glover begged not to be returned to Macon. The officers decided to hold him in the Griffin city jail overnight. This, they reasoned, would give tempers time to cool off in Macon, and spare them the headache of driving the long distance in the dark.[52]

Less than an hour later the police were informed that a lynch mob was heading for Griffin in a caravan. Panicking, the officers put Glover in a patrol car and tried to take a back road to Macon. Their car was quickly mired, and as the caravan headed toward Griffin, the mob saw its headlights. The night stalkers plowed through the mud, seized

Glover, and tied him to a pine tree. After shooting him almost a hundred times, they decided to burn him up. Someone extinguished the fire after it was suggested that the body should be taken somewhere else so the town wouldn't have a lynching investigation to contend with. Glover's body was thrown into the back of a pickup truck, and the caravan headed back toward Forsythe, which was halfway between Atlanta and Macon. At Forsythe, Glover's body was dumped in a lumber yard, and the caravan headed back to Macon.[53]

A group of white men from Forsythe saw Glover's body being dumped, and retrieved it moments after the caravan disappeared. They loaded the corpse onto another pickup truck and drove to Macon. As they were leaving Glover's bullet-riddled body in front of Hatfield's Poolroom, a man shouted: "Here's your nigger. You killed him."[54] Many of the men who had been in the caravan gathered again in front of the pool hall. This time, Glover's clothing was cut to shreds that were sold as souvenirs to the lynch mob. His nearly nude corpse lay in the street as a new campaign of violence began. Dozens of blacks were assaulted and randomly shot at. Charles H. Douglass, one of the wealthiest black men in Georgia and the owner of a popular theater in Macon, was warned to leave the city within twenty-four hours or face lynching. Fearing a race riot, the sheriff set an immediate curfew on Macon's black residents. Every black-owned business was ordered to close, and remained closed the next day.[55]

For Elija, having to keep within the four walls of his home to avoid being lynched was too much to bear; he had had it with Georgia and with the South. Although it took months, he and Clara finally saved enough money to finance their journey to the "Promised Land," as the black-owned Chicago Defender newspaper called the North. While Elija was making a decent living—he was earning $12 a week by March 1923, and was working as a tramroad foreman—Glover's lynching and the racial discrimination he faced on the job were pushing him beyond his threshold for abuse. He was afraid that he would injure or kill his white supervisor or a co-worker if he stayed at Southern Railway much longer.[56]

The North in those years sounded too good to be true—particularly in New York City, where the Harlem Renaissance was blossoming like apple trees in Eden. Ultimately, Elija was overcome by temptation, and he and Clara decided to settle in Detroit, where, as his father had written in one letter, the automobile industry was booming and the wages were incredible. (Willie Poole had moved to Detroit in late 1922.) Besides, Detroit was one of the few major cities that had not experienced a major race riot. In April 1923, Elija put on his Sunday best, gave Clara and the children a parting kiss, and bought a one-way ticket to Paradise.[57]

CHAPTER THREE

PARADISE LOST

The mind is its own place, and in itself
Can make a heaven of hell, a hell of heaven.
—*John Milton,*
Paradise Lost, *book i, line 253*

Here was Islam, his own country, more than a Faith, more than a
battle-cry, more, much more . . . Islam, an attitude towards life
both exquisite and durable, where his body and his thoughts
found their home.

—*E. M. Forster,*
A Passage to India[1]

Christianity robbed us of the harvest of the culture of the ancient
world, it later went on to rob us of the harvest of the culture of
Islam. . . .

—*Friedrich Nietzche,*
The Anti-Christ[2]

The train ride from Macon to Detroit catapulted Elija from Dante's Inferno to Paradise. Detroit hardly qualified as the idyllic "Promised Land" trumpeted by the *Chicago Defender*, but to a newcomer the quality of life there seemed heavenly compared with the South. Though it sounds allegorical, Elija's new life really did begin in Paradise—Paradise Valley. That was the unlikely name for the black enclave in Detroit's Hamtramck area. Although it was segregated (except for black patrons of white-owned businesses), Paradise was not without its advantages and seemed to hold as much promise as its biblical namesake. Located only a few miles from the mercantile Detroit River, the Valley reflected a kaleidoscope of life in a modern metropolis. It was the epicenter of million-dollar playgrounds owned by such tycoons as Henry Ford, Walter P. Chrysler, and Ransom Eli Olds. Railroad tracks swirled around neighborhoods like lace on a Victorian corset. Days and nights were filled with whistles from assembly plants, the chomping of metal-stamping machines, the occasional roars of military and commercial planes, and peacocklike puffs of smoke from trains and boats and aging automobiles.

To new arrivals, the industrial noises were particularly soothing at night, as it reassured these transplanted Africans that they were growing economically along with the rest of America. Segregated areas such as Paradise Valley and Harlem challenged the African-American's creativity, his ability to make something where there appeared to be nothing, and he responded by creating a new culture. Elija was fortunate in that his arrival in Detroit coincided with this cultural revolution. Although the period is usually known as the Harlem Renaissance, the blossoming of black culture extended from Maine to California, and its exciting developments were not confined to literature, music, painting, and sculpture; there were equally revolutionary advances in the social and hard sciences. Black political and religious philosophies underwent a radical shift, and there were industrial breakthroughs at the hands of blacks as well as whites.

President Theodore Roosevelt may have piqued the nation's interest in black culture in 1906 when he noted the African-American influence on Antonin Dvořák's *New World Symphony*.[3] After reading Dvořák's article on how he had been influenced by black music, Roosevelt suggested that African-American music might inform the basis of an American school of music.[4] By the "Roaring '20s," the influence of blacks on American music was unmistakable. Scott Joplin, W. C. Handy, Gertrude "Ma" Rainey, and scores of musical prodigies gave the nation its first taste of the originality and innovation to come. Ragtime, the blues, and jazz blazed a trail from Basin Street in New Orleans to Harlem, the "Mecca of the New Negro."[5] One of the first musical teams to reap real financial rewards were songwriters Eubie Blake and Noble Sissle. Their song "I'm Just Wild About Harry," from the Broadway musical *Shuffle Along*, was an immediate hit.[6] A new assertiveness in black literature, apparent in the works of Langston Hughes, Jean Toomer, and Countee Cullen, found its visual counterparts in the paintings of Romare Bearden and the sculptures of Margaret Burroughs. The social theoretics espoused by Washington and Turner (both of whom died in 1915) were reshaped by Harvard-educated scholars such as W. E. B. Du Bois and Alain Locke and by self-educated philosophers such as Marcus Garvey and Noble Drew Ali.

After moving into his parents' crowded apartment for his first few months in Detroit, Elija found work at the American Nut Company, manually separating the steel shavings from the nuts and bolts.[7] The job paid well, but he hated it. As he cleaned the finished products, the tiny metal shards cut into his hands, leaving them swollen and painful. After six months, he quit and took a job at the American Wire and Brass Company. The work was also debasing and demanding, but at least he could move his fingers at the end of his shift. The pay also made the job more palatable. His weekly wage of $30 was more than double the $12 he had earned at Southern Railway (after three pay increases).[8] By the fall of

1923, he had saved enough money to send for Clara and the children, and was able to afford the rent on a matchbox apartment.

Elija had assumed that his huge pay increase would be sufficient, but after his family arrived, he realized that $30 in Detroit and $12 in Macon afforded him the same precarious standard of living. The family moved into a three-room house at 8483 Rockwood, a dwelling so close to the tracks that if you stuck your head out of the window at the wrong time, you'd lose it to a passing train.[9] An imaginary partition in the living room separated it from the master bedroom. As time went by, the narrow confines and incessantly noisy neighborhood had Elijah longing for the openness of the farm and its quietude after dusk, but going home again was just not an option. Failure was unheard of in the Promised Land. Besides, there was really nothing to go back for.

With two toddlers and a job that demanded every ounce of his energy, the grim realities of his new life gradually began to eat away at Elija's initial impressions of Eden. There was no Promised Land to own in the North, just landlords threatening eviction of those who fell behind in their rent. A better name would have been the "Promises Land." One of the promises Elija fell for was easy credit. The interest rates were so high on the household goods he bought on time that he was soon engulfed in debt and was chasing his paychecks like a dog chasing its own tail.

Despite the millions of dollars generated by central city industries, little of it profited the residents of Paradise Valley. Some African Americans did prosper in the North, but no more so than in the South, where at least there wasn't the pretense of racial equality. In the North, the newcomer lived like a greyhound gasping for an illusory reward at a dog race. Paradise Valley residents became modern Rip Van Winkles, sleeping in the same place for years, even though the size of most families doubled or tripled. Elija and Clara were no exception. Their second daughter, Lottie, was born on January 2, 1925, and another son, Nathaniel Paul, on June 23, 1926.[10]

Elija's strongest shock perhaps was the realization that white terrorist organizations were as big and powerful in the North as in the South. The KKK, which many Southern sojourners thought lived only in the lower half of the nation, proved a formidable enemy in the North as well. In Detroit alone, membership rolls exceeded 70,000 in the early 1920s.[11] In the summer of 1925, more than 50,000 Klan families attended a convocation (called a "Klanvocation") in Lansing, Michigan, and by that time national membership had surpassed 5,000,000, with the majority in the North.[12] In Indiana, their numbers were so great that the Klan and the Black Shirts (an anti-black group inspired by the Italian Fascists) routinely charged through black communities like Hell on horseback. They regarded the Great Migration as a plague on decent wages, good neighborhoods, and the American Dream. These Northerners, supposedly champions of egalitarianism, who had expressed shock at the horrors of black life during slavery, saw nothing wrong with discriminatory racial policies that led to dark ghettos in essentially every major city in the North.

Most African Americans turned to the church for respite, but the problems arising from the ghetto's squalor were far beyond anything that the church could deal with, and so the only institution that had made slavery bearable was found wanting by the slaves' grandchildren. The black clergy, who kept their people docile for a century by assuring them that everything would improve once they reached the Promised Land, quickly changed the promise. Now that they were in the Promised Land, the devout were being asked to believe that the land of milk and honey awaited them, not in the North, but in the hereafter. The faithful, who cooled themselves with cardboard fans bearing the image of a Caucasian Christ, read the Holy Bible with its pictures of Caucasians, while surrounded by statues and images of white angels, began to question the relevancy of Christianity.

Eventually, social organizations created or controlled by blacks began supplanting the church as the anchor in African-American life. Middle-class blacks found organizations such as the NAACP, the Congress of Racial Equality (CORE), and the NUL more socially progressive than the church, but these groups had little appeal for lower-class blacks, who lacked the free time, the economic means, and the patience for the pace of change countenanced by such organizations. They were tired of waiting for the hereafter; they wanted a better life here, now.[13]

From the ashes of incinerated dreams and the conflagration of Red Summer arose a leader who convinced African Americans that they held the keys to Heaven in their collective willpower. Marcus Garvey, a stout West Indian immigrant with classic Nubian skin color and facial features, preached that by uniting with a common goal against a common enemy, black people could create Heaven on Earth.[14] A Bible-toting Pan-Africanist, Garvey dismissed such leaders as Du Bois and Roy Wilkins as "blue-veined" mulattoes who were too wedded to integration to solve the problems of Africans of the diaspora.

Known as "Moses" to the millions who joined his Universal Negro Improvement Association (UNIA), Garvey infused his political rhetoric with enough spirituality to attract many blacks who felt as though their souls were homeless. For Garvey and his followers, who included the young Elija Pool,[15] black nationalism was as much a religion as a political philosophy. Indeed, a key propagandist in the UNIA was the Reverend James Morris Webb, who in 1919 published the book *A Black Man Will Be the Coming Universal King*.[16] Paraphrasing Webb, Garvey declared in 1922: "Look to Africa for the crowning of a Black King; He shall be the Redeemer." God, Garvey asserted, created man in Africa in the region now known as Ethiopia. Garvey espoused many concepts that Elija was introduced to as a child, and much of his philosophy echoed Turner. In 1922, Garvey convened UNIA's first international convention in New York, which was attended by representatives from twenty-five different countries. As the featured speaker, Garvey called for a new nation in Africa for African Americans, and said he envisioned a country much like America, one he called the United States of Africa. He also urged black people to hang pictures of a Black Madonna and Child in their homes. "Where is the black man's government?" Garvey asked rhetorically. "Where is his king and kingdom? Where is his president, his country and his ambassador, his army, his navy, his men of big affairs?"[17]

On special occasions, Garvey dressed as flamboyantly as the bejeweled Henry VIII, and he and his "army" wore colorful uniforms that reflected the British influence in the West Indies. He rode in a carriage during parades, surrounded by men dressed in maroon and yellow wearing hats with big white plumes. By 1921, Garvey was the chief executive officer of perhaps the largest black corporation in the Western world. He sold shares in his Black Star Steamship Line and created *Negro World*, the most successful black newspaper in the nation's history.[18]

In the midst of Garvey's rise as the champion of African culture, the greatest archaeological discoveries of the nineteenth century came out of Africa. After years of excavating, British adventurer Howard Carter found the ancient tomb in Egypt's Valley of the Kings that contained the sarcophagus of the fourteenth-century B.C. pharaoh Tutankhamen.[19] Carter also uncovered the tombs of Thutmose IV and Queen Hatshepsut. These discoveries illuminated a glorious past that until then had been the stuff of legend. African Americans beamed with pride as stories reached America's shores about the young pharaoh's dark complexion and the dark skin tone of other figures unearthed during Carter's excavations. Henrik van Loon's *Story of Mankind* was published around the same time, and his controversial thesis that civilized societies originated in Africa, spread to Asia, and came lastly to Europe made the book an immediate best-seller (it was released in America only weeks after Carter discovered Tutankhamen's tomb). Carter's discovery and van Loon's research gave African Americans their first real inkling that their history was ages older than the slave trade.[20]

Garvey's surprising success angered black middle-class intellectuals, who dismissed him as an amoral confidence man. He was amoral, Civil Rights leaders argued, because he had met with Klan leaders to discuss a peaceful solution to the racial animosity between blacks and whites. He was a confidence man, they contended, because he liberated money from his followers' pockets without actually sending them to Liberia or other African nations where he sought repatriation. Garvey's talk of returning them to Africa, critics charged, was that and nothing more. At least one prominent government official was equally angry about Garvey's success. J. Edgar Hoover viewed Garvey as someone whose sole purpose was to instigate racial discord,[21] and consequently made neutralizing Garvey and the UNIA one of his top priorities. He hired at least four

UNIA members as informants assigned to furnish the FBI with enough documentation about the organization to warrant a federal probe.

By the time Elija joined the UNIA, Garvey was caught in this counter-intelligence web. On Friday, January 13, 1922—some fourteen months before Elija left Macon—Garvey was arrested on charges of using the postal service to defraud his supporters in connection with the sale of stock in the Black Star Steamship Line.[22] The government alleged in its indictment that the campaign Garvey and his top aides launched to raise funds for an additional steamship was a hoax. The crux of the indictment rested upon allegations made by the informants. What few people knew then (or today, for that matter) was that the indictment was the real fraud. A government audit conducted while Garvey was incarcerated revealed gross prosecutory misconduct.[23] The prosecution had suborned perjured testimony, fabricated incriminating documents, and committed other acts of misfeasance to guarantee Garvey's conviction.

On January 16, the UNIA called a press conference to declare its confidence in Garvey, but by then the organization was mortally wounded. Detractors, primarily black leaders of the Civil Rights movement, saw the indictment as a chance to grab the reins of power from Garvey, and their public denunciations made it easier for the public to believe in Hoover's counterintelligence operations. On June 21, 1923, Garvey, who made the mistake of acting as his own lawyer, was found guilty as charged and sentenced to five years imprisonment. "I feel the dawn for the Negro race will come and my children and people will appreciate my sacrifice," he told the court after he was sentenced. "I am satisfied to serve any sentence the court may impose."[24] He was given four months to file an appeal. "Most of my troubles," Garvey told reporters during an interview from his cell at the infamous "Tombs" Prison in New York, "are the results of efforts of my opponents of the colored race. They are light-colored Negroes who think that the Negro can always develop in this country. They also resent the fact that I, a black Negro, am a leader."[25]

Garvey's fraud conviction was reaffirmed in March 1925, and the U.S. Supreme Court declined review. He was sent to the Atlanta federal penitentiary to serve the remainder of his time. The Justice Department, which had been trying to have Garvey deported as an alien enemy since Red Summer, finally had the law on its side. At the urging of influential black members of the UNIA, President Calvin Coolidge commuted Garvey's sentence two years later on the condition that he leave America and not return. In December 1927, Garvey was deported to Jamaica. With his deportation, the UNIA foundered under lackluster leadership and infighting. In the aftermath of his fall and the dissolution of the UNIA, land that the government of Liberia planned to sell to Garvey was leased instead to the Firestone Rubber Company, a direct result of economic pressure from the United States and Great Britain.[26] The erstwhile emanicipator's fall coincided with a congressional filibuster on the Dyer Anti-Lynching Bill. It somehow seemed appropriate that leaders who theorized about the efficacy of legal lynchings would also treat the issue of physical lynching with an equally inhumane attitude.[27]

As the UNIA spiraled downward, so did Elija. Strong drink became his communion wine and festering racial animosity the bread that sustained his dying dreams. He blamed white people not only for Garvey's downfall but for the bankruptcy of UNIA members who had invested their savings in Garvey's steamship stocks. Like a million other lost souls, Elija wandered from organization to organization seeking spiritual fulfillment. One of his first expeditions was into the esoteric world of Freemasonry. Since the mainstream Masonic organization, the Ancient Arabic Order of the Nobles of the Mystic Shrine of North America, was all-white, Elija enlisted in the all-black Ancient Egyptian Order of the Nobles of the Mystic Shrine of North and South America.[28] The Black Shriners, as these Freemasons were known, were a large bureaucracy with a virtually impenetrable hierarchy. Nepotism ruled. As Elija was too new to the North to know any high-ranking officials, he soon realized that he had little chance of ever being anything but a dues-paying drone and quit the organization after a few months.

To avoid his increasing marital difficulties and the screaming toddlers at home, Elija spent most Friday nights at local bars with friends. Gradually, he started spending more time with them than with Clara and the children, and Friday's revelry stretched into Saturday night. By Sunday morning, he was unable to account for his paycheck. Liquor was his refuge from the drudgery of work, where tired men were appendages of tireless machines, and a community where there was so much mindless violence that men lost their lives over pennies wagered in dice and card games. His drinking and unorthodox political views made it difficult for him to get along with white plant managers, and he found himself getting fired for the most nebulous reasons. By early 1926, the family's meager income consisted of the money Clara earned as a maid and the pay from occasional odd jobs that Elija stumbled into. He had to hold down two jobs, and sometimes three, just to keep his family from going cold or hungry. By the end of the year, his luck really began to sour. He was scrambling for work, often gladly grabbing a single week or even one day of work wherever he could find it. "I worked for various companies" during that time, he said later, "including the Detroit Copper Company, Briggs Body, and Chevrolet Axle Company."[29]

On Friday, March 19, Elija went to the local bar as usual. When he left several hours later, he was so inebriated that he fell into a gutter and couldn't get up. A sharp-eyed policeman noticed him, put him in a paddy wagon, and took him to Detroit Receiving Hospital. Doctors quickly diagnosed him as intoxicated and handed him back to the police. Officer John Carlson of the First Precinct put him in an overnight "tank," after booking him for public drunkeness. He was convicted and sentenced the next morning, but the sentence was suspended.[30]

He swore off drinking after his encounter with the criminal justice system, and changed the spelling of his name to accompany his new resolve, calling himself Elijah Poole. Despite his best efforts, by autumn his memory of the arrest had faded, and though he tried to hide his addiction from his children, alcohol is a master who suffocates the shame of his servants. Elijah's reddened eyes, slurred speech, and malodorous belching betrayed him. His unpredictable behavior frightened Clara and the children. They lived their lives in fear of his explosive temper when he was in the house and worried about his accidental death when he was out. "I had become such a drunk that my own wife was ashamed of me,"[31] he remembered. As it happened, their fears were well-founded. During the Christmas holidays of 1926, Elijah got so drunk that he passed out on the railroad tracks a few yards from his house. Luckily, a neighbor had seen him reeling and alerted Clara, who ran outside to search for him with five-year-old Emmanuel. She spotted him sprawled on the tracks, and she and Emmanuel dragged him to safety and then carried him home. Although Elijah only weighed 135 pounds, he might as well have weighed a ton, since Clara tipped the scale at 100 pounds.[32]

Repentant, Elijah again promised to quit drinking and to give Clara back the proud man she had married. As part of his spiritual quest, he attended meetings of a local temple that called its religion "Islam" and whose members were called "Muslims."[33] The founder of the temple, he learned during his first visit, was a strangely dressed man by the name of Noble Drew Ali. According to the temple's teachings, Drew Ali was the seal of God's prophets, despite the word of the Holy Quran, the book that orthodox Muslims accept as the direct word of Allah. As did Muhammad of the seventh century, Drew Ali produced a holy book, this one called the *Holy Koran of the Moorish Science Temple of America*, in connection with that organization, which he founded in Newark in 1913. The frontispiece of the *Holy Koran* proclaimed that the book was "divinely prepared by the Prophet Noble Drew Ali, by the guiding of his father, God, Allah."[34]

Drew Ali believed that Morocco was the original land of African Americans, whom he called Moors and Asiatics. According to Drew Ali, he had been divinely inspired to go to Africa in the early 1900s. After visiting Egypt, he went to Morocco, whose people are said to be descendants of Bilal ibn Rabah, the African slave converted to Islam by the Prophet Muhammad, who was himself a Bedouin. While there, Drew Ali said, he converted to Islam. In Morocco (then under Spanish rule), for reasons that are unclear, he asked the king for permission to propagate Islam in America, which was readily granted. Upon returning to America, he met with President Theodore Roosevelt to apprise him of his meeting in Morocco and of his plans to convert African Americans to Islam. He assured the president, however, that Muslims would remain loyal to the American government. Roosevelt, he said, laughed at him because he felt his mission was foolhardy and doomed to fail. "Go ahead," Roosevelt is supposed to have replied. "Getting Negroes to accept Islam will be about as easy as getting horses to wear pants."[35]

The story, like nearly everything else about Noble Drew Ali, was fanciful. There is no record at all of his meeting with President Roosevelt or any Moroccan dignitaries, nor is there any evidence that he ever left the United States. What immigration records do reveal, however, is that thousands of Muslims from Asia arrived in America in the midst of the black cultural revolution, bringing with them Islam and other Eastern religions whose appeal to urban blacks was immediate. Among the immigrants was an East Indian missionary who came to the West to proclaim that the Mahdi, or Messiah, had returned to Earth. The Messiah, the missionary said, had come in the person of Hazrat Mirza Ghulam Ahmed of Qadian, India.

Hazrat Ahmed was a highly respected Muslim mystic and scholar who, in 1889, announced in India that he was the Messiah prophesied both in the Holy Bible and the Holy Quran. Ahmed had written a book, *Braheen Ahmadiyya*, which laid the foundation for the Ahmadiyya Movement in Islam, or the Ahmadiyya Community. His theology, like that of the Persian mystic Siyyid Ali Muhammad, founder of the Baha'i faith in 1844, was considered heretical by orthodox Muslims. Siyyid Muhammad had also proclaimed himself the Mahdi. Ahmed's followers in India, like those of the Bab (as Siyyid Muhammad is called by his adherents) in Persia, were mercilessly persecuted by orthodox Muslims.[36] Thousands were murdered; others were disfigured for life after being tortured. Ahmed died in 1908. After his death, his followers selected disciples, or missionaries, to travel throughout the world to spread the gospel of the man they worshipped as the reincarnation of Christ.

One of his missionaries, Mufti Muhammad Sadiq, arrived at Ellis Island around 1910, and, settling in New York City, opened a small mosque. He brought hundreds of East Indians and Arabs into the Ahmadiyya Community, and soon expanded his ministry to other large cities where there were high concentrations of immigrants from the East, notably Newark, Detroit, Dearborn, and Chicago. Sadiq was able to attract small numbers of African Americans to the Ahmadiyya Movement mainly because they looked favorably upon any alternative to Christianity, which they felt had failed them. Among the African Americans Sadiq converted was a New Jersey railway expressman named Timothy Drew,[37] who studied Islam under him for about a year, between 1912 and 1913. Drew quickly became disaffected with the Ahmadiyya Community, though, finding that it did not offer him the spiritual and psychological fulfillment he needed. In 1913, Drew, greatly influenced by the writings of white spiritualist Levi H. Dowling, author of *The Aquarian Gospel of Jesus the Christ,* formed his own sect, calling it the Canaanite Temple. After Dowling died in 1911, Drew plagiarized the book, combined it with the teachings of the Ahmadiyya Movement and material from freemasonry to produce his so-called *Holy Koran.*[38] He changed his name to Drew Ali, preceded by the title of "Noble," which he borrowed from Masonic ritual. Black Americans, Noble Drew Ali wrote, were actually Asiatics who descended from the Moabites. Besides his *Holy Koran,* Drew Ali gave his followers several manuals containing questions and answers that had to be memorized. One pamphlet posed the following:

Q-5: Who is Noble Drew Ali?

A: He is Allah's Prophet. . . .

Q-28: Why did Allah send Jesus to this Earth?

A: To save the Israelites from the iron hand of oppression of the pale-skin nations of Europe who were governing a portion of Palestine at that time. . . .

Q-57: Who were Adam and Eve?

A: They are the mother and father of the human family—Asiatics and Moslems.

Q-58: Where did they go?

A: They went into Asia.

Q-59: What is the modern name given to their children?

A: Asiatics. . . .

Q-81: What is the name of the person into who Jesus was first reincarnated?

A: Prophet Mohammed, the Conqueror. . . . [39]

Noble Drew Ali's combination of black nationalism and religion proved as popular as Garveyism, and within ten years there were chapters of the Moorish Science Temple of America (MSTA) in cities in the Northeast and Midwest. By 1928, Drew Ali had established seventeen temples in fifteen states, the one in Chicago being the largest and most profitable. From his office there, he manufactured oils and herbal remedies for countless ailments, among which were Old Moorish Healing Oil, Moorish Purifier Bath Compound, and Moorish Herb Tea for Human Ailments.[40]

While he had never personally seen nor heard Marcus Garvey deliver a speech, Elijah did attend a lecture given by Drew Ali in Detroit and was profoundly impressed. He was soon among the thousands of blacks who joined the Moors. Because of their odd dress, employers had no problem singling the Moors out for discrimination: the maroon fezzes (which men were required to wear at all times) and goatees were a dead giveaway. As Moors held themselves superior to white people, their religious beliefs frequently resulted in hostile encounters on the streets and in the workplace. Things reached a point where Noble Drew Ali felt compelled to issue an edict warning members to stop assaulting whites and to avoid incendiary speeches on the job.

In 1928, Elijah was working as a forge helper at the Chevrolet Motors plant in Detroit.[41] While the pay was good, the forge job was one of the most dangerous and physically debilitating in the plant. The heat alone was suffocating, and the helpers often went home sick, many of them coughing up black mucus for hours after the shift because they constantly inhaled vapors from red-hot metal. Elijah stayed on the job for as long as he could, but quit after several months, complaining of breathing difficulties and persistent asthma attacks. He returned to working odd jobs, but devoted most of his time to spreading Islam, at least as the MSTA understood it. As he moved up through the ranks of the organization, he was given several names in short succession: Muhammad Ah, Elim Ah Muhammad, and finally, Muhammad Ah Fahnu Bey.[42] For the first time in his life, Elijah was moving in the same social circles as the black middle class. Many officers of the MSTA were college-educated professionals; others were pillars of their communities because they earned good wages working for wealthy whites. One high-profile member of the Chicago temple was Aaron Payne, a former assistant state prosecutor;[43] still another was butler to a generous Chicago multimillionaire.[44] At election time, some candidates paid tribute to Drew Ali, particularly in Chicago, where his endorsement guaranteed thousands of votes. Among them was Oscar S. DePriest, a popular city alderman representing Chicago's South Side. With Drew Ali's help, DePriest was elected to the U.S. House of Representatives in 1928, the first African American from a northern state to make it to Congress.[45]

Drew Ali's success in sending DePriest to Washington aroused envy within his inner circle. Chief among his detractors was Sheik Claude Greene, the butler in the mansion of philanthropist Julius Rosenwald.[46] Rosenwald was highly regarded by African Americans, particularly in Chicago, where he was one of their most generous benefactors. He had given millions of dollars to black colleges, was on the board of trustees of Tuskegee Institute, and had financed construction of the first YMCA in Chicago's black community.

Apparently unaware of Greene's membership in the MSTA, Rosenwald purchased a building at 3640 Indiana Avenue on his butler's behalf. The building, named Unity Hall, immediately became the cult's main mosque and national headquarters, and in 1928 was the site of the first MSTA annual convention. By early 1929, Unity Hall was the center of Drew Ali's own multimillion-dollar empire. Female members paid dues of $1 a month, while men paid $2. Temple records showed national membership peaked at 15,000.[47] Drew Ali made a profit of between $15,000 and $18,000 a month from his various temples and businesses, which afforded him a lavish lifestyle—one that Greene and other high-level temple businessmen began to question. The questions evolved into hostilities. Greene accused Drew Ali of wasting MSTA revenues on himself and a succession of women. Drew Ali "married" whomever he wanted, sometimes living with two or more women at the same time, wisely paying for separate homes for each. When he grew tired of one "wife," he would quietly "divorce" her and "marry" another. One woman he married was the apple of Greene's eye, and when she moved in with Drew Ali, the cruel Fates moved in with them. Greene made it clear to Drew Ali that he wasn't motivated by jealousy alone; unless he received a larger piece of the MSTA's economic pie, Greene said that he would publicly denounce Drew Ali as a gentleman of leisure and expose how he squandered the cult's wealth. Since the bookkeeping records were kept inside a safe in Greene's office, he clearly could carry out his threats. Drew Ali, perhaps too enamored of his own ego to sense impending scandal, rebuffed Greene's demand.[48]

On March 11, 1929, Greene dumped the contents of Drew Ali's offices in the Unity Hall on the sidewalk. Three nights later, several of Drew Ali's "enforcers" attacked Greene at the headquarters as he was locking up, shooting him once and stabbing him several times, leaving the body to be discovered by a janitor the next morning.[49] Drew Ali, who had been out of town on the night of the murder, was arrested upon his return and charged as an accessory to homicide. Police alleged that he, his wife, and a group of Moors were celebrating Greene's death at the time of his arrest.[50] Drew Ali hired Payne and William Dawson-el to represent him. A grand jury handed down an indictment after a hearing on May 20, 1929.

While Drew Ali was out on bail, a man by the name of David Ford joined the MSTA in Chicago, and it seemed that he was a godsend. With the trial pending and his followers abandoning the MSTA in droves, Drew Ali desperately needed someone capable of overseeing his organization. Ford, who seemed to fit the bill, was renamed David Ford-el and promoted to Sheik. He rose rapidly to Grand Sheik and was put in charge of the Chicago temple.[51] Less than a month after naming David Ford-el acting head of the Chicago mosque, Drew Ali died. Rumor had it that he died of injuries inflicted by the police while in custody for Greene's murder or from a beating by MSTA members as retribution for Greene's death. Other MSTA members, including Hamid Anderson-el of Newark, claimed that he died because of poor health. "He was gravely ill in the weeks preceding his death," Anderson-el recalled.[52] In any event Drew Ali was found dead in his home on July 20, 1929. Black newspapers attributed his death to tuberculosis, a verdict never accepted by most Moors.

Arguments erupted over the issue of a successor. David Ford-el claimed Drew Ali had left him in charge, and declared himself the "re-incarnation of Noble Drew Ali" on July 29.[53] Those who had been loyal to Greene, on the other hand, argued that David Ford-el had not been with the MSTA long enough to succeed Drew Ali, and insisted that Charles Kirkman Bey, one of Greene's closest allies, had the authority by virtue of his seniority to assume the mantle of leadership. Still another faction, headed by Ira Johnson Bey, claimed that Kirkman Bey was unfit to sit on the Supreme Prophet's throne. In September, the arguments degenerated into a war between the two factions.[54]

On the morning of September 25, four of Johnson Bey's lieutenants went to Kirkman Bey's Elm Street home and kidnapped him. They did not harm Kirkman Bey's wife, Peasie, but threatened to kill her if she called the police.[55] Nonetheless, the minute the abductors left, Peasie summoned the police and led them to Unity Hall, where two of her husband's kidnappers were interrogated. They admitted that Kirkman Bey was being held at the home of Ira Johnson Bey. Chicago Police Sergeant John O'Toole called for backup en route to the Johnson Bey home.

By noon, over 1,000 policemen had the place surrounded. A gunfight broke out when Johnson Bey refused to release Kirkman Bey. By the time it was over two police officers and one cult member were dead, and two other police officers and a cult member were seriously injured. When Johnson Bey finally surrendered, sixty MSTA members were taken into custody. Johnson Bey was charged with murdering a police officer. On September 29, he and William Johnson-el were charged with Claude Greene's murder. The deployment of 1,000 police officers in a single block of the black community evoked outrage. The fact that it all started with the kidnapping of Kirkman Bey got lost in the flood of rumors of police brutality and conspiracy theories about police plans to kill every member of the MSTA.

As retribution for what he called the "unjust" attack on the MSTA, Ford-el swore that he would bring "America to its knees in the very near future." On October 29, one month to the day after the shootout, the stock market crashed, and Ford-el said that the crash proved he was the reincarnation of Noble Drew Ali.[56]

While the crash caused panic in America in general, it induced a state of euphoria among those who believed that Ford-el really was what he claimed to be. Thousands of Drew Ali's followers swore allegiance to him, but the more educated members of the MSTA rejected his prophecy as coincidence and decided to stay under Kirkman Bey's leadership. In November, Ford-el moved from Chicago and headed for Detroit. Using the names Wallace D. Fard and Wallace D. Fard Muhammad, the former Moor renamed the faction he controlled the Allah Temple of Islam (ATI).

Two weeks before Fard arrived in Paradise Valley on July 4, 1930, the head of the Moorish temple there sailed for Turkey in search of a homeland for members tired of the factional disputes. Ali Muhammad Bey (whose given name was James Lomax), head of the Detroit temple who had joined with Greene to topple Noble Drew Ali, thought that he would be in jeopardy if he remained in America. He arrived in Constantinople on May 24, where he hoped to gain an audience with President Mustapha Kemal Pasha, whom he regarded as a "fellow Muslim."[57] What he found instead was red tape about diplomatic protocol, and he cooled his heels in Turkey for more than a month before his presence was even brought to Pasha's attention. On June 29, he delivered a petition to the Turkish president in which he requested permission "in the name of 28,000 Muslim Negroes suffering from racial prejudice in America" to found a colony in Anatolia, Angora, or any other underpopulated farming area. Although President Pasha was cordial, he denied the request.[58]

By the time Lomax returned from Turkey in July, Elijah and thousands of Moors had left the MSTA. America was in the throes of the Great Depression, and like millions of others who find solace in alcohol, Elijah started drinking again, this time more heavily than ever. Rather than being Clara's partner, he became another dependent. To keep body and soul together, Clara worked in several places as a domestic, while nine-year-old Emmanuel went "up and down alleys with my little wagon" to collect cardboard, milk bottles, brass, copper, and anything else he could sell at the junkyard.[59] He also climbed into the trash bins behind grocery stores searching for anything remotely edible. Despite their efforts to avoid the shame of public assistance, Elijah and Clara took turns standing in the welfare line as the nation's economy skidded rapidly downhill. While frantic whites reportedly jumped from windows on Wall Street, Elijah hushed his fears with bootlegged liquor. To worsen matters, Clara gave birth to two more children during the Depression: Herbert was born on April 16, 1929, and Elijah Jr. on June 29, 1931.[60]

When Fard first arrived in Paradise Valley, he attracted little attention. Starting by using fine silks as a come-on, he made his way into people's homes. A gifted salesman, he would lace his sales pitch with talk of the advantages of his dietary habits and religious beliefs. As some of his customers noticed an improvement in their health after following his dietary guidelines for a few weeks, Fard soon acquired a reputation as a healer and miracle worker.[61] Within two months of his arrival, people were crowding into basements to hear him preach about Islam and how it could improve their lives. The Messiah had returned, he said, but few people realized it because he wasn't espousing Christianity anymore. Rather, he was gathering his people under the wings of a religion called Islam. While some were drawn to Fard, others saw him as another false prophet in what was a growing cottage industry. The number of people— mainly men—claiming a divine kinship had multiplied to such a degree that it was difficult to distinguish one prophet from another. Around 1925, for example, another group whose members regarded themselves not only as Moors but as Jews as well was established in Harlem. Members of the cult, which was called the Zionist Temple of the Moorish Jews, studied Hebrew and used the Torah and the Talmud and as their religious guides. However, unlike the MSTA, the cult was confined to New York and its membership never rose above a few hundred.[62]

Nor was Noble Drew Ali the only African American professing to be God's last messenger. Perhaps the best-known was Father Divine. Born of the Gullah tribe of blacks on Hutchinson's Island off the coast of North Carolina, Divine was a maverick Baptist preacher who moved to New York in the late 1920s and proclaimed himself "The Messenger" and the "Son of God."[63] Like Fard, initially Divine taught his tens of thousands of followers that blacks were superior to whites. Blacks were attracted to his cult, it seemed, as much by his religious teachings as by the free food, clothing, and shelter he offered. Divine renounced his black superiority claims during the Depression, when he realized that he could attract white people to his churches as well as blacks. In fact, he eventually married a white woman whom he renamed Mother Mary.

Charles Manuel "Sweet Daddy" Grace was another young black man who rose to prominence as the "Messenger of God" in the early 1930s. Grace, who claimed at times to be God in person, took credit for ending the Italo-Ethiopian War in 1936 after his disciples prayed for a month for the war's cessation. By 1934 he had established some eighty-five chapters of the "House of God" along the Eastern seaboard.[64]

It was during the ebb in Elijah's life that began with the Great Depression that his wife first heard about the silk peddler who was offering salvation to his "lost uncle in the wilderness of North America," a phrase Fard used to describe the African American. Elijah was usually either too inebriated or too ill (owing to a chronic asthmatic condition) to attend meetings sponsored by the mysterious traveler, so Clara went without him. After a particularly inspiring sermon, Clara concluded that the stranger was what he said he was—a prophet. She rushed home to tell Elijah about him and the incredible message he had delivered that evening, but Elijah was too ill to think of anything but his own health. Since Elijah wouldn't go to meet the prophet, Clara decided to bring the prophet to meet Elijah.[65]

CHAPTER FOUR
LORD OF THE FLIES

At the reading of the sentence, all the Foulahs shouted, "Glory to Allah and Mahomet his Prophet!" Then, coming forward again to the chief, I laid my hand on the Koran, and swore by the help of God to accept the invitation of the great king of Futa Jallon.

—Capt. Theodore Canot,
Adventures of an African Slaver (1854)[1]

Son, you are always with me, and all that is mine is yours. It was fitting to make merry and be glad, for this your brother was dead, and is alive; he was lost and is found.

—Luke 15:32

It was part of the economy drive in preparation for Hate Week. . . . On each landing, opposite the lift shaft, the poster with the enormous face gazed from the wall. It was one of those pictures which are so contrived that the eyes follow you about when you move. BIG BROTHER IS WATCHING YOU, the caption beneath it ran.

—George Orwell,
1984[2]

Although Clara Poole had explained to Elijah that Master Wallace D. Fard's appearance was deceptive, nothing could have prepared him for the shock of their first meeting in the spring of 1931. Fard, who had accepted Clara's invitation to dinner, arrived promptly at six o'clock.[3] Accompanied by his chief assistant, Eugene Ali, he sat in the sparsely furnished apartment while Clara prepared dinner. Elijah tried not to stare, but he was transfixed by this stranger, who looked like an East Indian or perhaps a Caucasian with an enviable tan. His neatly trimmed hair was ebony black, with every strand in place. His dark pupils were so hypnotic that few women were willing to settle for a mere handshake. His perfect white teeth were framed by a captivating, gentle smile. He dressed like a fashion model: his dark blue pinstriped suit appeared to be tailor-made, and a maroon fez gave him the look of a distinguished diplomat.

"I know you think I'm white," Fard said after introducing himself, "but I'm not. I'm an Asiatic black man. I have come to America to save my long lost uncle [the African in America]." Elijah was familiar with the concept of the "Asiatic black man" from his days in the MSTA, and he knew black people who "passed for white," so it wasn't the color of the stranger's skin that had him mesmerized. Rather there was something different—even otherworldly—about Fard's appearance, though few could explain exactly what it was. Elijah looked in vain for Fard's "Negroid" traits; his facial features were simply not those associated with Africans. As for his heritage, Fard said he and the Prophet Muhammad shared a common ancestry, both being from the tribe of Quraysh. Fard said that he had been born in the holy city of Mecca on February 25, 1877, had received his undergraduate degree from Oxford University, and had completed his postgraduate work at the University of Southern California in Los Angeles "in preparation for a diplomatic

73

career in the service of the kingdom of Hejaz."[4] His conversation with Elijah was interrupted at that point by Clara announcing dinner. Although Clara was a wonderful cook, Elijah was ashamed of the meal they had that evening because "we didn't have good food to eat."[5] After dinner Fard insisted, much to Clara's embarrassment, upon clearing the table with Elijah so that she could get her children ready for bed. Elijah and Fard then returned to the living room, where the latter resumed his lecture about his mission. The discourse, capsulated here, lasted over three hours.

According to Fard, after completing his studies in California, he returned to the home of his wealthy parents in Hejaz to tell them that he had come to bid them farewell, as he had found a mission far more important than being a diplomat. While in America, he said, he had discovered "his uncle who was lost for four hundred years in the wilderness of North America."[6] He always used the term "uncle" as a euphemism for the African American. "You know me as Master Wallace D. Fard," he said, "but in truth I am the Mahdi whom everyone expected to come two thousand years after Christ, who was crucified at Jerusalem."[7]

He had, he said, assumed the physical features of a Caucasian so as to be able to mingle easily among whites; by living as a white man, he could keep abreast of their secret plans to eliminate all people of color from the face of the Earth. His mission in America had begun July 4, 1930, the anniversary of the day on which America broke the chains binding her to Europe. That day was chosen, he said, because it was symbolic of his freeing of African Americans from their dependence upon whites and what whites represented to blacks—"slavery, suffering and death."[8]

Fard likened Caucasians to Shakespeare's Caliban. They were "human devils," he said, the sons and daughters of Beelzebub. Caucasians were not superior to black people, Fard assured Elijah; they were inferior to them. The white race had been grafted from the black race thousands of years ago in a gene-manipulation experiment conducted by an evil genius, "a big-headed black scientist named Yakub."[9] Yakub, he said, was born near Mecca more than six thousand years ago, and had founded his own cult by the time he was seventeen. He taught his followers that there was no God but him, and that they would rule the world through a newly created religion-based science known as "tricknology."[10]

Fard described tricknology as the "science of deception." During a genetics experiment, he explained, Yakub discovered that while white people had only a single gene for pigmentation, black people had two, "a black germ [sic] and a brown germ [sic]."[11] This genetic discrepancy explained why a black man could create a white man through selective interracial reproduction, but a white man could never create a black man in the the same way. White people knew that they would eventually be eliminated from Earth if interracial marriages became routine, he said, so they had a survival imperative to maintain a social system of racial separation. Yakub initiated the genetic experiment on his followers without their knowledge, by deciding who could marry whom and through the secret practice of infanticide. Gradually, Yakub's tribe became brownish-red in appearance, then red-skinned like Native Americans, then yellow-skinned like Orientals and, in the final stage, white.[12]

Yakub, he said, observed one side effect to the experiment: the further away from the color black his tribesmen grew, the more immoral they became, until they were so evil by the final stage that the rulers of his nation drove him and his followers—some 60,000 people—away from the Holy City of Mecca. Eventually, Yakub's people sailed to an island in the Aegean Sea called Pelan, which in the Holy Bible is referred to as Patmos.[13] These people lived like wild animals in the caves of northern Africa and Europe, while Asiatic blacks lived in palatial homes in Africa and Asia and, yes, even in the Americas.

The cavemen (Fard called them "cavies") lived, he said, like the wild beasts that they slaughtered for dinner. Sometimes, he maintained, the cavemen had carnal knowledge of animals before they killed them. The two practices had not only tainted the white man's blood but had led to the appearance of virtually every disease and sexual perversion that plagues the Earth today.[14] Even now, white people like their meat very rare and it is served that way in the finest European restaurants, he said;

the taste for raw meat is a genetic trait of his caveman past, when he failed to understand and master the nature of fire. Moreover, it was among the caveman's descendants that bestiality was still practiced. Because warfare was a way of life for the caveman, his descendants could conquer peace-loving African and Asian nations, and his offspring now ruled nonwhite people all over the world, just as Yakub had predicted. If Elijah were a white obstetrician, Fard said, he would know the best-kept secret of Caucasians: some white babies were born with a tail, or the stub of a tail, which was surgically removed in the postpartum room.[15]

Fard usually carried several books around with him, including the Holy Bible and the Holy Quran. He also recommended that Elijah read Henry Ford's writings, particularly the auto magnate's reprinted version of the *Protocols of the Learned Elders of Zion*. All white people were devils, Fard told Elijah, but Jews represented Beelzebub, Lord of the Flies. Ford was the target of a smear campaign by the international Jewish cabal because he had exposed the "truth" about them, Fard asserted.[16] Elijah had heard about Ford's book; every black nationalist in Paradise Valley had.

As Fard continued to talk, Elijah stopped asking questions and just nodded his head in agreement, as this was the wisest man he had ever met. In the alcohol-blurred haze through which Elijah viewed reality, the whole encounter must have seemed surreal. Here he was living in Paradise, tempted by the vices of big-city life—most of them controlled by whites. Whites were always using tricks to keep black people half-free and half-slave, Fard said, and blacks had been so brainwashed and so certain of man's basic goodness that they fell for the same tricks over and over again. According to Fard, the poverty of Paradise Valley and Elijah's addiction to alcohol were proof positive of the white man's inherent evil nature. Whites, the mystic contended, used the black media to lure black people to the North, only to leave them locked into communities so crowded that violence was inevitable. Elijah wasn't responsible for his alcohol addiction, Fard said; the white man was responsible, because he had created a situation where drugs were the only balm that made life livable. Black people had fallen from grace, but he, Fard, had been sent by God to redeem them, just as Jesus was sent to redeem the descendants of Adam. As for Adam, Fard said, he wasn't the original man; the black man was the original man.[17] Adam, he said, was the first white man and Eve the first white woman, and they were born six thousand year ago, but no one knows when the first Asiatic black man was born. Scientists and archaeologists, he said, could dig until the end of time and never discover the age of the black race.[18]

Fard's theocracy was a burst of blinding light to those "wandering in the wilderness" of Paradise Valley. Of course, true to the axiom that there is nothing new under the sun, nearly all of his ideas, were based on religious beliefs that stretched back to antiquity. His theory that man was God's earthly manifestation, for instance, was borrowed from the ancient African concept of the God-king, in which the pharaoh was considered to be a divine being.[19]

Similarly, there was nothing unique about the notion that the devil could be human. The Egyptian man-god Seth, for example, was one of the earliest incarnations of Satan. In the fourth century, Cyril, bishop of Jerusalem, wrote of the Antichrist who would mislead men into believing that he was the Christ.[20] Saint Cyril of Alexandria theorized that Jesus Christ "was two separate persons, one divine and the other human." By the seventeenth century, volumes of literature focused solely on the notion of devils assuming human form. King James I, who hired a group of England's most brilliant writers to assist him in rewriting the Holy Bible, was also the author of a book about devils. In his treatise *Demonology*, James argued that Satan could take human form (in this case, Dr. Fian in 1591) just as blithely as he could assume the form of a serpent or any other creature in God's kingdom.[21]

During the same period, an Ambrosian monk named Francesco Maria Guazzo wrote *Compendium Maleficarum*, a scholarly work on the nature of witchcraft and demonology in which he argued that Satan was capable of assuming human form and impregnating normal women as well as witches. Another highly respected theologian,[22] a Franciscan named Lodovico Maria Sinistrari, wrote *Demonality*, in which he argued that creatures called Incubi were devils, masters of witchcraft and black magic, and could assume any form they desired.[23] He wrote of a devil who had tried to seduce a fair maiden through deception:

I might not impertinently relate many other most amazing tricks and naughty japeries which that Incubus played on her, were it not wearisome. . . . Now, it is undoubted by theologians and philosophers that carnal intercourse between mankind and the Demon sometimes gives birth to human beings; and that is how Antichrist is to be born, according to some doctors.[24]

One hundred years after Shakespeare's demonic Aaron had English audiences enthralled, the notion that evil spirits could inhabit people's souls caused the dark drama in American history known as the Salem witch trials, after which professed witches and warlocks went underground for 150 years.

So the concept of evil beings inhabiting human bodies was not Fard's invention. What was unique about his doctrines, at least in terms of American religion and philosophy, was his demonizing of all white people. Even Hitler's categories were vague and had exceptions. For instance, he believed the Germanic superrace descended from Aryans, thus overlooking the Asiatic roots of Aryan civilization. In addition to satanizing all black people, he included Jews and Gypsies, as well as others who are normally categorized as Caucasians. For Fard, all white people were devils—no exceptions. This idea, incidentally, was separate and distinct from the view of many African and Indian cultures that the color white represents evil and death. As these cultures had never seen a Caucasian, that concept never extended to human beings.[25]

Fard's blanket indictment of Caucasians was shocking, yet it took very little to convince Elijah and Clara of its veracity. They had both witnessed enough hate crimes to make Fard's assertions sound logical.

As for separation of the races and returning to Africa, Fard had borrowed his philosophy from Garvey and his predecessors. Moreover, the idea of separation was a cornerstone of the American Communist Party's presidential platform in 1928 and 1932, the latter marking the first time in the history of America that a black man was on a presidential party ticket. James W. Ford was nominated to run for vice president on presidential candidate William Z. Foster's ticket.[26] In 1930, the Communist Party's Election Campaign National Committee advanced the following proposals: "[W]e propose to break up the present artificial state boundaries . . . and to establish the state unity of the territory known as the Black Belt, where the Negroes constitute the overwhelming majority of the population. . . . [W]e demand that the Negroes be given the complete right of self-determination; the right to set up their own government in this territory and the right to separate, if they wish, from the United States."[27] The party also courted young African-American intellectuals, and among those who joined was a gifted young writer named Langston Hughes, who was appointed director of the League of Struggle for Negro Rights formed in 1930.[28]

While the FBI was well aware of the American Communist Party's programs to inculcate its ideology into African Americans, it remained unaware of the rapid rise of the ATI as a political force in the black community. Then, in 1931, President Herbert Hoover asked J. Edgar Hoover to provide him with information on the MSTA after he had received a formal invitation from the sect's national headquarters to address the group at its annual convention in Chicago. The president eventually declined, first because the FBI director concluded that the MSTA no longer had any real membership (a colossal example of the FBI's early shortcomings in investigating black groups), but also because the attempt by members of the cult to relocate in Turkey a year earlier had been damaging to America's international image. During the investigation for the president, FBI agents learned about the group called the ATI, but as it had done with the MSTA, it dismissed the cult as much ado about nothing.[29] Elijah thought otherwise.

Despite his lack of originality, Fard's scope of knowledge seemed encyclopedic to Elijah, who was an enthusiastic listener. There was nothing that Elijah asked about for which Fard didn't have a ready reply. When queried about the pyramids at Giza, the only one of the Seven Wonders of the World still extant, Fard spoke in graphical terms of how they "were built with hydraulics that they don't have in use now."[30] Fard claimed to speak sixteen languages and to have a firm grasp of etymology. The word "Europe," he explained, meant "false rope," being composed of "eu," meaning false, and "rope," which he said suggested encirclement.[31] According to Fard, white people were "roped in" or landlocked in the Caucasus Mountains by what were known as the Gates of Caucasus, "towering walls built to keep whites from crossing back over into civilization." Some armed guards stood watch high atop the walls, flanked by steep cliffs and insurmountable barriers of rock and ice, while others patrolled surrounding sections of the border."[32]

Elijah thought that Fard's knowledge of the Holy Bible and Holy Quran was even more impressive. Jesus wasn't white, Fard said matter-of-factly, nor was he born on December 25. He was rather an Asiatic black man who "was born between the first and second week in September."[33] It was a devil named Nimrod who was born on Christmas Day, and he later ruled Iraq and its infamous city of Babel. Fard described Christmas as a pagan holiday that grew out of Satanic worship.[34] He called the Holy Bible "the poison book" because it had been rewritten by so many who were unqualified. It was, he said, originally a book of prophecy, but wicked leaders who wanted to rule the world changed it so that people would think of it as a history book.[35] However, with proper guidance, the essence of the truth in the Bible could be distilled and put before the faithful. By the time Fard left the Poole home that night, Elijah was ready to follow him to the ends of the Earth. In reflecting upon that evening, Elijah said: "I was a student of the Bible. I recognized him to be the person the Bible predicted would come two thousand years after Jesus' death. It came to me the first time I laid eyes on him."[36]

Elijah's epiphany was so intense that he imagined Fard to be more than the Christ—he was God in the flesh. After Elijah had known Fard for several months, he waited until they were alone one day in the temple before asking his teacher about his identity. "Are you the God that's supposed to come and separate the righteous from the wicked and destroy the wicked?" Fard reddened with embarrassment and anger. He thrust his finger in Elijah's face and replied sharply: "Now, who would believe that but you?"[37] After regaining his composure, Fard cautioned Elijah against teaching that he was Allah. He was the Mahdi, he said, not God. "When I am gone, then you can say whatever you want about me," Fard said smiling, taking the edge off his harsh words and defusing a very tense situation.[38]

Elijah's craving for alcohol subsided after Fard's visit, and within a few weeks he stopped drinking entirely. Islam renewed his vigor, and after working two and sometimes three jobs in one day, he still had enough energy to spend the evening proselytizing. Fard rewarded his industriousness by allowing him to preach in their rapidly growing temple. Despite poor pronunciation skills, Elijah delivered a powerful sermon. Slowly, he started to understand what Fard meant when he said that Islam was more than a religion—that it was a way of life.

Fard's proscription on pork—he described the pig as part rat, part cat, and part dog—came as a shock to his followers, for most of whom pork was a staple. If they would abstain from eating pork and limit themselves to one meal a day, Fard told his followers, they would be free of most diseases.[39] Given the circumstances of the Great Depression, it was easy advice to follow, and the drastic improvement in the health of many of his acolytes after a few months convinced them that Fard was a miracle worker. In fact, the members' dramatic weight loss became a recruitment tool in much the same way that advertisers use before-and-after photos of dieters to sell products today.

Elijah never tired of listening to the man he called Master Fard, the Shaman of Shabazz. "He used to teach me night and day. We used to sit sometimes from the early part of the night until sunrise and after sunrise . . . all night long for about two years or more."[40] Elijah had finally found his calling. In early 1932, Fard gave him permission to propagate Islam in Paradise Valley, cautioning him not to frighten potential converts away by exposing them to too many new ideas at once. He warned him to be particularly circumspect about Fard being the Son of Man. "You can't give babies meat," Fard said. "Give the little baby milk."[41]

The gradual approach worked well. Elijah, who seemed possessed by his newfound faith, converted his immediate family and close friends. Among those who joined him in accepting Fard's guidance was John Lee Hatchett, an old friend from West Point, Georgia. Both Hatchett (who was renamed John Hassan) and Willie Pool Sr. became officers of the sect, which Fard officially called the Lost-Found Nation of Islam in the Wilderness of North America. "We are a nation within a nation," Fard preached. The sect had its own flag—a white star and crescent on a red field to symbolize "freedom, justice, and equality." Later, the first letters of those three words were added to the corners of the flag, along with the letter "I" for Islam.[42]

Hatchett converted his daughter Pauline and his son Raymond, both of whom Fard groomed for leadership. In August 1932, Fard had a surprise for the faithful in the Detroit mosque, located at 283 East Hancock Avenue. As he stood before a crowd of several hundred, he announced that he was promoting Elijah to Supreme Minister of the ATI and renaming him Elijah Karriem. Elijah's brother Jarmin was renamed Kallatt and was made Supreme Captain, while John, Elijah's youngest brother, was elevated from usher to acting principal of the newly created University of Islam. Despite its lofty name, the "university" was started as an unaccredited elementary school attended by children of members of the sect.[43]

As Supreme Minister, Elijah pounded away at Christianity as he lectured on Wednesday and Friday evenings. He also spoke on Sunday afternoons when Fard was out of town. Besides Christianity, Fard seemed to have a virulent hatred for Hinduism. His views on Hinduism, in fact, were remarkably similar to those of Muslims in India before it was partitioned in 1947. "The true religion of Allah and His prophets Noah, Abraham, Moses, and Jesus was Islam, and it is to overcome all religions," John wrote of Fard's teachings. Citing a passage from the Holy Quran, he taught that Islam would reign as the supreme faith one day, even though polytheists would be slow to accept a monotheistic religion. "That is why the white race and Indian Hindus had always been and are now the enemies of Islam and Muslims."[44]

"Hindus have been on this planet for untold ages," he said later.

They are an Original people. They have been here for a long, long time. For 35,000 years, they have been worshipping other than the Real God. . . . God let the Hindu go astray and worship whatever he wants to. Today you find the Hindu with more gods than he can mention. Everything is a god to the Hindu. He is far worse than any religious people you know of. He makes his God, and when he gets out of ideas how to make them [sic], he starts worshipping himself. That's the Hindu.[45]

On another occasion, Fard told Elijah that there was a law among Muslims, a ruling, as he called it. "If the Hindu and the Christian are walking together, kill the Hindu first because the Hindu is more poisonous than the Christian."[46]

As one would expect of someone professing divine qualities, Fard frequently made prophecies before the faithful. He predicted in 1933 that a war between the United States and Japan would erupt in the near future. He was eager to establish a temple in New York City because, he said, "some very wise men" would come from it.[47] He made a prediction expressly for Elijah in the spring of 1933, saying that the first-trimester fetus Clara was carrying was a boy, and that the child would prove to be special, so special that he would be the one to lead the ATI when he became a man. When Elijah and Clara asked what they should name the child, Fard carved his own initials on a doorframe. "There is your name for him," he said. Pressed further, Fard suggested that the child should be his namesake.[48]

From the outset, Fard preached that Islam would supplant Christianity as the predominant faith of African Americans, a prediction that seemed incredible at the time. He would raise the African American from mental death just as Jesus raised Lazarus from a physical one. The day would come, he said, when the work of the ATI would be on the minds of everyone in America. Like his alleged prediction of the stock market crash and the gender of Clara's seventh child, the prophecy about the ATI being the topic of national conversation proved accurate as well, but clearly not in the way that his followers thought it would.

In the fall of 1932, Fard's work was revealed to America. But instead of marveling at his ability to raise the dead, Americans were profoundly disturbed by the cult's practice of slaying the living. In his book *Secret Rituals of the Lost-Found Nation of Islam*, Fard had carefully worded several passages that, when interpreted by him during sermons, were understood by the faithful as "coded" rituals for human sacrifice. According to Fard, not only white devils were to be targets for ritual slayings, but also African Americans who placed their loyalty to the American government before their loyalty to the temple and God. Fard referred to these blacks as "imps," meaning they were "impersonating" white people in their thinking and behavior. Most of Fard's followers preferred to forgo the rewards he promised for carrying out ritualistic murder, but there was a handful for whom the salvation he assured them meant everything. Robert Harris, whom Fard had renamed Robert Karriem, was one of them. His desire to please Fard led him into an unspeakable act that had the city of Detroit in shock during Thanksgiving week of 1932.[49]

Karriem, a forty-four-year-old unskilled laborer, built a makeshift altar in the living room of his row house apartment on Dubois Street. He placed a single chair in front of the altar and set up some rows of chairs several feet away. At eleven forty-five on Sunday morning, he told his twelve-year-old son, Hasaba, and nine-year-old daughter, Ruby, to remain in his bedroom until they were told to come out. He and his wife, Bertha, then began seating twelve members of the temple who had come to witness a warped version of hero worship. Ten minutes later, James J. Smith, a former member of the MSTA who had become friends with the Karriems before they had sworn allegiance to Fard, emerged from the bedroom he rented in their home and was asked to sit on the single chair near the altar. "It's twelve," Bertha whispered to her husband, who then told her to fetch the children and seat them behind the twelve adults. Flashing the blade of his eight-inch knife, Karriem stood behind Smith, who thought he was being inducted into the ATI, and asked him whether he was still willing to sacrifice his life for Islam. Smith nodded nervously in the affirmative.[50]

"Stand up and lay on the altar," Karriem told him, and as Smith complied, the Karriem children suddenly ran toward their father, crying, "Please, Daddy, don't do it, don't do it!" They grabbed their father's arms, sobbing as they pleaded with him not to go through with his plan.[51]

Karriem implored them to try to understand that he was doing God's work, and that Fard, the God of Islam, had demanded that the entire family be present in addition to exactly twelve nonfamily witnesses. He told two of the adult males in the room to restrain his children, and, as they screamed in horror, he plunged the blade into Smith's chest, narrowly missing his heart. Smith fell from the altar and tried to stand up.

Having anticipated that Smith might change his mind about sacrificing himself, Karriem had hidden part of a rod from an automobile axle under the wrinkled white sheet that covered the altar. He bent down, grabbed the rod, and hit Smith once over the head, crushing the front part of his skull. Smith hit the floor hard, but he was still alive. Karriem plunged the knife into Smith's chest four more times, and then he and several male witnesses put their victim back on the altar, where he stabbed him eight times more. Blood from severed arteries spurted from the wounds, turning the white sheet red and dripping onto the caramel-colored carpet. When it was clear that Smith was really dead, the witnesses left hurriedly, most of them in a daze.[52]

Alarmed by the children's frantic screams, some of the neighbors peeked from their doorways into the hall, and watched as the witnesses vanished. Upon seeing the Karriem family leave with some of the guests, the neighbors called the police. After arriving at the bloody scene and interviewing the neighbors, police went to the ATI branch on Hastings Street, where they secured the names and addresses of the witnesses to the crime and promptly paid each a visit. They found Karriem and his family with one of them who lived on nearby Clinton Street. Halabas and Ruby were placed in protective custody, while Robert and Bertha were taken in for questioning. Karriem, who kept referring to himself as "King Karriem" and to Fard and Ali as the "gods of Islam, confessed to having murdered Smith, saying "I had to kill somebody. I could not forsake my gods."[53]

He also admitted that his wife had initially opposed the sacrificial slaughter, and that he had to beat her into submission. The reasons Karriem gave for murdering his boarder convinced the Detroit police that he was certifiably insane. Smith, Karriem said, was the first of four people he planned to kill in order to "gain his reward."[54] Each murder, Karriem said, would move him closer to Allah. Among Karriem's other prospective victims was Gladys Smith (no relation to James Smith), a twenty-one-year-old Detroit social worker who had recently terminated welfare benefits to the Karriem family after determining that they had other means of financial support. He also planned to murder two Detroit lower-court judges, the Honorable Edward J. Jeffries and Arthur E. Gordon.

When police questioned Karriem further about these "gods" from whom he was trying to get rewards, they realized that the "gods" were in fact men, leaders of the cult to which Karriem belonged: Wallace D. Fard and Ugan Ali, Ugan being the "Arabic" name Fard gave to Eugene Ali.[55] While Karriem and his wife were in custody, detectives searched their home. In a copy of Fard's *Secret Rituals*, found near the bloody makeshift altar, police found the following words underlined in blue ink: "the believer must be stabbed through the heart." Karriem's knife was protruding from Smith's heart when his body was found.[56]

The police immediately initiated a manhunt for Fard and Ugan Ali. The day after the murder, detectives Oscar Berry and Charles Snyder went to the ATI branch on Hastings Street, which was above an apparel store, accompanied by twenty uniformed policemen. In a room whose walls were adorned with Islamic and ancient Egyptian religious symbols and photos of famous black men, the detectives saw a frail, short black man wearing a maroon fez lecturing to some one hundred black men wearing similar fezzes sitting on black folding chairs. The room fell silent as Berry and Snyder approached the man at the lectern. Snyder asked him whether his name was Fard or Ali. "Why are you interrupting our service?" the man countered, without bothering to identify himself. Snyder apologized for doing so, and again asked the man what his name was. "My name is Ugan Ali," he replied. Snyder asked Ugan Ali if they could speak with him privately for a moment, and the three of them left the meeting room and went into an adjoining area.

"Have you ever taught a colored man named Robert Harris or Robert Karriem?" Berry inquired. Ugan Ali flew into a rage. "I don't teach colored people anything! We are not colored—nobody colored us! We are Asiatic!"[57]

Berry, trying to conceal his surprise over what he regarded as an exaggerated reaction to a simple question, rephrased it. "Is Robert Karriem a member of the Allah Temple of Islam," he asked.

"Yes," Ali said firmly, "Brother Karriem is one of my students."

"Then you're under arrest," Berry replied. Ugan Ali said nothing as the detectives handcuffed him and led him through the crowd sitting in the meeting room. After handing him over to two policemen, Snyder and

Berry joined the other officers in frisking the group in the room before ordering that the building be cleared.

The temple was searched from top to bottom, and accounting and attendance records were confiscated along with membership lists, copies of pamphlets authored by Fard, and antisemitic books and pamphlets bearing the Kansas City address of Gerald B. Winrod. As Berry approached the lectern where Ugan Ali had stood a few minutes earlier, he noticed a book open to a page with the passage: "Every son of Islam must gain a victory from a devil. Four victories and the son will attain his reward."[58] Turning to the cover, Berry saw that the book was titled *Secret Rituals of the Lost-found Nation of Islam*, by Wallace D. Fard Muhammad, and showed the passage to Snyder. Now they understood why Karriem planned to murder three more people. Fearing that other lives were at risk, Berry and Snyder quickly left the temple and resumed their search for Fard with renewed intensity. Acting upon information they received from the on-the-spot interrogation of Ugan Ali and others in the temple, they went the next day to the Fraymore Hotel, where Fard was known to be staying. After checking with the desk clerk, the detectives, accompanied by several uniformed officers, rushed upstairs, where they found a dapper, distinguished-looking gentleman leaving Fard's room.[59]

"Are you Wallace Fard?" Berry asked.

"I am Master Wallace Fard Muhammad," the man replied. The detectives were flabbergasted. They were expecting to find a black man, perhaps even a light-complexioned man like Ali, but the individual they saw seemed to be a white man. "You're Fard?" Fard replied in the affirmative. The detectives, still startled, asked Fard if Ugan Ali and Karriem were his followers. They were indeed his students, he said. They also asked him whether he was aware that Karriem had committed murder, and whether he had written the book advocating sacrificial killings, copies of which they had found at the temple and at Karriem's house. He had written the book in question, Fard said, and was also aware that Karriem had been charged with murder. Asked by the detectives if he condoned the murder of his enemies, Fard said no. "They apparently misunderstood my teachings." While it was true, Fard said, that the precepts of Islam as he taught it demanded the death penalty for anyone "who disturbed the peace in our temples, human sacrifice is not tolerated under Islam." He also denied profiting from selling names and other items to his followers. "In fact," Fard told them, "I have had to ask the brethren to contribute to a fund for the payment of an overdue electric light bill in the temple."[60]

Unconvinced, Berry took Fard into custody. During his interrogation, Fard was questioned repeatedly about some of the passages in the *Secret Rituals*. His explanations were deemed wholly unsatisfactory. In fact, the detectives wondered whether Fard was as unstable as Karriem, so they called in Dr. David Clark, a psychiatrist at the Detroit Receiving Hospital, who administered a battery of psychological tests to Ugan Ali and Fard individually for more than an hour. He recommended that both men be placed on the hospital's psychopathic ward along with Karriem, where they could undergo further observation. A judge signed an order to that effect. Like Ugan Karriem, Ali and Fard were enfolded in white straitjackets and confined to padded cells.[61] More than 500 members of Detroit-area temples milled about the halls of the Recorder's Court during Karriem's arraignment on November 25. Karriem pleaded guilty to the charge of first-degree murder. He killed Smith, he said, because it was "crucifixion time."[62]

"I killed this man with the crucifixion," the glassy-eyed suspect said. "I said 'Ali-kerslump' and he fell dead." When he finished relating his version of the murder, Karriem looked at Judge John A. Boyne and said seriously, "Well, I've got to go now." As he tried to leave the courtroom, several police officers restrained him. "Let me go!" Karriem demanded. "I'm the king here and everywhere!"[63]

Karriem's plea was of no value, however, as his incriminating but inconsistent testimony as well as his bizarre behavior left Judge Boyne in no doubt that he was psychotic. At the start of the hearing Karriem entered the court wearing his maroon fez. When asked by the bailiffs to remove it, he refused, replying that he was king in the courtroom. The scene was reminiscent of a "Three Stooges" routine as the bailiffs kept taking Karriem's fez off, and he kept putting it back on. Eventually the exasperated bailiffs let him keep the fez on.[64] At the conclusion of the hearing Karriem was returned to a holding cell, while Fard and Ugan Ali remained in the hospital, and police continued their investigation of the cult. It was during this investigation that the Detroit police realized that the ATI, about which the department had received only a handful of complaints before the Karriem incident, had grown from a small cult to a large sect with about 10,000 members across the country. An estimated 7,000 followers lived in the Great Lakes area alone.

Detective Berry met with Detroit's police commissioner, James K. Watkins, to request that a special squad be assigned the task of destroying the cult.[65] The request, which Watkins approved immediately, was readily granted because the cult had been on the enemies' list of virtually every African-American organization in Detroit. At the first conference sponsored by the special squad and held at the YMCA building, representatives from the Detroit office of the NAACP and the NUL, as well as local ministers and social workers, all portrayed the ATI as a cancer in the black community and a threat to the white population. Several Caucasian speakers at the meeting, including *Detroit Free Press* reporter Sherman Miller, concurred in the views expressed by the black representatives, and speaker after speaker warned the packed auditorium that Muslim children were being taught that white people were devils who deserved death. Social workers complained that welfare payments made to members of the ATI were handed over to the leaders of the sect instead of being spent on the children and the needs of the family. A prominent black psychologist testified that he had among his patients several members of the cult who had suffered nervous breakdowns shortly after joining.[66]

In the meantime, Fard's followers were growing impatient with the anti-Muslim hysteria that gripped the city. They felt that black organizations and the legally segregated white-controlled city government were overreacting to a single bizarre incident. When Fard and Ugan Ali were still in custody on Friday—five days after Smith's murder—Elijah, leading over 200 members of the cult, marched to the Recorder's Court Building and staged a protest on the main floor. It took police an entire day to get the last demonstrators to leave.

Miller continued to write sensationalist front-page stories for the *Detroit Free Press* about the ongoing investigation of the ATI. The headline that provoked the Friday morning picket was dire: "New Human Sacrifice with a Boy as Victim Is Averted by Inquiry; Frenzied Father Sought by Police."[67] The shocking nature of the headline not only guaranteed that Ugan Ali and Fard would remain in their padded cells on the psychopathic ward, but also meant that the police might charge the cult's leaders as accessories to murder, if for no other reason than to reassure the public that matters were under control. In those days, when journalistic and privacy issues were still legally gray areas, Miller managed to see the confidential psychiatric reports on Fard and Ali, and he quoted the most damaging portions in his front-page exclusive.

"The mental processes" of Ugan Ali, Miller's story quoted, "are radically deviated. His sanity is extremely doubtful. . . . His case must be handled with the utmost caution, as the slightest word or phrase, used inadvertently, seems to enrage him for no apparent reason."[68] What Miller's account failed to mention was that Ugan Ali vehemently protested being called "colored," and reacted angrily when police and psychiatrists used the term. This protest was noted as a sign of his irrationality. The verdict on Fard was equally ominous. Fard, Dr. Clark wrote in his report, which Miller excerpted, "is suffering from delusions that he is a divinity. He has a pattern of religious precepts and patterns which, taken literally, are dangerous to those influenced by them." Dr. Clark recommended that both men be confined in the psychopathic ward until further notice. The court approved his recommendation without debate.[69]

During a hearing before a special sanity commission on December 6, 1932, three white psychiatrists testified that Robert Karriem was legally insane. Detroit Recorder's Court Judge John P. Scallen committed him to the Ionia State Hospital for the Criminal Insane, where he remained until he died on June 19, 1935.[70] Ugan Ali, threatened with possible criminal charges stemming from the sacrificial slaying, told the commission and Judge Scallen that he now realized "the danger of my teachings" and promised to use his "influence to disband the Allah Temple of Islam." Fard, also facing possible aiding and abetting charges in the Smith case, made a similar confession. In exchange for dropping the charges, Fard agreed to leave Detroit forever as a condition for his

release from the psychopathic ward and immunity from possible criminal charges. On December 7, detectives Berry and Snyder put Fard on a
train bound for Chicago.[71] As far as they were concerned, the special
squad had achieved its goal, which was to destroy the ATI. On the same
day, in an attempt to capture some of Fard's disillusioned disciples, Mit-
tie Maud Lena Gordon, head of the Chicago branch of the UNIA, broke
with the Garvey movement to start the Peace Movement of Ethiopia
(PME). Like Garvey and Fard, Gordon said her main goal was the repatriation of African Americans to Africa.[72]

Gordon, however, had seriously underestimated Fard's determination
to spread Islam among African Americans. To be sure, Ugan Ali kept his
promise. But the trouble with promises is that they may mean one thing
to the maker and something quite different to the taker. For Master Wallace Fard Muhammad and Ugan Ali, the very idea of disassembling an
organization with nearly 10,000 dues-paying members nationwide was
about as savory as a slaveship's stench. Neither man had the slightest
regard for the American judicial system and, as they were discovering,
the Detroit courts held an equally low opinion of them and their cult.

Acting upon the earlier order of Commissioner Watkins to disassem-
ble the cult, in the days following Fard's banishment police arrested at
least 100 members of the ATI. Nearly all of the arrests were pretextual,
the objective being to make it difficult for temple members to congre-
gate. They were arrested on the streets, on their jobs, and anywhere
else that might cause them public embarrassment. To bolster the law-
enforcement campaign, social workers whose caseloads included ATI
families unilaterally ended welfare payments for many, which affected
nearly one-third of Fard's followers in the Michigan area. Many of the
Muslims with young children were devastated, as welfare was their sole
sustenance.[73] Families formed food pools to survive. On some days
males over thirteen had as little as three slices of bread to eat. To allevi-
ate the harshness of the food crisis, Fard established the "Poor Fund,"
through which money donated to the temple was doled out according to
a family's needs.

Though spared the harassment that their fathers faced from police
and their mothers from welfare workers, the Muslim youngsters also

had a harsh life. At school, they were ostracized by their black teachers and taunted mercilessly by schoolmates for the peculiar way they dressed and for practicing what the public regarded as "that voodoo religion."

Ugan Ali and his wife, Lillian, disappeared after his release, and Elijah became Fard's chief aide. Elijah's children got into street fights so often that he finally took them out of the public schools, and, with Fard's permission, reorganized the fledgling school. Located in the Hastings Street temple, the University of Islam accepted its first forty students in January 1933.[74] Although the ATI was disbanded, signs reading "Nation of Islam" started cropping up in Paradise Valley, and Fard gave Elijah Karriem another name: Elijah Muhammad.[75]

CHAPTER FIVE
BITTER FRUIT

These children had, by the age of ten, learned to reject the Negro category totally. No favorable quality was ascribed to Negroes more often than to whites. In effect, whites had all the virtues; Negroes none.

—*Gordon Allport,*
The Nature of Prejudice[1]

Nepalese women are favored by Indian men because of their [European] facial features and light skin. . . .

—Washington Post *(1995)*[2]

Lead the Negro to believe this [that he is inferior] and thus control his thinking. If you can thereby determine what he will think, you will not need to worry about what he will do. You will not have to tell him to go to the back door. He will go without being told; and if there is no back door he will have one cut for his special benefit.

—*Carter G. Woodson,*
The Mis-Education of the Negro[3]

When Wallace Fard sneaked back into Detroit to assess the crisis in January 1933, he announced a new survival strategy for his cult. The ingenuity of his plan was a clear sign of his native intelligence and cleverness, which in some measure explain why people were so attracted to him. At a clandestine meeting at the Hastings Street temple, he told his devotees that they were in the first phase of the War of Armageddon. Likening Caucasians to Lestrigons, Fard said that government agencies were using their police powers and social service institutions to devour the self-confidence of members of the ATI. If the tactics against Muslims were successful, he warned, the second phase of Armageddon would engulf all black people in America. It would be of no use to quit the cult, he cautioned them, since there would be nowhere to run to once the second phase started. Unless the so-called Negro was careful, Fard prophesied, welfare checks would come to symbolize the African-American's demise in the same way that the buffalo represented the decimation of Native Americans. He also reminded the gathering that the Holy Bible was a book of prophecy, that the trial and crucifixion of Jesus was symbolic of what would happen to Black Muslims in the final days, and that those who survived persecution would witness the Kingdom of Heaven on Earth after the Apocalypse.[4]

As he summarized what was described as his final sermon, Fard revealed a strategy modeled after the myth of Phaedra. First, he changed the name of the Allah Temple of Islam to the Nation of Islam (NOI); that way, leaders could not be arrested for violating the court order to disband the ATI. Semantically speaking, he was following the letter of the law. In short order, cult members returned to welfare benefits offices, where some swore to caseworkers that they were no longer members of the ATI. Again, semantically speaking, they had not breached their religion's proscription on lying. As soon as their benefits were reinstated, they gave a tenth of it to the NOI treasurer to beef up the Poor Fund. All members were told to use their "slave names" when dealing with the public, but to use their Arabic names or interim names (like John X Jones or Mary 2X Magruder) while at the temples or when addressing fellow Muslims in private. Elijah used his new name, Elijah Muhammad, but to make it difficult for authorities to track him, he also used two aliases: Mohammed Rassoull and Ghulam Bogans.[5]

Fard went back to Chicago for a few weeks, returning to Detroit in May 1933. As police officers in the Hamtramck area now knew what Fard looked like, it didn't take long for them to realize that the light-skinned man preaching on street corners in Paradise Valley was the banished founder of the Black Muslims. On May 25, police arrested him on the pretext of disturbing the peace.[6] He was booked and photographed the next day, then ordered to leave the city. A few days later, Elijah Muhammad and a large group of Muslims gathered around Fard as he stood beside his sleek black Ford automobile. "Don't worry," Fard said to the crestfallen coterie. "I am with you. I will be back for you in the near future to lead you out of this hell." He singled out Muhammad and continued his final speech. "Tell them, Elijah, I love them." After hugging Muhammad and others, Fard got into his car and drove away.[7]

No one heard from Fard for months. Rumor had it that he really had returned to Mecca. He was, in fact, living in Chicago and using various aliases to avoid attention from the authorities. In September 1933, however, he cast caution to the winds and plastered posters on the West Side of Chicago urging African Americans to come hear his divine message. As he was addressing a group in a rented hall near the intersection of 48th and Calumet on September 25, police raided the building and arrested him on charges of disorderly conduct. At his arraignment the next morning, the arresting officers told the judge that Fard was arrested after citizens complained that a confidence man was preaching hatred near the intersection and was thereby disturbing the peace.[8] The charges were dismissed.

Upon his release, Fard made another self-described farewell visit to Detroit. He had returned, he told believers, to bring good news about the impending war between blacks and whites. "The white man will be destroyed this year," he said.[9] Everyone was afraid to ask him how he could be so certain, but he explained anyway. The unidentified flying object sighted in Canada recently, he said, was really the Mother Plane, a vehicle that resembled the description of Ezekiel's wheel in the Holy Bible. The Mother Plane was designed and built in Japan by "our Asiatic brothers," Fard said, and when he gave the signal, the airship would release smaller ships inside its bay that would drop poison bombs on America. Only 144,000 people would survive, and all of those would be Muslims of color, the only "true" Muslims.[10]

He was returning to Mecca soon, Fard said, but he wanted to reshape the infrastructure of the "Lost-Found Tribe of Shabazz" so that it could survive both his absence and Armageddon. He announced the formation of several new institutions. The first was the Fruit of Islam (FOI), a para-military training unit that all male members were required to join. They were taught self-defense, including karate, and the leaders were assigned military ranks. A similar unit was created for women, though for different objectives. The Muslim Girls Training (MGT) class was designed to teach all females basic home economics. Members were urged to remove their children from the public schools for the school year beginning in the fall of 1933, and to enroll them in the University of Islam. Each satellite temple in Detroit would house a school. To create the impression that Fard's sect had been replaced in Detroit by a different one, each temple removed signs identifying it as a branch of the ATI and substituted others reading "University of Islam." It was the decision to expand the schools, however, that proved Fard's undoing, for while the new signs may have allayed suspicions about the cult's continued existence, the hundreds of children withdrawn from the public school system became conspicuous by their absence.[11]

In January 1934, truant officers raised questions about the high dropout rate among juveniles in Paradise Valley. As they looked for a pattern, they realized that nearly all of the dropouts had attended schools where there was a high concentration of "temple children." They also noted that the parents of some absent children had given "Mohammedan" names on the enrollment forms. Under school board guidelines, the removal of juveniles from the school system without authorization was tantamount to child neglect. But as Fard saw it, a separate school system was the only way to free the Tribe of Shabazz from the savage nature of self-hatred.[12]

Three months later, truant officers parked across from the Hastings Street temple observed over forty children going in with schoolbooks. They drove directly to the office of Archibald Henniger, director of attendance of the Detroit Board of Education, to inform him of their discovery. Henniger took the information to the city's chief prosecutor, George Schudlich. Alarmed that the cult had violated the dispersal order, Schudlich notified the Recorder's Court, and asked the judge to issue an injunction to close the Hastings Street school immediately. On Tuesday, March 27, the cult was back on the front page of the *Detroit Free Press*. Under the headline "Voodooist Cult Revived in City; Negro Children Found in Islam School," the reporter wrote that Judge W. McKay Skillman had given Schudlich permission on Monday to instigate legal action to close the University of Islam. Armed with the judge's order, Schudlich, Henniger, and several of the latter's aides arrived unannounced at the school. They were denied entrance by FOI soldiers guarding the door. Two of Henniger's aides drove to the Canfield police station to get help, returning moments later with eight patrolmen. This time, the FOI guards allowed them entry. In a large, all-purpose room on the main floor, the group saw forty-six children going through what newspapers later described as a "military drill."[13]

When asked why the children were not in a state-approved school, the principal replied that Muslims did not have to follow the rules of the Detroit Board of Education. Schudlich assured the principal that they did and then demanded a list of all students registered at the school and a copy of the curriculum. The principal refused to comply. One student, fifteen-year-old Sally Ali, was separated from the rest of the class and questioned. She confirmed what Schudlich already suspected: the teachings of the supposedly dissolved ATI had been interwoven into the general studies of each course, including science and mathematics. After leaving the school, Schudlich returned to his office with Henniger to compile a summary of their investigation, which they gave to Judge Skillman on Tuesday morning. The report indicated that not only was the school's curriculum a threat to the community, but that "no pre-pared course of study was followed" and that the teachers were appar-ently not licensed by the state. The most alarming allegation raised in the report, though, was an assertion that the students were being trained to kill.[14]

While Judge Skillman was studying the report, Schudlich and Hen-niger fielded telephone calls from members of the public disturbed by the cult's continued operation in the city and its implications. The ritualistic murder of James Smith had people wondering if the children in the school were being taught voodoo. Virtually every black organization in Detroit contacted city officials in charge of the investigation, most of them expressing support of the measures taken to close the school. The organizations selected a black evangelist, the Reverend Jeremiah Jack-son, as their official spokesman. Jackson went to Schudlich's office on March 27 and signed an affidavit in which he affirmed that the black community considered the cult a threat to public safety. Jackson stated further that the cult was a "reversion to paganism and ought to be halted at once."[15]

When Henniger and Schudlich went before Judge Skillman on Tues-day afternoon to submit Jackson's affidavit and other material support-ive of their case, the judge asked Henniger what the Detroit Board of Education planned to do about the school. "I have given them until April 3 to provide me with a list of all students, as well as a list of courses taught," Henniger replied, "and the qualifications of its teachers and directors." Henniger did not receive what he considered an ade-quate reply from the University of Islam until April 8. According to the packet provided him at that time, the curriculum included a list of twenty-three subjects. Some of them were what he expected—English, arithmetic, and the like. Others were surprising—trigonometry and astronomy, for instance, But most were esoteric and, to Henniger, dis-turbing. There were courses labeled "General Knowledge of the Spook Being Displayed for 6,000 Years," "Prophecy," and "General Knowl-edge of Spook Civilization." Of the thirteen instructors and officials run-ning the Hastings Street school, not one was licensed to teach by the state of Michigan. It was therefore doubtful, Schudlich told the reporters gathered outside Judge Skillman's courtroom, that any of the teachers were "equipped to teach school" on the most rudimentary level, let alone higher mathematics and science.[16]

On Friday, April 13, Judge Skillman ordered the University of Islam closed at once. The following Monday afternoon, Schudlich, Henniger, his assistants, and fifteen police officers conducted a raid on the school's Hastings Street campus. The thirteen teachers and administrators were arrested and charged with contributing to the delinquency of minors. Only two students were in the school at the time of the raid, seventeen-year-old David Sharrieff and Sally Ali. The two were taken to a local juvenile detention center for questioning, and Schudlich ordered that they remain in custody there as state's witnesses. During the raid, police seized pamphlets, textbooks, and school attendance records. To the prosecutor's astonishment, there were over 400 students enrolled at various campuses of the University of Islam throughout Paradise Valley. Each campus was inside a storefront temple. When he realized the size of the presumably disbanded cult, he contacted federal prosecutors to determine whether the group's leaders could be charged with federal offenses.[17]

"One of the children has informed me that they were taught that the American flag means nothing to Muslims," Schudlich told reporters at a press conference regarding the raid. "The only flag they are taught to respect is the flag of Islam," he said. "Such practices might be considered as anarchism and syndicalism." Among those arrested were Elijah Muhammad, his brothers James and John, and Abbass Rassoull, general secretary of the sect. Joseph X Gravitt-el, a Muslim who had been a close friend of Muhammad since their days in the MSTA, was also arrested. They were all subsequently released on personal recognizance.[18]

To Elijah's coreligionists, the raid was interpreted as a threat to the NOI's very existence. That night, Elijah began mobilizing his followers for a march on police headquarters. The purpose of the march, scheduled for Wednesday morning, was to protest the arrests and the boarding up of the University of Islam's campuses—in effect, all the NOI's premises in Detroit. On Wednesday morning, 500 of Fard's disciples, many of them armed with sticks, bricks, knives, and straight razors, filled the streets leading to the Canfield police station, which was only a few blocks away from the Hastings Street temple. When police cars cruising the area saw the crowd, they quickly drove back to the station, and within minutes, there was a cordon of police guarding the building. A shoving match ensued as Elijah and his father led the protesters to the front entrance, and several Muslims were hit with nightsticks. Police charged into the melee and tried to pull Elijah out of the group and arrest him.[19]

Suddenly, someone yelled, "Get the coppers!"

Within seconds, the Canfield station had a riot on its hands. A Muslim snatched a bucket of green paint from a man repainting rails alongside the building and dumped it on a police officer's head, then struck the officer in the face several times with the dripping can. Another slashed an officer in the face with a straight razor. The officer and fellow patrolman Roy Carmer, who was cut across his left temple with a pocket knife, were rushed to a hospital. Pandemonium reigned until forty mounted policemen managed to disperse the crowd. When the disturbance was finally quelled, thirteen police officers required medical treatment. Forty-two Muslims were arrested, among them nine women and four children. Elijah and his father, as well as his brothers John, James, Willie Jr., and Kallatt, were among the twenty-nine men. Abbass Rassoull also was arrested again, as was William X Gravitt-el (Joseph's brother). This time bond was set for each at $500. Elijah refused to post it, saying he'd rather sit in jail than post what he considered an outrageous "ransom" for defending his faith and his followers. The group protested the high bail by mounting a hunger strike.[20]

They were arraigned on April 21, the third day of the strike. Cult members testified that the riot started when police tried to force Elijah Muhammad and other Muslims into the police station. The patrolmen who gave rebuttal testimony did not refute these allegations, but contended that they tried to arrest the leaders of the march only to prevent mayhem. At the conclusion of the hearing, the judge, fearing more violence from the Muslims if those arrested on April 18 were convicted, dismissed all charges. The trial on the school-related charges, however, proceeded upon the incident of March 25. Sally Ali was called as the state's key witness.[21]

"What are you taught at the University of Islam about white people?" Schudlich asked her.

"I was taught that . . . if I cut off the heads of four devils . . . I would win a trip to Mecca and a button with Allah's picture on it," she replied.[22]

Judge Arthur Gordon, who earlier had been targeted for murder by Robert Karriem, interjected: "Who is Allah?"

"W. D. Fard," she said proudly.

"And when is the last time you saw Allah?" the judge inquired.

"Oh, about two months ago."

Schudlich then resumed his questioning. "What else are you taught about Caucasians?"

"That Caucasians would be put off the planet in 1934—destroyed," Sally said.

"How destroyed?" Schudlich asked.

"By poison gas," Sally answered, "and fighting."

When Schudlich concluded his direct examination of the young girl, Muhammad, who had no legal training whatsoever, acted as his own lawyer. During his cross-examination of the girl, he tried to subdue the sting of her testimony by asking her whether only white people were considered devils. "No," she answered, "all wicked people are devils." By the time he finished cross-examining the girl, it was obvious that he had done little to elevate his defense. Against a seasoned prosecutor, his performance all but guaranteed a judgment against him. During Schudlich's closing argument, he emphasized that the children were being trained not only to decapitate whites but also to murder blacks whom they considered enemies. Schudlich warned that there had already been at least one black victim of the "voodoo cult rituals," and said there were bound to be others unless Elijah Muhammad was put behind bars and the cult outlawed for good. He reminded the court that Fard was still operating in the city even though he had been banished, and that not even the police were safe from attacks by the fanatical followers of Fard and Muhammad.

It was a stunning performance. Nonetheless, Judge Gordon was mindful of the large number of Muslims both inside and outside the courtroom, and that his own life might be threatened again if he convicted the chief defendant. At the same time, he recognized that the community demanded satisfaction. As a compromise, perhaps, he found Elijah Muhammad guilty as charged, but placed him on six months probation with the proviso that he close all campuses of the University of Islam and re-enroll his own children in public schools.[23]

"I also want you to talk over things with those misguided followers of yours who marched down here a week ago," Judge Gordon said. Since most of the Muslims in the march were in the courthouse, his comments were clearly intended not only for Muhammad but for the others as well. "I advise you, if you want a school, to get a faculty entitled to teach under state law."

As he left the courtroom, Muhammad realized that the real trouble was just beginning; he could tell by the glaring grimaces on the faces of the police officers sitting in the courtroom. Harassment of Muslims, which had begun only hours after the incident at the Canfield station, escalated after the trial. On the street, the rumor was that the police wanted Muhammad and Fard, and they wanted them either dead or out of the city of Detroit. Fearing for his life, Muhammad had himself whisked away from the courthouse by a large entourage of FOI soldiers, and left immediately for Chicago. Upon his arrival, members of the main Chicago temple who welcomed him mentioned that they, too, had been badgered by local policemen since the Detroit incident.[24]

Fard was never seen again by most Muslims in Detroit. Though it took several months for Muhammad and other leaders to accept his permanent departure, a leadership crisis forced ministers to take measures to ensure organizational stability. Kallatt thought that the sect should be run by committee since no one could fill the void left by Fard. For a while, Elijah agreed. With the aid of his father and brothers, he began publishing a weekly tabloid titled *The Final Call to Islam* in August of 1934, the first official newspaper of the sect.[25]

According to the paper, Fard clearly had not preached that he was

Allah, but rather that he was only a prophet. In a front-page article of the third issue, dated August 25, Muhammad wrote emphatically that "there is no God but Allah and his Prophet [is] Fard Muhammad."[26] In another article inside the paper titled "Warning to the Black Man of America," Muhammad wrote: "Prophet Fard Muhammad came to North America teaching us of Allah and showing us things that will shortly come to pass upon this present wicked generation. . . . The Prophet will tell you the truth of all things and let the Jews and all the devils see their mistakes in not receiving Islam from Jesus when he was here two thousand years ago."

Nor did Muhammad's brother John believe that Fard was Allah. In an article titled "A Happy Muslim," John wrote that he was

happy to give honor to the great Prophet Fard, knowing that I cannot thank him enough for the wonders that he has done for me and all Muslims. . . . [I was] like a lion walking to and fro in a cage seeking a way out, but the door was not found until 1930 upon the arrival of Prophet Fard. I myself was like one that was sick unto death. And in one day, all sickness vanished from me, when the Prophet began calling his Lost-Found Brothers of Asia, returning the wisdom of themselves, healing them with their own Freedom, Justice and Equality, giving them their original names which they had been deprived of for more than 379 years.[27]

Despite the reluctance of any one individual to attempt to replace Master Fard, Elijah Muhammad decided to act upon what Fard had said to him in jest on a single occasion: that he could teach whatever he wanted to after he, Fard, was gone. In late 1934, a new rallying cry was heard in the Detroit branch he controlled: "There is no God but Allah, and Muhammad is His Prophet." He claimed that Muhammad of the Holy Quran was not really a prophet but an "enthusiast." Elijah of Cordele was the real prophet, he said. In proclaiming himself Elijah of the Holy Bible's Book of Malachi and himself as the Seal of the Prophets, he combined two central tenets of Christianity and Islam.[28]

Muhammad's decision resulted in a fight for power that turned brother against brother and lifelong friends into homicidal enemies. The bitterest fight started between Kallatt and Elijah. Kallatt considered Elijah's new theory—that Fard was God and that Elijah was his prophet— heretical. Kallatt's views and the views of those who supported him were summarized by his nephew Imam Wallace.

> I am convinced that he himself never told anyone that he was God in the flesh. . . . When he left in 1934 his successor, the Honorable Elijah Muhammad . . . quickly began to erect Professor Fard Muhammad as the second coming of Christ. Gradually he introduced him as Allah, God manifest.[29]

Other members, however, believed Elijah Muhammad when he said that Fard had personally appointed him as his heir. Their view, as expressed by his son Emmanuel, was that Kallatt "was envious of my father's position. He became an enemy of my father."[30] But it was Elijah who had changed the teachings, not Kallatt. As the differences between the brothers became irreconcilable and rumors of plots to kill Elijah proliferated, Kallatt moved out of the home that they shared.

Ministers who had once put their lives on the line for Elijah Muhammed now talked openly of taking his life. Others simply grew weary of all the negative attention the NOI was calling down upon itself. Among the latter were William X Gravitt-el and Joseph X Gravitt-el. The brothers returned to the MSTA, where Joseph, who headed the Newark temple, became one of the most powerful black nationalists on the East Coast. Osman Sharrieff, a well-regarded minister in the NOI's Chicago temple, quit as well, taking several hundred Muslims with him into his new organization, the Moslem Brotherhood. Sharrieff, who had joined the NOI in 1932 and was personally trained as a minister by Fard, insisted that Fard never claimed to be Allah in person, and that neither he nor anyone he knew had heard Fard designate Elijah as the new "prophet" of the sect. To Sharrieff, Elijah was a hypocrite.[31]

To Elijah's dismay, Kallatt joined forces with two of his chief rivals.

One was Abdul Muhammad (no relation to Elijah), a former minister who left the NOI following a dispute with Fard. Although Fard knew of Abdul's theological disagreement with him, he was unaware that Abdul had aligned with a controversial Japanese radical by the name of Satohata Takahashi. Thus, it came as quite a shock to Elijah and Fard when they visited Abdul at home on December 11, 1933, and found the two of them having dinner. Abdul didn't mince words. He had grown disillusioned with Fard's drastic departure from the philosophy and moral guidelines established by Noble Drew Ali. With financial assistance from Takahashi, Abdul said he planned to establish an organization whose aim would be keeping Drew Ali's vision alive.[32]

The group Abdul created with Takahashi's aid was called the Society for the Development of Our Own (SDOO). Incorporated in Lansing, Michigan, on October 5, 1933, it threatened to have the same devastating impact upon the NOI that Fard's arrival had had upon the membership of the MSTA.[33] By design, there was little to distinguish the SDOO from the NOI. Like the NOI, the SDOO flag featured a white star and crescent moon on a red background. The NOI flag had four letters on it: F,J,E,I, representing the words "Freedom, Justice, Equality" and "Islam." Similarly, the SDOO flag had one letter in each corner: F,J,E,L. The letters represented the words "Freedom, Justice, Equality," and "Liberty." These represented four of what Takahashi called his "Five Guiding Principles." The sum of the four equaled the fifth principle, Honor. Takahashi scheduled his meetings within an hour of Fard's services on Wednesdays, Fridays, and Sunday afternoons. That way, potential converts did not have to choose one over the other. By making the groups as similar as possible, Takahashi felt he could pull followers away from the NOI. He was right.[34]

Though Fard knew little about Takahashi's background, the federal government had been on the radical's trail for years. He had come to America in 1930 to promote the aims of the Kokuryukai, or Black Dragon Society (BDS). Established in 1901 by a Buddhist monk, Ryohei Uchida, the BDS assisted in Japan's invasion of Korea in 1910 and in the seizure of Manchuria in 1931.[35] The global ambitions of the BDS brought some members to America, although the U.S. Department of Justice had difficulty in determining the ones among them who were actual agents of the ultranationalist society and those who were just petty opportunists. At any rate, Takahashi entered the United States from Canada in 1929. He lived in Tacoma, Washington, then briefly in Seattle, where he created the first cell of a pro-Japanese cult dedicated to "sabotaging American businesses" and committing acts of terrorism. In July 1930, Takahashi received a letter from someone who signed himself Augustus Muhammad, who asked him to come to Detroit to help him establish a new organization. Augustus was Abdul Muhammad's given name. Takahashi agreed.[36]

With access to seemingly bottomless coffers for organizational capital, Takahashi attracted over 5,000 followers to the SDOO by early 1931, most of them of African-American, Filipino, or East Indian descent. As part of an ongoing investigation into the activities of Japanese agents in America, the Department of Justice learned from its informants that Takahashi had become a major political force in Paradise Valley, where he was called Major Takahashi.[37] An investigation opened in 1932 resulted in the ATI and the SDOO being added to the list of "subversive" organizations collectively referred to as the "Fifth Column." The extent of Takahashi's influence upon the ATI became clear in lectures given at the NOI temples during the mid-1930s and 1940s. Repeated references to the superiority of Japan were made in virtually every speech. "The Japanese will slaughter the white man," Elijah Muhammad said in numerous sermons, transcribed copies of which later fell into the hands of the FBI. "It is Japan's duty to save you; they have been given the power by the Asiatic nation to save you in the West," he said in another address to his followers in Chicago. "The Asiatic nation is prepared to destroy the white man."[38]

And in still another sermon, Muhammad said:

Our brothers in the East [Japan] did not know that we [blacks] were here until sixty years ago. After finding out we were here using the names of the devil, they at once went back and told the Asiatic nation. . . . Then they knew where their lost brother was. Now, they are only waiting on the word of the Prophet [Fard]. The Japanese army and navy are already strong enough to destroy this devil.[39]

While Fard continued to make guest appearances at the ATI, he reportedly spent time visiting Takahashi's group as well.

Sensing an opportunity to widen his base of support in Detroit, Takahashi nurtured a friendship with Fard and Muhammad at the same time that he was laying the groundwork for Abdul's new organization.[40] His interest in Fard intensified as he discovered the extent of the latter's associations with Japanese radicals in Oregon, California, and Washington State. Fard took an interest in Takahashi only after the African-American press started covering the Asian's activities and Takahashi allegedly offered him financial assistance. Photographs of him lecturing to hundreds of minority members who joined SDOO made the front page, and his wedding to a young black woman caused a scandal. The young woman, a Tuskegee Institute graduate named Cheaber McIntyre, had left her husband for the much older Takahashi. Takahashi had abandoned Pearl T. Sherrod, another black woman, to marry McIntyre, which made matters even worse. The wedding made the front page of the *Detroit Tribune*, a leading African-American newspaper.[41]

Takahashi, of course, had ulterior motives in offering Fard money; it soon became apparent that the Japanese rebel was trying to take over. In August 1932, Takahashi talked to Fard about his vision for the future of the ATI. Speaking in language suggesting that his takeover was inevitable, he asked Fard to become his chief minister. Fard declined. In his view—to paraphrase a favorite Marxist saying—Fard had nothing to gain and everything to lose if he went along with Takahashi's grandiose dream. Nonetheless, this ideological confluence marked the beginning of the federal government's monitoring of Muslims in America.

The Office of Naval Intelligence (ONI) discovered Takahashi's group by accident. In March 1932, Captain Hayne Ellis, director of ONI, sent a classified memorandum to J. Edgar Hoover to alert him to the activities of an alleged Japanese student on the campus of a prestigious university in Baltimore:

> Mr. Ashima Takis, Japanese student at Johns Hopkins University, has been lecturing or speaking in a manner calculated to arouse the colored citizens of America against their government. I am further informed that he has caused quite a lot of trouble among the colored employees of the steel companies in the Gary, Indiana, steel district. The importance of this district in times of peace as well as in times of war suggests that Mr. Ashima Takis may have had a special purpose in visiting that region.

In his reply the next day, Hoover acknowledged the navy's concern, but was noncommittal regarding an investigation of the student.[42]

On December 7, 1932, the day Fard was run out of Detroit, Takis filed incorporation papers for the Pacific Movement of the Eastern World (PMEW), a pro-Japanese group whose sole aim was to recruit African Americans to support Japan in the event of a war against the United States.[43]

At the same time that Fard was prophesying war between America and Japan, Takahashi and Takis were talking in a similar vein around the country. During a rally sponsored by the Communist Party in St. Louis on June 22, 1933, at which Takis was the featured speaker, an FBI agent transcribed the following portion of the heated address:

> Negroes of the United States: You are the most oppressed people on Earth. If you will join the Japanese and other colored races, you will be in command of the whites. In case of war between the United States and Japan, you must divorce yourselves from the whites, the United States commanding bosses, and join the Japanese yellow race, your only friends![44]

Takis gave an equally inflammatory speech four days later at a rally sponsored by the PMEW:

Negroes, you are too easy to be fooled by anybody and especially white people. The white man pushes you ahead as cattle in any war and uses you as a shield. But when the spoils of war are to be divided, the white man is in front and if any Negro raises only a finger of disapproval of the white man's action, the white man cuts off not only the Negro's finger but his whole hand. The white man has been, and is, pushing you Negroes into the background if he does not need you, so why should you respect the white man when the white man has nothing for you but a bloody whip?[45]

Like Fard and Muhammad, Takis was a man of many names. He was known in St. Louis and Washington as Mimo de Guzman, and in New York, Baltimore, and elsewhere as Ashima Takis. His real name was Policarpio Manansala, and he wasn't Japanese at all, but Filipino. Dishonorably discharged from the U.S. Navy in 1920 for insubordination, he was appointed Takahashi's chief aide in September 1931.[46] Since blacks believed Manansala was a well-educated, high-ranking Japanese soldier, Takahashi suggested that he use a name similar to his own and append a professional title to it in order to elevate his stature among the North's functionally illiterate minority groups. Overnight, the naval reject became "Dr. Ashima Takis." The rapid development of the Harlem branch of the PMEW encouraged Takis to move on to Washington, D.C., to start a second chapter. Within six months, Takis had established groups in St. Louis, Chicago, Detroit, San Francisco, Los Angeles, and Dallas.[47] During a visit to St. Louis, the leader of a pro-Axis group went to hear Takis lecture. Their meeting following the lecture led to a shady business venture that Fard found himself a party to. Gerald B. Winrod, a Kansas City evangelist and the pro-Nazi publisher of a magazine called *The Defender*, and one of his staff writers, Hudson DePriest, began selling Axis propaganda to Takahashi's new movement. Winrod, who later ran unsuccessfully for a U.S. congressional seat from Kansas, sold bulk orders of the *Protocols of the Learned Elders of Zion* to Takahashi, who in turn passed along copies to the NOI and the PMEW.[48]

Unfortunately for the fifty-eight-year-old Takahashi, his health started declining just as the SDOO reached its zenith. Half-blind and suffering from ulcers, he was forced to hand over the reins of leadership to Abdul Muhammad.[49] This move sounded the death knell for the SDOO because Abdul Muhammad, who was five years older than Takahashi, lacked the money and organizational skills to keep the organization stable. In the summer of 1932, the ailing Takahashi again moved into Abdul Muhammad's home to help him in the leadership takeover. The house had been purchased with Takahashi's money, but as he was in the United States illegally, its title was in Abdul Muhammad's name.

Notwithstanding repeated pleas and the American incentives, Takahashi was unable to persuade Abdul Muhammad to renounce his American citizenship. Abdul was steadfast in his allegiance to the teachings of Noble Drew Ali. The only reason he had left the MSTA to begin with was that he opposed the theory among its members that John Givens-el, Drew Ali's former chauffeur, was the reincarnation of Drew Ali. Abdul and Takahashi argued continuously as the group evolved over the next nine months, the main point of disagreement being a suggestion by Takahashi that SDOO members murder white people as a token of their faith in him.[50] Abdul Muhammad dissented vigorously, but Takahashi held firmly to this notion. Exasperated, Abdul ordered Takahashi out of their shared abode and threatened to summon the police if Takahashi ever showed up again at either the house or any of the five SDOO branch offices. Takahashi packed his things and left.

In a matter of months, he re-emerged as head of the Onward Movement of America (OMA), while also playing a pivotal role in the development of the PMEW, whose members accepted his proposal to commit terrorist acts against Caucasians in exchange for cash and special "bonuses" in heaven. Takahashi's plan was strikingly similar to Fard's, which may have been more than coincidental. The Japanese radical was popular with Fard's group, and there were persistent rumors that he was partially bankrolling the NOI.

This suspicion was enhanced when a random attack against whites occurred on November 24, 1932, in Seattle, where Takahashi had a small but fanatical cadre of disciples.[51] The attack took place only four days after the murder of James Smith in Detroit. The Filipino suspect who murdered six whites and wounded fifteen more before being subdued by police was believed to be a member of the PMEW. The FBI took an active interest in the investigation, concluding that the Seattle attack and reports of a similar episode in Detroit involving Fard's followers suggested that the two cults were engaged in a conspiracy, thereby posing a threat to national security. In cooperation with the FBI, the Detroit Police Department conducted a manhunt for Fard and Takahashi. Finding the latter proved quite difficult, as, in spite of his poor health, he traveled so frequently among the various chapters of the PMEW that he eluded a special FBI squad for more than a year. On December 2, 1933, he was arrested during a raid on the PMEW headquarters on Congress Street East in Detroit. Fard was arrested five days later.[52]

After a volatile trial, Takahashi was deported to Japan in February 1934 for entering the United States illegally. Abdul Muhammad in the meantime had contracted tuberculosis and was seriously ill. After he died in 1938, Kallatt was unable to hold the organization together, and the SDOO soon crumbled.[53] As it disintegrated, so did Kallatt. He began drinking heavily, and before long liquor became his master and his religion. "My uncle lost his mind,"[54] Emmanuel said. According to Elijah, Kallatt's troubles were the result of a curse cast upon him for doubting that Master Fard had designated himself as his prophet:

Many of the Chicagoans saw the chastisement upon that brother of mine at that time. Almighty God, Allah, gave him the name, Kallatt Muhammad, and who had pretended that he was with me and turned overnight and became my enemy and a hypocrite of Almighty God, Allah, and the Nation of Islam. That faithful month of June [was] when he fell prostrated by the hand of Almighty God in my own house, at my feet, unable to move his hands and feet, unable to blink his own eyes. There he became like a dead man ready for the grave. . . . This condition often struck him from time to time until death took him away. . . . Every time he was released [from the hospital] he'd go right back trying to oppose me and the truth that Almighty God brought me. [55]

Kallatt's predicament, Muhammad said, was Fard's chastisement for going astray. At least one-third of the NOI's members accepted Muhammad's argument that his brother's fate and the inability of his detractors to harm him, Muhammad, were proof positive that he was divinely protected. Intoxicated by his power, Elijah Muhammad gradually convinced himself that he had emerged from the Book of Malachi, that the countdown to Armageddon had begun, and that one day he would guide the Tribe of Shabazz through parted seas, through valleys of fire, and beyond the Apocalypse.

Devoted to Freedom, Justice and Equality for the so-called Negro. The Earth Belongs to Allah

Muhammad Speaks

Vol. 3—No. 24 — AUGUST 16, 1963 — 15c—OUTSIDE ILLINOIS 20c

Nation Of Islam Offers Hearst

$100,000

Beware of Phony Claims

To Prove Charge

By Elijah Muhammad

I, Elijah Muhammad, Messenger of Allah, told the Los Angeles "Herald-Examiner" Office on Monday, July 29, 1963, that my followers and I will pay the Los Angeles "Herald - Examiner" Newspaper $100,000.00 (one hundred, thousand dollars) to prove the headline charge ("BLACK MUSLIM FOUNDER EXPOSED AS A WHITE") made against us; that we are following one Wallace Dodd with many aliases including the name, Fard; that he is the man that I r m representing to my people as being Master Fard Muhammad (Allah in Person) who appeared among us in Detroit, Michigan, in 1931 and is the same person (Wallace Dodd).

The Los Angeles "Herald-Examiner" also printed his prison history in San Quentin Federal Penitentiary on a charge of peddling dope, and that he admitted he was teaching us.

If he (Dodd) was teaching for money in those panic days in Detroit, he did not get it from us. Mr. Dodd, undoubtedly, must have been teaching the white people if he received any money at all, because we did not have any.

WE DID NOT pay Mr. Fard any money to teach us and there are many who will verify this statement who are yet alive. We could hardly pay the rent of a hall in those days.

Sometimes they (the Be-

Continued on page 3)

The Phony

The Savior

At left is the dug-up convict, Wallace Dodd, alleged by the sensation-seeking and anti-Negro white Hearst newspaper to be founder of the Nation of Islam in North America. At right, however, is the real and rightful Master Farad, of Mecca, who gave all to black people in America before returning to Mecca. The Honorable Elijah Muhammad has not only offered to confront the phony imposter invented by the Hearst press, but has exposed the deceit and has offered to pay $100,000 if they can prove their fraudulent claims. (See Mr. Muhammad's Column)

The Messenger offered $100,000 to anyone who could prove that Wallace D. Fard was an alias of Wallace Dodd Ford. But when Hazel Ford, the former wife of the Nation of Islam's founder, stepped forward with the evidence, the Messenger refused to pay.

Fard borrowed the name "Shabazz" from the famous Lal Shahbaz Qalander mosque *(left)* in Pakistan. Another indication of his Pakistani heritage was the name he gave Elijah Muhammad's brother: Kallatt. Kalat is a small town in what was the ancient Mauryan empire. Fard's father lived among the Maori (an Anglicized spelling of Maury) people of New Zealand. *(Map by Brad Wye. Photo courtesy of MIT/Harvard University Archive)*

The FBI learned in 1943 that the founder of the NOI was a man named Wallace D. Ford of Los Angeles. Ford had an extensive criminal record, and was sent to San Quentin in 1926 for selling narcotics to an undercover agent. Note that his prison identification number is 42314. *(California State Archives)*

Fard was joined in San Quentin by his sidekick, a Chinese American named Edward Donaldson. It was the second offense for Donaldson, who was convicted in San Francisco in June 1921 for possession of narcotics. Note that his prison identification number is 42313. Fard's departure from the NOI coincided with Donaldson's parole.

(California State Archives)

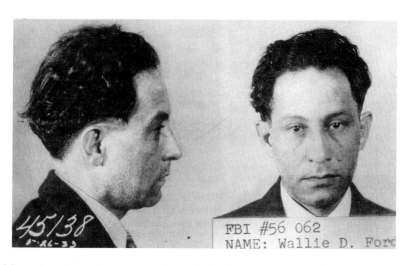

Although Elijah Muhammad denied that Wallace Dodd Ford and Wallace D. Fard were the same person, FBI agents knew otherwise. Note the similarities in the hairline, shape of the lips, protruding ears, arch in the chin, and the mole next to the left nostril in this photo and the Ford photo from San Quentin *(above left)*. Also note that the FBI photo of Ford is dated "5-26-33," which is the date Muhammad admitted was the last time Fard was arrested in Detroit. *(FBI/Detroit Police Department)*

The views of South Carolina senator Benjamin "Pitchfork" Tillman and Georgia bishop Henry McNeal Turner dominated debates on race during Elijah Muhammad's youth. Tillman *(left)* constantly warned the nation of a "race war" in the early 1900s, while Turner *(right)*, who preached that God was black, saw the return of blacks to Africa as a solution to "the Negro problem." *(Tillman: Dictionary of American Portraits, Dover Publications Inc. Reprinted with permission. Turner: Bishop Henry M. Turner Papers, Courtesy of Moorland-Spingarn Research Center, Howard University)*

Noble Drew Ali, founder of the Moorish Science Temple of America, was among the first African-American converts to Islam. Elijah joined the Moors briefly, then joined a new sect called the Nation of Islam, headed by Wallace D. Fard. Like Fard, Drew (*right*) was deeply influenced by Islam as practiced by the Ahmadiyya Movement. *(Courtesy of Moorish Science Temple)*

Satohata Takahashi, a Japanese radical who greatly influenced the Nation of Islam in its formative years, sits handcuffed to a chair after his arrest on June 29, 1939. Kallatt Muhammad, Elijah's brother, was among NOI members who defected to Takahashi's Detroit-based Society for the Development of Our Own. Takahashi was interned along with many other Japanese Americans in April 1942. *(UPI/Corbis Bettmann)*

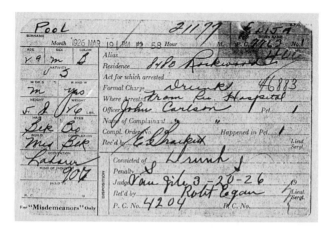

Elijah Muhammad used his given name, Elija Pool, until the early 1930s, as this Detroit Police Department crime report reveals. Pool was convicted following his arrest for public drunkenness in Paradise Valley on March 19, 1926.

Despite denials by Black Muslims, the Nation of Islam was an offshoot of the Moorish Science Temple of America. Elijah Muhammad is shown here wearing a fez nearly identical to those worn by the "Moors" in the lower photo. He proscribed the wearing of the fez in 1935 because it made it too difficult to distinguish one group's members from the other. *(Courtesy of the Library of Congress)*

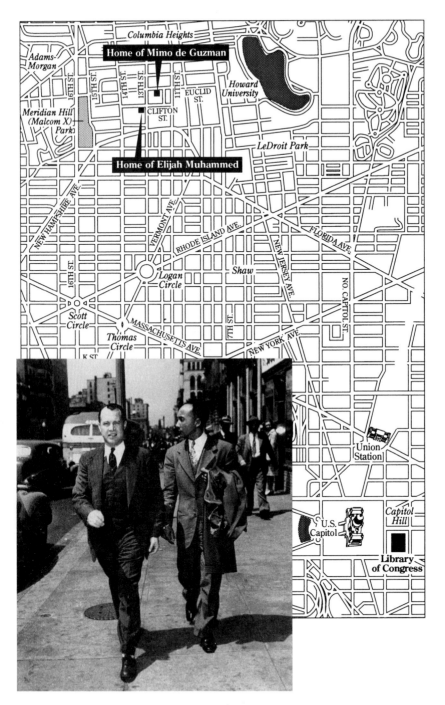

During a 1941 probe of pro-Japanese groups, the FBI discovered that the Messenger and Mimo de Guzman, a functionary of the Black Dragon Society, lived less than a block apart in the Clifton Terrace section of Washington. A year later, the Messenger was arrested and taken into custody. *(Map by Brad Wye. Photo UPI/Corbis Bettmann)*

CHAPTER SIX
ELIJAH THE PROPHET

Then said Elijah unto the people, I, even I only, remain a prophet of the Lord; but Baal's [Satan's] prophets are four hundred and fifty men.

—*I Kings 18:22*

Attack on the United States itself will follow when the Japanese position in the Orient has been consolidated. The same people who fifteen years ago decried and ridiculed prophecies of Japan's present war of aggression against China will doubtless scoff at Japanese conquest of America as an impossibility.

—*Chinese Premier H. H. Kung,*
October 16, 1939[1]

All the talk by Elijah about the last days of the devils and of Japan's impending attack on America was overwhelming for most of his followers. By the end of December 1934, Black Muslims were in an apocalyptic frenzy. Many were ready to go into the streets to expedite the removal of white people from the planet when Muhammad dropped a bomb of his own on December 30. With a single day left in the year, he managed to shake off the spell that Fard had cast on him long enough to see how improbable it was that all Caucasians would vanish within the next twenty-four hours.[2]

In his final lecture of the year, Muhammad injected a new theme into his sermon, a theme that caught Chicago temple members by surprise. "This is the last of the devil," Muhammad told them. "He will have no more power." But in the next breath, he said that "the devil will live awhile physically. Several [of you] have heard that this is the end of the devil and by 1935 there will be no devils on the planet."[3] Alas, he said, it wasn't so.

That was the last thing the congregation wanted to hear. What, in the name of Fard, had the devils done to deserve a reprieve, they wanted to know. Muhammad explained that Fard had given whites a "one-year extension" on life. The extension wasn't granted because Fard believed Caucasians were suddenly salvageable, but merely to give those African Americans still lost in the wilderness of North America a little more time to accept Islam. Despite the regrettable reprieve, Muhammad said, 1935 would be a year that white people would suffer such economic and environmental adversities that they would wish they were dead. Fard "is now withholding the rain from America and Great Britain. He is smiting these two countries with plagues as often as he wills."[4]

As the new year opened, Muhammad remained confident that Fard's prophecy would be fulfilled. "This is the day of Armageddon," he declared at a meeting on January 16, 1935, in Chicago. "There will be no more prosperity here, brothers and sisters. This year will seem like night to day. In the next few days, the bottom will fall out. . . . 1935 is here, so keep your tongue in your mouth if you want to see the hereafter."[5] The assembled knew exactly what Muhammad was referring to: many of their homes had been visited by police in recent weeks because some overanxious members had told their white employers that the white race was as good as dead.

Interpreting such loose talk as a threat, white foremen fired quite a few Black Muslims and occasionally called in police to arrest NOI members to discourage any on-the-job violence. Other NOI members simply quit their jobs, despite being urged by Muhammad to continue working: What was the point in working for a race that would be eliminated any day now?

The days and the weeks marched on toward spring and then summer, but there were no earthshaking changes in Paradise Valley or in the country as a whole. When the floods and plagues and earthquakes that Muhammad predicted failed to materialize, Black Muslims began to lose faith in their leader. Some naturally concluded that it was unlikely that white people would be destroyed in 1935 or 1936 or any other year in the foreseeable future. The anger that this realization provoked against whites became apparent to Muhammad in February 1935. On February 24, as Black Muslims were preparing to mark Fard's birthday, Chicago temple member Rosetta Hassan was riding on a streetcar with her husband, Zack, and their nine-year-old son, Zack Jr., when she became embroiled in an argument with a white female rider. The white woman, a Greek immigrant named Athenasia Christopolous, made an undiplomatic remark about Mrs. Hassan's manner of dress, whereupon the latter adjusted the Greek woman's eyeglasses by punching her in the face. Ms. Christopolous got off the streetcar at the next stop and walked to the nearest police station, where she filed assault charges. A hearing was set for March 6.[6] That day, the normally quiet halls of the Chicago courthouse were abuzz with chatter as Mrs. Hassan entered, for walking closely behind her was a posse of some sixty Black Muslims. They had come to court with her, an NOI spokesman said later to reporters, to guarantee that "justice and freedom and truth" prevailed. The show of support paid off handsomely. The hearing lasted less than half an hour, with the arbitrator ruling that no charges would be filed against Mrs. Hassan.[7]

The Muslims clapped as a bailiff tried to restore order in the courtroom. He instructed the cultists to leave by a door at the rear. But as the group marched proudly toward that exit, another bailiff who was escorting ten black women into the courtroom for another hearing yelled at the Muslims as though they were his disobedient children. "You people turn around and use the other exit!" he shouted, unaware that in the midst of the sixty Muslims was the bailiff who had told them to use the rear rather than the front exit. That's when all hell broke loose.[8]

Women in the non-Muslim party tried to escape by intermingling with the Muslims, which resulted in a scuffle among the two black groups and the two bailiffs. Police standing guard in the courtroom ran to the aid of the bailiffs. In self-defense the Muslims started swinging chairs at the officers. One policeman, a seventy-three-year-old captain, tried to subdue King Shah, the official leader of the Muslim group. Shah pushed him and as he fell to the floor, other Muslims began hitting and kicking him. As the captain lost consciousness, bailiffs and police officers stationed elsewhere in the courthouse finally got to the courtroom and joined the fray. One of them shot King Shah in the right shoulder. Another Muslim, Allah Shah, was shot in the left foot. A bailiff, Phillip Branton, was shot in the chest. Once order was restored, police noticed that the elderly captain was still unconscious, and after checking for a heartbeat and a pulse, they realized that he was dead.[9]

Immediately, 150 policemen and bailiffs took forty-three Muslims into custody. The seventeen Muslim children that were with the group were released. King Shah and Allah Shah were charged with shooting the court bailiff and with the captain's murder. At the pretrial hearing the next morning, however, doctors testified that the captain had died not as a result of the pummeling he had received but rather from the "strain of too much excitement" during to the fracas. It was also determined that none of the Muslims had been carrying knives or guns, and that all of the gunshot wounds were caused by police fire. Fearing another riot if any of the Muslims were retained in custody, Municipal Court Judge Edward Scheffler dismissed all charges against them.[10]

The euphoria among Muslims over their courthouse victory was so all-consuming that Fard's apocalyptic prophecy was forgotten, at least for the moment. As word of the Muslim "miracle" (in the sense that no one paid a price for the officer's death) traveled through black communities in Chicago and other cities where temples were located, blacks sought to join the NOI. Most were eager to get their "original" names and have them entered in Lamb's "Book of Life," the official Muslim registry. Muhammad, who still harbored the hope that Fard would return, advised them that he could not give them their original names; only Fard could do that. Instead, he told them that they would receive an "X" as a surname. The "X" represented their unknown true nature, just as it represented the unknown in algebra. The new recruits were advised to write a "letter of submission" to Islam addressed to W. F. Muhammad, reading as follows:

As Salaam Alaikum: (Freedom–Justice–Equality)
Dear Savior and Deliverer:
   I have been attending the Temple of Islam for the past two or three meetings, and I believe in the teachings. Please give me my Original name. My slave name is ——————.[11]

By August, however, the upward spiral in membership had peaked. Riots in Harlem and Chicago had whetted the Muslims' thirst for the penultimate showdown with Caucasians. Sensing this growing disenchantment, Muhammad announced at a temple meeting on August 16 that he had just received another sign from Fard that the War of Armageddon had entered a new, critical phase.

This sign, he said, was the passage of the Social Security Act, which decreed that all adults would be issued a six-digit identification number from the federal government. This six-digit number, Muhammad contended, was the "mark of the beast" mentioned in the Holy Bible's Book of Revelation. "Roosevelt gave you a Social Security number just to hold you, and now he's getting ready to call in these numbers and give you a stamp," Muhammad warned his congregation in lectures and in *The Final Call* newspaper. "He's going to put a stamp on you, the mark of the beast."[12]

Muhammad was convinced that the numbers were a clear sign that the nightmares visited upon the biblical Daniel and retold in Revelations were coming to pass. He instructed his followers to dispose of all their worldly possessions. "The end of the world is here."[13] He forbade them to read any newspaper other than *The Final Call* or to listen to the radio. The purpose of the prohibition, he said, was to protect them from the devil's tricknology in the final days of white civilization.

Any Muslim caught listening to the radio suffered draconian consequences, including excommunication and even permanent expulsion from the sect. Because of this harshly enforced prohibition, most Muslims didn't know that the prophecy relating Social Security numbers to the Book of Revelation had not come from Fard to Muhammad through the powers of divinity; it had come rather from the radio addresses of Joseph Rutherford of the Jehovah's Witnesses.[14] Muhammad always listened carefully to Rutherford's broadcast sermons. In fact, without Fard as his guide, Muhammad became increasingly dependent upon Rutherford's broadcasts and writings for his own interpretations of scripture and for ways to lure underclass African Americans to his temples. Once the unconverted entered his temples, Muhammad found that he could keep them interested for a few months by relating to them the triumphs of ancient black civilizations, both real and mythical, and by promises of a glorious future once the NOI membership reached a certain figure, which he cited, based on the Holy Bible and Fard's instruction, as 144,000.[15]

An example of this phenomenon occurred in the early months of 1935 when membership began to plunge. The decline was due, of course, to Fard's failure to destroy all white people as he had promised. Without Fard to help him, Muhammad started using fear tactics as a recruitment and retention tool. He claimed that the story in the Holy Bible's Book of Ezekiel was in reality a description of what was happening at that very moment. "Ezekiel's wheel is already hovering over the United States,"[16] he said in what became one of his standard sermons. However, the wheel was visible only to him, by virtue of the "special vision" he had received from Fard:

> The Asiatic Nation has the Ezekiel wheel ready to destroy this devil in six hours time. . . . They are just waiting to hear the name of the Prophet W. D. Fard Muhammad. . . . This plane is a wheel-shaped plane known as the Mother of Planes. It is one-half mile by a half-mile and is the largest mechanical man-made object in the sky. It is a small human planet made for the purpose of destroying the present world of the enemies of Allah.

The plane was built in Japan, he said, on the island of Nippon. According to Muhammad, the flying saucers people had reported seeing were actually "escort planes" from the Mother of Planes. In all, 1,500 escort planes had accompanied the Mothership. "One bomb from this plane will destroy fifty square miles and if it doesn't kill a person—that is, if it only breaks his leg—the poison gas does the rest," he warned his audience.[17]

In late 1935, the Messenger pointed to several more catastrophes as evidence that Armageddon was approaching. Hitler's denunciation of the Versailles Treaty and the construction of concentration camps in Dachau were seen by him as evidence of the end of the international "Jewish conspiracy" that Fard had preached about. The assassination of Senator Huey "Kingfish" Long of Louisiana on September 10 was hailed by him as another sign of the decline of the American empire, as the presidential aspirant (his book, *My First Days in the White House*, had just been published) was seen as a symbol of the moral decay in the national government. The third omen was a hurricane in Florida in September that killed 436 people. Most of the fatalities were passengers on a Florida East Coast Railroad train that was mangled by winds of over 125 miles an hour.

These tactics worked for a while, but were of questionable value in the long run; after a few weeks, new recruits became bored by Muhammad's monologues and his constant cries about the big, bad wolf in white skin. Membership in the NOI continued to plummet. By Christmas, it was clear to all but the desperately devout that no plagues were on the horizon and that the year-long physical death of the white man that Muhammad described was a rather enjoyable life as far as anyone could tell. The American economy, despite Muhammad's dire forecast, was improving steadily under President Roosevelt's New Deal program. Many African Americans, Muslims included, were able to find gainful employment on Detroit's auto assembly lines and under programs created by the government under the National Recovery Act (NRA). Muslims were doing so well, in fact, that a sociologist who conducted the first formal study of the NOI reported that there wasn't "a single case of unemployment" among Muhammad's followers, and that most Muslims enjoyed a fairly fortunate lifestyle.[18]

One of the axioms of political science is that few people favor a change in a system of government when its economic policies are working to their advantage. The Muslims were no exception. Some members of the NOI who had joined as early as 1931 stopped attending Muhammad's thrice weekly sermons; it was simply too depressing to listen to his "the sky is falling" sermon over and over again, especially so soon after the worst years of the Great Depression.

When the War of Armageddon failed to materialize and the Mothership failed to land, there was a growing feeling among the NOI membership that Muhammad was a fraud. How could a real prophet have made such a colossal miscalculation, they wondered. The faithful, who had had few worldly possessions to begin with, now, since obeying Muhammad's injunction to dispose of them, had nothing, nothing at all—no chairs for sitting or tables for eating. Some were homeless, having given up their apartments. If the message was wrong, perhaps the Messenger was a false prophet. "The enemies, hypocrites, united to drive me out," Muhammad recollected.[19] Narrowly escaping several attempts on his life, he bid farewell to his wife and children, as he had done when coming to the Promised Land, and headed for Washington, D.C. He found a room for rent in a row house owned by Benjamin and Clara Mitchell.[20]

"Call me Evans . . . Mr. Evans," Muhammad said when he introduced himself to the couple. (Evans, as may be recalled, was his wife's maiden name.) The house was near Howard University, a repository of some of oldest and rarest books on Africans of the diaspora. Accepting him at his word, the Mitchell's extended a hearty welcome to the newcomer at 1602 13th Street Northwest (the city's streets all carry a directional quadrant), which was in a well-maintained black neighborhood within walking distance of the Library of Congress, where Muhammad planned to study the books on the list Fard gave him. He quickly befriended his landlords, who allowed him to use their home as a makeshift temple. After converting the Mitchells and about thirty other Washingtonians to Islam, Muhammad began holding meetings in a storefront building on U Street, the center of black economic power in the nation's capital.[21]

Despite his moderate success in Washington, NOI national membership had fallen from 20,000 to fewer than 5,000. In a desperate measure to beef up the membership rolls and increase the revenues for his dwindling sect, Muhammad reinstated some of the ritualistic practices Fard had introduced in the cult when he was under Takahashi's influence, including human sacrifice. In January 1937, Muhammad decreed that it was the moral obligation of every Muslim head of household to convert his entire family. The demand was not to be taken lightly, either. Any man who failed to convert his family within one year of joining the NOI was threatened with expulsion. For most Muslims, the isolation associated with expulsion was the equivalent of a death sentence.[22]

Verlen McQueen (renamed Verlen Ali by Fard in 1933), a member in Detroit, had been unable to convince his wife and daughter to join the cult. Although he had been a member since 1932, he had never been under any pressure to convert his family until Muhammad's mandate was handed down. McQueen's brother, Tata Pasha (his slave name was Todd McQueen), was an assistant minister at a satellite temple in Detroit. On January 16, 1937, Pasha, who had converted his own family, ordered McQueen to either convert his wife and daughter or sacrifice them in the name of Allah.[23]

McQueen pleaded with his wife, Rebecca, and their eleven-year-old daughter, Dorothy, to join the cult. But his wife refused, citing McQueen's promise to her that if she came back to him—they had been separated for seven years—she would not be forced to join. McQueen knew that his wife's recalcitrance would cost him his membership in the NOI. His salvation was suddenly slipping away, his entire lifestyle threatened. On January 18, he invited twelve witnesses to his home. Pending their arrival, he prepared a ten-gallon pot of boiling water to be used as "holy water" during a noon ceremony in which he planned to murder his wife and daughter.[24]

McQueen refused to tell his wife why he was boiling the water, but she had only days earlier overheard Pasha tell him that he would sacrifice his own family if that was what it took to ensure his standing in the NOI. Fearing for her life, Rebecca McQueen called the police while her husband was in the kitchen. When they arrived and questioned Verlen, he admitted that he had planned to kill his family. When asked why, he replied that his family had to die because "they were unholy." He was arrested on charges of attempted murder. Rebecca and Dorothy McQueen were put in a "safe house" pending McQueen's trial to protect them from being harmed by other members of the cult.[25]

Newspaper headlines about the McQueen case caused many Muslims to rethink their commitment to the NOI. The overriding fear was that Muhammad would order other non-Muslim family members put to death. Rather than risk facing such a dreadful dilemma, over five hundred families quit the Detroit and Chicago temples within weeks of the McQueen incident.

The return to the idea of sacrificial slayings rekindled memories of the macabre murder of James Smith in 1932. NOI faithful wondered why Muhammad had suddenly reinstated the archaic rituals, when the practice had resulted in widespread discrimination against Muslims and had led to an economic deprivation so severe that it had nearly destroyed the sect. The riddle was sufficiently solved when they discovered that Takahashi had returned to Detroit just weeks before Muhammad issued the membership mandate. He had sneaked back into Paradise Valley, where he had been seen with his common-law wife. His return to Detroit could not have come at a more propitious time, for all four of the black organizations that he had helped either establish or finance were disintegrating.[26]

The setbacks Muhammad suffered after the McQueen affair left him scrambling for a way to hold on to his cult. He was receiving so many death threats that he spent most of his time shuttling back and forth between Chicago and Washington. In Chicago, he used several aliases, among them Ghulam Bogans (Bogans was the surname of his brother-in-law, Aaron).[27] In Washington, he used another set of aliases, including Charles Evans, Mohammed Rassoull, and the Prophet, as well as Ghulam Bogans. Although he had established a small temple in Washington and held on to a small following in Chicago, neither provided him with enough money to feed his own family, let alone to help less fortunate members of the NOI. In 1938, he suffered the indignity of having to apply for welfare assistance, and gave his name as Ghulam Bogans. As the Social Security system was still in its infancy, welfare workers had little reason to doubt him, and even fewer means of verifying his identity.[28]

Although Takahashi was personally responsible for some of Muhammad's woes, he provided support that caused Muhammad to quickly forget his grievances. Besides, Muhammad knew that he would have lost followers even without the controversy surrounding the sacrificial slaying episode. He had simply been unable to come up with anything to replace Fard. In an attempt to reinvigorate and usurp the leadership of the NOI, Takahashi began circulating flyers around Paradise Valley that echoed Fard's prophecies regarding the War of Armageddon.

"Japan's new policy," he wrote in one flyer, "is to establish a new epoch in world history by leading the darker majority of mankind to a new life founded on international justice."[29] He promised Muhammad's followers that in exchange for the NOI's support of the Japanese war effort, Japan would build a single-family detached home in Hawaii and provide lifelong employment for every family as soon as America was defeated. Like the NOI, the SDOO had also fallen on hard times. A third black organization, based in New York and headed by Sufi Abdul Hamid, competed with Muhammad and Takahashi for members in Harlem. The *New York Times* and other mainstream media had labeled the politically astute Hamid "Harlem's Hitler"[30] because of his economic boycotts of white and Jewish merchants who refused to hire blacks. From a small band of followers who joined his organization in

1935 after a Harlem riot that he was accused of instigating, his group had grown so large that by 1937 it was second only to Father Divine's Peace Movement in membership.[31]

Three months before he was killed when his J-5 Cessna crashed near a Long Island highway, Hamid relocated his cult, the Buddhist Universal Holy Temple of Tranquillity, Inc., into a spacious office building that he had bought for cash. But even before his death on July 31, 1938, his appeal to blacks had been ebbing. He had surrounded himself with a group of white advisers, notably Fred Burkhardt and Kay Price, the latter serving as his personal secretary, with whom he was rumored to be having an affair. In the days following his death, his organization started to fall apart amid media speculation that the source of his wealth was payoffs from Harlem merchants for calling off picketing against their establishments.[32] Hamid had been the last obstacle that Takahashi had to overcome in his effort to garner the support of Harlem's black nationalists.

The other roadblock in Harlem, Father Divine, was eliminated in April 1937, when Divine's estranged wife, a Caucasian known as Faithful Mary, called a press conference in which she labeled Divine a confidence man.[33] She told reporters that she planned to write a book in support of her claim that Divine's movement had been a fraud from its inception. She said that Divine had never really been concerned about helping the poor, and that he was only using them to enrich himself. Recently, she said, he had tried to coax her into turning over the deeds to the sect's hundreds of acres of land in Ulster County called the "Promisedland." Divine wanted her to promise the land to him exclusively, she said, leading to a violent argument and her decision to break away from his movement.[34]

Even more serious allegations followed closely on the heels of the dissolution of Divine's marriage. One of his senior assistants, John the Revelator, had been indicted in Los Angeles for Mann Act violations. According to the indictment, he had forced a juvenile member of the sect into becoming his concubine and into prostitution by telling her that she was the reincarnation of Mary, Mother of Jesus, and that she would give birth to a messiah. At the same time, Divine was facing prosecution on criminal charges that he knowingly used coal that had been stolen from a supplier in Pennsylvania to drive the furnaces in some of his buildings.[35]

Finally, an elderly woman by the name of Jessie Birdsall had filed a civil complaint in New York against Divine in which she alleged that he had bilked her out of her life savings of $2,000 by promising to provide her with "social security" payments for the rest of her life. When she confronted him after the first payment failed to arrive as promised, he told her that she had misunderstood him and that her $2,000 was gone, but that he would make good on his promise to care for her.[36] But this time she didn't buy his line.

On April 20, 1937, a process server attempted to serve a summons on Birdsall's lawsuit while Divine was delivering a sermon to a crowd of 2,500 at his Harlem Heaven church. When several ushers were unable to prevent the server from approaching the pulpit, one of them pulled a knife and stabbed the man while Divine watched from the pulpit. Divine escaped through a rear exit, but police found him the next day after receiving a tip that he was hiding out in Milford, Connecticut. According to press accounts, Divine first tried to "invisibilize" himself by hiding behind a furnace in the basement of the Milford house.

At a court hearing after his arrest, Divine told the judge that he had never professed to be God or any supernatural being. His public confession proved too embarrassing even for his most devout followers. The movement survived, though membership—particularly among black males and whites—decreased significantly.[37]

The way was thus open for the rise of the PME, the Pan-African organization founded in 1935 in New York by a group of West Indians who were former high-ranking officials in Marcus Garvey's UNIA. The two chief leaders of the PME were Leonard Robert Jordan, a former officer in the Japanese navy, and the Reverend William Gordon (Miltie Gordon's former spouse), former assistant president general of the UNIA. In reality, the group was an unwitting front for the Black Dragon Society (BDS); most of its operating expenses came directly from the Japanese consul generals in San Francisco and in New York, with Ashima Takis acting as intermediary.[38] While Jordan and Gordon were well aware of the BDS's role in bankrolling the PME, they were initially given the impression that they could set their own agenda. However, by late 1938, with Takahashi out of jail, they realized that that was not the case. Takahashi was soon running the organization.

Like the pro-Japanese sermons that Elijah Muhammad was delivering in the Midwest, speeches by the leaders of the PME were bitterly anti-American and seemed to focus more on the plight of Japan than on the international oppression of nonwhites. The speeches that Muhammad and Jordan delivered all had the same central theme: As soon as Japan defeated America, it would help all people of color achieve full independence and prosperity. "I'm going to have President Roosevelt picking cotton after Japan crushes this government," Jordan promised in one speech, "and Secretaries [Frank] Knox and [Henry] Stimson riding me around in rickshaws."[39] In another lecture, one which would help the FBI send him to jail, Jordan declared:

> No one should be afraid to join this movement. We are protected by big people. This is an international setup. Our present main office is in Hawaii. We are connected with the Black Dragon organization in Japan.[40]

With the support of many of America's most committed black nationalists, Takahashi was well on his way to creating a national underground network of revolutionaries to assist Japan's war effort against America, but his personal relationships proved to be his undoing. When she moved in with him, Cheaber McIntyre was still legally married to Nathaniel McIntyre, a black Detroit auto worker and father of her four children.[41] At first McIntyre ignored his wife's politics and philandering, but after she moved in with Takahashi he began seething with resentment. In the course of filing for divorce in March 1939, he contacted the Detroit police to see if they knew about the Japanese radical who was conducting subversive activities in Paradise Valley.[42] Detroit police responded in the negative, but notified the FBI's Detroit field office.

In April, Pearl Sherrod, the black woman Takahashi jilted in favor of Cheaber McIntyre, also sought revenge. She contacted the Detroit field office and told FBI agents that her former paramour was hiding in Paradise.[43] To solidify their case against Takahashi, the FBI collected data on every black organization he was rumored to be linked with. To the complete astonishment of the Detroit police, Takahashi had been operating out of a luxuriously decorated home on Canfield Avenue, within blocks of the Canfield police station. They also discovered that he had five branches of the cult in Detroit alone, with at least 3,000 card-carrying members. On June 27, 1939, immigration officials, assisted by Detroit police, raided a branch of the OMA on Washburn Avenue and arrested Takahashi for immigration violations.[44]

On the way to the courthouse for booking, Takahashi offered immigration inspectors Edward Carpenter and Roy Stevens $1,500 in cash if they would allow him to escape. They declined the offer. "I'll give you $2,000," Takahashi said, raising the ante. They declined again.[45] When they took him before U.S. Immigration Commissioner J. Stanley Hurd that afternoon, the inspectors advised Hurd of the attempted bribe. The commissioner set Takahashi's bond at $2,500 on the illegal entry charges, and instructed Detroit police to bring criminal charges against him for attempted bribery of a federal officer. At the conclusion of the trial on bribery charges on September 28, it took the jury three minutes to find Takahashi guilty. The next morning, he was fined $4,500 and sentenced to three years in the federal penitentiary at Leavenworth, Kansas.[46]

Cheaber McIntyre sat quietly through the trial, but on the morning the sentence was announced, she sobbed uncontrollably. She was sitting with another black woman in the front row near the jury. As Takahashi was led away in handcuffs, a juror overheard one of the women say that "they were going to get the judge."[47] After the court was adjourned, the juror informed the bailiff, who told Judge Frank A. Picard. Picard asked the prosecutor to notify the FBI of the threat immediately.

A few weeks after Takahashi's conviction, Hoover berated Americans such as McIntyre, whom he accused of aiding America's enemies.

> It is known that many foreign agents roam at will in a nation which loves peace and hates war, a country which has proclaimed neutrality in a strife-torn world. . . . There are even native-born American citi-

zens as well as aliens who have sold their birthright for less than the proverbial "mess of porridge."[48]

While investigating the threat against Judge Picard, the FBI's Detroit field office uncovered information suggesting that Takahashi was the mastermind behind a national network of anti-American activities. In early 1940, the Detroit special agent in charge (SAC) recommended that sedition charges be lodged against Takahashi.[49] After conferring with U.S. Assistant Attorney General Wendell Berge, who indicated that no grounds existed for further prosecution, Hoover sent a letter dated April 6 to the Detroit SAC ordering him to close the investigation.[50]

Even before Takahashi's arrest, the FBI and military intelligence units had been investigating and attempting to inhibit anti-American activities by Japanese espionage agents in black communities. To this end, Hoover joined other top government officials who were pushing for passage of the Alien Registration Act, and on June 28, 1940, Congress adopted the legislation Hoover had been clamoring for. The Alien Registration Act (also known as the Smith Act) made it a federal offense to advocate "the overthrow by force and violence" of the U.S. government.[51] The first peacetime national sedition law since the Sedition Act of 1798, the Smith Act in the first instance curtailed the right of free speech of the Communist Party, the Socialist Workers Party, and other progressive political parties, and denied free-assembly rights to those who believed that the country was on the road to war, as well as to those who felt that a social revolution was needed in America. In late September, the first anniversary of Takahashi's bribery conviction, the FBI recorded the first of nearly 100,000 pages of war-related documents on the NOI.[52] Hoover also added two new names to more than 6,000 on the Bureau's "custodial detention list," a list of Americans who were considered dangerous enough to pose a threat to national security in case of war. One of the names was a "John Doe," whom the Bureau's Washington field office had under close surveillance. The other was Elijah Muhammad, who was under close scrutiny by the Chicago Field Office.[53]

On September 20, 1940, an intelligence report noted that "a Japanese in Washington, D.C., has been going around addressing a group of colored people in homes and at other places. . . . In these addresses his major promise is that if the colored people will help the Japanese out, the Japanese will take care of the colored people."[54] The possible presence of Japanese espionage agents at the FBI's front door evoked a strongly worded order from the director. On October 16, Hoover sent a memo to the Washington SAC in which he emphasized the importance of the alien's apprehension:

> He is reported to have told listeners that the Japanese were building thousands of nice homes on islands near the United States for the colored people to pay them for their assistance. . . . You are instructed to conduct the necessary investigation to determine the identity of this individual to see if he is violating the [Alien] Registration Act.[55]

Around the same time that the October 16 memo was being written, Congress passed the Selective Training and Service Act, which required all men between twenty-one and thirty-six years of age to register for the draft; an amendment expanded the upper draft age to forty-four. The next day, Congress passed the Registration of Certain Organizations Act, more commonly called the Voorhis Act, which required all foreign-controlled organizations and groups espousing a violent social revolution in America to register with the Justice Department. Although it had agreed—on paper—to close its investigation of Takahashi, the Detroit office kept an eye on the SDOO and the OMA. On December 23, 1940, the Detroit office asked Hoover for permission to reopen its investigation of the groups, noting that "Information received from the Chicago office indicates that [Takahashi] is a direct representative of a powerful Japanese organization whose aim is to overthrow the White Race."[56]

On March 3, 1941, Hoover forwarded the reports of Japanese espionage activities to Berge. Once again, Berge found no grounds on which to base a federal prosecution. On March 7, Hoover told the Chicago and Detroit SACs of Berge's decision. But one month later, he took a verbal swipe at Berge:

It is highly important that the Federal Bureau of Investigation be unhampered in its authority to conduct investigations into situations involving potential danger to the government of the United States, particularly as it relates to the obvious menace and danger to the internal security of this Nation by foreign agents such as Takahashi.[57]

In July the War Department issued a general memo advising all divisions of the intelligence community that Japan appeared to be involved in a nationwide campaign to "use" African Americans as part of its plan to take over the United States. The Japanese agent spotted in Washington was but one of many who made up the Fifth Column. On December 4, the ONI's Counter Subversion Section issued a report of its own about Japanese sympathizers among Americans. The twenty-six-page report noted that African Americans were particularly susceptible to Japanese overtures and propaganda. Hoover's arguments for more investigatory authority and the ONI's report went unnoted by the legislative and executive branches—for seventy-two hours.[58]

On December 7, 1941, which happened to be the eighth anniversary of Fard's last arrest in Detroit, the unthinkable happened. The War of Armageddon that Elijah Muhammad had believed in since Bible school, the race war that he had feared as a young man in Macon, and the cataclysmic destructive power of the Mother Plane that Fard had preached about in his final sermon moved nightmarishly close to reality: the Japanese—"Allah's Asiatic army"—bombed Pearl Harbor, the U.S. naval base in Hawaii. The attack—which occurred, incidentally, in the Year of the Snake (the biblical representative of Satan) on the Asian calendar[59]—was the first aggressive act by a foreign power on American soil since the American Revolution, and took the lives of 2,345 men in a matter of hours.[60] In an impassioned national address, President Roosevelt decried the surprise attack calling December 7, 1941, "a day that will live in infamy."

Congress declared war on Japan the following morning. The media and the military brass faulted Hoover for failing to pick up warning signs days before the attack, and Hoover, in turn, castigated the armed forces for the same reason. Both the FBI and the military had erred, so both redoubled their efforts to prevent another catastrophe. At the time that Pearl Harbor was struck, the United States was nowhere near being prepared for a global conflict, let alone a war on two fronts, as Germany and Italy declared war on America on December 11. In the fall of 1941 the War Department had reported that "it did not have more than two (of thirty-six) divisions trained and equipped to take part, if needed, in an overseas landing against opposition."[61]

For its part, the FBI immediately launched a probe of Takahashi and his contacts in America. Hoover also requested an update on Takahashi's legal status. He was advised that Takahashi was incarcerated in the Federal Medical Center in Springfield, Missouri (under the alias of Naka Nakane), but was scheduled to be released in January 1942.[62] On December 23, 1941, the attorney general ordered him detained under a presidential proclamation for the duration of the war. The proclamation was initially used against radicals, but its scope broadened rapidly as the Japanese victories escalated. President Roosevelt signed Executive Order 9066 on February 19, 1942, designating the West Coast a military area. More than 100,000 Japanese Americans were ordered from their homes and herded into internment camps. Takahashi, who was nearly blind and suffering from stomach ulcers, was removed from the hospital and placed in an internment camp by the order of U.S. Assistant Attorney General Frances Booth on April 2. Three weeks later, General John L. DeWitt posted public notices ordering all "persons of Japanese ancestry" living in Seattle to report to internment camps by May 1. Similar orders were issued to Japanese Americans elsewhere on the West Coast.[63]

After most Japanese Americans were corralled on these makeshift reservations, the intelligence agencies started discussing the possibility of arresting African-American radicals who supported Japan, and even broached the idea of placing them in internment camps as well.[64] On April 21, Berge finally gave Hoover the go-ahead for a witchhunt aimed at the NOI. Berge wrote regarding the possible prosecution of Muhammad and David Jones:

It is the view of the Criminal Division that these subjects have violated Section 11 of the Selective Service Act in that they have counseled evasion, and there appears to be no reason why these subjects should not be apprehended based on the warrants presently outstanding against them. The United States Attorney for the District of Columbia is authorized to proceed with the prosecution of these subjects under said Section 11.[65]

CHAPTER SEVEN

MOLES IN THE MOSQUE

Thus it comes about that all armed prophets have conquered and unarmed ones failed. . . . .

—*Machiavelli,*
The Prince[1]

May it be possible that foreign hire
Could out of thee extract one spark of evil
That might annoy my finger? 'Tis so strange
That, though the truth of it stands off as gross
As black and white, my eye will scarcely see it.
—*William Shakespeare,*
Henry V[2]

While America trembled in fear of another Japanese attack, the NOI celebrated the bombing of Pearl Harbor as the beginning of the hellfire. Many Muslims wondered how soon the ships would come to take them to their promised new homes in Hawaii, and when they would get their first glimpse of the Mother Plane. Others wrote letters urging their families to join the NOI before it was too late. On December 9, two days after the attack, Milwaukee minister Sultan Muhammad wrote an effusive letter to the Messenger:

> The end of the enemy truly has come, and at this time they should able to see it. All Praise is due to Allah; it [Armageddon] truly has come, my Loving and most Faithful Apostle. Oh, how happy am I to see what I am seeing! If I only could speak like I desire to speak.[3]

In a follow-up letter on December 16, Sultan, who was the Messenger's cousin, beamed proudly as black Milwaukeeans were suddenly beating down the door to join the NOI.[4] His weekly report of February 3 was equally euphoric:

> Old Satan is really silent in his Hell. They are just as quiet and never have anything to say concerning his war in our presence on the train or in the gasoline stations. All Praise is due Allah alone, the Great God of the Universe. What is the matter with the Devils? Why are they carrying such long faces? Ha! Ha! They have discovered their ends and what they have carried into practice. Blessed be the name of Allah, Who promised through His prophets that He would overtake the Devil and his host![5]

The NOI was clearly confident of a Japanese victory, but no one felt as assured of the war's outcome as Japan. Sensing its ultimate triumph, the Japanese government printed currency it planned to use in Hawaii, the Philippines, and other Pacific islands once its flag was raised in those places. Germany was also certain that Japan would crush America; after all, Tojo had Mussolini and Hitler on his side. "Exceptionally happy news came during the night about a great naval victory of the Japanese in a battle in the Coral Sea which still continues," Third Reich propagandist Joseph Goebbels wrote in his diary on May 8, 1942. "That, of course, means that the Anglo-Saxon East Asiatic fleet sustained an irreparable loss."[6]

At Temple No. 4 in Washington, D.C., Muhammad and his followers reveled in newspaper accounts of Japan's exploits, though not for long. As the war entered its sixth month, the FBI's intelligence reports forced Hoover to take a closer look at the NOI, as they indicated that the Muslims and other black nationalist organizations were receiving carbine rifles and sophisticated military weaponry from Japanese espionage agents. These weapons, several field offices reported, were stockpiled in black ghettos in nearly every major American city.[7] On the afternoon of May 8, two FBI agents went to the rooming house at 1306 Girard Street Northwest, where Muhammad had moved most of his belongings. The home belonged to one of his followers, a Mrs. Williams. Muhammad, sensing that he would soon be apprehended, traveled and changed residences frequently to avoid arrest.[8] One week he'd visit the temple in Philadelphia, then spend the next week in Chicago or Detroit. He was using so many aliases that it's a wonder that even he was able to keep track of them all. The Mitchells called him Mr. Evans and Mohammed Rassoull, while Mrs. Williams at the Girard Street address was told to call him Ghulam Bogans.

Despite his aliases and fancy footwork to dodge the draft, the FBI picked up his trail. On May 8, agent Frank J. Holmes knocked on Mrs. Williams's door. Holmes knew Muhammad was there because one of the FBI's moles in the local mosque had seen him go in but hadn't seen him leave, and his car had been parked out front for several days. When Mrs. Williams answered the door, Holmes asked whether Bogans was inside. Mrs. Williams said that indeed he was, but asked Holmes the nature of his visit. Holmes identified himself as an FBI agent, and said he had come to see Bogans, who he said also used the aforementioned aliases. Williams nervously summoned Muhammad, who came down the stairs wearing a pinstriped suit and freshly shined duckbill shoes. When Holmes asked to see his draft registration card, Muhammad informed him that he did not have one.[9]

"Did you register on February 16 at Local Board Eleven?" Holmes asked.

"No," Muhammad replied, nor had he any intention of doing so, he added. "Then you're under arrest," Holmes said. Muhammad knew how this hand was going to be played. Though it was a warm, sunny day, he carried his overcoat, for he expected his stay in jail to be a long one. Passersby stared as Holmes led him down the busy street. One could hardly blame them for staring, as it was rare to see a well-dressed black man walking down U Street—the center of a black community— with a white man. Those who stared long enough saw what press photographers captured for posterity. Holmes's left arm and Muhammad's right moved in unison because they were connected at the wrist by handcuffs. Muhammad turned his head away, but the cameras kept clicking as the photographers in front of him walked backwards. Each time he looked forward for a moment to see where he was walking, shutterbugs snapped feverishly.

That evening, the paparazzi devoted their attention to Paul Robeson, a true Renaissance man, who was in Washington to give a concert. The son of a fugitive slave, Robeson was a Phi Beta Kappa graduate from Rutgers University and the first black All-American football player (he played professional football before graduating from the prestigious Columbia Law School). He also was a gifted actor and a superb baritone. As Muhammad was being taken to the D.C. jail, Robeson was across town in a studio rehearsing *Elijah,* the oratorio composed in 1846 by Felix Mendelssohn.[10]

Shortly after ten o'clock that same evening, FBI official D. Milton Ladd dictated a memo addressed to Assistant Director Edward A. Tamm regarding Muhammad and the mysterious Japanese agent mentioned in the intelligence report of September 20, 1940:

SAC McKee of the Washington field office telephonically advised that they had picked up Mohammed Rassoull on a warrant. . . . As a matter of interest in connection with this matter, Mr. McKee advised that Rassoull had in his possession a newspaper clipping, which was yellow from aging, relative to the Japanese Takahashi (phonetic). Mr. McKee further advised that Rassoull had been living in Chicago, [and] that although he is a Georgia negroe [sic], he looks like a Japanese, having slant eyes.[11]

Days after this embarrassing admission, the FBI updated its records to reflect that the so-called Japanese agent its Washington field office had been trying to identify for two years without apparent success was none other than Elijah Muhammad.

Muhammad's bail was set at $5,000, but he had less than one-tenth of that at his disposal.[12] Clara learned of his arrest from radio reports at her home in Chicago, where she started a fund-raising drive for bail money. Meanwhile, the prophet of the NOI sat in a musty cell at the D.C. jail. On May 14, Minister Sultan Muhammad arrived at the jail with Minister Willie Muhammad Jr. of Detroit to see what they could do about securing the Messenger's release. A prison official quickly but quietly notified the FBI's Washington field office of their presence. Agents arrived at the jail within minutes to interview the two men, who admitted that they were of draft age but had not registered for the draft. When asked if they preferred to do so immediately, they replied in the negative. The agents consulted with Assistant U.S. Attorney John Conliff in Washington, who called prosecutors in Milwaukee and Detroit.[13] Sultan and Willie Jr. were detained overnight in the D.C. jail. The next morning, formal complaints were lodged against them in their respective hometowns, and they were extradited the next day. With their arrest, there were only a few prominent ministers still free, and on May 19, one of the others lost his freedom, too. David X Jones, the regular minister of the Washington temple, was arrested at his 9th Street home on draft evasion charges. He was placed in a cell near Muhammad's in the D.C. jail. When U.S. Commissioner Needham C. Turnage asked him why he had failed to register for the draft, he replied, typically, that he had "already registered with the Nation of Islam."[14]

"When there is a conflict between the law of Allah and any other law," explained Jones, who acted as his own legal counsel, "the law of Allah will be followed by the Nation of Islam."[15] The defendant's speech clearly angered the commissioner, who ended up sounding like a prosecutor. "Real Muslims have been fighting for hundreds of years, Mr. Jones," Turnage said sardonically.[16] With that, he ordered the marshals to take Jones back to his cell. On June 4, over thirty Muslims (more than half of them women and young children) from the Washington temple marched to the jail to protest the Messenger's incarceration. They demanded to be jailed with their leader, a spokesman said, because they were equally guilty of failing to register for the draft.[17] A few local newspapers noted their protest with a paragraph here and a photograph there, but their efforts proved futile. After fourteen grueling hours of standing and squatting on the jail's cement steps, the last of the demonstrators went home. Muhammad, David, and others who had been apprehended remained in the jail for several more weeks.[18]

Two days before the demonstration, a senior FBI official wrote in a memo to Hoover that there was a direct link between Takahashi's groups, the NOI, and the MSTA. Under the title "Development of Our Own, aka the Onward Movement of America," Assistant FBI Director Percy E. Foxworth wrote:

> When this cult [SDOO] was founded, it was directed toward the extermination of the White Race and this motto still stands, as during meetings and services a large sign is always displayed bearing the inscription, "The Paleface has to go."

Among at least five nationally prominent leaders who reported to Takahashi, Foxworth stated, were Walter Davis-el of the MSTA and Elijah Muhammad.[19] A follow-up memorandum added Emmanuel Pharr of Detroit as the leader of the OMA in Takahashi's absence and also listed Kallatt Muhammad as a high-profile member of the movement. Kallatt "said that he has had no connection with the organization recently, but it was informant's opinion that he is still connected to the group."[20] The informant also said that Kallatt was employed at the Wheel Mill of the Carnegie Illinois Steel Corporation in Gary, Indiana, as were many OMA members.

It took nearly three months, but Clara finally secured enough cash to bail her husband out of jail. She waited for an hour on July 23 while a clerk counted the $5,000 she had brought along, much of it in small bills.[21] Several hours later, Muhammad was taken before a U.S. District Court magistrate. Instead of the expensive hand-tailored suit he was wearing when arrested, he was dressed in a long white robe and a white turban, apparel that Clara had brought to the jail along with the money. She was similarly attired. The Messenger was freed and greeted by cheering supporters as he and his wife left the modern-day dungeon.[22]

Before Muhammad was released, Hoover approved a counterintelligence plan by which professional makeup artists were hired to apply cosmetics and even shoe polish to the skin of white FBI agents (at that time the agents were all white) so that they would appear to be black. After they were made up, these agents were assigned to various NOI temples to determine whether the speakers were violating the Smith Act. While they discovered that it was possible to fool a few attendees in the darkness outside the temple, the agents complained about looking wholly unconvincing as black men once the sun rose or if they encountered blacks in well-lit areas. Their problem was summarized in a memo dated August 21, 1942, from FBI official Alex Rosen to Tamm:

> While talking with SAC Johnson of Chicago regarding an investigation presently being conducted on the above group, he mentioned a matter which I thought might prove of interest. Johnson stated that this particular meeting was in a colored district and it was extremely hard for the agents to operate without being detected. He said, however, that when the meetings have been held, arrangements have been made to have the agents made up by professional make-up artists so that by wearing dark glasses, the agents could mingle unnoticed in a group of colored people. He advised, however, that under strong sunlight this make-up does not prove to be so effective.[23]

Contrary to Tamm's belief and some of the agents' own illusions, few were ever deceived for long by the Al Jolson routine. On September 4, for instance, four agents in blackface arrived at the Washington temple for the Friday night service. According to Dorothy X, who headed the temple in David Jones's absence, the agents were stopped at the door and asked why they were there. After giving her a song and dance about how much they were "interested in the teachings," the agents were told to get lost. The next day, the incredulous secretary mailed a letter to the Messenger to tell him how "four devils attempted to get into the temple."[24]

Out of exasperation or embarrassment, or both, Hoover asked the chiefs of the New York Police Department, the Metropolitan Police Department of Washington, and the Chicago Police Department, among others, to release black police officers for temporary assignment with the FBI for counterintelligence work. Among the officers placed on loan were Raymond Weaver of the Metropolitan Police and several officers from the New York City force.[25] The wisdom of having African Americans as agents—a move Hoover opposed because he regarded blacks as intellectually deficient—became readily apparent in the first weeks of Weaver's assignment. Weaver alerted the Bureau to the connection between the NOI and Ashima Takis (Mimo De Guzman), who fled Washington only days after Muhammad's arrest on May 8. Takis was arrested in Harlem on July 27, then extradited to Washington to face draft evasion and sedition charges.[26] Upon being questioned, prior to being bound over for trial, Takis admitted that he had founded the St. Louis chapter of the SDOO, and had done so upon the orders of Takahashi.

Muhammad was indicted two weeks later on several counts, the first charging him with violating the Selective Service and Training Act of 1940. His arraignment, along with those of eighty-one other Muslims, was set for August 25. Most of those expected at the arraignment that day were present, but not the Messenger. After Clara had posted bail on July 23, he had fled to Chicago. The court declared him a fugitive, and notices were circulated that the Messenger was wanted by the FBI.[27]

On September 1, a complaint was lodged and a warrant issued against Elijah Muhammad and his top aides, charging them with violation of the draft registration laws. The government had planned to indict Nannye Beverly, the third most powerful woman in the NOI (after Clara Muhammad and Pauline Hatchett Bahar), but she fell ill before the grand jury heard the full case against her. She died of tuberculosis at Gallinger Hospital in Washington a month before the second warrants were issued.[28] A grand jury sitting in Chicago handed up yet another indictment against Muhammad on September 15. Five days later, FBI agents found the fugitive from Washington hiding in a carpet under his mother's bed.

On September 21, Albert Johnson, the FBI's Chicago SAC, called a press conference to confirm media reports of a nationwide raid on black nationalists and pro-Japanese organizations. Johnson, who said that the Bureau had evidence that the NOI, the PME, the PMEW, and an organization known as the Brotherhood of Liberty for the Black People of America were all were linked to BDS. The FBI's three-day search for Pauline Bahar ended where it had begun on September 20, at her home.[29] She was one of eleven black nationalist leaders seized that day, and one of the few females among the seventy people apprehended over the weekend. What baffled FBI investigators was the large amounts of money that many suspects had on their persons at the time they were arrested, and how well they all dressed. "The leaders we took into custody on Sunday and yesterday have lavish and expensive costumes, and have plenty of money," an FBI spokesmen told reporters. "Even their followers," he continued, "many of whom are poorly dressed, seem to have some means."[30] Another federal agent added that the search for Japanese expatriates believed to be financing the black organizations was continuing:

> We have only scratched the surface. . . . It seems certain that Japanese money has been going to these organizations. None of these people have any visible means of support. There have been Japanese who have had contact with these people. We are looking for them.[31]

"They should call him J. Edgar Herod," Muhammad said of the FBI director upon discovering the extent of the raid. For him, what Hoover had done in trying to imprison all the male members of the NOI was similar to—and it must be borne in mind that he viewed the Holy Bible as a story of things to come—King Herod's murder of male babies in Nazareth in his search-and-destroy mission against Jesus. "The King, Herod," Muhammad wrote upon reflection some years later, "desired most of all to kill Jesus in his infancy." He compared Herod's action to the story in the Book of Revelations about the dragon who stood before the woman. "The woman here represents the Messenger of God," the Messenger said. "The child [Jesus] represents the followers of the Messenger."[32]

During his interrogation on September 20, Muhammad admitted that he knew Takahashi, but denied being one of the Japanese agent's subordinates and refuted allegations that the NOI and the OMA worked together. He claimed that he had first met Takahashi in 1932 or 1933, when the latter visited him at Temple No. 1 in Detroit,[33] at which time he had asked about the philosophy and aims of the NOI, but had not offered financial aid or other enticements for cooperation. He also recalled meeting Takahashi at Abdul Muhammad's home, but denied having seen him since then. The agents were unconvinced. If there were no links between Takahashi and the NOI, the agents asked, why were the philosophies so similar? Why was Muhammad so pro-Japanese? Why, they asked, was he walking around with a three-month old newspaper clipping about the arrest of Takahashi in his wallet?[34] Why had Takahashi and Takis been invited to lecture at Muhammad's temples? Why was the NOI flag so similar to Takahashi's flag? Why, finally, had Takis been seen at the Washington temple, and how could Muhammad explain the fact that Takis lived right around the corner from him—in an all-black community, no less? Muhammad's hesitancy and inability to answer the barrage of questions made the agents even more suspicious. To prevent Muhammad from jumping bail again, the prosecutor asked the court to deny him the privilege of posting bond, a request that was readily granted.

On October 1, 1942, Takis was sentenced to three years in prison by a federal court in St. Louis, where he had pleaded guilty to forging a postal money order.[35] Facing further charges and the possibility of more time in prison, he decided to turn state's evidence against the NOI and other black nationalist organizations. Three weeks later, a grand jury sitting in Chicago indicted Muhammad, Linn Karriem, and his wife, Pauline Bahar, for conspiracy to commit sedition.[36]

The sting of Muhammad's indictment was all the more painful because of the conviction of his eldest son, and the psychological impact on him was not overlooked by the Bureau. FBI official Ladd wrote in a memo to Hoover on October 5:

> I thought you would be interested to know of the 38 negroes who were indicted for Selective Service violations in connection with the captioned case [Allah Temple of Islam; Sedition] in Chicago . . . six entered pleas of not guilty and will be tried beginning October 12, 1942. . . . The thirty-one others entered pleas of guilty and thirty of them were sentenced to three years each. One, Emmanuel Muhammad, with aliases, who is the son of Elijah Muhammad, one of the individuals indicted for sedition, was sentenced to five years on his plea of guilty.[37]

On October 22, Elijah Muhammad was sentenced to three years on draft evasion charges, as was Linn Karriem.[38]

Owing to a procedural error (the indictment was void for being too vague about the acts constituting the crime), the indictments were quashed, and the government took its cause before another grand jury, which quickly handed up another indictment in November. This second indictment was more specific than the earlier one. It alleged that the three defendants in the April indictment conspired with Sultan Muhammad and David Jones to

> commit sedition contrary to Section 33 of Title 50 in that the United States being then at war they willfully attempted and did cause insubordination and refusal of duty in the military and naval forces of the United States to the injury of the United States, and the United States, being at war, they willfully obstructed recruiting and enlistment services of the United States.[39]

The pleading said that evidence would prove that the conspiratorial acts occurred in Chicago, Milwaukee, and Washington, D.C.

The Messenger suspected that the government had infiltrated his group, but he was stunned by the volume of evidence entered against him. In addition to documents from the sixteen boxes seized from his home in Chicago, prosecutors presented witnesses who testified about pro-Japanese lectures delivered inside the temples and witnesses who had seen suspected enemy aliens with Muslim ministers. Not only had the informants taken down parts of speeches; some had transcribed statements made by the Messenger and the others, and noted the time, date, and location where such statements were made. In its case against the Messenger, the government introduced a large collection of damning statements by him and his ministers, most of them from informants who had joined the seven temples. It also produced letters in which Muhammad and others had gloated over the imminent fall of America. One item submitted as evidence was a lecture the Messenger had delivered at the Chicago temple on August 9, 1942, which read in part:

> The devil [referring to the white men in charge of administering the Selective Training and Service Act] will trick you into believing that you will have to fight for him, but don't pay any attention to him. His time is up. You should pay no attention to what he says about registering for the draft because he can't force you to do a thing. His laws don't mean a thing. You shouldn't fear the devil when he tells you that you must go and fight in this war. You should refuse to fight. . . . The newspapers are lying when they say that the Japanese are losing. We are going to win.[40]

His sermon from August 16, 1942, was also introduced in evidence. In that one, the informant reported the Messenger as saying:

> The Japanese are the brothers of the black man and the time will soon come when from the clouds hundreds of Japanese planes with the most poisonous gas will let their bombs fall on the United States and nothing will be left of it.

On August 30, the court was told, the Messenger said:

The Asiatic race is made up of all dark-skinned people, including the Japanese and the Asiatic black man. Therefore, members of the Asiatic race must stick together. The Japanese will win the war because the white man cannot successfully oppose the Asiatics.[41]

In view of the evidence, the only question remaining at the conclusion of the trial was not how much time he would serve—most Muslims received the maximum sentence allowed by law—but where he would serve it. Presentencing procedures began on November 23. A continuance was granted the next day because a writ of habeas corpus was issued for his return to Washington. After a one-day trial in the U.S. District Court in Washington on November 25, Muhammad was again found guilty of violating draft registration laws. He was sentenced on December 18 to one to five years in federal prison.[42]

On the same day, Takis was called to the witness stand in the New York City sedition trial of Leonard Robert Jordan, leader of the PME. Takis gave damaging testimony about Jordan's political and economic ties to the Japanese consulate in New York and his affiliation with the OMA. His depiction of Jordan as a traitor was seconded by that of George D. Buchanan, a black detective in Harlem assigned by the FBI to infiltrate the PME. The final important witness against Jordan was Herbert S. Boulin, another New York detective working for the FBI as an ad hoc agent.[43]

As counterintelligence campaigns against black nationalists continued, the FBI explored ways to ensure that the NOI would not be revived in the Messenger's absence. Since nearly every major leader but one—Master Wallace Fard—was in custody, officials in the Chicago field office deemed his capture central to their goal of smashing the NOI.

The next group targeted was the House of Israel, a Newark sect that proclaimed, as did Muhammad, that African Americans were the "real" Jews, the true Chosen Few. Reuben Israel, the sect's founder and leader, was arrested on January 13 on draft evasion charges. Owing to similarities between Reuben's sect and the NOI, the FBI wondered if Fard was linked to the House of Israel.[44] Reuben was offered his freedom if he agreed to divulge where Fard was hiding. He insisted that he knew nothing about Fard, but the agents remained unconvinced. On January 15, 1943, Muhammad was again interviewed by several agents, at which time he insisted that it was Fard's idea, not his, that black people should not serve in the armed forces of the United States. He was made to recount his years with Fard repeatedly, mainly because the agents were certain that he would unwittingly provide clues that might lead them to the fugitive.

The next day, agents interviewed William Gravitt-el, head of the MSTA at 270 Court Street in Newark. Even though Gravitt-el was very close to the Messenger and was acquainted with Reuben Israel, he denied any knowledge of the NOI, Fard, or Muhammad.[45] On February 9, the Chicago SAC formally requested the director to place a "wanted notice" in the files of the Identification Division for Wallace Don Ford, with the alias of W. D. Fard.[46] Ten days later, Reuben Israel was sentenced to one to four years imprisonment for violating draft registration laws. Israel's was one of many wrongful convictions in this prelude to McCarthyism.

On June 7, 1943, John D. Owens, an assistant federal prosecutor, told Judge John P. Barnes that the government was dropping all remaining charges against Elijah Muhammad, Linn Karriem, David Jones, Sultan Muhammad, and Pauline Bahar. Bahar, Owens told the court, had only a "passive part" in the NOI, and the other four defendants were already serving time.

The decision to drop the charges came at a time when racial tensions were as high as the temperatures in Paradise Valley. The NOI was already experiencing internal bickering over leadership—some men opposed Clara's taking control—and the FBI was still hounding suspected members of the sect. White workers instigated most of the confrontations by demonstrating against the hiring of black women, and the KKK provoked several riots in and around Detroit. Then on June 15, a white mob attacked several black youths with stones after they tried to enter Eastwood Park.[47]

Five days later, the simmering hostility between the races reached the boiling point. At the Forest Club, an all-black operation at 700 East Forest Avenue that was the center of performing arts in Paradise Valley, a dance turned into the flashpoint for a riot. On the humid Sunday evening of June 20, Belle Isle was teeming with Detroiters out for family fun. Nearly 100,000 people, most of them African Americans, were rollicking there when a rumor started that a black woman and her baby had been deliberately drowned by a white mob.[48] Since there had been other racial disturbances earlier in the week—and indeed, earlier that evening—the rumor rang true. In a matter of minutes, it had spread from Belle Isle to the Forest Club.

The club was a block or so away from the Hastings Street temple. It was also less than two blocks from the home of Takahashi's chief assistant in Detroit, George Ohki, who lived at 961 East Forest, a gathering place for members of the OMA.[49] A party was in full swing at the club when a patron grabbed the microphone and repeated the rumor of the drowning. People swearing revenge ran out into the nearby streets, where whites were driving by as they made their way from Belle Isle. The angry mob threw stones at the white motorists, and at least one man was stabbed as he tried to escape on foot. White-owned businesses in Paradise were firebombed, pillaged, and otherwise vandalized. By sunrise, Paradise was a shambles. By the next evening, the rioters were virtually in complete control of the city, so President Roosevelt ordered federal troops to the area. The riot was ended less than two hours after the troops arrived, but by then, more than thirty people were dead.[50]

The government immediately began looking for someone to blame. Initially, it blamed black-owned newspapers for fanning hatred by constantly drawing attention to racial discrimination. A. Philip Randolph also was faulted, merely because he had written an article decrying racial discrimination; ironically, the article was published six months before the riot. In an article in the *Detroit Tribune* on January 2, Randolph argued that justice "is never granted, it is exacted. It is written in the stars that the darker races will never be free until they make themselves free. This is the task of the coming year." In its report on the causes of the riot, the commission charged that Randolph's article "clearly constitutes an appeal to extract justice by violence." In fact, Randolph had suggested a march on Washington to protest racial injustice.[51]

Though the governor's riot commission concluded that the riot was not the result of subversive influences, it did implicate the NOI and the Klan:

> This report would be incomplete without some reference to factors which have created and inflamed that tension. That certain misinformed people have relied upon their peculiar racial characteristics in asserting alleged superiority over another race is unfortunate. . . . Of present concern to this committee, however, is the increasing tendency among certain hoodlum elements in Detroit, both white and Negro, openly to flaunt the established social order in combating this animosity.[52]

While the report did not mention the NOI or the SDOO by name, media reports implied that Muhammad's draft troubles and Takahashi's internment played a part in sparking the riot. Thurgood Marshall, a brilliant young lawyer for the NAACP, was outraged because, he said, the riot commission blamed the riot primarily on blacks. He poured his passion onto the pages of *Crisis* magazine. Under a headline reading "The Gestapo in Detroit," he accused the police of enforcing the law

> with an unequal hand. They used "persuasion" rather than firm action with white rioters, while against Negroes they used the ultimate in force: nightsticks, revolvers, riot guns, submachine guns, and deer guns. As a result, 25 of the 34 persons killed were Negroes. Of the latter, 17 were killed by the police. . . . This record by the Detroit police demonstrates once more what all Negroes know only too well: that nearly all police departments limit their conception of checking racial disorder to surrounding, arresting, maltreating, and shooting Negroes.[53]

Eight days after the bloodiest riot in the history of Detroit, a riot erupted in Harlem after a white policeman shot an African-American soldier during a scuffle.[54]

On July 23 Muhammad began serving his sentence at the Federal Corrections Institute in Milan, Michigan, where his son Emmanuel also was incarcerated. Several months after he was imprisoned, his son-in-law, Raymond Sharrieff, was found guilty of violating the Selective Service Act. Sharrieff had retained Frank C. Eskridge to represent him,[55] but he nonetheless receieved the same kind of sentence as Muslims who came to court without counsel. The humiliation Muhammad felt was almost unbearable. He fell into a deep depression, blaming himself for the fates of his son and son-in-law as well as other families facing trial or already in prison on draft evasion charges.

However, the predicament that Emmanuel and others he had influenced found themselves in was only one of several reasons for the Messenger's dark mood. Japan's global ambitions were being thwarted by defeats in the Coral Sea and at Midway, and Germany's assault on Russia had become a nightmare, with many soldiers on both sides dying of hypothermia before ever firing a shot. The reality slowly set in that even if Japan started winning again, it wouldn't do him or the NOI much good. If Tojo's forces had stormed the California beaches in 1943, or if the Mother Plane had landed as Muslims thought it would, there would have been no way to tell the Tribe of Shabazz from the Sioux or Navajo nation or any other tribe or brown-skinned minority group.

With Takahashi's internment and subsequent deportation, the promises he had made in the name of Japan were as empty as those that had lured Elijah Poole from Macon. He had been so busy running from his enemies and from the law that he had never really taken time to assess his blind devotion to Japan or, for that matter, to assess his own life. Prison provided him with an opportunity, however unwanted, for introspection and retrospection, and what he saw haunted him.

Kallatt, the brother he had been closest to, had become an alcoholic after Takahashi was interned and the OMA collapsed. He would come by the house inebriated, shouting obscenities as he staggered around outside the door, angering Elijah and frightening his children.[56] Elijah saw his brother sliding down a treacherous slope but did nothing to try to help him. It was only a matter of time, he knew, before the little brother he had once been so close to joined the other Pool children who died young. Charlie had died in a sanitarium in early 1939, and Hattie had died in the winter of that same year. Sam died the following year of unknown causes. Another sister, Lula, had been only twenty-two when she died in 1918.[57]

With his siblings dead or facing sedition charges and his organization in ruins, Muhammad appeared to a prison psychiatrist to be a man harboring tremendous hostility. He told a social worker that if prison officials released him right now, he still would not register for the draft—even if the military "assured him he would not be called for military service." He spoke derisively of the government, citing the many injustices his family had suffered in 1941 at the hands of the Chicago Welfare Association.[58] A prison sociologist wrote:

> He apparently accepts his present situation with the attitude of a martyr, but it is felt that he will adjust here without difficulty. Prognosis for future adjustment will be dependent upon the status of the war.

The prison psychiatrist was less optimistic. On July 26, 1943, Dr. W. S. Kennison wrote:

> His mental trend and thought content revealed that he does have a marked persecutory trend, both against himself and his race (Negro). He does admit having visual hallucinations, visions as he called them, in which the supreme Allah would come to him and talk with him. He also reveals that, on numerous occasions, he has had the feeling that he is being followed and that people are talking about him. In general, his attitude is that of his own superiority.[59]

He recommended that Muhammad be interviewed by a psychiatrist at frequent intervals:

> While it is felt that this individual is suffering from paranoid schizophrenia, he is what is classified as an ambulatory type who has made an adjustment to his psychosis that will not probably render him into any adjustment difficulties.

The irony of the suggestion that Muhammad felt that he was being followed was that he had been under FBI surveillance for three years, and he was being talked about. The FBI agents who kept tabs on him were obvious, as were the notepads they jotted in. Muhammad had seen them writing in them on many occasions as they interviewed men he had just finished speaking with.

On the admissions summary dated August 20, officials wrote that the Messenger's name was Elija Bogans and that he was forty-six years old. His eligibility for parole was set for December 17, 1943, and his full term would expire on December 17, 1947.[60] A conditional release date was set for August 24, 1946. A prison physician determined that he was generally in good health. With the exception of his asthmatic condition, the doctor wrote that his only health problems were an "inguinal hernia and some cavities." Upon admission to the prison facility, he was placed on medium security status and assigned to the "Number 2" detail. Prisoners assigned lower-numbered details were considered co-opted in the view of fellow inmates. Those who protested conditions were given more demeaning assignments. "When I was teaching, I spent most of my time building pig pens," one dissenter recalled. On September 27, 1943, Muhammad was assigned to work as a janitor in the administration building's bookkeeping section, and remained in that job for two years. He "willingly devoted many hours of overtime work," an evaluator wrote.[61]

While he was, indeed, a model prisoner, Muhammad's dietary demands on the staff at Milan made him a pariah. He recalled:

They deliberately put swine, or the essence of the swine, in everything, and the assistant warden made mock of it when I told him my followers lived on nothing but bread to avoid swine. He said that even the bread had swine in it.[62]

He made at least one attempt to further his education while at Milan. Because he was a model prisoner, in early 1944 Warden C. J. Shuttlesworth approved his petition to take remedial education classes offered through the director of education. Shuttlesworth, whose career included executive posts at Alcatraz and Leavenworth, held a strong resentment against conscientious objectors. "I'll be glad when we get rid of all you goddamned COs," he once told a group of prisoners, "so we can get some real prisoners in here."[63]

After Muhammad was accepted into the education program, Roger Axford, a white Methodist minister who had graduated from Nebraska Wesleyan University with a degree in political science and psychology, was assigned to teach him the fundamentals of English. Axford had refused on religious grounds to fight for his country, or any country for that matter: "To me war was wrong, so I sent my draft card right back to where it came from."[64] In Axford's case, the card had come from a draft board in Lincoln, Nebraska. Ironically, Axford remembered, that office was headed by the father of the girl he was dating. He had very vivid memories of that period, and of his initial encounters with Muhammad.

"He was very resentful of the whites over him, around him, and beside him," Axford said. "He called me a devil on several occasions." Despite his hatred for Axford and other whites, Muhammad remained in Axford's course for several months. The class met two or three times a week. "He made it clear almost from the outset," Axford remembered, "that he was more interested in learning Arabic than English. I told him as politely as I could that he should try to better understand English before trying to learn another language. Besides, I didn't know Arabic." Elijah resented this notion, and dropped out the course before summer.[65]

Shortly after leaving the course, the Messenger began proselytizing among the black inmates. His son, Emmanuel, recalls:

He set up a temple in the prison despite the difficulties he experienced with the blackboard and all. He set up classes right there in prison. He would teach on Wednesday and Friday evenings until the bugle was blown for us to go to bed. He also taught on Sunday afternoon at two, and made many, many converts in prison.[66]

Emmanuel's memory of the Messenger's recruitment activities is juxtaposed to those of Axford:

There were never more than a handful of them at Milan. Three of them would always eat together, and I never saw the group expand while I was there.

The three Axford remembered seeing were the Messenger, Emmanuel, and Robert X, a Muslim chef.

The experience of Wallace Nelson, another black inmate at Milan during Muhammad's incarceration, is instructive concerning the lack of success of the NOI appeal among the prisoners. Nelson was a thirty-two-year-old conscientious objector who was serving a five-year term for refusing to be drafted. A Quaker, he had initially been in a conscientious objector (CO) camp in Ohio, but had deserted and fled to Detroit, where he joined a Quaker-run commune.[67] Unlike Muhammad, who merely objected to fightng a war for white people, Nelson, like all Quakers, opposed war on principle. Muhammad's arguments for refusing to register for the draft were closer to those of a group of Italian conscientious objectors in the prison, who weren't opposed to war per se but refused to fight for America against their relatives in Italy.

Nelson and Muhammad shared similar backgrounds—both were the sons of ministers, both of their parents were born in Georgia, and during their youth, both had witnessed the most nefarious forms of racism. Despite this, Nelson never let the experiences he suffered as a black man in America tarnish his view of whites. "If the course of history had been turned, if the wheel, the damning wheel, had fallen upon people with dark colors, they'd behave just as stupidly as the white ones," Nelson said. "So I didn't blame them because of their white skin."[68] But Nelson probably had never run into anyone quite as convincing or charismatic as Master Fard, which may be one reason that he and his fellow Georgian took such different roads in life. In prison, Nelson was among many black inmates who viewed the Messenger not as a prophet or even a man of the cloth but as someone poisoned by ignorance and hatred.

While Muhammad spent much of his time sunk in melancholy, Clara juggled her time between doing whatever she could to keep up his morale and Emmanuel's, raising her younger children, and running the

NOI. "She held the family together all the while he was on the run," Emmanuel recollected, "and while he was in prison. She gathered and sent or brought to my father and me whatever literature the prison permitted. She also typed verses from the Holy Quran and sent them to us."[69]

In his absence, Muhammad designated Clara as the Supreme Secretary for the NOI. He would mail instructions and guidelines to her almost daily. "The orders came from him to her to the ministers and captains," his son Wallace recalled. "Actually, she was like his second [in-command] while he was in prison."[70] As a nine-year-old, Wallace said, he would watch in awe as his mother managed things, particularly how she handled Muslim ministers, most of whom were used to dealing with women only in subservient roles. "I saw her give instructions to ministers. They would sometimes be in doubt about how they should carry them out, [so] she would give them insights. She was a very strong woman and she believed in him."

Although Muhammad's relation with prison officials got off to a shaky start, even the warden had kind words for him as his sentence neared its end. "Elijah," Warden Shuttlesworth wrote, "was one of our many Selective Service violators who made an excellent adjustment at this institution."[71] On April 23, 1945, he appeared before the parole board. When asked about his plans upon parole, he said that he planned "to reform my people and put them back into their own. At the present time my followers and I plan to buy a farm upon which to raise food for ourselves and the market. . . . I will live with my family at 6116 South Michigan Avenue in Chicago."[72]

As for earning a living, Muhammad told the board: "Allah takes care of me and my family through my followers." While the answer seemed sufficient for him, the parole board was not satisfied. His parole adviser informed the board that Arthur Caruthers, the proprietor of a plumbing supplies store at 2372 Cottage Grove Avenue in Chicago, would employ him. The board designated the Messenger a ward of Charles W. Fisher, a probation officer assigned to the U.S. Court House in Chicago. A few days after the parole hearing, Muhammad received some bad news.

Kallatt, the brother with whom he had hoped to repair his relationship, had died during an apparent epileptic seizure, leaving a wife with six children to raise without insurance benefits or other sources of income.[73] Muhammad wasn't permitted to attend the funeral. He left Milan on August 24, 1946, and headed back into what he regarded as the larger prison, the one he called the "wilderness of North America."[74]

CHAPTER EIGHT

KAABALLAH

For a nation with this start in culture and efficiency to sit down and await the salvation of a white God is idiotic. With the use of their political power as consumers, and their brain power . . . Negroes can develop in the United States an economic nation within a nation. . . .

—*W. E. B. Du Bois,*
"*A Negro Nation Within the Nation*"[1]

It was a little thing, but piled on all the other little things it broke something in me. Suddenly I had had enough [of being black]. Suddenly I could stomach no more of this degradation—not of myself but of all men who were black like me.

—*John Howard Griffin,*
Black Like Me[2]

Store windows were smashed and several clashes erupted during the morning between bus drivers and their passengers. The papers listed similar incidents that exploded during the night. The mirrored face of one store on 125th Street was smashed and I passed to see a group of boys watching their distorted images as they danced before the jagged glass.

—*Ralph Ellison,*
Invisible Man[3]

For Jews, the gripping terror that began with Kristallnacht, the Night of Broken Glass, the degradation and abuse that being forced to wear the yellow Star of David subjected them to, and the ultimate horror of the gas chambers in Dachau and Auschwitz came to an end with Hitler's suicide and the Allied victory in Europe in June 1945. In August a small-scale Armageddon in Hiroshima and Nagasaki led to Japan's unconditional surrender; and World War II was over. Two years later, in November 1947, a fledgling international organization known as the United Nations voted to partition the British Mandate of Palestine into a Jewish and an Arab state, and Herzl's dream of Zion became a reality. It had taken fifty years, just as Herzl predicted.

Elijah Muhammad was livid over the fact that one of the central figures in the negotiations for partition was an African American, the debonair Dr. Ralph Bunche. He felt that Bunche, who had a part in drafting the U.N. Charter (and who in 1950 was the first African American to win the Nobel Peace Prize), was misusing his time and his talents in the advocacy of a Jewish homeland while his own people, who Muhammad said were the "real" Jews, remained homeless. In the late 1940s he wrote:

> The Christian whites claim nearness to Allah and make Jesus a member of their wicked race and ascribe Sonship unto him. The Jews also claim to be God's "beloved ones.". . . These sayings of theirs have deceived the so-called Negroes in America one hundred percent, and many black people throughout the earth. The Jews and Christians are not really the "beloved ones."[4]

According to Muhammad, only the African American fit the biblical description of God's Chosen Few who would be enslaved in a strange land for four hundred years. The first African was enslaved in America in 1555, he said.[5] The four-hundred-year period of their enslavement would end in 1955, presumably with the creation of an all-black nation in America or repatriation to Africa. "The Jewish people are not the ones referred to [in the Book of Genesis] who would serve a strange people for four hundred years," a minister paraphrasing Muhammad wrote. "This people who would be lost and enslaved cannot be the Jews, as the Jews have never been lost and in the enslaving grip of another people for four hundred years."[6]

The NOI's leader wasn't alone in demanding international assistance for African Americans. On October 23—a full month before the United Nations adopted the partition plan for Palestine—the NAACP compared the plight of African Americans to that of Jews by presenting "An Appeal for Redress" to the United Nations.[7] The book-length document, compiled by W.E.B. Du Bois, Walter F. White, Jewish labor-rights activist Milton Konvitz, and attorney William R. Ming Jr., among others, asked the United Nations to consider the plight of African Americans with the same urgency and gravity it had given to oppressed Jews. In his opening statement, Du Bois said that he spoke for 14,000,000 citizens of the United States who believed that America's racial problem was as much an international problem as it was an American one.[8]

Howard University professor Rayford W. Logan, another author of the petition, said that the U.N. General Assembly had "the obligation to initiate studies and make recommendations for the protection of human rights and fundamental freedoms" for everyone. Unlike a similar petition filed with the League of Nations by Garvey in the 1920s, the NAACP's petition avoided any mention of sanctions.[9] Rather, it focused on the economic plight of African Americans, which they argued would change if racial segregation was abandoned. Owing to the imposing power of the United States in the United Nations, the petition never advanced beyond the filing stage.[10]

Clearly, the NAACP's remedies weren't remotely related to those the Messenger had in mind. Logan and Du Bois were well-regarded historians and, as such, were familiar with the saga of Africans who went home in the 1800s with assistance from the federal government. The African

Colonization Society repatriated former American slaves to Liberia, while Great Britain repatriated many of its former slaves to Freetown, Sierra Leone. Nonetheless, the Messenger insisted that America remained obligated to create a state for Africans still living in America, and that a new nation in Africa was required for the unique Tribe of Shabazz.[11]

A major difference between the Lost-Found Tribe of Shabazz and the wandering Tribes of Israel, of course, was that Israel had enough Jews to people Jerusalem and Tel Aviv and other cities and towns in the new nation. The Messenger, by contrast, barely had enough followers to fill a storefront church in Chicago on his fiftieth birthday in 1947. A year after his release from prison, the NOI had fewer than 400 members in the whole country, and all told, there were only about forty members of Temple No. 1 in Detroit.[12] Still, Muhammad felt that Bunche, as an undersecretary of the United Nations, owed it to black people to improve their lot now that he was in a position to do so. If Bunche could push aside Palestinians to create the state of Israel, Muhammad preached in the late 1940s, why couldn't he remove white people from four or five Southern states to make way for the Blackstone Nation?

Blackstone Nation was another term Muhammad used to describe African Americans, as he believed that the Kaaba stone in Mecca was their symbolic manifestation:

> I am the Elijah of your [Holy] Bible and I am the Muhammad of your Holy Quran. Not the Muhammad that was here nearly 1,400 years ago. I am the One that the Holy Quran is referring to. The Muhammad of 1,400 years ago was a white man. Then they put up a sign of the real Muhammad. It's there in Mecca, Arabia. They call it the Little Black Stone. . . . People in the past have worked and made the pilgrimage to Mecca and have returned to their people as teachers to teach them of this sign, but I say the American so-called Negroes are the end of that sign. A pilgrimage there will not help him become a great and righteous Muslim, but bowing down to that Last Messenger [Elijah Muhammad] . . . is the real Mecca to which they should make pilgrimage. . . . The finding of this people [African Americans] and the choice of God for this people to be His, and making them the founda-

tion, a stone for building the kingdom of heaven on Earth, absolutely is the end of all pilgrimages. . . . I am the end of prophets.[13]

One of those who accepted the Messenger as the Seal of the Prophets was Wilfred Little of Detroit. Wilfred, the son of former prominent Garveyites, was waiting for a bus when a well-dressed black youth approached him. After introducing himself, the young man started talking about black nationalism and religion. He invited Wilfred to visit the Temple No. 1, an invitation to which he nonchalantly replied. It took Wilfred time to follow through, but when he did, the introduction to Islam as taught by the Messenger was like finding a long-lost friend. The blending of black separatism with the concept of black-skinned biblical characters reminded him of his childhood, listening to his father, Earl Little—an itinerant Baptist minister—preach about how white people bleached the characters in the Holy Bible to prevent Africans of the diaspora from knowing their glorious past.[14] Earl Little, it turns out, had once lived in Reynolds, Georgia, and had preached on occasion in Perry, the birthplace of Clara Muhammad's parents. Another coincidence Wilfred stumbled upon was that Ella Little, his half-sister, knew both Clara and the Messenger.

Wilfred joined the temple after a matter of months, becoming Wilfred X Little. His brothers Philbert, Reginald, and Wesley also joined, as did his sister Hilda. "We didn't have to be converted," Wilfred said in explaining why so many of his family members joined. "You see, we were already black nationalists." The family agreed that Reginald should be the first one to visit Malcolm, their wayward brother who had gotten himself into trouble with the law, to tell him about Muhammad. As Malcolm felt the closest to Reginald, the others assumed that he would be more receptive to the idea if it came from him. While Reginald and Hilda made frequent visits to Malcolm at Norfolk Prison Colony in Massachusetts, Wilfred opened his home to the Messenger. Whenever Muhammad came to Detroit to sermonize or take care of business, he stayed in Wilfred's home. This gave the Littles—who called Muhammad the Holy Apostle—an opportunity to ask him to write a letter of encouragement to Malcolm, which he finally did.[15]

Muhammad had always said that men with Malcolm's background—hustlers, pimps, and confidence men—made excellent servants of the people once they were reformed.[16] They were ideal ministers because they understood human nature better than most psychiatrists and psychologists. There was something about hustlers that made people listen to their stories, no matter how outlandish, and to invest in them—emotionally and financially.

From what Muhammad heard about him, he felt that Malcolm would make a perfect minister if he could be persuaded to use his God-given talents for good. Malcolm eventually joined the Messenger, but he was a tough convert. Despite appeals from his siblings, Malcolm cast a jaundiced eye toward clergymen, seeing almost all of them as "pulpit pimps." His father was an exception, obviously, but generalizations about ministers had made it easier for him to justify his own immoral conduct. His distrust of authority, including the ministry, was understandable given his difficult childhood and victimization by a malfunctioning social welfare system. His father was reportedly lynched in Michigan when Malcolm was six.[17] At the time, the Black Legion was very powerful in Lansing (where the family lived), and Malcolm's parents were prominent members of the UNIA. His mother, Louise Helen Norton Little, suffered a nervous breakdown not long after her husband's death, and was sent to Michigan State Mental Hospital at Kalamazoo.[18]

The orphaned Malcolm and his siblings wound up in America's well-intentioned but primitive foster-care system after their mother was institutionalized. Malcolm attended Pleasant Grove Elementary School in Lansing from 1932 through 1938, and then went on to West Grove Junior High,[19] but he was a rebel and was often in trouble. After putting a thumbtack on a teacher's chair, he was expelled from West Grove and sent to a juvenile detention center in Mason, Michigan, where he remained a year. In 1940, at the age of fifteen, he enrolled in Mason Junior High School. A trip to Boston in the summer of 1941 to visit his half-sister, Ella, opened his eyes to an enchanting nightlife. He dropped out of Mason and moved in with Ella, where he quickly blended in among the vermin of street life. Like many young hustlers, he made several missteps while selling stolen goods to support his drug addiction, and was sent to prison following a conviction for burglary in 1946.[20]

After converting to Islam as taught by Muhammad in 1948, Malcolm wrote dozens of letters to the Messenger. Beyond swearing off alcohol, cigarettes, and narcotics, he also stopped eating pork. By 1950, he was a new man. His new faith put him on the front page of an issue of the *Springfield Union* that year after he and several other Muslims staged a protest over the poor quality of the food in the Norfolk Prison Colony and the denial there of religious freedom.[21]

Upon being paroled on August 7, 1952, Malcolm Little—now Malcolm X—went to Detroit to live with Wilfred, who helped him find a job at a local factory. After a brief stint as assistant to Minister Lemuel (Anderson) Hassan, Malcolm became a student minister, and his rapport with the disbelievers was nothing short of phenomenal. In the first few months, Hassan endorsed nearly everything his student proposed, and by 1954 membership in the Detroit mosque had tripled. Muhammad was so impressed that he made Malcolm the assistant minister in Detroit.[22] Hassan—whose brother, James (Anderson) Shabazz, was one of Muhammad's chief aides in Chicago—soon grew jealous, for just as the surge in membership showed the potential of an industrious minister, it also exposed Hassan as a mediocre one. Hassan guessed that it was only a matter of time before he was replaced as head of the temple, and he guessed correctly. In November 1957 the Messenger shipped him off to lead a new temple Malcolm X had started in Cincinnati. At the same time, he appointed Wilfred X Little as minister of the Detroit temple and sent Malcolm X to Boston to open yet another one.[23]

In giving the NOI new life, Malcolm also gave new life to the Messenger. As the two men sat together at Wilfred's or in Muhammad's home in Chicago, the Messenger fondly assured him that there was nothing the two of them could not accomplish.[24] He would listen to Malcolm X deliver a sermon, then offer constructive criticism. In his early speeches, for example, Malcolm would begin by castigating white people without taking the time to lay a foundation for his assertions. The Messenger offered several suggestions. He told Malcolm to give his audience examples of the bad behavior of white people before condemning them as devils. That way, the audience had a frame of reference and would be more inclined to agree with him. Secondly, the Messenger urged him to curtail criticism of black behavior. Instead of blaming black people for cultural diversions (drinking, smoking, and gambling, for example), he should lay the blame for the objectionable behavior at the white man's door. The suggestions apparently helped Malcolm to remember what he had learned as a member of the debaters' club in junior high school. Whatever the reason, there was a dramatic turnabout in his sermons.[25]

During a meeting in the winter of 1952, the Messenger gave Malcolm X the first of many special assignments. Joseph Gravitt-el, the Messenger's friend from his days in the MSTA, was at his wits' end over his son, Joseph Jr., who had recently completed a stint in the army as a marksman, during which he had been awarded the World War II Victory Medal. After an honorable discharge on October 15, 1947, Joseph Jr. had a very difficult time adjusting to civilian life. He drank heavily and was unable to hold a job for long. Within a year of his discharge, he was a drug addict as well as an alcoholic.[26] On November 30, 1949, the stocky street urchin was so inebriated that he relieved himself on a busy street corner in Detroit. Several women out with their small children saw him and called the police, who arrested him on a charge of "involuntary molestation of women." The charge was later changed to "indecent and obscene conduct in a public place."[27] He was sentenced to thirty days in jail and given a year's probation. Following the trial, his father asked Muhammad for help. He wanted to get his son away from Detroit, he said, before he overdosed or someone killed him over a drug deal. Joseph Sr., then head of the Detroit branch of the MSTA (while his brother William led the Newark temple), had been unsuccessful in his efforts to involve his son in the group. Perhaps, the Messenger said, the boy would listen to the dynamic new minister who was the talk of Detroit. As a former alcoholic himself, Muhammad empathized with his old friend. He told Malcolm X to go get Joseph off the streets and to drag him into the temple if he had to. "I literally found him in the gutter," Malcolm X recalled.[28]

Muhammad suggested with all the force of an order that Joseph Jr.

spend seven weeks with Malcolm X. If after that time he wasn't convinced that the NOI was the way to a brighter future, he would be free to return to the streets. Joseph was enchanted with Malcolm X from the moment he heard him preach. There was something magical about what he said, Joseph recalled, and the truth of it struck him like rain on a thirsty field.[29] Although Joseph joined the NOI, the Messenger and Malcolm both knew that it would take at least six months before he would be free of his addictions. Muhammad assigned Joseph to Malcolm X's security detail, and gave him a job in the Shabazz restaurant in Detroit.[30] With his entire lifestyle wrapped up in the NOI's activities, Joseph had neither the time nor the desire to think of the past. Joseph X Gravitt was only one of about two hundred Detroiters converted during a twelve-month period beginning in late 1952. In the summer of 1954, the Messenger rewarded Malcolm by appointing him minister of Temple No. 7 in Harlem, and he promoted Joseph X from a cook at the Muslim-owned restaurant in Chicago to captain of the New York temple.[31]

Shortly before his departure from the NOI, Master Wallace D. Fard prophesied that "some very wise men" would come from the Harlem temple.[32] Among the wise men who befriended the new minister was Ernest 2X McGee. McGee, who joined the Harlem temple in 1951, possessed many leadership skills and the educational background that the Messenger sought in his ministers, which allowed him to rise quickly through the ranks. Born in Gary, Indiana, in 1922, McGee had attended Purdue University after graduating from Gary's Roosevelt High School in 1940.[33] In 1943, he transferred from Purdue to the Mid-Western Conservatory in Chicago, and in 1948 he enrolled at the City College of New York. For the next three years, his musical talent gained him a place with some of the most popular jazz bands in the world, among them Bud Powell, Charlie Parker, Max Roach, Billie Holiday, and J. J. Johnson. In 1954, at Malcolm X's suggestion, the Messenger named McGee the first national secretary of the NOI, and sent him to Chicago to head the University of Islam.[34]

By a strange coincidence, a man thought to be Fard appeared at the Harlem temple in 1951.[35] Few saw him, but those who did doubted their own vision and sanity. One witness kept it to himself for two years, but on August 31, 1953, walked nervously into the FBI's New York field office to report the sighting. He told an agent the terrifying secret and said that he feared the loss of his sanity if he didn't confide in someone. The agent asked him if he was certain that the man he saw was Fard, and he said yes, he was sure of it. The agent then pulled a mug shot of a Wallace Ford out of a file cabinet drawer and showed it to him. Although the man was "visibly startled," he refused to positively identify Ford as the man he had seen two years before. He hurried from the office and never returned.[36]

Three weeks after that encounter, the FBI began a major investigation of the NOI. On September 18, the Chicago SAC recommended to the director that the Messenger be placed on a Security Index Card (SIC).[37] Simultaneously, he was added to another list of individuals considered national security risks, this one known as DETCOM, an acronym for "Detention of Communists."[38] "The subject is being tabbed for DETCOM in view of his position as national leader of the Muslim Cult of Islam," the agent noted on his file. The next day, the SAC sent a follow-up memorandum to headquarters noting that the Messenger "has been tabbed for DETCOM and is being made a key figure in the Chicago office." This meant that in the event of a national security incident, the FBI would arrest the Messenger and other "key figures" of the NOI, suspend all due process rights as the government had done to Japanese Americans during World War II, and detain them until the threat had abated.[39] Copies of the memo were sent to G-2 (the Army's domestic intelligence division).[40] Malcolm X, Wallace Muhammad, and other top NOI officials also were added to the SIC and DETCOM lists in the following weeks.[41]

On August 10, 1954, William F. Tompkins, an assistant attorney general in the Internal Security Division of the Justice Department, wrote to Hoover to request his aid in the possible prosecution of the Messenger and key Muslim officials. "Under the direction of its 'prophet' Elijah Mohammed [sic]," Tompkins wrote,

the Muslim Cult of Islam (MCI) has established temples in approximately sixteen leading cities. . . . The fanaticism of MCI members appears to be of such an extreme degree as to render possible an outbreak of violence by cult members, which might be similar in nature to the recently attempted assassination of members of the House of Representatives by Puerto Rican nationalists.[42]

Tompkins was referring to the wounding of five members of Congress by Puerto Rican terrorists who fired into the Capitol Building in March 1954. The attack came three years after an attempt by nationalists to assassinate President Harry S. Truman. The second attack occurred directly across the street from the White House. Both assaults revealed national security shortcomings and increased government attempts to head off potential incidents by domestic groups. In furtherance of his plans, Tompkins requested that the FBI give him access to a list of witnesses and confidential informants that it had inside the NOI.[43]

The Bureau's investigation was without subtlety, perhaps intentionally so. White agents in suspicious-looking cars parked near the homes of Muslim leaders, homes which for the most part were in predominantly black neighborhoods. The agents' crew cuts, drugstore-issue sunglasses, and cheap suits had "police" written all over them. In November 1954, Malcolm X and others told the Messenger that FBI agents were tailing them constantly.[44] Not only were they interviewing Muslims in their homes, but they were also interviewing their neighbors. They frequently visited Muslims' places of employment to interview them and their supervisors, thus jeopardizing their livelihoods; after all, few white employers wanted trouble from the FBI, especially over someone suspected of being a Communist.

As the FBI's interest in the NOI escalated, the New York Police Department Bureau of Special Services (also called BOSS and BOSSI) assigned its own agents to investigate leaders of the Harlem temple.[45] There was little difference in the investigative techniques because BOSSI agents, as well as select officers in the police departments around the country, were trained at the FBI academy.[46]

Even as the FBI aimed to undermine Muhammad by disrupting his sect, federal courts and social progress weakened the appeal of black separatism by finally pursuing a course the NAACP had recommended in its 1947 U.N. petition. On May 17, 1954, the Supreme Court handed the Messenger bad news in the landmark case of *Brown v. Board of Education of Topeka.* The High Court agreed with NAACP lawyers, led by Thurgood Marshall, that the legal doctrine of "separate but equal" in public education was unconstitutional.[47] The decision had little to do with the sudden enlightenment of the Court; rather, it was the result of growing social pressure against America's version of apartheid.

In 1951, DuBois had joined the Civil Rights Congress (CRC) in calling for action from the United Nations on behalf of African Americans. On a petition signed by a host of prominent activists, including author Howard Fast, Communist Party leader James A. Ford, attorneys George Crockett Jr. and Paul Robeson, and William L. Patterson, the CRC charged the United States with genocide against black Americans.[48] Although the United Nations did not respond to the petition, the CRC had disturbed a hornet's nest. In retaliation for their roles in preparing the petition, Robeson and Patterson were targeted for counterintelligence measures by the intelligence community. Their passports were revoked, and Robeson was blacklisted in Hollywood. Nonetheless, at least one member of the United Nations felt that the organization had a legitimate complaint. S. P. Demtchenko of the Ukraine stood before the General Assembly on February 2, 1952, and charged that segregation in America was inherently repressive.[49]

Sensing a changing tide, President Dwight D. Eisenhower met with leaders of the NAACP in January 1954 to discuss race relations.[50] In April, Republican Party advisers urged the president to move toward dismantling segregation as a means of securing the "Negro vote for the party" in November's congressional elections.[51] With the executive and legislative branches of government taking the lead, action by the judicial branch seemed inevitable. *Brown* and the string of desegregation cases that followed (*Plessy* was overruled two years later in *Gayle v. Browder*) contradicted a central tenet of Muhammad's theology: that whites had no intention of integrating with blacks. Muhammad labeled these decisions as cheap tricks. Just as the advantages of separatism were beginning to bear fruit, he argued, the white man was using "tricknology" to keep blacks as pawns within his powerful economic and social structure.[52]

Despite these apparent setbacks for black separatism, the delay in implementing the objectives of the desegregation rulings provided the Messenger and his ministers with persuasive evidence that laws alone could not eradicate America's racial problems. Indeed, one repercussion of the decisions was the birth of the White Citizens Councils, organizations formed specifically "to fight desegregation and civil rights."[53] One of the first places to feel the impact of the white backlash was Detroit, where racial violence erupted after the NAACP won a lawsuit calling for the integration of public housing in the largely Polish Hamtramck area.[54]

By 1955, the FBI's interest in the NOI had risen significantly. Percentage-wise, the sect was among the fastest-growing black organizations in the country. The sudden growth was largely attributable to one minister: Malcolm X. "I need more ministers," the exasperated Messenger told Malcolm. People were signing their names in the "Lamb's Book of Life" (a registry of all individuals who joined the NOI) so fast that there weren't enough facilities to hold them all or ministers to shepherd them from Christianity to Islam.

During the Saviour's Day convention in Chicago in 1955, the Messenger targeted a young singer from Boston for possible recruitment as a minister. Women said the singer, Louis "the Charmer" Walcott, was handsome. Men, perhaps out of jealousy, were less charitable. (A former associate of Walcott's said the singer reminded him of Jerry Lewis with a terminal tan because of his protruding front teeth.) In any event, Walcott and his wife were in Chicago during the convention as part of a traveling musical revue and went to hear the Messenger speak.[55] Midway through his sermon, the Messenger looked directly at Walcott and said, "Brother, don't pay attention to how I speak. Pay attention to what I'm saying." To Walcott, it seemed as though the Messenger was reading his thoughts. How, for instance, did the Messenger know he was in the audience? How did he know where he was sitting in the cavernous auditorium? As it turned out, Muhammad was told before he started his lecture that Walcott was in the audience, and knew exactly where he was sitting.[56] He was also advised that Walcott had gone to college, this at a time when fewer than 5 percent of all Black Muslims did so. What Walcott would later describe as a miraculous encounter was nothing more than a ruse—and it worked like a charm. Walcott's wife joined the NOI that same day, and Walcott himself joined the Boston temple a few months later after hearing Malcolm X lecture. Walcott's older brother, a dyed-in-the-wool hoodlum by the name of Alvan, joined the Boston mosque the following year.[57]

Walcott, who was given the name Louis X, was ordered to give up his career as a nightclub singer once he joined the NOI, but he continued to sing and play the violin and ukulele.[58] To bridge the gap between the rituals of Christian churches and his temples, Muhammad gave Walcott and others permission to sing Islam-inspired gospel songs. One popular song was "Pharaoh, Let Us Go." Another contained this chorus:

> So let us fight, ye Muslims
> Fight for your own.
> Fight, oh ye Muslims, fight for your own.
> Fight for your nation
> And we will all be free.
> Fight for your nation, fight for your own.[59]

Owing to Muhammad's ties to the Japanese during World War II, FBI officials felt that its skyrocketing growth made the NOI ripe for exploitation by the Communist Party; this wasn't all that usual, as the Bureau believed that every major black organization was a Communist Party target.[60] Hoover's convictions about Communist influence on the NOI deepened after the Bandung Conference, a 1955 gathering of non-white—and mostly Muslim—nations to discuss ways to end colonialism in the Third World. His suspicions were also heightened when the Messenger embraced the conference as a sign of the "fall of the white man."[61]

In an attempt to develop informants within the group, agents approached Lucille X Rosary of the Boston mosque on June 9, 1955, ostensibly for a routine interview. From the line of questioning, however, it was patently clear that they were more interested in cultivating her as an informant than in mundane matters at the mosque.[62] In October, Malcolm X was contacted. The FBI suggested that Malcolm could make a great deal of money as their man inside the NOI, but the minister advised them that his hustling days were over; for Malcolm, the idea of being a government stool pigeon was no more tempting than a pot of pigs' feet.[63]

On December 5, 1956, FBI agents requested permission for wiretaps on Muhammad's home telephone and on any other phone that he might use regularly. Hoover examined the request, and sent it on to the U.S. attorney general on December 31. He wanted to install telephone surveillance devices (or "tesur") and microphone surveillance devices (or "misur") in two locations inside Muhammad's home.[64] On January 2, Attorney General Herbert Brownell sent Hoover a letter granting permission for a wiretap on Muhammad's telephone and electronic eavesdropping devices (or bugs) in his home at 4847 South Woodlawn Avenue. The tap was installed two days later.[65]

Like programs in operation against other groups considered subversive, this one came under the umbrella of COINTELPRO, an acronym for Counterintelligence Program. Its aims were manifold, but its central premise was that certain Americans could not be trusted with the freedom to think and act independently. For these individuals, the Bureau believed that the government had to monitor and even direct their political destiny as they lacked the intellectual ability to act in their own best interests. Although COINTELPRO was new, the motivations went as far back as World War I. One of the targets of government surveillance then was the Reverend A. D. Williams of Atlanta.[66] In 1917, the War Department's Military Intelligence Division began spying on Williams, who was head of the Atlanta branch of the NAACP. Williams, who also was the Reverend Martin Luther King's maternal grandfather, was labeled an "agitator" and Communist dupe because he fought for the creation of a black high school at a time when most Americans were deemed sufficiently educated after completing intermediate school.[67]

Besides interference from the FBI, Black Muslims also had to deal with a society unaccustomed to people who practiced faiths other than Christianity. Their distinct attire and appearance—most of the Muslim men sported a bald head while many inner-city black men wore "the process" (a hair-straightening method using lye)—made them easy targets for harassment. The first in a spate of major incidents occurred aboard a train in Maryland on February 23, 1951. A group of Muslims from the Harlem temple were en route to the Saviour's Day convention in Chicago when they got into an argument with a train employee. The train stopped while FBI agents and local police boarded. During a search, the agents found pamphlets in which whites were portrayed as devils. When the Muslims protested an attempt by the authorities to arrest them, a fight resulted and several policemen were injured. The Muslims sat in jail until Muhammad sent lawyers to bail them out two days later.[68]

On February 22, 1957, another incident occurred in the temple in Pensacola, Florida. It was raided by police during a service. The police chief was injured during the melée, which resulted in the arrest of several Muslims.[69]

Two months later, there was a conflict between police and members of the Harlem mosque. Johnson Hinton, a Muslim who was employed by a local dry cleaner, was assaulted after yelling at two policemen who were brutalizing a young black man. Insulted by the interloper, the officers attacked Hinton with a vengeance, and the back of his head was split open during the beating. Even though he was gravely injured, Hinton was thrown into the back of a paddy wagon and taken into custody.[70]

At sundown, Malcolm X led a crowd of about 100 Muslims to the 28th precinct. By the time they reached the police station, more than 5,000 sympathizers and onlookers had gathered. Upon seeing Hinton's wounds, Malcolm demanded that he be taken to a hospital immediately. Police acquiesced, but only after Malcolm agreed to disperse the crowd first; they were afraid that if the crowd saw Hinton's condition they would charge into the police station and trigger a riot. Malcolm stood before the growing throng. Like a catcher using sign language to communicate with his pitcher, he gave the Muslims a cue to disperse. Within minutes, the crowd had vanished. New York Inspector William McGowan was astounded. If a man could dispatch a crowd that fast, what was there to prevent him from summoning one with equal swiftness, he wondered. "No man should have that much power," he said.[71] Malcolm X went to the hospital and waited while doctors rushed Hinton into surgery. The largest wound to his head was so severe that a sizable silver plate was placed inside his skull. Despite the doctors' efforts, Hinton suffered permanent brain damage and filed a $1,000,000 lawsuit, which was eventually settled out of court for less than a tenth of that.[72]

The legend of Malcolm X and the "fearless Black Muslims" was born as stories about the incident snowballed, and coincided with the birth of another legend: Dr. Martin Luther King Jr. and the Southern Christian Leadership Conference (SCLC). Born Michael Luther King into a middle-class family in Alabama, King (who changed his name in homage to Martin Luther) was thrust into the national limelight after helping to organize a bus boycott in Montgomery in December 1955.[73] Just as blacks in the North weren't expected to contest police brutality, blacks in the South rarely resisted segregation. That changed on December 1, 1955, when a civil rights activist, Rosa Parks, refused to give her seat to a white man and move farther to the back of a public bus. Her defiance sparked a strike by blacks that nearly bankrupted the city's public transit system, and resulted in an indictment against King.[74]

The strike was part of the impetus for the Southern Manifesto, a bill signed by more than 100 Southern congressmen, which labeled the desegregation cases as a "clear abuse of judicial power." The measure went nowhere, however, as it lacked support from President Eisenhower and Senate powerbrokers Albert Gore of Tennessee and Lyndon Baines Johnson of Texas. In fact, Johnson joined Massachusetts Senator John F. Kennedy in an effort to pass legislation to hasten integration, much to the dismay of Harry Byrd, chief advocate of the Southern Manifesto.[75] The end of the Montgomery bus boycott in 1957 and passage of the Civil Rights Act signaled the end of legal segregation. By the same token, these changes diminished the appeal of the NOI to African Americans in the South, where it had been slowly opening temples. Muhammad's Temple No. 15 had opened in Atlanta, Georgia, in 1956 and Temple No. 24 in Richmond, Virginia, a year later.[76]

The rapid rise in the NOI membership above the Mason-Dixon line gave the Messenger his first opportunity to generate wealth for his budding nation. Despite constant talk of going back to Africa and of creating a nation in several Southern states, his first major investments were a small farm in Whitecloud, Michigan, and, in 1957, some real estate in Chicago: a home at 4847 Woodlawn, and apartment buildings at 7143 Indiana Avenue, 8201 South Vernon Avenue, and 616 East 71st Street. Another property, at 6116 South Michigan, was sold for a tidy profit to the Chicago Housing Authority after only a few months in Muhammad's portfolio. A second property on 71st Street was converted to a Shabazz grocery store and a restaurant, and a large building at 5335 South Greenwood was turned into a temple and a University of Islam campus.[77]

In a precursor to tactics used by today's televangelists, the Messenger strongly encouraged elderly followers to will their homes and other real property to the NOI, which many did. Although he lacked access to radio and television to spread the message, the Messenger became a newspaper columnist in the spring of 1956.[78] Under the title of "Islamic World," his message found its way into black homes across the country through the popular *Pittsburgh Courier*. In October 1957, the column was renamed "Mr. Muhammad Speaks." With the NOI's assistance, the *Pittsburgh Courier* (also published in New York as the *New York Courier*) became the largest-selling African-American newspaper in the country. In June 1957, for instance, NOI members sold nearly 100,000 copies, or an average of 25,000 extra papers each week.[79] Thrilled by its skyrocketing sales, the newspaper added another Muslim columnist: Minister Malcolm X wrote an article titled "God's Angry Men."[80] After financier S. B. Fuller bought the *Courier* in 1959, the Messenger's column was dropped, but by then it didn't matter; other black-owned newspapers were happy to welcome him aboard.[81] Both the Messenger's and Malcolm X's columns ran in the *Los Angeles Herald Dispatch* before Fuller completed his purchase of the *Courier*. Though published in California, the *Dispatch* was sold in every major American city by early 1960. Its owner, Sanford Alexander, was investigated by the FBI after it received reports that he had become a Muslim.[82]

Though he was prospering financially, Muhammad's personal life was in chaos. While young Americans danced ecstatically to Elvis Presley's "Jailhouse Rock," the song had totally different connotations for twenty-four-year-old Wallace Muhammad, who was indicted in August 1957 for refusing to register for military service as required by the Selective Service Act of 1948.[83] Wallace, who was targeted under COINTELPRO because he was the Messenger's heir-apparent, told his father that he had no intention of fighting for America. He also made it clear that dancing in the penitentiary was not his idea of a good time, either. After his indictment, Wallace was exploring alternatives to incarceration when draft board officials advised him that he could work at Elgin State Hospital instead of going to prison.[84] Comfortable that he had found a solution to satisfy his father and his own sense of justice, Wallace told the Messenger that he would serve time at Elgin.[85] At first his father told him calmly that whatever he decided would be all right, but then he made it clear that he hoped Wallace would do the "honorable thing" and go to jail instead of compromising with the "devils at the draft board." Wallace protested that he wasn't compromising at all; being forced to work at the hospital was like serving a prison sentence.

Wallace married and had his first child while his case went through the appeals process. As it dragged on, he tried several times to convince his father that helping out at the hospital was as honorable and sensible as sitting in a cell doing nothing. The implications of the son's statement (that his father had erred in going to jail in 1942) were not lost upon the father. "You're too cooperative! You're nothing but a coward!" the Messenger screamed.[86] Wallace was dumbfounded and humiliated, but was too angry to respond. His father's accusation was so hurtful that it permanently altered their relationship. Chicago attorney William R. Ming Jr. fought Wallace's conviction to no avail. After his appeals were exhausted, with the Messenger having spent $20,000 in legal fees over four years of legal jousting, Wallace surrendered to his father's wishes and chose prison over the less onerous alternative. He was sent to the Federal Correctional Institution at Sandstone, Minnesota.[87]

The showdown between father and son may have had less to do with Muhammad's insistence upon his own infallibility than with a brewing

scandal that threatened his thriving theocracy. After Wallace's indictment, one of Muhammad's personal secretaries, a teenager from Michigan, became the talk of the Chicago temple after her pregnancy started
to show.[88] Everyone knew that she wasn't married and wasn't dating
anyone regularly. The only two men she spent time with, at least as far as
anyone knew, were Malcolm X, who was frequently in town to confer
with Muhammad, and Muhammad himself. The consensus was that
Malcolm X was the child's father; after all, to the best of everyone's
knowledge he wasn't married and wasn't seeing anyone regularly.

When the rumors made their way to Captain Joseph, he was furious
with Minister Malcolm.[89] Joseph told members of the Chicago mosque
that he was certain that Malcolm X was the one who had impregnated
the young woman. In September, he sought and was granted a meeting
with the Messenger. Seeing this as a once-in-a-lifetime power play, a
chance for one-upmanship against Malcolm X, Joseph told the Messenger of his groundless allegations. The Messenger, who seemed shocked,
promised to launch his own investigation. A week or so later, the secretary was notified by the Messenger that she would have to face a trial for
violating the laws of Islam.

Around this time, Malcolm X began to notice a change in the way the
members of the Chicago mosque treated him whenever he was in town.
Young women snickered as he passed by, and he caught contemptuous
glances from the men. By the time Malcolm saw that the secretary was
pregnant, she was in the third trimester. He felt sorry for her, and also
guilty: sorry because he concluded that some young non-Muslim gigolo
had seduced the young woman, and guilty because he had secured the
job for her. He knew that she would soon be drummed out of the NOI
and given a one-way ticket home.[90]

As Malcolm looked further into the matter, he discovered that he, not
some outsider, was rumored to be the child's father. After discovering
that Joseph had spread lies about his private life, Malcolm immediately
complained to the Messenger. He told the Messenger that Joseph had,
without a scintilla of evidence, accused him of impregnating the girl, and
he wanted the Messenger to reprimand the captain. At the secretary's
trial, at which the Messenger acted as judge and jury, she refused to

divulge the name of the child's father. She would only say that he was not a *follower* of the Messenger, which, of course, was true. At the conclusion of the hearing, the secretary was expelled for promiscuity, and ordered to leave the NOI forthwith. The Messenger paid for her one-way ticket back to Michigan; the baby's father was never identified.[91]

Ordinarily, the Messenger would have excommunicated a Muslim for spreading lies about another person, particularly another Muslim. But Joseph wasn't just any Muslim; he knew where the Messenger's skeletons were buried, at least those regarding the origins of the NOI. Owing to the virtual dissolution of the NOI in the early 1940s, Joseph was one of the few members who knew about Muhammad's past, about his years as a member of the MSTA with his father, Joseph Sr., and uncle William Gravitt-el.[92] As the Messenger always adamantly denied any affiliation with the MSTA, Joseph's revelations would have been scandalous. Hence, circumstances dictated that the Messenger should mete out a punishment mild enough to prevent Joseph from becoming hell-bent on revenge, but severe enough to make Malcolm X feel that Muslims understood that there was a heavy price to be paid by those who spread lies.

The Messenger summoned Joseph to his office. They discussed old times, about how Joseph Sr. was once among the Messenger's chief assistants. He reminded Joseph, too, that he, Elijah, had personally sent Malcolm X to Detroit to save him from the early death toward which he was surely headed. Joseph couldn't deny this; he agreed with the Messenger that he would have to be punished so as to keep order in the NOI. There was a noticeable tear in his relationship with Malcolm X after Joseph returned from his brief suspension. He had lost Malcolm X's trust, while Malcolm X had the Messenger's complete confidence. Without an endorsement from Malcolm X, Joseph knew that there was no hope of his fulfilling his dream of one day becoming a minister as his father was, and that as long as the Messenger kept him assigned to Malcolm X, he would never be more than what he was in the camera's lens—a bloated Boy Friday. To appease Joseph, and over Malcolm X's objection, the Messenger appointed him supervisor of the FOI on the East Coast. While it did not seem to be such a prestigious position, the appointment made Captain Joseph the third most powerful enforcer in the NOI, with Elijah Muhammad Jr. being the first and Raymond Sharrieff the second. It put Joseph in a position to establish his own fiefdom, which he did. From his office tiny in the Harlem temple, he would later devise a scheme to extract vengeance against not only Malcolm X but against the Messenger as well.[93]

CHAPTER NINE

ARABESQUE

If we consider how greatly he [the Jew] has sinned against the masses in the course of the centuries, how he has squeezed and sucked their blood again and again. . . .

—Adolf Hitler (1925)[1]

In America, the Jews sap the very life-blood of the so-called Negroes to maintain the state of Israel, its armies and its continued aggression against our brothers in the East.

—Malcolm X (1960)[2]

Jews are the bloodsuckers of our community. They take tractor-trailer loads of money out of our community on a daily and consistent basis.

—Khallid Muhammad, leader,
Million Youth March (1998)[3]

Although he had long taught that the people known as Jews today were not the "original" Jews, and believed that the *Protocols* was an authentic document, Muhammad rarely voiced his views on the subject before the media. That changed with the start of his newspaper column in the fall of 1956. After the first several columns generated little comment, he became more strident in his tone. During the holy days of December 1957, he wrote disparagingly of Jews and Jesus Christ. Jews, he said, were part of the white race of devils. "If God was your father, you would love me," the column began, citing a passage from the Holy Bible's Book of John:

> Surely, if the Father of the two people (black and white) was the same, the two would love each other. In a family where the children are of one father, they love each other because they are of the same flesh and blood. . . . The argument here between Jesus and the Jews is, the Jews claim they all were the same people (children) of one God or Father, but this Jesus disagreed with and proved they were not from the same Father (God). He, having a knowledge of both Fathers, knew their Father (Devil) before his fall, and before he had produced his children (the white race) of whom the Jews are members. Here, in this chapter (John 8), it shows there was no love in the Jews for Jesus.[4]

Perhaps because of the Messenger's unorthodox opinions on race and religion, the column quickly came to the attention of the FBI. Ostensibly out of concern that Islamic nations were financing the NOI, the Bureau placed a "mail cover" on Muhammad's home in Chicago.[5] "Mail cover" is an oxymoron, since what the Bureau did was to open the mail. Sometimes it made summaries of a letter's contents; at other times, a letter was photographed or otherwise copied in its entirety. The issue often came up when Muhammad spoke to ministers around the country. One minister's suspicion was aroused when he received a letter from Muhammad that had been opened and resealed with cellophane tape. He called to ask Muhammad if he had tampered with the package after sealing it, but the latter couldn't recall having done so.[6]

The Messenger made some of his harshest statements about Jews during the Saviour's Day Convention of 1958. The crowd of nearly 3,000 inside Tabernacle Baptist Church in Chicago rose to its feet as the Messenger made his way down the aisle toward the stage. Visitors and Muslims stood and clapped for nearly fifteen minutes before the Messenger could deliver his address. "Jesus was not a Jew," he said to the astonishment of many non-Muslims. "Jesus could not have been a Jew because he was born in Palestine," and claimed that no Jews were born in Palestine at the time.

> The Jews are not God's chosen people nor the seed of Abraham because Jesus said the Jews did the work of the devil and not the work of Abraham. The Jesus who died 2,000 years ago will never return. We must follow the teachings of Master Wallace Fard Muhammad, who is our God and who was born on February 26, 1877, in the holy city of Mecca. . . . If you can accept Abraham and Moses and Jesus as prophets, why can't you accept me? I am here to do as Moses did—to tell Pharaoh to let my people go. All prophets before me were persecuted and finally killed, but no one can lay a hand on me because I am protected by Allah. All the other prophets had seen a revelation and were only revealing what they saw, but none besides me was taught directly by God.[7]

For many of the Christians and even the agnostic visitors in the auditorium, much of what the Messenger said sounded like the blasphemous rantings of a man overcome with delusions of grandeur. Some left after Muhammad's speech, while others trickled out over offense taken from statements of the ministers who followed on the program, among them James (Anderson) Shabazz, Malcolm X, and Wallace Muhammad. Malcolm asked rhetorically in his introductory speech: "How can you worship a man who doesn't look like us, who doesn't act like us, who doesn't talk like us and who doesn't walk like us or even smell like us. There are over 17,000,000 so-called Negroes in America, but still we have to look to the white man for everything."

A few weeks before the convention, Malcolm X had made similar remarks in a speech taped by the FBI. Echoing a statement Elijah Muhammad had made many times about President Eisenhower, Malcolm X told a filled temple that "a Jew is in the White House, Jews are in the State House, and Jews run the country. You and I can't go into a white hotel down South, but a Jew can."[8]

The Bureau's suspicion that foreign money was behind the spurt of antisemitic statements being made by Muslim leaders was heightened by a cablegram from an Arab head of state. As Malcolm X read the cablegram, which he had sent to black-oriented newspapers as a public relations measure, a hush fell over the conventioneers; no one wanted to miss a word. Dated January 23, 1958, the message from President Gamal Abdel Nasser of the newly formed United Arab Republic read:

Mr. Elijah Muhammad
Leader, Teacher and Spiritual Head of
the Nation of Islam in the West
I have received your kind message expressing your good wishes on the occasion of the Afro-Asian conference. I thank you most heartily for these noble sentiments. May Allah always grant us help to work for the maintenance of peace which is the desire of all peoples. I extend my best wishes to our brothers of Africa and Asia living in the West.[9]

Nasser despised America as much as he hated Israel. A veteran of the 1948 Arab-Israeli War, he was convinced that the only reason that Israel survived the conflict was because of European and American arms support:

Israel got all the arms and ammunition she wanted, and her Arab foes were denied them. Imperialism conspired to turn us into weaklings who seek its protection. But how could we seek protection from those who created Israel and turned it into a menace against us.[10]

His hatred of America was further inflamed by America's attempt to block Arab nations from forming a Middle East version of the United States, which Nasser called the United Arab Republic (UAR).[11] While the Saviour's Day convention was in progress, Nasser was in Syria working out details of that country's decision to join with Egypt to create the UAR when he learned of a CIA plot to have him assassinated. According to Syrian Colonel Abdel Hamid Serraj, the CIA had conspired with King Saud's family to overthrow or kill Nasser to prevent the Egyptian-Syrian union.

The plot was part of Operation Omega, launched in 1956 by American and British intelligence units. Both President Eisenhower and British Prime Minister Sir Anthony Eden agreed that "Nasser must be got rid of," but only Eden favored assassination.[12] "It is either him or us, don't forget that," Eden told intelligence officials. Eisenhower favored a plan that called for a coup and for King Saud to replace Nasser as head of the growing United Arab Republic. Serraj produced documents revealing that the two nations had offered King Saud the presidency of Syria and $60,000,000 for disposing of Nasser. Upon his return home, Nasser denounced the Eisenhower administration and labeled King Saud a traitor who had been "bought by United States money."[13]

Back at the convention, James R. Lawson, president of the United African Nationalist Movement in Harlem, read a similar message from Nasser to the congregation and another message from President William Tubman of Liberia.[14] On the final day of the convention, Muhammad unveiled his "Blueprint for the Blackman's Future." With the support of African Americans and Muslims throughout the world, the Messenger said he hoped to build a $3,000,000 complex in Chicago that would include a "religious, educational, and business center" by 1961.[15] He told the gathering that newly acquired apartment buildings and the Temple grocery and market were an infinitesimal indication of the economic power in the hands of African Americans. Under his guidance, a new nation could be established within America, he said. The only reasons similar empire-building plans by Booker T. Washington and Marcus Garvey failed was because of "the lack of knowledge of self."[16] During the convention, Louis X sang, "Pharaoh, Let Us Go,"[17] which was appropriate given what was transpiring outside the convention hall. While Louis X was singing about freedom from oppression, FBI agents and local police were conducting a "fisur," an acronym for physical surveillance. Essentially, agents and police roamed the parking lot and noted the license plate number of every car. Some took photographs of anyone who might be a dignitary, while others monitored eavesdropping equipment set up to record the speeches inside.[18]

The exchange of messages between Nasser and Muhammad was part of the Messenger's attempt to establish a relationship with the Muslim nations emerging from colonialism. His first step in this regard involved a contract with Abdul Basit Naeem, a Pakistani journalist living in Brooklyn. In May 1957, Naeem signed a contract with the Messenger to produce a glossy ninety-page booklet, *The Moslem World and the USA*, focusing on international Islamic affairs but featuring the last Saviour's Day convention as its centerpiece.[19]

In July 1957, Malcolm X met with Achmed Sukarno during the Indonesian's visit to Adam Clayton Powell Jr.'s Abyssinian Baptist Church in Harlem. Sukarno, who hosted the Bandung Conference in 1955, was highly impressed with the NOI, particularly with Malcolm X. Malcolm, who had journeyed from a prison cell to the halls of the United Nations in five years, was equally enamored of the world leaders he was beginning to meet regularly. During Sukarno's visit, Malcolm said publicly to Powell:

> You show great wisdom and foresight, inviting these leaders from Asia into Harlem to study the conditions here firsthand. . . . The 80 million Muslims in Indonesia are only a small part of the 600 million more in other parts of the dark world, Asia and Africa. . . . We here in America were of the Muslim world before being brought into slavery, and today, with the entire dark world awakening, our Muslim brothers in the East have great interest in our welfare.[20]

Just as Malcolm X had assumed the mantle of diplomat, Naeem filled the role of publicist. He contacted Muhammad again in June to see whether he was interested in publishing a second edition of the magazine to cover the upcoming Afro-Asian Festival at the Park Palace Recreation Center in New York City.[21] This time, Muhammad seemed reluctant. The 100,000 copies of the first issue had not sold well, and he was reluctant to make another questionable investment. First, he would have to see how the festival turned out. More than 2,000 New Yorkers participated in the affair, and a few of America's most highly regarded black celebrities were on hand, including bandleader Noble Sissle, president of the Negro Actors Guild.[22] Although the affair was long on speeches—it was one of the rare occasions when Clara Muhammad addressed a large audience—no one complained. Clara received sustained, thunderous applause, but the person who won the day was Dr. Thomas N. Matthews, the neurosurgeon at Coney Island Hospital who had performed a series of successful operations on Johnson X Hinton's skull. Matthews, who sat next to his white wife, received a ten-minute standing ovation. Foreign dignitaries also were on hand, including Rafik Asha of the Syrian Mission to the United Nations, A. S. Chauvize (editor of *Al Islaam*), and Ahmed Zaki el-Borai, Egyptian attaché to the United Nations.[23]

Aside from the highly publicized attack on Hinton, the thing that alerted Muslims at the United Nations to the NOI's presence was Muhammad's newspaper column, which ran in the *New York Amsterdam News* under the title "Islamic World," and featured a small photo of the Messenger. Some dignitaries mistook the Messenger for an Asian, just as the FBI had a decade earlier. Malcolm X tried to correct this perception by addressing the issue of Muhammad's race in one of his columns. "The Messenger might pass as an Oriental. But his sympathies and outlook are those of a Black Man."[24]

Ambassador Asha was in search of American allies of whatever hue as his diplomatic battle with Israel over the Lake Hula area grew more contentious. The dispute involved the lake and a small tract of land in the demilitarized zone between Syria and Israel. According to Syria's formal protest, Israel had violated the recent truce by building a bridge there and evicting Muslims from the Lake Hula area, which the Israeli government wanted to convert into farmland.[25] While Israel denied that it was trying to occupy the land, Asha noted that the bridge was built to be strong enough to carry heavy military vehicles. Israel refused to rebut the Syrian charge directly. Rather, it claimed that the bridge was needed to get construction equipment to the location. The Israeli ambassador also conceded that three Israeli settlements had already been established in the area from which Muslims had been evicted. The mainstream media's reports on the dispute seemed to favor Israel's interpretation of the issue. To level the playing field, Asha and Nasser looked to the NOI (which, given the word "Nation" in its title, a foreigner might have mistaken for a genuine province or territory within the United States) as a possible vehicle for airing Arab concerns. "Nasser . . . has confirmed the importance he attaches to American Nationalist Negroes to serve as a minority pressure group," a BOSSI report noted. "The Egyptian diplomatic people have been instructed to show courtesies to Negro Nationalists."[26]

Muhammad's column suggested that he would make a good ally in a country where the word "Muslim" was rarely mentioned in a favorable light. When a Jewish writer complained about the tone of the column, for example, Muhammad wrote an unapologetic reply:

> Mr. Emmanuel Rosenfeld . . . who fears that my articles in this paper (which teaches my people the truth) will stir up hatred in the hearts of my people towards the White people would like to see my articles discontinued. Let us ask Mr. Rosenfeld: Who stirred up hatred of the White Race against we so-called Negroes? The Bible says: Do unto others as you would like others to do unto you. This mistreatment of our people by the Caucasian Race will be given back to them in full. A token of it is now going on.[27]

In April 1958, the NOI broadened its international appeal to Muslims by hosting a conference in Los Angeles to celebrate Third Pakistan Republic Day.[28] The gathering, which also focused on the upcoming tenth anniversary of Israel, featured Mohammed Mehdi, head of the Arab Information Center, Pakistani government officials and students, and several Muslim ministers from the West Coast. Mehdi argued that there would never be peace in Israel:

> If the Zionists, as they claim, have not forgotten Palestine over the last 2,000 years, it is reasonable to assume that the Arab refugees of Palestine, who were born in Palestine . . . will not forget their home. The return of the Arab refugees, as resolved by the United Nations, will be the first vital condition for peace.[29]

Mehdi charged that the reason Americans had not heard the Palestinian side of peace equation was "the complete control the Zionists have over the media of communication in America." Malcolm X, who said he was speaking for the Messenger, concurred:

> It is asinine to expect fair treatment from the white press since they are all controlled by Zionists. . . . Arabs must—if they are to escape Atomic death and destruction—make an effort to reach the millions of people of color in America who are related to the Arabs by blood.[30]

Sepia, a progressive black-oriented magazine, was first to make the charge of Arab influence on Muhammad. In October 1957, it ran a story implying that the NOI's growth was the result of financing by Muslims from the Middle East. "Mr. Muhammad's new temples of Islam are more closely connected to foreign sources and are believed to be a carefully plotted campaign by Moslem leaders to get a foothold in America."[31]

The FBI had come to a similar conclusion. Officers in the COINTELPRO section thought initially that the key to crippling the NOI was the removal of Wallace Muhammad from under his father's wing. In January 1958 the Chicago field office sent a letter to the director suggesting that it was woefully mistaken in this assessment, and that it now believed Malcolm X would replace the Messenger should the ailing leader die suddenly.[32] The Bureau was caught off-guard by these concerns, as it felt certain that Muhammad would hand over the reins only to one of his sons, and that the one he preferred was prison-bound. The effort to disrupt the NOI by removing Wallace had been for naught, the Bureau discovered, because the Messenger was seriously mulling over the idea of cultivating Malcolm X as his heir.[33] Marie Pool, the Messenger's mother, began calling Malcolm X her "son" soon after she met him because she sensed there was something special about him. Following her lead, Elijah and Clara also began referring to Malcolm as their "son." The endearment moved the former orphan deeply, though he feared that it rankled Muhammad's real sons.[34]

The secret to disabling the movement, therefore, lay in neutralizing Malcolm X. Four months after the FBI's re-evaluation of his importance, Malcolm X's home resembled a scene from an Ian Fleming novel. On the morning of May 14, 1958, two BOSSI detectives went to the East Elmhurst apartment building that Malcolm X and his wife, Betty Shabazz, shared with three other couples: John Ali and his wife, Minnie, and John X Mollette and his wife, Yvonne, who owned the property. Neither Malcolm nor John Mollette was home. The detectives said they were there to arrest a postal fraud suspect named Margaret Dorsey. They were informed that no such person lived there. The detectives, who had no search warrant nor an arrest warrant for anyone, then asked if they could come in and look around. When their request was denied, they left angrily, promising to return.

By the time the detectives returned with a postal inspector, Mollette was home. He inspected the warrant for Dorsey's arrest, which indicated that Dorsey lived in a first-floor apartment of the Mollette house. Mollette assured the officers that they had the wrong address. At that point, one of the detectives pushed Mollette aside and barged into the house.[35] Another ran up the back stairs leading to Malcolm X's office on the second floor, although, according to the warrant, Dorsey lived on the first floor. After shattering a rear window, the officers fired several shots into the office. One bullet lodged in a bedroom wall where the women and children were huddling. Betty, who was pregnant with her first child, opened the bedroom door after one officer threatened to continue firing. After they opened the door, Betty and Minnie were placed under arrest.

"If you don't move faster," a detective said as they walked down the rear steps, "I'm going to throw you down the steps."[36]

By the time the detectives returned to the first-floor apartment, where Mollette was struggling with one detective, a crowd of Muslims and their neighbors had the house surrounded. Two detectives were hospitalized after being beaten senseless. The melee ended with the arrival of additional police, who arrested Betty, the Mollettes, Minnie Ali, and another couple. They were indicted in June on charges of assault, conspiracy, resisting arrest, and obstructing a police officer in the performance of his duty.[37]

The savagery of the attack raised many questions, but none more disconcerting than why police shot through the walls when they could clearly hear the cries of terrified children. Muhammad hired Edward W. Jacko, a talented New York attorney, to represent his chief minister, but had no time to focus on the incident because his mother was on her deathbed in his home in Chicago. She died three days later.[38] The funeral, which was held in Chicago on May 21, was one of the largest the city had ever seen. Malcolm X, who was very close to the matriarch—he called her Mother Marie—took her passing especially hard. While Muhammad spent the next several weeks in mourning, Malcolm X poured his energy into a media campaign against the New York Police Department. In an open letter to New York City mayor Robert Wagner, Malcolm warned the city of the international impact on its image:

Outraged Muslims of the African Asian World join us in calling for an immediate investigation by your office into the insane conduct of irresponsible white police officers. . . . Representatives of Afro-Asian nations and their press attaches have been besieging the Muslims for more details of the case.[39]

As the Messenger moved closer to Muslims from the Middle East, Ernest 2X McGee introduced the idea of the NOI embracing Islamic orthodoxy. That was an outrageous suggestion, the Messenger replied, as it negated everything he stood for. Furthermore, Islam in the East had been corrupted by devils. Once he finished converting his own people to Islam, the Messenger swore, he would send ministers to the Middle East and re-educate Muslims there about the "true" Islam, the NOI's Islam.[40] The conversation sounded the death knell for McGee. When the Messenger informed Malcolm X that he needed someone to replace McGee, whom he characterized as an infidel, Malcolm X recommended John Ali of the Harlem temple. McGee had never really gotten along well with Wallace or Herbert, so replacing him was of little moment. After some discussion with Malcolm X, McGee was demoted and transferred to New York, and John Ali was appointed national secretary. Feeling betrayed by Malcolm X, McGee quit the NOI.[41]

Without changing his core philosophy, Muhammad used every possible opportunity to attract the attention of Muslim diplomats. The Hinton incident was highlighted not only as an example of racism but as evidence of America's anti-Muslim environment. This perception was enhanced by the bizarre break-in at Malcolm X's home. Though he needed little encouragement, Sanford Alexander made every effort to give front-page exposure to stories about the mistreatment of Muslims at a time when blacks were still being lynched, and when visiting African and Asian diplomats—many of whom were Muslim—were experiencing racial discrimination for the first time in their lives.[42]

By 1958, the discrimination against dark-skinned foreigners by white businesses in America had become the talk of the United Nations. There were many instances of diplomats being thrown out of certain restaurants because of Jim Crow laws and because they were mistaken for African Americans. Another investigation revealed that diplomats were denied access to restrooms while traveling to and from New York and Washington by automobile.[43] These insults, however, were trifling compared to what Muslims found to be the biggest disadvantage for them: the lack of Islamic houses of worship. Only seven cities in the country had orthodox Islamic mosques at the time. Most were quite small and in need of repair, such as the popular mosque in Dearborn (built in 1934). The largest was the Islamic Center in Washington, which had been erected in 1956.[44]

The Messenger sought to build upon this budding brotherhood and America's cultural inadequacies by repeatedly expressing his desire to be of service to Third World Muslims. A second conference between American Muslims and Muslim delegates at the United Nations was held on July 12 at the Park Palace.[45] This time, over 13,000 people participated in the weekend gala. Prominent Third World personages were present, including Mahmoud Boutiba of the Algerian Nationalist Front, Ahmed Z. el-Borai, and dozens of area African-American politicians. J. A. Rogers, an influential black historian and columnist for the *Pittsburgh Courier*, was among the special guests as well, and his command of ancient history made him one of the few black men that Muhammad held in awe. In his lecture, the Messenger sounded every bit as revolutionary as the African leaders sitting before him. "Don't ask the president for jobs. Ask the president to either let us go or give us a few of these forty-eight states," he said.[46]

On August 2, the Messenger traveled to Pittsburgh, where he addressed a crowd of 3,000 at the Syria mosque. Much of the speech was reminiscent of Washington's Harlem address of 1912:

> The white man has been taking care of you. He's listened to your begging, but things are getting tough for him now. He's about ready to ask you to get off his back, and when he does, what are you going to do?

Picking up on a theme that J. A. Rogers had explored in New York, he told the audience that there was no advantage in integration; on the contrary, he said, there were many disadvantages:

> Negroes have been working hard for integration, but we're not ready yet. Give me the same textbooks and I'll teach my children not only what's in the books, but about the history of our great race. I'll make them proud to be so-called Negroes. I'll tell them about their heritage, derived from African and Asia.

In explaining why blacks had made little progress since slavery, he said that slavery had taught them to rely on white people for their existence, and blacks had not reshaped their thinking yet to break the cycle of dependency:

> We are too extravagant, too wasteful, too ignorant. We have no property, no land. We grow nothing. We depend on the white man for our livelihood. We are too rich with nothing in our pockets. Quit blaming others when we ourselves are guilty of many shortcomings.[47]

After receiving Muhammad's consent, Malcolm X accepted an invitation to join the Welcoming Committee of the 28th Precinct Community Council. The group's primary function was to welcome foreign dignitaries to New York. In that capacity, Malcolm X and John Ali were at the airport on August 1 to welcome Prime Minister Kwame Nkrumah of Ghana to America. When John Ali handed Nkrumah several pamphlets about the Messenger, Nkrumah smiled and thanked him, saying he was "most interested in the plight of my people in America."[48] As one might expect, the strengthening bond between Muhammad and the Middle East angered some Americans who considered Muhammad's actions unpatriotic.

In the first week of December, Captain Joseph and John Ali brought a letter to the mosque in which the author threatened to kill Malcolm and the Messenger unless $50,000 in cash was left at a drop site in the black-owned Hotel Theresa in Harlem. "Murder is not new to us," the letter stated. "We could have killed Elijah Muhammad in Boston when he got off the plane." If Muhammad appears in Newark on December 14, the writer warned, "it will be his last time." Muhammad was frightened by the letter.[49] He told John Ali to notify the police and the FBI, which he did. The problem with the letter, police told him, was that it bore no postal stamp to indicate its origins, nor did it mention any organizations, or have any distinctive marks or detectable fingerprints.

The inability of the police to intervene had Muhammad rattled. On December 10 he called his wife, who was in Cordele visiting relatives, and asked her to return home immediately. "My blood pressure is sky high," Elijah told her. "I need you here."[50] Clara rushed home immediately. After police assured him that the letter was probably nothing but the idle ranting of a harmless lunatic, Muhammad regained his composure and decided to speak in Newark as planned. "I have no fear," he said boldly before a crowd of several thousand. "If I'm shot down, you stand up. What is there to be afraid of? We are greater than our enemies who enslave us."[51]

On Saviour's Day 1959, the Messenger and Malcolm X held a joint press conference at which the former announced plans to build a $20,000,000 Islamic Center on Chicago's South Side. The center, he said, would have a modern hospital, a traditional mosque (as opposed to the shabby storefront temples located in most cities), and an expanded University of Islam.[52] The NOI didn't have the money then, but given the increasing number of attacks on Muslims, someone was bound to win a big judgment sooner or later. The first potential windfall was a $24,000,000 civil suit filed against the New York Police Department, the officers involved in the Dorsey incident, and the state. Betty Shabazz and the other defendants went on trial in New York for allegedly assaulting the police officers who broke into their home. They were acquitted of all charges after a two-week trial that began on March 2, 1959—the longest assault trial in New York City's history. After their acquittal the Muslims filed a suit, but it was settled out of court for an amount too meager to call it a victory.[53]

More likely sources of funding that Muhammad hoped to tap into were the newly independent Islamic nations. While he dismissed the *Sepia* report as baseless rumors, the article was accurate about his desire to obtain some financing from the Middle East. On April 20, 1959, Muhammad co-sponsored a major gathering of Pan-Africanists in the New York area. Held in New York City at the Bishop Law Refuge Temple, the African Freedom Day rally demonstrated that newly independent African and Arab nations were immensely interested in alliances with American Muslims.[54] Dozens of prominent African Americans attended the event, including J. A. Rogers, Dr. Henrik Clark, and jazz vocalist Dakota Staton, who provided entertainment at the extravaganza. Diplomats were spotlighted as well, among them Liberian ambassador Charles T. O. King, who emphasized the special kinship between his nation (populated by freed American slaves who had returned to Africa a century earlier) and those Africans who remained in America after slavery. CBS-TV covered the event, but focused on Malcolm X and the NOI. In his speech, Malcolm X called for a "Bandung Conference" of Harlem leaders and urged civil rights groups to support a rally in Washington in May that was being sponsored by the NOI.[55]

The overtures from Middle Eastern and African countries to the NOI also attracted the attention of the B'nai B'rith Anti-Defamation League (ADL) and other Jewish organizations that were concerned about the widening influence of Islam in America and the NOI's antisemitic inclinations. On May 6, 1959, Detective Anton Weidinger of BOSSI notified his commanding officer that he had obtained a copy of the ADL's file on the NOI. According to Weidinger, he had obtained the file from Milton Ellerin, director of the National Fact Finding Board of B'nai B'rith. The document claimed that "A. Z. Borai, third secretary in the United Arab Republic Mission to the UN, is the most active and effective of Arab agents to the Negroes. Basheer of the Mission [is] also active among Negroes."[56]

The Messenger's courtship of Arabs paid off handsomely. In May 1959, Nasser invited him and his family to visit Egypt as official state guests. The invitation, which was delivered by Borai, included a chance to make the hajj.[57] Muhammad immediately started making plans for his first trip abroad. Besides his wife, he planned to take his son Akbar along as his interpreter (Akbar spoke fluent Arabic), and Herbert as the official photographer. Muhammad made airline reservations through Hilton G. Hill, Inc., a black-owned travel agency on 42nd Street, which hired Naeem as a means of securing a contract with the NOI.[58]

When the FBI and CIA learned about the trip, they mounted a COINTELPRO to abort it. First, the CIA contacted the ambassador from Egypt in Washington to determine if he knew what an "unsavory" character Muhammad was and that he preached an adulterated form of Islam.[59] The clock kept ticking as the CIA put up new roadblocks to prevent Muhammad from traveling. Similar contraventions of the Constitution had been used successfully in 1951 against Paul Robeson and William L. Patterson, who had lodged charges of genocide against the United States with the United Nations. Just as the intelligence community played hide-and-seek with their passports, Muhammad found it next to impossible to get his.[60] The Chicago field office SAC wrote in a memo to FBI headquarters:

> It is requested that the Washington field office contact the passport office . . . arrange to place a stop on Elijah Muhammad, Clara Muhammad, his wife, Wallace D. Muhammad, his son, and Raymond Sharrieff, his son-in-law, in the event they make application for a passport. It is requested further that this stop be placed for a three-month period and that it be allowed to expire automatically at that time.[61]

Not to be thwarted, Muhammad decided that Malcolm X should go on to Egypt while he and his lawyers battled the federal government. Malcolm also was instructed to inform Nasser that his, Muhammad's, will to make the hajj would ultimately triumph over the will of the American government to prevent him from doing so. When his lawyers told him that the circumstances surrounding his passport trouble suggested high-level government involvement, Muhammad began to look at every measure involved in traveling abroad with a wary eye. His suspicion that white physicians could not be trusted, for instance, was heightened in late May when he went for the injections that were required for traveling abroad. The doctor wanted to inoculate him against smallpox and give him the two cholera shots together. Hesitant, he first called Malcolm X, who had gone to a different doctor, about what his doctor recommended. The shots should not be given together, Malcolm told the him, because there was a high probability of side effects. His doctor, Malcolm said, recommended that the "second cholera shot be taken a week later."[62] That Malcolm's physician thought the shots would be harmful seems to have made Muhammad think that the physician was part of the plot to prevent him from visiting Nasser. He asked Malcolm in a follow-up call about the race of the doctor who gave him his shots. He was white, Malcolm said. When Muhammad asked about finding a black physician to administer the shots, Malcolm replied that he didn't think there were any black doctors in the office where the shots were given. "They were all devils," he said.[63]

On June 5, 1959, the FBI sent the CIA's deputy director of plans a memorandum regarding Muhammad's pending trip. According to the memo, the FBI had discovered that the main objective of the trip was to "impress his followers in the United States who contribute to his support by showing that he is a well-known Moslem and has connections in the Moslem world."[64] For its part, the CIA contacted Ambassador Mustafa Kamal of the United Arab Republic. After discussing the matter, Kamal was reported to have said that "it is religiously and politically unwise to give Muhammad any recognition when he visits Egypt." But Kamal refused to speak out publicly against Muhammad's trip, which probably was a wise move. He had been an ambassador for a little over a year and had not been in the country long enough to be well acquainted with the NOI. Besides, it would have been political suicide to speak out against the wishes of Nasser. Without being able to get Muslims to publicly denounce Muhammad, the intelligence community had to resort to other measures.[65]

The State Department's shell game with Muhammad's passport came to a halt after William R. Ming Jr., a formidable attorney who also represented Dr. Martin Luther King Jr., lobbied to get the passport approved. In a conversation monitored by the FBI on June 19, Ming told Muhammad that he had contacted the Chicago offices of Illinois senators Everett M. Dirksen and Paul Douglas. Ming complained that his client was an upstanding American citizen who was being unconstitutionally deprived of his right to travel. The office promised to look into the matter immediately. The mere mention of Dirksen, who had just been named Republican minority leader, quickly got the State Department's attention. When an aide called on June 19 to determine what the holdup was, an official in the passport division said that there "appeared to be no overriding political reasons which preclude issuance of a passport" to Mr. Muhammad.[66] Five days later, Muhammad received Passport Number 1677936. By the time everything was in order for the trip, it was too late for Muhammad to properly prepare for the complete hajj. In the meantime, he told Malcolm X to go to the Middle East without him, as the invitation from Nasser was not an opportunity to be wasted.[67]

Malcolm X, a gifted thinker and the NOI's cynosure, left the country on July 12, and the very next day, Muhammad got the national exposure that he craved. On the evening of July 13, Mike Wallace, a former game-show host and commercial pitchman who anchored a new, provocative television show on WNTA-TV called *News Beat*, ran the first segment of a five-part series on the NOI.[68] The research for the program was primarily the work of Louis E. Lomax, a well-respected black journalist who worked with Wallace. The packaging, however, was vintage Mike Wallace (now a veteran anchorman of CBS-TV's *60 Minutes*). The series, which was called "The Hate That Hate Produced," ran on Channel 13 in New York, but its impact was nationwide because news wire services spread it in frightening terms. Wallace, a Jew, narrated in a somber, ominous tone. When he featured James Lawson of the United African Nationalist Movement calling Roy Wilkins an "Uncle Tom" and Arthur Spingarn, president of the NAACP, a "Zionist Jew," Jewish immigrants who still bore numbers that were tattooed on their arms during the Holocaust surely recognized what Wallace was implying: Hitler had been reincarnated as a little black man from Chicago, and the NOI was a diabolical cult of "250,000 fanatical Muslims" dedicated to the destruction of Jews and Gentiles:

> While city officials, state agencies, white liberals and sober-minded Negroes stand idly by, a group of Negro dissenters are taking to street-corner stepladders, church pulpits, sports arenas, and ballroom platforms across the nation to preach the gospel of hate that would set off a federal investigation if it were to be preached by Southern whites.[69]

The documentary was repackaged as an hour-long show and rebroadcast elsewhere on July 22, placing the NOI among the most controversial topics in the media. Much of the media's interest was induced by the uniqueness of the group—it had never occurred to most white people that some blacks rejected Christianity, and it certainly was never suspected that anyone black could believe that Caucasians were inferior to the country's former slaves. Some footage that CBS-TV shot of black Americans commiserating with Arabs and Africans during the Africa

Unity Feast was incorporated into the documentary; the overall effect was to suggest that black Americans pledged allegiance to their race instead of their nation.

For Muhammad, the program couldn't have been aired at a worse time. Malcolm X was in Egypt that week as Nasser's guest. The inferences drawn from the visit were that the NOI was being financed by Arabs who, like Muhammad, were dedicated to dismantling the eleven-year-old state of Israel. Only four days after the second broadcast, Nasser made comments that seemed to corroborate media implications of an international Muslim conspiracy. "We are awaiting aggression by Israel and any supporters of Israel," Nasser told a large crowd gathered in Alexandria in celebrate the seventh anniversary of the coup dethroning King Farouk. "We will make it a decisive battle and get rid of Israel once and for all."[70]

Fallout from the broadcast was swift, uniform, and international. Nearly every prominent civil rights leader condemned the Messenger and his philosophy. "We must not stoop to the low and primitive methods of some of our opponents," Dr. King told attendees at the National Bar Association (the African-American counterpart of the American Bar Association) on August 28. The NOI is but one of the "hate groups arising in our midst which would preach a doctrine of black supremacy. Black supremacy is as bad as white supremacy."[71] The Reverend Ralph Abernathy, a top assistant to King, had expressed similar sentiments. "We are not working for black supremacy, for I happen to know that it is worse than white. We are working for a world of brotherhood."[72] At least one civil rights leader, however, fell into a trap set by Wallace, an originator of "ambush journalism." When asked about the NOI, Roy Wilkins, national director of the NAACP, pretended not to know very much about the group, not even the names of its leaders. Footage showed Lomax asking Wilkins whether he had read Muhammad's newspaper column. "I do not read the *Los Angeles Herald Dispatch* at all and I must say that in reading the *Pittsburgh Courier*, I have never read a column by . . . Mr. Who?"[73]

"Elijah Muhammad," Wallace replied.

"Elijah Muhammad? No. No."

After the clip ended, Wallace returned to the camera and announced that he found it "incredible that Roy Wilkins was unaware of the existence of Elijah Muhammad. Every other responsible Negro leader in the city knows about the Muslims, about Elijah Muhammad, and about Minister Malcolm X. . . . Then our research staff unearthed these pictures." The camera panned to a photo of Wilkins talking to Malcolm X, then of the two men smiling at each other and shaking hands. As if the audience didn't get the message, Wallace made it plain:

Maybe Mr. Wilkins does not know that there are about 250,000 of these people [Black Muslims] in the United States. Maybe he does not know that the members of the black nationalist movement have taken to the street corners to preach hatred of the white man . . . but I think he should. As leader of the NAACP, he not only should know these things, but he and his colleagues should begin to do something about it.

Kenneth B. Keating, a powerful U.S. senator from New York, immediately threatened a congressional probe of the NOI:

A very disturbing development has been the emergence of a new hate group in the United States which calls itself Moslem and whose leader preaches a cult of racism for Negroes and extreme antisemitism. . . . The name adopted by this fanatical organization is an insult to the members of the Moslem religious faith, which has absolutely no relationship to this group. . . . These developments require the attention of Congress.[74]

Five days after the initial broadcast, S. B. Fuller, the black Chicago multimillionaire, bought a controlling interest in the *Pittsburgh Courier*. He immediately advised Muhammad that he was dropping his column from the newspaper, effective in thirty days. Fuller's entrance into the picture signaled the end of Muhammad's influence on the paper and the beginning of Dr. King's reign.[75]

The documentary was the first crisis in a decade that the Messenger faced without the able assistance of Malcolm X. The fact that Malcolm X's fiery rhetoric was edited to make the Muslims sound like antiwhite pit bulls didn't help matters, nor did the fact that Malcolm X received more time on camera than the Messenger and all the other ministers combined. Several ministers who were jealous of Malcolm X and who had urged Muhammad not to cooperate with Wallace and Lomax cited the uproar after the show as evidence that Malcolm X was grandstanding. While Muhammad fumbled for a way to blunt the show's impact, Malcolm X was thousands of miles away, trying to finesse his way through the rituals of diplomacy and prayer. The trip began on a sour note, as he had made no reservations for lodging. He had assumed that the Egyptian government would accommodate him as Muhammad's emissary.[76] The Egyptians quickly resolved the misunderstanding by reserving a suite for him in a luxurious hotel in Cairo.

Most of Malcolm X's time was spent with Anwar el Sadat, vice-president of Egypt. During one meeting with Sadat and prominent businessmen and religious figures, an architect was deeply impressed by Malcolm's interpretation of Muhammad's dreams of an Islamic empire in America. The architect volunteered to draw blueprints for any size mosque Muhammad wanted to build anywhere in America.[77] Malcolm was also offered a chance to make the hajj, but he declined. He was embarrassed in the first phase because he didn't know the words to the Holy Quran's daily prayers. He also avoided discussing Muhammad's theocracy because he knew it "would be regarded as blasphemy by the devout."[78] He developed dysentery on the third day of the trip, which kept him in his hotel room for three days. "Something I ate just before leaving Cairo gave me a serious siege of upset stomach," he wrote self-effacingly in his weekly column.[79]

Malcolm X returned to Harlem on July 22, the day the documentary was rerun as an hour-long special. The fallout from the show angered Muhammad, who had maintained his silence about the broadcast. When he spoke at the St. Nicholas Arena in Harlem on July 26, he seemed angry with Malcolm X. He had been opposed to allowing Lomax to attend a Muslim rally because the latter wanted to bring in white men with fancy television cameras. The NOI, Muhammad argued, had no control over how the videotape would be edited, and he warned Malcolm that the show could backfire against the NOI. Malcolm, on the other hand, argued that the benefits were greater than the risks. He believed the broadcast would put Muhammad closer to getting the 144,000 members he was aiming for.

Events proved that each man was half-right. When Malcolm X and Muhammad, whom the *Courier* described in a news story as the "spiritual leader of more than a quarter-million black Americans," finished castigating Wallace for using "tricknology" in editing the show, whatever hostility the Messenger had against Malcolm disappeared. Further, when Malcolm X told the crowd about his recent trip, and how fond Anwar Sadat and Nasser were of Muhammad, the surrogate father smiled proudly. God, the Messenger often said, never closes one door without opening another. The standing-room-only crowd proved that the broadcast had broadened the NOI's appeal. Membership was growing so fast that there was no room in the temples for many. In Los Angeles alone, 500 people joined the NOI the week after the rerun.[80]

Imam Talib Ahmad Dawud, Dakota Staton's husband, was enraged over Mike Wallace's failure to include the Moslem Brotherhood in what he called a "one-sided" special report that defamed all Muslims who were African American. In a front-page article of the August 1 edition of the *Chicago New Crusader*, Dawud denounced Muhammad as a "fake" and a "confidence man" who taught a "perverted form" of Islam. On the same day, his wife gave an interview to the *Pittsburgh Courier* in which she said that the documentary was a "vicious misrepresentation as well as a slander against the religion of Islam. . . . He [Wallace] acted in a very bigoted manner when he refused to present the side of orthodox Islam, although he had taped an interview with the representative of the Moslem Brotherhood."[81]

Two days later, *U.S. News and World Report* ran a three-page spread on New York, which it said was sitting on a "powder keg" of racial unrest. The article said that while the "sect claims to deplore violence," its inflammatory teachings often led to violence. It also included two photographs taken at the scene of a Harlem demonstration against police brutality that nearly turned violent. The only reason calm was restored, it noted, was because boxer Sugar Ray Robinson pleaded with the crowd to disperse. The demonstration, the article noted repeatedly, occurred on July 13—the first day that "The Hate That Hate Produced" was broadcast.[82]

On August 10, a *Time* magazine reporter who had been given a copy of the FBI's dossier on the Messenger ran a damaging article, citing the most salacious data from the file, and made it appear that he was a career criminal. The Messenger, the writer stated, had an "extensive" FBI record.[83] Yet the article cited only two instances in which the Messenger had been arrested. It highlighted his 1934 arrest for "contributing to the delinquency of a minor," a charge that most people associate with pedophilia or other types of child abuse when in fact it stemmed from the home schooling issue. It also described, much to Muhammad's embarrassment, the circumstances of his arrest in Chicago on sedition charges during World War II. "When FBI agents tracked him to his mother's Chicago home in September 1942, they found him rolled up in a carpet under her bed." That was the first time most Muslims knew about the episode because it had not been mentioned in the media since the day after his arrest. With the exception of Muhammad's immediate family, no one in the NOI knew about the actual circumstances of his arrest. *Newsweek* ran a similar story in its August 11 issue.[84]

When Muhammad asked Malcolm X where he supposed the magazines were getting their information, the minister replied that someone he knew had evidence that the FBI and the ADL were conspiring against the NOI. Malcolm's source appears to have been BOSSI or FBI agents because it was someone who knew him well enough to broach the subject, and it was someone with access to BOSSI's files (they even offered to show Malcolm X the BOSSI account of his trip to Africa). "I'll tell you actually who's supposed to be putting out all this information—it's a Jewish organization called B'nai B'rith. They have agents all over the world and they've supposedly got a complete set of information on everything."[85] Malcolm said his source had shown him the files on which the *Time* magazine story was based. "They had a so-called file on you from the Chicago Police Department, the Federal Bureau of Investigation, and from B'nai B'rith. They had all these files and they let me read it and I told them outright that all this information is not even true."[86] For the Messenger, Malcolm X's statement about a worldwide Jewish cabal corroborated his belief that the *Protocols* was an authentic document.

CHAPTER TEN

COMPROMISED

He was full of the most tantalizing thoughts about how wonderful it would be if only he were permitted to hold her close, kiss her mouth, bite her, even. . . . She would look at him at moments with deliberate, swimming eyes, and he actually felt a little sick and weak—almost nauseated. His one dream was that by some process, either by charm or money, he could make himself interesting to her.

—*Theodore Dreiser,*
An American Tragedy[1]

The marriages of the Holy Prophet have furnished his critics with the chief implement of attack on him. . . . Therefore, I give below the full particulars regarding the Prophet's marriages. . . . Briefly these are: (1) a celibate life up to age twenty-five. (2) A married state with one wife from 25 to 54. (3) Several marriages from 54 to 60. (4) No further marriage after 60. . . . Thus it will be seen that all marriages of the Prophet were due either to feelings of compassion for the widows of his faithful followers or to put a stop to bloodshed and ensure union with some tribe.

—*Holy Quran, Commentary*[2]

No sooner had Muhammad doused one fire than another one started, each burning more fiercely than the last. His next setback involved a former theater building housing the University of Islam in Detroit. On August 13, 1959, the Detroit State Police and the Michigan State government building engineers raided the school after receiving reports of building code violations. The *Detroit Free Press* was tipped off about the raid and had photographers on hand to record the event.[3] A story appeared in the next day's paper, flanked by photos of the dilapidated dwelling. News services covered the raid as well, resulting in national exposure; the *New York Times* was among those who printed a version.[4] By the time the apologetic minister called the Messenger to apprise him of the "bad publicity," word of the raid was on the airwaves and in the Chicago newspapers. The minister claimed that the raid was unfair because the fire marshal and city health officials found that the violations did not warrant a shutdown. Muhammad told the minister that considering the source, they had nothing to be overly concerned about. "That paper [*Detroit Free Press*] has been against me and my followers since the early 1930s," he said.[5]

Up until that point, all the negative publicity had come from the popular media, a source that the Messenger and his followers easily dismissed as the work of "white devils," but the next fire flared up in Muhammad's own back yard and scarred him for life. "White Man Is God for the Cult of Islam," read a banner headline in the *Chicago New Crusader* on August 15, 1959. The story that followed claimed that the Messenger taught his "70,000-odd Negro followers scattered across the U.S. that a white man, called 'Master W. D. Fard Muhammad,' who was a Turkish-born Nazi agent [who] worked for Hitler in World War II, is their God!" According to the article, Fard was a Muslim from Turkey who had come to the United States in the early 1900s. He had met

Muhammad in prison, the author alleged, where the two men plotted a confidence game in which followers were charged a fee to become Muslims. After joining, converts contributed 10 percent of their earnings to Fard and Muhammad. Parts of the story were true, as it was based on information culled from a recent FBI investigation of Fard's past, but the large number of errors in the story tainted even its truths. On a humorous note, the author's name was Mohammed Yakub Khan. Yakub, of course, was the name of the "big-head scientist" who created white people, according to the NOI's eschatology. The fact that the author's middle name was Yakub, Muslim ministers taught, was a sign from Allah that the "devil" was behind the error-filled story.

FBI agents listened in as Muhammad and Malcolm X discussed what they considered to be a media conspiracy against the NOI.[6] The Messenger felt that the media were printing false information to get him to make public rebuttals revealing what he knew about Fard's life and to divulge personal data about himself. Initially, he was determined not to provide any information to the media. "They will take the honesty and the fairness of the thing and mix it up, so the best thing to do is to stay away from it. That was one of the dirtiest tricks in the world,"[7] he told Malcolm, adding that he considered the owners of the *Crusader* as brothers who had betrayed one of their own so as to appease white advertisers who kept their papers afloat. Until the *Crusader* story, Muhammad and the paper's owners had been on friendly terms, but the Fard story changed that and altered his perception of all black journalists. Not only was the story wrong, but the *Crusader* had never even bothered to invite Muhammad to reply to the allegations. Scores of black-owned newspapers printed some version of the story. Like the *Crusader*'s reporter, few bothered to seek Muhammad's reply.

There was a conspiracy involved, as Muhammad surmised, but the media were not involved. The campaign of disruption was hatched by FBI agents in Chicago, Detroit, and New York and at FBI headquarters.[8] Most of the accurate material in the story had been in the Bureau's files for a little more than two years. The reporter did not attempt to conceal the source of his story. "Washington records of the Justice Department," the fifth paragraph stated, "show that Elijah Muhammad (alias Elijah

Mohammed, alias Gulam Bogan, alias Mohammed Rassoull) was arrested during World War II by Chicago police on a sedition charge." In the context of the story, the Justice Department was synonymous with the FBI.[9]

In his August 20 column of the *Los Angeles Herald Tribune*, Muhammad castigated the media for printing unsubstantiated material as fact:

> The average Negro has been so thoroughly changed into the devil that the only way to distinguish the real devil from his imps is by color. . . . The Negro press knows it all, but as soon as their white God wrote false charges against me three weeks ago, the so-called Negro press carefully picked out all the false and evil things said, and wrote against me and my followers. They made headlines out of it for their papers to show the world their love for the enemy, and their hate for the leader among them.[10]

The African-American media's blind acceptance of the leaked FBI file on Fard as the gospel truth may have been a blessing in disguise, as it served as the impetus for the Messenger to recharge sales of the NOI's two magazines, *Muhammad* and *Salaam*. More importantly, Malcolm X started a house organ for the sect in his basement. The first edition was called *Islamic News,* but it was later renamed *Muhammad Speaks.*[11]

In the midst of the media's pummeling of Muhammad, a white bigot from Kentucky entered the ring. In early August, Jessie B. Stoner had sent a bellicose letter to New York City police commissioner Stephen P. Kennedy.[12] Writing on stationery of the Christian Knights of the Ku Klux Klan, Stoner, who had been charged with bombing a black church in Montgomery, Alabama, in 1958,[13] offered the commissioner some ideas on how to deal with the NOI:

> I am an expert on the black Muslims. The only thing that can stop Elijah Muhammad and his black Muslims from conquering New York is for my Christian Knights and your New York police to join hands and work together to uphold White Christian Supremacy. . . . You need to

learn more about that evil genius, Elijah Muhammad, or you will never stop him and his niggers from taking over your city.... He claims to be the reincarnation of that infidelic 7th Century prophet, Mohammed, who almost conquered the known world and he may be him because he is much more clever than the other niggers ... the Muslim religion of Islam is a nigger religion which appeals to the nigger's black racial instincts. That is why Muslims grow stronger every day even though every nigger that becomes a Muslim will go to hell when he dies. If we fail to stop the Muslims now, the 16,000,000 niggers of America will all soon be Muslims and you will never be able to stop them. Reports from Christian missionaries say that Islam is sweeping over all of Africa, so don't underestimate the Muslims ... there is a bad nigger at the head of the Muslims.[14]

Stoner's letter was dated August 6, 1959. On August 7, the Bureau had started its own racist letter-writing campaign. FBI official James F. Bland suggested that a pseudonymous letter be sent to leading newspapers and magazines in the Middle East countries that Muhammad planned to visit.[15] If foreigners realized that "Muhammad" was not Elijah's given name and that he taught an impure form of Islam, Bland argued, then they might keep their distance from him. The COINTEL-PRO was approved by Alan H. Belmont, one of Hoover's chief assistants, on August 20. Constructed as a story about an Arab father and son, the letter warned that "true Moslems have all been alerted to stay away" from Muhammad during his tour because he "teaches hate and deceit for the purpose of extracting millions from his gullible followers for his own personal gratification, whereas the true Moslem believes in love and respect for all mankind." The letter alerted readers that the Messenger's real name was "Elijah Poole," a man who "hasn't done a day's work since about 1930 when he started spoofing the Negroes in Detroit, Michigan, with his own butchered version of our beloved Moslem faith."[16]

While the Bland letter made its way overseas, another letter, dated August 29 and written by Stoner, landed on Muhammad's desk.

Infidel, I have you black Muslims on the run and will soon put you out of business. That being the case, why don't you dissolve your Muslim niggers organization of Islam and tell your darkies to go home and be good niggers and stay in their place? . . . You will have to admit that I kept you from speaking in Indianapolis recently . . . when I heard you were planning to speak in Indianapolis, I drove over to Indianapolis and had a conference with local Klan leaders. . . . They then got prominent people to call on Rev. Hardin and other leaders of the nigger community in Indianapolis and headed you off. . . . If you will dissolve your temples of Islam and publicly say that the great White Race is a superior race and that all niggers should stay in their place . . . I will help you get a good job on a farm.[17]

Muhammad was shaken up by the letter, perhaps because of its insight on the Indianapolis cancellation, or maybe because Stoner stirred up memories of the lynching of his childhood friend, Albert Hamilton. In light of Stoner's villainous reputation, Muhammad sought to ensure his safety by mailing a copy of the two-page letter to the *New York Amsterdam News,* which reprinted it in its entirety on the front page of its September 19 edition. Thus, if anything happened to him, Stoner would be high up on the list of suspects. He also sent a copy of the letter to the federal agency responsible for investigating notes like the one from Stoner and Bland: the FBI.[18]

The Messenger's troubles continued to mount as he prepared for his trip to the Middle East. On Friday, September 18, the University of Islam in Detroit was shut down again for building code violations. He was informed that it would require a minimum of $10,000 to bring the building up to standard. Rather than invest more money in the old structure, he took out a $50,000 loan to purchase a new building.[19]

Negative media reports continued to proliferate. A most damaging remark came from Thurgood Marshall, who had become a folk hero after successfully arguing the *Brown* case. Marshall, who had indirectly defended Muslims against police brutality during the 1943 riot in Detroit, joined the chorus of dissenters. "The Black Muslim movement," he said during a speech at Princeton University, "is run by a bunch of thugs organized from prisons and jails and financed, I am sure, by Nasser or some Arab group."[20] Malcolm X immediately denounced Marshall as a "20th-century Uncle Tom," while an editorial in the *Los Angeles Herald Dispatch* labeled the lawyer a "Zionist" and an "Uncle Tom." The Messenger's response was less visceral, almost apologetic in tone. Marshall's charges, he said, "are completely false. I have no knowledge of what other Muslims are doing in America and I am only speaking for my group. We are not and have not received so much as a penny from the Arab nations, nor any others than ourselves."[21]

Like Muhammad, Malcolm was certain that the "Zionist media" were trying to sabotage the Messenger's relationship with Arabs and Africans. His anger boiled over on September 23 while he was at Muhammad's temple in Connecticut recounting his African trip: "The Honorable Elijah Muhammad does not teach hate. . . . The Bible and Negro leaders teach that men should love each other, but if one ever asked a Jew if he loved Hitler, he would probably have a spasm. Do Americans love Khrushchev? Do white people love black people?"[22]

The Mike Wallace/Louis Lomax special on the NOI had catapulted membership into the tens of thousands during the next year. As one would expect, the sudden notoriety of the NOI made it attractive to the downtrodden. Criticism from men such as Marshall and Wilkins and King enhanced the NOI's appeal, as the thinking among inner-city blacks was that Muhammad must be good if white people and "Uncle Tom Negroes" condemned him. At the time, the NOI simply was not equipped to handle thousands of new recruits—it was like forcing a dozen people to live in an apartment designed for three. The strain of trying to accommodate so many new adhereents at once frustrated ministers, and also strained Malcolm's relationship with the Messenger. Malcolm X often called Muhammad to let him know how well a recruitment drive had gone in a given city, only to hear him reply that what he really needed was for Malcolm X to train more men for ministerial duties. "I could have a million followers if I had more ministers," the Messenger kept telling him.[23]

The NOI's rapid growth also fomented fights for power and turf. Louis Farrakhan became embroiled in one such struggle in the fall of

1959, not with Malcolm X, but with Ella X Little, Malcolm's sister, who lived in Boston. The dispute over the leadership of Temple No. 11 in Boston came to a standoff in July.[24] As it was known that Ella was the person Malcolm X had relied on for guidance from his teens onward, members of the temple habitually came to her for instruction instead of going to Farrakhan. After all, she served as counsel to the second most powerful person in the NOI. Angered over Ella's rising authority in the temple, Farrakhan called the Messenger to complain that Ella was undermining him and ought to be disciplined. She was acting as though she was the minister, he said.[25] When Ella discovered what Farrakhan had done, she confronted him, calling him a "Momma's boy" who had let a little power go to his head. The charge stung Farrakhan, an outwardly bold man who never knew his father, and who was said to have a worse Oedipus complex than Norman Bates. In her anger, Ella telephoned the Messenger in Chicago on July 16 to tell him that Farrakhan was incapable of managing the mosque. "He's young, and he wants everyone to bow to him," she said.[26]

Ella was one among many women who had written to Muhammad to complain about Farrakhan. She, like the others, wanted him to reprimand Farrakhan and to make her the first female captain, as he had promised he would. When Malcolm X called him later that day, Muhammad mentioned his discussion with Ella. He wanted to placate her, he said, but was most reluctant to remove Farrakhan as minister because he felt things were going well in Boston, particularly in terms of membership. He asked Malcolm if he could solve the crisis for him. "I'm afraid she'll use me to get people to side with her," Malcolm said.[27]

"Go to Boston," Muhammad replied, "and try to settle the troubled waters, but don't side with either one." He told Malcolm to call them together and listen to each one's story. Even though she was Malcolm's sister, Muhammad said, Ella had to recognize and respect Farrakhan as the leader in Boston, while Farrakhan should recognize that he should not dismantle programs or "tear things down" just because Ella devised them or merely to "show he is in charge."[28]

Malcolm followed the instructions to the letter. He told Farrakhan to reinstate some programs that Ella had created for women and children.

Dismantling the programs had been ill-advised and was the chief source of acrimony among the men and women in the temple. Similarly, he told Ella that she would have to stop undermining Farrakhan by usurping his responsibilities as minister. The treaty met with Farrakhan's approval, but Ella signed on reluctantly. She told her siblings that the Messenger had betrayed her and that he never had any intention of making her or any woman a minister or captain of the mosque.[29] After several weeks of trying to go along with the compromise, Ella stopped coming to the temple. When Malcolm asked her about it, she replied that she could not remain in a mosque under the leadership of "a minister who lacked backbone and vision." Besides, Ella said, she had only joined the NOI to please Malcolm. She had never really believed that the Messenger was a prophet—she knew him when he was a scrawny little teenager in Georgia, she said—nor did she believe for one second that Master Wallace D. Fard was Allah. "The only reason she did so [joined]," her son Rodnell Collins said, "was because she felt it was the best program for black people since the Marcus Garvey movement."[30]

Muhammad's problems persisted. On October 27, one of his secretaries, Evelyn Lorene X Williams, started calling him at home to complain that he was not giving her enough money.[31] She reminded him that she was carrying his child, and suggested that she could cause trouble for him if he didn't meet her demands. Muhammad accused her of trying to blackmail him, and dared her to try to get more money out of him. "You must think I'm a fool or Santa Claus," he said.[32] Evelyn's call had come at a most inopportune time. Not only was his bronchial condition giving him trouble, but his right hand was still bandaged owing to a mishap with his 1956 Cadillac. He had slammed the door on his hand on October 2, and had ripped off a fingernail and torn most of the muscles in his thumb, which put him in the hospital for three days.[33] The pain left little room for aggravation. In a conversation with a minister after hanging up on Evelyn, he said, "It looks like she will have to be put down."[34] As the minister listened closely to learn how the Messenger wanted him to deal with Evelyn, FBI agents listening in on the conversation made notes that would soon help the Bureau deal with the Messenger.

Meanwhile, Muhammad readied himself for Mecca. The COINTEL-

PRO concerning the bogus letter of August 7 had had little or no impact at all because its "camel jockey" humor was as repulsive as the derogatory portrayal of Muhammad.[35] Thus, the FBI kept close tabs on Muhammad, noting on November 20, 1959, that "Special Agents of the FBI observed Elijah Muhammad and entourage depart from [Chicago's] Midway Airport . . . at 12:00 noon via United Airlines Flight Number 632 en route to New York City." The next day, two agents from the New York field office "observed Elijah Muhammad and sons depart on SAS [Scandinavian Air Lines] Flight 912 to Copenhagen, Denmark." The Bureau had already coordinated surveillance of Muhammad's activities abroad with the CIA and the intelligence divisions of the armed services.[36]

After a brief stop in Denmark, the family boarded a plane bound for Istanbul. The Turkish government was only vaguely familiar with Islam among African Americans. Members of the MSTA had come before the Turkish government in 1930, and the same group periodically appealed to Turkey to allocate land to Moorish Americans. Perhaps the intelligence community expected Muhammad to make a similar move. "The two sons visited the American Consulate, Istanbul, on 24 November 1959," U.S. Army Colonel Martin L. Green wrote from his office at the American embassy on December 30. The memo, titled "Movement of Elijah Muhammad (U),"[37] was addressed to the assistant chief of staff for army intelligence at the Pentagon. "They discussed any possible difficulties they might have in obtaining visas for the rest of their trip. Mr. Burke, the Visa Officer, described them [Herbert and Akbar] as American Negroes, approximately twenty-five years old." Similar cables were sent to Washington from the Foreign Service, the CIA, and naval intelligence.[38]

After several days of sightseeing in Turkey, Muhammad and his sons moved on to Lebanon for two days, and then to Jordan. The much anticipated stay in Egypt began on November 29. Nasser rolled out the red carpet. He was quite taken with Akbar, because of his fluent Arabic. The Messenger also discovered that he and Anwar Sadat had similar backgrounds. For starters, both men were named Muhammad: Sadat's full name was Muhammad Anwar el Sadat. Both believed that Hitler was a brilliant military leader—Sadat even considered him a hero.[39] Both went to prison in 1942 over military issues: Muhammad for refusing to fight for America, and Sadat for collaborating with the Nazis. Finally, Sadat and Muhammad believed that Zionism was racist and felt that the United Nations had erred in creating the state of Israel.[40]

At two weeks, the Egyptian segment of the trip was the longest. Sadat's earlier meetings with Malcolm X and Nasser's conversations with Muhammad convinced the United Arab Republic's dynamic duo that the NOI was the key to promoting Islamic causes in America. According to Muhammad, Nasser first appealed to him to resettle in Africa to propagate Islam. "Millions of Africans are ready to listen to you overnight. You have a million-and-a-half people in French West Africa." But Muhammad declined, telling Nasser that God placed him in America for a divine purpose, just as God had placed Nasser in Egypt.[41]

From Egypt Muhammad and his sons went on to Ethiopia, and by then Muhammad really began to miss Clara. On one hand, the geographical distance symbolized their marital relationship. On the other, she was his childhood sweetheart. Being so far away from her became nearly unbearable. He began calling her in Chicago at every opportunity. Clara received a letter from Akbar on the day after Christmas, dated December 19, in which he wrote that they were in Ethiopia, and that it was much colder than they had expected. He asked her to send them some warmer clothing as soon as possible, but by the time the package arrived they were already in Saudi Arabia. They landed in Jidda, army intelligence agents stationed at the American embassy there noted, "from Cairo 24 December, visited Mecca, Medina."[42] Muhammad wrote in the notes of his trip that,

Mecca is the only city on our planet that is divinely protected and made sacred and inviolable. . . . On entering that holy and magnificent place, [the guide] proceeded with us to the court where stands the Kaaba and that prophetic sign—the Black Stone that the builders rejected, placed in one corner of that great black veiled monument that stands in a circle. . . . There were between five to ten thousand Muslims inside the court of the mosque. Such a prayer service I have never witnessed before being with these thousands of sincere worshipers of God, His religion, and Muhammad His Prophet.[43]

After the hajj, Muhammad went to Pakistan, the first nation founded exclusively for Muslims. On December 29, he called Clara from Karachi to remind her that he would be back in Chicago on the first Wednesday of the new year. He spoke effusively about the unforgettable experience of the hajj, but mostly he listened to Clara. The sound of her voice was comforting for an old man who had never been in a foreign country. Africa was not as Muhammad had imagined it, he told her. Some of the places they visited lacked modern conveniences that Americans took for granted—basic things like indoor plumbing and lighting, reliable public transportation, and abundant clean drinking water. When it came to Africa, the words of Thomas Wolfe rang true for African Americans. It was true of Africa for Muhammad, and it was true of America when he returned. When he landed in New York City shortly before ten o'clock on January 6, the first person he got in touch with was Malcolm, but only to use Malcolm's telephone to call Clara. "Don't tell anyone we're back," he told her, because "we've been on the road for three days and look awful."[44] Herbert was with him; Akbar had remained in Egypt to attend college.

Muhammad recounted his trip to Africa in his column of January 14. There was an oddity about his recollections: the column made no mention of the thousands of white Muslims he saw in Mecca. Ironically, at the end of the column his standard closing appeared: "Hurry and join onto your own kind. The end of this world is at Hand." And in each temple—which he designated as a "mosque" on Saviour's Day—three lessons remained unchanged: (1) the white man was still the devil; (2) Elijah was still the synthesis of the Prophet Elijah and the Prophet Muhammad Ibn Abdullah; (3) Master Wallace D. Fard was regarded as Allah.[45]

While Elijah sat around recounting the glories of the hajj, Clara did everything she could to refrain from putting arsenic in his coffee. Within a day of his return home, he was barely speaking to her. He spent most of his time in Apartment Number 1 at 8205 South Vernon Street, which he used as an office and love nest.[46] When she asked for an explanation for his absence, he said that he was staying there "to study and rest." Clara retorted, in so many words, that he was studying Evelyn's anatomy while "resting" with her.[47] It wasn't simply his affair with Evelyn that upset her, but all of the affairs whose existence she had denied for so long. She had seen evidence of her husband's infidelity as early as 1955 but had turned away from the realities. In July 1958, a secretary who had left their home abruptly in March started calling Muhammad repeatedly. During one call, she told him that he had treated her unfairly by covering up their relationship, and that she wanted a trial "by the Nation" so she could restore her good name. "I am the Nation," he said sharply, "and I have already told you that it has been decided and therefore there is no need for any further discussion." With that, he hung up on her, then vented his anger by arguing with Clara.[48]

On January 18, 1960, a minister called Muhammad's home. Clara answered the phone. "I haven't seen him since yesterday," she said despondently. "He doesn't sleep here now." The reason Elijah hadn't been home, she discovered, was that Lucille X Rosary, one of his secretaries, had borne his child on January 17.[49] On January 23, Lottie called, wanting to come over to visit her parents. Clara replied that she would be disappointed if she hoped to see her father because he was never home. When Lottie asked her mother whether she had done something to anger him, Clara replied, no, that it was just the opposite. "I got hold of one of them things I got before," she said, referring to a love letter to her husband from one of his secretaries. Lottie asked her how she had found the letter. "He meant to put it in his suitcase when he went to Detroit," she said, but by mistake he had left it lying on the bed. When Clara asked him about it, "he got mad at me because Allah let him leave it where I can see it."[50] Elijah had asked her to give him the letter, which had been addressed to his private apartment, but she refused. She was keeping it as evidence of his infidelity, she said, which he had denied. Since her refusal, her husband had stopped talking to her. "I don't know what he thinks my heart is," she said sadly, "flesh and bone or a piece of wood or what." She had an open invitation to go to California, Clara said, and given the way things were going, she just might take her friends up on their offer one day.[51]

Clara, it turns out, had also discovered that Evelyn was scheduled to give birth to Elijah's child in March, and that a third young secretary, Ola X Hughes, would have a child he sired in April.[52] As if that weren't bad enough, Elijah started spending an inordinate amount of time with a June X, another of his secretaries. The FBI taped a conversation on January 27 in which Muhammad and one of his mistresses discussed his plans to redecorate the apartment.[53]

The annual Saviour's Day convention of 1960 couldn't have come at a worse time for Clara. She was so upset with her husband that she didn't want to be with him in private, let alone play the role of the innocent, ignorant wife before an assembly of thousands. On February 13 she and Elijah got into a bitter argument, and he grabbed his coat and stormed out of the house. When he left, Clara called one of her daughters. "I'm sick and tired of it," she protested. "I'll try to stick it out until the 26th [Saviour's Day], but that's it."[54] Clara had threatened to skip the event entirely because things were so bad between her and her husband. When Lottie called the Chicago residence on Monday, February 22, to speak to her father, Clara sounded deeply depressed. "All he ever says to me is 'As Salaam Alaikum,'" Clara confided, "and it's all because of that bitch in Detroit." Her daughter knew immediately to whom Clara was referring, as Elijah had been spending a great deal of time with a young woman from Mosque No. 1. "You need a long rest, Momma," her daughter said. "I thought that stuff was all under the rug."[55]

"No," Clara replied, "I'm sick of being treated like a dog. After Friday [Saviour's Day], I'm going to leave here." She burst into tears and hung up the phone before Lottie could say another word. What Clara had kept to herself was her greatest shame: her husband had taken the virginity of a young female relative.[56] She made good on her threat a week later. On March 9, she left Chicago and headed for Jacksonville, Florida, to visit a relative for a few days.[57]

Clara wasn't the only person close to the Messenger who was upset with him on Saviour's Day. A few days before the event, Farrakhan called him to request permission to sell his first recording, "A White Man's Heaven Is a Black Man's Hell," during the convention. "No," the Messenger replied, "it's too inflammable." The lyrics would frighten the unconverted away from the open convention instead of luring them inside, he said.[58] Sensing Farrakhan's dejection—the record was very popular and the convention was the perfect place to market it—the Messenger tried to make Farrakhan feel better by telling him that while he couldn't sell the record on the first two days of the weekend-long affair, he could sell it on the last day.[59]

Among those who bought a copy was a lanky youth who was in town to attend an annual athletic exhibition. He played the record night and day upon returning to his home in Louisville. Though his father was horrified by the antiwhite, anti-Christian lyrics, he kept his anger to himself. After all, his namesake, Cassius Clay Jr., had won all of his bouts at the Golden Gloves tournament and was a shoo-in for the 1960 Olympics boxing team. Though Clay Jr. was regarded as a "good boy" by whites in town, the *Louisville Courier-Journal* listed him as among those burned by hot water thrown on civil rights demonstrators in the spring of 1960. An aunt warned Clay after the demonstration that he was "being brainwashed" by Farrakhan's recording.[60]

Another of Farrakhan's customers was Dr. Lonnie Cross, chairman of the department of mathematics at Atlanta University. From the moment he heard the record playing on a jukebox in a black-owned restaurant, Dr. Cross recalled, he knew he had found his mission in life.[61] Dr. Cross was the kind of convert—a highly educated, middle-class black—Muhammad dreamt about. Speaking to Clara in Atlanta in late March, Muhammad proudly told her that "the class we have been after is waking up! We're finally taking Chicago at last . . . they [African Americans] are all in our corner either openly or secretly."[62] Within a year, Dr. Lonnie Cross was Minister Lonnie X Cross of the Atlanta mosque.

On May 20, 1960, James Bland came up with another COINTEL-PRO suggestion that he believed would destroy the Messenger and the NOI. In a memo to Belmont, he wrote:

Elijah Muhammad is the national leader of the Nation of Islam (NOI) and Evelyn Lorene Williams is one of his secretaries. Both are on the Security Index. Williams disappeared from Elijah's home during January 1960, and was subsequently located in Los Angeles. Los Angeles [field office] recently ascertained that she had been a patient at St. Francis Hospital at Lynwood, California, and had given birth to a child on March 30, 1960. She is unmarried.[63]

Bland asked that a fictitious letter be sent to Clara and a select group of ministers. The letter began:

Despite the highly stated aims . . . spouted by Elijah Muhammad, there appears to be a tremendous occupational hazard in being a young unmarried secretary employed in the household of Elijah Muhammad. . . . One of Elijah's secretaries recently disappeared from the fold. When next heard of she was a patient at a Los Angeles hospital. . . . Could this have been the reason Elijah cut short his visit to Los Angeles, canceled his speaking engagements and announced he had to return to Chicago "due to pressing business"? . . . Elijah Muhammad has . . . preached against extramarital relationships but he doesn't seem to be able to keep things under control in his own household.

The COINTELPRO was approved by Assistant FBI Director Cartha DeLoach on May 22. In the meantime, the Messenger had impregnated June X, and she was one month pregnant when Evelyn was delivered of her child.[64]

The Chicago field office also wrote the director to request permission to renew the wiretaps and electronic bugging devices inside the South Vernon Street apartment. Muhammad was spending most of his time there, the request noted, with several young women:

Muhammad, feeling he is secure in his "hideaway," may converse more freely with high officials of the NOI and his personal contacts. Through this it is hoped to obtain policy and future plans of Muhammad both personally and for the NOI. It is felt that only confidants of Muhammad will have this listing available.[65]

Besides his troubles with Clara, Muhammad's relationship with Malcolm X was becoming combative. By mid-May, more than seventy radio stations across the country were broadcasting speeches by Malcolm X and Muhammad at least once a week. Malcolm felt that his radio addresses should be as candid and fiery as those he usually gave in public. Their addresses, he felt, could make them the Islamic version of Billy Graham. Having the advantage of age and experience, Muhammad was mindful of how Father Charles Coughlin's unrestrained enthusiasm on his national radio program proved to be his undoing.[66] A radio advertising agent had warned him, Muhammad said, that most stations will not carry the broadcast if it contains "our harsh radical stuff" because they would lose advertising revenue.

> He told me to tell you that the best way of winning [converts] is to not go into any of that raw stuff in the open. He said to take it very soft and not to hit those hard places like we do in the temple . . . put great emphasis on the good of doing in unity regardless of what religion or faith one belongs to. . . . Just tell them that our main trouble is disunity and disunity is caused by lack of knowledge of self.

If this compromise was agreeable, Muhammad said, the agent was willing to sign the two of them to a thirty-six-week contract. Malcolm agreed, of course, since the Messenger was "infallible."[67]

In view of the successful national radio program, the FBI accelerated the number of COINTELPRO actions against Black Muslims. While the letter it produced about Muhammad's marital problems had some impact in Chicago, any loss in membership was quickly offset by people lured into mosques after hearing Malcolm X on the radio. His voice entranced them like the Sirens or the Pied Piper. No one articulated the despair and the dreams of black people better than Malcolm. No black leader confronted white people the way he did, made them appear so ignorant during debates the way he did, or made being Caucasian sound like such a tremendous burden the way he did. Blacks routinely witnessed police grabbing and punching Dr. King and throwing him into the back of a paddy wagon; they never saw police cast a cruel eye at Malcolm, even when he stood before officers and called them devils. Malcolm's voice sprang from the radio like light from the birth of a new day. At the rate the NOI was growing, the FBI would need an everlasting total eclipse to block Muhammad from his goal of 144,000 converts.

The years of wiretaps suddenly began to pay off. The Bureau knew from its 1959 investigation of Fard that among the aliases the Muslim mystic used were "Fred Dodd" and "James Dodd," and "Wallace Dodd Ford."[68] If there were any doubts regarding whether Muhammad knew that Wallace Dodd Ford and Wallace D. Fard were the same man, they were erased in the summer of 1960. On August 8, 1960, the Messenger—or someone on his personal staff—called American Airlines and made a reservation in the name of J. Dodd at telephone number HUdson 3-6531.[69] That was the phone number at Muhammad's home in Chicago. The reservation was for a three o'clock flight to Cincinnati, Ohio, from Midway Airport and Muhammad was the one who boarded the plane under that name. The use of the name J. Dodd raised questions for several reasons. Whether Muhammad personally made the reservation or an FBI informant on his staff made it for him, it suggests that he was aware of Fard's identity. Moreover, he had seen boxes in Fard's hotel room that were addressed to "Mr. Dodd" or "Mr. Fred Dodd." It seems unlikely that anyone other than Muhammad would have approved of making the reservation in that name for obvious reasons: (1) it would have been embarrassing when he arrived at the airport without knowing under whose name his reservation was made, and (2) if a staffer used the name of Dodd without Muhammad's knowledge, it would have immediately exposed the staff member as a government informant. This suggests that the use of the name Dodd was Muhammad's idea. This link was interesting, but like much of the data the FBI accumulated in the COINTELPRO against Muhammad, it had to be set aside until the timing was right to use it. A congressional probe held promise as the ideal opportunity.

While the Messenger focused on reorganizing his empire—he was training John Ali as the new NOI national secretary—and cuddling up with his newborns, Malcolm busied himself creating the monthly newspaper *Muhammad Speaks*.[70] He patterned the paper after *Negro World*, the official news organ of Marcus Garvey's UNIA, and the *Pittsburgh Courier*, the premier African-American newspaper of the 1950s. The content of *Muhammad Speaks* was a careful balance of news about the NOI, international events affecting people of color, accounts of horrendous injustices inflicted upon African Americans, and a splash of photographs from recent social events.

Among the highlights in the fall was the induction of a dozen Third World nations into the U.N. General Assembly. Although Malcolm was no longer on the city's official welcoming committee, the NOI's reputation among Arab and African nations was such that no one dared to exclude the Harlem minister from welcoming ceremonies. With Muhammad's approval, Malcolm and a phalanx of Muslims were on hand to receive Kwame Nkrumah of Ghana, Sékou Touré of the Republic of Guinea, Gamal Nasser of Egypt, and Dr. Mahmond Yousse Shawarbi of Yemen, a nation that had recently joined Nasser's United Arab Republic. When Nasser arrived at Idlewild Airport on September 30, a Muslim honor guard of 150 men were on hand to welcome him.[71] Their uniforms—red bow tie, white shirt, and blue suit—symbolized one of many paradoxes of the NOI. Though Muhammad claimed to hate everything America stood for, he had chosen the colors of the American flag as the official colors for the honor guard who welcomed foreign heads of state who also professed hatred for the United States.[72]

The only head of state whom Muhammad had qualms about being associated with was Fidel Castro, the Cuban revolutionary who, with the aid of the Soviet Union, had overthrown the right-wing Batista regime in 1959. Besides, Muhammad was uncertain of Castro's racial background; all of the other heads of state were Asian or African. Muhammad saw Castro as a white devil, as did several other black nationalists. Castro's government, Harlem activist Carlos Cooks declared, represented a "return to white supremacy."[73] The other thing that bothered Muhammad was Castro's ties to the Soviet Union. Castro's relationship with the United States bore too many resemblances to American-Japanese tensions in the 1930s. Muhammad had grossly miscalculated American strength during World War II and ended up in jail. This time, he wanted to select his bedfellows more carefully.

Castro had expressed a desire to meet Muhammad before his arrival in the United States in September 1960; when he invited several black activists to Cuba in early 1960, someone suggested that the Muslims would make valuable American allies. On August 11, the FBI intercepted a phone call between Muhammad and his personal secretary, Tynetta Nelson, regarding Castro's impending visit. Muhammad had been fretting about Malcolm X's desire to meet Cuba's new head of state, but Nelson suggested that a meeting with Castro might actually be advantageous. "You know," she said, "I had a funny dream last night. In the dream, Fidel Castro came to see you."[74]

"There may be something to that," Muhammad replied. "I got a message that they would pay all expenses of a number of my followers and myself to come there for a visit." Changing the subject, he asked her whether she had bought a gun yet, as he had advised her to do. "But won't I need a license?" she asked.

"No," Muhammad replied. "Just don't let anyone else know about it."[75] After notifying FBI headquarters of the conversation, particularly about the Messenger's advice on the gun, the Chicago SAC sought permission to share the information with the Chicago Police Department as a COINTELPRO maneuver. The suggestion was rebuffed, however, since it carried the risk of exposing the FBI's wiretap as the source of the information.[76]

Muhammad was taken aback when Castro and Malcolm X held an impromptu meeting at the Hotel Theresa, where the Cuban leader was staying. After the meeting had generated barrels of ink from pundits and members of Congress, Muhammad told Wallace Terry of the *Washington Post* that Malcolm X had overstepped his bounds. "If I had known Malcolm was going to visit Castro, I would have prevented it. The Muslim world is against Communism. I don't like it because it's atheistic. But Communism has its place in Allah's program. It was raised to destroy the whites."[77] The Messenger's suspicion that Hoover would try to use

Malcolm X's affiliation with Communist delegates at the United Nations was well-founded. On September 9, Hoover—having learned of Nelson's discussion with Muhammad—wrote to J. Walter Yeagley, the assistant U.S. attorney general, to explore the possibility of prosecuting the Messenger, Malcolm X, and other leaders of the NOI pursuant to Executive Order Number 10450.[78]

Yeagley replied:

The available evidence concerning the activities of the leaders of this organization falls far short of the evidentiary requirements sufficient to meet the standards set forth in the [Supreme Court's] *Yates* decision . . . the First Amendment would require something more than language of prophecy and prediction and implied threats against the Government to establish the existence of a clear and present danger to the nation and its citizens.

Hoover was infuriated. "Just stalling!" he scribbled at the bottom of the letter.[79]

Despite the censuring of Senator Joseph McCarthy in 1954 for trampling upon the Constitution in the name of national security, Hoover remained a practicing McCarthyite. In his 1958 book, *Masters of Deceit*, he explained why African-American political activity had to be watched closely:

The [Communist] Party's claim that it is working for Negro rights is a deception and a fraud. The Party's sole interest, as most American Negroes know, is to hoodwink the Negro, to exploit him and use him as a tool to build a communist America. The Party has made vigorous efforts to infiltrate the National Association for the Advancement of Colored People.[80]

To protect blacks from what he regarded as their childlike immaturity when it came to politics, the FBI maintained a file on nearly every prominent African American.

Two weeks after Ethel and Julius Rosenberg were sentenced to death in 1951, for example, the Bureau was investigating Nat King Cole. Cole, the Los Angeles field office SAC wrote in a memo to Hoover on April 20, had been a member of "the Communist Party and the Communist Political Association" during the mid-1940s.[81] The Bureau conducted another inquiry on the native Alabamian in 1960 after learning that he was the treasurer of the Committee to Defend Martin Luther King, then under indictment in Alabama for alleged income tax evasion.[82] In March 1959, the New York field office investigated another wildly successful African American, Lorraine Hansberry. "Captioned individual is the author of the play entitled, *A Raisin in the Sun.* At the request of the Bureau, an investigation has been conducted to determine if this play, in any way, is controlled or influenced by the Communist Party, or in any way follows the Communist line."[83]

In other cases, files were maintained on individuals for years, even though they had denounced Communism. A classic case in point is Edward Kennedy Ellington, better known as Duke Ellington. In May 1938, Ellington endorsed the first All-Harlem Youth Conference, an organization whose sole aim was to generate jobs for unemployed young people. The Bureau, however, was among the government entities that labeled the conference a "Communist front."[84] For the next twelve years, Ellington participated in social activities that the Bureau classified as Communist or Communist fronts. For the next ten years, the Communist-run *Daily Worker* newspaper periodically ran articles mentioning Ellington's name. Ellington didn't complain until the *Daily Worker* reported in 1950 that he had signed the Stockholm Peace Petition. Ellington denied the report and demanded a retraction. Seeing how minor allegations had ruined the Hollywood Ten and scores of others, Ellington wrote a newspaper article in which he emphatically expressed his opposition to Communism. Yet in 1960, an FBI agent made the following comment in a memorandum to a State Department official as Ellington was embarking for a concert tour in France:

For the information of the Legal Attache [in Paris] . . . Bureau files indicate that Ellington has had some affiliation with numerous Communist front groups such as the All-Harlem Youth Conference, the

Hollywood Chapter of the Veterans of the Abraham Lincoln Brigade, the American Committee to Save Refugees, the Artists' Front to Win the War and the National Committee to Abolish the Poll Tax. . . . He is a well-known Negro musician who is presently traveling abroad, according to information received by Bureau from the State Department in memorandum received 12/21/60.

Despite Ellington's persistent efforts to distance himself from Communism, this notation sadly remained on the loyal American's file at the Bureau: "Subject—Edward Kennedy Ellington; Security Matter—C[ommunism]."[85]

On April 16, 1960, Muhammad was talking to his attorney, William R. Ming Jr., about his income taxes—which were already a day late—when the lawyer told him that he would have to wait until he finished filling out some forms. "Don't worry," Ming said, "I always do Mahalia Jackson's report and she usually gets hers in late." With that brief mention, another document was added to the Bureau's file on the gospel music legend from Louisiana.[86] Files were also kept on Josephine Baker, Sammy Davis Jr., the Reverend C. L. Franklin (Aretha Franklin's father), Miles Davis, Langston Hughes, Billie Holiday, Richard Wright, James Baldwin—well, the list is endless.[87] While racism played a part in the Bureau's compulsive spying, a greater influence was Hoover's fear of Communism. His preoccupation with stamping out that political philosophy was one reason the Bureau maintained files on Lucille Ball, Elvis Presley, Albert Einstein, and thousands more both famous and obscure.[88]

Two days after Hoover's letter to Yeagley, Muhammad, Malcolm, and other high-level NOI officials arrived in Atlanta, where the Messenger was scheduled to deliver a lecture at a rally in the Magnolia Ballroom. Two of the topics of his lecture, ironically, were childbirth and hypocrisy. "Christianity is false because it teaches that Jesus was born with a spirit for a father, and everyone knows that is impossible. If the spirit of God could make a woman pregnant, then all Christian women would have spirit children."[89] In another part of his speech, Muhammad, who had fled Macon's "Negro town" out of fear of racial violence, told Georgians: "People told me that I should not come to Georgia as it would be a waste of time because the black man in Georgia is scared of the white man. I want to tell the black man in Georgia that he has nothing to fear from the white man because in unity there is strength." After the rally was over, the Messenger was chauffeured to the home of Minister Jeremiah X Pugh. Clara was already there, but not in anticipation of seeing her husband. Her father, Quartus X Evans, was in poor health. Minister Jeremiah's family cared for him in his home as a way to please the royal family. Later that evening, Jeremiah, Malcolm, and other top officials left the house for a top-secret rendezvous.[90]

Several months passed before Malcolm realized that this meeting, now known derisively as the Muslim Compromise, was a mammoth miscalculation. With the Messenger's approval and at Jeremiah's suggestion, Black Muslims met with a group of prominent Klan leaders in Atlanta—the scene, ironically, of the Atlantic Compromise of 1850. There have been several accounts of what transpired, none of which is fully rational. Given the Klan's domination in Georgia, Muslims were hesitant to man the farms owned by the NOI for fear of being lynched. They would do so only with assurance that the Klan would not attack them. According to one participant, the Klan agreed not to molest Muslim farmers if Muhammed agreed not to purchase farmland in "non-Negro" areas. That was, in essence, the nature of the contract. Malcolm X gave a slightly different account. Muhammad had received land in Georgia and several other states from Muslims who assigned it to him in fee simple in their wills, but it wasn't nearly enough acreage to mount agribusinesses, which is what he envisioned. To fulfill his vision, Muhammad said, he wanted to purchase a "county-size tract of land in Georgia or South Carolina" where he could then "induce Negroes to migrate and make it appear that his program of a segregated state or separate state was feasible."[91] The meeting was arranged to offer the Klan financial incentives to leave Muslims alone and to help the NOI purchase the tract. Malcom, who declined to participate in subsequent negotiations, had already begun to regret following the Messenger's command to attend even the first meeting. As far as he knew, the Klan had murdered his father in 1931 and was still lynching black people; since 1882 white racists had lynched more black people in Georgia (492) than in any other state except Mississippi (536).[92] Albert Hamilton, the Messenger's childhood buddy, was one of their victims, a fact that he allowed no one to forget. Every mosque in the country owned a blackboard with a tree painted on it. The black figure dangling from the rope was said to represent Albert.

How, then, could Black Muslims break bread with the Klan? If the Messenger could compromise with "devils," with whom would he not negotiate? Wasn't the Muslim Compromise of 1960 as repugnant as the Atlantic Compromise of 1850? For Malcolm, the Messenger's bargain with Satan's sinews was a turning point. It was more than a betrayal of Muslims and of black people in general; it was a crime against common sense and a sin against God.[93]

CHAPTER ELEVEN
BLACK MACBETH

MALCOLM: It is myself I mean; in whom I know
All the particulars of vice so grafted
That when they shall be opened, black Macbeth
Will seem as pure as snow, and the poor state
Esteem him as a lamb. . . . .

— Macbeth,
act IV, scene iii[1]

How can anyone who abhors the oppression of Negroes be in favor of degrading classes of white people? Our progress in degeneracy appears to me to be pretty rapid. As a nation, we began by declaring that *all men are created equal.* We now practically read it, *all men are created equal except Negroes.*

—Abraham Lincoln
August 24, 1855[2]

uslims revered the Messenger as a god-king, though most of them were treated like knaves and serfs in his monarchy. According to Muhammad, 30 percent of the people under any system of government are always dissatisfied.[3] For some reason, he failed to heed his own thesis, and thus was unable to sense the rising degree of discontent with his kingship. For the first two decades after his release from prison, there were no outward signs of dissension, or at least none that made it into print, but the media attention Muhammad craved and had finally won was about to change that. By early 1960, rumors of oppressive disciplinary practices, deviations from the moral code, and financial irregularities were seeping through the NOI's façade of perfection.

In one case, a prominent female officer of the Chicago mosque accused Raymond Sharrieff of misappropriating the mosque's money.[4] When she was given a "trial" at the mosque on January 13 on charges of making false accusations, Sharrieff served as one of the judges. After she was found guilty, she was suspended for ninety days. Upon her return on April 20 for a reinstatement hearing, the original complaint committee voted to accept her back into the temple, but Sharrieff vetoed its decision. "You talk too much," Sharrieff told her, then announced that she was suspended for another ninety days. If she returned in ninety days, he said, she would be placed under a special probation for six months. His accuser reluctantly accepted the ruling.[5]

Men under the supervision of Sharrieff and Muhammad's sons didn't fare much better. In the summer of 1960, for example, they were required to buy each week at least thirty-five copies of the *Los Angeles Herald Dispatch* at eleven cents a copy and a minimum of twenty copies of the *New Chicago Crusader* at ten cents a copy.[6] After a Sunday afternoon open service ended on August 28, 1960, Sharrieff instructed the

250 FOI members to remain behind for a special briefing. After the visitors, who had listened as the minister painted a rosy picture of life in the NOI, departed, the veil was lifted. Sharrieff announced that it had been decided that each male would have to pay $20.00 into the mosque as soon as possible. This money would be used to cover the cost of producing Farrakhan's play titled *Orgena* ("A Negro" spelled backwards), which Sharrieff said would be $2,800. He assured them that a profit of $8,000 was expected from the production, as if they would get a share.[7]

Elijah Muhammad Jr. subjected the FOI to equally arbitrary measures. For instance, on November 21, 1960, he was conducting a drill of 150 members when he noticed that a few men were not impeccably dressed for the exercise. He singled out one man and accused him of being sloppy and of appearing sleepy. At first, he ordered the man to stand at attention for the remainder of the meeting, which lasted nearly four hours. Junior then subjected each man to a thorough inspection. Unless they improved in their personal hygiene and appearance, he said, "a new procedure requiring each of you to drop your pants to make sure you're wearing clean underwear" would be instituted.[8] Women also had their burdens. On October 6, 1960, for example, MSG lieutenant Elizabeth X of the Chicago mosque announced that every member had to buy a white "uniform" before Saviour's Day 1961. Anyone who had not acquired a uniform by February 14 would be suspended. The real snag was that the dresses had to be bought from Ethel Muhammad, who ran a for-profit clothing store. Although the business was financed by the NOI, the profits went into Ethel's personal piggy bank.[9] Ethel's spending habits were another source of jealousy. While most women in the NOI were criticized for being overweight, no one remarked too loudly about the Messenger's own daughters being on the hefty side. But what galled everyone, particularly in Chicago, was Ethel's penchant for diamonds and furs while the rank-and-file women were expected to live frugally.[10]

Mounting organizational disputes between Malcolm and Muhammad were taking their toll on Malcolm's marriage. During one argument, Betty accused Malcolm of being less than intelligent for living like a peasant while the royal family was spending money like there was no

tomorrow.[11] Like many marriages, theirs was stressed by financial difficulties, a situation made worse by Malcolm's refusal to allow Betty to
take a job.[12] Unless things changed, Betty said, she was going to leave
him. She had left briefly during their first year together, so Malcolm
knew that she wasn't bluffing.[13] On the other hand, he had taken a vow
of poverty and he hadn't any intentions of breaking it.

Another area of contention between Malcolm and Muhammad was
deceptive recruiting practices. Essentially, new recruits were given the
impression that all they had to do was abstain from eating pork, smoking tobacco, and consuming alcoholic beverages. After the probationary
period, however, the "hidden" Minister Hyde replaced Minister Jekyll.
Suddenly, recruits were expected to attend every meeting, sell every
newspaper, and do everything they were told without question. This led
to a high attrition rate. The only way to control the NOI's needless over-
growth, Malcolm contended, was to have a uniform system of discipline.[14] If new converts regarded membership as a cakewalk, there was
little or no incentive for them to improve their lives. By introducing them
to its rigid discipline early, the NOI could reduce the rate of attrition
because those who weren't seriously committed to Muhammad would
quit during the trial period.

The Messenger disagreed:

I know Allah's design better than all of you [ministers] put together,
and the things I am doing I am doing according to his way, that he
gave to me, and his wishes. Some things that I do may seem odd to you
all but nevertheless in the future you will learn that they were right.[15]

The Messenger insisted that Malcolm X hold off on putting too many
restrictions on the followers because it might deter others from joining.
He wanted to bait the trap as attractively as possible, he said. "Once the
game is trapped and in the cage, I'll put more restrictions on them."[16]

By April 1960, the NOI was bursting at the seams. Much of the over-
crowding was caused by Muslim ministers who portrayed the mosque as
a hospital where people entered in the advanced stages of "Steppin'

Fetchititis" and exited as pious clones of John Shaft. "Everybody knew that the Muslims were some bad brothers," author A. Peter Bailey recalled.[17] "Nobody bothered them. That's what made the Nation so appealing." While Bailey resisted the temptation to join, thousands of African Americans applied for the "X" surname in early 1960. One great influx came after a young writer named Alex Haley wrote a favorable feature story on Muhammad for the March 1960 issue of *Reader's Digest*. "He's with us," Muhammad told one of his ministers. That comment, captured on a reel of tape by the FBI, prompted the Bureau to start a file on Haley.[18]

More than 5,000 came to hear the Messenger at the Chicago Coliseum on July 24, 1960, many of them poor blacks anxious to get their names listed in Muhammad's so-called "Book of Life." Whites were allowed in, too, but only because local governments notified Muhammad that he could not ban people from a public building solely because of their race. George Murray, a white columnist for the *Chicago American*, was alarmed by what he heard. "Muhammad doesn't shout with the harsh accents of Adolf Hitler, but his message is the same," Murray wrote after the convention:

> It is hate and envy for the rich minority. . . . I cannot imagine the Coliseum being rented to the Ku Klux Klan without a public outcry. . . . His meetings today are about like Hitler's must have been in 1932. You may laugh today—and wonder tomorrow why you took it so lightly.[19]

Ben Holman, a black reporter for the *Chicago Daily News*, also condemned the Muslim rally, held on the same day, incidentally, that the NAACP was holding a convention a few blocks away.[20]

To further complicate matters, corruption crept into Mosque No. 7 while Malcolm X was on the road. While he assumed that Captain Joseph was running the FOI as a tight ship, its members were actually running wild—breaking nearly all the rules. When Malcolm returned to his mosque in early December, he discovered that some new recruits were not only smoking marijuana but selling it as well.[21] Some were selling other drugs, including cocaine and heroin, and members were engaging in adultery and fornication. On December 23 Malcolm told a recruit who had sold heroin near the mosque that he was lucky the NOI caught him instead of the police because the police would "blow this up and use it against the Honorable Elijah Muhammad." When the purge was over, the violators were expelled for periods lasting from three months to five years.[22]

Though skyrocketing membership put the NOI in a position to affect the outcome of some elections, particularly in New York, Detroit, and Chicago—as Noble Drew Ali had done in the 1920s with Oscar DePriest—Muhammad forbade his followers to vote. For him, voting implied that America had a future. Voting would contradict everything he preached as gospel. If the white race was going to lose all of its power by 1970, what sense would it make for Muslims to prolong the days of a terminally ill government?[23] On October 30, the Messenger lashed out at Dr. King over his endorsement of Democratic Party presidential candidate John F. Kennedy of Massachusetts:

Martin Luther King is a fool for wanting integration. It makes no difference in the coming election who is elected as neither candidate will do anything for the so-called Negro because it is against their nature to do so.[24]

The next day, the IRS's Intelligence Division contacted the FBI about the results of a COINTELPRO aimed at sending Muhammad back to prison. Given that the same attorney, William R. Ming Jr., represented both King and Muhammad, there was a chance that Muhammad could be indicted for "alleged evasion of income taxes for the years 1954 through 1958."[25] A similar gambit was used against King in February 1960, resulting in extensive negative media attention and a disruption of his leadership of the SCLC. After a six-month probe, the tax COINTELPRO was closed due to insufficient evidence of evasion. The tax COINTELPRO against Dr. King also failed.[26]

Despite the feature article in *Readers' Digest* and Wallace Terry's five-part series in the *Washington Post,* the lion's share of publicity went to Malcolm X, much to Muhammad's dismay. Even when *The Black Muslims in America,* the first book-length treatment of the NOI, was published in early 1961, the invitations to speak were addressed to Malcolm, not to Muhammad. For white college students particularly, listening to Malcolm was daring, like playing the "race records" of Little Richard and Chuck Berry. He was as popular on predominantly white campuses as he was at colleges founded for African Americans. Unlike Khallid's crude oratory, Malcolm's was refined; he knew how use the King's English. Watching Malcolm debate was as electrifying as watching Jack Johnson box or Jesse Owens run: part of the audience was there to watch him win, and another part was there to see the expression on his face if he lost. Many respected thinkers tried to outwit him, but few succeeded. One of the more memorable matches was between Malcolm and Arthur M. Schlesinger Jr., a Harvard graduate who was part of the Kennedy clique called by David Halberstam the "best and the brightest."[27] "Nothing can obstruct American life and the recognition of the brotherhood of the human community more than the racist doctrines preached by the White Citizens Councils, the Ku Klux Klan, and the Black Muslims," Schlesinger said during a speech at Atlanta University on February 3, 1961.[28]

Unbeknownst to Schlesinger, Malcolm X and Professor Lonnie X Cross were among dozens of Muslims in the audience. When the floor was opened for questions, Malcolm X challenged Schlesinger's arguments, leading him to make a hasty retreat. He apologized to the audience after admitting that he had "insufficient evidence" to support his assertions about the NOI.[29] It seemed that every invitation Minister Malcolm accepted generated two more invitations, and middle-class black students slowly joined the NOI. A prominent black intellectual was horrified when his son announced that he intended to become a Muslim. He contacted Malcolm secretly and asked him to dissuade his son from doing so because he feared his white colleagues wouldn't understand. Malcolm assured the intellectual that he would do everything within his power to discourage the boy from joining. Among the middle-class youths who did convert was Thomas Wallace of New York. Wallace was the younger brother of Ruby Wallace, better known as Ruby Dee, one of the country's most prominent actresses, who starred on Broadway in 1959, in *A Raisin in the Sun,* along with her husband, Ossie Davis, and Sidney Poitier.[30]

The black intelligentsia's fear of Malcolm X was highlighted by an incident at Howard University, proudly referred to by its students as "the black Harvard." In early February 1961, the NAACP chapter on the Howard campus invited Malcolm X to speak. When Carl E. Anderson, director of student activities, heard that Malcolm X was coming, he moved quickly to quash the invitation. Citing a procedural formality, Anderson said that the Faculty Committee on Student Organizations and Activities had not approved the invitation as required.[31] Owing to the demands of his schedule, Malcolm was unable to come to the campus once the matter was rectified. Then, in May 1961, the NAACP tried to minimize the embarrassment it suffered during debates by "prohibiting an appearance of NAACP staff members on the same platform as Muslim representatives."[32]

Howard University students finally won their battle with Anderson over inviting Malcolm X to speak on campus, and on October 30, 1961, he and Bayard Rustin debated in Cramton Auditorium. The debate signaled that the Messenger was slowly abandoning not only his call for a return to Africa but even the demand for separate states. Rather, Malcolm X said, Muslims would follow the advice of DuBois, who suggested that blacks separate economically from white America. The Messenger would expand his "Buy Black" campaign from the NOI to all African Americans. As part of the campaign, blacks were urged to deposit their money in black-owned banks, to buy their goods from black-owned businesses, and to invest their money in black neighborhoods. That, he said, was the only way to create wealth.

The campaign began on the heels of economic studies showing that a dollar earned by an African American changed hands only once before leaving the black community, whereas a dollar earned by a Caucasian changed hands four or five times before leaving the community. Malcolm X also scored with the students by pointing out that the NAACP has never in its 51 years elected a Negro as head of the organization and therefore must have doubts about Negroes. The [National] Urban League is similarly headed by whites and the head of the Council on Racial Equality dishonored his feelings about equality by marrying a white woman.

The students loved it. FBI agents monitoring the debate reported, "His attacks on the white man's treatment of Negroes sparked the most enthusiastic response."[33]

Outwardly, the NOI appeared to run as smoothly as a new Rolls Royce. But the goings-on behind the scenes were a different matter. On February 17, 1961, a secretary called Muhammad and told him that she was onto his philandering. She knew of at least seven other secretaries that he had been romantic with and she felt that he was abusing his power. "Little people like myself are sacrificed for your pleasure because you're not suffering like my friends are suffering." She warned him that he had better give her more money to take care of their new baby. Everyone knew the child was his, she added, because the baby "looks just like you when you were a baby."[34]

Adding to Muhammad's woes was a traffic mishap in late spring. On June 10, 1961, Muhammad was driving near his home when two small children suddenly ran from behind a bread truck and into the path of his Cadillac. They were both hit and fell in front of his car. Panic-stricken, he ran to their aid. Neither child was moving, and he feared that they were dead. But after a few seconds, they regained alertness and sat up. Muhammad and passersby tried to comfort the crying children as the sound of an ambulance siren grew louder. The ambulance driver assured the crowd that the children were all right; they had only suffered a few minor scrapes, but were going to be taken to Cook County Hospital as a precautionary measure.

As the crowd dispersed, a policeman on the scene took Muhammad to the police station to record his account of the accident. The incident had so rattled him that he could barely speak, let alone recount the accident. After the patrolman concluded his questioning, Muhammad called his son Herbert and told him to come and get him. A few minutes later, Muhammad was in his study calling the hospital to check on the children. To his relief, they had both been patched up and sent home.[35] Although that was the end of the matter as far as police were concerned, the sixty-four-year-old patriarch considered himself lucky, and rarely drove after that. The accident forced him to face problems with his vision that he had tried to ignore. Upon his doctor's recommendation, he began wearing dark glasses to reduce the pain caused by bright light.

On June 25, the Messenger flew to Washington to deliver a speech in the famous Uline Arena. Three months earlier, he and Malcolm had discussed how to attract 30,000 to Washington for the event. On the day of the so-called Freedom Caravan, only 3,000 showed up. The low turnout was no surprise, however, as Muhammad complained to one minister that he was having trouble filling six buses leaving Chicago for the event.[36] The low turnout should have served as a warning to the Messenger that he was bleeding his followers dry, but apparently it didn't. The harsh economic burdens imposed by the god-king of the royal court continued.

In the aftermath of the unsuccessful income tax probe, the COINTELPRO against Muhammad took a different approach. On August 1, 1961, the FBI tried to nail down reports from the Chicago field office that Muhammad "has in the past or is currently converting Nation of Islam (NOI) funds to personal use."[37] Two days later, FBI agents received more information that they hoped to use against him. Muhammad had suffered a mild heart attack in 1958, but had kept the episode a secret from everyone, including Malcolm. In July, however, he started experiencing heart problems, which he discussed on the phone with a physician. That was the kind of information the Bureau found extremely valuable, as it was making plans to maneuver some of its informants into positions from which they could disrupt the NOI upon Muhammad's death. The Chicago SAC wrote to FBI headquarters:

Based on information [recently received] . . . it is possible Muhammad's health is worse than previously received information had indicated and may involve a heart condition along with the bronchitis. This matter will be closely followed and any pertinent information received will be promptly furnished the Bureau in suitable form.[38]

The FBI knew that with Wallace Muhammad headed for prison, Malcolm would instantly assume leadership of the NOI if Muhammad died suddenly. At the time, it had only two men it considered reliable informants in Muhammad's inner circle. One of them—Abdul Basit Naeem—had influence with Muhammad but not with Malcolm X.[39] If it was going to disrupt the NOI, it would have to figure out some means of discrediting Malcolm or causing a split between Muhammad and Malcolm.

As the Bureau mulled over its options, Muhammad returned to his home at 2118 Violet Drive in Phoenix to get some rest. His bronchitis had become so severe, Malcolm recalled, that "when he talked with anyone, he would unpredictably begin coughing harder and harder, until his body was wracked and jerking in agonies that were painful to watch."[40] One doctor told him that he might have tuberculosis, and another said he had acute bronchitis. The difference of opinion only heightened Muhammad's distrust of white physicians. He obtained several books on respiratory ailments, and then told several aides that he was believed he was actually suffering from "acute bronchitis asthma." He also mentioned that he was switching to an Arab physician in whom he had more faith. "But my only real faith is in Allah."[41]

After resting for about two months, Muhammad resumed the life he had enjoyed before the coughing spells had become so severe. In October 1961, Chicago notified FBI Headquarters that wiretaps had intercepted calls between Muhammad and at least five women with whom he was having adulterous affairs. Two of the women were sisters. In a telephone conversation on October 7 with a young secretary identified as June X, Muhammad urged her to be discreet about their relationship because he didn't "want anyone to find out about us."[42] Two days later, he was taped as he told Evelyn X that he wanted to have "Sweet and Honey come and stay with me for two or three months . . . or years." He also talked about buying a large house where all of his illegitimate

children could be raised by only one of the mothers. When he asked Evelyn if she would be interested in being a mother to all of his children
under such an arrangement, she replied that she would. Then he asked
her if she would like to live on the West Coast. Again, she said yes.[43] A
few months later, the FBI identified the five women with whom Muhammad was committing adultery: Evelyn X Williams, June X, Lucille X
Rosary, Bernique Cushmeer, and Ola X Hughes. Moreover, he was also
making sexual advances to a sixth, Tynetta Nelson.[44]

Like his father, Wallace Muhammad was leading a complicated
domestic life. After two years of dating Shirley X Allen, he married her
in Chicago on April 28, 1959.[45] At the time, he was free on bond while
appealing his conviction for violating the Selective Service Act of 1948.
Their first child, Laila, was born seven months later, but the marriage
was stormy and ended before the child was a year old. While separated
from his wife, Wallace began dating Lorraine X Washington, another
member of the Chicago mosque. On September 16, 1961, Shirley was
granted a divorce on the grounds of desertion, and Wallace was ordered
to pay her $100 a month for child support. On October 27, Wallace
married Lorraine at the Cook County courthouse, and three days later,
he was in the Cook County jail. He had gone there as required by the
U.S. Supreme Court, which on October 9 denied him a writ of certiorari
on the draft conviction. The Court ordered him to surrender to the U.S.
marshal in Chicago by November 1, 1961. Wallace complied on October 30—his twenty-eighth birthday.[46] After a nine-day incarceration, he
was taken to Sandstone to begin serving his sentence. The day that Wallace remarried, his father had told him that he shouldn't surrender. "You
should make them come and get you," he said.[47] That's what he himself
had done in 1942, but it was for naught. Wallace let him have his say,
and quickly departed with his new bride for a brief honeymoon.

Emotionally exhausted at the conclusion of a three-year battle to keep
his heir-apparent out of prison, Muhammad returned to Phoenix the
week before Wallace turned himself in. His bronchitis worsened, and
even when he was medicated and under an oxygen tent, he had difficulty
sleeping. Bernique and Clara were there with him, though the combination proved as troublesome as the inclement weather. On November 1,

he was suffering from a cold with a high fever. Wallace's former wife, Shirley, called to speak to Clara. She cried and cried about Wallace's fate, as though she was somehow to blame. "Don't worry about Wallace," Clara said reassuringly, "because this is something he has been in for years" and so has had time to prepare himself for the eventuality.[48]

Three weeks later, it was Clara who was depressed and crying. On November 21, her husband was talking to a paramour in Chicago about a diamond ring he was buying for her from the Zales Jewelry Store. He had deposited $500 toward the $1,300 ring. "Are you happy?" Elijah asked her. Yes, the young woman replied, saying that "the only jewelry I've ever owned was quartz." They bantered about other rings he had considered for her but rejected because the stones were too small. As he hung up, Clara burst into the room and accused her husband of betrayal. She said that she was sick of him writing letters to his secretaries all over Creation and talking lovey-dovey on the phone and of catching him and Bernique in compromising situations. Elijah denied all the allegations. He had not received any letters from any women, nor had he been talking with them by phone. As for Bernique, well, that was all a misunderstanding.[49]

To avoid any further misunderstandings, Clara decided to leave. "I can't stay in the same house with that woman," she told her daughter during a call to Chicago.[50] Bernique stayed with Muhammad, playing the role of secretary, nurse, and homemaker. After several weeks, he was beset with melancholy. He had no appetite and sustained a seventeen-pound weight loss, a lot for a frail man in poor health. Doctors urged him to go to the Mayo Clinic for treatment, but he refused.[51] As if the loss of weight and missing the companionship of Wallace and Clara weren't enough, the California State Senate Fact-Finding Subcommittee on Un-American Activities released a highly unfavorable report on the NOI, characterizing it as an un-American organization that operated schools for "the indoctrination of young Negroes with race hatred." In a long rebuttal printed in *Muhammad Speaks,* the Messenger charged that the sole aim of the report was to "frighten already frightened so-called Negroes from coming to Allah."[52] American dictionaries, he wrote in his column, described an American as "one not belonging to one of the aboriginal races." That, Muhammad contended, ruled out African Americans, Hispanic Americans, and even Native Americans. "We were brought here not to be made Americans, nor American citizens, but rather, to be slaves or servants for the true American citizens—whites who originally came from Europe."[53] Muhammad had the last word in the matter, or so it seemed. Given his fragile health, it is doubtful that he wrote the reply at all. Examined closely, the column read suspiciously like Malcolm's rhetoric. At any rate, the report was nothing more than that; it was in a government warehouse somewhere before the ink on the last page was dry.

After Muhammad was feeling better, he accepted a call from an aide in Chicago who complained that Clara was so hostile that working inside Muhammad's home was nearly impossible. She was argumentative and overbearing. They had to beg her for keys to get into parts of the house where she had locked the doors, and she refused to give even her household helpers keys to the car so they could go grocery shopping. "My wife is a very nervous woman," Muhammad said, amused. He asked the aide to be patient with Clara, whom he characterized as a good woman having a bad time. After some coaxing by her daughters, Clara relented and flew back to Phoenix, and remained there with Elijah until early January.[54]

For some reason, Chicago NOI officials placed an unusual advertisement in several black-owned newspapers as the organization prepared for Saviour's Day 1962. The advertisements challenged anyone with an "opinion and solution on the future of the so-called Negro" to attend a special gathering in Chicago on Sunday, February 25.[55] As expected, none of the major civil rights leaders accepted the challenge. After a number of local black activists had their say at the convention, a Caucasian male in the audience stood and asked permission to speak. He identified himself as George Lincoln Rockwell, leader of the American Nazi Party. Rockwell, who ran unsuccessfully for governor of Virginia in 1960, said he had decided to take advantage of the advertisement, which stated that "all leaders" were invited—not simply all black leaders.[56] The audience, some of whom had been saving money all year to come to Chicago and see Muhammad, was shocked that this cartoonish character was wasting time that would be better used by the man they called "Dear Holy Apostle." Booing filled the room as Rockwell waited for a microphone. John Ali, the national secretary, pleaded with the audience to permit Rockwell to speak. Instead hundreds left.[57]

"I believe Elijah Muhammad will solve the race problem," Rockwell shouted over the groans of his reluctant audience. His bodyguards, each of whom wore an armband bearing a swastika, surrounded him as he continued:

> We don't want to integrate. When we come to power, I promise you we will help you get what you want. . . . Elijah Muhammad has done some wonderful things for the so-called Negro. Elijah Muhammad is to the so-called Negro what Adolf Hitler was to the German people. He is the most powerful black man in the country. Heil Hitler![58]

The booing quickly changed to thunderous applause as Rockwell and the neo-Nazis made their way back to their seats. They weren't cheering for Rockwell but for the Messenger, who slowly made his way to the microphones up on stage. "We don't need no help from you. We want to help you keep your race all white. We also want to keep ours all black."[59] The crowd gave him a standing ovation as he made his way back to his seat.

Some Muslims concluded that Rockwell's presence was planned as a means to divert the attention of Muslims visiting Chicago from another drama being played out right under their noses. Members of the Chicago mosque were venting long pent-up anger against the royal family. Knowledge of Muhammad's extramarital activities was no longer limited to an elite cabal; almost everyone in Mosque No. 2 knew. There were jokes about so-and-so carrying a little message from the Messenger, about how divine seed was sprouting all over the secretarial pool, and even a double entendre about secretaries spending most of their time in Muhammad's office taking dictation.[60]

Clara sat anxiously through the annual ceremony. She knew that cruel things were being said about her, but felt economically enslaved to the Messenger. She made many long-distance calls to Akbar in Cairo before the convention about spending some time with him. When she found out that Elijah was involved with yet another woman, she felt she had to get away from him, from their homes in Phoenix and Chicago, from everything related to the NOI. On April 23, after still another argument with Elijah, she applied for a passport, which was issued the next day. According to the U.S. Passport Office, Clara indicated that she would be visiting her son in Cairo for approximately two months.[61] The talking walls in her house, however, revealed another plan: that she wanted to leave her husband, and that she was thinking of remaining in Cairo permanently. On April 26, 1962, the Bureau began discussing ways to use the information it had gathered on Muhammad's extramarital affairs as a COINTELPRO ploy. In a memo from FBI headquarters to the Chicago field office, a high-level FBI official wrote:

> Bureau continues to receive information through investigation conducted by Chicago and Phoenix and the sources available to these offices that Elijah Muhammad is engaging in extramarital activities with at least five female members of the Nation of Islam (NOI). This information indicates Muhammad has fathered some children by these women and that his wife, Clara, has become aware of his infidelity which has resulted in domestic strife. Apparently, Muhammad is furnishing financial support to at least some of these women and their children and contemplates a nursery to get his illegitimate children under one roof. . . .
>
> Chicago and Phoenix should make recommendations concerning the use of information thus obtained to discredit Muhammad with his followers. This could be handled through the use of carefully selected informants planting the seeds of dissension through anonymous letters and/or telephone calls and through various other selected actions. . . .[62]

While agents dreamt up ways to implement the suggestion from FBI headquarters, Clara and Herbert made final arrangements for their trip to Egypt. On April 30, a source at Trans World Airlines told Chicago

FBI agents that Clara and Herbert were leaving on TWA Flight 800 from O'Hare International Airport at three o'clock on the afternoon of May 3.[63] Clara's ticket was one-way to Cairo, the flight's final destination after several stops in Europe. The day after Clara left, Muhammad's mistresses flooded him with phone calls. All of them wanted the same thing: money. Muhammad refused, telling one that the money he gave her in April was enough to last until October. Another threatened to go to his house in Chicago and cause a disturbance if he didn't relent. "Go wherever you want because it won't make any difference," he told her. "You can't prove anything."[64]

"Are you going to send the money or not?" the former secretary asked.

"No," he replied.

"Then I'm going to call your family and tell your daughter just how you are."

"Listen," he said softly, perhaps realizing that he had overplayed his hand, "now is not the time for anything like—"

"I'm going to tell her," she said, then quickly hung up.

When he told the secretary that he didn't have time to deal with their personal relationship just then, he assumed that she would understand why, though clearly she didn't. He was deeply involved in a major crisis: a Muslim had been murdered in cold blood six days earlier, and nearly every Muslim in the country was ready to declare war. The fatal disturbance involved the Los Angeles Police Department and Ronald X Stokes, the popular secretary of Muhammad's Mosque No. 27 at 5606 South Broadway. On April 27, Stokes was handing freshly cleaned clothing to another Muslim when a police officer took an interest in the transaction.[65] According to the officer, he thought that Stokes was selling stolen clothing from the trunk of his car. The officer approached Stokes's vehicle with his weapon drawn. He asked Stokes to show him his business license. As Stokes tried to explain that he worked at a local cleaners which gave him a discount for bringing it so much business (he personally picked up and delivered clothing to his coreligionists), the officer assumed he was lying. The next words out of the officer's mouth were guaranteed to provoke a fight: "Nigger," he said, "turn around and put your hands up against the car and spread-eagle."

"We didn't do anything," Stokes protested. He offered to take the officer to the cleaners to prove that the clothing wasn't stolen, but the officer wouldn't hear of it. Stokes grew nervous as he faced the officer's drawn gun, and he accused the policeman of harassment at the same time that he was trying to reason with him. Several onlookers ran a block or so to the mosque and alerted the Muslims to what was happening. By the time they arrived, Stokes had been felled by a bullet to the chest. His blood colored the sidewalk as the officer, who had summoned reinforcements, joined other officers in beating the handcuffed victim. The back of Stokes's head was crushed from the impact of the blows. When the Muslims saw what had happened, a few fought with the police while others ran back to the mosque to protect the women and children. Those who stayed with Stokes were seriously injured, two so severely beaten with nightsticks that a hospital spokesman said they were not expected to live. Another was shot in the groin, and one was shot in the lower back, leaving him permanently paralyzed.[66]

By the time the police invaded the mosque, most of the women and children had escaped through a rear entrance. The men, who had been trained to protect the sanctity of their temple with their lives, found themselves in circumstances harkening back to slavery. Though the police knew that Muslims did not keep weapons in the mosque (Muslims frequently made a point of this in an attempt to avoid violent confrontations with police), they ransacked the place on the pretext of searching for them. Once they were absolutely sure the Muslims were unarmed, police ordered them to form a single-file lineup. "We shot your brother outside," one officer yelled at them. "Are you going to do something about it?"[67] The Muslims stood there, saying nothing. The officers then conducted one of the most bizarre strip searches in the annals of law enforcement. First each man's jacket was ripped up the middle, and then while some officers held the group at gunpoint, others pulled each man aside for a more thorough search. The officers used their hands and a sharp object to cut each man's pants to shreds, exposing their underwear. Several men accused of acting "belligerent" were poked in the rectum with nightsticks. As a final act of humiliation, they were made to walk slowly outside and get into police cruisers. Hundreds of witnesses watched as the Muslims were taken away in shame. Fourteen Muslims, including Minister John Shabass, were booked for assaulting a police officer and other charges.[68]

As word of the assault traveled eastward, Malcolm X and others were considering means to take an army of Muslims to Los Angeles to go into battle. But when he asked Muhammad for approval, the Messenger was aghast. "There's already been one bloodbath. Why do we need another?" Malcolm was angry, he said later, but abided by Muhammad's decision. "I told you we would lose some good soldiers in the war with the devils,"[69] Muhammad added, "and we will lose more. Allah is the Best Knower. He will settle the score." He instructed Malcolm to tell the Muslims to go back to their homes, and asked his national representative to fly to Los Angeles as soon as possible. For the first time in recent memory, civil rights leaders heard Muhammad asking for their help in the name of brotherhood. The conciliatory note came after Dr. King, Roy Wilkins, and other civil rights leaders called or sent telegrams to Muhammad to express their condolences and to denounce police brutality.[70]

"In these crucial times we must not think in terms of one's religion, but in terms of justice for us black people," Muhammad said at a press conference in Chicago. "This means a united front for justice in America. It would have been more safe on the 27th of April for our people in Los Angeles to be among wild lions than in civilized America. What happened to us on April 27 could and is happening to you and me throughout America."[71] Malcolm X joined several black leaders in Los Angeles for a rally at the Second Baptist Church on May 17. The highlight of the rally, which drew 3,000, was an announcement from the NAACP that it would support the NOI's call for an investigation into the raid on a house of worship. Malcolm X controlled his anger during the press conference, but later told his top aides in New York that the lack of direct action for the murder of Stokes was one of several indicators that the

Muslims were seen as "all talk and no action."[72] Malcolm's speech at Second Baptist evoked comments from Mayor Sam Yorty, who portrayed it as an incitement to violence. When a second rally was scheduled, Muhammad privately expressed fears about what Malcolm X might say next. "I don't know who's to control Malcolm," he said to a member of the Los Angeles mosque. "Just tell Malcolm to cool his heels."[73]

Muhammad gave several speeches in the weeks after the assault that were filled with talk of fire and brimstone, but suspiciously silent on self-defense. He was starting to sound like the Christian preachers whose "turn-the-other-cheek" philosophy he ridiculed. An airline tragedy on June 4 served to bolster Muhammad's claim for divine retribution. "The airplane crash in France in which 130 people from Georgia was killed was the work of Allah for what the white man had done to the so-called Negroes," he said at McCormick Place on July 15. "More of this will come."[74] With the exception of the six-member flight crew, everyone on board was from Georgia, the state for which he harbored the most hatred. Muhammad's contention about the loss of innocent lives in the airplane catastrophe did little to assuage the anger of Muslims in Los Angeles, as the officer who shot Stokes testified that the fatal wound was struck only after Stokes moved his hands "menacingly." A jury agreed, and held that it was a case of "justifiable homicide."

While Muhammad vented his rage against injustices in America, his harem of secretaries were meeting in Chicago to vent their rage against his personal injustices. On May 10, several of them discovered the curious and coincidental nature of their relationships with the Messenger. Except for the two sisters, the secretaries were unaware that Muhammad had given each of them the same spiel about his sperm being "divine seed." He had been lying to all of them about his affections and marital intentions. None seemed to take the revelation harder than Tynetta X Nelson. On May 17, 1962, she called the Messenger at his home in Phoenix. As agents monitored and recorded the conversation, she argued with him about his promiscuity and asked him about rumors that he was involved with the other secretaries. "I don't know what you're talking about," the Messenger replied. "Don't tell me you don't!" Tynetta yelled. "It's a lie, the biggest one I've ever heard . . . I'm not going to have it!" If he kept seeing anyone besides her, she said, she was going to have to have another man's arms around her. "Oh, you don't have anyone else," he said. "Come on," he pleaded, "don't talk to me like that."[75]

"All right," Tynetta snapped, "but if you try a trick like that again—" Without completing the thought, she hung up.

As the Messenger was whirled around in a cyclone of trouble, Clara was in Egypt enjoying peace of mind for the first time in years. Time flew by. Her eight-week stay extended to ten, then twelve, then to four months, and Elijah began wondering whether she had finally made good her threat to leave him. As he had done when he was in Egypt in 1959, he made frantic calls to her, telling her all the things a neglected woman needs to hear. Several love letters later, Clara relented and agreed to return to him. She arrived in New York on August 2, then took a flight to Chicago later that evening.[76]

What Clara discovered upon returning home extinguished whatever remained of love in her marriage of four decades: word of Elijah's escapades had spread throughout the NOI faster than an Asian flu. The real trouble began on July 12, when Evelyn called Muhammad to demand more money. When he balked, she accused him of treating his illegitimate children like mangy stray dogs. "You don't allow your other children to live on $300 a month. . . . All I want is money to pay the rent and to get some food and clothing." But Muhammad remained unmoved. "You're trying to blackmail me and therefore I won't speak to you or give you one red cent!"[77] Evelyn called again the next morning. If Muhammad wasn't at her door by three o'clock that afternoon, she was coming over to his house. He replied that he was too busy, but gave in a little by promising to meet her demands before dusk. During the dinner hour, when they knew Muhammad would be entertaining, Evelyn and Lucille took their children over to his house. They banged on the door, but no one answered. Reluctantly, they left the toddlers at the front entrance and started to walk away.[78] When Raymond Sharrieff called to the women to come back and get their children, they refused. Muhammad didn't give them enough money to raise his children, they said, so let him raise them. To avoid a scene at the Messenger's front door, Sharrieff waited until the mothers left, then called the police and told them that someone had abandoned several young children on his doorstep. The children were taken to the precinct and handed over to social workers for investigation.[79]

Muhammad called Evelyn the next morning to complain about her actions. She tried to reason with him, she said, but he had ignored her. "From now on, I'm not going to protect you in any way, shape, or form. If you want trouble, you'll get it."[80] While in custody, Evelyn told Chicago policemen that she had gone to the house to collect child-support money. Although she refused to divulge his name to the policemen who interrogated her about the father of her children, she told Elijah that she was through protecting him. Calling the police on his own children, Evelyn said, "was the dirtiest thing you could do." From now on, he would have to deal with her lawyers. "I'm not going to be pushed around anymore." No charges were leveled against Evelyn and Lucille for abandoning their toddlers, but the police department's juvenile section put them on notice that the penalties would be severe should there be another child-neglect incident.[81]

In a memorandum dated July 14 to William C. Sullivan, FBI official Fred J. Baumgardner wrote that the incident could be the break the Bureau was waiting for. The Bureau could use its contacts within the Chicago Police Department to "conduct an independent investigation directed toward bringing the incident to public attention and causing a bastardy charge to be filed against Muhammad."[82] On July 31, Sullivan authorized the Chicago SAC

to prepare and mail an anonymous letter to Clara Muhammad upon her return from Egypt. Chicago is also authorized to prepare and mail similar anonymous letters containing substantially the same information as the letter mailed to Clara Muhammad to selected individuals listed on page 3. . . . These letters should be mailed at staggered intervals using care to prevent any possibility of tracing the mailing back to the FBI.[83]

Despite the letters that Clara had found earlier and her repeated pleas to her husband to reform, the anonymous letter made it obvious that the sixty-four-year-old Elijah was continuing his indiscretions. In August 1962, Robert 5X, a member of the Boston mosque, was considering proposing to Evelyn X, but first he wanted to know how, as a good Muslim, she could justify having two children out of wedlock. After being evasive for a long while (she routinely claimed her "husband was away"), she reluctantly told her suitor the truth. The reason she had not married the father of her children, she said, was because the father was already married. His name was Muhammad—Elijah Muhammad.[84] Robert 5X was shocked. He loved her, but found what she was saying simply impossible; it was blasphemous, the product of a sick or defective mind. Robert rushed to Captain Clarence X Gill for advice. Gill told him that he would look into her allegations, and also said that he would have to tell Minister Louis Farrakhan immediately. Shortly after Gill told Farrakhan, Evelyn X was transferred from Boston to Chicago. Another secretary from the Boston mosque, Lucille X Rosary, was transferred back to Chicago around the same time. She, too, had borne a child out of wedlock while working in the Messenger's office in Chicago.[85]

While Muhammad was enmeshed in his personal crises, Malcolm X was kept busy managing the empire. In mid-August, he produced a special edition of *Muhammad Speaks* that focused on the Stokes incident. Using autopsy photographs, photos taken of Stokes as he lay in a pool of blood, and photos taken of the other victims, he brought the special edition out on the heels of a grand jury's finding that the death of Stokes was "justifiable homicide." One photo revealed powder burns on Stokes's chest, suggesting that he was shot at extremely close range.[86] The outrage sparked by the publication led to minor civil unrest in Los Angeles, and police feared that conditions were ripe for a riot. On August 14, 1962, Charles Nicodemus of the *Chicago Daily News* broke a story about a pending probe of the NOI:

The House Rules Committee Tuesday recommended a congressional investigation of the Black Muslim movement. A resolution adopted by the powerful House unit asked that the investigation probe into possible subversive or un-American activities of the black supremacy cult be conducted by the Committee on Un-American Activities.[87]

The resolution, introduced by South Carolina Congressman L. Mendel Rivers, alleged that a lower-court judge had erred in finding that the NOI practiced a legitimate faith. At a press conference on the steps of the Capitol Building on August 14, Rivers promised to

open up the unsavory history of the Black Muslims for all America to see. We know that the organization is dedicated on a national level to violence, bloody deeds, hatred, and death. We need to look at this group because it is tailor-made for a Communist takeover.[88]

After picking up support from Francis E. Walter, head of the House Un-American Activities Committee, Rivers persuaded the House Rules Committee to endorse the probe. "It appears to be clear that on the simple basis of what the Muslims teach, they are subversive to our form of government and pose a growing danger to our internal security," Walter's statement for the *Congressional Record* read on September 4. There was evidence, he added, that the "Communist Party tried to work for united-front type of operation" with the Nation of Islam.[89] A resolution demanding the investigation was passed in early September, and subpoenas were issued ordering Muhammad, Malcolm, and other top officials to come to Washington to face the House Un-American Activities Committee.

If Rivers sounded like a man with a card up his sleeve, he was. Weeks before the August 14 press conference, he had conferred with top FBI officials about the NOI. During the discussions, Hoover assured Rivers that the information in the Bureau's files would "make Elijah Muhammad look ridiculous." The Bureau gave Rivers a copy of its files on Wallace D. Fard. In summaries, agents described Fard as a white confidence man with an extensive criminal record. It also gave Rivers its file on Muhammad, which emphasized that he was once convicted of "contributing to the delinquency of a minor."[90] The decision to haul Muhammad before HUAC generated numerous letters of protest from civil rights groups, but the hearings moved ahead. The threat of the probe, the Bureau learned, frightened Muhammad, who was determined at all costs not to return to prison.

On September 14, Muhammad ordered Malcolm X to cancel all of his pending appearances on college campuses on the grounds that the appearances won them "no new converts" and college officials "blast us in public" as soon as the visit is announced.[91] In truth, not only were Muhammad and his sons jealous of Malcolm's popularity, but Muhammad was concerned that he was losing control over Malcolm—he often bragged to his secretaries about how Malcolm was his little lap dog. Malcolm had become the media star, while Muhammad played second fiddle. If he was going to regain any control over Malcolm, he knew that the time to do it was before the hearings began. Ordering him to stop speaking on college campuses—something Malcolm enjoyed as much as his daily sundae for dessert—was one way of tightening the reins on the Muslim maverick. Malcolm complied and sent a letter to selected colleges advising them that "because of a recurring throat problem," he had to cancel all college and university appearances for the next few months.[92]

Muhammad condemned Malcolm for being publicity-hungry when he himself loved publicity as much as Malcolm—as long as it was positive, of course. When Haley's piece ran in *Reader's Digest,* for instance, Muhammad boasted about it for week. And when the *Chicago New Crusader* ran his column with a photo he disapproved of, he threatened to withdraw the column—and Muslim salesmen—unless a more flattering picture was substituted.[93]

Having just purged itself of the excesses of McCarthyism, Congress was perhaps hesitant to demand prosecution of the Muslims, and Rivers chose to back away from an extensive probe because several black congressmen, Charles C. Diggs of Michigan, Adam Clayton Powell Jr. of New York, and Robert Nix of Pennsylvania, criticized the hearing as a waste of money. *Muhammad Speaks* reprinted a letter from Nix in which he wrote that Muhammad's teachings on liberty and freedom were "consistent with statements by Thomas Jefferson, Benjamin Franklin, John Adams, and other founders of this republic. They were legal. The source of authority to speak as he spoke is granted in the Constitution of the United States."[94] Since the issue of the probe was dividing along racial lines, Rivers satisfied himself by revealing the information he had received from the Bureau, and the hearings ended after several hours.

Just when it seemed that things were settling down for the Messenger, a scandal involving his son Herbert provided the banner headline on the *Chicago Defender*'s edition of October 13. According to the story, Herbert had been arrested for battering his mistress, who was described as a twenty-five-year-old white woman. According to the woman, Herbert, who was still married and living with his wife and their children, had somehow obtained a key to her apartment. After concluding in March that he had lied about being separated, she broke off their relationship. On October 10, Herbert hid in her apartment and waited for her. When she arrived he beat her so badly that he broke her jaw.[95] Herbert, who ran his own photography studio, was arrested for aggravated battery but released on bond. His trial was set for November 19.

The story ripped through the NOI like Hurricane Agnes. A week after his arrest, an NOI spokesman labeled the charges false, insisting that there was "no white girlfriend." The spokesman claimed, and the *Defender* agreed, that the woman involved was the "daughter of a well-known Negro photographer." A lawyer for the victim insisted that she was a Caucasian. Herbert's defense was, of course, completely illogical. Whether the woman was white or not, he did not deny having an extramarital affair, an offense that had resulted in the expulsion of dozens of rank-and-file Muslims; and the color of her skin did not mitigate the central allegation of extreme domestic violence.[96]

The federal probe and problems in his personal life had taken their toll on the Messenger. Having become seriously ill by the time of Herbert's trial date, he returned to Phoenix to get away from the stress of governing, but it did him little good. The telephone rang constantly.

Although Chicago officials assumed control of the kingdom, they were ineffective since Sharrieff and others were afraid to make decisions without consulting the king. At the conclusion of the federal hearings, for example, the Committee on Un-American Activities of the Louisiana state legislature launched its own probe of the NOI.[97] The investigation stemmed from a police raid on Muhammad's mosque in Monroe, Louisiana, on March 5, 1961. After the raid, the minister and eight others were arrested for assaulting police officers. While awaiting trial (all were found guilty as charged) Minister Troy X Cade was indicted on charges of "criminal anarchy" and other subversion-related counts. When the minister called officials in Chicago for advice, they said that they would consult with Muhammad and then get back to him. The secretary of the Monroe mosque called Muhammad on November 20 and said she was calling for legal advice on the probe. Muhammad, who was feeling very ill that morning, was enraged. "Do you think I'm so silly as to call and give you information on such as problem as that? I will not tell the minister what to say. It is up to him."[98] The secretary apologized profusely. The only reason she called, she said, was because the minister was so hysterical over receiving the subpoena that he was unable to call for himself. But what she was asking the Messenger to do, in effect, was practice law (by giving her legal advice) without a license. Besides, he was paying lawyers to handle the problems in Louisiana. At the culmination of the investigation, the committee concluded that the NOI posed a threat to the country's internal security, and that Troy was the ringleader of a "Communist conspiracy." Despite appeals, the minister went to prison along with others convicted in the aftermath of the raid, and the mosque in Monroe was boarded up.[99]

After a series of legal defeats, the Messenger finally had something to celebrate as the holiday season neared. Several federal courts ruled that Muslim inmates were denied their First Amendment right to freedom of religion by prison officials who banned Muslim clergymen (but not rabbis and Christian ministers) and forbade Islamic worship services. The rulings coincided with an article in the influential *Columbia Law Review* titled "Black Muslims in Prison: Of Muslim Rites and Constitutional

Rights."[100] The authors supported recent court opinions favoring Muslims. Then, the Messenger learned that a very special prisoner—his son Wallace—was about to be released after serving only a year of his three-year sentence. That was good news. That, he would soon discover, was also bad news.

CHAPTER TWELVE
SONS AND LOVERS

Stone walls do not a prison make,
Nor iron bars a cage.
Minds innocent and quiet take
That for a hermitage.
    —*Richard Lovelace*,
        "To Althea: From Prison"[1]

Clara wanted to run. She looked round. There was the black, re-echoing shore, the dark sky down on her. She got up terrified. She wanted to be where there was light, where there were other people. She wanted to be away from him.

—*D. H. Lawrence*,
Sons and Lovers[2]

The parting of the ways between the NOI's heir apparent and his father, who had ruled with impunity for thirty years, started on the highway home. In prison, Wallace was detached from the scandals that were destroying Elijah's reputation and threatening his kingdom. Upon his release from Sandstone, he had to be briefed on the dramatic changes in Chicago, and Elijah Jr. was selected as the family's emissary. Marital strife marked every day in Elijah's house, and several of the more recent incidents had been tinged with the threat of violence. Junior picked Wallace up at the prison and the two of them engaged in brotherly banter until Wallace asked how his parents were doing. "Things are pretty bad at home," Junior replied.[3] Wallace recalled that he hadn't had the foggiest notion of what Junior was referring to because he had "rejected things my own mind was telling me." He asked Junior for details. Slowly, Junior told him that their parents were bickering worse than toddlers, that Clara was constantly complaining about Elijah's gallivanting with impressionable young women in his employ, and that she was ready to end the marriage. All she talked about was leaving Elijah and moving back to Georgia or perhaps going to Africa to live with Akbar. As for their father, he was behaving like the men across town at Hugh Hefner's place.

During the holidays, Clara and Elijah had had an argument over Bernique. When Clara returned to Phoenix after Elijah's persistent pleading, she walked in unexpectedly and caught Bernique and Elijah in an embrace.[4] At first she said nothing about the incident, but when Elijah continued to act like a nursing-home Casanova after returning to Chicago, she started to make a fuss about it. Borrowing a page from Ovid's treatise on love, Elijah denied that anything amorous was afoot. He even tried to gain the upper hand by berating her for not showing him any affection when they were in Phoenix. "You didn't kiss me once when I was sick!" he shouted.[5] Clara was dumbfounded. Here was a man who, in forty-two years of marriage, had never been the cuckold, who made only the most modest attempts to shield her from his extra-marital endeavors, questioning her loyalty and devotion. Perhaps the reason he was having so many health problems, Clara retorted, was that "Allah is punishing you for the way you mistreat me." She again threatened to leave him and return to Egypt or to relations in Georgia.[6]

"Go ahead! I didn't ask you to come back here from Egypt anyway," Elijah barked. Clara was crying as she gathered her things to pack a suitcase: "Go ahead! I ought to lock you out of the house. I'd rather stay in a motel than in the same house with you."[7] With that, Elijah gathered his own things and left for his Vernon Street apartment. After Wallace had spoken to his other siblings and heard about the argument and his father's contemptuous behavior, he was more receptive to the things that Junior had confided to him; and when he saw how weary and worn out his mother looked, Wallace was ready to believe almost anything about his father. That was his frame of mind when Ola X Hughes, one of his father's secretaries, came into the picture. Power had ruined the Messenger, Ola told him.[8] The stories circulating in the Chicago mosque about the illegitimate children were true. Evelyn and Lucille were not the only ones he had seduced; there had been at least a dozen victims, Ola said, including herself.[9]

At the same time that Wallace came to believe the allegations against his father, he discovered that the Messenger had changed his mind about naming him as the next ruler of the NOI. Malcolm was the favorite now. That's what everyone was saying—even the Messenger. Two days after Wallace came home, his father was having a pleasant telephone conversation with Malcolm when one of his sons overheard him praising Malcolm for a recent sermon. "Allah will keep you courageous and with wisdom. You are a modern Paul."[10] Being dethroned wasn't exactly the reward that Wallace had anticipated for going to prison just to satisfy his father's idea of manhood. All of his life Wallace kept hearing that Master Wallace D. Fard—God—had decided that he was the son who would succeed the Messenger as head of the NOI. Now that the hour of heirship was approaching, he was hearing another story. If his father saw

Malcolm as the NOI's Paul, how did he perceive Wallace—as a forgotten leftover?

The man Wallace had once worshipped he now looked upon with derision and scorn. Elijah criticized him for not developing wings large enough to support his flight into manhood, yet he did everything within his power to stunt Wallace's growth. His father had been constraining him since high school, Wallace recalled. He had gone to his father and asked for tuition to enroll in a technical school, but he was refused on the grounds that he was being primed for the ministry. After graduation, Wallace had tried to strike out on his own, but his father jumped on his back again, threatening to prevent him from obtaining employment outside the NOI. Like his brothers and sisters, he was a slave to his father's money and power and a prisoner of his own desires.[11]

Wallace's animosity toward his father was heightened by remarks from his brothers, who warned him that Malcolm had a blueprint for taking over the NOI.[12] Malcolm's having appointed his wife, brothers, and close friends to powerful positions was cited as evidence of his ambitions. This, too, must have had the ring of truth. Much had changed in the NOI in the year that Wallace had been incarcerated, and most of the changes were the direct results of Malcolm's impressive ideas and hard work. Since Haley's articles had appeared in *Reader's Digest,* dozens of mosques had opened. By January 1963, there were at least 120 mosques across the country, most of them so new that only one-third had been assigned numbers. Another 30 were nearly large enough to warrant a number, Muhammad said, but he would wait a few months more to test their durability before assigning them a number. The remaining ones were "small places teaching ten to fifteen" converts. Between Malcolm's proselytizing and media attention, he added, there was no telling how large or how fast the NOI would grow.[13]

While Clara and Wallace tried to sort out where they fit in the scheme of things, Malcolm moved closer to the royal crown. Given the Messenger's continuing ailments, most of the executive decisions fell to Malcolm. On February 16, he sent a telegram to Attorney General Robert F. Kennedy concerning a recent police raid on the NOI mosque in Rochester.[14] The telegram was passed on to Burke Marshall, assistant attorney general in the Civil Rights Division. The gist of the complaint was that the January 6 raid by the Rochester Police Department was unjustified, that the brutality of the police provoked the Muslim assault on several officers, and that the indictment of thirteen Muslims was foul.[15] The raid followed the same pattern as the ones in Los Angeles and Monroe. Local police, under the pretext of trying to protect Muslims and to avert violence, forcibly entered a house of worship and arrested worshippers, who were startled by their sudden invasion. The pretextual circumstances varied—in the Rochester case, police alleged that an anonymous caller said that a man with a gun was in the mosque—but the results were always the same, with Muslims being shot or killed or facing criminal charges. Money that might have gone toward building the Islamic Center that Malcolm was working toward ended up in the pockets of lawyers hired to defend Muslims on frivolous charges.

Malcolm was so preoccupied with the daily business of running the NOI that he wasn't aware of the discord in Chicago. When he came to Chicago for Saviour's Day 1963, Wallace informed him of the lurid charges that had been made by Ola X Hughes. The convention that year was the shortest in NOI history—lasting only one day whereas they usually extended over a long weekend—because Muslim officials in Chicago were trying to keep the rumors about Muhammad from spreading. They reasoned that if the visitors stayed longer, they would certainly hear about the scandals, which thus far had been "quarantined" in Chicago.[16] Muhammad missed the convention completely. The more than 3,000 people who attended the celebration were told that he was too ill to appear.[17] Malcolm was assigned to run the event, which triggered anger and hostility on the part of Muhammad's children. A few members of the disappointed crowd asked to hear Wallace speak, but Malcolm said that there was no time, as the program was running late and people would miss their buses and planes if it was extended any further. As it turned out, four chartered planes from the East Coast were delayed anyway, as someone had phoned in bomb threats.[18]

Malcolm was thankful that few Muslims outside Chicago had heard about the Messenger's indiscretions. He remained in Chicago for several weeks after the convention while Muhammad recuperated from stress related to family matters. During his stay, he tried to discern how much of what Wallace had told him made sense, only to discover that almost all of the allegations were true. All of the women who had worked for the Messenger as personal secretaries and who had become pregnant were young, unmarried, and fascinated by his supposed divine powers. Some of these young women had joined the NOI in the first place in hopes of marrying Malcolm. Two of them, Evelyn and Lucille, had even dated Malcolm in the 1940s, and he and Evelyn had once seriously considered marriage.[19] In fact, when it was announced that Malcolm was marrying Betty X Sanders in 1958, Evelyn jumped up from her seat and ran screaming out of the mosque. A further irony was that Malcolm had personally recommended most of the young women involved for the secretarial jobs, and Muhammad had offered to give Betty a secretarial position just a few days before she and Malcolm eloped.[20]

There was a time when Malcolm had prided himself on being a procurer, a hustler so popular that they called him "Detroit Red." Now, all he felt was shame and guilt for having placed so many eager young girls in a situation where their innocence was exploited.[21] In putting so much faith in Muhammad, Malcolm failed to heed a primary rule that street hustlers learn: No one hustles a good hustler, because he reserves a share of mistrust for everyone. Malcolm said he never trusted anyone completely; later, he had to admit to himself that he had made an exception of Muhammad, an exception that proved the value of the rule. Now he was paying the price. "All the wind was taken out of his sails when he realized what the Messenger had done," Wilfred Little recalled.[22]

Malcolm quietly contacted three of the former secretaries to verify what was being said, and discovered that one of the Messenger's affairs was incestuous.[23] After hearing their accounts, he wrote Muhammad a long letter about the matter and asked for an appointment to discuss it.

In April 1963, Malcolm went to Phoenix to confront his surrogate father. He spoke candidly with him, and Muhammad was equally blunt. Yes, Muhammad confessed, he had done all the things of which he stood accused. Malcolm suggested that the scandal be broken to the faithful gradually and in biblical terms, and the Messenger seemed pleased with that: "You always have had such a good understanding of prophecy and of spiritual things," he said in a slow, soft, way. "You recognized that's what all of this is—prophecy. You have the kind of understanding that only an old man has. . . . I'm David," the Messenger went on. "When you read about how David took another man's wife, I'm that David. You read about Noah, who got drunk—that's me. You read about Lot, who went and laid up with his own daughters. I have to fulfill all of those things."[24]

Malcolm was shocked by Muhammad's admission of guilt and his frightening fatalism. He went to Wallace to see if they could come up with some plan to rescue the NOI from what now appeared to be its certain demise. Wallace, however, was as pessimistic as his father. He had already tried to discuss the matter with him, he told Malcolm, but "my father doesn't want to be helped. He doesn't want to mend his ways."[25] Wallace also told Malcolm that Elijah was so angered by his [Wallace's] questions that he suspended him as minister of the Philadelphia mosque.[26] When Malcolm asked Wallace why he supposed that his father felt that way, Wallace's answer was chilling in both its simplicity and its implications: Muhammad had been worshipped as the final prophet of God for so long that he had convinced himself it was true.

Though dispirited, Malcolm could not free himself from his need to believe in Muhammad's divinity. He turned to the Holy Bible and Holy Quran to study the lives of prophets whose weaknesses were recorded there for all time. He found dozens of stories in the Holy Bible about prophets and their imperfections. A few were murderers, others were adulterers, and some were both. Malcolm again suggested that it would be a good idea to confide in some of the top ministers and to begin delivering sermons about the shortcomings of biblical prophets. That way, when the rank and file of the Messenger's flock found out about the illegitimate children, they might be able to put it into some kind of perspective. Muhammad told Malcolm that he could tell select ministers. "But don't tell Brother Louis," Muhammad cautioned, referring to Louis Farrakhan of Boston. Malcolm returned to New York, saying nothing to temple officers of his troubling conversation with the Messenger. The only one he confided in was his wife, Betty.[27]

After Malcolm left Phoenix, Clara was the first person Elijah called on for comfort. "He doesn't weigh as much as a little boy," a secretary told Clara once when she called to check on his condition. "He can hardly talk and just stumbles around." He was coughing incessantly, she said, and "spitting up big black spots which he says is just mucus." Part of his trouble, she told Clara, is that he doesn't have anyone there in Phoenix—meaning Clara—"telling him how much they love him." Once, when she went to check on him after a coughing spell, she said, the Messenger looked at her and said, "I feel like blowing my brains out."[28]

As much as Clara hated how her husband had mistreated her, she still cared about him. She immediately left Chicago for Phoenix. She was not prepared for what she found. She noticed that all the while she was there, two secretaries coddled Elijah, caressing him the way a wife would. His health improved surprisingly quickly after Clara's arrival, and he gained weight rapidly, but the minute his strength returned, he started taking Clara for granted again. Her resentment grew over his cavalier treatment and his flaunting of his infidelity. She told one of her daughters that she had blinded herself to his behavior and was falling for the same old tricks. This time, she said, she was leaving him for good. She transferred money she had managed to save to banks in Cairo and Switzerland, and on July 17, she returned to Akbar's house in Cairo, where he lived with his wife, an Egyptian of the Christian faith.[29]

In Washington, FBI officials handling the COINTELPRO campaign against the NOI were given to understand that finally the timing was right to demolish the sect. Several field offices had COINTELPRO operations ready, any combination of which had the potential to bring Muhammad down. It could exploit the extramarital scandal or aggravate hostilities between Wallace and his father and Malcolm's budding disenchantment. It could release its most recent findings on Wallace D. Fard, information of such an explosive nature that it was bound to rattle Muhammad. While agents mulled over the first two ideas, the third was launched. In July, newspapers suddenly ran stories about Fard's "true identity." The first to break the story was the *Los Angeles Herald-Examiner*, part of the Hearst-owned chain. "Black Muslim Founder Exposed as a White," the large headline read.[30] According to the story, accompanied by mug shots and a copy of a birth certificate, there was exceptionally strong evidence that Fard was in fact a Los Angeles confidence man named Wallace Dodd. It also alleged that Fard had bilked black people in the name of religion. The article, which was carried in other Hearst-owned papers across the country, was among the most successful COINTELPRO actions against the NOI.

Through its wiretap on Muhammad's telephone and other surveillance devices, the FBI determined that the July 28 story had infuriated him. One agent noted that he was ranting and raving about the story and had ordered national secretary John Ali to contact the "finest lawyer" they could find to file a defamation lawsuit.[31] Meanwhile, Muhammad sent a letter to the *Los Angeles Herald-Examiner*, in which he promised to pay the newspaper $100,000 if it could prove that Wallace Dodd and Wallace D. Fard were the same person:

> If he [Dodd] was teaching for money in those panic days in Detroit, he did not get it from us. Mr. Dodd, undoubtedly, must have been teaching the white people if he received any money at all, because we did not have any. . . . If Mr. Dodd was The Mr. Wallace Fard Muhammad, why did not the F.B.I. arrest him for this teaching of truth? Let this paper prove these things before it headlines us as liars and worshippers of white devils.[32]

Two days later, three Muslim officials went to the offices of the *Herald-Examiner* and asked to speak to Ed Montgomery, who wrote the story. "When we walked into his office he turned on his tape recorder. He looked and acted nervous," one recalled. "He was given . . . the offer [of $100,000] in plain words. That devil . . . never tried to prove what he knows was and is a lie."[33]

Montgomery couldn't prove the charges to the satisfaction of the Muslims because the dossier on Fard had come from the FBI. In basing his story on Fard's FBI file, which revealed that agents had conducted one of the most exhaustive and expensive searches on a noncriminal matter in its history, Montgomery placed himself at the mercy of the Bureau. The FBI wasn't about to expose its role in the episode. In the

days and weeks following the exposé, many Muslims wrote letters to
Hoover asking about the veracity of Montgomery's charges. Hoover
replied that the Bureau's practice was to decline comment. Montgomery's story accurately related the data in the Bureau's file, but he
made one glaring error in referring to Fard as "Wallace Dodd" throughout the story, whereas the files noted that his name was "Wallace Dodd
Ford." Montgomery did note, however, that Dodd had named his son
"Wallace Dodd Ford."[34]

The influential *Washington Daily News* ran the story on August 20.
"Did Muhammad Come from Mecca or from Jail?" the headline read.
Malcolm X, who had been critical of President Kennedy's attempts to
derail the March on Washington, which was scheduled for August 28,
accused the administration of planting the story "to enhance the image
of the so-called civil rights leaders."[35] The leaked information about
Fard had a negative impact on the NOI but didn't achieve what the
Bureau had hoped for. Without corroboration from the FBI, the story
had no more credibility than those in some supermarket tabloids, and
for Muslims, the story was further proof that Caucasians were the masters of deceit and "tricknology." The story died down with little long-
term effect on the NOI, but the Bureau had succeeded in the sense that it
had planted another seed of doubt in the minds of some Muslims—perhaps even Malcolm.

The FBI also regarded its COINTELPRO aimed at ending Muhammad's marriage as a minor victory. While the anonymous letters to Clara
had caused problems, FBI agents noted ruefully that it was unlikely that
Clara would leave Muhammad permanently because she was too economically dependent upon him. Besides, Muhammad was doing a good
job of destroying his marriage without interference from the Bureau.
The only sure means of destroying the sect, agents concluded, was
through internal bickering among the leadership. If it couldn't discredit
the Messenger, agents wrote, the Bureau would try to provoke a war
between the Messenger, Wallace, and Malcolm X.[36]

On August 28, Dr. King and a throng of 250,000 had the FBI's undi-
vided attention. The March on Washington, at the time the largest
demonstration ever held in the nation's capital, attracted black people

from every religious group in the country—except the NOI. Muhammad forbade Muslims to participate in the protest, which Malcolm derided as the "Farce on Washington."[37] Malcolm accused King and five other black leaders of compromising their principles to please President Kennedy. Kennedy, Malcolm said, had arranged for the "Big Six" to receive financial rewards for making sure the crowd was "out of town by sundown."[38] But in private, Malcolm confided to select associates that while he disagreed with King's methods, he admired him for at least taking a stand. Muhammad's isolationist policy had outlived its practicality in a period when black people were losing their lives not so much for the right to be treated civilly as for the right to be treated as human beings. Medgar Evers wasn't assassinated in Mississippi for begging to sit at a lunch counter next to a Caucasian; he was gunned down in Jackson for the same reason that Ronald Stokes was gunned down in Los Angeles: for defending his God-given right to be treated as a human being.

Malcolm's reluctant admiration for King was one more indication that Muhammad's influence on his spokesman was waning. The Muslims talked tough, but people were beginning to have their doubts. The assault on Hinton, the raids in Rochester, Monroe, and elsewhere, belied Muhammad's claim that white people were afraid to touch his followers; and in some Southern states, Muslims stayed "in their place" just like everyone else with black skin who placed a premium on staying alive. "The Muslims talk a good game," Louis Lomax told Malcolm, but "they get their asses kicked" just like King's followers.[39] At least King's movement was improving the lives of millions of African Americans by tearing down the social and psychological wall between the races and the inequality it generated.

The benefits of being in the NOI, in contrast, seemed to be limited primarily to Elijah and his family. The rank and file were better off healthwise, but were as poor or poorer (from extensive tithing) than before they had become Muslims. Moreover, the emergence of radical young black men such as Stokely Carmichael made King's movement more progressive and realistic than the NOI, and it came without all the baggage of reverse racism. To hate Caucasians merely because they were white was unequivocal nonsense to African Americans who were trying to show the stupidity of being hated just because they were black.

King and the SCLC were a distant thunder to Muhammad and the cause of black separatism; a more immediate danger lay in the spreading web of COINTELPRO. On October 18, 1963, FBI agents approached Lucille Rosary, Muhammad's former secretary and presently disgruntled mistress. They just wanted to ask some general questions, they said, like whether it was true that the Messenger was the father of her children.[40] There was nothing the agents couldn't tell her about her personal life. They knew the date of her birth and the size of her feet, her telephone number, and how many times she called Muhammad each week. She was afraid of them in the way one is afraid of anyone with the power to violate one's privacy. But her fear of Muhammad was greater; the FBI would have to look elsewhere for a turncoat.[41]

Malcolm was alarmed when Lucille told him about the FBI's visit because he suspected that the Bureau planned to use the Messenger's excesses to destroy the NOI. He visited Wallace in Philadelphia and told him what was going on, asking him again if there was anything they could do to head off the FBI's exploitation of the scandal. Not only was his father continuing to engage in extramarital activities, Wallace said, but "things were getting worse."[42]

If Muhammad wouldn't help himself, Malcolm decided, perhaps he and certain ministers could help him. Malcolm approached several ministers to advise them that a storm was headed toward the NOI. He told Captain Joseph Gravitt and mosque secretary Maceo X Owens that the NOI was about to face its greatest challenge. A few days later, he discussed it again with Wallace, then told Minister Lonnie X Cross of Washington (following his shift from Atlanta) and Minister Isaiah X Edwards of Baltimore. "I thought those babies looked like the Messenger," Edwards replied.[43]

The sixth and last person Malcolm discussed the scandal with was Louis Farrakhan, and he was mystified by the fact that Farrakhan did not seem surprised by the allegations. It turned out that Farrakhan wasn't surprised because he had known about the scandal for more than seven months, as two of the young women the Messenger had seduced were from the Boston mosque. When Muhammad asked Malcolm not to tell Farrakhan, he was only testing his loyalty; he knew that Evelyn had told Farrakhan about their illicit relationship. If Malcolm X told Farrakhan about the scandal against the Messenger's orders, it would be a sign that he could no longer be trusted. Farrakhan warned Malcolm that he intended to tell the Messenger that Malcolm had told him about the scandal. "He asked me to give him a little time to write a letter to the Messenger,"[44] Farrakhan said, to explain why he had told Farrakhan despite the admonition not to do so. Farrakhan told Malcolm that he would give him time to mail his letter to the Messenger, but that Malcolm "had better write fast," as he had already arranged to go to Chicago. The greatest reward, NOI officials knew, went to the first tattletale.

Meanwhile, Joseph was making his own plans to tell the Messenger what Malcolm was divulging about his private life, seizing the opportunity to retaliate against Malcolm for having him punished in 1958. After Malcolm told Joseph and Maceo about Muhammad's indiscretions, Joseph called together select FOI officials, confiding to them that Malcolm was spreading such malicious rumors about the Messenger that he ought to be silenced. In the parlance of the NOI, that was not just an idle suggestion; it was an order to kill. Fortunately for Malcolm, one of the men in whom Joseph had confided warned him that his life was in jeopardy.[45]

Predictably, Farrakhan was the first to contact Muhammad. If Malcolm X was ousted, Farrakhan was most likely to succeed him as national spokesman. Moreover, Farrakhan was looking for an opportunity to impress Muhammad with his trustworthiness, particularly after Tynetta had told Muhammad that she was the one who first expressed the intention to write the play *Orgena*. Once over dinner, Muhammad asked Farrakhan whether it was true that he had stolen the idea for the play from Tynetta.[46] Farrakhan said no. The Messenger asked him again, and again Farrakhan said no. "Are you sure you didn't take the sister's idea?" Muhammad asked him a third and fourth time. Farrakhan, sensing the Messenger's doubt, assured him that he had not taken Tynetta's idea.

The conversation moved on to other topics, but it was clear that

Muhammad had some doubts about Farrakhan's integrity. Bringing Muhammad the story about Malcolm X was a sure way to impress him with his purity of purpose. Malcolm had told him everything, Farrakhan said. The Messenger wasn't surprised, though; what Malcolm knew was too much for any mortal to keep to himself. Farrakhan was godfather to Malcolm's children, who called him "Uncle Louis," and Muhammad knew that if Malcolm were to confide in anyone, Farrakhan was the most likely candidate.

When Muhammad realized that the bond was broken between him and his favorite minister, he began to contemplate homicide and even suicide. He knew that the hurt Malcolm was suffering made him as dangerous as the blinded Samson, and just thinking about what Malcolm might do in his anger made him ill. By mid-May, the Messenger was bedridden. His health had deteriorated to the point that he talked openly of suicide. On May 14, he suffered a severe bout of bronchitis. He had lost so much weight again that his staff was afraid that he was going to die of self-inflicted starvation.[47] Apart from being despondent over the publicity Malcolm X was getting and grappling with his marital crisis, he had to face the fact that Wallace had turned against him for his terrible treatment of Clara.

In early November 1963, Clara was again threatening to leave—to get away from Muhammad and his descent into decadence. The FBI tried to take full credit for the marital breakup, but the phony letters were no more significant than one flea on a cat; what was happening between the couple would have happened without the Bureau's interference. The Bureau noted, though, accurately enough, that Clara probably would return to the Messenger. Her age, lack of commercial skills, and temperament made her a prisoner of home economics.

Muhammad had become so accustomed to Clara's idle threats of leaving that he dismissed them.[48] Ironically, he called one of his mistresses the day after Clara threatened to leave him and told her that her flirtatiousness was jeopardizing their relationship. "You have to control your sex desires," he said. "Every time you're around a man, you can see the desire to sleep with him in your eyes." If she wasn't careful about being so obvious, he warned, Clara was going to "blow the whole thing wide open."[49] On November 21, the Chicago field office filed a routine memorandum entitled "Justification for Continuation of Technical or Microphone Surveillance" of Muhammad's home and apartment in Chicago. In the request, the SAC noted:

> This surveillance has proven extremely valuable in covering the overall activities of the NOI, which is considered potentially dangerous to the security of this country. Information has been furnished regarding changes in NOI leadership around the country; contact with sympathizers in the British West Indies; contact with the NOI by World Heavyweight title contender, Cassius Clay; publicity by *McCall's* magazine; and traveling of Elijah Muhammad's son to Cairo, Egypt. This information is furnished on a current basis and greatly facilitates the handing of this case by the Chicago office.

The request for continuation was approved in a matter of hours, and marked the beginning of major intelligence gathering by the Bureau on Clay.[50]

The day after the wiretap was reapproved, President Kennedy was campaigning for reelection in the homestate of Vice President Lyndon B. Johnson. The sunlit streets of Dallas were filled with people on their lunch break and schoolchildren who had been released from their classrooms to witness history in the making. But somewhere lurking in the shadows was a gang kindling a fire for the devil. President Kennedy, the youngest president in American history and one more well-regarded by African Americans than Abraham Lincoln, was assassinated in Dallas shortly after noon on November 22, 1963.

Though his Muslims were quietly celebrating the president's death as evidence that the white man's rule would end by 1970, Muhammad was suddenly and curiously mute. He wanted to make sure that none of his ministers—meaning Malcolm X—said anything that would provoke a white backlash against Muslims, so he quickly issued an edict calling for silence on the subject of the president's death. Malcolm X was in the Shabazz Restaurant in Harlem when news of the shooting hit the airwaves. As the radio announcement ended, everyone looked at Malcolm. There wasn't a smile or a frown on his face, friends recall, but the same expression of disbelief that millions of Americans wore that afternoon. The dazed Malcolm said quietly: "That devil is dead."[51]

In spite of his caution, the Messenger was caught on tape making what the average American would consider a horrific statement about the late president. "This isn't a day of mourning for Muslims," he said when an official called about closing the University of Islam the next day to demonstrate that Muslims shared in the country's loss. "That devil's death doesn't concern us; it's time for the Christians to mourn, not the Muslims."[52] Despite everything that they were taught about white people, some Muslims believed that John Kennedy was an exception, that he was a man with genuine empathy for the underclass. "You know," a former lieutenant from the Harlem mosque said, "I never really believed all that devil stuff in the first place . . . and I certainly didn't think President Kennedy was a bad man."[53] It was probably sentiments like this and the sight of black chauffeurs and black millionaires shedding tears in public over the end of Camelot that forced Muhammad to reassess how Muslims would respond to the president's death. If his and Malcolm's words about the Georgia plane crash had prompted a congressional investigation, how would the nation react to Muslims making light of the murder of the president?

Muhammad, who generally approved each page of *Muhammad Speaks* before it was printed, called the editors and ordered a new front page for the December 6 issue. He wanted his column on the front page, he said, along with a large photograph of the slain commander-in-chief. "After all," he said, "he wasn't so bad for a devil."[54] FBI agents monitoring his telephone calls noted that he laughed upon making the statement. His own revelry over Kennedy's assassination must have conjured up images of Malcolm making a press statement, because he suddenly called his son into the room and told him to call Malcolm. Muhammad dictated the exact words he wanted the national spokesman to say in the likely event that he would be asked to comment on the president's assassination. "My father said that we should say that we are sorry about the death of our president," Malcolm was told as he listened in disbelief, and then hung up the phone.[55] His reddish skin paled as he looked at his portly protégé, Joseph, and he told him what the Messenger wanted him to say to people. To Joseph, Muhammad's statement made perfect sense; to Joseph, anything the Messenger said made perfect sense. To Malcolm, though, the statement—one that the Messenger did not even believe—represented the prophet's final stumble in the fall from grace. The statement was a lie—nearly everyone in the NOI felt that the death of Camelot was a sign of the end times. It was the biggest lie that Malcolm had ever been asked to tell, and he couldn't do it.[56]

"How can I say that after what I've been saying [about Kennedy and the fall of America]?" Malcolm asked Joseph rhetorically. Joseph said that ministers have no choice in the matter; it was an order, not a wish or plea.[57]

"Well," Malcolm said sadly, "you just don't understand."

The Messenger was scheduled to speak in New York on Sunday, December 1, at Manhattan Center, but he fell ill a few days after the assassination and was unable to travel. Naturally, Malcolm was the designated replacement. There was nothing out of the ordinary about the speech. What was unusual, officials from the Harlem mosque recalled, is that Malcolm used extensive note cards that evening. He wanted to make sure, he told several of them, that he didn't stray from the message that the Messenger wanted him to impart. At the conclusion of his talk, Malcolm was surrounded by reporters eager to know what he personally felt about Kennedy's death. Malcolm stuck to the script for a few minutes, but his need to be true to himself overpowered his inclination to blindly obey Muhammad's order hold his tongue. No national figure had spoken out about America's role in the gruesome assassination of Patrice Lumumba of the Congo. No black leader had addressed the American public regarding American war crimes against the people of Vietnam. No black leader had criticized the Kennedy administration for its bullying of Castro and attempts by the CIA to have him assassinated. That night Malcolm, who believed that his own father was killed for his allegiance to political views at odds with the mainstream, believed that the moment had come to speak for those who could not speak for them-

The Messenger *(left)* and Minister Malcolm X, national spokesman for the Nation of Islam, share a light moment during a Muslim gathering in Chicago in 1961. To Muhammad, Malcolm was the ideal son, while the Messenger served as an idealized father figure for the minister, whose own father was killed in 1931. *(The New Crusader. Reprinted with permission)*

Elijah Muhammad *(standing next to the groom)* poses with his family at the wedding of his daughter Lottie. Marie Muhammad, his mother, is at the far left *(in dark dress)* next to her husband, Willie Muhammad.

The Messenger *(above left)* poses proudly with his son and heir apparent, Wallace D. Muhammad, in this photo taken in 1960. A glamorized depiction of Wallace D. Fard hangs on the wall behind them, and Wallace holds a copy of the Holy Quran in his left hand (as does Fard in the painting). Wallace was sent to prison less than a year later on draft evasion charges. When her marriage to the Messenger soured because of infidelity and mental cruelty, Clara Muhammad *(right)* confessed to her son Wallace that she—not his father, Elijah—was the first to meet Wallace D. Fard, the man worshipped as Allah by members of the NOI. Wallace later denounced his father and his misinterpretation of Islam. *(Elijah Muhammad: Schomburg Center for Research in Black Culture, New York Public Library. Reprinted with permission. Clara Muhammad: The Washington Post. Reprinted with permission)*

Newly crowned world heavyweight boxing champion Cassius X Clay
(renamed Muhammad Ali) holds photos of the Messenger and Wallace D.
Fard at a press conference prior to the rematch with Sonny Liston in May
1965. "I am afraid of only two men," he said, as he showed the photos to
the media. Internationally renowned singer Joe Tex shocked the recording
industry and his fans by announcing that he was forsaking his entertainment
career to become a Black Muslim minister. He is shown here after delivering
a lecture on the NOI at Howard University in July 1972. *(Cassius Clay: AP/Wide
World Photo. Joe Tex: Tom Allen/The Washington Post. Reprinted with permission)*

Elijah Muhammad, accompanied by his son-in-law Raymond Sharrieff (to his left) and other Muslim officials, holds a press conference in 1961 to protest an unprovoked attack on members of the NOI's temple in Watts by the Los Angeles Police Department. *(AP/Wide World Photo)*

Elijah Muhammad's attempt to forge an understanding between himself and Dr. Martin Luther King Jr. proved futile. This meeting in February 1966 was their last public appearance together. *(UPI/Bettmann)*

"When I saw that cartoon," Wallace Muhammad said of this one from the caustic inkwell of NOI artist Eugene Majied, "I knew they were trying to get him killed." Malcolm X was killed a few weeks after the cartoon ran in *Muhammad Speaks*, the nationally distributed newspaper of the NOI. *(Muhammad Speaks/Muslim Journal)*

Three months before Malcolm X was killed, Minister Louis Farrakhan of Boston lambasted him in *Muhammad Speaks* as the NOI's "chief hypocrite," and as "worthy of death." The denunciation came on the heels of Elijah Muhammad's declaration that Malcolm X had to be neutralized "at all costs."

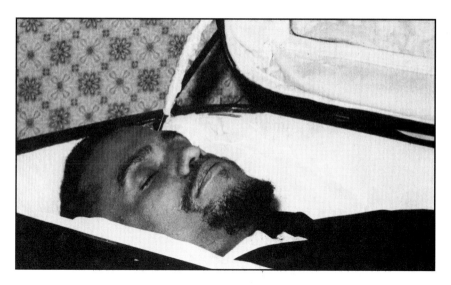

On January 12, 1965, Black Muslims held a dinner at the Audubon Ballroom in Harlem, where Malcolm X's splinter group sponsored meetings every Sunday. The dinner gave the NOI a chance to familiarize itself with the building's floorplan. Malcolm X was murdered in the Audubon Ballroom five weeks later. *(Courtesy of the Library of Congress)*

The Black Muslim mosque in Harlem went up in flames two days after the assassination of Malcolm X on February 21, 1965. Someone also set fire to Muhammad Ali's Chicago apartment, but the boxing champion was away from home at the time. *(AP/Wide World Photo)*

Hamaas Abdul Khaalis, former national secretary of the NOI, ties his shoe as a young Hanafi Muslim guards him. Khaalis's family was brutally murdered by Black Muslims in Washington in 1973. In 1977, he declared war on Jews and others, leading to the death of a black reporter and wounding of D.C. councilman (later mayor) Marion Barry. Khaalis is serving a life sentence. *(UPI/Corbis Bettmann)*

The Messenger used a $3,000,000 interest-free loan from Libyan leader Muammar Gadhafi to purchase a church in Chicago in the early 1970s. The church was converted into the NOI's largest mosque in America. *(UPI/Corbis Bettmann)*

At the University of Islam, which was actually a grade school, Black Muslim children were taught that Jesus was a metaphor for African Americans. Elijah Muhammad also taught that the Kaaba stone in Mecca represented black people, and that he was both Elijah the Prophet of the Bible and the Prophet Muhammad of the Holy Quran. *(The Washington Post. Reprinted with permission)*

One year after the death of Elijah Muhammd, Dorothy Dorsey became the first white woman to integrate the Nation of Islam. Wallace D. Muhammad had declared in 1975 that the sect would abandon its race-based religion for orthodox Islam. *(UPI/Corbis Bettmann)*

selves. A part of what he said entered the lexicon of infamous quotes: "It was a case of the chickens coming home to roost."[58]

Joseph's eyes nearly popped out of his head when he heard what Malcolm said. John Ali, who was also in the auditorium, looked at Joseph in horror. While Malcolm chatted with reporters, Joseph and John hurried to the nearest telephone to call the Messenger and tell him about what Malcolm had said. Back in Chicago, Muhammad had just finished recording a message of condolence to the Kennedy family, a blatantly insincere piece about how broken up members of the NOI were over the assassination. It was played on many stations that carried his Sunday sermons, but unfortunately, it was played along with the comments Malcolm had made to reporters at Manhattan Center.[59]

A Los Angeles radio station reporter had called for his comments, and the Messenger said that members of the NOI, like their fellow Americans, were "deeply shocked by the assassination of the president, and shared the nation's grief." When the reporter asked him what he thought about Malcolm X's comments, the Messenger was aghast, and wouldn't reply because he couldn't believe that Malcolm had spoken out about the president's death in a direct contravention of his order. When John confirmed what the reporter claimed that Malcolm said, Muhammad knew that Malcolm had finally freed himself from the chains that made him an intellectual prisoner. It was the first time that anyone had so brazenly ignored one of his orders since the murderous years after Fard's departure. Since then, Muhammad had denounced his brother Kallatt for refusing to worship him as God's last messenger, had broken Clara's heart, crippled her children by denying them their right to an independent adulthood, and denied his illegitimate children their birthright. When he realized that Malcolm had followed his own conscience and disobeyed him, he began plotting the destruction of his surrogate son.

Time would prove that Malcolm X had offered an accurate if poorly phrased assessment of what had been going on in the world. There was already strong evidence that the CIA was the moving force behind the toppling of the leaders of several African and Asian nations who refused to follow American mandates, and occasionally the agency had resorted to arranging assassinations.[60] Besides, the truth is like a nine-month-old fetus: if its deliverance depended upon good timing, there would be zero population growth. Its unpredictable arrival is the essence of its character. Hadn't the Messenger been teaching that terrible things would befall America in its last days? What could be more horrific than the televised slaying of the king of Caucasians? What sign was more demonstrative of God's power and the Messenger's prophetic abilities than a single event that paralyzed the nation and the world for weeks?

But the Messenger was right as well. In politics, as in truth-telling and nearly everything else, timing is everything. Perhaps Malcolm should have been more diplomatic; one can be right, after all, without being self-righteous. Most black people loved the charismatic Catholic as much as most whites and Indians and Latinos did. There was something about Kennedy that made minorities feel like Americans. He had not yet done great things for blacks, but they sensed that he would if given a chance and given time. An incident between President Kennedy and Dr. King helps explain his enormous appeal for black people. In 1962, Kennedy was walking in the Rose Garden with King when he made a startling admission. King should be very cautious about what he said on his home and office telephones, the president said in hushed tones as they strolled slowly, because Hoover had them wiretapped.[61] The director planned to use information gathered from the telephone surveillance to prove that King was under the influence of Communists, the president warned. What King didn't ask, and what Kennedy didn't mention, was who had authorized Hoover to place the taps on his phones; they had been sanctioned by none other than the president's younger brother, Attorney General Robert F. Kennedy.[62]

On December 4, John Ali called a press conference to put the NOI's official view on Kennedy's murder on record:

Minister Malcolm Shabazz, addressing a public meeting at Manhattan Center in New York City on Sunday, December 1, did not speak for the Muslims when he made comments about the death of the president, John F. Kennedy. He was speaking for himself and not the Mus-

lims in general, and Minister Malcolm has been suspended from public speaking for the time being. The Nation [NOI] still mourns the loss
of our president.[63]

During a short telephone conversation, the Messenger had told Malcolm only that he intended to suspend him for ninety days for appearance's sake, that the punishment would be moderately enforced, and
that things would go on as usual; after all, he knew of the Messenger's
dislike for the president. So Malcolm was stunned when he heard talk
about his "indefinite suspension" over the airwaves. He immediately
called the Messenger for confirmation. "Yes, they have it from here, that
you have been suspended for the time being . . . that you will not be
making any public speeches for the time being. There is no definite time
set. . . . This is for the best."[64]

The suspension from public speaking would not affect Malcolm's
administrative and ministerial functioning at the mosque, Muhammad
said. The punishment was limited to public speaking, including lecturing
at the mosque. "Everything else will be the same. . . . I'm only referring
to public speaking." When Malcolm called back later that evening,
Muhammad again gave vent to his displeasure about the statement:

> You should have known better than to talk about the president like
> you did. . . . I told you to lay off because it was too hot. There is a time
> for everything. . . . I don't like to do a thing like that [suspension], but
> I had no alternative.[65]

The Messenger reminded him that the radio stations were playing a
tape on which he talked about his sadness on the loss of the president
and following it with an excerpt of Malcolm saying how Kennedy's
death was cause for celebration:

> You made me look like a fool. People are looking to me to see if I
> would back you up. Such talk as that could get us into trouble when
> the man is not even cold in the grave.

When another minister called to discuss the news reports about Malcolm's suspension, Muhammad commented:

Papa has to spank his son, and if he accepts his punishment, he will be okay. But if he sticks out his lip and starts popping off, he will get a worse beating the next time. . . . I was more surprised than anyone because I didn't think Malcolm would say such a thing.[66]

On December 6, James Bland sent a COINTELPRO suggestion to Sullivan. He composed a phony news release for the media, which he believed would heighten tensions between Malcolm and Muhammad, noting:

The data in the enclosed memorandum is set forth in the most general terms and its release will not prejudice your investigation of the NOI. The suspension of Malcolm X by Elijah Muhammad should not be taken as an indication that the NOI is in any way tempering or softening its vicious antiwhite teaching. It only indicates that Elijah Muhammad is more politic than his disciple, Malcolm X. . . . Maybe this is Muhammad's way of taking Malcolm X down a peg as well as taking steps to insure that a successor to his mantle will come from among his own large family. . . . It is no secret that Muhammad's immediate family had considered Malcolm X to be a threat to their own positions in the NOI.

The release of the fake news item had the desired impact. The day after receiving the bogus document, reporters called Muhammad to determine whether his comments on Kennedy's death—which appeared on the front page of *Muhammad Speaks* on December 3—meant that he "had backed down on his stand regarding white people" being devils. He spent most of the day telling white reporters that yes, they were still devils as far as he was concerned.[67]

One reporter pointed out the obvious inconsistency in Muhammad's labeling of white people as devils, then suspending Malcolm for commenting on the death of one. "Minister Malcolm was suspended for ignoring orders," Muhammad said. But he remained evasive about whether he agreed with the gist of Malcolm's comments. In a follow-up question, the reporter asked about rumors of a rift between himself and Malcolm, and he replied:

> Malcolm and I are still brothers. . . . I hope such rumors don't get too far out of hand. . . . Malcolm and I have not split by any means. We are still brothers and I still think Malcolm is a wonderful worker of mine. But the way I say, we have rules; we must obey them.[68]

When Malcolm called Muhammad on the evening of December 7, they talked like two close friends who hadn't seen one another for months. Malcolm told him that Betty was pregnant again, and Muhammad congratulated him. He also indicated that he really appreciated the things that Malcolm had told the *New York Times* about the wisdom of his suspension. "That was very nice," he said. Malcolm told him that things were going well at the Harlem mosque, and that he had arranged for Farrakhan to lecture the next day and planned to have Dr. Lonnie X Cross speak on the following Sunday. Muhammad approved of the choices and told Malcolm to get some rest, and that he looked forward to seeing him soon: "We [Muslims] don't act like Christians seeking revenge and so forth when something goes wrong. . . . Islam makes us true brothers and we have true unity."[69]

The FBI was most unhappy to hear that. On December 13, the Bureau applied for reauthorization on its microphone surveillance ("misur") of Muhammad's homes. The application by the Phoenix SAC noted that the two microphones installed at the Violet Drive address—one in the front of the building and one in the rear—had captured volumes of valuable intelligence about the Messenger. On November 14, the SAC noted, the microphones picked up information about a letter from the president of Mexico announcing that Muhammad had been made an honorary member of the Academy of Human Science and Relations. On November 17, the microphones recorded Muhammad discussing plans to visit South Africa in 1965. On the final page of the application, the SAC credited the microphones for picking up conversations between Malcolm and Muhammad regarding Kennedy's death and Malcolm's suspension. This type of intelligence, the SAC pointed out, was essential to the Bureau's "subversive control" objectives. The "misur" was reauthorized immediately.[70]

The next week, the FBI uncovered evidence that Clara had, for all intents and purposes, left Elijah. She had been living at a place in Washington and had been spending a fortune redecorating it—which Elijah reluctantly paid. At the same time, informants and surveillance devices planted in Philadelphia revealed that Wallace was extremely unhappy with his father and was contacting Malcolm regularly since the latter's suspension. According to the intelligence reports, Wallace was providing Malcolm with salacious details about his father's extramarital affairs.[71] Whether Wallace was motivated by a desire to cause a permanent split between his father and Malcolm, as Bland's memorandum hinted, or whether he was merely crying on Malcolm's shoulder, as Malcolm believed, was not clear.

Whatever his motives, the FBI was determined to exploit each man's weaknesses. In late December, the Bureau began issuing bogus news stories about a deepening leadership crisis in the NOI. Most of the stories focused on allegations that Malcolm was trying to take over by spreading rumors about Muhammad's private life. Though it's impossible to know how many phony letters actually reached his hands, Muhammad relied on the advice of two men whom the FBI considered reliable sources: John Ali and Abdul Basit Naeem.[72]

For the Messenger, who thought that the issue of his extramarital affairs had been hushed, the rumors about Wallace were heartbreaking. Upon receiving irrefutable proof from other officials in the mosque, he knew he had to suspend him. He was angrier at him than he was at Malcolm. In Harlem, members were told that Malcolm was no longer in charge, and they should avoid associating with him. Though Muhammad had said that Malcolm's suspension was for a ninety-day period, what members of the Harlem mosque were told about his status after his suspension ended made it clear that the Messenger did not want him to return to the NOI. "We were told that if Malcolm came back to the temple after the suspension," his former assistant remembered, "we should give him a job washing dishes in the restaurant." Curiously, that was Joseph's job in Detroit before he was elevated to assistant cook.[73]

Although she was quarreling with her husband, Clara told her daughter Lottie that Wallace was a bad influence on Hassan Sharrieff, Lottie's son, who had been speaking ill of his grandfather. "It's terrible the way he's trying to confuse the boy that way," Clara said forlornly. "Wallace is out of his mind," Lottie added, to which Clara agreed without hesitation. Clara, who had turned her back on Wallace after hearing that he was siding with Malcolm, said she felt that Wallace had begun sinking in dark waters when he made "certain mistakes" with his first wife.[74] Wallace had rejected her advice then, Clara said, and now he was paying a punishing premium. Tragically, Clara's allegiance to her husband was for naught; he still treated her like God's stepchild. "I've tried many times to help him," Clara said sadly, "but he treated me just like a housecat, kicking me from one door to another." From now on, she said, she was going to try to stay away from him, as she was tired of being mistreated.[75]

On January 2, 1964, Muhammad called Malcolm X from Chicago and read him the riot act. "I've been hearing about Malcolm this and Malcolm that, and even Malcolm being the leader," he said as Malcolm listened on his home phone in New York. "Now this one [minister] and that one is getting jealous. You are my property and I am your property."[76]

"Yes, sir," Malcolm replied.

"You made an error," Muhammad said sternly. He was referring to Malcolm X's discussion with other East Coast ministers about his extramarital activities.

"I asked your permission in a letter before I said anything, and I understood that it was all right," Malcolm said.

"I certainly didn't say such a thing!" Elijah shouted. "I can't understand why you took this poison and poured it out and told them [the other ministers]. . . . You can't use fire to fight fire. One must carry a basket of water and not fire. . . . I thought you were referring to something else. I thought you had a sly scheme or shrewd plan to undermine me, but it won't work, sir, not this time."

Dumbfounded, Malcolm X said nothing. Muhammad had very clearly admitted to certain moral transgressions when Malcolm was in Phoenix, and he implied then and in a subsequent letter that it was okay for Malcolm X to prepare the NOI for the scandal. Now, he was refuting everything. Muhammad paused to catch his breath, then continued his harangue. "If anyone had told me that you were going to use things like that, I wouldn't have believed it. If you love Allah, then you must love me as the Messenger of Allah."[77]

"I would rather be dead than say anything against you," Malcolm said. "I didn't say anything to anyone about you. I spoke in parables."

"Then how could Isaiah, Lonnie, and Joseph have gotten the wrong impression from what you said?" Muhammad countered. "They all wrote to me and said about the same thing." After pausing again to catch his breath, he went on with the tongue-lashing. "Why are you checking into my personal affairs?"

Malcolm replied that he hadn't inquired into the illicit relationships. "I heard about it in Chicago [during Saviour's Day 1963]. I talked to Wallace about it and he already knew about it."

Farrakhan's name came up a few times, but never as the one who flew to Chicago to personally deliver his version of what Malcolm had said about the secretaries. After receiving the proverbial pieces of silver—in the form of a pat on the head from the Messenger—Farrakhan was so inflated with self-importance that he could have flown himself back to New York—as his own hot-air balloon.[78]

The FBI followed the play-by-play of the dispute between Muhammad and Malcolm through a host of surveillance techniques. Muhammad was heard bragging about how he was going to bring Malcolm to his knees for consulting with Wallace, and laughing about a two-hour tape that Malcolm had mailed to him seeking forgiveness for speaking out on Kennedy's assassination and for speaking to the press during his suspension. He was also heard to vow to break Wallace for daring to question his lifestyle.

Armed with these insights, FBI agents called Malcolm on January 15 and asked permission to visit him regarding an alleged plot by Muslims to assassinate President Johnson.[79] Sensing that the Bureau was up to no good, Malcolm invited them over, but placed a tape recorder under the sofa in his living room before they arrived. When the agents knocked on the door, Malcolm activated the recorder, then opened the door and invited them in. It became apparent in minutes that the visit was designed solely for the purpose of recruiting Malcolm as an informant. They tried to motivate him by stoking his anger over his suspension. When that failed, they suggested that there would be money and other amenities for his cooperation. Malcolm accused them of insulting his intelligence and asked them to leave. It was the last time they would bother him with such nonsense.

Bland was furious when he received the report on the interview. On February 7, he wrote to Sullivan for permission to spare no expense to guarantee that Malcolm's suspension was made permanent:

> Little is probably the most dynamic and forceful Nation of Islam (NOI) spokesman in the movement and the attached memorandum, which is worded in the most general terms, could possibly widen the rift between Muhammad and Little and possibly result in Little's expulsion from the NOI.[80]

After approval from Sullivan, another fake news story was mailed to mainstream newspapers and prominent African-American-oriented publications, including *Muhammad Speaks*. A copy of the story was also sent to Muhammad:

> Little has not taken this disciplinary action gracefully and he has attempted to develop sympathy and backing for his position among other leaders of the Black Muslims in various sections of the country. He evidently feels that Elijah Muhammad is in his declining years and that he is slipping. . . . Muhammad is reportedly fuming at the temerity Little has exhibited in questioning the "Messenger's" judgment and

it would not surprise anyone at all familiar with the works of the NOI to see Little summarily expelled from this organization if he continues to buck the orders and wishes of Elijah Muhammad.[81]

Ministers began calling the Messenger to see whether he had been interviewed for the contrived news release. He had not, so he and others suspected that someone white—and probably in the employ of the FBI— had concocted the story because no one in the NOI, or in the mainstream press, for that matter, referred to Malcolm X as "Little." The use of the name "Little" was a dead giveaway. "We are going to put a stop to all that kind of talk," the Messenger told an editor at *Muhammad Speaks* during a monitored phone call. He was suspicious of the letter, he said, and wanted to print something in his newspaper to head off any talk of divisiveness within the leadership. Regardless of how the editor phrased it, the Messenger said he wanted to make it clear that

there is no discord in the Nation. We don't take Malcolm for no enemy nor are we enemies of him. . . . Make sure that the article states the following: "We believe Malcolm is a believer as he has always preached that he was. It is not true that Malcolm is trying to ruin or run Muhammad's family, and we don't believe Malcolm is against us or that we are against Malcolm."[82]

Muhammad spent the next two weeks preparing for the annual convention. For the first time in twelve years, Malcolm would not be there to introduce him. When Muslims looked toward the stage for the man most likely to succeed the Messenger, they wouldn't be reassured by the presence of either Malcolm or Wallace. And so, for the first time, the Messenger faced the most joyful occasion of the NOI's year with trepidation and dismay.

CHAPTER THIRTEEN
DEVIL'S DISCIPLES

Envy is so troublesome because it causes the individual who possesses it to literally grow to hate the person whom he or she envies. The end product of this hatred is the desire to murder the person that is envied. Envy makes its possessor a devil. . . . .

—*Louis Farrakhan (1996)*[1]

I have so much respect for the traffic which you have engaged in, and I regard it as so perfectly legitimate, that I am willing to deduct twenty-five copecks from the price which you usually give for each dead soul, simply so as to enjoy the pleasure of assisting in the success of your operations. . . .

—*Nikolai Gogol,*
Dead Souls[2]

aving alienated the three people dearest to him—his wife, his son, and his chief confidant—Muhammad was in an uneviable condition. He realized that unless something miraculous happened, Saviour's Day 1964 was going to be a disaster. People were coming to see the man they believed had been personally taught by God, but even Muhammad was realistic enough to know that most of them wanted to hear Malcolm X. The suspended national spokesman was at home in Elmhurst preparing for a vacation in Florida, the family's first.[3] A few days before they left, Joseph called Harlem FOI member Anas M. Luqman, a Vietnam War veteran and an explosives expert, into his office and told him to attach a bomb to Malcolm's car that would detonate when the key turned in the ignition. Luqman immediately quit the NOI, told Malcolm, and then gave the details to the *New York Amsterdam News*. The failed scheme convinced officials in Chicago that Joseph was too inept to orchestrate the assassination.[4]

In Chicago, the Messenger had chosen Farrakhan as Malcolm's replacement for the convention. The obliging orator had mastered the sound of his mentor ("I styled my delivery and whatnot" after Malcolm, he said),[5] but lacked his fury and brilliance. The real McCoy was in Florida with his family, his thoughts as far away from Chicago as his body. Malcolm was in Miami against Muhammad's wishes but at the invitation and as the guest of the young boxer Cassius Clay, who at the time had fought only twenty professional bouts and was destined, pundits said, to lose his battle for the heavyweight title. Ordinarily, that would have been of no concern to Muhammad. The problem, as he saw it, was that Clay was one of his followers who idolized Malcolm. Although Clay had been a supporter of the NOI for five years and a member for three, Muhammad had kept his distance because he opposed professional boxing. But he had another, more selfish reason:

he didn't want the NOI's name associated with failure after the February 25 fight with Sonny "the Bear" Liston, which he felt certain Clay would lose.[6]

When Malcolm asked for permission to attend the fight, Muhammad objected. If you go to the fight, he told Malcolm, "you will not be representing us, because it's impossible for him to win."[7] Malcolm went anyway. Clay wanted Malcolm to be with him so desperately that he paid for the Shabazz family's round-trip plane tickets, hotel accommodations, and other amenities. It was, Clay said, a wedding anniversary present. At Malcolm's request, Clay also got the ticket for seat number 7 in the arena. He considered 7 his lucky number, and he earnestly believed that just being in that seat would enhance his young friend's chances for an upset. Clay went along because everything Malcolm had suggested up to then had worked to his advantage. Malcolm was one of the few high-ranking officials in the NOI who believed that Clay would win. On a night when everyone was telling him that he was going to lose, well, there was simply no question but that he wanted Malcolm there.[8]

Back in Chicago, people wondered why Malcolm and Wallace hadn't been reinstated, and why Clara seemed so miserable. She sat stonefaced throughout the NOI's holiday ceremonies. Photographers snapped pictures of her rolling her eyes at her husband when he tried talking to her, forcing him to back off with a sheepish smile. When Muhammad rejected Malcolm's request for reinstatement in late February, Malcolm feared that their relationship was over. "You have not converted a man by silencing him," Malcolm wrote in a note to Alex Haley during his suspension.[9] And when journalist Louis Lomax asked him on the heels of Saviour's Day how much longer his suspension would last, Malcolm replied: "It better not last too long. I'm thinking about making a move on my own."[10]

When Clay defeated Liston for the heavyweight boxing title no one was more astonished than Clay, happier than Malcolm, or luckier than Muhammad. A tug of war between Malcolm and Muhammad for Clay's loyalty began within hours after the fight's dramatic finish, which saw Liston lying on the canvas unable to continue the seventh round. There were several rumors about the bout; one was that Liston took a dive on the instructions of organized-crime figures to whom he was heavily in debt; a second was that he threw the fight because members of the NOI had threatened him.[11]

Suddenly rejuvenated by Cassius X Clay's triumph, Muhammad called him and offered him the Islamic name of Muhammad Ali, telling him it was a name that Fard had used during his years in Detroit (Fard had once used the alias Wali Fard Muhammad Ali). On Saviour's Day, Muhammad proudly told Muslims that the rumor about Clay being a member of the NOI was true. "I have renamed him Muhammad Ali," he said to thunderous applause.[12] Clay felt guilty about accepting the name because the Messenger said that no "original names" (meaning Arabic) would be given out until the Second Coming of Master Fard, and also because he knew that there were men and women who had been faithful members of the NOI for more than forty years, yet none of them had ever received their holy names. They were still listed in Lamb's "Book of Life" under their slave names. If Clay felt guilty about accepting the new name, the media soon made him fight to be recognized by it. Many newspapers refused to refer to him as Muhammad Ali. He was accused of rejecting America when he rejected his surname. It was an odd argument, as Howard Cosell pointed out, because hundreds of celebrities had changed their names without any fuss at all. Only one person in the media called him by the name he had adopted. "I did this instantly," the over-modest Cosell recalled:

How selectively we apply our righteous indignation. Nobody calls Betty Perske by that name. She's Lauren Bacall. Cary Grant was a stilt walker at Coney Island named Archie Leach. Ever hear anyone call him Archie? As part of the sickness of the decade, and as part of the dugout mentality of a certain portion of the press, they would ceaselessly refer to Ali as Cassius Clay. But he knew my position and respected me for it.[13]

Muslims readily called Ali by his new name, though many considered him a clown who would fade with yesterday's headlines once he stepped into the ring with Floyd Patterson or another well-known fighter; the fight with Liston was seen as a fluke to be enjoyed until the next bout.

Despite Ali's pledge of devotion to Muhammad, the golden boy spent several days after Saviour's Day in New York with Malcolm. A host of Third World Muslim diplomats were eager to meet the first Muslim to win the heavyweight championship of the world. When Ali asked Malcolm when his suspension would be lifted, Malcolm told him that he believed it would end very soon. Ali had continued to associate with Malcolm X for that very reason. On March 2, the new heavyweight boxing champion of the world told reporters that his outrageous statements (about how the Messenger was divine and so forth) were nothing compared to those they'd hear from Malcolm X in a few days, when his ninety-day suspension was to end.[14] Muhammad was furious when he heard about Ali's comments on the suspension. On March 6, he called Ali and told him that he should not be spending time with Malcolm X, as he was suspended indefinitely. If he ever wanted to become a minister himself, Muhammad said, he would be wise to avoid Malcolm. Ali promised to sever their relationship immediately.[15]

On March 7, Elijah went through the motions of celebrating his forty-fifth wedding anniversary even as Clara made plans for a separation. That same evening, Malcolm X met with several confidants whose opinions he trusted to discuss plans for the immediate future. The next morning, he announced on the *Today Show* that he had broken with the NOI because its leader was morally bankrupt. When the Messenger learned that Malcolm had gone public with their problems, he was flabbergasted. "I could hardly believe it at first," he said during a monitored phone call, "but actually it turned out to be the truth." What made it even more insulting, he said, was that Malcolm had chosen to air their dirty laundry on what Muhammad termed "the white man's television."[16] After seeing part of the broadcast, he instructed an aide to call Minister Philbert X Little, one of Malcolm's brothers, in Lansing. Once Philbert was on the line, the Messenger dictated a list of questions and told him to call Malcolm for his responses. Malcolm assured Philbert during the call that he had not forsaken Islam, nor did he regret having served under the Messenger. As for returning to the fold, however, it was now completely out of the question. Upon hearing Malcolm's replies, Muhammad told one official:

> I wrote him a letter last week and told him that he is drunk over publicity and leadership. I don't intend to give him the place [Mosque No. 7] back, no matter what he did [sic]. If I did, he'd set up a crew that's one hundred percent behind him and not with us. He wants to oppose us. He thinks he's smart, but I have too much experience.[17]

The Messenger wasn't being honest with the public about his relationship with Malcolm, and Malcolm had not told Ali and others the whole truth, either. Though hoping otherwise, Malcolm suspected before Saviour's Day that he would not be returning to the NOI. He had called Muhammad on February 21 to ask for reinstatement, but had been told that he could not return because he had refused "to submit." During another call that day, Muhammad warned Ali that "all good Muslims should stay away from Malcolm" during his suspension.[18]

On March 8, 1964, the same day on which Malcolm X broke the chains that kept him in political and intellectual bondage, the Messenger began touting Farrakhan as Malcolm X's replacement as the NOI's national spokesman. Of the hundred or so ministers and student ministers in the sect, only a few came close to being a second Malcolm. Farrakhan, whose relationship with Malcolm was stronger than that of any other minister, stood out in Muhammad's mind as the best of the lot. Another gifted orator was Larry 4X Prescott, a protégé of Farrakhan's whose skills rivaled Malcolm's but who was regarded as "too dark-skinned" to attract recruits as the lighter-skinned Farrakhan and Malcolm did. Muhammad selected ministers based on a ranking system which included intelligence, oratorical skills, and physical features.[19] The whole skin-color issue was among the NOI's more bizarre standards, as it dated back to the era when the treatment of a slave depended upon how close his skin shade was to the master's whiteness.

The Messenger assigned Farrakhan to speak in Malcolm X's stead that afternoon at the Harlem mosque, where he addressed a crowd of nearly 1,000. The Messenger was also advised that 400 people had attended services in Brooklyn, and that other mosques had had similar turnouts. In a subsequent telephone call to Farrakhan, Muhammad complimented him again for the "excellent job" he was doing.[20] Merely mentioning Malcolm's name seems to have made Muhammad angry, and he suddenly launched into a venomous invective against "that no good, long-legged Malcolm." "The only way to stop him" from spreading salacious stories about the NOI, Muhammad said menacingly, was "to get rid of him the way Moses and the others did their bad ones."[21]

"You have to make an example out of the bad ones," Muhammad told Farrakhan. "When you try to be peaceful and nice and love them, they just jump up and try to take over," he added angrily. "With these hypocrites, when you find them, cut their heads off."[22]

When the Messenger called him a "hypocrite," it was a signal that hunting season was about to open for all mammals named Malcolm X. "The Quran teaches Muslims to kill hypocrites wherever they may find them," former Harlem mosque member Benjamin Karim said.[23] In an telephone interview on March 8, the Messenger accelerated Malcolm X's martyrdom by repeatedly calling him a hypocrite. "Anyone who deviates from Islam is a hypocrite," the Messenger told James Booker of the *New York Amsterdam News* during a telephone interview. "They both [deviators and hypocrites] are the same. There is no weeping and moaning for that person by the believer. We are glad to know a hypocrite. There is no weeping and moaning over one that leaves Islam as a hypocrite or deviator or one that would not like to live under the guidance of God's Messenger."[24]

"Well, sir," the reporter inquired, "what is finally your feeling about what Malcolm has done so independently?"

"I am absolutely surprised at the man," the Messenger replied.

"Why are you so surprised, sir? He was boxed up for ninety days."

"He didn't have ninety days," the Messenger retorted. "He had an indefinite suspension."[25]

While Muhammad had angrily said during a telephone call that the suspension was indefinite, Malcolm and nearly everyone else who knew about the conversation considered the statement to be words spoken in the irrationality of anger and not to be taken seriously. Muhammad had personally told Malcolm that the suspension would be lifted before Saviour's Day, mainly because he wanted Malcolm to be there to excite the crowd. Now that Malcolm had opened the Messenger's Pandora's box and quit the NOI, the Messenger was talking like a jilted juvenile lover; he didn't quit me, he seemed to say, because I quit him first.

On March 9, the Messenger held a press conference at his home in Phoenix. Asked for his reaction to Malcolm's new organization, he stared at the reporters sadly and said, "I am stunned. I never dreamed this man would deviate from the Nation of Islam. Every one of the Muslims admired him." Cameras snapped away as crocodile tears welled in the Messenger's eyes. Ali was deeply moved.[26] When asked for his reaction to the split and his mentor's new organization, Ali replied: "I don't know much about what Malcolm X is doing, but I do know that Muhammad is the wisest."[27] During a call that day, Muhammad asked Farrakhan whose name was on the deed to Malcolm X's house and who was paying the mortgage. The NOI was paying the mortgage, Farrakhan replied, so the NOI owned the house. The mosque had put down $5,000 at the time of sale and was paying the mortgage each month. Title is actually in the name of the mosque, as is Malcolm X's car, Farrakhan said. "Send a letter or have the secretary send one to him and tell him he must give up the house. Have Captain Joseph and the others sign the letter. I want you to demand that Malcolm vacate the house and give up everything that belongs to the Nation." Once Malcolm X is evicted, the Messenger told Farrakhan, "you can move into it if it doesn't interfere with anything. It's a seven-room house and you have four children. But don't say anything until Malcolm is out," he cautioned.[28]

The next morning, Malcolm received what amounted to the Messenger's "Dear John" letter. "Dear Brother Malcolm," it began,

You have several items such as letters, mosque film, Negro documents, etc., relative to the Muslims and their affairs . . . the laborers and believers hereby request your cooperation in turning these items over to Muhammad's Mosque #7 immediately. Also, you are residing in a building which was purchased by Muhammad's Mosque #7 for the use by a laborer as designated by . . . the Honorable Elijah Muhammad . . . who may serve in ministerial capacity. . . . Since you no longer hold this position we . . . request that you vacate premises located at 2311 97th Street, East Elmhurst 69, New York, upon receiving this letter. . . . This letter will also serve notice your car insurance is [paid by] Muhammad's Mosque #7. . . . We are requesting that you discontinue using the name of Muhammad's Mosque or the Nation of Islam for your personal effects. . . . This letter also serves notice that Muhammad's Mosque #7 will discontinue handling expenses on utilities at said 2311 97th Street.

The letter was signed by Captain Joseph and several other Harlem mosque officials.[29]

Malcolm was furious. With no income and everything he possessed in the name of the Harlem mosque, he was suddenly on the verge of bankruptcy. Even though the Messenger had told him the house was his, the deed said something else. With everything at stake, Malcolm challenged Muhammad's right to the Elmhurst house. He also announced the formation of a new religious group called Muslim Mosque Inc., which would be a haven for African Americans who wanted to convert to Islam but who wanted no part of the NOI.[30] Within weeks of the announcement, the NOI lost roughly 20 percent of its membership to Muslim Mosque. Unlike the members of NOI, Muslim Mosque members were not required to make heavy financial contributions.

Organizational costs and personal finances pushed Malcolm closer and closer to bankruptcy. He was forced to seek more advance royalties from his publisher for the autobiography he was writing with Alex Haley's assistance.[31] When that was spent, he borrowed money from his half-sister, Ella Collins, who ran a day-care center in Boston and owned several pieces of real estate there. He also secretly consulted with his brother Wilfred, minister of Muhammad's first mosque in Detroit. Wilfred, who was ordered by Elijah to have no contact with Malcolm, strongly urged him to take some of the money he borrowed from Ella to get out of the country.[32] Muslims in Detroit were obsessed with talk of killing the Messenger's tormenter, Wilfred warned; perhaps things would cool down if he disappeared for a while. Malcolm respected his brother's wisdom; he had never misled him, and Malcolm still trusted him even though he had remained in the NOI. As it happens, Malcolm and Muhammad Ali had discussed making the hajj together while they were in Miami before the big fight. They also planned to visit several African and Asian nations during the trip, since Nasser, Nkrumah, and other heads of state had invited them to be their guests. Now that the two had parted ways, Malcolm hastily made plans to travel alone.[33]

On March 16, Muhammad poured more fuel on the fire. During a conversation with one of his ministers, he said that he had heard a rumor that the "other fellows [ministers] are out to get him [Malcolm]."[34] When Muhammad did not say anything about being opposed to someone bringing harm to Malcolm, the minister understood what the Messenger wanted done. As the first step toward isolating Malcolm, Muhammad ordered Philbert X Little to appear at a press conference where he would denounce Malcolm. The statement, which John Ali handed to Philbert and told him to read, caught the latter by surprise. Without looking through it first, Philbert read the statement as the press took notes. "I am aware of the great mental illness which besets, unfortunately, many in America and which beset my mother whom I love and one of my brothers, and which may now have taken another victim . . . my brother Malcolm."[35] He had a perturbed expression on his face afterward, because he did not realize that the statement called upon him to victimize his own mother. Malcolm dismissed Philbert's statement as a product of someone else's envy. "We've been good friends all our lives. He has a job he needs; that's why he said what he did. . . . I know for a fact that they flew him in from Lansing, put a script in his hand and told him to read it."[36] Besides, Malcolm quipped, if he was mentally deranged, why hadn't his brother or the Messenger or someone else noticed it when he was out making a ton of money for the NOI?

On April 4, 1964, Muhammad discussed a letter he had received about his indiscretions with his secretaries with one of his ministers. The letter had come from the FBI, but Muhammad suspected that Malcolm had written it because it bore the marks of his writing and speaking style. Muhammad told the minister, who had also gotten a copy, that he wasn't worried about the letter. People said nasty things about Jesus in his final days, Muhammad said. Malcolm, he said, "is like Judas at the Last Supper."[37]

Four days later, Muhammad's lawyers were in court for a hearing on the ownership of Malcolm's residence. By now, Malcolm's refusal to give up the house had Muhammad enraged. The matter was set for trial on April 17. However, Malcolm left for a three-week tour of Africa on April 16, which made Muhammad even angrier when he was told that the court had approved a request for a continuance. "We're having some trouble with the house in New York with the big man," he said sarcastically during an April 22 conversation.[38] At the same time that he was quibbling with Malcolm over the matchbox house in Elmhurst, Muhammad was spending a fortune on homes for his mistresses. On April 23 he and Clara got into an argument over the lavish way he treated the young women. Clara complained to Lottie:

> He lets these girls have everything just the way they want it and he fixed everything up very nice just the way he wants it, and he comes back and raises all this trouble about where she [one of his mistresses] is supposed to live all this time. If he keeps it up, I'll set fire to the place.[39]

Malcolm was treated like royalty during his time in Africa. When he appeared at the summit of the Organization of African Unity, he introduced a petition charging the United States with violating the rights of African Americans.[40] The Muslims were receptive, and those listening to him for the first time were impressed with how knowledgeable he was in international law. Now that he was free of Muhammad's ball and chain, some suggested, perhaps he could serve as an American spokesman for their grievances as well. Subsequently, several African and Arab diplomats, notably U.N. General Assembly president Alex Quaison-Sackey of Ghana, arranged for Malcolm to open an office off the same corridor where the other "provisional governments" (such as the Palestine Liberation Organization) had space.[41] Upon his return to New York on May 21, Malcolm announced at a press conference that several African and

Asian nations stood ready to support his U.N. petition.[42] Within days of his return, five members of Muhammad's Mosque No. 25 in Newark were recruited to kill him. Wilbert X Bradley, Robert X Ben Thomas, Wilbur X McKinney, Talmadge X Hayer, and Leon X Davis met with a party who remains unidentified but who allegedly trained them in the art of assassination and paid for their time.[43]

On another front, Wallace's denunciations of his father made him a moving target for Muslims eager to prove their allegiance to the Messenger. Wallace's phone rang incessantly with callers threatening to do him bodily harm or to take his life, including, of all people, his brother Junior and his brother-in-law Raymond Sharrieff.[44] To say that Wallace was unnerved by these conversations is an understatement. On June 1, he was driving in Terre Haute when an Indiana state trooper pulled him over for driving without license plates. According to the trooper, Wallace initially refused to get out of the car, and when he finally did, he was holding a club. Another trooper approached him as the first one tried to take the club from him. Wallace allegedly bit the trooper during the scuffle, but was finally subdued. When asked why he was driving without plates, Wallace replied that putting plates on the car—and by that allowing police to keep track of him—"would make me a slave to the state."[45] Perhaps Wallace was trying to get arrested to remove himself from the volatile environment in which he was living. He had felt safer in prison than he did now in Chicago. Malcolm was also being terrorized by prank calls, some of them from FBI agents, but most of them from angry Muslims. Joseph authorized the NOI's harassment campaign. "Every five minutes," a former member of the Harlem mosque recalls, "a different soldier would go to the telephone and call Malcolm's house. Sometimes we would say something threatening, sometimes we would just hold the phone and hang up. The idea was to unnerve Malcolm and Betty and maybe push them to the breaking point."[46]

On June 5, James 67X Warden called Malcolm from Phoenix to advise him that he had obtained signed statements from Lucille Rosary and Evelyn Williams in which they said that the Messenger was the father of all of their children.[47] He intended to take the information to Gladys Towles Root the next day, he said, to try to get a paternity warrant issued against the Messenger. Root was a well-respected lawyer in Los Angeles, where Lucille and Evelyn were living in seclusion. Since the FBI was trying to intensify the hatred developing between the two factions, a summary of the conversation was sent to all domestic and military intelligence agencies, including the Secret Service.

Things were also getting more and more difficult for Wallace. On June 10, 1964, his wife, Lorraine, called Clara. She was frightened because Wallace had not yet returned home after several hours as he said he would. "I'm ready to call the police," Lorraine said, "because Wallace was threatened by Junior and some other members who called him a hypocrite." Clara cautioned Lorraine to be careful, particularly about calling the police, because she might find herself being targeted by diehard followers. Lorraine said she would get the proof to show police that her husband's life was in jeopardy. "I can't go on living like this because every day I'm afraid that someone is going to jump him. All he's trying to do is go to school and better himself."[48]

"Go ahead and let people talk," Clara cautioned her. "Trust in Allah. He will take care of everything." Two days later, Lottie called Clara to tell her that Junior and Raymond had consulted with the Messenger the day before, and that threats had been made against Wallace. "Don't look into all this trouble," her mother warned her, "because things are bad. The only thing we can do is leave it all up to Allah."

"If we don't stop clowning, I'm going to be ashamed of being a Muslim," Lottie said. [49]

Ironically, the Messenger cut a special tape that same day, which he ordered Sharrieff and Junior to send to the head of every mosque with instructions that it be played at male-members-only meetings. The topic of the speech was "Hypocrites," but it unmistakably referred to Malcolm X. "The white man has offered reward for people to lie on the Messenger of Allah," Muhammad intoned. "This hypocrite is going to get blasted clear off the face of the Earth." Those who doubted that Malcolm X would be killed, Muhammad said, should keep their eyes on the events of June 24. "I'm going to show the world."[50] Later that evening, Sharrieff and Junior called Louis 3X Carr and John 21X Garrison of Mosque No. 2, and demanded their presence at a hastily arranged meeting. Carr and Garrison, who were considered the best practitioners of karate in the Chicago mosques, were told to get ready for a special assignment in Detroit.[51] Other NOI enforcers, Malcolm would soon discover, had received a similar order.

On June 13, Malcolm spoke by telephone with Jerry Williams, host of a Boston radio program. During the broadcast, he went into great detail about Muhammad's extramarital escapades. He was scheduled to be in Boston the next day for an organizational meeting of the Organization of Afro-American Unity (OAAU), a political coalition he was modeling after the Organization of African Unity. Inspired by the Messenger's tape, a squad of Muslims from the Boston mosque made plans to assassinate Malcolm. "Rumor had it that Malcolm would not be returning from Boston alive," Benjamin 2X Goodman recalled. "Malcolm still wanted to attend the meeting, but we objected."[52] Goodman filled in for Malcolm. He took an Eastern Airlines flight from New York and was picked up from Logan Airport in Boston by Rodnell Collins, Ella's adopted son. As Rodnell and Goodman got out of the car and headed inside, they saw Captain Clarence 2X Gill and a goon squad. Gill was about as sorry an excuse for a human being as one is ever likely to encounter. The resident Bluto of the Boston mosque, Gill had joined the NOI in 1957.[53] Despite his reputation, the Messenger thought very highly of Gill, primarily because he was a faithful soldier who followed orders and only asked questions later, if ever. "He is one of my best," the Messenger once said of Gill. "In some areas he is my best."[54] According to men who were members of the Boston mosque under Farrakhan and Gill, the former's authority was often trampled on by his underling. Gill was "arrogant, suspicious, [and] dictatorial," members said, the prototype of an ignorant man with too much power.[55]

In October 1962, for example, Gill ordered the Muslim men in Boston, some of whom ran their own small businesses, to put selling *Muhammad Speaks* above the interests of staying financially afloat. The businessmen rebelled. Their businesses were their livelihood, they told Farrakhan, and if they closed shop to go out on the streets and sell *Muhammad Speaks*, they would be bankrupt in no time flat. While Farrakhan searched for a compromise, Gill called Junior and told him that the businessmen were refusing to obey orders. Junior came to Boston and told them: "If you don't sell the paper, then don't even bother to come in here." He suggested that they would be killed if they remained in the NOI and refused to follow orders. A few days later, forty-two of the fifty men quit the Boston mosque.[56]

With their leaving, the mosque fell into disarray. Farrakhan's ability to run the mosque without them became a major concern and once again called his leadership into question. After a few weeks of chaos, he issued a "general amnesty," and invited all of the businessmen to return, assuring them that things would improve, as Gill had been expelled. But Gill wasn't expelled for riding roughshod over Farrakhan; he was punished for rushing into a marriage that ended after only three days. When the businessmen returned, Farrakhan told them that Junior had ordered Gill's ouster for failing to "provide a glittering example of marital success."[57]

Only days after the businessmen returned, Farrakhan told them that their newspaper sales quota was no longer in force, and that the days of Gill's harsh discipline were over. As it turned out, however, Gill hadn't been excommunicated at all. "He had merely been directed to stay away until his marital problems were straightened out," a member recalled. Upon his return, Gill wrote to Chicago officials accusing Farrakhan of undermining Junior by abolishing the sales quota. Farrakhan was called on the carpet for his insubordination, and was forced to go before his congregation with his tail between his legs. "Some of you seem to have misunderstood me," he said. The businessmen would have to sell 200 copies of *Muhammad Speaks* each week just like every other male member; there were no exceptions. In the face of Farrakhan's turnabout, most of them quit.[58]

Some of the disenchanted businessmen were at Ella's house on the afternoon of June 14. As dusk neared, Rodnell and several others got into Rodnell's Cadillac and headed for Logan Airport.[59] Upon driving away, they noticed that a 1962 white Lincoln was tailing them. Once Collins got onto the Southeast Expressway, the Lincoln pulled in front of him and slowed to a crawl. Recognizing the men as members of the Boston mosque, Collins quickly swerved to the left and sped away as fast as he could go without losing control of the car. As he neared Callahan tunnel, however, he was met by a second carload of Black Muslims in an old Chevrolet. Once inside the two-lane tunnel, Collins was forced to slow down to avoid hitting cars in front of him. The Muslims in the Chevy forced their way ahead of him, then made a forty-five-degree turn so as to block both lanes, bringing traffic to a standstill. At the same time, the men in the Lincoln pulled up behind him, sandwiching him in. Two men got out of the Chevy and two emerged from the Lincoln. The men with Collins recognized the driver of the Chevy as James X Cook and the driver of the Lincoln as Don X Straughter. As the four men walked toward the Cadillac, a woman in a car between the Cadillac and the Lincoln started screaming at the top of her lungs, fearing she was about to be assaulted by a gang of menacing-looking men.[60] Cook told her to be quiet as he stuck his right hand in the right pocket of his suit jacket. He pulled out a nickel-plated revolver and continued toward Collins's car.

"Get the shotgun!" Collins yelled to Gilbourne Busby, a former Muslim who was sitting in the back of the car with Goodman. Goodman and Busby were old army friends who hadn't seen each other in a while, and had hoped to use the ride to the airport to catch up on old times. "It's in the rug on the floor," Collins said "Put the shells in it . . . hurry up!" Busby unrolled the rug and grabbed the shotgun and the shells, but couldn't figure out how to load the gun. The four came closer. "Where you goin'?" Cook asked rhetorically. "Ya'll ain't leavin' here. Ya'll gone die!"[61]

Dying certainly wasn't on their agenda. Pretending that the gun was loaded, Busby rolled down the window and aimed at Cook, then at Straughter, then at the other two. As Straughter came within three steps of the rear door, Busby turned the gun around and jammed the butt into Straughter's chest. When Straughter bent over in pain, Busby reversed the gun again. Cook peered into the car and saw that Malcolm wasn't even in it—they had risked their lives for nothing. Following Cook's lead, the would-be assailants turned around and ran back to their own cars. Collins shifted the Cadillac into drive and rammed the Chevy, nearly ripping off its front fender.[62] As the car emerged from the dim tunnel, Collins pressed the palm of his left hand against the blaring horn and held on tight to the steering wheel with his right as he drove at 90 miles an hour, sure that his speed or noise would attract the attention of the Massachusetts State Police, but there wasn't a policeman in sight. On reaching the airport, he stopped the car near an airstrip and he and his passengers ran to the Mohawk Airlines terminal's entrance.

In the excitement, Busby must have imagined that he was back in Korea, because he carried the shotgun—now fully loaded—into the terminal. Someone notified police as the group ran toward the Eastern Airlines terminal. Several state troopers intercepted them there and placed them under arrest. It was probably the first time in their lives that the men had prayed to be arrested. Ella posted bond for Collins, Goodman, and the others, and Goodman rushed back to New York to tell Malcolm what had happened.[63]

At a meeting for men only on June 21 at the largest Chicago mosque, Raymond Sharrieff announced that his son, Hassan Sharrieff, and Wallace Muhammad had "deviated from the teachings of the Honorable Elijah Muhammad and were therefore hypocrites."[64] Since Hassan was a lieutenant, he knew that he and Wallace would be targeted for assaults, as that's what happened to hypocrites. Fearing for his life, Hassan called the FBI field office in Chicago on June 23 and advised the Bureau about the meeting and its implications. He also asked the agent there about procedures for legally carrying a handgun for protection, and about the requirements for becoming an FBI agent.[65] Neither Hassan nor Wallace was ever actually attacked.

When Malcolm arrived in Detroit on June 24 to organize a chapter of the OAAU, Carr and Garrison were among those in the auditorium. Since they were from out of town, it would have been difficult for anyone in Malcolm's security detail to recognize them as potential troublemakers. They tried getting near him to attack him, but to their dismay Malcolm was surrounded by a wall of bodyguards; after the Boston incident, Carr and Garrison didn't stand a chance of getting within a hundred feet of him, but their strange behavior attracted the notice of Malcolm's security detail.[66]

The Muslims who sat around waiting for something dramatic to happen on June 24, as the Messenger had predicted, were sadly disappointed. What made matters even worse was that Malcolm, whom Muhammad had accused of plotting to kill him, extended an olive branch on June 26. That morning, the *New York Post* printed a letter from Malcolm in which he pleaded with the Messenger to agree to a truce before innocent people were harmed or killed. To the Messenger, Malcolm's letter was a sign of cowardice. On June 28 he delivered an angry address to an audience of Muslim men at the armory in New York City, declaring, "The ten-year rule of Malcolm X is over."[67] If the men, who had come to New York from all over the country, had doubts about what the Messenger meant, Junior cleared it up when he spoke. Malcolm X, he said, was a "red, no-good dog." He implied that Malcolm X's reddish complexion was appropriate, as he was just like a devil. "He will be killed by a Muslim or a white devil," Junior said, "or Allah will put a plague on him." One way or another, he added, Malcolm X was going to die. "If we decide to kill Malcolm, no one can help him."[68] Among those in the audience was Leon 4X Ameer, a karate expert who served as one of Muhammad Ali's personal bodyguards when the champ was on the East Coast. Ameer loved Elijah, but the things he heard Elijah Jr. say that day sickened him: "Malcolm should have been killed by now. . . . All you have to do is go there and clap on the walls until the walls come down and then cut out the nigger's tongue and put it in an envelope and send it to me. And I'll stamp it 'approved' and give it to the Messenger."[69]

Though it learned from wiretaps and informants of the murder conspiracy, the FBI made no attempt to intercede. Instead, it explored means to exploit a potentially lethal situation. The CIA had become involved because Malcolm's proposed human rights petition was considered a matter of national and international security. The day after Muhammad issued the unmistakable order to kill Malcolm X, the FBI's Domestic Intelligence Division (also called the Internal Security Division) sent a memorandum to all U.S. intelligence agencies, which described the June 28 meeting and added the following:

Muslim Mosque, Inc., (MMI) is black nationalist group formed by Malcolm X Little, former New York Nation of Islam (NOI) leader who has been attempting to discredit Elijah Muhammad, head of NOI.

Attached reports formation of group by Malcolm X Little called "Organization of Afro-American Unity," which has announced purpose of sponsoring a reform program aimed at getting racial problems before United Nations. We have been following this development very closely. Dissemination is being made to [Justice] Department, State, CIA, Secret Service and Military agencies.[70]

The conflict that the FBI had hoped to exploit rapidly intensified a few days later. On July 3, a UPI reporter covering the Los Angeles courthouse filed this item: "Elijah Muhammad, 67-year-old leader of the Black Muslim movement, today faced paternity suits from two former secretaries. . . . Miss [Lucille] Rosary and [Evelyn] Williams charged they had intimacies with Elijah Muhammad from 1957 until this year."[71]

The next day, a group of FOI soldiers arrived at the Harlem mosque under the command of Gill of the Boston mosque and John X of Mosque No. 13 in Springfield. Joseph had been expecting Gill, since after the rally many Muslims were eager to be the ones to kill Malcolm X in order to please the Messenger. Joseph's failure to carry out the execution had led to his demotion, and Gill had replaced him as the Muslims' overseer on the East Coast. "They were calling us punks and sissies," Thomas 15X Johnson recalled, because Joseph and the Harlem FOI men failed to murder Malcolm X in the days following the Messenger's tirade.[72] After they arrived, Gill went to talk to Ameer and asked him where they could get a silencer. Ameer said he didn't know. When they left, he got in touch with Malcolm X and gave him the news. Later that evening, a group from the Harlem mosque devised a plan to please their "divine leader and teacher."

Malcolm X was working at home that evening, with a babysitter in the house to watch the children. At around ten o'clock, he decided to go outside and move his car from in front of his home to a less conspicuous location. He suspected that NOI members would attempt to kill him after the sex scandal became public, and he was right. He showed the babysitter how to operate his rifle. After he was sure she understood, he opened the front door and peered outside. Satisfied that the coast was clear, he dashed toward his car, opened the door quickly, and revved the engine. But before he could get out of the parking space, two men he recognized as enforcers from the Harlem mosque approached the car and tried to open the front door on the driver's side. Malcolm quickly locked the door and drove away. He circled the block a couple of times, each time looking at his front door to make sure the enforcers were not there. The door was just as he had left it, and there were no signs that the pursuers had entered his home. On the third cycle Malcolm parked the car down the street from his home, went back inside, and called the police emergency number. After taking a statement from Malcolm and the babysitter, they left.[73]

On July 5, Raymond Sharrieff and John Ali held a press conference on Elijah Muhammad's behalf to refute reports that he had fornicated with his secretaries:

> We hereby give answer to the false charges made against our leader . . . by evil-saying two former secretaries, namely Evelyn Williams and Lucille Rosary. . . . As to who is [sic] the fathers of Evelyn and Lucille's children, Allah is the Best Knower. These two women and their babies have been and are still being cared up to the present time from No. 2 Mosque's Poor Treasury for their food, shelter, clothes, and spending money. . . . Messenger Muhammad says his conscience is clear.

Then John Ali made a startling admission: "Evelyn has a five-room furnished apartment in the Nation Apartment Building [at] 8201 South Vernon Avenue." It was the same building, of course, where FBI agents had secretly recorded the Messenger's meetings with the two women and with other secretaries on any number of occasions. The apartment was only a door away from the one occupied by the Messenger.[74]

Hassan Sharrieff called a press conference the next morning in Chicago to announce that he had quit the NOI. He denounced his grandfather as "a fake and a fraud" who bilked black people of their money under the guise of helping them. Wallace made similar charges against the Messenger.[75] In a story published in the *Chicago Daily Defender*, he described the Black Muslims as fanatics who "will kill you" if they feel that someone has criticized Muhammad. Not only were leaders of the NOI guilty of criminal misdemeanors and felonies, he suggested, but they also smoked cigarettes, abused alcohol and drugs, and routinely engaged in embezzlement.[76] On July 7, 1964, Wallace and Malcolm X discussed the financial maneuvering of Muhammad and his wife—about how Muhammad allegedly had been depositing money in a Swiss bank account, while Clara was putting money in banks in Beirut and Cairo. Malcolm X also mentioned that in going through the financial records in Chicago a year earlier, he had uncovered evidence that H. L. Hunt, the Texas billionaire oilman who was so thrifty that he took his lunch to work in a paper bag every day, "had been giving the Messenger money for several years."[77]

On July 13, Wallace placed a call to the FBI's Chicago SAC, and he told him that he had been receiving threatening phone calls for the past two or three nights.[78] The agent asked him to describe the nature of the calls. One of the callers, Wallace reported, had called him "a dirty rat," while another caller had warned him to "be careful," as his life was in jeopardy. Did he have any idea who made the calls? the agent asked. Wallace said that he did, that one voice sounded like his brother Junior and another like his brother Herbert. When asked if he knew whether the calls were made in interstate commerce (across state lines), Wallace replied in the negative, whereupon the agent said that unless the calls were coming from out of state, it was a matter for the local police. Wallace replied that he had already had someone file a report with the local police, but the agent urged him to file the report personally since he was the one who had received the calls. After Wallace advised the agent that he was recording the phone calls, the agent explained that it was still a matter for local police, and the conversation ended.[79]

The combination of Wallace's calls to the FBI, the failed attempts on Malcolm's life, the paternity suit, and his marital problems plunged the Messenger into a deep depression by late September. He returned to his home in Phoenix for relief, but the weather proved adverse and aggravated his bronchitis. "I'm under oxygen some five times a day," he told a female caller on September 20. He also talked about the deterioration of his marriage, but used a parable. If a married man takes carnal knowledge of many women, he told her, but always returns to his wife because he truly loves only her, then "there's nothing wrong with that."[80]

"I do mean good," Muhammad assured the caller, "and I do have love for my people." But he also chided his children as greedy sloths. There was enough money tucked away, he told her, for all of his children to continue living lavishly for the next twenty years. The woman acknowledged that, and added that none of his children had ever found a job on their own. "I can't remember when they've worked," she said.[81]

"It's a shame," Muhammad said, adding that he was particularly angry with Wallace, whom he called his "foolish son." The only person worse than Wallace, he said, was Malcolm X. "I didn't think," he said bitterly, "that Allah had given me such a son."[82] At the end of the month, Muhammad sent orders by mail to a select group of FOI soldiers telling them to report to Chicago for another special meeting. As the meeting was highly confidential, the recipients were also told not to mention the letter to anyone, not even their superiors in the mosque. Each man had been carefully chosen; he either possessed special training in how to kill or was a minister in whom the Messenger placed a great deal of trust. Two of those summoned came from the mosque in New Haven. Leon 4X Ameer was captain of the FOI there, but also was a highly regarded expert in karate. Ameer was accompanied to Chicago by his superior, Minister Abdullah Karriem.[83] Muhammad's health was poor, but he knew that he was in a fight for the very survival of the NOI, and managed to garner sufficient energy to address the special squadron for nearly eight hours.[84] He spent the entire time haranguing the captive audience about the dangers posed to the NOI by hypocrites, whom he defined as anyone who had left the NOI after the expulsion of Malcolm X, the "chief hypocrite."

"He [Malcolm] is the greatest hypocrite the NOI has ever seen," the Messenger said. "He must be stopped at all costs."[85] Other hypocrites were to be taken care of, by either beating or murder, but the attacks were to be carried out carefully. The men were to make sure that there were no witnesses to the attacks so that there would be no repercussions with the police. Ameer left the meeting in a daze, not so much from exhaustion (though that certainly was a factor), but because he was having difficulty digesting what he had just heard. He had known of the rumors that some officials at the Chicago headquarters wanted Malcolm X dead, but he never imagined that he would hear the Messenger order the assault and murder of his own followers. Although he feigned agreement with what Muhammad had said as he and his superior headed back to New Haven, he knew that he couldn't remain in the NOI. Ameer, who acted as Muhammad Ali's press secretary when the champion was on the East Coast, told Malcolm about the Messenger's harangue.[86] He was equally protective of Ali. In October 1964, the boxing champion had started complaining about the large sums of money he was required to give the NOI. When he gave an exhibition match at Santos' Gym in Boston, for example, Santos charged spectators a fee of which he received half. Instead of the other half going to Ali, Chicago had ordered him to "donate" his half to the Boston mosque. Ameer had told the Messenger that Ali was unhappy about this.[87]

That same month, Clara told Elijah that she wanted to return to Cairo. The frequency of her visits finally made him realize that she was thinking of leaving him; she kept testing the waters, and stayed in the pool longer with each visit. When she asked for several thousand dollars for the trip, he erupted in anger. "There's other places to take a vacation," he said angrily. "You could stay here and take a vacation. It's a big country, you know."[88] In November 1964, the FBI discovered from wiretaps that Clara had left Elijah. She was planning to move to Cairo permanently, but had not told her husband. Since the marriage seemed to be over, the Bureau wrote if off as another successful COINTELPRO.[89]

The Messenger took possession of *Muhammad Speaks*, the vehicle

Malcolm X had created in his basement, and used it to run over his heir designate and his former right-hand man. In one edition, Herbert, who was then assigned to a piddling little mosque in Mansfield, Ohio, also castigated his brother Wallace and Malcolm X:

> But for our Holy Prophet's teachings, which he received from Allah, I would have been surprised at the vicious scheming and treachery of Malcolm X, Wallace D. and their followers in an effort to do harm to our beloved Holy Apostle, Messenger Elijah Muhammad. . . . The hypocrites envy the success of Mr. Muhammad and the Nation of Islam and the acclaim and recognition the Messenger has received from all over Allah's earth.[90]

Next to Herbert's article, the Messenger issued his own admonition to the dissidents:

> The hypocrites and devils are now united against me and my followers, and wish to make a concerted attack on us with many false charges as well as planning actual death for us. But Allah, too, has planned. . . . I have Allah on my side, while the hypocrites have the devils—and they cannot defend the followers on their side who are against Allah. I knew what the enemies and hypocrites were going to do long ago, because Allah had told me of them and the evil, deceitful plans they would try to carry out. He will bring them to naught before your very eyes.[91]

On December 12, twenty-five-year-old Akbar flew in from Cairo with his wife, Suhare, and their one-year-old daughter. Elijah sent for him for two reasons: first, to clear up stories he had read in the media about Akbar's plans to disavow the teachings of the Black Muslims, and second, he wanted to know if Akbar was aiding Clara in her plan to leave the marriage. If Akbar was still in his father's corner, Elijah said, he had a special assignment for him. The conversation began slowly in the dining room that Elijah also used as a conference room. Akbar sat patiently at first, listening to his father rant and rave about how Malcolm X was about to bring down the proverbial walls of Jericho—or in this case, the pyramid of pure profit that the Messenger had built. After nearly five hours of discussion, though, it was clear that they would never agree about Malcolm X, Islam, or much of anything else. Elijah, nonetheless, ordered Akbar to visit every major mosque throughout the country and deliver speeches depicting Malcolm X as "an ingrate and a hypocrite."

"And what if I refuse?" Akbar asked his father.

The veins around Elijah's forehead bulged as he stared in disbelief at his youngest child. "If you refuse, you get out of the Nation and stay out," he said. "I don't want to see you again."[92]

By the end of 1964, a section of the Audubon Ballroom, which had once housed a synagogue, served as Malcolm's mosque. Everyone in Harlem knew that if you wanted to hear the "new" Malcolm X speak, you had to go to the Audubon. And go they did. The destitute sat side by side with wealthy, prominent African Americans, and it was not surprising to walk into the ballroom and find a homeless drifter sitting next to trumpeter Dizzy Gillespie or actor Ossie Davis or saxophonist John Coltrane. These artists and other black celebrities caught the attention of adoring fans—and of FBI agents monitoring Malcolm's new organization. Their names were entered into the FBI's domestic intelligence files alongside Miles and Lady Day and Satchmo. While not every celebrity who went to an OAAU meeting publicly endorsed Malcolm's message, Coltrane and others made no attempt to disguise their admiration. Coltrane had studied orthodox Islam years before Malcolm X's break and had played at the Audubon a dozen times. "I thought I had to see the man," Coltrane said when asked by a reporter about why he attended Malcolm's lectures. "I was in the [Theresa] hotel. I saw the posters, and I realized he was going over there [to the Audubon], so I said, well, I'm going over to see this cat, because I have never seen him. I was quite impressed."[93]

The Messenger was impressed too—and envious. On a second trip to Africa, which began in late August and lasted until November, Malcolm had effectively replaced Muhammad as America's preeminent Muslim power broker. He had become acquainted with nearly every prominent African and Arab leader and had not come home empty-handed.

Kwame Nkrumah of Ghana tried enticing him to stay by offering him a cabinet post.[94] Ben Bella of Algeria, Egypt's Nasser, and the government of Ethiopia all promised to make room for him in their governments.[95] Ethiopia, which had a human rights petition against South Africa pending in the United Nations, was most interested in having Malcolm mention its petition when he spoke publicly about his own.

Saudi Arabia gave him twenty-five scholarships for American Muslims interested in studying Islam and eventually becoming teachers, or imams. It also assigned Ahmed Hassoun, a highly regarded Islamic scholar, to return to America with Malcolm to instruct members of Muslim Mosque, Inc., on practicing and propagating true Islam.[96] Last, but most important, it promised to construct a multimillion-dollar mosque anyplace in America for Malcolm. A lavish new mosque would have spelled the end of the NOI and Muhammad's empty promises; despite its wealth, the NOI had never laid the cornerstone for a single genuine mosque or the Islamic Center that the Messenger had been promising since the late 1950s.[97] When Malcolm announced that the mosque probably would be built in Los Angeles, he also announced that Akbar, the Messenger's youngest child, would be a teacher there. In the New Year's Day edition of *Muhammad Speaks*, Muhammad kept his word about disowning Akbar. Throughout the column, he called his son the worst epithet in Islam: hypocrite.[98]

CHAPTER FOURTEEN

THE PEN AND THE SWORD

To everything there is a season, and a time to every purpose under the heaven.
—Ecclesiastes 3:1–8
—The Byrds, "Turn!Turn!Turn!"
Billboard's #1, *Christmas Eve, 1965*[1]

The words of the prophets are written on the subway walls, and tenement halls.
—Simon and Garfunkel, "The Sounds of Silence,"
Billboard's #1, *New Year's Day, 1966*[2]

"They're not scared of you. They're scared of what you represent."
—Easy Rider,
#1 Box Office Movie 1969[3]

Faced with Malcolm's international success, prominent members of the NOI took turns taking pot shots at him; one envious minister called him "an international hobo." Like Goering and Hess and other Nazi officers tried at Nuremberg, they blindly followed orders—from a man credited with divine powers that no one had ever witnessed. Muhammad had never parted the waters, fed the multitudes, or even performed a classic trick like pulling a rabbit out of a hat. Nonetheless, some of his Muslims—particularly those faring well financially—were ready to kill to keep the scandals from reaching the rank and file. Certainly many knew about the paternity lawsuit, but ministers claimed it was bogus, the result of a plot involving Malcolm and white devils. The most provocative attacks on Malcolm came from Louis Farrakhan, the godfather of Malcolm's children. On December 4—the first anniversary of Malcolm's suspension—in an article for *Muhammad Speaks* in which he condemned Malcolm as a "chief hypocrite," Farrakhan wrote:

> If any Muslim backs a fool like Malcolm in building a mosque, he would be a fool himself. . . . Only those who wish to be led to hell, or to their doom, will follow Malcolm. The die is set, and Malcolm shall not escape. . . . Such a man as Malcolm is worthy of death. . . .[4]

Years later, Farrakhan would sheepishly suggest (to broadcast journalist Barbara Walters) that his words were "wolf tickets," a form of bluffing by which one tries to intimidate another by describing in detail how badly the bluffer plans to mangle the target of his anger. But in the climate of 1964, they were anything but that.

One of Malcolm's followers had already been murdered by Black

Muslims. In late October, Kenneth Morton was returning from his job as a professional house painter when he was ambushed by members of the Harlem mosque. According to an eyewitness, the attackers took cans of paint out of Morton's truck and beat him until he fell unconscious. After he died from his injuries on November 5, two Muslims from the Harlem mosque were charged with his murder.[5]

On Christmas Day, another man who chose Malcolm over Muhammad was targeted for death. Leon 4X Ameer, the karate expert who had heard the Messenger's eight-hour monologue in September on the necessity of killing Malcolm, was staying in a Boston hotel when members of the Boston mosque discovered his whereabouts. Led by Clarence 2X Gill, they went to the hotel and beat Ameer senseless as terrified guests looked on. The assault was stopped by a police officer who just happened to drop by the hotel.[6] As Ameer was preparing to check out of the hotel later that evening, a second group of Muslims burst into his room and beat him so badly that they assumed that he was dead. They dumped his bloody body in the bathtub and left. Once again, a policeman just happened to drop by after the damage was done. The officer claimed that he had come to arrest Ameer on embezzlement charges filed by Minister Abdullah Karriem. The policeman went into the hotel and up to Ameer's room and followed the trail of blood to the bathroom. Ameer was rushed to the hospital, but remained in a coma for several days. He later testified against Gill and others, who were convicted on minor assault charges.[7]

When Wallace saw the cartoon accompanying Farrakhan's December 4 indictment of Malcolm X, he feared that Malcolm's days were numbered. Drawn by Eugene Majied, the drawing showed Malcolm's decapitated head bouncing over headstones in a cemetery where the bones of infamous traitors—Judas, Brutus, Benedict Arnold—rested. Majied added the name "Malcolm: Little Red," to the headstones just above a bed of bones, and drew horns on Malcolm's forehead. Wallace recalled:

What stays in my mind is a picture [cartoon] . . . and they were calling him a Judas. . . . The language of ministers in the paper—I know Farrakhan was one of them, but there were other ministers, too—I read their language and said to myself, "They're trying to get him killed. They want him dead."[8]

Malcolm knew that Muhammad was trying to drag him into a dog-fight, but he refused to take up the challenge. The Messenger's Muslims, however, were relentless. When Malcolm arrived in Philadelphia on December 29 to appear on a radio program, he and his bodyguards were met by a group of them led by Sterling X Hobbs, a man the FBI described as a "gangster" for Minister Jeremiah X Pugh. Hobbs, one memo said, "is the individual usually called upon by mosque officials when the need for physical force is anticipated."[9] The memo was filed in October after Hobbs had attacked a group loyal to Wallace. As the guards opened the door to the station, the Muslims attacked them to get at Malcolm, but a detective suddenly appeared and interceded. When Malcolm arrived at the radio station, he called Betty and told her what had happened: "Be careful. . . . Have those things [a reference to his shotgun] near the door and don't let anyone in until I get home." The FBI agents transcribed the conversation and noted, curiously, that the "Army and Secret Service" had been advised of the attack.[10]

Malcolm concentrated on building a coalition with prominent civil rights leaders, particularly Dr. King, with whom he had become friends after a brief meeting in Washington in March 1964.[11] Clarence Jones, a civil rights activist who practiced law in New York, had been a go-between for Malcolm and King since the March meeting. By January 1965 he had finally arranged for the two men to have a serious discussion about Malcolm's human rights petition, which King had expressed interest in backing, and on ways to involve Malcolm in the vanguard of the civil rights movement.[12] When the Messenger learned about the planned meeting, he told Chicago lawyer Chauncey Eskridge that he wanted to meet with King. Eskridge, who represented King and Muhammad, arranged for the two of them to talk by telephone, but King was clearly more interested in teaming up with Malcolm, who was philosophically more progressive than the Messenger, who was still expounding racial separatism and the long-ago discredited "scientific racism in reverse."[13]

Based on wiretaps, the FBI surmised that Muhammad was trying to quickly develop a friendship with King in hopes of having him appear on stage with him at the next Saviour's Day ceremonies.[14] The possibility of such a meeting prompted a flurry of activity in the "Racial Matters" section of the FBI:

> Information has been received that efforts are being made to arrange a meeting between King and Muhammad which meeting will possibly take place at Chicago, Illinois, on 2/26/65. This meeting may include Roy Wilkins, Executive Director of the [NAACP], and James Farmer, National Director of the Congress of Racial Equality. . . . We have authority to institute technical coverage of Elijah Muhammad from the [Justice] Department which provides that this coverage may be extended to any location to which he may move. . . . It is felt that this additional coverage in Chicago is extremely desirable since it is expected to provide coverage of the meeting between King and Muhammad and also provide additional coverage of the Annual Muslim Convention which will take place in Chicago 2/26-28/65.[15]

Eskridge did everything possible to arrange the meeting, but failed. Jones was also unsuccessful in his attempt to get King and Malcolm together. They spoke by telephone several times, but scheduling conflicts and politicking by King's associates, who were afraid that such a meeting would damage the civil rights leader's reputation with liberals, kept the two apart.[16]

Ameer, who had been transferred to the Boston mosque after he raised questions about bookkeeping practices in the New Haven mosque, was ordered to call Joseph after he was released from the hospital. As East Coast FOI overseer, Joseph informed him that Farrakhan wanted to meet with him at the Harlem mosque.[17] Farrakhan was spending a great deal of time there after Malcolm quit the NOI. His brother, Alvan, was Joseph's right-hand man. Alvan, an officer in the

Harlem mosque confided, was well known as a subspecies of hooligan.[18] This officer had been present when Alvan threw a man down a flight of steps over a minor transgression and had seen Alvan beat other members with apparent pleasure. Despite being fearful, Ameer followed the order to meet Farrakhan on January 5 at the mosque. Upon arriving at Mosque No. 7, Ameer was taken to Joseph's office. Two men with worse reputations for violence than Alvan—Lieutenant Thomas 15X Johnson and Norman 3X Butler—stood guard outside the door.[19] Ameer knew something was wrong when the office door closed because Farrakhan was nowhere to be seen. When he asked where Farrakhan was, Joseph replied that the minister—who shuttled among the mosques in Harlem and Boston and Newark to preach—had had a sudden change of plans and would not be coming to the meeting after all.[20]

Suspecting that he had been set up, Ameer asked why the henchmen were standing outside the door. Joseph replied that they were there to take care of a hypocrite who had quit the NOI and established his own storefront mosque. The defector had angered Muslims because he had placed a photograph of the Messenger in the window of an unauthorized mosque. That evening, Johnson, Butler, and other Muslims surrounded the Universal Peace Mosque run by Benjamin X Brown. According to an eyewitness, a Molotov cocktail was thrown in a side window of the building, forcing Brown and his group out into the street.[21] Johnson accosted Brown as the minister stood out front and asked him why he hadn't taken the photo of the Messenger out of his window as he had been ordered to do earlier in the week. When his answer, that he wished to show his continued loyalty to the beliefs of NOI, failed to satisfy Johnson, he pointed a shotgun at Brown's chest and fired, hitting him just above the heart. As Brown fell to the sidewalk, the would-be assassins scattered, leaving him for dead just as Ameer had been left in Boston. Once again, the victim survived. Johnson and Butler were arrested, and police recovered the shotgun from a closet in Johnson's apartment.[22] Ameer, upon hearing of Johnson and Butler's arrest, finally understood what Joseph had meant at their last meeting. When Ameer told Malcolm, he replied, "If my life is worth two cents, yours is worth one." Ameer left the NOI after the incident and joined Malcolm's new crusade.

One week later, male Muslims from across the country, particularly the East Coast mosques under the control of Gill and, nominally at least, Joseph, arrived in Harlem for what was billed as "A Night with the FOI."[23] In the advertisement, which ran in *Muhammad Speaks*, attendees were promised that Muhammad Ali would be the guest, and that Raymond Sharrieff, the Supreme Captain of the FOI, would be the featured speaker. What was so unusual about the evening was the location. Muhammad's Mosque No. 7, formerly headed by Malcolm and now run by Farrakhan, was holding the event "at the beautiful Audubon Ballroom," where Malcolm held meetings every Sunday. It is unlikely that the Audubon was selected for its architectural splendor; whatever the reason, the long evening gave NOI enforcers ample opportunity to study the building's floorplan. When the two women who had filed paternity suits against the Messenger learned about the gathering, their lawsuit suddenly seemed like a bad idea. Their Los Angeles Superior Court hearing was scheduled for January 11, but neither woman showed up for the hearing.[24] Their failure to appear gave the judge no alternative but to remove the case from the court's calendar until there was an explanation lodged for their absence. Malcolm, who was scheduled to testify for the women, grew nervous when he heard about the delay, saying, "If this case doesn't get to trial soon, I won't be alive to testify."[25]

On January 24, muckraker Jack Anderson revealed that the intelligence community—particularly the CIA—was getting nervous, too, about Malcolm's pending petition before the United Nations.[26] High-level government officials were concerned, the *New York Times* reported, because the petition stood a good chance of being scheduled for review if a single government threw its support behind it.[27] As it turned out, Malcolm had the firm support of several African nations. Lobbying out of his tiny office in the U.N. building, Malcolm had convinced Nkrumah and others that he and King could form an alliance to bring pressure on the American government to stop fomenting coups in

Africa. Other supporters, a CIA memorandum noted, included Egypt's Nasser, Abdul Rahman Babu, the newly appointed head of Tanganyika, and John Karefa-Smart, the former foreign minister of Sierre Leone. John Karefa-Smart was the older brother of Frank Karefa-Smart, who was dating (and later married) James Baldwin's sister Gloria.[28] By early 1965, FBI agents were closely monitoring Baldwin's activities, and noted that he was meeting frequently with Frank and Malcolm. Even more troubling, though, was the appointment of Alex Quaison-Sackey of Ghana as president of the U.N. General Assembly. Quaison-Sackey, who had experienced American racism firsthand (a bigot had torched his home in a predominantly white neighborhood) and was a staunch supporter of Ethiopia's petition against South Africa, was also viewed as a powerful supporter of Malcolm's petition.[29]

While Malcolm's influence grew from national to international, Muhammad's world shrank. Membership in the NOI continued to drop since no one else had Malcolm's organizational skills—or his integrity when it came to handling large sums of money. Malcolm's resilience and success pushed the Messenger closer to the brink of homicidal madness. He and Malcolm had had a hundred discussions about the day when emissaries from the NOI would break bread with Muslim diplomats. That day had come, at least in terms of diplomatic contact—but it was Malcolm who was being wined and dined. Muhammad's attempts to break Malcolm through economic and psychological ploys had failed. Had it not been for growing outside interference, it would have been only a matter of time before the NOI met the same fate as Garvey's UNIA.

Alas, the army came to the rescue—literally. When Malcolm arrived in Detroit on January 17, agents from the army's G-2 intelligence corps were there to monitor his movements, as were FBI agents and local undercover policemen.[30] Moreover, the FBI was working with major city police departments to keep tabs on him. "Elijah seems to know every move I make," Malcolm told journalist Louis Lomax. What Malcolm later guessed was that the Messenger's Muslims knew his itinerary because the FBI, through a chain of reliable informants, told officials of the NOI where Malcolm would be at any given moment.[31] On January

28, for example, Malcolm went to Los Angeles for a meeting with attorney Gladys T. Root and the two secretaries involved in the paternity suit against the Messenger. He was caught completely off guard upon arriving at the Los Angeles airport when he saw John Ali, the Messenger's chief aide and a man who reportedly had ties to the FBI, waiting inside the terminal.[32] After Hakim Abdullah Jamal, Malcolm's cousin and a former Muslim, alerted airport security that they were being stalked, John Ali and his henchman quickly departed.

John Ali and Basit Naeem weren't the only people whom FBI agents portrayed as "reliable sources" close to Muhammad. Surprisingly, Wallace and Hassan were also considered allies, though they may not have been aware of it. Essentially, anyone who consistently gave FBI agents reliable information was pegged as a reliable source or reliable informant. Wallace and Hassan fit the bill because they had provided the Bureau with information it considered crucial to inciting violence between Muhammad's camp and Malcolm X.[33]

Despite unmistakable cracks in the walls of his castle, Muhammad was in Phoenix carrying on as usual. A young secretary who was there with him was startled in late January when he approached her and tried to French kiss.[34] She noisily recoiled in shock, attracting the attention of other people who were there. Embarrassed, Muhammad feigned outrage. "I have kissed millions of believers!" he shouted. "You can't work here any longer."[35] The secretary gathered her belongings and went back to Los Angeles. When she told her fiancé what had happened, he was ready to wring Muhammad's neck. Instead, the couple did the next best thing: they told everyone they trusted about the episode. On February 1, Minister John Shabass from Mosque No. 27 called Muhammad to ask him about the incident. It had happened, he said, but not in the way that the young woman had described. It was an innocent little kiss that the secretary had taken for something more. He declared that her behavior had dishonored him and that she should have known that telling her fiancé would cause problems. But the kiss, he said, was not the only reason that he fired her; she was a very poor secretary. "She could hardly do three to four letters a day. . . . It's just wicked. . . . People like her that build this fire will regret it." Before hanging up, Muhammad told

Shabass to sentence the secretary to ninety days in "Class F" and to expel her fiancé and her mother.[36]

Malcolm retaliated against Muhammad for the attempts on his life by revealing as many of the NOI's false teachings as he possibly could. When he appeared on the *Irv Kupcinet Show* on January 30, he described the Messenger as a liar and a coward. Malcolm dismissed the notion that the white media was using him to discredit Muhammad; as he saw it, the Messenger had done a bang-up job of discrediting himself. "What Elijah Muhammad is teaching is diametrically opposed to the principles of Islam and the Muslim world itself," he said. "The religious officials at Mecca . . . and those at the top authority on Islam theology totally reject what Elijah Muhammad teaches as being . . . Islam. On the other hand, what he is teaching can easily be defined as a religion, but it cannot be labeled Islam." As there were so few Islamic scholars and mosques in America, Malcolm said, it was easy for "any phony or faker to come along with a concocted, distorted product of his own making and say that this is Islam."[37]

"Are you by inference saying that Elijah Muhammad is a faker and a phony?"

Malcolm explained that he had once believed in the Messenger more than the Messenger believed in himself, but that changed when the Messenger

was confronted with a crisis in his own personal life and he did not stand up as a man. Anybody could make a moral mistake, but when they have to lie about it and be willing to see that murder is committed to cover up their mistakes, not only are they not divine—they are not even a man.[38]

Malcolm's words stung Muhammad worse than African honeybees.

On February 14, Joseph took on his Al Capone persona and began his version of the Valentine's Day massacre. Malcolm's phone rang so often that day that Betty Shabazz, then four months pregnant with her fifth and sixth daughters, said she felt as if she was having a nervous breakdown. Led by Lieutenant Edward X, Joseph's death squad hid in the darkness outside Malcolm's house.[39] Once the last electric light went out, the house was like a duck in the middle of a small pond. There was an alley at the rear of the house and walkways on either side. The darkness gave the death squad ample opportunity to torch the house with Molotov cocktails without being seen by the neighbors. Qubilah Shabazz, Malcolm's four-year-old daughter, was awakened by the sound of shattering glass and the smell of smoke in the bedroom she shared with her six-year-old sister, Attallah. Qubilah woke her sister and the two dashed to their parents' bedroom. By the time Malcolm and Betty realized what was going on, the fire was out of control. Malcolm rushed his wife and four daughters (Ilyasha and Amilah were toddlers) to safety on the front lawn—and only afterward did he realize that he was standing outside in subzero weather in his underclothes.[40]

Later that morning, Joseph went to the scene of the firebombing while his lieutenant, Alvan X Farrakhan, remained at the temple.[41] He went, he said, to assess the damage to what he called "the Honorable Elijah Muhammad's property." To Joseph, it was his finest hour; he finally had succeeded at something—something that anyone with common sense would have been ashamed of. Had it not been for Qubilah's quick thinking, four little girls in Elmhurst would have suffered the same horrible fate as the four little girls trapped inside the Sixteenth Street Baptist Church in Birmingham when the Klan torched it in 1963. Joseph had often railed against the "devils" who committed that crime. It never occurred to him that he had become the thing he hated.

James 3X McGregor, acting minister of the Harlem mosque, joined Joseph in telling fire marshals that the NOI had nothing to do with the blaze. Malcolm "probably set the fire himself,"[42] he said, because he was angry over the eviction lawsuit. Fire investigators lent credence to McGregor's statement by releasing a statement claiming that a whiskey bottle filled with gasoline was discovered on top of a dresser in a child's bedroom. Malcolm called the allegation ludicrous; a black firefighter later told him that the bottle was planted during the investigation by a man wearing a policeman's uniform.

Although Malcolm knew that Muhammad had had nothing to do with France's decision not to permit him entry into Paris a few weeks before the fire,[43] the fireman's revelation provided further evidence that the Messenger had bedfellows in law enforcement circles. The day after the bombing, Malcolm moved what remained of the family's belongings out of the house. Juanita Poitier (Sidney Poitier's wife), Ruby Dee, Sammy Davis Jr., and others collected money for the uninsured Shabazz family.[44]

Thomas X Wallace, Ruby Dee's brother, who was viciously beaten after he quit the Harlem mosque to follow Malcolm, invited his hero's family to live with him until things settled down. Malcolm reluctantly accepted the offer. Ordinarily, he would never have accepted, but the constant harassment had worn him down. "I'm just about at the end of my rope," he told a colleague. He was tired, tired of arguing with his distraught wife, tired of staying up all night to keep the Messenger's maggots from eating his children, tired of playing "double jeopardy" with the FBI. He knew that he could not escape; his only prayer was that his children and wife would. So, he prepared himself for the inevitable.[45]

"It's a time for martyrs now. And if I am to be one, it will be in the cause of brotherhood. That's the only thing that can save this country. I've learned it the hard way—but I've learned it," Malcolm told photojournalist Gordon Parks on February 19.[46] On February 21, Malcolm went to the Audubon Ballroom shortly before three o'clock to discuss his plans for the OAAU. With his wife and four children looking on, he approached the podium and welcomed those who had come to see him. Before he could begin his lecture, two men in the audience created a disturbance. As Malcolm tried to restore calm, he was shot by three men standing near the stage. The sound of gunfire turned the Audubon into a scene from a war veteran's nightmare.

A blast from a shotgun knocked Malcolm backward. As he went down, Betty and others rushed to his aid. One witness recalled hearing the sound of his choking on blood. Gene Roberts, a bodyguard who was actually an undercover agent for the New York Police Department's BOSSI division, hovered over him and appeared to administer mouth-to-mouth resuscitation.[47] The gunmen ran for their lives. "The police and press were unfair," Betty Shabazz told the reporters waiting at the entrance of Bellevue Hospital. "No one believed what he said. They never took him seriously. Even after the bombing of our home, they said he did it himself. Now what are they going to do—say that he shot himself?"[48]

On the evening that Malcolm X was assassinated, the Messenger gave a rare interview, this one to WVON-AM radio's popular black radio personality Wesley South. "We understand that there is a group coming from New York who intends to try to assassinate you and leaders of your organization," South said. "What is your reaction?"[49]

"It is Allah who has chosen me to do this work," the Messenger replied in his trademark deliberate drawl. "I rely solely upon him. My trust is in him, and if he gives me up to the hands of some wicked one, then I am still satisfied. So long as it pleases Allah, I do not run, nor am I afraid of the consequences." Notwithstanding the Messenger's assertions of faith, South noted that police and hundreds of members of the FOI had formed a human shield around the Messenger's mansion. He also observed that the interview was being conducted by telephone, and that the Messenger had not ventured outside his home since Malcolm's murder. But the Messenger had anticipated the question and offered a stock rebuttal. "We don't teach violence," he said. "We are not to be the aggressor. But if anyone attacks us, we will try to protect ourselves."

Although South tried to enliven the debate on his call-in show, a technical snafu at the telephone company prevented any calls from getting through after the first one, so South was on his own. Having run out of prepared questions, he started to stammer a bit and complained about the phone service. While he waited for the technical problem to be solved, he ran repetitious commercials urging listeners to buy "healthful, zestful Joe Louis Milk." When it became apparent that the telephone company could not repair the problem anytime soon, South started asking the Messenger some very general questions about the NOI.

Q. Do you hate white people?

A. I will say, as I have always said, they could have been any color they wanted, or God wanted to make them. They could have been blue, green, yellow, or any color. It is not so much their color; it is the characteristics or nature of the person. I do not teach race hate, I teach truth. When we say devil, it means a wicked person. They [white people] are that because by nature they were made that. You can't call truth hate.

Q. How many followers do you have in your organization?

A. This is not an organization; it is a resurrection. I have an estimated two hundred to three hundred thousand throughout the country.

For some in South's audience, what sounded perfectly logical to Muhammad reminded others of Father Coughlin's radio ranting and Hitler's diatribes against Jews. An irate caller who finally made it through—the only one to get through that night—pointed out the irony of all the attention the media were giving such a relatively small religious group:

> There are twenty to thirty million Negroes in America today, so the fact that you have only two hundred to three hundred thousand followers indicates that the majority of Negroes do not accept your program because it breeds hate. Your organization is just about the same as the KKK.[50]

Despite Muhammad's statements about divine protection, he was free-falling into the hell of paranoia—the Harlem mosque had gone up in flames at nightfall on February 21, and someone had tried to set fire to Muhammad Ali's apartment in Chicago.[51] He was surrounded by so many guards on Saviour's Day that it was nearly impossible for his Muslims to see him; those in the "nosebleed section" had a good vantage point, but only if they had brought along binoculars.

"He criticized, he criticized, he criticized," the Messenger intoned as Farrakhan, Junior, and other ministers on stage grinned, laughed, or otherwise cheered him on. "There is no chicken about Muhammad. . . . Malcolm got what he preached . . . he was a star as long as he was with me. Now he is a man, his body on the way to the middle of the earth."[52] Malcolm's brothers Wilfred and Philbert were on stage, too. They hadn't attended Malcolm's funeral for fear of being labeled "hypocrites" and ending up like Malcolm. Philbert had let his love for Muhammad come between him and Malcolm, but not Wilfred. "He was my little brother and I loved him," Wilfred ruefully reminisced, "and nothing Muhammad said or did could ever change that."[53]

To deflect the tension in the Chicago Coliseum, Wilfred told the assembly that the murder of his brother should not be the focus of the convention. Rather, he said, they should focus on "the one who got us into this condition in the first place." As for Farrakhan, an intellectual bulimic (he regurgitated half-digested ideas), his warning that Malcolm X deserved to die had come to pass. Seemingly oblivious to his tendency to provoke violence, Farrakhan spotted Ben Holman, a black reporter who joined the NOI, quit, and then wrote a first-person account of what it was like inside the group for the *Chicago Daily Press*. Holman, who was covering the convention for CBS, froze when he saw Farrakhan looking in his direction. Suddenly Farrakhan shouted: "We have a traitor in our midst." As he pointed toward Holman, every eye in the building followed the accusing finger. "There he is!" A small group headed toward Holman as Muslims booed him, and guards escorted him from the auditorium while Junior ordered the crowd to remain calm.[54] When it was his turn to take the lectern, Farrakhan could not think of a single kind thing to say about the man who was the only father he had ever known. When he first heard Malcolm X, Farrakhan had said, "The thought came to my mind that if this man was not God, he was very close to it." Nine years later, he had joined the confederacy of dunces that condemned Malcolm as Satan. Little wonder, then, that the Messenger distrusted someone who vacillated to such extremes so easily.[55]

Another individual Malcolm had once trusted also appeared at the convention. Wallace, the wayward son whose allegations helped trigger the schism, made a cameo appearance as the Oz-like Cowardly Lion. He had run back to his father the day Malcolm was assassinated and begged forgiveness. The choice was not his, Muhammad said. If he wanted shelter, he would have to go before the throng on Saviour's Day (which he did) and ask them to accept him (which they did).[56] Wallace embraced his father, then took a seat. As the crowd started to thin out, Muhammad tried to hold them with tales from the Twilight Zone. "Allah takes pictures of people on Mars. They're tall and skinny. They're about seven to nine feet tall . . . not as intelligent as we are."[57]

Everyone who visited the Messenger's mansion in the weeks after the assassination was searched by members of the FOI and the Chicago Police Department, and the police examined every arriving letter and parcel thoroughly. The fear of retaliation from Malcolm's group sparked more violence by Muhammad's loyalists. On March 3, *Muhammad Speaks* ran its version of the old Western "Wanted" poster. Although it did not say that the three followers of Malcolm X were wanted "dead or alive," it might as well have, as it accused them of plotting to assassinate the Messenger. Under a heading reading "Editorial: Wanted," Donald Washington, Omar Ahmed, and Leon 4X Ameer were shown in mug shots obtained from the New York Police Department. The men, the editorial claimed, were part of Malcolm X's "vengeance" squad who "are headed for Chicago to assassinate the great Islamic leader, the Honorable Elijah Muhammad."[58] Two days later, someone in a fast-moving car fired two shots through a window of the Messenger's home in Phoenix. Several police were standing guard around the house, but oddly, they did not give chase, so the assailants were never apprehended.[59] The Messenger was still in Chicago.

Talmadge Hayer was the only one of Malcolm's five assassins who was caught at the time of the killing. He, like the others, was recruited in the Newark area a year earlier (Hayer later identified his four accomplices as the men recruited along with him in May 1964).[60] According to a witness that prosecutors planned to call during Hayer's trial, John Ali had met with Hayer at the Americana Hotel in New York the night before the assassination, and flew back to Chicago in time to join Muhammad's press conference the next day.[61] Another mystery involved Farrakhan. The FBI's investigation of his activities revealed that he left Boston at one-thirty on the morning of February 21 and was at the mosque in Newark at the time of the assassination. The assassins had left Newark on February 20 and conferred with men linked to the Harlem mosque, where Alvan X Farrakhan was chief underling to Joseph. When asked about his disappearing act, Farrakhan's story was that he had gone to Newark as part of his regularly scheduled ministerial program. For the next several months, the FBI's investigation of Malcolm's death centered on three mosques: Mosque No. 7 in Harlem, Mosque No. 11 in Boston, and Mosque No. 25 in Newark.[62]

The national media had never even heard of Farrakhan until February 27, the day that Malcolm was buried at Ferncliff Cemetery in Hartsdale, New York. He did have one shining moment in 1953 when he appeared on the *Ted Mack Amateur Hour,* but that was as Louis Eugene Walcott, violinist. His debut in the February 27, 1965, edition of the *Saturday Evening Post* did not constitute the kind of attention one welcomes. The article, titled "The Black Muslims Are a Fraud," was written by Aubrey Barnette, a former member of the Boston mosque, and portrayed Farrakhan as a man without convictions.[63] Barnette recounted in detail how Farrakhan was dominated by Gill and how readily he backtracked whenever his opinions were challenged, particularly by anyone close to Muhammad. The article's description of Junior's brutish behavior, by contrast, reminded one of the adage that "even the devil can quote scripture."

Meanwhile, the investigation into Malcolm's murder continued, though the FBI said publicly that it was an open-and-shut case. Since a firebomb had been used to destroy Malcolm's home on February 15 and to burn Benjamin Brown's mosque on January 5, Thomas 15X Johnson and Norman 3X Butler became prime suspects. Suspicions about their involvement intensified because a shotgun was used in the fatal attack (Johnson had hunted deer in Pennsylvania as a youth), and because Butler wore a tweed coat that fit the description of the coat worn by one of the assassins. Butler was taken into custody on Saviour's Day.[64]

Betty Shabazz was astounded when she heard that Wallace had gone crawling back. What she hadn't realized, however, was that the constant harassment from his own family and COINTELPRO had Wallace living the same way that she and Malcolm had, like deer dodging a hunter's scope.

Even civil rights leaders who disagreed with Malcolm's philosophy agreed that the black community had suffered a tremendous loss with his murder. Just days after the assassination Roy Wilkins said,

Certainly I do not agree with most of what Garvey or Malcolm X preached. But I do think Malcolm X's most significant contribution to the Negro was his unswerving insistence that Negroes develop good, sound family relationships. He campaigned against drugs and whiskey, and he spoke up for self-respect among black people. . . . He also encouraged Negroes to develop their own businesses and to seek a certain amount of independence. Every American must admire this side of Malcolm X. In this regard, he represents a great loss.[65]

Dr. Martin Luther King, who was interviewed in Selma as he was leading a voter registration drive, said somberly that the assassination of Malcolm "revealed that our society is still sick enough to express dissent through murder."[66] The assassination shook King up because he himself had been warned only weeks earlier by a high-level government official that there was "authoritative evidence of a plot taking place in Selma and Dallas County to take my life." Several days after the interview, King nearly joined the growing list of assassination victims. While he was in Los Angeles for a movie premiere, police discovered that a white segregationist had planted dynamite in the theater. The dynamite was traced to a young gun dealer who was awaiting trial on a charge of trying to kill another black man in September 1964. Police discovered boxes of dynamite and other explosives during a search of the suspect's apartment.[67]

Although the mainstream American media had few kind words for Malcolm X, he was hailed as a fallen hero in many countries in Africa and Asia. Several African nations flew their flags at half-mast. Some moved quickly to incorporate Malcolm into high school history lessons about racism and political oppression in America. Others created postage stamps bearing his likeness. When Ella Collins approached African and Arab dignitaries for aid to Malcolm's family, not one of them turned her down.[68] They preferred to refer to him by his Arabic name, "El Hajj Malik El Shabazz," but they also got a kick out of calling him "Mr. X." On May 19, which would have been Malcolm's fortieth birthday, Ethiopia and Liberia filed their final arguments with the International Court of Justice at the Hague on the issue of South Africa's violation of the human rights of its black citizens.[69] It was a fitting posthumous birthday gift to a man who had dedicated the last twelve years of his life to emancipating people of color everywhere. He had shown them how the United Nations could be coerced into doing part of its job through embarrassing it in the media, and they had taken his lessons to heart. However, despite convincing arguments, their appeals were ultimately unsuccessful.[70]

Ameer, who had vowed that Malcolm's death would be avenged, feared for his own life after someone's apparent attempt to shoot Elijah in Phoenix. He contacted several reporters in New York on March 10, the same day that Thomas 15X Johnson was arrested for his alleged role in the conspiracy to murder Malcolm. During Ameer's interview, he charged that Muslims loyal to Muhammad had filed false embezzlement charges against him in order to discredit him "before they come out and kill me."[71] He repeated his story to FBI agents the following afternoon. But he told the agents something that he had withheld from the reporters: he could positively identify another one of Malcolm's assassins. On March 12, a housekeeper at the hotel where Ameer was hiding out opened the door to his room after he failed to respond to her knocking. She turned the knob to see if the door was unlocked, opened the door, walked over to the bed, and discovered Ameer's lifeless body.[72]

The OAAU and Muslim Mosque, Inc., fell apart after Ameer's death. The randomness of the mayhem within the Black Nationalist movement and the discovery that police informants and agents provocateurs had penetrated a number of civil rights organizations unleashed an avalanche of mistrust. College-educated members of Malcolm's groups were suspected by less-educated members as probable government informants.[73] On the other hand, some less-educated members who wanted to govern were ill-equipped to do so, leading to inertia. Making matters worse, Ella Collins and Betty Shabazz became entangled in a bitter dispute over Malcolm's papers after an OAAU member reportedly saw Betty putting them into the trash bin in her yard. Some documents—Malcolm's letters, drafts of speeches, and other material—were retrieved and sold to a small publishing company.[74]

Betty had given birth to Malika and Malaak Shabazz on March 10, and was in desperate need of funds since she had no health insurance.

Muhammad was at this time in the throes of a severe diabetes crisis and fighting to stay alive. After running several tests, his doctor warned him that he had an "extremely high blood-sugar and acetone count." Even though he was on the verge of lapsing into a diabetic coma, he was too much afraid to go to the hospital. If he didn't get insulin and fluids fast, odds were that he would die, his personal physician said. He didn't seem to care. He told the doctor that he would probably die even if he did go to the hospital, and hinted that his sudden death would be convenient for a society that blamed him for the assassination of Malcolm X.[75] The doctor did what he could for him, then left. When he returned in the first week of June, Muhammad's ankles were swollen because of excessive salt in his system, and his blood pressure, the doctor noted, was "grossly elevated." He was as listless as he had been since shortly after Malcolm's assassination.

By the time the Messenger was up and about again a month or so later, Clara had to return to Georgia to help care for her ninety-four-year-old senile father. Seeing her father in his demented state was devastating. One minute he was fine, she told Elijah. The next, he was tearing off his clothing and complaining of being too hot. Mercifully, the torture of his illness ended on July 28.[76] When she called Elijah to tell him, he replied that he was unable to attend the funeral because he was experiencing severe asthma attacks.

Funeral preparations and the burial had taken so much out of Clara that she was reluctant to return to Chicago, where nothing but trouble awaited her. Going home meant returning to a spouse who mistreated her, and who had shamefully confessed that he knew of plans by Chicago NOI officials to kill Wallace. The whole nightmare—from Barnette's beating to Malcolm's murder to threats against Wallace—was the result of careless rhetoric, words that led to deeds that could not be recalled any more than a mother could return her premature baby to the womb. Her struggle to keep Wallace from being harmed in the weeks before and after Malcolm's murder had also worn her out. Six weeks after losing her father, Clara learned that Tynetta Nelson had borne yet another child by Elijah. (Two years later, Tynetta gave birth to another son sired by the seventy-year-old Messenger, who by then was the father of at least twenty-one children.[77])

If Malcolm's death proved anything, it was that there are no winners in war. Even the FBI, whose Chicago field office bragged about fomenting the deadly conflict between the Messenger and his messenger, realized too late that Malcolm was the symptom of urban unrest, not the cause. The long hot summer that Malcolm predicted in early 1964 erupted in seven Eastern cities that year. In August 1965, urban violence shifted to the West Coast. Cynicism became fashionable, triggered in part by the hasty passage of the Voting Rights Act of 1965 after Malcolm's murder, the Warren Commission's whitewash, the doubling of the number of American soldiers in Vietnam. The counterculture preferred Eldridge Cleaver's socialism over Ward Cleaver's romanticism. For once, a generation of black and white teenagers were united in a fight against political leaders who desecrated the Constitution while passing laws against desecrating the American flag.

The Watts riot and similar outbreaks forced King to acknowledge that nonviolent protest had nearly run its course. In desperation, King asked the Messenger to join him on August 17, 1965, in issuing a public statement condemning the violence in Watts, then in its sixth day.[78] Muhammad refused. He felt that King had snubbed him by refusing to join him at the previous February's Saviour's Day ceremonies, and now was time for a payback. As Muhammad saw it, Watts and the lynching of Schwerner, Chaney, and Goodman were signs of "the fall of America." He insisted that his prophecy that the government would collapse by 1970 was on target. William R. Ming, the lawyer who represented King and Muhammad, took steps to bring the two together, and King went to Chicago and met with Muhammad for an hour on February 23, 1966.[79] Afterward, the two told reporters that they had "mutual areas of concern" and planned to confer again soon. "One point of agreement was that Negroes are trapped in deplorable slums because of an evil system," a spokesman for King said.[80] *Muhammad Speaks* portrayed the discussion as a meeting of the minds: "We must concentrate our energies on a united solution to the problem [of racism]. We now must know and act according to the time. Our work must correspond with the changing needs of the times. The world of white rule over blacks is at an end. . . . Our people want no more licking of the white man's boots." King's response reflected his growing militancy: "I know we are in absolute agreement on that. We suffer domestic colonialism like the black people in Southern Rhodesia. We must achieve self-determination." From the article, one would have concluded that King was moving toward the Messenger's philosophy of separatism, and that the two agreed on a host of issues. In truth, the meeting had not gone well; King had agreed with Muhammad on only one or two issues, namely the housing crisis and self-determination. Muhammad tried to coax King into attending the convention but King wouldn't even consider it. "I do hope we can get together again and have a more extensive discussion," King replied, making it clear that he had no intention of attending the Saviour's Day celebration.

During the convention, Muhammad praised the New Jersey Supreme Court for ruling that Black Muslim school children could not be forced to salute the flag. He also praised Muhammad Ali for refusing to fight "the little brown people" in Vietnam. "The white man hates to go to war, even to fight for his country. If he wants us to help fight, he should give us something to fight for." In reference to the Army's unprecedented release of Ali's intelligence-test records, the Messenger said: "You classified him as unfit and then you call him. You tell him that if he won't go to Vietnam, he can't fight and make money." For its hypocrisy, Muhammad said, America would pay a terrible price. "The Vietcong will fight you for twenty years."[81] Despite the Messenger's prediction that Ali would win in court, the boxer was found guilty of draft evasion four months later. On June 20, he received the maximum sentence of five years in prison and a $10,000 fine.[82]

Much to King's dismay, leaders of the Student Nonviolent Coordinating Committee (SNCC) were moving toward the black nationalist views of the NOI and the revolutionary rhetoric of the Black Panther Party. During a meeting in Chicago on July 28, SNCC chairman Stokely Carmichael declared that it was time for "Black Power. . . . We are the only people who are powerless. We have to protect ourselves from our protectors. If they touch one more black man in Mississippi and Los Angeles, we are going to disrupt the whole country."[83] At the conclusion of the rally, Carmichael told reporters that he planned to meet with Muhammad soon as many of their goals were the same.

The antagonism between Muhammad and King flared again in the fall. On August 28 Muhammad denounced King after the civil rights leader announced plans for an "open city" in Chicago. The NOI wanted no part of the project, Muhammad said, because he was opposed to anyone who "loved the white man so much they want to fight to stay with him."[84] While condemning King's move for integration in housing, in the job market, and in government, Muhammad announced at the Saviour's Day 1967 convention that he was endorsing Adam Clayton Powell for Congress. "I ain't no politician, but he's the strongest one of them all . . . all black politicians should get behind Harlem Congressman Adam Clayton Powell!" Since he forbade Muslims in New York to vote, however, the endorsement had no value. Powell, who was facing a possible impeachment hearing, was defeated by a newcomer, Charles P. Rangel. The Messenger had prophesied that Powell would win—a presumably safe prediction given his longevity in Congress and popularity in Harlem. But times were changing, and again the Messenger had missed his mark.[85]

Muhammad Ali's pronouncements on Vietnam triggered more antagonism. His comments ("no Vietnamese ever called me 'nigger,' ") made him a hero even to young whites who opposed the draft, but may have been the impetus for the increasing number of acts of violence against the NOI. On July 29, the Los Angeles Police Department raided Muhammad's Mosque No. 27 for the second time in five years. The justification for the raid, Mayor Sam Yorty said at a press conference called to issue an apology to Muslims, was an anonymous call to the police that "submachine guns, rifles, dynamite, and hand grenades" were stored in the building. Still, that didn't explain why the police waited until a religious service was in progress—which meant the mosque was full—to raid the premises. "If I had been informed," the embarrassed mayor swore, "it might have been avoided."[86] Less than a month later, the Chicago Police Department raided a Muslim-owned business across the street from the Messenger's mansion. When questioned about the raid, police produced a box of dynamite, which they said was discovered in the building. Assault charges were subsequently dismissed against nineteen Muslims arrested during the raid.[87]

No one knew about COINTELPRO practices then, but people sensed that the government was behaving peculiarly. There were too many unexplained things going on in minority enclaves—police raids resulting in deaths, mysterious letters, and arrests of activists on phony drug charges—which hinted of widespread government misconduct. On October 12, members of the NOI, the Black Congress, the Black Panther Party, CORE, and SNCC joined with Hopi Indians and Hispanic American activists to work out a pact aimed at preventing misunderstandings between minority groups. Reies Tijerina, leader of the Political Confederation of Free States (a Mexican-American organization), met with Muhammad before the pact was announced.

Tijerina was a colorful character in his own right. He accused the United States of illegally stealing 100,000,000 acres of land in the southwestern part of the country from Mexico, and he wanted it back.[88] Muhammad, on the other hand, wanted a mere four or five states in the southeastern part of the country. "I suggested," Tijerina told reporters, "that we reach a common agreement on a treaty of peace and harmony and respect for each other's culture. He agreed." The pact was ratified by the organizations two weeks later, thereby putting a major dent in the FBI's plan to cultivate disputes between minority organizations, and forcing the Bureau to shift gears.[89]

On February 12—Abraham Lincoln's birthday—in 1968, the sanitation workers of Memphis, 90 percent of whom were black, launched a protest against working conditions, particularly job safety, racial discrimination, and wages. King arrived in Memphis on March 28 to lend leadership and moral support. Three days later, Hoover sent out a six-page directive to the field offices in every major city. "By letter dated August 25, 1967, the following offices were advised of the beginning of a Counterintelligence Program against militant Black Nationalist-Hate Groups," Hoover wrote. Under a section titled "Goals," he noted that the Bureau must "prevent the *coalition* of militant black nationalist groups. . . . An effective coalition of Black nationalist groups might be the first step toward a real 'Mau Mau' in America, the beginning of a true black revolution." Under other items, he argued that the intelligence community must "prevent the rise of a 'messiah' who could unify, and electrify, the militant black nationalist movement. Malcolm X might have been such a 'messiah'; he is the martyr of the movement today. Martin Luther King, Stokely Carmichael, and Elijah Muhammad all aspire to this position."[90]

The primary targets, the memorandum stated, were "leaders, members, and followers of the Student Nonviolent Coordinating Committee (SNCC), Southern Christian Leadership Conference (SCLC), Revolutionary Action Movement (RAM), and the Nation of Islam (NOI)." Of the four, only RAM was considered radical by the African-American community, and only because some of its members espoused a bloody revolution in this country. At the conclusion of the memo, each field office was ordered to assign agents to the new COINTELPRO, submit a list of radical black organizations in its territory, and submit practical counterintelligence suggestions to FBI headquarters by April 4, 1968: The memo stated:

> Thereafter, on a ninety-day basis, each office is to submit a progress letter summarizing counterintelligence operations proposed during the period, operations effected, and tangible results. . . . Because of the nature of this program each operation must be designed to protect the Bureau's interest so that there is no possibility of embarrassment to the Bureau. Beyond this the Bureau will give every possible consideration to your proposals.[91]

Pursuant to this new directive, agents invented scenarios aimed at undermining King and the Messenger and, in the process, precluded any chance of success for the Washington Spring Project (WSP), more commonly called the Poor People's March on Washington. The memo read in part:

It is noted that during an SCLC retreat held in Atlanta in the middle of January 1968 regarding the WSP, King stressed that obtaining jobs or income for Negroes would represent a mere fraction of that which America owes the Negro throughout its history. He declared America owes an incalculable sum to the Negro. . . . This language suggests some degree of adherence to [the] teachings of Elijah Muhammad. It is suggested the proposed [COINTELPRO] publicity might be slanted to convey the thought that the apparent alliance between SCLC and the NOI possibly grew out of the former meeting between King and Muhammad [in February 1966]. It is felt King's reaction to the proposed technique would be positive for counterintelligence purposes. King considers himself a devotee of the nonviolent philosophies of the late Mahatma Gandhi. To publicly align him and/or SCLC with the NOI should trouble him on this basis. It is further conceivable that Muhammad may see fit to respond to this publicly, which should embarrass King further.[92]

From the outset, Hoover, the president, and other high-level officials expressed fear that the march might get beyond King's control. On March 12, in a memo concerning the march, a Bureau summary expressed fear of a revolution starting in the streets of the nation's capital. There had been so many demonstrations and riots in recent years that military experts at the Pentagon believed anything was possible. The memo stated:

It is King's contention that the government of the United States does not move until it is confronted dramatically. To add to the dramatic confrontation, King has boasted [that] he and his entourage are coming to Washington to stay; that his followers will conduct sit-ins, camp-ins, and sleep-ins at every government facility available including the lawn of the White House. He has bragged that he will fill up the jails of Washington and surrounding towns.

One serious danger in the confrontation lies in the proposed action of the black nationalist groups, which plan to attempt to seize the initiative and escalate the nonviolent demonstrations into violence. King has met with black nationalists and attempted to solicit their support. . . . The combined forces of the communist influence and the black nationalists advocating violence give the "Washington Spring Project" a potential to be an extremely explosive situation.[93]

The allegations raised in the memorandum were based upon a conversation between King and Carmichael that was intercepted by Army intelligence. After undercover agents trailed the two men to a hotel in Washington where H. Rap Brown was staying, a bug picked up a conversation in which Brown and Carmichael were urging King to use the march as the flashpoint for the second American Revolution.[94]

"We stop the fuckers right here, right here," Brown said.

"No more Uncle Tom, dammit. This let-them-shit-on-you shit ain't working. You know it," Carmichael said, staring at King, "and so does everybody else."

"Is killing and burning buildings in your own people's streets your answer?" King replied rhetorically.

"It's time," Carmichael, who had coined the phrase "Black Power" (much to King's dismay), retorted. "We can't wait anymore, and the people supporting us are tired of waiting."

"Nobody is as tired [of waiting] as me."

"Then let's shut the honkies down," Carmichael implored his mentor. "They bring the Army, we fight the fuckers with ours. We got guns. Marching for peace . . . shit, you've seen it. What's it got us?"

CHAPTER FIFTEEN
APOLLO FIRES

...I believe that, despite their follies, these young centaurs deserve to win their encounter with the defending Apollos of our society.

—*Theodore Roszak,*
The Making of a Counter Culture[1]

And they sung as it were a new song before the throne, and before the four beasts, and the elders: and no man could learn that song but the hundred and forty and four thousand, which were redeemed from the earth.

—*Revelation 14:3*

The army personnel following King in specially equipped surveillance vehicles parked outside the Vermont Avenue Baptist Church after King entered with Brown and Carmichael an hour after their heated exchange.[2] During his speech, King made a statement that quickly landed on President Lyndon B. Johnson's desk. "We seek to say to the nation in our campaign that if you don't straighten up, then you're writing your own obituary."[3] The revolution in the streets of Washington didn't happen that day, but clearly the angry young men around King were ready to die to bring about change.

On March 4, 1968, FBI officials in the "Racial Matters" division proposed to destroy the two most influential black leaders with one stone. Hoover signed off on a plan designed to discredit King and the SCLC by linking them to the Messenger and the NOI.

On March 25, Hoover sent a memo to the Chicago SAC regarding a

telephone conversation with you during the past week giving instructions concerning Martin Luther King's Washington Spring Project. This is to personally urge you to do everything possible in carrying out the instructions given you in referenced telephone calls and to carry out these instructions as soon as possible.[4]

Plans for the march, which was scheduled to kick off on April 22, fell into murky waters in the weeks following this enigmatic conversation. What was clear, though, was that the Bureau was sparing no expense to derail the project. Toward this end, it recruited more that 3,000 black and Hispanic informants to report and otherwise wreak havoc in the planning.[5] Some informants were agents provocateurs. In Memphis, informants inside the Invaders, a local black militant group, were paid to cause violent incidents during local marches as a means of frightening members of Congress into taking measures to cancel the Poor People's March on Washington.

The inference drawn by the media and the government from the violence was clear: if King couldn't control several thousand marchers in Memphis, how could he prevent hundreds of thousands from fomenting a riot outside the White House or in the halls of Congress? To make matters worse, there was the problem of the King-Carmichael tape from army intelligence. What if Carmichael betrayed King and deliberately started a riot? How many casualties would result and how would the nation respond? At high-level meetings, army intelligence officers agreed with Hoover's assessment that the march had to be stopped. The outbreak of violence in Memphis was cited by the Bureau (whose informants sparked it) as proof that King could not control men like Brown and Carmichael.[6]

On March 29, 1968, COINTELPRO official George C. Moore recommended to Sullivan that a fake letter accusing King of being an "Uncle Tom" be sent to "friendly media contacts." The two-paragraph letter read:

> Martin Luther King, during the sanitation workers' strike . . . has urged Negroes to boycott downtown white merchants to achieve Negro demands. On 3-29-68 King led a march for the sanitation workers. Like Judas leading lambs to slaughter King led the marchers to violence, and when the violence broke out, King disappeared. The fine Hotel Lorraine in Memphis is owned and patronized exclusively by Negroes but King didn't go there from his hasty exit. Instead King decided the plush Holiday Inn Motel, white-owned, operated and almost exclusively white patronized, was the place to "cool it." There will be no boycott of white merchants for King, only for his followers.[7]

The March 30 edition of the *Commercial Appeal,* the largest daily newspaper in Memphis, ran a story highlighting where King was residing. King left Memphis that afternoon for an appointment in Washington. When he returned to Memphis on April 3, he and his entourage checked into the Lorraine.[8] Later that evening, he was joined by Reverend Ralph Abernathy and Jesse L. Jackson, among others, at the Mason Temple. "Like anybody, I would like to live a long life," King told the standing-room-only crowd in the sweltering hot building. "Longevity has its place . . . but I'm not concerned about that now. I just want to do God's will. . . . I may not get there with you, but I want you to know tonight, that we, as a people, will get to the Promised Land."[9]

At six o'clock the next evening, King and the other ministers made plans to go out for supper. As King stood on the balcony of the Lorraine Hotel, a blast from a shotgun shattered the evening's calm. King fell backward. Aides rushed to him as he lay on his cement deathbed, blood spurting from severed vessels in his neck with each beat of his failing heart, dripping over the edge of the balcony and down to the earth below. Medics arrived after several minutes and rushed the mortally wounded civil rights hero to St. Joseph's Hospital. African Americans who admired King and Malcolm did not realize then how much the two men had in common. Both died within an hour of being wounded by shotgun fire. Like Malcolm, King was only thirty-nine years old. Like Malcolm, King had taken a vow of poverty early in his career and stuck to it, and each followed the philosophy of an Asian mystic. King dedicated himself to Mohandas Gandhi's philosophy of passive resistance, while Malcolm subscribed to Wallace D. Fard's "eye for an eye" philosophy.

Five days after he was assassinated, King, as Nicholas von Hoffman wrote so eloquently, "led his last march." A horse-drawn carriage carried his body from Ebenezer Baptist Church to Southview, a cemetery opened by blacks for blacks because racial segregation excluded their dead from other cemeteries in Atlanta. In terms of racial unity and the aspirations of African Americans, King's murder was the most devastating blow to the country since the assassination of John Kennedy. No one gave voice to the effect of his loss better than gospel singer and political activist Mahalia Jackson. Although she believed in God with every fiber of her being, King's murder had profoundly shaken her faith, she said, reflecting the sentiments of nearly every American who believed that King was the country's last and best hope for salvation. "I'm oppressed," Mahalia told reporters with a faraway look in her tear-filled eyes. "I'm burdened and I'm hurt. Since the shock of his death, I have tried to think reasonably that this is God's will. But the pressures weaken its effectiveness. Thus, I've faltered."[10] She was exhausted, she said, but nothing would stop her from singing "Precious Lord, Take My Hand," Dr. King's favorite hymn, at his funeral that morning. James Baldwin was equally despondent. When Malcolm was killed, he felt like something sacred had died in the world. "The hand that pulled the trigger did not buy the bullet. That bullet was forged in the crucible of the Western World." When King was killed, friends remember that he acted as though something sacred had died in him: his sense of hope. Black Americans, he said, were facing the possibility of a holocaust. "For saying this I may be dismissed as paranoiac. So were those unhappy [Jewish] people (shortly to be reduced to corpses) who saw the real significance of the Reichstag Fire."[11]

Eyewitnesses to the assassination wondered why local police and the FBI never bothered to interview them. Earl Caldwell, a prominent *New York Times* reporter who was staying in a room on the lower level of the Lorraine Hotel, believes that inconsistencies in the official version of the assassination, and the fact that crucial witnesses were never interviewed, bespeak the evil surrounding King's death. Worse, much of what was uncovered by the congressional probe of King's murder will remain classified until the year 2023.

About the only segment in the black community who saw an advantage in King's murder was the leadership of the NOI. No one knew better than the Messenger how deeply disillusioned African Americans were after King's death. He understood from watching the ebb and flow in his membership rolls that whenever African Americans were in a collective despair, thousands turned to the NOI to cope with their rage. Others vented, resulting in riots in 125 cities after King's death, and at least forty-six homicides.[12] Each time it seemed that things could not get worse, things got worse. Most black Americans mourned for King as though they had lost a member of their family.

Another death that week also devastated Black America, though few people beyond a neighborhood in Oakland knew the victim. Two days after King was murdered, seventeen-year-old Bobby Hutton got caught up in an ill-planned ambush on police by Black Panther Party leader Eldridge Cleaver. Before carrying out his plan, Cleaver got out of the car to urinate at the side of the street. A police cruiser just happened to come down the street, and police saw Cleaver violating public health laws. When the police got out of their vehicle and approached the car, Hutton and the other Panthers grew nervous and one of them fired his weapon, provoking a gun battle. The Panthers dashed from the car and ran toward nearby houses. Cleaver and Hutton hid in an old abandoned building. Police suspected some of the Panthers were hiding inside the building and yelled at them to come out. When no one did after several warnings, police threw tear gas through the broken windows. Hutton and Cleaver removed their shirts and covered their faces, but the burning sensation was becoming unbearable. As the suspects held out, police sprayed the building with at least 200 bullets, two of which hit Cleaver. Suddenly the house was engulfed in flames (started, it was believed, by sparks from the bullets igniting the gas).[13] Overcome by fumes and fearing he would be killed if police thought he was still armed, Cleaver removed all of his clothes and tried to leave the basement, yelling to the officers that they were surrendering. Hutton, who could not bring himself to march out completely nude, kept on his pants. Since Cleaver could barely walk because one of the bullets had struck him in the leg, Hutton assisted him as they emerged from the building and walked toward the police. Policemen ordered Hutton to step away from Cleaver and to run toward the police cruiser parked at the curb. As he reluctantly moved slowly toward the car, a fusillade of hot metal tore into him. The noise of gunfire and Cleaver's screams had attracted a crowd, which converged only seconds after police ordered Hutton to run. Cleaver stood there, dazed, until police threw him into a cruiser and took him away. News of Hutton's execution was featured in black-oriented newspapers while King was being buried. For millions of African Americans, King's murder and Hutton's execution were all the proof they needed that the Messenger was right and that white people were beyond redemption.

Instead of capitalizing on that empathy, Muslims cited King's call for brotherhood as the main reason for his murder. On April 7, Farrakhan and Muhammad Ali (who remained free pending appeal of his draft conviction) addressed an audience of some 1,000 at Muhammad's Mosque in Brooklyn, Farrakhan saying self-righteously,

> Martin Luther King died because he had no vision. He was a brother and I'm not against him, but the Bible told him the white man is our enemy. I don't get mad at a white man because of what he does because I know it is his nature to be unrighteous. There was no need for Dr. King to die if he had vision.[14]

Farrakhan's statement about King was as callous as the one Malcolm X had made following Kennedy's assassination, yet neither the public nor the Messenger seemed bothered by this blind declaration of dumbness. Indeed, his comments were similar to some made by the Messenger two months earlier. On Saviour's Day 1968, Muhammad condemned Malcolm as "a wicked hypocrite. He did not die an unjust and unrighteous death."[15] He was angered by Malcolm's elevation to martyrdom. *The Autobiography of Malcolm X*, published by Grove Press within days of the Messenger's first book, *Message to the Blackman in America*, sold a thousand times as many copies in the first year. When the *Saturday Review* published a joint review of the two books on November 20, 1965, the reviewer clearly preferred Malcolm's book. The *Autobiography* was followed in 1967 by George Breitman's book *The Last Year of Malcolm X: The Evolution of a Revolutionary*. The small publisher could not keep this book in stock, while copies of Muhammad's *Message* were gathering dust in a Chicago warehouse and in the closets of Muslims who couldn't sell it.

With the silencing of two of the country's most influential black leaders, the FBI turned its attention to its third major target. On the day of King's assassination, Sullivan and Moore, the main overseers of the "Hate Group" COINTELPRO, launched a two-month-old plan involving a mass mailing to disrupt the NOI's growth by destabilizing the Harlem mosque, the most profitable one in the Messenger's empire:

New York is authorized to anonymously mail these booklets to the Nation of Islam members as set out in referenced letter [of February 27, 1968]. Use commercially purchased envelopes and all other necessary precautions to insure this mailing cannot be traced to the Bureau. The Bureau appreciates this suggestion and the imagination and enthusiasm exhibited by the New York Office.[16]

The program was clever for its simplicity alone. It called for a comic book bearing a 10¢ sales price to be mailed to every member of the Harlem mosque. "Once upon a time there was a good Muslim who gave $12.00 dues to [leaders of the Harlem mosque]. He made these men very, very happy. . . . In order to do this, the good Muslim had to deny himself and his family necessary food, clothing, and good times," the booklet read. In one illustration, Captain Joseph was shown saying "This pile is mine," as he ogled a large stack of paper money. "I got this pile," a figure representing Farrakhan says as he holds another large stack of bills. A stack of bills about half the size of the other stacks is set aside "for Elijah," according to the cartoon. The booklet then described how the mosques in "Manhattan, Bronx, Brooklyn and Corona take in over $70,000 each month,"[17] which was an estimate based on 500 members paying $48 dues each month, and 500 members selling $96 worth of *Muhammad Speaks* every month. When regular, special, and Saviour's Day collections were figured in, the booklet alleged, the mosques in New York City were taking in nearly $72,000 a month. The books were mailed April 8.[18]

Copies of the booklet wound up on the Messenger's desk. If he suspected that the FBI was responsible for it, he seemed more concerned that top officials in the Harlem mosque were embezzling funds. He ordered Chicago officials to conduct an independent investigation. Not surprisingly, most of the allegations in the booklet proved true; the COINTELPRO worked magnificently for the Bureau. The book was so accurate that mosque officials suspected that there were high-level informants in their midst. The suspicions about misappropriation of funds led to the first significant dispute between Farrakhan and Captain Joseph.

As the probe went on, officials in Chicago went looking for a scape-goat and chose Joseph. Although he drove an old station wagon to the mosque and dressed shabbily, the probe revealed that he enjoyed an upper-middle-class lifestyle outside the temple. Not only did his home have all the creature comforts, but he drove a new Cadillac when he was away from the mosque. "Everyone knew Captain Joseph was living a double life," a former high-ranking officer in the Harlem mosque said. "We knew others were, too. We just didn't realize the extent of it until that little book opened our eyes."[19] Farrakhan, who was the first to run to the Messenger to accuse Malcolm of betrayal, fingered Joseph as the new chief offender. "Said I stole a million dollars," Joseph said. "We aren't all Farrakhan now, and that's all right."[20] Muhammad expelled Joseph, but money gathered by the New York mosques continued disappearing along the road to the coffers in Chicago. Yet another COINTEL-PRO, launched one month after King's assassination, was aimed at Herbert, the Messenger's son who was Muhammad Ali's manager. On May 7, Moore wrote to Sullivan about targeting Herbert for harassment from the IRS.

> Herbert Mohammad [sic] is involved in several businesses and is the manager of former heavyweight boxing champion Cassius Clay. Herbert Mohammed has been described as money crazy and one who will do anything for money. A review of his income tax returns might indicate he is vulnerable in this area. If Herbert Mohammad could be removed as successor to the leadership of the NOI, it would place our top-level NOI informants in a better position to neutralize this extremist cult. . . . A first step would be to review his tax returns.

The subsequent lengthy IRS probe proved futile.[21]

The Messenger and Farrakhan were at their philosophical best on King's death, but were silent after the June 6 assassination of Democratic presidential candidate Robert F. Kennedy in Los Angeles. Given that Robert Kennedy had admitted publicly in 1962 that the NOI was under heavy surveillance by the federal government, their silence was strange.

Muhammad Ali was proving to be an ineffectual magnet for the NOI. He was an excellent entertainer, but his sermons about white people being devils didn't ring true. There were white trainers and assistant managers in his corner even after Herbert became his chief manager. When he lectured at colleges, he was paid to speak about his battle with the draft board and his views on Vietnam, not his beliefs as a minister for the NOI. At the end of a lecture to a mainly white audience at American University in Washington in May 1968, for example, Ali was warmly embraced by the students. He made it a point to touch the hands of as many of them as possible, and was so affectionate toward his so-called evil white enemies that some believed he was using religion to avoid induction into the armed services. His abhorrence of racial violence was another strong point. When asked his opinion of H. Rap Brown, Ali quipped, "Hide the matches!" His jovial nature made him a top-earner on the college lecture circuit, which was his main source of income during his suspension.[22]

Ali's popularity was one reason that the FBI intensified its COINTELPRO actions in late 1968. After the Honorable James Benton Parsons of the Northern District of Illinois wrote an article condemning the NOI and black nationalism, the Chicago SAC sent an unusual suggestion to FBI headquarters:

As the Bureau is aware, approval was given for [redaction] a high-level counterintelligence program against the NOI by Bureau letter dated November 11, 1962, entitled "Nation of Islam: IS-NOI." This program was initiated by Chicago and resulted in a nationwide counterintelligence program which showed the fallacies and weaknesses of the NOI to the public. It was conducted on an extremely high level and avoided name calling, mudslinging, etc. This program continues. . . . It is suggested the Bureau in this program may well desire to canvas various field offices in an effort to determine if they have some responsible Negro leaders who could participate in a high-level program designed to expose the disadvantages extremist black nationalists groups can have on their community and especially their children.[23]

COINTELPRO or no, by 1969 the Messenger's message was reaching black communities as never before. His speeches were broadcast on black radio stations across the country. While some only carried his program once or twice a week, others such as KTYM-FM in Los Angeles aired them six days a week. Farrakhan of New York, Yusef Shah of Chicago, and Clyde X Jones of St. Louis were but a few of the powerful orators who were attracting a new generation of African Americans to the NOI.[24] The sounds from street corners and factory loading docks where black men gathered to sing "doo-wop" or listen to music from cheap transistor radios had changed radically. Reverend Ike, Mahalia Jackson, the James Cleveland Choir, and the Dixie Hummingbirds had been replaced on Sunday evening by Farrakhan's clear, charismatic voice.[25] His fiery rhetoric wielded such a tremendous influence in the ghettos that budding black revolutionaries mimicked his speaking style much as they did that of his mentor, Malcolm X, and the style of the Panther from Oakland, Huey P. Newton. Farrakhan wasn't as intellectual or handsome or muscular as Newton, but his oratorical thunder and powerful position in the NOI gave him a presence every bit as menacing to white society as the Black Panthers.

The response to Farrakhan's popularity and his propagation of the Messenger's theology began to have an impact on African-American music. In what was perhaps the most dramatic shift in black culture since the Harlem Renaissance, the recording industry retooled its lyrics and the sartorial symbolism of its artists. James Brown, the "Godfather of Soul," suddenly abandoned his painful pompadour (called a "process") and paid homage to the new black consciousness with the hit song "Say It Loud (I'm Black and I'm Proud)." But the clearest indicator of the Messenger's growing influence came from Motown Records in Detroit, founded by Berry Gordy, a man who, like Muhammad, had roots in Cordele, Georgia, and who now headed a million-dollar empire founded in Detroit.[26] In 1969, the Temptations had a million-selling record with "Message from a Black Man," a song whose title was a paraphrase of the title of the Messenger's book, *Message to the Blackman in America*. Intentionally or not, the song's refrain echoed what

Farrakhan and Muhammad were saying on the radio: "No matter how hard you [white people] try, you can't stop me now." Lest anyone miss their point, the album also included a seven-minute song called "Slave." Baritone Otis Williams wore a dashiki for the cover shot, and the other Temptations were clad in bell-bottoms and other attire associated with the "revolution."

The most ominous new forces in the African-American recording industry hailed from Harlem, where in 1969 a small ensemble of poets gave birth to a new form of black music called rap (though it was a mix of jazz and poetry). The group, which was officially formed on May 19 (Malcolm X's birthday), called itself The Last Poets. Lyrics on their self-titled album, which soared to the top of the charts that year, further illustrated the growth of the Black Power movement.[27] With national sales of *Muhammad Speaks* topping the million mark, people were listening to the NOI's message even when they could not accept the Messenger.

Another aspect of the NOI that appealed to blacks was the dietary regimen and healthy look of its members. In economically depressed areas where dental and health insurance were rare, home remedies and prayer were often the only answers to a health crisis. Members of the NOI seemed to radiate good health (Farrakhan, who looks twenty years younger than his age, is a prime example). To capitalize on the growing interest in the Muslim diet, Muhammad published a book titled *How to Eat to Live*,[28] advertised in *Muhammad Speaks* for $1.25, in which he suggested radical changes in the African-American diet. Though he was in poor health himself, Muhammad's book argued persuasively that people would live a lot longer if they ate fewer meals, restricted their diets primarily to fruits and vegetables, and avoided alcohol and tobacco. Health would improve significantly in less than a month, he wrote, if pork products were taken off the table.[29]

This renewed respectability of the NOI created serious concerns at FBI headquarters. On January 7, the Chicago SAC received a memorandum from headquarters regarding the role it might play in neutralizing the NOI.

Although the Nation of Islam (NOI) does not presently advocate violence by its members . . . the membership is organized and poses a real racial threat. The NOI is responsible for the largest black nationalist newspaper, which has been used by other black extremists. The NOI appears to be the personal fiefdom of Elijah Muhammad. When he dies a power struggle can be expected and the NOI could change direction. . . . In this connection Chicago should consider what counterintelligence action might be needed now or at the time of Elijah Muhammad's death to bring about such a change in NOI philosophy. . . . What are the positions of our top-level informants in regard to leadership? How could potential leaders be turned or neutralized? The alternative to changing the philosophy of the NOI is the destruction of the organization. This might be accomplished through generating factionalism among the contenders for Elijah Muhammad's leadership or through legal action in probate court on his death. Chicago should consider the question of how to generate factionalism necessary to destroy the NOI by splitting it into several groups.[30]

On January 22, 1969, the Chicago SAC sent a boastful reply:

Over the years considerable thought has been given, and action taken with Bureau approval, relating to methods through which the NOI could be discredited in the eyes of the general black populace or through which factionalism among the leadership could be created. Serious consideration has also been given toward developing ways and means of changing NOI philosophy to one whereby the members could be developed into useful citizens and the organization developed into one emphasizing religion—the brotherhood of mankind—and self-improvement. Factional disputes have been developed—the most notable being Malcolm X Little.

After taking credit for the split between the Messenger and Malcolm, the SAC focused on the future.[31]

It appears the NOI is on a collision course for a factional split after the death of Muhammad. The power struggle could well develop among members of the "Royal Family" and could well involve some of the more prominent NOI ministers who could well align themselves with a certain member of the "Royal Family" or could entertain illusions of "ruling" a segment of the NOI. It is not beyond the realm of possibility that any one of Muhammad's more prominent ministers could make a power play on Muhammad's death. At present, however, Muhammad seemingly has all of them totally subservient to him. . . . As mentioned earlier, the spiritual aspects of the NOI must be maintained to keep the group going. It is recalled that when Malcolm X Little defected and later was murdered, many dissenting NOI members sought out Wallace Muhammad for spiritual leadership. When Wallace Muhammad returned to his father on another occasion and was presented to NOI members gathered at the Annual Muslim Convention in Chicago he was wildly acclaimed. It is felt Wallace Muhammad is still warmly thought of by his father and he is the only son or daughter who is not monetarily motivated. It is known Muhammad still asks about Wallace.[32]

On February 4, the feared chief of security for the NOI was discredited in a nearly lethal fashion. Three gunmen forced their way into Raymond Sharrieff's mansion and made him lie face-down on the living room floor. After they tied his hands, they asked him where he kept his money. Sharrieff told them that there was money in his office on the third floor. After tying up Sharrieff's family as well as the maid, the gunmen went to the office and took $23,000, jewelry, and business papers from the safe. Asked to explain why he had such a large sum in the house, Sharrieff said he had planned to use the money to buy new spring clothing for a store he owned on East 51st Street on the South Side.[33] The Chicago media had a field day with the robbery. "One well-known Chicago TV news commentator compared the robbery on the air as being comparable to that of a police chief's home being robbed," the Chicago SAC reported to FBI headquarters on February 17. At the Saviour's Day convention, Sharrieff insinuated that the gunmen were somehow tied to supporters of Malcolm X. Before a crowd of thousands at the Chicago Coliseum, Sharrieff railed that "Malcolm was an enemy to us. . . . He was an enemy to our cause. We don't like him. Our enemies are those who are sympathetic to Malcolm's cause. Stay away from us and we will stay away from you."[34]

Sharrieff was believed to be directing his comments to Charles 37X Morris, Malcolm's former chief bodyguard. Morris had founded an organization in Harlem called the Mau Mau Society after he was expelled from the OAAU.[35] Using the name Charles Kenyatta (in tribute to Jomo Kenyatta), he took the name of his organization from Malcolm's quip that the Mau Mau was needed in America. Kenyatta's group was composed mainly of dishonorably discharged Vietnam War veterans who could not find jobs. Well-known in Harlem, Kenyatta was one of several activists who accompanied New York mayor John Lindsay to Dr. Martin Luther King's funeral.[36] A few months after the funeral, Kenyatta received a grant from the Urban Task Force to help contain violence in Harlem in the wake of the assassination. However, according to press reports, the Mau Mau also engaged in extortion, robbery, and other illegal activities. The group had a small chapter in Boston and one in Chicago, and it was the Chicago chapter that Sharrieff seemed to suggest was behind the robbery.[37]

The Messenger's comments on Saviour's Day in 1969 were more disconcerting than ever. After ridiculing African Americans for worshipping a Caucasian image of Christ, he said: "You don't find in America a little black nigger God."[38] It was an exceptionally vile statement, which may have been directed at Clarence 35X Smith, another former Black Muslim who had established a rival organization in Harlem.

Like Kenyatta, Smith, whose real name was Clarence Smith Jowers, was a former member of Malcolm's security detail. His group was called the Blood Brothers in early 1965, but the name was changed to the Five Percenters after Malcolm's assassination—a reference to Fard's belief that 85 percent of black people were easily led like cattle, another 10 percent would always be Uncle Toms, and the remaining 5 percent were so intellectually advanced that they were like gods on Earth. As "born warriors," they had a duty to liberate the other 95 percent. Smith wasn't a mere prophet; he taught his teenage followers that he was Allah.[39] After King's assassination, Smith allegedly used his association with Kenyatta to contact Mayor Lindsay about funding for a so-called street academy, which was essentially a night school for intermediate and high school dropouts. On June 13, Smith was shot at four o'clock in the morning while sitting in the lobby of the Martin Luther King Towers apartment complex.[40] "Brothers, first I hope you know the sadness in my heart at Allah's death," the mayor said (making him the first sitting mayor to state publicly that God was dead), "His contribution was an important one these last few years, most especially in the world of education."[41]

Ordinarily, the NOI would not have been on the list of suspects. But Smith was killed less than a week after members of the NOI attempted the murder of Kenyatta, who was shot on Valentine Avenue. "The Black Muslims are out to get me," he mumbled to paramedics as they treated bullet wounds in his left arm and the left side of his chest.[42] Media accounts linked both shootings to the NOI, as there were rumors that the Messenger had ordered his Muslims to eradicate all splinter groups. When the rumor was given credence by a front-page story in the *New York Daily News,* Farrakhan accused the government of complicity in the violence:

> We, the Muslims, are extremely outraged by the vicious, wicked deliberate sowing of divisive, slanderous seeds by the *Daily News,* which appears to be designed to cause black people to fight and kill each other . . . it appears the police and the white power structure are tired of the Muslims and black militants and would like to rid themselves of both [by] instigating, provoking, and inciting innocent black people to fight and kill each other through false accusations.

The NOI, he claimed, had a cooperative relationship "with the Five Percenters and many other black groups who disagree with our views."[43] However, given Smith's claim of being God, it was unlikely that the NOI had any relationship with that group, and they clearly did not cooperate with Wallace Muhammad's quasi-religious Afro-Descendant Upliftment Society. Wallace had remained at his father's side until the threats of violence subsided after Malcolm's death, and then broke away in late 1965 to reorganize his own group.[44]

With so many defections, only two nationally recognized ministers remained with Muhammad by late 1969—Farrakhan and Muhammad Ali—and Ali wanted out. When the boxer, whom the mainstream media insisted upon calling Cassius Clay four years after his name change, confessed that he was considering a return to the ring, the Messenger was furious.[45] His debts were mounting, Ali said, and he needed to box, at least temporarily, to make an honest living; boxing was the only means he had to earn the large sum of money he needed. The implication of what Ali was saying did not dawn on the boxer, but it struck the Messenger as an insult. When Ali made a statement to the press that he was considering returning to boxing, the Messenger immediately ordered him to come to Chicago. Once Ali and Minister Jeremiah X Pugh arrived at the Messenger's home, it was clear that the Champ was in big trouble.[46]

"I don't want to be involved with anyone who was so weak as to go crawling on hands and knees to the white man for a little money," the Messenger told Ali during a heated harangue on April 4.[47] His most illustrious acolyte could not serve the NOI as a minister and at the same time earn a living from a primitive, violent sport. Islam represented peace, the Messenger told Ali, and for him to consider returning to the ring conflicted with the teachings of the Holy Quran. "We, the Muslims," Elijah wrote later in *Muhammad Speaks,* "are not with Muhammad Ali in his desire to work in the sports world for the sake of a little money."[48] The Messenger suspended Ali for a year, and told him that he was taking his Arabic name back and that Ali was to resume using his slave name, Cassius Clay. The Messenger didn't realize that expelling Ali was the best thing he had ever done for the impressionable young man. The boxer stuck with his new name in spite of Muhammad's edict. Wallace, the troublesome heir, returned to his father after Ali's expulsion.

During his suspension, Ali's lawyers received good news on their appeal of his draft conviction. In late March 1969, Eleanor Holmes Norton and Chauncey Eskridge won a review of his case after discovering that prosecutors may have used information gathered from the wiretap on Muhammad's telephones as evidence during the trial. At a hearing on June 5, FBI agent C. Barry Pickett testified that he had been part of a team of agents in Phoenix who listened to all of the Messenger's conversations—on the phone and in the bedroom—from 1962 to 1966. "My instructions were to monitor conversations both in the home and by telephone and make notes of conversations by Elijah Muhammad."[49] Pickett also testified that FBI agents intercepted King's conversations from 1964 until the day that he was assassinated. Robert Nichols, another FBI agent called to testify, corroborated Pickett's testimony, and other evidence established that the wiretaps extended as far back as 1960.[50]

Ali's chief counsel, Charles Morgan Jr., introduced into evidence transcripts of calls between his client and the Messenger, and others between the latter and King. It was the first time that the government had publicly admitted to intrusive investigations of the two black leaders. Attorney General Ramsey Clark told reporters that when he asked Hoover every three months for a list of all authorized wiretaps, "the names of Dr. King and Muhammad never appeared on such a list."[51] When asked to comment on the revelation, Muhammad dismissed it as old news. He had known for some time, he said, that his phones were bugged. That was true, but he also had let down his guard on enough occasions that the federal government, were it so inclined, could have indicted him on any number of charges, from tax evasion to accessory to murder. The only reason it hadn't was because high-level officials feared that the outcry from Muslims and sympathetic religious groups would make him a martyr.[52]

The Messenger prided himself on keeping Muslims safe from the violence that was taking the lives of so many black nationalists as the decade drew to a close, and attributed his success in this to his refusal to permit them to bear arms. By and large his strategy worked, but there were exceptions. On June 7, a young Muslim in Macon was killed by two white detectives. Charles 7X Fambro's apparent offense was selling *Muhammad Speaks* on a downtown street corner after being told that he was violating laws against loitering. A scuffle ensued as the detectives tried to subdue Fambro, who was joined by other Muslims standing nearby. Someone pulled a gun—police said it was the Muslims—and Fambro was fatally wounded.[53]

Incidentally, the National Society of Afro-American Policemen honored the Messenger eight days later at their annual convention in New York City. During the ceremony at the Waldorf Astoria, Leonard 12X Weir, president of the society, said the Messenger was being honored for his successes in "business, education, communication through various self-help programs, and for his effectiveness in lifting the black man out of the servant class among the races of the world."[54] On September 14, 1969, the NOI held its Educational Benefit Banquet at the same hotel, and the Messenger hired Duke Ellington and his band for the event, advertising it with a full-page ad in *Muhammad Speaks*.[55]

No matter what the Messenger did, he could not escape Malcolm's shadow. World War II had Betty Grable as the quintessential pinup; the Black Revolution had Malcolm. Muhammad's harshest blow came with the fall school semester, when he discovered that the Crane campus of Chicago City College was going to change its name in memory of Malcolm X. Writing in the October 3 issue of *Muhammad Speaks,* John Ali condemned school and government officials for the decision:

> A great affront has been made to the black people of Chicago and America by naming a school after Malcolm right in the home[town] of the Honorable Elijah Muhammad. . . . This effort throughout the country to glorify Malcolm by the former slave master and his puppets is a great attempt to weaken the leadership position of Messenger Muhammad or to embarrass him. . . . We are well on to this trick of picking dead men (Jesus, Booker T. Washington, Martin Luther King, and now Malcolm) . . . for black people to follow. . . . The black man of America will not be fooled by all this glorification and elevation of Malcolm.[56]

However, notwithstanding the NOI's vociferous protests, the school was renamed as planned.

In spite of the appearance of expanding wealth, the Messenger's fortune was actually contracting. In November, the media discovered that the NOI had quietly purchased farmland in Alabama. When white citizens in rural Ashville learned that Muhammad had already bought 1,000 acres in their community and was making similar purchases in Georgia, they declared a "legal war" on the land sales.[57] The war was successful in part because a 1961 state law made it illegal for a Muslim to remain in Alabama more than a few days without registering his presence and disclosing "such matters as finances and membership roll."[58] Progressive Land Developers, which was owned by Herbert, John Ali, and former Cleveland Browns football star Jim Brown, had also failed to register as an out-of-state corporation before buying the land. "This deal is a threat to Christianity and is un-American," the local KKK Imperial Wizard said. "It's part of a concentrated effort to take over the eight states of the Bible Belt."[59] The "Muslim Registration Law" was later overturned after a court fight, but the problem of violence against Muslim farmers remained unsolved. After 63 out of 225 head of cattle were poisoned or shot, the Messenger abandoned the farm project. "This proves what the white people are," he said in a statement released to the media. "They don't want the black man to have any freedom to do for self. . . . We don't want to be anywhere where we're not wanted." The land, most of it purchased from a white businessman in violation of the Muslim Compromise of 1960, was put up for sale. A Muslim official said Muhammad would sell it to anyone, even the Klan.[60]

The irrational fear of domestic intelligence experts that America was being overrun by enemies reached its predictable conclusion two months later. On May 4 a Vietnam War protest rally suddenly turned violent at Kent State University, where 97 percent of the students were from Ohio and 94 percent were white. When the smoke from the rifles of the National Guard cleared, four students were dead. Neil Young's musical eulogy, "Ohio," was in the stores eight days later, and on the Billboard charts for months. The Messenger had predicted that the American government would fall in 1970, and in a way he was right, because Kent State represented "the final breach of the generation gap."[61]

The pervading loss of innocence was symbolized by skepticism about Apollo 11, which many regarded as a hoax staged in the Arizona desert to divert attention from the war.[62] There was a growing sense that "the end" really was near, that the presidency of Richard Nixon was morally bankrupt. Dick Gregory, the comedian and social activist who was the only man with enough courage to tell Malcolm that Muhammad "was nothing but a pimp," also spoke candidly about the murders at Kent State, suggesting that they were, in reality, a modern lynching.[63] After Kent State, the powers that be recognized that the "new nigger" coming to dinner wasn't the Black Knight trying to capture the White Queen. Gregory said, only half in jest, that the "new niggers" were the white teenage sons and daughters of a nation in the grip of a social revolution.[64] Kent State proved, he argued, that if you crossed the power structure, bullets fired to protect the "industrial–military complex" would not slow down to determine the color of your skin.

On November 7, 1969, Deputy Assistant to the President for Domestic Affairs Egil Krogh Jr. wrote to the FBI to inquire about foreign funding received by "revolutionary groups" in America.[65] The Bureau sent its reply on February 26, 1970, as tens of thousands of Muslims gathered in Chicago for the Annual Saviour's Day convention, listing more than a dozen "revolutionary groups" whose funding was possibly from foreign sources. Among them were the Republic of New Africa, a black separatist group formed by Milton Henry, a prominent Detroit lawyer once allied with Malcolm X; the Black Panther Party; and the NOI.[66] Under the heading "Nation of Islam," the FBI noted:

Approximately 100 temples or mosques of this fanatical all-Negro cult exist in the United States today with a total membership in excess of [number redacted]. The membership supports this organization. Principal income is derived from member dues, special membership assessments and from sale of its official publication, *Muhammad Speaks*.[67]

On March 12, Charles D. Brennan, a high-level FBI official, made a point of bringing his correspondence with Krogh to Sullivan's attention:

By letter dated 2/26/70, in response to a specific request, we furnished the White House with material concerning income sources of revolutionary groups. Such an inquiry is indicative of the high-level interest in the financial aspects of revolutionary activity.[68]

Had the FBI done its homework, it would have discovered that the Messenger's money wasn't coming from overseas, at least not directly. Most of the funds came from the nickels and dimes of his followers, but at the time of Krogh's inquiry, some of the money lining the coffers of the NOI bore the taint of organized crime. The main point of criminal entry into the NOI was the Philadelphia mosque. After a government crackdown on black street gangs, a peace treaty was signed between all the gangs except for the one known as Twentieth and Carpenter Street. Since the treaty made it difficult for that gang to operate, scores of its members joined the Philadelphia mosque with the intention of hiding its felonious activities behind a religious façade.[69] Known alternately as the "Muslim Mafia," "Black Incorporated," and the "Death Squad," the Muslim Mafia engaged in the distribution of illicit drugs, primarily cocaine and marijuana, and later, a drug known as PCP.[70]

Among the ringleaders were Robert X "Nudie" Mims, Sam X Christian, Ronald X Harvey, Herschel X Williams, and Lonnie X Dawson. These weren't foot soldiers, but key members of the Philadelphia mosque. Harvey, for instance, was an assistant minister, while Christian was captain of the FOI and Mims was the secretary (and later an assistant minister). The Muslim Mafia developed ties to major crime families on the East Coast, including the Gambino and Scarfo syndicates.[71] Mims and Dawson worked out one deal that allowed organized crime figures to sell heroin in certain sections of the Philadelphia ghetto, and Dawson arranged another deal for PCP to be sold in the same areas. Harvey had a reputation as a hit man, while Christian made a living stealing and reselling cars.

In early January 1971, eight members of the Muslim Mafia robbed Dubrows Furniture Store after the owners refused extortion demands.[72] During the robbery, one customer was killed, another burned, and several customers tortured. During the subsequent investigation, Mims fled to Chicago, where, instead of handing him over to the authorities, NOI officials made him one of the Messenger's personal bodyguards. When the FBI finally arrested Mims, he was working as the manager of a hardware store owned by the Messenger's family.[73] Police seized his customized Cadillac, for which he had paid $17,000 in cash. They also found pieces of identification in eighteen different names in his wallet.[74]

Mim's reassignment was done at the request of Jeremiah X Pugh, the minister of the Philadelphia mosque at the time and the NOI's high priest of hypocrisy. Pugh was the minister who, over Malcolm's objections, struck a deal with the KKK while he was minister of the Atlanta mosque in 1960. In Philadelphia, he sold his people a bill of goods about how Islam would awaken them, then turned his head while gatekeepers sold narcotics to lull them back to sleep.

The advent of organized crime into NOI affairs made it easy for the FBI to provoke violent disagreements between Muslims and the police and between Muslims and other black organizations. On June 26, 1970, Moore recommended to Sullivan that the Bureau increase disruption in black communities by triggering a war between the NOI and the Black Panther Party.[75] The primary purpose of the proposed COINTELPRO, Moore wrote, was threefold: it would make both groups less attractive to potential new members, it could result in the arrest of high-level officials in both groups, and lastly, it could help stem the spread of the Black Panther's newspaper, which advocated a political revolution instead of a religious one. It could "curtail circulation of the Black Panther newspaper," the memorandum stated, "by inducing retaliatory reaction by the NOI for loss of revenue" owing to that paper's competition with *Muhammad Speaks* in the black community. If it were brought to the Messenger's attention that his newspaper was losing sales to the Black Panthers, it "might well be the spark to ignite the fuel of conflict between the two organizations," Moore observed in another memo to Sullivan, "both [of which] are extremely money conscious. . . . Elijah Muhammad . . . might well be influenced to take positive steps to counteract the sale of Black Panther Party newspapers."[76]

This COINTELPRO was another one with predictable results. On February 15, 1971, a Panther and a Muslim got into a fistfight over newspaper territory. Other Panthers and Muslims joined in, causing a

melee in Atlanta's business district. Within twenty minutes of the outbreak, one hundred policemen in riot gear were at the scene. Twenty-one
people were arrested, and there was thousands of dollars in property
damage.[77]

Moore's memo was written a few weeks before Huey P. Newton's
release from prison for allegedly killing a police officer. The ultimate
irony, however, was that of all the black nationalists and revolutionaries
who were targeted by COINTELPRO either by trumped-up charges
(Geronimo Pratt, Newton, Bobby Seale) or FBI provocation (California
Black Panthers John Huggins and Bunchy Carter, and Malcolm X),
apparently only one escaped unscathed: Louis Farrakhan. When the FBI
decided in 1964 to promote a violent schism between the Messenger and
Malcolm, Farrakhan played a pivotal role in creating the circumstances
that led to Malcolm's murder. And less than six months after Moore
received approval to start a war between the Black Panthers and the NOI,
Farrakhan proved again to be a most valuable player. Just as Newton was
beginning to reorganize the West Coast chapters of the Black Panther
Party, Farrakhan "began running around the Northern California Bay
area, where our base was being built, incorporating foul little formula-
tions subtly denigrating the party into his speeches," Panther leader
Elaine Brown remembers bitterly.[78] "We in the Nation say that a man is
what he eats. . . . We say that if a man eats pig, he must be a pig," Farrakhan would say. What Farrakhan had done was intellectually dishonest, and no one understood that better than Newton, a philosopher who
knew Farrakhan was preaching pretzel logic. The Panthers had altered
the derogatory line "the only good Indian is a dead Indian" to read: "the
only good pig is a dead pig." And of course, the rallying cry was "Kill the
pigs," referring to the police. The Panther's barbecue picnics were not
only symbolic of its quixotic triumph over the police but also were an
inexpensive means of feeding hungry people. Angered by Farrakhan's
provocations in an area that had already seen too much bloodshed, Newton invited him to his apartment for a philosophical discussion. Newton
reminded the Muslim minister that while the Black Panthers "appreciated the teachings of the Honorable Elijah Muhammad," the party lived
by the "principles taught by Minister Malcolm X."[79]

Then, with the precision of a panther, Newton began verbally cornering his prey. He asked Farrakhan if he really believed that a man is literally what he eats, and the Muslim minister told him that it was the gospel truth.

"Are you a man?"

Farrakhan assured him again that, verily, it was so.

With that, Newton moved in for the kill. "If man is what he eats, and you are a man," Newton said, pausing for effect, "what part of the man do *you* eat?"[80]

CHAPTER SIXTEEN

AND MERCURY FALLS

The words of Mercury are harsh after the songs of Apollo.
—Love's Labours Lost, *act V, scene ii*

Faith, zeal, curiosity, and more earthly passions of malice and ambition kindled the flame of theological factions, whose conflicts were sometimes bloody and always implacable.
—*Edward Gibbon,*
The Decline and Fall of the Roman Empire[1]

Having averted a violent confrontation with the Muslims, the five-year-old Black Panther Party soon had more chapters than the forty-year-old NOI. By late 1971, the FBI backed off from the idea of fomenting a war between the two groups. Attempts to start turf wars over newspaper routes were too costly and inconsequential, and it would, in any case, have been difficult to trigger real violence when one side (the NOI) refused to go armed. The Panthers' growth was due to a consensus in the black community that the Nixon administration's harsh domestic policies reduced the underclass African American's options for survival to rejecting everything America stood for and joining the NOI or similar self-help organizations that sprouted like crabgrass across the urban landscape.

While the Black Panther Party was in the forefront of such self-help groups, it inspired at least two dozen similar organizations in nearly every major city in the country, among them a radicalized CORE, the Black P Stone Nation in Chicago, Percy Greene's ACTION in St. Louis, the Black Liberators, and on college and high school campuses, the Black Student Union. All became major targets of COINTELPRO campaigns that resulted in frameups, shootouts with police and rival organizations, and murder.[2] A memo from Moore to Charles D. Brennan began: "To recommend that attached airtel to all offices be sent regarding discreet preliminary inquiries on all Black Student Unions (BSU) and similar groups on college campuses."[3] FBI officials also made it a point to note that laws could be broken if necessary to destroy the effectiveness of the organizations. As early as the summer of 1966, Cartha DeLoach was made aware that Sullivan had authorized burglary as a means of obtaining information on COINTELPRO targets. The Bureau used "black bag job" as a euphemism for burglary. In a "Do Not File" memorandum on July 19, 1966, Sullivan explained:

The following is set forth in regard to your request concerning what authority we have for "black bag" jobs and for the background of our policy and procedures in such matters. We do not obtain authorization for "black bag" jobs from outside the Bureau. Such a technique involves trespass and is clearly illegal; therefore, it would be impossible to obtain any legal sanction for it. Despite this, "black bag" jobs have been used because they represent an invaluable technique in combating subversive activities of a clandestine nature aimed directly at undermining and destroying our nation.[4]

As a primary target of COINTELPRO in which the government used every possible means—legal and illegal—to undermine it, the NOI started to unravel by the early 1970s. National Secretary John Ali had controlled the purse strings of the organization for over a decade and had become a wealthy man. In addition to his part ownership of Progressive Land Developers, he incorporated a company in his own name and was part owner of Main Bout Inc., a firm that managed Muhammad Ali and negotiated his boxing matches.[5] His regime ended abruptly in May 1970, when he was summarily dismissed from his position. One rumor had it that the Messenger had grown suspicious of John Ali's loyalty as he had been publicly identified as someone with connections to the FBI.[6] "The Messenger thought he was an FBI informant," a top aide to Farrakhan confided (author Louis Lomax described John Ali as a former FBI agent in one book, and as someone with ties to the Bureau in a sequel).[7] Another rumor held that the dismissal was due to "mishandled funds." After weeks of speculation, Raymond Sharrieff told reporters that Ali was "relieved of his duties as national secretary" because the Messenger had found "someone more competent."[8] Abass Rassoull was named as his replacement. The reason for his suspension was never fully explained, and John Ali wrote in *Muhammad Speaks* that the allegations resulting in his expulsion were false.[9]

The Messenger's inner circle was now nearly completely destroyed. Wallace was gone again, Herbert was too involved in managing Muhammad Ali's revived boxing career, John Ali had lost his trust, and he had reservations about Farrakhan. The only key player remaining was his son-in-law Raymond Sharrieff. In October 1971, someone with a shotgun fired five rounds into Sharrieff's Chicago mansion. Sharrieff and his wife Ethel were visible in a window facing the street at the time of the attack, and he was hit in the arm by several pellets.[10] In late December, there was another attempt against Sharrieff when someone driving down the Dan Ryan Expressway fired a shot through his office window, narrowly missing his secretary. According to a reporter who was in the office when Sharrieff arrived, the latter began to shake at the thought of what could have happened.[11]

The Messenger also felt threatened by Chicago's Jesse Jackson, president of Operation Breadbasket and People United to Save Humanity, or PUSH. Jackson's trademarks were his mod attire, fondness for rhymes, and an Afro hairdo as big as a small child. The Messenger called upon Jackson several times for religious discourse, and the meetings were, by all accounts, cordial. There was never a meeting of the minds, however. For one thing, Jackson made what the Messenger considered heretical comments about the biblical David, which he attributed to Jackson's lack of seminary training.[12] After one meeting ended on a sour note in early 1972, the Messenger denounced Jackson just as he had Dr. King when he had failed to sway King to his way of thinking six years earlier:

Take Reverend Jackson, poor boy. Making a fool out of himself to be called Reverend Jackson by the devil . . . Jackson is the name of devils. If he'd come over to me, I'd give him an honorable name. . . . We talked together a few times, but he just loves to be called Reverend by the blue-eyed devil. . . . They will dump him after a while, like they do all who follow them. The devil acts as though he's worshipping Martin Luther King. After Martin Luther King visited my house, he [white agents] sat out there in his car and tuned in on what we were talking about. I guess he heard him [King] say that he agreed with me, that he is the devil. He saw that Elijah was winning their disciple over, so they shoot him and set up a hypocrite for Elijah, and that was Malcolm.[13]

For a man who claimed to know the exact date of birth of the first Caucasian, the Messenger's knowledge of recent history was somewhat wanting.

The source of the Messenger's jealousy was simple: while Muhammad was out trying to net bluefish, Jackson snared a blue whale. By the early 1970s, Jackson's organizations had received several large grants from the federal government for poverty programs. Muhammad's people were doing the same work—converting "unemployable" inner-city youths into productive members of society—but were doing so with the nickels and dimes collected from members. In the summer of 1970, the Messenger decided to follow Jackson's lead. For the first time in its history, the NOI requested government aid for financing job-training programs. On July 29, fourteen government representatives visited Muhammad's home in Chicago "to work out a program that may yield the Muslims $40,000,000 in matching funds."[14] According to the reports, the NOI's program would be open to all races, and would train recruits in automotive repair, printing services, and similar blue-collar vocations.

When Barbara Reynolds, an outspoken Chicago-based reporter, noted the paradox of the antiwhite, anti-American leader suddenly groveling for money like others labeled by pundits as "poverty pimps," Muhammad vented his rage in the pages of *Muhammad Speaks*:

> You like to make light of each other. A Black brother whom you think the white man does not like, you like to make mock of him in order to get the white man to like you. I will never let a black man nor a black woman interview me any more for a white man, for they love to say something evil and false against me for the sake of the smile of the white enemy of all of us Black people.[15]

The Messenger accused Reynolds of putting quotes in his mouth, an accusation which proved groundless. After the brouhaha subsided, the NOI went ahead with filing the proper applications for government grants.

In January 1972, after years of activity that had resulted in harm to almost everyone who had been close to him, Muhammad was targeted for assassination by a group of Muslims who felt that he had betrayed them. Following a complicated roadmap, the dissidents set out to eradicate corruption in the NOI. They planned to stop in Louisiana, where a Muslim minister was known to associate with prostitutes,[16] and to end their jihad in Chicago, where they reportedly planned to kill Muhammad and other members of the royal family.[17] In any event, the plans went awry before they could get out of Baton Rouge. On January 10, the group got into a gun battle with police that left two white officers and two Muslim vigilantes dead. Governor John J. McKeithen, who called the Muslims "a bunch of damn maniacs," called out 800 National Guardsmen to restore order in the black section of the city.[18] Several black eyewitnesses to the shootout said the Muslims fired first.

The Messenger accused the rising number of discontented Muslims of hypocrisy. In his *Muhammad Speaks* column, he charged that "white devils furnish the crazy, savage black brother of the Muslims with the deadly weapons with which to kill his black brother."[19]

His "let them eat cake" attitude, however, blinded him to the wrongs he committed with abandon. The Baton Rouge Muslims, like other splinter groups, believed that Muhammad was squandering the wealth of his organization. This belief gained credence several days before the shootout when Muhammad revealed (after media reports of the obvious) that he was constructing a new $500,000 mansion for himself and four additional mansions for his children and aides at a cost of $250,000 each.[20]

On Saviour's Day 1972, the Messenger proudly paraded his accomplishments before a crowd of 15,000 at the armory in Chicago. The NOI, he said, now owned about 25,000 acres of land.[21] When its importing business and other concerns were tallied, its net worth was $75 million. While that sounded like a great deal to the menial workers who formed the core of the NOI's membership, the more educated members knew that it was a mere pittance compared to what the NOI should have been worth after nearly twenty years of regular tithing and business revenues. Some Muslims also recognized signs that Muhammad was reverting to ideas that had landed him and his followers in jail in 1932. Near the end of his speech, the Messenger declared that God was "beginning to change me into Himself."[22]

The Messenger had also begun to move more toward Sufism and the notion that each man has the potential to be a god. "God and I love you so much that He sent me to tell you that which is to make gods out of you. You say, 'I know I will never be a god.' You already are a god."[23] If anyone knew the inherent danger in teaching a functionally illiterate and angry man that he is a god, it was the Messenger. But when he announced that God was "turning me into Himself," it was obvious that he had forgotten his own past. It was only a matter of time before some of his followers gave a literal interpretation to his words.

While he was in Chicago asserting his divinity on February 26, police in Trinidad made a gruesome discovery involving former Black Muslims. In the garden of a commune run by Michael Abdul Malik and Hakim Abdullah Jamal, investigators unearthed the body of Hale Kimga, a white woman permitted into the compound only because she was Jamal's lover. Her adopted name was an anagram for "Gale and Hakim." Jamal's given name was Eugene Allen Donaldson.[24] A former member of the NOI, he quit in 1965 to join Malcolm X's new organization. He was married to Malcolm X's cousin, a relationship that he exploited to the fullest. In March 1968, while seeking funds to start the Malcolm X Foundation in Los Angeles, Jamal told the *Los Angeles Sentinel* that he was proposing a "Malcolm X Holiday" law to bring awareness to the people of Malcolm's contributions to black history. "Malcolm X was my cousin. He was one of the greatest teachers of black people this world has ever known."[25] Kimga, whose real name was Gale Ann Plugge Benson, was the daughter of Leonard Plugge, a former member of Great Britain's Parliament. She was also the half-sister of Jacqueline Bouvier Kennedy, as Gale and her twin brother Greville were actually the result of an affair between Leonard's wife, Ann Plugge, and Jack Bouvier, Jacqueline Bouvier Kennedy's father.[26]

Jamal was a man of divided loyalties: he was one of many black militant leaders whose behavior gave birth to a new expression during the Black Power movement: "talking black and sleeping white." The phrase referred, of course, to black men who spent the morning giving inspiring speeches about the beauty of black women, but spent the night whispering sweet nothings into the ears of white women, women who made room for these wild and dangerous "black stallions" in spacious Malibu boudoirs. The Los Angeles Police Department's Domestic Intelligence Division leaked its dossier on Jamal to Hillard Hamm, publisher of the *Metropolitan Gazette* in Compton.[27] The LAPD (which kept Muhammad Ali and other celebrities under surveillance during their visits) had received the FBI's hefty COINTELPRO file on Jamal.[28] Included in the information were numerous reports revealing that Jamal was having an affair with Jean Seberg, one of Hollywood's most popular actresses (she starred in Otto Preminger's *Joan of Arc*). Hamm's revelation badly damaged Jamal's credibility among black militants, so he took off for Europe, leaving his wife, Dorothy, and his children behind. He said he was going there to write his autobiography. What he omitted to say was that he was going to live with Seberg in Paris.[29]

When the relationship soured, Jamal took Gale Benson as his new lover, and the two moved to London, where Jamal sold his memoirs, *From the Dead Level,* to Andre Deutsch, a small publishing concern. He was also having a passionate affair with his editor, Diana Athill.[30] "He was a very intelligent man by nature and good-looking," Athill remembered. The affair ended after Jamal started referring to himself as Allah and insisted that Benson call him God: "The man was mad and the girl was mad." The last time Athill saw him, Jamal was dangerously paranoid. Gale and Jamal left London for Trinidad along with Michael Abdul Malik (known as Michael X in London).[31]

In the first week of January 1972, Jamal and Gale Benson got into a violent argument. No one knows what happened immediately after the argument, except that Jamal left suddenly.[32] While he was away from the compound, Benson decided to take a walk in the garden. She saw some of Malik's "soldiers" digging a ditch. Nervous about being there without her protector, she stopped near the large hole and asked them why they were digging. They were following orders, one of them replied; she had nothing to worry about. When the hole was about six feet deep, Malik sneaked up behind Benson and squeezed her neck, using his left arm as a vise. He released her quickly, so that she fell to the ground next to the hole. Before she could get up, Malik took a machete and stabbed her dozens of times in the throat and chest. As she pleaded for her life, Malik and his men pushed her into the hole and buried her alive.[33] Jamal hastily left Trinidad for America, settling in Boston's Roxbury district, where he was born in 1931.

When Benson's body was discovered, the scandalous story was on the front page of every tabloid in Great Britain.[34] On March 3, Malik was arrested for murdering Benson and for the murder of Joseph Skerritt, a cult member whose body was unearthed on February 24 in another grave in the compound. Both, it transpired, had been murdered because they were suspected of being informants.[35] Malik was hanged for the crimes. When investigators tracked down Jamal and questioned him, he denied any knowledge of the murders. By the time stories of Jamal's relationship with Benson had faded from the American media, the NOI was stirring up trouble for him over statements in his book regarding Malcolm X's assassination.[36] Members of the Mau Mau also were angry with Jamal. They blamed him for neglecting Malcolm's cousin and accused him of being a traitor for leaving his wife for a white woman. On May 2, eight members of the Mau Mau shot Jamal to death in Boston. Five were accused of his murder and later convicted.[37]

At the time of Jamal's murder, the Mau Mau organization had cells of terrorists across the country. Between May 3 and August 4 of 1972, the Chicago cell killed nine white people in the Illinois area. Six of the assassins were arrested on October 15, but the wars of the self-actualized black gods continued.[38] Another cult inspired by Fard launched a six-month killing spree in San Francisco in late 1973. Saying that they were sacrificing "blue-eyed devils" to Allah, the Death Angels had attacked twenty-three white people (fourteen of whom died) before seven members of the cult were arrested on May 2, 1974.[39] The Death Angels, it turned out, were members of Muhammad's Mosque No. 26 in San Francisco. The NOI posted bond for them and hired their lawyers. The ultimate irony of the murders was that one victim, Saleem Erakat, was a Muslim whose skin happened to be white.

The case became known as the "Zebra Murders" after the police radio band set aside for tracking the killers. But the description was pop-ularized because all the victims were white and the assailants were black. During the trial, attorney Edward W. Jacko tried explaining to the jury that the defendants had taken too literally the lessons about a Muslim having to kill four white people in order enter heaven. The defendants denied that their cult even existed, but four were ultimately convicted.[40]

Although the NOI was self-destructing, COINTELPRO actions con-tinued, and some resulted in deadly backfires. On April 14, 1972, two New York City police officers invaded the new Harlem mosque after receiving a bogus distress phone call from a man who identified himself as a detective trapped inside the mosque.[41] When the officers rushed into the building, they were attacked by at least ten Muslims. Within minutes of the surprise invasion, one officer was shot with his own gun and the other was beaten with his nightstick.[42] When the ordeal was over, Far-rakhan said at a press conference that he believed the attack was pre-meditated. "People saw patrol cars lined out in the streets minutes after the incident. They had submachine guns, automatic weapons, every kind of handgun imaginable and they were wearing bulletproof vests." The rapidity and scope of the response, Farrakhan said, suggested that the invasion was pretextual.[43] The attack dispelled Muhammad's theory that police would exempt the supposedly unarmed NOI from the types of attacks that had led to the assassination of Fred Hampton, Mark Clark, and other black revolutionaries. But it also gave him another chance to highlight the importance of unity among black organizations.

In July, the Messenger thought he had discovered a powerful new preacher. Joe Tex, an internationally recognized black entertainer at the zenith of his career, called a press conference to reveal his membership in the NOI. "You can call me Joseph X now," Tex said smiling.[44] A high school dropout in 1955, Joe Tex was earning as much as $500,000 by 1970 with a string of hits, among them "Skinny Legs," "Chicken Crazy," and "Hold On to What You Got," which sold more than a mil-lion copies. Tex announced in early 1972 that he was forsaking his music career to follow his heart. "I had wanted to get out a long time before this," he said during a national tour for the Messenger that brought him to Howard University that July. He confessed that he had joined the NOI in Miami in 1967 after attending meetings with his road manager, who was a Muslim. The only thing that had kept him from quitting the entertainment industry sooner, he said, was that he wasn't sure of what he would do after he revealed his allegiance to the Messenger.[45] "I did not want an ordinary job under the white man. I had that as a young man, picking cotton where it was 'nigger' this and 'nigger' that."

After discussing his dilemma with the Messenger, Tex said, he was advised that he could become a minister. "Being a minister is the highest you can go," he said euphorically. "I am very happy that the Honorable Elijah Muhammad is giving me a chance to get out of the song and dance business." One of the most successful crossover artists in history, he stunned white and black fans alike with his announcement. It was eerie to think that a man so frequently seen on television entertaining predominantly white audiences could suddenly start screaming "devil" and "savage" at them. Joe Tex's revelation had a tremendous impact on black teenagers, but like Muhammad Ali, he had a credibility problem. Most people simply refused to believe that he was serious. Whatever his intentions, the singer's stint as a minister was short-lived; he returned to the recording studio in 1974 and churned out at least five more albums.[46]

Although Muhammad Ali was not attracting the hordes of converts that Malcolm would have, he offered the Messenger access to foreign heads of state who literally worshipped the first Muslim athlete to become an international icon. When Ali was a young boxer, he won the admiration of a Muslim student who had participated in human rights demonstrations as a youth (including a protests against the French government's alleged involvement in Patrice Lumumba's assassination) and who worshipped Ali after meeting him once after a boxing match.[47] The student, who was the same age as Ali, shook his hand and tried to explain what a hero Ali was to him and to young Muslims throughout the world. When the student, Muammar Gadhafi, became premier of Libya, he offered the Messenger a $3,000,000 loan, negotiated by Muhammad Ali, to build a mosque in Chicago.[48] The U.S. State Department was furious, but the loan was not in violation of any laws so there was nothing the government could do. When the State Department contacted Abdalla Suwes, the Libyan ambassador in Washington, to complain about Gadhafi's "interference in domestic affairs," Suwes replied that Libya had no intention of doing so. "We are merely helping to build a church, and this is something American missionaries have done in many countries."[49]

African Americans beamed with pride that a foreign ruler had trusted one of their own enough to lend that much money, and had refused to back down in the face of an implied threat from the big, bad United States. Muhammad used the money to purchase the Saints Constantine and Helen Greek Orthodox Church on Chicago's South Side.[50] When Muhammad had wanted to buy the church in 1970, representatives of the government of Saudi Arabia had offered to pay nearly half the cost. Despite his desire to acquire the building for an Islamic Center, Muhammad was reluctant at that time to accept loans from the Saudis for fear of becoming "beholden" to the lenders. The original asking price was $3,000,000. But when the Messenger was the highest bidder, the seller hiked the price to $4,000,000.[51] It was an odd business move since no one else had offered anything near $3,000,000 for the building in a neighborhood that had gone from being all-white to 70 percent African American.

Gadhafi's loan was by far the most generous, but soon other Muslim heads of state joined in the philanthropy, the logic being that anyone who opposed Zionism can't be all bad. In late October 1972 Prince Abdalla Aziz Khalifa Althani of Qatar gave the Messenger a check for $100,000 during a visit to his Chicago mansion.[52] That was followed by a $125,000 loan from the government of Abu Dahbi "to aide the cause of Islam" in America.[53] Less than a year after the $3,000,000 Gadhafi loan, the Messenger asked for another one. This time, Gadhafi hesitated. Arab students had complained that the Muslims were an apostate group who denied the brotherhood of man.[54] The Messenger had hoped to get approval of the loan before Saviour's Day 1973, but was not successful. On the other hand, Gadhafi received such favorable publicity in black newspapers that he announced his intention to donate the money of the first loan instead of lending it.[55]

Not to be outdone, FBI official Moore wrote in a report for the Bureau's file on the NOI that the "Tax Division of the [Justice] Department currently has a tax claim suit pending against Elijah Muhammad [over the loans from Libya]."[56] The Bureau agreed to cooperate, but would not reveal the entirety of its file on the Messenger, which was well over a million pages. There were nearly 100,000 pages from the 1942 draft-evasion investigation alone.[57] Besides the tax investigation, the intelligence community was called upon during the OPEC crisis to investigate reports that Kuwait and Libya were considering "giving the NOI oil tankers to transport oil to the United States and a possible visit by Colonel Gadhafi, premier of Libya, to the United Nations in the near future and, at that time, possibly meeting with Elijah Muhammad in New York City."[58]

Two weeks after Moore wrote the memorandum, President Nixon told Congress that while the United States had "only six percent of the world's population, we consume one-third of the world's energy output." The energy crisis that had been choking American motorists since January was showing no signs of abatement, and a little black man in Chicago suddenly seemed like a potential ally instead of a threat. The results of the investigation remain classified, but it's a safe assumption that the idea of talks between Kuwait and Libya and the NOI never advanced beyond the theoretical stage.

During the same week in 1972 that the Libyan loan was granted, Clara Muhammad returned to her physician, complaining of a painful burning sensation in her stomach. She was hospitalized and given a battery of tests. The diagnosis was advanced cancerous growths in her abdomen, and the prognosis was grim: she probably had less than three months to live.[59] On July 14, the Messenger wrote in *Muhammad Speaks* that Clara was progressing from her recent illness. From the tone of the article, he seemed confident that his wife would make a miraculous recovery. Whether he was hiding the truth about Clara's condition to reassure the women in the NOI for whom she was a heroine, or merely blinding himself to it, is unknown. In all probability, it was a little of both. On August 12, 1972, Clara's battle with stomach cancer ended. There was no autopsy, but her death certificate showed that she had cerebral thrombosis, generalized arteriosclerosis, and carcinoma of the stomach with general metastasis. She was buried at Mount Glenwood Cemetery in Thornton, Illinois.[60]

Clara's painful death after two decades of painful life seems to have awakened Muhammad's dulled sense of justice and mortality. It was one thing to pretend to be a divine man who could live to be a thousand with the proper diet and lifestyle; it was quite another for him to see the stilled body of a friend who had been beside him for nearly all of his life, who bore his children and raised them well, and who loved him when others saw nothing worth loving. Clara was the one who picked him out of the gutter when he was an alcoholic. She opened his mind to Islam, then led Master Fard to him. She wrote to him constantly while he was in prison, and held the NOI together while trying to do the same for her own family. And through it all, she had been faithful. She put up with his philandering and his verbal abuse. She left their home when he ordered her to leave, then returned whenever he begged her to come back. While rumors started going around after Clara died that Elijah was planning to marry Velora Najieb, one of his personal secretaries,[61] or Tynetta Nelson, they were unfounded. As his health declined, Elijah seemed to have come to the realization that a hundred concubines couldn't give him what he and Clara had had together. Faced with his own mortality, the Messenger began saying things he really believed instead of things to perpetuate a faded façade. The first indications of this came during an interview while Clara was ill.

"Some Muslims, or former Muslims, wonder why you employ so many white people?" The question, posed to the Messenger during a press conference in 1972, was one that had troubled members of the NOI for a long time.[62] The Messenger's first significant contract was with the Lerners, a Jewish family whose company printed *Muhammad Speaks.*[63] By 1970, Muhammad worked daily with Caucasians he was forced to hire to handle the NOI's growing wealth. The question, and the conspicuous integration of his staff, had Muslims wondering whether Muhammad had changed his racial views. "Because I can get along with both," Muhammad answered defensively, "and the white people know their country, know their government, know their buildings, their material. And if my people would build those houses over there [referring to his new mansions], they would have to buy the material from the white people."[64]

The reporter had raised the issue because he was struck by the obvious contradiction of labeling Caucasians as inferior to black people and then hiring them to manage the NOI. The Messenger's wish to have it both ways became the focus of a report released by the American Jewish Committee, which accused the NOI of being a major source of "anti-Semitic infection in the black community." It had been prepared by Milton Ellerin, who had given a similar report on the Muslims to BOSSI agents in 1959. "*Muhammad Speaks*," Ellerin wrote, "frequently indulges in overt anti-Semitism . . . [and] stereotypes reminiscent of the Nazi propaganda diet crop up from time to time." The report stated further that the paper habitually referred to "international bankers" and the "international economic conspiracy" supervised by Jews. The report noted that the group's views were troubling because it was the most influential black separatist group in the nation, and that *Muhammad Speaks* had a verified paid circulation of over half a million.[65]

Muhammad's vision of a significant influx of members from the new black middle class—created largely through affirmative action and other integration efforts promoted by civil rights groups—never materialized. In early October, 500 black professionals chartered six planes to Chicago for a "unity meeting" requested by Muhammad. In the invitation they received from Farrakhan, they were told that they would not be required to join the NOI in order to handle the group's growing bankroll. "We have reached our level of expertise in handling it and we now need the help of black professionals to maintain it and carry it forward," a spokesman for the Messenger said.[66] Among those who attended the meeting were Leonard Jeffries, head of the Black Studies Department at the City University of New York; educational consultant Preston Wilcox, and Carlos Russell, dean of the School of Contemporary Studies at Brooklyn College. The meeting was a complete disaster. Instead of pleading for their cooperation, the Messenger denounced them for two hours. Most were so outraged that by the end of the meeting, fewer than fifty were ready to cooperate with the NOI.[67]

With their departure, Muhammad reluctantly recognized that he would have to hire even more Caucasians to help manage his burgeoning antiwhite NOI. A further sign of deteriorating conditions in the organization was the decision in late October to expel every Muslim in New York who was a policeman. "You can't be a Muslim and a policeman at the same time," Leonard 12X Weir was told when he arrived at the Harlem mosque for a religious service. The irony of the expulsion for Weir was that he had personally presented the Messenger with an award from black policemen three years earlier. The blanket expulsion order was issued after Gene X Roberts revealed during the trial of the so-called Black Panther 21 that he had infiltrated Malcolm X's organization and the Black Panther Party.[68]

The most serious threat to the NOI wasn't misfeasance by the FBI or the growth of black nationalist organizations, but came rather from the Philadelphia mosque headed by the Messenger's lifelong friend, Jeremiah X Pugh. Emboldened by the Dubrow robbery and the Messenger's acquiescence in hiding Mims from the law, members of the Muslim Mafia decided to take over certain drug markets in Philadelphia's ghetto. On June 9, 1973, Major Benjamin Coxson was found shot to death in his home in Cherry Hill, a New Jersey suburb fifteen miles outside Philadelphia.[69] Coxson, who grew up in Philadelphia, was a pivotal player in the East Coast Black Mafia. Although he had no visible means of support, he lived in a mansion a few houses down the road from Muhammad Ali.[70] He was so well-respected that when he ran for mayor of Camden, Ali campaigned for him.

Coxson learned how to operate as a drug kingpin while running a popular nightclub in Philadelphia, from one of his regular customers who was a member of a prominent crime family. A quick study, Coxson helped the Muslims establish a number of dummy corporations for laundering drug money and money coming in from credit card fraud and extortion. The Muslim-owned Crescent Furniture Company was a front, as were Pyramid Enterprises Inc., the Barry Goldstein Agency, Fairmont Foods, and nearly a dozen other companies.[71] Checks drawn on the corporations were later discovered to have been made out to Muhammad's Mosque No. 12 in Philadelphia.[72] The investigation of

Coxson's murder revealed that he had introduced the Muslim Mafia to his drug syndicate contacts in New York and Jamaica. Once the Muslims felt they had learned all they could from Coxson, they killed him because "his penchant for publicity" and knowledge of corruption within the NOI had become a liability. The Philadelphia Muslims' Ronald Harvey and Sam Christian were charged with the murder.[73]

Another corrupt Muslim leader ended up on the wrong side of the gun a few months later. James 3X McGregor (also known as James Shabazz), who was transferred from the Harlem mosque and replaced by Farrakhan, was now in charge of Mosque No. 25 in Newark, whence came the assassins of Malcolm X. During a drenching rain on September 4, McGregor was getting out of his 1971 Cadillac in his driveway when members of a rival Muslim faction ended his life in a hail of gunfire.[74] The Newark mosque was second only to the Philadelphia mosque in terms of corruption, and investigators felt certain that McGregor's death was gang-related. On September 18, two more Muslims, twin brothers Roger and Ralph Bankston, were found shot to death in a car near an auto assembly plant in Newark.[75] A copy of *Muhammad Speaks* was reportedly placed over their faces. Exactly one month later, the heads of Warren X Marcello and Michael X Huff, both members of the Newark mosque, were found in a vacant lot less than a block from McGregor's home (their bodies were found four miles away).[76] Decapitation, investigators noted, was a trademark assassination technique of underworld fraternities.

While police theorized that the murders were the result of a fight for power between McGregor's mosque and a group calling itself the New World of Islam, they noted that the suspects arrested were involved primarily in extortion rings and murder-for-hire. McGregor's funeral was attended by 3,000 mourners, among them Newark mayor Kenneth A. Gibson and Farrakhan.[77] Farrakhan and McGregor were among the ministers who suggested in 1965 that Malcolm deserved to die for telling the truth about the Messenger. McGregor was the Harlem mosque official who told the media that Malcolm had set fire to his own house on Valentine's Day, though he knew that it was members of the Harlem mosque who had set the blaze. Slowly, it seemed, all of those who had conspired against Malcolm were dying or falling on hard times. "Malcolm's not through with them yet," Ella Collins once said of the men who betrayed her brother.[78]

In the aftermath of the Dubrow robbery and rumors that the NOI's thriving fish-importing business was being used to smuggle drugs into black communities, the Messenger should have shut down the Philadelphia mosque and set more stringent investigative procedures. But because he was so indebted to men like McGregor and Pugh, he turned his head and pretended not to notice what was going on. His silence resulted in one of the most heinous crimes in American history.

CHAPTER SEVENTEEN

IN THE NAME OF ALLAH

Thou shalt not kill.
—*Exodus 20:13*[1]

"I loved Elijah Muhammad enough that if you attacked him, I would kill you. Yesterday, today, and tomorrow."

—*Minister Louis Farrakhan,*
February 20, 1993[2]

8. And there are some people who say: "We believe in Allah and the last Day"; and they are not believers.

9. They seek to deceive Allah and those who believe, and they deceive only themselves and they perceive not.

10. In their hearts is a disease, so Allah increased their disease, and for them is a painful chastisement because they lie.

—*"Lip-Profession,"*
Holy Quran[3]

On January 14, 1972, Muhammad granted a rare press conference to reporters from the mainstream media. The interview, held at his Chicago headquarters, lasted nearly two hours, and touched on a range of subjects, from theocracy to his personal health.[4] During the press conference a reporter asked him how he would like to be remembered a century from that day. "I would only want to be remembered for the work that I do, in the Name of Allah. That is what I want to be remembered for."[5] He might have gotten his wish but for two missives from a former high-level Black Muslim official. Both letters arrived during the early days of 1973.

Ever since his ouster in the late 1950s as the first national secretary of the NOI, Ernest 2X McGee had harbored a consuming contempt for the Messenger. If Malcolm X was the Messenger's right-hand man, McGee was his left hand, or so he thought. That someone so indispensable could suddenly become expendable seemed incongruous and irrational. So he was quite naturally angry when the Messenger replaced him with John Ali. After leaving the NOI McGee, who had changed his name to Hamaas Abdul Khaalis, studied Islam as practiced by the followers of Abu Hanafa.[6] Hanafa, who died in 767, founded one of the four schools of the Sunni branch of Islam, and its students were called Hanafi Muslims.[7] Although he blamed Malcolm X for the Messenger's decision to replace him with Ali, Khaalis insisted that he and Malcolm X had patched up their differences after the latter was forced out of the NOI in 1964.[8]

At the time Malcolm X was assassinated, Khaalis was working as director of community relations for the NUL in New York City. Following his layoff a year later he spent most of his time organizing his own mosque.[9] The mosque, which was located in a rundown building in Harlem, attracted few members, most of them being from his own growing family. His luck changed, however, when he converted a twenty-four-year Milwaukee Bucks' star rookie named Lew Alcindor.[10]

In 1970, Alcindor (the Michael Jordan of his era) was renamed Kareem Abdul-Jabbar by Khaalis, whom Abdul-Jabbar called the Khalifa (or guide). His conversion and the controversy it generated caused the national spotlight to focus briefly on the Hanafi sect, but its membership failed to grow. Basketball wasn't the attraction it is today, and Abdul-Jabbar lacked the charisma and magnetic personality of Muhammad Ali. The only things Ali and Abdul-Jabbar had in common were Islam and a religious leader whom they followed with blind faith. Like Ali, Abdul-Jabbar gave freely of his wealth to his teacher. Although perturbed by some of the advice Khaalis gave him, Abdul-Jabbar followed it to the letter. So profound was Abdul-Jabbar's faith in Khaalis's infallibility that he married a woman his teacher suggested instead of the woman he loved.[11] A year later, Abdul-Jabbar paid $78,000 for a large home in Washington for Khaalis. The house, which would serve as the sect's headquarters and home for Khaalis, was located in an upper-class, predominantly black neighborhood known as the Gold Coast.[12]

While the Hanafi sect remained stagnant, the NOI found new vigor. Perhaps it was the growing popularity of the NOI that drove Khaalis mad with jealousy. Or it might have been his failure to recruit more than a few dozen people in Washington, a city with a predominantly black, progressive population. Or maybe, as Abdul-Jabbar suggested, it was a combination of these factors and megalomania that prompted Khaalis to record his distaste for the NOI in two torrid letters during the first days of 1973. "To Hamaas, who believed that he was the only person sincere, educated, and immersed deeply enough in Islam to lead the entire population of Muslims in America," Abdul-Jabbar recalled, "all other communities were a joke."[13] The letters, which were mailed to the Messenger, most of his ministers, and to the media, hint that Khaalis had begun to perceive himself as a messianic figure.

"Ministers," the second letter began in a tone of comeuppance, "you have received your first lesson in Allah Ta'Ala's Deenu-L-Islam, not W. D. Fard's Islam."[14] In the opening paragraph, Khaalis called Elijah a "lying deceiver," and implied that both the Messenger and Fard were frauds. Blacks had been better off "from a psychological point of view," Khaalis wrote, before Fard and the Messenger ever came along, because both had weaned them from one religion (Christianity) that was bad for them only to replace it with a fabricated form of Islam that was equally bad. Khaalis wrote:

> Just because his given name is Elijah, that doesn't give him the right to lay claim to being the minor prophet in the Bible. What madness is in your leader and teacher, what kind of minds do you have to be deaf, dumb and blind to everything?

Even worse than the things Khaalis wrote about the Messenger were his barbs concerning Fard:

> Was this god the Pope of Rome? The Archbishop of Canterbury? Or John Walker, a.k.a. W. D. Fard, the slightly cockeyed man who came from Greece, and was a Greek that came to this country at the age of twenty-seven years of life, and who served seven-and-a-half years in jail in America for stealing a carload of junk in Gary, Indiana, and for raping a seventeen-year-old so-called white girl? This man died in Chicago, Illinois, at the age of seventy-eight. Your Captain Raymond Sharrieff knows this. Do you?[15]

After revealing more of what he knew of Fard's alleged parentage and his life in Gary under the alias of John Walker, Khaalis accused the Messenger, his family, and his ministers of hiding the truth about Fard's life from the flock. "So, this is your W. D. Fard," Khaalis wrote. "Refer to Supreme Captain Raymond Sharrieff or any of Elijah Mukammad's [sic] children by his late wife. Make them tell you the truth. They know that their father is a deceiver." He had intentionally misspelled the Messenger's surname, and pointed out in a footnote that "Mukammad" means "sad, grieved, and blackened; to be laden with sin; sorrow-bound because of evil committed through ignorance (error)."

The Messenger's phone was ringing off the hook for days after the letters were received, as most ministers had never heard of John Walker or Khaalis, and didn't know what to make of the allegations.[16] While officials in Chicago urged the ministers to ignore them as the ravings of a disturbed former follower, the allegations made in the letters didn't remain a secret for long. Low-level officials obtained copies, and within weeks nearly the whole membership had heard rumors about what was contained in them. It also wasn't long—a matter of days, in fact—before a team was formed to kill the man who sent the letters to the Messenger.

Just as a lieutenant from the Harlem mosque had orchestrated the Valentine's Day firebombing of Malcolm X's home, Lieutenant John 38X Clark of Muhammad's Mosque No. 12 in Philadelphia was designated to deal with Khaalis. On January 10, just three days after the Philadelphia minister received the second letter, Clark recruited seven other members of Mosque No. 12 to help him carry out a diabolical scheme. William Christian, Theodore Moody, James Price, Thomas Clinton, and Ronald Harvey agreed to drive to Washington in two cars to rob and kill Khaalis. Robbery was Harvey's idea; since Abdul-Jabbar bought the house and it was the sect's headquarters, Harvey assumed that trunks and safes filled with money were hidden there.[17]

Several members of the conspiracy made a scouting trip to Washington on January 12 to locate the Hanafi headquarters on Sixteenth Street, study visible security systems, and examine possible escape routes. The easiest part, they concluded, was escaping. The house was located near the District of Columbia–Maryland border and was within a half-mile of four main streets that could put the hit squad back on state highways within fifteen minutes. The house was on a corner, making it accessible from any number of nearby streets. The toughest part, then, would be overcoming the internal security system. At the time of the visit, there were no visible signs of outside security.[18]

Satisfied that the killing and the subsequent escape could be accomplished without much difficulty, Clark called his team together on January 17. "Bring your shoes," he told them, a signal that they should meet him at his home with their weapons.[19] The group had problems finding hotel accommodations because the city was full of the Republican Party faithful in town to celebrate the second inauguration of President Nixon, but they finally found a room at the Downtown Motel. At eight-thirty the next morning, a man who said his name was "Tommy Jones" called the Hanafi headquarters to ask about buying books written by the Khaalis. Amina Khaalis, the Khalifa's twenty-two-year-old daughter, told the caller that two books were available.[20]

"What's the best time to pick them up?" the caller wanted to know. Amina asked the man to hold on while she checked. She handed the phone to her twenty-five-year-old brother Daud, who told the caller that he should stop by the house between one-thirty and two o'clock that afternoon. Around two o'clock, Amina heard the doorbell ring once, followed by three hard knocks at the front door. From a window of the big, oddly shaped house, she saw two young black men who were neatly dressed and had close-cropped hair. Assuming that one of them was Mr. Jones, she called Daud, then returned to the kitchen. Leaving the chain-linked lock on the door, Daud discussed the purchase with the two strangers, both of whom requested a single copy of *Look and See*, a slender volume on Islam written by Khaalis. The book sold for one dollar, but Mr. Jones handed Daud a five-dollar bill.[21]

"Hold on a minute," Daud said as he excused himself. He closed the door and went to the kitchen to ask Amina if she had change. When she answered no, Daud ran upstairs to get some singles, then rushed back downstairs to his customers. When he opened the door to hand Mr. Jones his change, Jones put a gun in his face and told him to move back. The minute Daud complied, the two strangers broke the chain and forced their way into the house. One kept Daud covered as he forced him into the dining room, while the other turned his pistol toward the entrance to the kitchen.

"This is a holdup!" he yelled as he saw Amina and a little boy. "Come on, come on," he added as he ordered them into the dining room. Two-year-old Abdullah, Amina's little brother, was shivering with fear, so she held his hand gently as the gunmen led them into the dining room, where they saw Daud lying nearly motionless on his stomach while a gunman held his weapon against his hostage's head. After the two gunmen collected their hostages in the dining room, they pushed them into the living room.

"Lie on your stomachs," one growled.

"Is there any money in the house?" the other asked. "Are there any leather gloves around here?" he asked after a short pause.

"I have three dollars in my pocketbook," Amina replied, telling them that it was on the dining room table. "We don't have any leather gloves," she said in response to a repeated query. As one gunman went into the dining room and took the money from Amina's purse, he spotted a small pile of clothing on the floor in the den. The gunmen took two shirts from the stack, placed one over Daud's head and the other over Amina's. As the shirt was pulled down over her face, Amina heard loud knocking at the front door again. One of the gunmen opened the door and six co-conspirators rushed in. Clark was with them.

"Who else is in the house?" Clark asked the first two intruders. Daud volunteered that there was a lady on the second floor, three children in the room next to hers, and a ten-year-old boy on the third floor. Clark ordered several of the men to go upstairs and subdue the other occupants.

"Is there any money in here?" Clark inquired. When Daud and Amina said no, Clark grew angry. "Come on, in this big-ass house you have to have some kind of money in here." When Daud and Amina insisted that there was none, Clark ordered his soldiers to take the hostages to the basement. Amina, Daud, and Abdullah were taken into the laundry room and again ordered to lie on the floor face down. Moments later, another gunman led Bibi Khaalis, one of the Khalifa's two wives, downstairs and into the laundry room, along with her one-year-old daughter, also named Bibi.

"Are you sure you didn't call the police?" Clark asked the Khalifa's wife as she tried to comfort her namesake.

"No, I didn't call the police," Bibi replied. As she answered, two gunmen came down the steps with the last hostages. One, eleven-year-old Rahman, was pushed by one gunman while another held the youngest hostage, nine-day-old Khadyja Tasibur, in his arms. Amina was Tasibur's mother.

Clark bombarded the adults with questions. "When is this Mr. Hamaas going to be home? I want to meet this Mr. Hamaas." He paused a minute, then continued: "Where do you hide the money in this big-ass house? If we don't find any money, one of these babies may get hurt."

When the burglars were upstairs, one of them noticed a locked closet in a large bedroom. Clark, when reminded about it by one of his underlings, asked the hostages where the keys were. Daud told him that it was on the keychain around his neck. Daud was briskly lifted off the floor and forced to go upstairs with seven of the gunmen; the one remaining thug stood guard over the unarmed hostages. The nine-day-old baby began crying loudly, annoying the gunman, so he untied Amina's hands, removed the shirt from her head, and told her to hold her baby. Amina hadn't realized just how tightly her hands were bound until they were freed. She looked at Rahman's hands. The knot was so tightly drawn that his hands had already turned purple.

"Could you please loosen my little brother's hands?" Amina pleaded. "The knot's so tight that it's cutting off his circulation."

"No!" the thug said sharply. A second later, he heard his accomplices coming downstairs. He ordered Amina to put the baby down on the floor. Then he put the shirt back over Amina's head and retied her hands. "Face down!" he yelled. Amina quickly complied. As any caring mother would do, Amina tried to remember the sound of each man's voice who touched her newborn baby. She heard the gunman say he was taking the newborn upstairs.

"Why are you taking her upstairs?" she asked helplessly.

"We're just taking her upstairs," he assured her. "Nothing's going to happen to her." A moment later, Clark returned to the basement. He helped Amina get up from the floor, then ordered her to come upstairs with him. Slowly, Amina climbed the first flight.

"Why did your father write those letters?" Clark said in a taunting tone of voice. "Shouldn't he have known better than to write those letters to the Honorable Elijah Muhammad?" At first, Amina said nothing. She was too weak from childbirth to argue with him. And besides, he seemed to be trying to provoke a response to heighten his anger, something that would justify his eminently ill intentions.

"Didn't you know this was going to happen?" he asked. Once he said that, Amina knew her fate was sealed, so she finally gave in to his taunts. "Well, my father knows best," she said as the man pushed her toward a closet in Rahman's bedroom on second floor.

"Oh, yeah?" the gunman angrily replied. "Get in there. Get on your knees." Amina obeyed him at once. As she steadied herself on her knees, the demon raised the gun and put its cold steel barrel against the left side of her head. "Well, this is what's best for you," he said as he shot her at point-blank range. A loud noise reverberated through her head, but, miraculously, she survived. She was in such a state of shock that she didn't realize she had been shot. The gunman, who assumed she was near death, left the closet door slightly ajar and went looking for his next victim.

The assassins forced ten-year-old Rahman into the bedroom the boy shared with Daud, the same one where Amina lay bleeding in the darkness. "Lie on the bed," he told the boy. Above the unreal ringing in her head, Amina heard the nightmarish cries of her little brother. "I'll do anything you say!" Rahman begged the giant-looking gangster holding the big gun. "Just don't hurt me."

"All right," Amina heard the thug tell the ten-year-old, but when the boy lay face down on the bed, the gunman shot him twice in the head. He died in a matter of seconds. After he killed Rahman, he and another assassin returned to the closet to make certain that Amina was dead.

"Man, she's still breathing!" one of the astonished assailants said. The other one put the gun to the right side of her head, and pulled the trigger six times. Amina rolled onto her side after the sixth shot, her eyes wide open. Satisfied that she was dead, the gunman left the room. As the two went downstairs, a car pulled up to the house. Two of the thugs kept an eye on the car's driver (its only occupant) while several of them dragged two-year-old Abdullah into a closet. The little boy struggled as valiantly as any man, but his gargantuan abductors quickly subdued him. As the third and final bullet entered his head, he submitted his life to God.

Abdul Nur, the man who had just parked his car outside the house, couldn't tell that anything was amiss. He had just come from a nearby grocery store because Khadyja Khaalis (the Khalifa's other wife) had forgotten to bring her money. Nur volunteered to rush home and get it. As he opened the door, three of the gunmen ambushed him and rapidly tied him up and gagged him. They carried him upstairs to Rahman's room and shot him twice in the right temple. He vomited as the second bullet pierced his brain and killed him.

Harvey told two of his accomplices to start running water in an upstairs bathtub.

"Why do you have to kill the babies?" Price asked. He and his wife, Josephine, also a member of the Philadelphia mosque, had three young children, and what modicum of conscience he had suddenly troubled him. The little children were too young to identify them, Price told Harvey, so why couldn't they simply be left in the house alone but alive?

"Because," Harvey answered angrily, "the seed of the hypocrite is in them." If Price didn't follow orders, Harvey warned him, his body would be found among the dead, too. With great reluctance, Price went upstairs and started filling the bathtub. In the meantime, several gunmen went downstairs to execute Bibi Khaalis, the last adult in the house. As she lay bound and gagged, they fired eight bullets into her at almost point-blank range. They left her in a pool of blood and went back upstairs.

One-year-old Bibi was then sent to follow her mother into the Afterworld. They turned off the water in the bathtub and held the baby under as she struggled for air. Her body convulsed for a moment or so, but the assassin held her under until the final air bubble burst. Amina's nine-day-old baby became the seventh and last victim of Elijah's emissaries. After the bathroom sink was filled with water, the tiny infant was submerged. The baby shook violently as she choked on water. A trail of bubbles came from her nostrils. Then the water and the baby were still.

Back at the grocery store, Khadyja Khaalis was growing frantic. Nur had not returned from a trip which should only have taken five or ten minutes at most; nearly half an hour had passed. She tried calling home several times, but got a busy signal. She sensed something was terribly wrong. She left her bags of groceries at the checkout counter and started walking home as fast as she could. Before she reached the house, however, she remembered that the Khalifa was visiting a neighbor's house nearby. She knocked frantically on the door. When Khaalis came out, she told him about Nur's failure to return to the Giant Food store where she had been shopping, and about the constant busy signal at home. They rushed to the house and saw Nur's car parked in front. As they passed an open window on the right side of the massive structure, Khadyja saw a stranger's face, and immediately told Khaalis.

"Who is it?" Khaalis yelled in desperation as he turned toward the window. "Who is it?"

"It's Tommy," Harvey replied, hoping Khaalis would think that he was a friend of the family. But Khaalis wasn't aware that anyone was coming by, and he didn't recall anyone named Tommy. As Khaalis ran toward the front door, Harvey opened it suddenly and tried to pull the main target of their madness inside. A powerfully built man, Khaalis shook off his assailant, and Harvey ran to the rear of the house. As Khaalis pursued him, the other murderers hastily departed. Khaalis jumped into his car and tried to catch Harvey, but the car was no match for a criminal accustomed to running through alleyways and cracks between tenement houses in Philadelphia to escape police. The lack of security at the Hanafi headquarters allowed all of the assassins to elude immediate capture, and they were back on the streets of Philadelphia by sundown.

The gang from Philadelphia had come to Washington to kill Khaalis slowly, as he begged for his life and, they hoped, to cart off thousands of dollars they assumed were kept in the headquarters, just as the Messenger kept thousands at his Chicago mansion. They had returned to Philadelphia having hardly caught a glimpse of the Khalifa, let alone taking his life. As for the cash, they never found it because it didn't exist. Ransacking the beautiful mansion netted the assassins a total of roughly $1,000, about $100 apiece, with the remaining $200 going for a donation to Mosque No. 12. They had come to Washington in the name of Allah, or so they thought; they left, for certain, as the devil's advocates.

Shakespeare wrote that every crime has its witness, and the Hanafi massacre certainly confirmed his belief. Whether it was due to the will of Allah, as Hanafis believe, or defective bullets, Amina and Bibi Khaalis survived the carnage. As the Khalifa returned home in a daze from the fruitless chase, he saw the swirling crimson lights of police cars and ambulances all around his home. City detectives and federal agents were helping police put up yellow tape to cordon off the crime scene when Khaalis saw Amina. She was sitting on the front steps, in silence, wiping streams of blood from the bullet holes in her head. She helped police sort out the crimes as best she could as she lay in an ambulance rushing her to the hospital, but for the next several days at least, the police and the FBI were pretty much on their own in trying to solve the biggest mass murder case in the history of the nation's capital.[22]

Media coverage of the ghastly crime committed by Muslims against Muslims continued for weeks. On January 26, Khaalis appeared on several nationally syndicated television and radio shows, including the *Today* show on NBC-TV, in which he labeled the Messenger and his malevolent minions as "executioners of babies" and "backshooters of women."[23] The massacre of his family, he said, only confirmed the opinion of many that the NOI had become "debased and depraved," and he pointed out the sickening behavior of a small group of Black Muslims who had gathered outside the funeral home where services were held for his slain children. "They began jumping up and down and rejoicing," Khaalis said, while the family was conducting last rites.[24] Top officials of the NOI weren't any better. Instead of apologizing for the massacre, prominent ministers, including Farrakhan, sought to lay blame for the atrocity elsewhere. Perhaps mindful of the bitter repercussions the NOI faced after trying to incinerate Malcolm X and his wife and babies in 1965, Farrakhan tried to point a finger at the federal government.[25]

Muhammad Speaks staff writers dismissed Khaalis as a "modern day Uncle Tom" who "would sell out his own brother for the favor of the devil." Another article accused Khaalis, without an iota of proof, of accepting large amounts of money from white people "to gain enough nerve to appear on television and tell these outrageous lies against Messenger Muhammad and the Nation of Islam." For a paper that had won the John B. Russwurm Award for its objective coverage of national and international events affecting nonwhites, *Muhammad Speaks* suddenly read like something produced by the son of Satan—a better name might have been *Mephistopheles Speaks*. During the same week that *Muhammad Speaks* and Farrakhan accused Khaalis of lying about the NOI's involvement, police revealed that two suspects in a multiple rape and armed robbery case in Philadelphia had also been involved in the Hanafi massacre. One of the guns used in the massacre, police said, had also been used in the Philadelphia case. Another suspect in the Philadelphia case had a copy of the second letter Khaalis had written to the Messenger in his pocket when police arrested him.[26]

The mujahedin who murdered the Khalifa's family continued to leave clues and evidence of their identities almost everywhere they went. Besides using the same weapons to commit other barbaric crimes, they made suspicious telephone calls from their own homes, used obvious aliases at hotels, and made other mistakes that led police directly to the Philadelphia mosque. In June, in the face of a mountain of incriminating material, Price confessed to his role in the massacre and agreed to turn state's evidence. Six Muslims whom Price identified were indicted (the seventh, Thomas Clinton, died of leukemia before the indictment was handed up).[27]

After Price agreed to become a state's witness, he was labeled a hypocrite by powerful people in the NOI, people who, had they had any moral integrity or sense of honor, would have apologized for such unfathomable evil. Farrakhan, the NOI's national spokesman, the same man whose writings and speeches helped create the conditions that led to the assassination of Malcolm X, made comments that many felt "could only have directed toward one person."[28] During a nationally broadcast radio sermon, his howl bouncing off the walls of the prison cells where Price and some of the other thugs were detained, Farrakhan said:

Let this be a warning to those of you who would be used as an instrument of a wicked government against our rise. . . . Be careful, because when the government is tired of using you, they're going to dump you back in the laps of your people. And though Elijah Muhammad is a merciful man and will say, "Come in," and forgive you, yet in the ranks of the black people today there are younger men and women rising up who have no forgiveness in them for traitors and stool pigeons.[29]

On the subject of the Hanafi murders, Farrakhan implied that the crime was part of a government conspiracy to deny the Messenger, whom he called the "Messiah," the privilege of "acceptability and respectability." But it may have been the final words of Farrakhan's speech that day that most affected Price. "And they will execute you," Farrakhan warned, "as soon as your identity is known. Be careful, because nothing shall prevent the rise of the messiah, the Nation of Islam, and the black man the world over."[30]

Shortly after the half-hour speech, Price changed his mind about testifying. Prosecutors felt that, besides Farrakhan's radio broadcast, visits from Black Muslims claiming to be Price's lawyers also played a role in his change of mind. Procedural matters delayed trial for months, but Price was steadfast in his refusal. In fact, he insisted that by keeping him separated from his codefendants, the government was placing his life in jeopardy by making it appear that he was still cooperating. Over the state's objections, Price was granted his wish for a transfer to the Philadelphia Detention Center. Although he was warned by prison officials that it was in his own best interest to be segregated, he insisted upon joining the general population. Clark, who arrived at the center on the same day as Price, specifically requested to be put in the same cell as Price. Clark was removed from the cell ten days later. However, another assassin—Moody—was also in the cell.[31]

Price believed that being in the same cell with his codefendants would assure them that he was on their side, but his judgment couldn't have been more faulty. The three men were later transferred to Holmesburg Prison in Philadelphia, where once again they shared a cell. "They're killing me! They're killing me!" a non-Muslim inmate heard Price scream four days after Christmas. An hour or so later, guards finally answered Price's call for help. By then, of course, it was too late. Price had been mutilated and lynched in a way that made Klan violence seem sparing by comparison. His testicles were crushed, and his rectum was ripped open by a prison shank or another very sharp object. After essentially castrating a black man and a fellow Muslim, the Black Muslims hanged him with his own bedsheet. Moody and John Griffin were subsequently convicted of that murder.[32]

On February 25, as tens of thousands of Black Muslims from across the country convened in Chicago for the Saviour's Day 1973 celebration, the two-month-old Hanafi massacre was still very much on the minds of African Americans. The Messenger had been silent about the atrocities commited by the automatons from Philadelphia, who killed innocent babies out of a perverted desire to please him. Would he use this gathering, many black newspaper editorials asked, to air his views on the crime? Would he apologize to the Khalifa's family, and to African Americans for the depraved actions of his madmen? As he approached the podium to address his brethren, Farrakhan and his sidekick, Abdul Karriem (formerly Larry 4X Prescott) led the crowd in a deafening chant: "Long live Muhammad! Long Live Muhammad!"[33]

The topic of his speech, the Messenger said, was "A Saviour Is Born."

"Who is lost that we have to have a Saviour's Day?" he asked the assembly. The answer, of course, was that the so-called American Negro was lost until 1930, when Fard came to find him. For those listening with a critical ear, the Messenger's message that day made very little sense. He told his followers that Fard—that is, God in the person of Fard—so greatly loved America's former slaves that he vowed to search the entire Earth until he found the lost Tribe of Shabazz. But his argument begged the question: if Fard was indeed Allah, and God is the All-Knowing and All-Wise, as the Holy Quran teaches, then it would follow that God, knowing everything, would know where the lost tribe was. While the Messenger was deadly serious during most of his speech, he cleverly injected some humor into it. "They tell me that over at the hospital," he said, some of the white infants are born "with little monkey tails." They roared with laughter because he had reversed a contention whites made about blacks that was popular during the era of scientific racism: black people were descended from apes, and black babies were often born with tails.

For the most part, though, the Messenger focused on disproving the allegations raised in the two letters from Khaalis. This decision rendered his speech a landmark for a very special reason: it was the first time in the forty-three-year history of the NOI that outsiders learned something substantive about Fard's parentage, at least his parentage according to the Messenger. "Fard said his father was a black man," Elijah said, his eyes hidden behind his trademark dark tinted spectacles, "and his mother was a white woman." Silence swept over the auditorium.

The Messenger then tried to explain how the "black man's saviour" could be "part devil" and why (though he never explained how God could have parents). Fard's father concluded that his son could not come to America and resurrect the African American if he was a full-blooded black man. Too many roadblocks would be placed before him, black people would never accept a black man as the Mahdi, and he needed to be "fair-skinned enough to be accepted by white people as one of them," Fard told him, he said. To succeed, Fard's father reasoned, his son would have to be dark enough to be accepted by blacks and light-skinned enough to be accepted by whites. In making his son a mulatto, Fard's father later told him, he had made it possible for him to fulfill the biblical prophecy of the Messiah who comes as undetected "as a thief in the night."

The Messenger went on to explain that there was one problem: Fard's father was very dark-skinned, as were all of the women in his village. To find a wife, he "went into the mountains and found himself a white wife" (though Elijah neglected to say which mountains). But before marrying her, the father had to "cast the devil out of her," meaning that he converted her to Islam. After he converted her, the father left his village because his wife was rejected for being a white woman. They settled elsewhere (the Messenger would not say where), and soon a daughter was born to the couple. The next child was a boy, the one his father planned to make into "a saviour for us."

For the next two decades, the Messenger went on, Fard's father schooled his son in all the great books, taught him about his own rich heritage, and generally prepared him for his sacred mission. Around 1910, the son arrived in America. "The black man is the only man created by God," Muhammad said in the meandering message. "All the other races were man-made, made by black people."[34]

His halting speech and rambling delivery had some scholars concluding that the Messenger was getting senile. During one segment of his
address, for instance, he couldn't seem to recall something as basic as the
year Fard was born: "So on this day in 19 . . . 19 . . . February 19, 1926,
we are face to face with the truth, that truly we can say today that the
man who was born in 18 . . . February 26 is here with us, to do what?
To save us from the destruction of our enemies."[35]

"This [man] came to us . . . his birth . . . 1870 . . . 1877, February
26 . . . A Saviour was born on this day." The Messenger repeated that
phrase more than sixty times, but only mentioned the year of Fard's
birth once. He apologized after realizing how badly he had stumbled
over a rote-learned element of the NOI's beliefs, but his confusion raised
obvious questions about his clarity of thought. In another part of his
address, he claimed that he and Fard had once discussed the "lynching"
of a poor man in Indiana who was accused of raping a white woman in
1930. Why, one wondered, did he inject such an irrelevant statement
into his lecture?

The only way to understand why the Messenger raised such seemingly unrelated issues that day is to bear in mind Khaalis's second letter,
in which he wrote that Wallace Fard died in Chicago around 1971 at the
age of seventy-eight.[36] The Messenger addressed the allegation by claiming that Fard was born in 1877. Not only that, but he claimed that Fard
"is still with us today,"[37] and by so doing refuted Khaalis's claim about
his death in Chicago. The Messenger said that Fard was ninety-six years
old that day, though he failed to produce him or even a recent photograph of him.[38] In fact, the NOI had no photographs of Fard other than
the one taken on May 26, 1933, by the Detroit Police Department. The
second issue—the rape case—was a reference to Khaalis's charge that
Fard was charged with raping a white girl in Indiana. In addressing the
issue indirectly, the Messenger said that the "poor man" was innocent of
the charge. Was Fard the poor man he was referring to?

Any doubt that the Messenger was alluding to charges in the Khaalis
letter was removed by the final issue addressed in his speech. "The reason black people can do unrighteous things," he continued, "is because
the weak germ [sic] from which springs white people" is still part of the

black man's genetic code.[39] He never mentioned the Hanafi massacre during the two-hour lecture, but he really didn't have to. Everyone understood that the reference to "unrighteous things" was his indirect way of rationalizing the demonic transgressions of his misguided acolytes. In raising the issue of a seemingly irrelevant rape case, in claiming that Fard's father "cast the devil out" of the Caucasian woman who bore him two children, and in claiming that Fard was still alive, the Messenger invited an investigation into the founder of the NOI's past. The truth about Fard was, as they say, stranger than fiction.

CHAPTER EIGHTEEN
KEYS TO THE KINGDOM

So far as I know, there is still no certain identification for Fard, whether as to his nationality, race, background, education, or even his age.

—Harold Bloom,
The American Religion[1]

Those who cannot remember the past are condemned to repeat it.

—George Santayana,
The Life of Reason[2]

Yes, Malcolm's gone,
but he's not forgotten.
He died to save me,
gave me my dignity.

—Leon Thomas,
"El Hajj Malik El Shabazz"[3]

In its attempt to destroy the NOI in 1963, the FBI spent a fortune trying to find out who Wallace D. Fard was and whether he was dead or alive. After the clandestine release of the Bureau's file on Fard failed to dethrone the Messenger, the FBI decided it had wasted enough money and labor on the COINTELPRO, signaling the third and final effort to expose the real background of the creator of the NOI. A decade later, it was the Messenger himself who provided critical clues that led to the uncovering of Fard's footprints. "I'm not going to tell what mountains" Master Fard's father found his wife in, the Messenger teased during his 1973 Saviour's Day speech, then implied that it was the Caucasus Mountains.[4] He also admitted that Fard's mother was a white woman; Muslims had been taught in the temples that she was a Russian Jew whose family moved to Azerbaijan when she was a small child. Though Jewish by birth (since her mother was Jewish), she was raised as a Muslim in her new homeland, where roughly 80 percent of the population practices Shi'a Islam.[5] The Messenger, who regarded Judaism as a corrupt faith, said that Fard's mother was kept in the Muslim society all of her life and "never mixed with her wicked people."[6]

Muhammad never adequately explained why Fard's father traveled all the way to the Caucasus Mountains to find a wife when there were plenty of white women in locales closer to Mecca, where Fard allegedly was born. Why didn't his father simply marry a white-skinned Saudi? That would have made infinitely more sense than asking converts to believe that Fard's father traveled from Mecca to Azerbaijan to find a white mother for his envisioned sacred son. The problem with having Fard's mother born in Mecca, of course, was that Black Muslims were taught that whites could not enter Mecca.[7] Thus, Fard's mother's origins had to be placed elsewhere. (Fard's decision to make Azerbaijan the place of her birth is significant, as we shall see shortly.) As Fard had recounted to Elijah and Clara Muhammad at their first meeting, he had remained with his parents in Mecca until he completed high school. He took his first trip to Europe that summer, and received his undergraduate degree from Oxford University four years later. He came to America to attend the University of Southern California in Los Angeles for graduate study in international affairs. Upon completing his doctoral work, he returned to Mecca to begin training as a diplomat for the kingdom of Hejaz (one of two kingdoms that were joined as Saudi Arabia in 1932). His memories of the terrible plight of African Americans made him restless, however, and he felt a calling to return to the United States to liberate them from their condition of being "half slave and half free." The year was 1930. The date was Independence Day, July 4.[8]

That was the myth. Government documents and public records tell a different story. Fard did not arrive in America in 1930. Nor did he ever visit the White House as an official guest (as Farrakhan's group claimed) or in any other capacity.[9] White House historians keep records of visits by dignitaries and common guests, and there is no record of a visit by Fard or by Noble Drew Ali. By the Messenger's own admission, Fard had actually come to this country nearly two decades earlier. "He had come in and out of this country for about twenty years before ever he made himself known to us," the Messenger said during an interview in 1972. "He . . . had enrolled in the California University there and he lived with a white family out there."[10] While many records were destroyed during the Civil War, record-keeping by federal, state, and local governments had vastly improved by 1900, and it was possible to compare the Messenger's biography of Fard with immigration records, birth records, and other public documents. For example, records at the University of Southern California for the period Fard would have attended—roughly anywhere from 1910 to 1929—failed to report even the enrollment much less the graduation of anyone named Wallace D. Fard, Wallace D. Ford, or any of the aliases Fard used.[11] Though most Muslims have refused to look at the evidence, the Bureau correctly concluded that Wallace D. Fard and Wallace D. Ford were one and the same. However, agents made errors in the details and were hindered by linguistics problems that threw their search off course. Using much of the same material the Bureau gathered on Ford together with modern research techniques provides a fuller picture of the founder of the NOI.

Master Wali Fard Muhammad Ali, Wallace Fard Muhammad, W. D. Fard, and dozens of other aliases all belonged to Wali Dodd Fard, a mulatto who immigrated to the United States from New Zealand in the early 1900s. He used two aliases upon his arrival in Portland, Oregon.[12] He anglicized his surname to Ford, and used the first name of Wallie or Wallace (to minimize confusion, he'll usually be referred to as Wallace D. Fard in this section). He used Dodd as a middle name when he used Ford as a surname. Wallace D. Fard was the son of Zared Fard, a New Zealander whose parents were East Indians from the area that became Pakistan. His mother, Beatrice, was part of New Zealand's minority British population. Judging from another alias he used—Fred Dodd— his mother's maiden name probably was Dodd. Wallace D. Fard was born in New Zealand on February 25, 1891. Zared and Beatrice Fard managed to get enough money together to send their twenty-year-old son to America in 1913. Fard must have entered the United States illegally through Canada, a common entry point for illegal aliens, who subsequently settled in Washington and Oregon. He gave conflicting accounts of his parents' place of birth. On some documents, he wrote that his parents were from Hawaii. On others, he wrote New Zealand. He also gave conflicting accounts of his own place of birth. On some forms, he wrote that he was born in New Zealand, and on others, he claimed that he was born in Portland.

Fard used the alias of Fred Dodd when he first arrived in America. His facial features, hair texture, and skin color were ambiguous enough for him to mingle among Caucasians, Asians, Latins, and African Americans; he presented himself as Caucasian. When he married Pearl Allen at the Multnomah, Oregon, County Courthouse on May 9, 1914, he said that he was white, as was his wife.[13] Their first child, a boy, was born the following year.[14] Within months of the child's birth, the marriage started to come apart. Like many young newlyweds, one party—in this case the husband—wasn't ready for marriage. He asked Pearl for a divorce, but she refused. Seeing no other way out of his domestic difficulties, he packed his bags and headed for California.[15] Using the name Wallie

Dodd Ford, Fard found work as a cook in 1916 in a small restaurant in Los Angeles.

An intelligent, industrious worker, Fard was managing the business for the owner within a year. Always a dapper dresser, he attracted the attention of at least one waitress, and they moved in together after a few months.[16] Once again, though, he was unlucky in love, and the relationship deteriorated when she realized that much about him was illusory. He had impressed her at first as a well-read gentleman who was going places. But after they started living together, she discovered that he was functionally illiterate.[17] She wrote letters to his parents for him occasionally because he lacked rudimentary reading and writing skills. Like many young men of his generation, he had learned how to feign literacy to such a degree that few ever noticed anything to the contrary, but in the intimacy of a personal relationship, his lack of education was obvious. The letters that Fard dictated during that period were always addressed to his parents in New Zealand as though their surnames were Ford. What finally destroyed the relationship was Fard's penchant for gambling and drugs, and his mercurial temper, which nearly landed him in jail.

On November 17, 1918, Fard was working in a restaurant at 803 West Third Street when P. W. Gillibrand came in. According to police reports,[18] Gillibrand ordered a meal, ate it, then refused to pay for it. Fard lost his temper and hit him with the butt of a handgun, knocking him to the floor. As Gillibrand tried to protect himself by curling into a fetal position, Fard struck him repeatedly with his fists. Other patrons pulled Fard off and restrained him until police arrived. When Fard told the arresting officers that his real name was Wali, they initially recorded it as "Wallei." Later, they spelled it as "Wallie," assuming that it was a nickname for Wallace (an assumption Ford encouraged). Fard was tried and convicted under the name of Wallie Ford of assault with a deadly weapon, but his sentence was suspended.[19]

The waitress Fard had been living with moved out after the trial, and several months later, Hazel Barton, a white woman from New York City, moved in with him. Hazel made it clear from the outset that she wanted to marry him, but Fard told her that that would be impossible, explaining that he was still married to a woman who refused to grant him a divorce. Hazel was so in love with him that she dismissed his erratic behavior and mysterious business dealings. In early 1919, twenty-six-year-old Fard and his twenty-five-year-old common-law wife moved into the home of an elderly white couple, Emmanuel Bushing and his Spanish-speaking wife, Annie, at 212 South Bunker Hill Avenue. On September 1, 1920, Hazel gave birth to Fard's son, whom they named Wallace Dodd Ford Jr. Fard's name appears on his son's birth certificate and on a United States census card for 1920 as Wallie D. Ford. His birthplace is listed as New Zealand on both documents. On the census report, Fard chose to leave the line for citizenship blank.[20]

As with his first marriage, Fard's behavior changed dramatically after the baby was born. Suspecting that Fard was having an affair, Hazel rummaged through his bureau one day while he was at the restaurant. To her horror, she discovered that she didn't even know the real name of the man she was living with. Hidden in one drawer was an old creased letter addressed to Fred Dodd. As she read it, she realized that Fred Dodd and her husband were one and the same.[21] The letter went into some detail about Fard's life in Portland, his first marriage, and his first-born son. When Hazel questioned Fard about his real identity, he insisted that his real name was Wallace Ford. But there were too many inconsistencies in his story, and she no longer trusted him. She waited until he left for work one day, then packed her belongings and left with the baby. Despondent, Fard sank deeper into drug abuse and gambling. In the winter of 1920, he and a close friend, a Chinese American named Edward Donaldson, moved to San Francisco.

Strong circumstantial evidence suggests that Fard used yet another alias there, that of George Farr.[22] According to ONI reports in late 1921, a man named George Farr got involved in the Theosophical Society, where he acted as an "advance man" for Brahmin Mohini Chatterjee, the East Indian mystic. Chatterjee's benefactor was Madame Blavatsky, the founder of the society who also is credited with sparking off Indian nationalism in the 1920s.[23]

In addition to his activities for the Theosophical Society, Farr also was a UNIA member. According to an ONI informant, Farr typically wore a beige military-style uniform with buttons advocating black nationalist themes espoused by Marcus Garvey, a fact which puzzled ONI investigators. Their summary stated:

> Though he claimed to be a Negro, his manner of talk, which had a little accent—not the Southern accent that is common to all Negroes, but the accent similar to that of an American-educated Hindu. He is rather small but stout. His facial color and the shape and structure of his face is also more like a Hindu than an American Negro.[24]

At the time the informant encountered Farr, Fard (which was, by the way, often pronounced "Farr" by Black Muslims interviewed by the FBI in the 1940s), he was living in the "Negro section" of San Francisco. According to ONI reports on Farr's philosophy, it was nearly identical to Fard's. Both men believed, for example, that the Holy Bible was a book of "prophecy," not a literal account of the history of the Jews. "All the prophecies in the Bible come true sooner or later," Farr told the ONI informant in December 1921. "Many of them have already become facts and others will. . . . That is one of the many things from the Bible we tell to the Negroes. They have to awaken to these possibilities."[25]

Just as Fard taught that black people were the victims of the white man's "tricknology," Farr told the informant that "the only thing for the colored people to do is to wake up and learn the tricks of the whites in politics, in warfare, and in industry and meet them with their own methods. Just look at Japan and what she has done and will do." Like Fard, Farr was described by the informant as vehemently antiwhite.[26]

"I do wonder," the informant said to Farr, "if there is any need of rousing racial hatred?" He replied:

> You bet there is justification [for racial hatred]. In certain sections of this country most work on farms and in factories is done by the negro—but what does the negro get in return? They get very little and hardly enough to maintain existence. . . . We negroes are tired of these things; we must get out and get away [from whites] so that we can develop ourselves freely somewhere by ourselves. And think what the

whites promised the negroes during the world war [World War I] and what they really gave them after the war was over. . . . Why should we work to death in peace times and kill ourselves in the trenches in time of war just for the white man's benefit?[27]

Clearly, Farr's views on blacks fighting for America were identical to Fard's, who regarded any follower of his who fought in America's armed services as a hypocrite. Farr, like Fard, argued quite persuasively that African Americans who lived in the South were for the most part "under slavery in reality, though not in name." Ten years after Farr was interviewed on the issue, Fard was in Detroit teaching that all black Americans were in a benign form of slavery.[28]

According to the informant, Farr lived at the Chicago Hotel on Pacific Street near Grant Avenue. The hotel was the center of black street life. It had a reputation for being a shady hangout, where blacks and whites gathered to trade and share illegal drugs and to play the Chinese lottery game known as Keno. What is particularly notable about Farr is that like Fard, he was the manager and a cook at a local café. Farr had a weakness for gambling and was a drug abuser. In fact, the owner had cautioned him about "shooting up" in the café or letting customers inject morphine on the premises. "Here is the queer thing," Officer J. J. Hanigan noted in one ONI report. "All the fellows in the game of working up racial and political hatred seem to carry with them some illegitimate business in forbidden drugs, bootlegging, or gambling."

According to the informant, Farr spent much of his free time at a Chinese café at 633 Pacific Street, where he mesmerized customers and curious onlookers with his pro-Japan, antiwhite harangues. Like Fard's friend, Farr's sidekick was a Chinese American.[29] If Farr was in fact Fard, then his Chinese-American friend noted by the ONI informant was in all likelihood Edward Donaldson, whom Fard first met in Los Angeles. Strengthening this probability even further is that in the summer of 1921, Donaldson, a waiter at the Pacific Avenue café, was arrested on narcotics charges. Since it was his first offense, he was sentenced to one year in jail, but it was suspended on condition that he stay out of trouble for that length of time. After the probationary period expired, he left immediately for Los Angeles.[30]

If Farr was another alias for Wallace D. Fard—and the evidence seems fairly convincing that it was—it would explain why descriptions of Fard's physical appearance, his philosophy, and his whereabouts in the early 1920s seem such an exact match for those of the man the informant identified as George Farr. It also would explain why Fard was so intimately familiar with the aspirations of poor African Americans, and why he formed such close ties to the Japanese political activists in America. Notably, the informant's reports on Farr ended in 1922, only a few weeks after Donaldson left San Francisco for Los Angeles. It is also suggestive that Fard's and Donaldson's encounters with the Los Angeles Police Department coincided, and that one of the arrests was narcotics-related.

Somehow, Fard raised enough money to open a restaurant in Los Angeles.[31] Judging from his arrest record, the source of his funding appeared to be bootlegging and drug trafficking, and the restaurant was apparently a front for his illicit enterprises. On January 20, 1926, Fard was arrested in Los Angeles for violating the Woolwine Act, also known as the California prohibition law, and the Volstead Act, the federal prohibition law. Specifically, he was arrested on four counts of possessing and selling alcoholic beverages.[32] On March 4, he was fined $1.00 or one day in jail for possession, and $400 or 180 days in jail for selling. He paid the fine and was released.

On February 15, while awaiting trial and sentencing on the violation of prohibition charges, Fard ran into more legal trouble. That evening, two white men came into his restaurant and asked waiter Donaldson if he knew where they could buy morphine. He told them yes, but it would cost them $225.[33] After haggling over the price for a few minutes, the two customers—actually undercover police officers—agreed to pay the full price. When one officer went into his pocket to get the money, Donaldson noticed handcuffs attached near the rear right pocket of his pants. Fard and Donaldson were suddenly apprehensive, but pretended that they had not seen the handcuffs. They told the prospective buyers that the deal was off. It was too late for that; the officers placed them under arrest and they were taken into custody. Three hours later, police returned to the restaurant with Fard to search for the drugs. Fard assured them that it was all a confidence game, that there weren't really any drugs on the premises. In the rear of the restaurant, the officers noticed a package rolled up in a newspaper.

"What's that?" the officer asked.

"That's just a bundle of old laundry," Fard replied.[34] The officer picked up the package and unrolled the newspaper. Instead of laundry, the newspaper was packed with vials of morphine, heroin, and cocaine. Faced with the damning evidence, Fard confessed that the drugs belonged to him and Donaldson. On May 14, 1926, a jury found Fard and Donaldson guilty of violating the California State Poison Act. Two weeks later, they were sentenced to a term of six months to six years, which they began serving at San Quentin on June 12. During the intake procedure at San Quentin, Fard said that his parents had been born in Hawaii. He also claimed that his father was employed as an machine operator at the Ford Bottling Works in Honolulu. A subsequent investigation found that there was no such plant in Honolulu, nor had there ever been. Fard also told prison officials that he was born in Portland on February 25, 1891. He resided there, he said, until 1913, when he moved to Los Angeles. The account omitted any references to his marriage to Pearl Allen. He listed his race as Hawaiian.[35]

Fard was a model prisoner, but declined to attend the first hearing for possible parole. He told the parole board that he would rather serve his whole sentence than be released on probation. After three years of working at the prison jute mill and on the chain gang, he was released. On May 27, one day short of his third anniversary at San Quentin, he was given a fresh suit, some spending money, and a one-way bus ticket to Los Angeles.

Fard hung around Los Angeles for about a month, then took a train to Chicago, where he soon found work as a traveling salesman. He bought doctors' supplies from the Marcellene Chemical Company in Richmond, Virginia, then sold them for a modest profit to physicians. The supplies were shipped to "W. D. Ford, General Delivery, Chicago,

Illinois."[36] Although Hazel had married, Fard wrote to her two or three times a year, mainly to inquire about his son. Her replies were always mailed to him at addresses in Chicago or Detroit—never anywhere else. Since the two main mosques of the NOI were in those cities, one would be hard-pressed to explain Fard's and Ford's presence in the same places at the same time as mere coincidence. Although Wallace Dodd Ford was using the name Fard, his letters were always signed with the name W. D. Ford, and that is how her replies were addressed. He also resumed his political activities. He joined the MSTA, but also spent time attending religious services at the Ahmadiyya Mosque at 4448 Wabash Avenue. Established in 1922, the mosque was the first one the Ahmadiyya Community opened in the United States, and it was financed by Ahmadis in India, the land of Fard's paternal ancestors.[37]

After the sudden death of Noble Drew Ali, Fard announced that he was the reincarnation of the MSTA leader. At least three others made the same claim, igniting a violent battle over leadership. Fard fled to Detroit, where he established the first branch of the Allah Temple of Islam in the fall of 1930. He returned to Chicago after things cooled down. Fard never mentioned the issue of reincarnation again, but held fast to his claim of being a prophet. Hundreds of disenchanted members of the MSTA believed him, and within a few months, Fard had enough income to open the second ATI temple. By 1933, he had opened temples in five more cities: Baltimore, New York City, Milwaukee, Cincinnati, and the District of Columbia. After a series of encounters with police in several states (his race-based religious activities made him an outlaw), he realized that he could no longer openly lead the Nation of Islam; police harassment had become too great.

In the summer of 1934, Fard packed his belongings and headed back to Los Angeles, showing up at Hazel's door in July. He was driving, she noted, a 1929 Model A Ford coupe with California license plates. Desperate to see Hazel and his twelve-year-old son, he paid little attention to the fact that her new husband was at home. Hazel was surprised to see him. His physical appearance caught her off guard as he was wearing his hair much longer than she remembered. She was also puzzled by what appeared to be white sheets on the back seat of the car. When she asked about them, he offered to let her have them. They were, he said, his religious garments, but he no longer had any use for them as he was on the way back to New Zealand. He also gave her a box of self-threading needles. The box, postmarked April 28, 1930, and addressed to W. D. Ford in Chicago, later became part of the FBI's bulky exhibits file as it searched for clues to Fard's whereabouts.[38]

During his brief stay in Los Angeles, Fard concentrated on things paternal. He tried to create some rapport with his son, but was unsuccessful and he remained just another stranger to the child. Hazel was puzzled by his apparent wealth and tried to determine its source, but most of the answers he gave her were riddles. While admiring the interior of the car, she discovered pamphlets that startled her. The father of her son, the man she believed was a Caucasian, was carrying around literature that denounced Caucasians as a race of devils and proclaimed himself to be a prophet. She asked Fard what he had been doing since his release from prison, but his replies were vague. Hazel offered him lunch on one occasion, but he declined, saying that he ate only one meal a day as part of his new way of life.

After Fard left, Hazel forgot about the pamphlets until Satohata Takahashi's arrest in 1939 made headlines. Fard's name was mentioned in many of the stories about Takahashi's pro-Axis activities, and she became concerned that her son would discover the unsavory truths about his natural father. To protect him from his father's shadow, Hazel petitioned the Superior Court of Los Angeles on July 10, 1940, for permission to change the boy's birth certificate. Permission was granted, and the birth certificate for Wallace Dodd Ford Jr. was changed to read "Wallace Max Ford."[39]

As far as anyone knew, Fard left the United States that same month. It is worth noting, however, that his return to Los Angeles coincided with Donaldson's parole from San Quentin.[40] Moreover, Elijah Muhammad and members of his family claimed that Fard was still in America, and that they were in contact with him. Wallace Muhammad claimed to have been in touch with Fard as recently as 1990. "Master Fard Muhammad is not dead, brothers and sisters," Wallace said during a speech on March 19, 1976. "He is physically alive and I talk to him whenever I get ready. I don't talk to him in any spooky way. I go to the telephone and dial his number." (In the early 1990s, Wallace confessed that the man he had represented as being Fard was someone else.)[41]

The Messenger always claimed that Fard had come from Mecca, but there were too many inconsistencies in the story, some of them geographical, others etymological, and still others historical. For example, while the name Fard is regarded as an Arabic surname, it is rarely used outside India and its neighbor countries. Notably, it's a very popular name in Pakistan, particularly among the Urdu-speaking population. Similarly, Zared, the given name of Fard's father, is an Urdu name.[42] A second word linking Fard to Pakistan is Shabazz, the name he used to label African Americans. There was no place on Earth called Shabazz before Fard invented it. The only place on Earth where a similar word was used during Fard's lifetime was in India. The name Shahbaz is as popular in Pakistan today as Lincoln or Washington is in America, as it carries great historical significance. A free-text search for "Shabazz" in nearly 900,000 documents contained in the news research database at the *Washington Post* revealed that it appears exclusively in stories about African Americans, most of whom were or had been members of the NOI.[43] In contrast, the same records produced only four stories containing the word "Shahbaz," and all four concerned Pakistan or Pakistanis.[44]

Another clue connecting Fard to Pakistan was the first names he chose to give Elijah Poole and one of his brothers. In 1932, Fard changed Poole's name to Ghulam Ali. In addition to being one of the names of the founder of the Ahmadiyya Movement, Ghulam is a commonly used name in Pakistan, meaning, in Urdu, "most humble servant" or "slave," the latter connotation resulting from the "slave sultans" period in India (roughly from 1192 through 1525).[45] A database search produced 148 references to "Ghulam." Two stories involved individuals living near the Afghanistan-Pakistan border and five were about the Ahmadiyya Movement, many of whose leaders have Ghulam as part of their name. The remaining 141 references all related to Pakistan. The final search of the database focused on "Kallatt," the name Fard gave Jarmin, one of Elijah's younger brothers. The name is unique and wasn't found even once in nearly a million records. Another search for "Kallatt" was pursued in the world's largest database, the World Wide Web. Using the MetaCrawler search engine in 1998 produced a mere dozen hits—and of the twelve, none was about a city or country, and only one was someone's name— that of Elijah Muhammad's brother Kallatt. The other eleven were German Web sites mentioning the word "Kalla" or "Kalata" or "Kala" within the same line as the letter "t." A search for "Kalat" produced fifty-five hits. Most were the names of men from Pakistan named Kalat, and one-third of these referred to the Kalat project, an archaeological dig under way in Italy. One reference was to a fish known as the "kalat" in some cultures. The search also turned up a single reference to the word "Khallatt," which, it turns out, is an Australian Web site run by orthodox Muslims who are outraged by the apostasy of Louis Farrakhan; it was their way of spelling Kallatt Muhammad's name.

If one bears in mind that Fard had poor language skills, it would explain why he often misspelled names and places—why he referred to Shahbaz as Shabazz, for instance, and why he spelled Kallatt with two extra consonants. Kalat is the name of a small town in a crowded corridor that wasn't on the map in 1932—Pakistan. It has an illustrious history, however, as it was once ruled by the powerful Khan of Kalat. When Great Britain was expanding its empire in India in the 1850s, its "armies marched through the lands of the Khan of Kalat to reach Qandahar."[46]

Still, the question remains why Fard chose Shabazz as the native land of his so-called lost tribe. The reasoning becomes clearer once his Pakistani roots are exposed. India, which has produced two contemporary world religions—Hinduism and Buddhism—was the home of advanced civilizations that have yet to be accurately dated, but are believed to have declined "around 1500 B.C. from uncertain causes." Although Zared Fard lived most of his adult life in New Zealand, he traced his lineage back to one of these ancient peoples. In New Zealand, he was listed as a Polynesian member of the cultural group called Maori Indians. Anthropologists discovered nearly a century ago that the word "Maori" is the Anglicized word for Maury. "Even the name Maori is an abstraction, created in the nineteenth century." Cook called them Indians, though the name New Zealanders was soon adopted.[47] Maoris in New Zealand interviewed by researchers in the early 1920s said that according to their lore, "they had come originally from a western land called Urdu and then migrated to Irihia which . . . was very like Vrihia, the Sanscrit [sic] name for India."[48] Chadragupta Maurya was the architect of the Mauryean empire, which existed in India at least four centuries before the birth of Christ. To the north of the Mauryan empire was the Kushan empire (there was, incidentally, a Cush kingdom in East Africa, though no anthropological nexus has been established).[49]

In 1177, a child named Usman Marwandvi was born into an upper-class family in Marwand, a small town in Azerbaijan. He was educated in the Sufi and Dervish tradition, and was a highly regarded religious leader by his early twenties. He joined the Order of Qalandria, an elite group of Sufis who gave up everything worldly to devote themselves to the propagation of Islam. As he rose to prominence in the order, his name was changed to Shahbaz Qalander.[50] "A Qalander is a saint whose actions are believed to be directly commanded by God and are based on love and devotion to God." Shahbaz Qalander is only one of three saints recognized by Islamic scholars. Today, his mausoleum, the Shrine of Lal Shahbaz Qalander, attracts millions of Muslims every year. Lal Shahbaz Qalander translates into English as "red falcon" or "king of the hawks (phoenix)."[51]

Since stories about Shahbaz Qalander are part of Pakistan's folklore, it should come as no surprise that Zared Fard familiarized his son with them, in much the same way that American children hear how young George Washington chopped down the cherry tree. Essentially, then, all Fard did was to transpose his own heritage onto African Americans, who were burdened with a psychological slavery induced by an inferiority complex. Significantly, Shahbaz Qalander's birthplace, Azerbaijan, was the same country that Fard claimed was his mother's homeland.[52]

When one juxtaposes the fact that Fard resembled a Hindu with the evidence that his father's roots are in Pakistan, one can draw several logical conclusions. First, Zared Fard or his parents were probably Muslims who were born in Sindh Province, perhaps near the town of Kalat.

Zared relayed his knowledge of the ancient civilization there to his son, Wallace Dodd. Finally, when Wallace D. Fard devised the eschatology of the NOI, he merely co-opted the history of his own people to African Americans. "The Madhi," the Messenger said of Fard, was

> a world traveler. He told me that he had traveled the world over and that he had visited North America for twenty years before making himself known to us, his people, whom he came for. He had visited the Isles of the Pacific, Japan and China . . . India, Pakistan, all of the Near East and Africa.[53]

The description of Fard's travels is interesting for one obvious reason. To begin with, if 1934 was the last time the Messenger saw Fard (his usual story), how could Fard have described his visits to Pakistan, as the state wasn't founded until 1947, some thirteen years after his alleged disappearance? Equally curious are several statements the Messenger made in 1972. When speaking about how he learned to read the Holy Quran, he said that Fard gave him a new one in September 1971. The first Holy Quran that Fard gave him was in Arabic, and "I couldn't read it. So he got me one in Arabic and English translated by Maulana Muhammad Ali of Pakistan." What he omitted to say was that the translator was, in addition to being from Pakistan, a prominent leader of the Ahmadiyya Movement, which opened its first mosque in Chicago near the site that Fard later chose to establish the NOI's second mosque.[54]

Yet another clue linking Fard to Pakistan comes from people who met him or saw unretouched photographs of him. Muslims who remember seeing photographs of Fard recall, without exception, that he appeared to be Pakistani. "This man didn't look like he was 'Afro-American,'" Elijah's grandson Ozier Muhammad recalled. "He looked like he was Pakistani, and we're thinking that this man is God, like Jesus, the son of God."[55]

"Everyone knew Fard was a Pakistani," Rodnell Collins claims.[56] "My mother, Malcolm, all the ministers knew." Malcolm's brother, Wilfred Little, took issue with his nephew's assertion that everyone knew, but he agreed that "Fard appeared to be a Pakistani." Wilfred Little said Malcolm X was too busy proselytizing to give Fard's origins much thought.[57] Even when the stories leaked to the media embarrassed the NOI, Malcolm X held firmly to his belief that Fard was from Saudi Arabia.

If Fard was the son of a Pakistani Muslim, that would explain his hatred of Hinduism. During his three-year education of the Messenger, Fard made only derogatory references to Hinduism and other East Indian polytheistic religions. When the Messenger condemned Hinduism in his pamphlet *The Supreme Wisdom*, he echoed Fard's sentiments:

> What a difference there is between the three religions [Christianity, Buddhism, and Islam]! The first teaches that there are three Gods, not one. . . . The second, Buddhism, requires belief in reincarnation, and contains many ignorant practices. . . . The true religion of Allah and His Prophets Noah, Abraham, Moses, and Jesus was Islam, and it is to overcome all religions. . . . That is why the race and Indian Hindus have always been and are now the enemies of Islam and Muslims.[58]

The Messenger's views on Hinduism are, not surprisingly, the same as those expressed by Fard.

For nearly forty years, the Messenger had insisted that Fard had come to America on Independence Day 1930. It wasn't until the early 1970s that he admitted that this was not true. "He had come in and out of this country for about twenty years before ever he made himself known to us," the Messenger said during a 1972 interview. "And finally he told me this: that he had studied every education system of the civilized world, and that he could speak . . . sixteen languages and write ten of them."[59] The interview was revelatory for several reasons. To begin with, it corroborated evidence that Fard was in California at the same time as Wallace D. Ford and the "Hindu" revolutionary an informant identified as George Farr. Fard understood a great many things—cabalism, theosophy, Freemasonry—but it seems highly doubtful that he studied every philosophy and education system. Moreover, since the Messenger spoke only English, he had no way of knowing whether Fard was feigning knowledge of certain languages or was really speaking them. To be sure, he probably spoke and understood several languages. One must bear in mind that his father spoke Urdu, he lived with a family in Los Angeles where the owner's wife conversed mostly in Spanish, and his best friend was Chinese. Clearly, then, he was familiar with perhaps four to six tongues. At any rate, and as Khaalis pointed out, a man whom one worships as the Almighty would be expected to speak more than sixteen languages; he would know them all.

In the course of its second major investigation of Fard, the FBI reexamined materials seized in the Messenger's home during the raid of September 20, 1942. "Bulky file" exhibits were removed from the Bureau's storage facilities to determine whether they offered additional insight concerning Fard. In one of the sixteen boxes was an item labeled "Exhibit Number 176." It was described thus: "steel cut on a wooden frame. Print of steel cut reflected a picture of Prophet Fard addressing a congregation." At the time the print was made, newspapers used heavy steel squares to print newspapers. Photos were processed on metal, pasted onto a piece of wood the same size as the photo, and inserted into the metal frame for printing. When the Bureau made a copy of the photo from the steel cut, it was very clear that Ford and Fard were the same person.[60]

A big breakthrough for the FBI came on October 17, 1957, when agents from the Los Angeles field office interviewed Hazel Barton, who was then known as Hazel Barton Ford Osborne Evelsizer, at her home at 4776 Hub Street. According to Hazel, Fard's son, Wallace Dodd Ford Jr., was in the U.S. Coast Guard during World War II. He was killed in a traffic accident, she said, on August 3, 1942, in Linhaven Roads, Virginia. She showed the agents documentation of Fard's son's death. Hazel told the agents that the last time she saw Fard was in 1932. On that occasion, she noticed that little had changed regarding Fard's outward appearance. The only difference, she told the agents, was that when she knew him, he always "had a short conventional haircut, but then he was wearing it long and full in the back.[61]

Three days before the visit to Hazel, the Los Angeles field office had checked the Los Angeles County Birth Index for the period from 1911 through 1927. On page 7850 of volume 173 for births in 1920, the

Bureau found the birth certificate of Wallace Dodd Ford, a male child born on September 1, 1920, at the MacDonald Sanitarium. According to the original birth certificate for Fard's son by Hazel, Fard listed his race as white, and said he was twenty-six years old, placing his year of birth between 1893 and 1895.[62] His occupation was listed as "restaurant keeper."

The Bureau honed in closer to the real Fard with the aid of other branches of the intelligence community. In November 1957, it asked the ONI to search its files for Wallace Don Fard, with aliases, but was informed on December 6 that nothing had turned up. The failure to find any data may have been due to the FBI's failure to note that, according to its own records, Fard was sometimes called Farr. Had the surname Farr been included in the search, ONI would have uncovered a man who fit Fard's profile. When the ONI search came up empty, Hoover asked the U.S. Army to search its G-2 files.[63] On December 9, G-2 agents notified the Baltimore Field Office that a search of the army's Central Records Facility was unproductive concerning Fard, but did produce files on eight individuals with similar names, physical characteristics, and political persuasions. Among the names were Emmanuel Pharr, leader of the SDOO, in Gary, Indiana, but ironically, this lead was rejected as irrelevant. Khaalis, however, argues rather credibly that Fard was not only in Gary during the mid-1940s, but that he was a key figure in the SDOO until his arrest on rape charges there. Moreover, the name that Khaalis swore Fard was using while in Gary—John Walker— appears several times in the FBI's declassified main file on the SDOO.[64]

On February 11, 1958, agents from the FBI's Detroit field office went to the home of Marion Kieber of Flint, Michigan. Kieber was the daughter of Erdmann D. Beynon, the sociologist who did the seminal study of the NOI between 1936 and 1937. Beynon had visited Temple No. 1, on Hastings near Wilkens Street, on dozens of occasions. He also had visited the University of Islam, often taking his daughter along. During those visits, Kieber saw both actual photos and glamorized portraits of Fard. There was absolutely no doubt in her mind, she said, that the man in the 1933 police print was the same as the man named Fard whose photos she had seen at the temple and the school.[65]

The final piece of evidence that the FBI had, which proved the dual identity beyond a reasonable doubt, was an interview from 1942 that had been buried in the Detroit field office file. On July 10, agents from that office interviewed a Muslim who had met Fard in 1931, and who, together with his family, had grown close to him over the next two years. After interviewing the man for over an hour, an agent pulled out a mug shot of Wallace D. Ford and asked him if he could identify the man in the picture. The Muslim, who looked as though he had seen a ghost, exclaimed, "My Sweet Saviour, My All Powerful Allah!"[66]

The man who positively identified Fard as Wallace D. Ford was eminently believable. After all, he was another namesake of Master Wallace Fard—Wali Muhammad Jr., formerly known as Willie Poole Jr.—the brother of Elijah Muhammad. The photograph he identified as being a picture of Fard was taken on May 26, 1933—of a man police identified from fingerprints and other evidence as Wallace Dodd Ford. On Saviour's Day 1957, the Messenger published the first half of *The Supreme Wisdom*, a pamphlet in which he stated the following about Fard: "He was persecuted, sent to jail in 1932, and ordered out of Detroit, Michigan, May 26, 1933."[67]

In speeches monitored by the FBI under its COINTELPRO against the NOI, the Messenger said that Fard went to Chicago in 1933 after his May 26 arrest. In May 1957, the Chicago field office contacted the Chicago Police Department's Records and Communications Section to determine whether it had any records relating to Fard's arrest in 1933. On May 8, that office advised the Bureau that its records contained "no information indicating any arrest for W. D. Fard." The records did, however, have an entry pertaining to the arrest of Wallace Dodd Ford in September 1933. According to documents in the city's records warehouse, "quasi-criminal complaint [number] 3227492" dealt with the arrest of Wallace Ford of Detroit on September 25, 1933.[68] Ford, who was delivering a typical sermon about the evils of the white race, was arrested at three o'clock after a citizen called to complain that a confidence man was stirring up African Americans who had gathered at a house near the intersection of 48th Street and Calumet. The intersection, by the way, is less than two square blocks from the Ahmadiyya Movement's first mosque in America. During the booking process, Ford described himself as a forty-year-old unemployed Negro from Detroit. The next morning, he was taken before Judge Dunn of Branch 34, at which time he waived a jury trial. After hearing the facts, the judge concluded that Fard was merely exercising his rights of free speech and told an embarrassed prosecutor that he was dismissing the charges. Upon his release, Fard went to Los Angeles and became the Invisible Man.

Elijah Muhammad moved to Chicago and became Elijah the Prophet. He tore down the pictures of a white-skinned Jesus from the temple walls and replaced them with his heretical white-skinned version of Allah.[69]

CHAPTER NINETEEN

A CON FOR A CON

An eye for an eye,
a tooth for a tooth,
Vote for me,
and I'll set you free!
    —*Temptations,*
        "Ball of Confusion"[1]

And it came to pass, as they still went on, and talked, that, behold, there appeared a chariot of fire, and horses of fire, and Elijah went up by a whirlwind into heaven.
                                            —*II Kings 2:11*

"Salaami . . . Salaami . . . Baloney."
                —Popeye *cartoon depicting Muslims at prayer*

The rumors about the Messenger's mind slipping took on more credibility after he spoke on Saviour's Day 1974:

Chicago white people are to be thanked for making it possible for us to obtain the Country Club and to get us to such a position where we can prove ourselves worthy. You do not disrespect people that are trying to respect you. Honor and respect the white man while his flag still flies over America. . . . The fault is not on the slavemaster any more since he said you can go free and we see that he is not angry with us. We are hindering ourselves. . . . It's time for us to stop calling white folks the devil because there's some black devils too. . . . Give justice to him when it is due. He cannot hold you as a slave. You are holding yourselves as slaves.[2]

These were strange words coming from a man who had grown wealthy condemning Caucasians for everything from lynching to lint in his hair in the morning. Times had changed, and Muhammad was finally getting the attention from white people that he had been craving for most of his life. On March 26, which was declared "The Honorable Elijah Muhammad Day in Chicago" by Mayor Richard Daley, a testimonial dinner was held at the Conrad Hilton by black civic and business leaders.[3] Among those who attended was President Nixon's special assistant for domestic affairs, Stanley S. Scott, who later received special appointments from Gerald Ford and George Bush.[4] A Pulitzer Prize nominee for his eyewitness account of the assassination of Malcolm X, Scott was the black reporter who integrated the staff of UPI, which certainly lent a touch of irony. Nixon was less negative about the Messenger after learning from FBI reports that the black leader was seriously considering attending the Republican National Convention in San Diego, and also considering letting Muslims vote.[5] The president was unable to attend the dinner owing to a pesky investigation called Watergate.

Muhammad published a book in May 1974 entitled *Our Saviour Has Arrived,* which was another compilation of columns from *Muhammad Speaks.* He also began traveling to Mexico, where he had purchased a home in Cuernavaca and opened a mosque.[6] He was usually accompanied by Tynetta Nelson, one of his mistresses and the mother of four of his illegitimate children. In August 1974, he bought a Lockheed Jet Star, which reporters for *Muhammad Speaks* said he needed to keep up with his hectic schedule.[7] In fact, the Messenger was afraid of flying and in actuality, he rarely left home. The plane was used primarily by a grandson who lived with him, and he himself only boarded the plane when it was absolutely necessary, such as flying back and forth to Mexico City for unorthodox medical treatment. Muslims paid for the plane in cash in response to a plea in *Muhammad Speaks* to raise $1,000,000 in ninety days to cover the cost of the jet.[8]

A trip to Mexico in September hadn't done Muhammad much good, so he returned to Chicago after several weeks. When FBI agents visited him on October 20, he was too ill to talk to them. But Velora Najieb, who described herself as his personal secretary, said she was authorized to speak on his behalf.[9] She told them that Muhammad was deeply troubled by the situation in the Philadelphia mosque. The agents said they were concerned about press accounts of bank robberies, extortion, and drug activities that were damaging the reputation of the Messenger and the NOI.[10] The agents went to his home to interview him again on November 12, and he said at that time that he could not be an informant on his own group, but promised to offer them any assistance he could.[11] The agents were utterly astonished at his final words. "The white man and the black man must learn to live together and to respect each other if America is to survive." They listened patiently as Muhammad rambled on and on, they reported, "about how much he loved America."[12] It must have been unnerving to hear the frail old black man who had grown wealthy preaching hatred for whites droning on endlessly in his twilight hour of his affection for "Babylon"—which is what he called America in his books, expressly *The Fall of America*.[13] He had come to terms, judging from their conversation, with the fact that changing his name and his religion did not make the genes he inherited from Middleton Pool disappear from his bloodline, nor multiply those he received from African ancestors of unknown origin.

If anyone still doubted that Muhammad had changed his thinking about Caucasians, his comments during an interview with William Brashler, author of *The Bingo Long Traveling All-Stars and Motor Kings*, left no more room for such doubt. Two non-Muslims who answered Muhammad's call for help from college-trained black middle-class professionals were Richard Durham and Leon Forrest, editors of *Muhammad Speaks*. Durham came into the room during the Brashler interview to get approval for several pages of the next edition of the paper. A troubled expression came over Muhammad's face. "This story here about the Second Ward Race."[14]

"Yes, sir," Durham replied.

"Oh, but Leon, we never get involved in politics."

"Yes, sir."

"And Leon, I've been thinking lately, what with things in the Nation taking a turn over the years, let's not talk no more about any blue-eyed devils."

In early January 1975, the Messenger flew to Cuernavaca in search of medical miracles. He was on oxygen continuously and his diabetes was out of control. The FBI legal attaché in Mexico City guessed that the aged leader would not last much longer, and the Bureau began speculating as to what would happen in terms of racial unrest if Muhammad died in a foreign country.[15] There were conspiracy theories that the CIA had poisoned Malcolm X when he was in Egypt in 1964. If Muhammad died, there were bound to be allegations of government complicity. After a flurry of memos back and forth across the border, the matter resolved itself. Muhammad suddenly returned to Chicago for what Muslim officials described as a "routine medical examination." In fact, the Messenger's health was deteriorating so rapidly that by the time he reached the hospital he was barely clinging to life. On February 8, he suffered congestive heart failure.[16] After emergency surgery he was moved to the intensive care unit and hooked up to a dizzying array of machines and intravenous tubing. His condition stabilized for a day or so, then worsened over the next two weeks. His dream of surviving for one more Saviour's Day was not fulfilled. At eight o'clock on February 24, Dr. Charles Williams, his personal physician, advised his family that the Messenger had died. His death, like that of Malcolm, had come only days before the holiest day in Islam, at least as it was practiced by most African Americans. On February 21, the tenth anniversary of Malcolm's assassination, the FBI issued an urgent message to the Secret Service and other intelligence agencies:

> The Nation of Islam is a Chicago-based black separatist organization considering whites to be devils, that has produced considerable violence in recent years. Chicago is following. In the event of Muhammad's death, there is the potential for violence among his followers battling for control of the Nation of Islam.[17]

Eulogies poured in. Mayor Richard Daley, who declared February 26 "Nation of Islam Day," described Muhammad's demise as "a great loss to the city and to the entire country. He was an outstanding citizen who was always interested in helping young people and especially the poor."[18] Vernon E. Jordan, executive director of the NUL, said that the Messenger's death "is to be sincerely regretted but his legacy of achievement remains as his eternal monument." Jesse Jackson, whose leadership the Messenger found lacking, was at his poetic best: "He turned alienation into emancipation. He concentrated on taking the slums out of the people and then the people out of the slums. He took dope out of veins and put hope in our brains." The most ambivalent comment was issued by Roy Wilkins: the Messenger "was a leader of the Black Muslims and will be missed by them and all those with whom the Muslims had business or social relations."[19]

Chaos reigned at the Saviour's Day Convention the next day. Muhammad died intestate, and had said repeatedly in his last interviews that he had no intention of designating a successor. "God chose me and if he wants a successor to me He will choose one. The work that I am doing . . . I don't think God needs one. What would another one do? There will be no successor. It will be an altogether new religion."[20] His family knew it wasn't quite that simple; someone had to be in charge. When the faithful gathered at Chicago's International Amphitheater on February 26, the royal family knew that they had better come up with a new leader, and fast. It was quickly decided that the best strategy was to name Wallace as his father's heir. After all, Muslims were still being taught the allegorical story about how Fard had prophesied Wallace's future when he was still inside his mother's womb. Naming someone else would have been illogical and might have led to the most serious erosion in membership since the murder of Malcolm X ten years earlier.

As the ministers stepped up to the microphone to eulogize the Messenger, each of them swore allegiance to Wallace. National secretary Abbass Rassoull told the congregation:

> Today we would like to inform the world that there is no leadership crisis in the Nation of Islam. Almighty Allah, in the person of Master Fard Muhammad, the Honorable Elijah Muhammad and the royal family have chosen Wallace D. Muhammad to lead the Nation of Islam. . . . We pledge to our royal family that we love you and we offer to you our very lives.[21]

Farrakhan could hardly deliver his eulogy for crying. People waiting for the NOI to split up through various bids for power will be disappointed, he said, dabbing tears away with a white handkerchief.[22] "The Honorable Elijah Muhammad did not teach his followers to think that way." Wallace Muhammad's reign, he declared, "is the will of God." That was all well and good, but Wallace did not trust Farrakhan. Neither did the Messenger. Tynetta's charges concerning Farrakhan's plagiarism of her play stuck with the Messenger, as did his hasty betrayal of Malcolm. Financial irregularities in the Harlem mosque had also been a sore point. Lastly, two of Farrakhan's sons became engaged to Muhammad's nieces in late 1974, when the Messenger was seriously ill. At that time, "My father told me to keep an eye on him because he was trying to use the family," Elijah Muhammad Jr. said.[23]

More than 7,000 people gathered in and outside Chicago's Mosque No. 2 on February 28 for the funeral service, and a procession of 500 cars escorted the body in its $20,000 silver casket to Mount Glenwood Cemetery in Glenwood, Illinois.[24] The casket was disinterred shortly thereafter, and Wallace announced that the family planned to build a shrine for the Messenger's body inside the NOI headquarters on South Stoney Island Avenue.[25]

In the weeks after the funeral, Wallace got wind of rumors that Farrakhan was contemplating a power play. National Secretary Abbass Rassoull suggested to Wallace that one way of preventing Farrakhan from even thinking about contesting his leadership was to move the popular minister from the Harlem mosque to Chicago, where Wallace could keep close watch on him, and to move other powerful East Coast ministers to mosques in the West and Midwest. Wallace took Rassoull's advice, and gave Farrakhan a hefty pay raise. But after relocating, Farrakhan realized that while he was at the center of the NOI's power, Wallace had no intention of sharing it with him. Gradually, Farrakhan became disillusioned with Wallace, particularly after Wallace began ridiculing Elijah, calling his father's teachings nothing more than gobbledygook, a hodgepodge of Islam, Christianity, Freemasonry, and heaven knows what else.

As Rassoull became more powerful, Farrakhan's authority diminished. After learning that the Church Committee Report on domestic intelligence operations mentioned that FBI informants had risen to powerful positions inside the NOI, Farrakhan and Larry 4X Prescott, his former chief in Harlem, began to suspect that Rassoull was an informant.[26]

Despite the professions of unity, the FBI had accurately predicted that infighting would start among the group's leaders upon the Messenger's death. On March 1, Herbert's son called the *New York Amsterdam News* and told the editor that the Saviour's Day message of unity was a complete farce. "I was a personal aide and attendant to my grandfather for six months prior to his death," Herbert Jr. said. He said further that

Wallace waited until the Messenger became comatose before he started planning his takeover of the NOI. After physicians told the family that there was almost no chance of Elijah coming out of the coma, Wallace, without consulting other family members, placed

> an article in the *Chicago Daily Defender* in which he made the statement that my grandfather . . . had groomed him and named him as his successor. This is a statement . . . based on a lie, for my grandfather did not groom him or name him to be his successor any more so than he had done [*sic*] for others of his family.[27]

Herbert Jr. revealed that Wallace and Elijah remained at odds until late October 1974, when the family was told that the Messenger could die at any time. Wallace had gradually eased himself back into his father's inner circle, but Elijah had remained steadfast in his decision not to select a successor, as he fervently believed that he was the Seal of the Prophets. During a meeting of Wallace, Herbert, Nathaniel, and Emmanuel on February 20, three agreed that Wallace and Nathaniel would jointly attend to spiritual matters, while Herbert would oversee financial concerns. Wallace disagreed, telling his brothers that he could carry the NOI alone. Although his brothers balked at such a plan, Wallace called a press conference and announced that his father had designated him as sole ruler of the NOI. The brothers remained silent, Herbert Jr. said, for fear of giving the "appearance of a power struggle within the family"; in other words, for fear of revealing the truth.[28]

Wallace moved quickly to distance himself from his father's teachings. On March 7, he announced that white people would no longer be referred to as "devils" because they had begun to treat members of minority groups more fairly in recent years, but that whites would still be barred from joining the NOI.[29] However, during an address to 40,000 at Madison Square Garden three months later, Wallace shocked his followers by urging Caucasians to join the new and improved NOI.[30] The first white woman to join the organization, which Wallace renamed the World Community of Al-Islam (the first of many name changes), was Dorothy Dorsey. Dorsey joined the group in early 1975 and became the immediate focus of media curiosity, much like Ota Benga in the Bronx Zoo in the early 1900s, but after a few months, she returned to obscurity. In the first few months of Wallace's rule, the Church Committee began holding hearings on the late J. Edgar Hoover's abuse of power. The discovery of the COINTELPRO program in 1973 caused a furor that did not subside until Congress began a public investigation. The final report revealed a massive counterintelligence campaign against both Dr. Martin Luther King and the Black Panther Party:

> The techniques used in COINTELPRO were—and are—used against hostile foreign intelligence agents. Sullivan's testimony that the "rough, tough, dirty business" of foreign counterintelligence was brought home against domestic enemies was corroborated by George Moore, whose Racial Intelligence Section supervised the White Hate and Black Nationalist COINTELPROs.[31]

To a lesser extent, it also focused on COINTELPROS against the NOI:

> I think as we have gone through the materials today, there might be some suggestion that the Bureau did not make any effort to secure guidance from the Department of Justice. While I think that may be true in some cases, we have others in which the effort was made, and which the Department is either unresponsive or merely takes a see no evil, hear no evil kind of approach, and at the same time nods to the Bureau, go ahead, or at least, go ahead if you wish to. The case in point is the effort initiated against the Nation of Islam, the so-called Black Muslims.[32]

Copies of documents released by the Church Committee were obtained by Farrakhan and later used to help bolster his break with Wallace. After quitting the NOI in 1978, Farrakhan wandered about the country trying to find himself. As his bankroll dwindled, he started to drift back into street life. He considered drinking to ease his troubles, then thought about leaving New York for Hollywood, where "blaxploitation" movies were being churned out like cars on a General Motors assembly line.[33] Then someone told him that declassified FBI documents mentioned a plot by Hoover to destroy the NOI by placing FBI informants in key leadership positions. After researching the allegations, Farrakhan obtained documents that corroborated the story. More importantly, he obtained pages from a declassified document in which agents talked of creating a situation whereby Wallace would succeed his father as head of the NOI. By late 1979, when Farrakhan launched his own newspaper, *The Final Call to Islam,* the reconstituted NOI was circulating a story about FBI documents that portrayed Wallace as an FBI spy.

The Bureau did consider Wallace and Hassan Sharrieff reliable allies during the period that Wallace and Malcolm were conferring on the bastardy scandal in 1964. But this characterization may have been made without their knowledge. Both men had given FBI agents highly valuable insights into the inner workings of the NOI, and both said to agents during wiretapped telephone calls that they were not opposed to speaking freely with them. As noted earlier, Hassan had even inquired about becoming an FBI agent. One must bear several points in mind, however. Hassan's query about becoming an agent was probably intended to flatter the agents interviewing him, for as far as one can tell he never raised the issue again. As for negative comments made by Wallace to the FBI about Malcolm and the Messenger, one might fairly conclude that he was trying to distance himself from both leaders since he knew that they were despised by the Bureau, and Wallace wanted more than anything for the FBI to protect him from his own family. Lastly, agents often exaggerated the importance of their informants—it's amazing how many were called "highly placed" or "highly reliable"—for self-promotion purposes.

The documents were circulated by parties opposed to Wallace's admission of whites into the World Community of Al-Islam. Wallace, however, did not help matters by leveling outlandish charges against his father, and by claiming that Imam Muhammad Abdullah of Hayward, California, was in fact Wallace D. Fard.[34] His move toward orthodoxy and his portrayal of the Messenger and Fard as misguided ignoramuses caused a significant backlash. Then, when he decided to sell nearly everything that his father had acquired—the newspaper and the commercial and residential real estate—he inadvertently gave further credence to charges that he was trying to destroy his father's little nation. In fact, he was forced to sell the holdings because the NOI was drowning in an ocean of insolvency.[35]

In the midst of the Church Committee hearings, Elijah's son Nathaniel, head of the Kansas City mosque, was indicted along with five other men by a federal grand jury for conspiring to possess and sell heroin during the first seven months of 1975. One conspirator was Juan Pablo García, a suspected drug kingpin from Mexico City. The indictment, which was handed up on September 25, accused Nathaniel of heavy involvement in the heroin and cocaine trade.[36]

On February 2, 1976, Wallace designated Farrakhan to announce that a decision had been made to rename the Harlem mosque in honor of Malcolm. The mosque was being renamed in Malcolm's honor, Farrakhan said at a press conference, "in recognition of the great work that Malcolm X did when he was among us."[37] In March 1998, Farrakhan announced that Norman 3X Butler had been named minister of Muhammad's Mosque No. 7 in Harlem, the one under the auspices of Farrakhan's NOI. There was a loud public outcry that Farrakhan had the effrontery to appoint a man who had served a life sentence for allegedly conspiring to kill Malcolm X to run the mosque named in memory of his martyred victim. In explaining the appointment, Benjamin F. Chavis Muhammad declared that Butler "was falsely accused, wrongly convicted, and unjustly imprisoned for twenty years, and to this day is unfairly the target of racial hatred, fear, ignorance and misinformation." Benjamin, who was himself wrongfully convicted and sentenced when he was a Christian activist, rightly pointed out that Butler might have been railroaded in the Malcolm X murder case. What was left out, however, was Butler's arrest during the investigation of the attempted murder of Benjamin Brown, and allegations that he was with Johnson on the night that another dissident was so badly beaten that he almost died.[38]

Farrakhan isn't just disliked by people who believe that he has played a provocative role in the civil rights movement. Captain Joseph, who died a few years ago, also accused Farrakhan of misrepresenting the Holy Quran by claiming that the Messenger was abiding by Islamic law when he seduced his secretaries. In an interview with movie director Spike Lee prior to the shooting of the film about Malcolm X, Joseph sharply disagreed. "That's not what the Holy Quran says. . . . Here's what the Holy Quran says: 'You are allowed four wives, but one is better for you, if you only knew.'"[39] But Joseph wasn't telling the whole story either; he was hedging in order to avoid facing the truth about Muhammad's obsession with nubile Nubians. He hadn't any intention of marrying any of them, nor had he planned to provide for them or his thirteen illegitimate children. He gave the women what he wanted, when he wanted, and while he wanted, and that was that.

Well, not quite. In June 1975 three of Muhammad's illegitimate children filed a lawsuit demanding part of what was believed to be a fortune. At a probate hearing in Cook County Circuit Court on October 13, 1978, Judge Henry A. Budzinski heard testimony from Emmanuel Muhammad, the Messenger's eldest son.[40] Emmanuel testified that all the children that Malcolm had accused the Messenger of fathering were acknowledged by the Messenger as his flesh and blood, and that there were thirteen of them in all. In his testimony, he gave their names, dates of birth, and the names of their mothers.

In Islam, as in any major faith, a good man does not lie about paternity. If the women were really the Messenger's wives, the paternity suit would have been unnecessary. Simply put, the Messenger had a series of affairs—with as many as five women at the same time—then threatened to kill them if they dared to tell the truth. Take, for example, this sworn statement from Lucille Rosary Karriem in her paternity suit, which was filed in the Superior Court of Los Angeles on July 6, 1964: "In June of 1959, defendant [Elijah Muhammad] stated to plaintiff that if plaintiff made known the fact that he was the father of plaintiff's children, some of his fanatic followers, disbelieving plaintiff's allegations, would seek to kill plaintiff."[41]

Finally, there was the undisputed truth of Emmanuel Muhammad's testimony on October 13:

Question: And did you have a conversation with your father concerning whether he was the father of those [13] children?
Emmanuel: Later, I came into the knowledge of that. Later on, not right away, that they were his children and also my brothers and sisters.
Question: When you say later, what do you mean, sir, in point of time?
Emmanuel: He tried to keep it a secret from the family.[42]

At the conclusion of Saviour's Day 1976, Salim Muwakkil, editor of *Bilalian News* (formerly *Muhammad Speaks*), revealed that the IRS was investigating the NOI because of suspected financial irregularities: "There was corruption in the Nation of Islam." Wallace was less tactful about the movement's dire financial condition: "It didn't catch me totally off guard because of the large volume of foreign products I saw coming from the [Muslim-owned] farm told me something was wrong." The Messenger, Wallace added angrily, "knew that some niggers would take the money and go off on vacation but when they came back there would be nothing."[43]

While Muhammad's children by Clara fought over the spoils with their half brothers and sisters, another former prominent Muslim got into a battle with Farrakhan over Muslims who were unhappy about Wallace's decision to abandon the theology of demonology. Silis Muhammad, who describes himself as the "Chief Executive Officer of the Lost-Found Nation of Islam,"[44] joined the Los Angeles mosque in the early 1960s. He met the Messenger a few years later through his wife, Harriet, who was a former daughter-in-law of the Messenger. Silis Muhammad's claim to fame was prodigious success in selling *Muhammad Speaks*. Muhammad, impressed by the young man's hustle, appointed him to the team overseeing national distribution of the newspaper.

According to published reports, Silis went to the Messenger one day and whispered in his ear about "a petty theft" and a "conspiracy" to topple him. The Messenger, apparently wholly unimpressed, suggested that Silis return to Los Angeles, which he did. Silis remained in the NOI after Wallace took over, but quit in late 1976 because of the radical changes.[45] In August 1977, he hand-delivered a letter to Wallace's home which he grandiosely referred to as the "Declaration of Spiritual War." A year later, Farrakhan formed another NOI. Both men agree that white people really are devils, but they had philosophical differences.[46] In 1995, Silis watched Farrakhan and the Million Man March from the comfort of his living room in Atlanta, where his cult is headquartered. Farrakhan, who learned how to preach at Malcolm X's knee, is the only high-ranking official in the NOI who has grown wealthy. Silis and others have sought to join him, but so far Farrakhan has chosen to keep all the pie for himself.

Those who underestimated Farrakhan are now clamoring to get into his good graces. Rassoull is another outcast who wants in; he had been dismissed by Wallace over financial irregularities. In a long letter of apology, he asked Farrakhan to join with him and others to reunite the NOI.[47] However, given the rumors about his loyalty, that isn't likely to happen. In the apology, Rassoull admitted that the reason he urged Wallace to destroy Farrakhan's power base in 1975 was to prevent the latter from mounting a serious challenge to the Messenger's son and heir. After Wallace consolidated his power base, one of his first actions was to summarily dismiss Rassoull and Raymond Sharrieff from positions of authority. Since then, Rassoull has denounced Wallace as a hypocrite. He believes that the Messenger will somehow eventually make Wallace suffer a terrible affliction similar to the one he claimed to have brought down upon his brother Kallatt, Malcolm X, and Muhammad Ali.[48]

Ali has said that he believes Elijah Muhammad was a decent man, but he rejects the idea that he was the Seal of the Prophets and that Fard was Allah. For this "apostasy," Rassoull contends, the Messenger has put a "hex" on the champion, who is afflicted with a form of Parkinson's disease:

Many of you remember that the Honorable Elijah Muhammad publicly took back the name Muhammad Ali and never gave it back to him. Muhammad Ali is under chastisement for his statements against and about the Honorable Elijah Muhammad. You can use any medical terminology that you wish, but the truth is that it is severe chastisement. Please understand that I have no personal malice toward Muhammad Ali. The man has helped me personally. . . . However, it does not change the truth. Cassius Clay is not beyond redemption, and if he wants a miracle, let him [begin by] recanting his statements against the Honorable Elijah Muhammad.[49]

And people wonder why police called the NOI's members the "voodoo people" in the 1930s.

Even Dorothy Dorsey has emerged from the rubble of the fallen temple. She defected from Wallace's group and joined a splinter group that preaches that all whites are devils. She has authored a book, which is now in its third printing, titled *Yakub & the Origin of White Supremacy: Message to the White Man & Woman in America*. What is even more surprising is that Dorsey, known now as Dorothy Blake Fardan, has earned a doctorate, which implies a certain level of reasoning ability. Her publisher, United Brothers & United Sisters, describes her as "the rare caucasian [*sic*] who is willing to brave the vicious, devious nature of her own people to deliver the truth to them and to Black [*sic*] people from a caucasian perspective."[50] For some reason, this all brings to mind the 1950s with its white Beatniks and black men with conked hair, the Jews for Jesus and the Black Hebrews of the next two decades, and the Beastie Boys and Michael Jackson as we approach the millennium. Once Farrakhan, Silis, and the others admit that the real NOI died with Elijah Muhammad, someone will get around to writing its epitaph. If past is prologue, perhaps its epitaph will be a phrase coined by a white guy named Hunter "Gonzo" Thompson and put to music by white guys called the Grateful Dead: "What a long, strange trip it's been."

VIRTUAL RELIGION

And ye shall know the truth, and the truth shall make you free.

—John 8:32

The demagogue, mounting his platform, like a slave in the market, is a slave . . . and because of the honors which he seems to receive, is the slave of ten thousand masters.

—Philo Judaeus,
Joseph[1]

Richard D. Heideman, president of B'nai B'rith International, said the [Malcolm X] stamp should "remind all Americans of the possibility of change and reconciliation between people previously divided by racial hatred."

—Washington Post,
November 20, 1998

"The Honorable Elijah Muhammad has returned!"[2] proclaimed a new home page on the World Wide Web on the centennial of his birth. "The Honorable Elijah Muhammad was introduced to his biological brother, Supreme Minister John Muhammad, for the first time since 1975," stated a caption accompanying the article. In the photograph, John, the youngest of the Messenger's twelve siblings, is holding the hand of a man who appears at least twenty years his junior. The man presented as Elijah Muhammad is dressed in white from head to toe. He has a blank look on his face reminiscent of Peter Sellers in the movie *Being There*. His resemblance to Elijah Muhammad is nil. Perhaps that is why John Muhammad is smiling broadly, and a woman standing behind them seems equally amused.

Accompanying this new and presumably improved Messenger is an equally odd fellow who calls himself Brother Solomon. But you don't have to call him Brother Solomon, as Mr. Johnson in a certain beer commercial reminded us: you can call him Solomon, or you can call him Allah, or you can call him God, but you don't have to call him Brother Solomon. He bears a slight resemblance to football legend Art Monk, but he swears to God that he really is God. Alas, Elijah Muhammad has risen from the dead and is inhabiting another man's body, and God has returned to his Earthly Kingdom, not as Master Wallace D. Fard or Wallace Fard Muhammad, but as Brother Solomon, leader and founder of the United Nation of Islam. Things have come to that in the African-American community of professed Muslims. The Nation of Islam, which underwent reformation in 1975 by Imam Wallace D. Muhammed, has become the carcass of a cat on a country road, its rotted flesh baked by the summer sun. Cultural vultures tear away its flesh in their futile search for its mythical remaining lives. Today, there are more groups called the Nation of Islam (or some variation of it) than bicycles in

434

China. The name no longer denotes a sect; it denotes a twisted virtual reality game in which the cat lives all nine lives concurrently.

Solomon's United Nation of Islam is headquartered in Temple Hills, Maryland. Right now, the only other branch is in Kansas City, Kansas.[3] Solomon says that the difference between his cult and the sect headed by Farrakhan is that the United Nation of Islam is run by God (that is, Solomon), while Farrakhan's group is headed by a mere prophet. On September 18, 1997, Abbass Rassoull, Brother Solomon's assistant, sent Minister Farrakhan a letter advising him that "the Honorable Elijah Muhammad has returned" and was interested in speaking at Mosque Maryam in Chicago, which is owned by Farrakhan's Nation of Islam. "I pray that you see the light of this."[4] Perhaps Farrakhan did, because he has been feeding a similar spiel to his followers for the past several years. "In spite of the controversy and clamor surrounding the Nation of Islam and its Divine Leader, Minister Louis Farrakhan," a recent article on the Farrakhan-sponsored World Wide Web site states, "we are forging ahead in the Spirit of Almighty God, Allah, to unite with all of humanity in the Oneness of God, where all people of goodwill of every race and of every nation may participate in the Universal"—something or other.[5] The article was written by Tynetta Deanar Muhammad, alias Tynetta Nelson, who describes herself as the "wife" of the Honorable Elijah Muhammad.[6] This misleading statement at the conclusion of the article is appropriate, given that the cyberspace feature begins with prevarications and has misstatements in its midsection, so that it is consistent in at least one respect. Like Elijah Muhammad, who taught that Fard was the Messiah and that he, Muhammad, was the Seal of the Prophets, Farrakhan claims now that Elijah Muhammad was a messiah, and that he, Farrakhan, is a prophet. More ghoulishly, Farrakhan and Tynetta Nelson both contend that Elijah Muhammad is alive today; reports of his death, his autopsy, his burial, and his headstone have been greatly exaggerated.[7]

The irony is that at the 1973 Saviour's Day Convention, where Farrakhan sat less than thirteen paces away from the Messenger for over two hours, the Messenger spoke specifically about the notion of the afterlife and reincarnation. "The Bible says that after Elijah there are no more prophets," he said over Farrakhan's yodel-like yelps of "Go ahead, Dear Holy Apostle!" "There is no coming back. After we die, there is no coming back. That's the end of all life." He said people who believed in the afterlife or reincarnation were practicing what he called that "crazy Christianity religion." Clearly, then, Farrakhan and others are knowingly attributing religious beliefs to the Messenger that he shunned shortly before his death. The same holds true for Tynetta. Her claim of being the "wife" of Elijah Muhammad is wishful thinking and nothing more. She was not married to him legally, illegally, or by common law. His death certificate, a copy of which appears on a Web site created by a rival Muslim faction, clearly reads that he was widowed.[8] The bitter truth is that she was one in a string of mistresses who bore his children, and that he was a father who publicly denied siring her children until the final months of his life. As this book has pointed out, her jealousy of the other mistresses was captured on tape by the FBI.

In a televised interview with a foreign journalist a few years ago, Farrakhan said he could not believe that one day soon people would regard him in the same way they think of the Prophet Mohammad of the Holy Quran, Jesus, and other major prophets. The journalist smiled nervously, and his look conveyed what students in a recreation room at a local college said aloud: Farrakhan was either joking or delusional when he made the statement. The assumption that he will eventually be regarded as a major prophet painted him in a stark shade of megalomania, and evoked lung-clearing laughter from the students watching the interview on Maryland Public Access Channel. As for Farrakhan's arguments about the resurrection of Elijah Muhammad, they have not gone unanswered. Minister Levi Karim, who belongs to yet another offshoot of the Nation of Islam, suggests that Tynetta and Farrakhan are "liars" and "deceivers."[9]

John Muhammad has repeatedly condemned Farrakhan, Tynetta, and others who he thinks are deliberately misleading young people about the Nation of Islam and the Messenger. Karim registered his complaints in cyberspace on the "Muhammad Speaks" Web page. "These deceivers and misleaders are actually trying to convince us to give up one spooky belief (that Jesus will return from the grave) for another spooky belief (that Messenger Elijah Muhammad will return from the grave). I say, NO THANK YOU, Brother and Sister. Been There, Done That," Karim wrote on the *Muhammad Speaks* Web site in 1996.[10] John Muhammad made similar arguments in *The Journal of Truth,* a slim volume of his recently published speeches:

> I can't see how Minister Louis Farrakhan, who sat under the Messenger's teaching for a few years, can now preach that the Messenger is alive. This doctrine has caused confusion among good people. . . . Sister Tynetta Deanar Muhammad should have a clear knowledge of the Honorable Elijah Muhammad's death or being physically alive. . . . There is no such thing possible as my brother [Elijah] and the Messenger . . . being still physically alive. . . . And there is no such thing as the return of one's spirit into another after physical death.[11]

To the bafflement of his family, John Muhammad seems to have become a party to the reincarnation show. John's nephew, Chicago broadcast journalist Wali Muhammad, was bewildered by the photograph of his uncle with the man posing as the Messenger. Asked what he thought John's motive was in participating in the charade, Wali's answer was simple and unequivocal: money.[12]

Money and celebrity may be the evil twins responsible for the proliferation of cults using the same or similar names and the Messenger as the lure. Malcolm X became a controversial celebrity during the zenith of the Black Muslim movement, but he shunned chances to grow rich. The Messenger grew rich, but he was unable to achieve celebrity status. Since the Messenger's death, only one Black Muslim—Farrakhan—has acquired both wealth and fame. Neither the Messenger nor Malcolm X appeared on the cover of *Time* or *Newsweek* (or any other mainstream national publication). Farrakhan has appeared on both. In March 1998, Farrakhan was among many "celebrities" at the seventy-fifth anniversary party held by *Time* in New York City.[13] Farrakhan, in the tradition of entertainers, had just concluded his "World Friendship Tour," which included a cordial meeting with Saddam Hussein's subordinates, and a controversial kiss with Winnie Mandela, the militant African National

Congress leader who is as suspect in South Africa as Farrakhan is in America.[14] At the time the kiss was captured by international photographers, both Mandela and Farrakhan were subjects of speculation about their involvement in misdeeds against their own people.[15]

The titles that he gives to his international escapades are perhaps the greatest reminder that Farrakhan, like a leopard, is incapable of changing his spots. Although he changed his name long ago, he remains Louis "the Charmer" Walcott at heart. His violin concerts and sound recordings attest to that, as do the rock-music-style labels he puts on his national and international travels. In a bid to share the national spotlight with Farrakhan, the new groups have descended from the sublime to the surreal. Silis Muhammad has accused Farrakhan of betraying the Messenger's mission. Before the Million Man March in 1995, Silis wrote Farrakhan a letter accusing him of violating Elijah Muhammad's teachings by, among other things, participating in the voting process. On another occasion, after Farrakhan refused to cooperate in Silis Muhammad's plan to unite their two groups, Silis derided Farrakhan as the "Second Beast of the Book of Revelations."[16]

What is one to make of this modern Tower of Babel? Essentially, each group is little more than a cult of personality. When their aging leaders are gone (both Farrakhan and Silis are sexagenarians), all that will remain is a storefront temple here and there. For the most part, members will scatter to the winds, as they did when Marcus Garvey was deported, when Satohata Takahashi was deported, and when Father Divine died. Mergers are unlikely, since there is little that groups using the Nation of Islam's flag in their coat-of-arms agree on. All agree that Master Wallace D. Fard was Allah in person. This belief persists despite a mountain of evidence to the contrary that has surfaced in the last ten years. Most also believe that Elijah Muhammad was the Seal of the Prophets, despite the inherent contradiction with the Holy Quran. Beyond that, there is nothing but babbling.

As a practical matter, the Nation of Islam is a mirage. It has become the stuff of legend, like the block of salt mistaken for Lot's wife. The Nation of Islam built by the team of Malcolm X and the Messenger has disintegrated and become a pool of gross mutations. During the twelve years of Malcolm X's ministry, it constantly progressed financially and philosophically. After Malcolm, the sect devolved instead of continuing to evolve. When the current crop of leaders depart, the sole victor may prove to be the one J. Edgar Hoover suggested was best suited to direct Muslims: Imam Wallace D. Muhammad. Though he, too, is a sexagenarian and is struggling financially, his followers are more concerned with their spiritual advancement than those of Farrakhan and Silis, who remain mired in a hybridized theology grounded in erroneous assumptions about race. There is none of the petty political sniping in Wallace's organization that is so characteristic of the other groups. Wallace's followers have not been accused of attacking members of other Islamic sects, as have the followers of Silis and Farrakhan. Finally, Wallace's coreligionists no longer have the need to demonize Caucasians or to promote themselves as God's Chosen. Wallace Muhammed has recognized such teachings for what they are: psychological bondage that blinds the believer instead of opening his or her eyes to the truth.

Unlike Farrakhan, who has retained much of his charisma for forty years, Wallace is no longer the forceful speaker he was when Malcolm X was his teacher. After a faltering start, during which he ridiculed his father, talked too freely to FBI agents, and behaved in a suspect fashion toward Malcolm, Wallace appears to be adjusting to the axiom about the impossibility of serving two masters: he often speaks of his need for money, but he doesn't let it blind him to his higher mission. He has single-handedly converted tens of thousands of African-American Muslims from a false Islamic faith to true orthodoxy. For the descendants of slaves who came to America as Muslims, that will prove to be Wallace's greatest gift to his father and to his country. History will remember him not as a prophet, as some imagine it will remember them, but as a decent man who struggled to remain true to the tenets of his faith.

Farrakhan's legacy is another matter entirely. "I'm not going to be a prostitute for anybody anymore," Farrakhan protested when Wallace Muhammed announced that he was transferring Farrakhan from Harlem to Chicago in 1977. "Why should I do it for anybody else when I can do it for myself?"[17] If, as his outburst implied, Farrakhan regarded himself as a prostitute for the Messenger, future historians would be wise to examine the implications of his outburst. Someone, a divinity student perhaps, may compare him to the sisters Ahola and Aholibah from chapter 23 of the Book of Ezekiel: "Yet she multiplied her whoredoms, in calling to remembrance the days of her youth, wherein she played the harlot in the land of Egypt." And they will surely look more closely at his statements regarding how he and the Nation of Islam "dealt with" Malcolm X, particularly after the FBI declassifies its files on Farrakhan. While we're on the subject, Farrakhan, who has been clamoring for the release of the FBI files on Malcolm X, could help allay suspicions about his youthful transgressions and perform a public service by requesting the release of his own files, which remain classified. That, of course, isn't remotely likely.

For now, Farrakhan will remain a world-class demagogue, one who broke bread with other demagogues, such as Saddam Hussein, Winnie Mandela, Idi Amin of Uganda, and Sani Abacha of Nigeria. He will be remembered for deliberately distorting the teachings of the man he professes to love more than anything in this world and abusing the religion he claims to practice. He will be remembered for the Rolls Royce in which he was chauffeured about town, the gauche jewelry and tailor-made clown suits, and, yes, the contrived militancy he summoned at the first sight of a television camera. He has successfully repackaged and marketed the Messenger. Books authored by Farrakhan sit alongside *The International Jew* by Henry Ford and the *Protocols of the Learned Elders of Zion*.

The Messenger's recorded speeches and old photographs are sold in stores run by Farrakhan's sect in nearly every major city, and are normally displayed side-by-side with Farrakhan's books, tapes, and photographs. The signs in the window don't say so, but "Idolatry for Sale" is the message one gets from visiting these establishments. One item for sale is a sticker reading "Don't Mess With Farrakhan." Shortly before his death, Captain Joseph offered another slogan: "Don't Listen to Farrakhan." Joseph agreed with what Muhammad and his children have long suspected, namely that Farrakhan could not be trusted to represent the man that the Messenger had become shortly before his death, the man who ordered those who worshipped him to stop calling white people "devils."

The words of Thomas Jefferson come to mind when one reflects on the proliferation of the Elmer Gantry type of Muslim ministers in the African-American community. The same greed and hypocrisy that soured blacks on Christianity will ultimately spill over into Islam at the rate things are going. The first omen of this was the confession of Omar Muhammad on the Christian Broadcasting Network.[18] Omar's father was a captain of the notorious New Jersey mosque who enjoyed "dinners with close friend and leader of the Nation of Islam, Minister Farrakhan."[19] After a series of unfortunate social encounters that tested his faith—at least as taught by the Messenger—Omar abandoned the Nation. He also abandoned Islam and became a Christian. "The spirit of Islam, I would like to say, put on me a spirit of ignorance and almost deafness and dumbness." It is understandable, though regrettable, that he blames a true religion for the shortcomings of dishonest, incompetent imams. As the Omars in the Nation of Islam realize that what they accepted as Islam is nothing more than a shell game designed to keep certain families in the lap of luxury, they will reject it and seek the truth somewhere else. They will curse the teachers who sold them into spiritual slavery instead of leading them to the liberation of true faith. Today, no one in her right mind names a child after Benedict Arnold or Adolf Hitler or Pol Pot. Tomorrow, no one will name a child in honor of the imams who have betrayed this generation. "I tremble for my country when I reflect that God is just" and "that his justice cannot sleep forever," Jefferson said in reflecting upon slavery.[20] That's a thought that pulpit pimps—and prostitutes—should keep in mind and take to heart.

APPENDIX A

I. REPORTED ALIASES OF THE MESSENGER

Author's Note: During the forty-three years that the FBI conducted surveillance of Elijah Muhammad's activities, agents discovered dozens of aliases allegedly used by the Messenger. Some of the names reflected philosophical growth and change as determined by Master Wallace D. Fard. A few were used to make it difficult for his rivals and police to discover his whereabouts. The majority, however, were noted by the Bureau merely because the agent or informant misunderstood what the source was saying. For example, when members of the NOI first began using a few Arabic words, they were required by Master Fard to attempt to pronounce them correctly. "Muhammad," they were taught, was actually pronounced "Muck-ah-Mud." Owing to differences in patois and vernacular among African Americans, this and other words were pronounced in myriad ways. As one might expect, mispronunciation led to misspellings. The best example of this, as pointed out in the main body of the book, was the mistaken belief that Elijah Muhammad was using the name "Ugan Ali" in 1932 when he was, in fact, using the name "Ghulam Ali." Similarly, Wallace D. Fard's surname was pronounced as "Far-odd" by some Muslims, and perhaps by Fard himself at some point. Fard and Farad are both rooted in Arabic.

Below is a list of most of the names the FBI cross-referenced to Elijah Muhammad from 1932 to 1975, as they appear in "Enclosure 203" of the Main File on Elijah Poole Sr., also known as Elijah Muhammad. Section II is a list of known and alleged aliases used by Wallace D. Fard.

443

FBI Headquarters
Elijah Poole, Sr.
105-24822-203

Enclosure 203

[Aliases of Elijah Poole Sr.]

(1) Elijah Muhammad; (2) E. Muhammad; (3) Elijah Muhammad; (4) Elijah
Poole Muhammad; (5) Elijah H. Muhammad; (6) Elijah Poole K.A. Muham-
mad; (7) Elijah Muhammad; (8) Elijuh Muhammad; (9) Elizah Muhammad;
(10) Elljah Muhammad; (11) Elijah Muhammand; (12) Elijah Muhammed; (13)
Elisha Mohammad; (14) Elijah Mohammad; (15) Elijah Mohammed; (16) E.
Mohammed; (17) Eli Mohammed; (18) Elija Mohammed; (19) Allah
Mohammed; (20) Prophet Mohammed; (21) Rassoul Mohammed; (22) Ras-
soull Mohammed; (23) Rassoull Elijah Mohammed; (24) Eli Muck Muck; (25)
Eli Muck; (26) Elijah Muck Muck; (27) Muck Muck; (28) Muck Eli Muck; (29)
Elijah Mahammed; (30) Elijah Poole (*true name*); (31) Eija Poole; (32) Elijah
Muhammad Poole; (33) Elijha Poole; (34) The Messenger of Allah Poole; (35)
The Prophet Poole; (36) Gulam Bogan; (37) Gulan Bogan; (38) Gullam Bogans;
(39) Gulam Bogans; (40) Gulan Bogans; (41) G. Bogaus; (42) Gulam Gogan;
(43) Gulam Gogans; (44) Gulan Gogans; (45) One Rassoul; (46) Mohamed
Rassoul; (47) Mohammed Rassoul; (48) Mohammed Rassouli; (49) One Ras-
soull; (50) Elijah Mohammed Rassoull; (51) M. Rassoull; (52) Mohammed Ras-
soull; (53) Muhammad Rassoull; (54) One Karriem; (55) Elijah Karriem; (56)
Mohammed Karriem; (57) Black Moses; (58) Bulam Bogans; (59) Elija Bogans;
(60) Elijah Bogans; (61) G. Bogans; (62) Mohammed Elijah; (63) Mohammed
Rassoull Elijah; (63) Muhammad Elijah; (65) One Much; (66) Elijah Much-
muhd; (67) One Muck; (68) Muck-Muck; (69) Elijah Muckmuck; (70)
Mohammed Muckmud; (71) Elijah Muhd; (72) Elijah Muck Muhd; (73) Elijah
Muk Muhd; (74) Muk Muhd; (75) Muhd Muck; (76) Elijah Muhd Muk; (77)
Elijah Mukmuhd; (78) Elijah Mut Mut; (79) One Mutmud; (80) Elisha Pool;
(81) Elizah Pool; (82) Prophet; (83) The Prophet; (84) Allah Prophet; (85) Muck
Muck Prophet; (86) Mohammed Rosoull; (87) Mohammed Elijah; (88)
Muhammad Elijah; (89) One Elijah; (90) Elisha Mohammed; (91) Elizah
Mohammed; (92) Muk Muhd Elijah; (93) "The Profit" Mohammed; (94)
Mohammed Ah; (95) Mohammed Elim Ah; (96) Ah Mohammed Elim; (97)

Elim Ah Mohammed; (98) Elijah Muhmuhd; (99) Elijah Maukmauhd; (100) Elijah Ford; (101) Robert Muhammad; (102) Robert Pool; (103) Robert Poole; (104) Robert Takahashi; (105) Robert Takis; (106) Elijah Muhammads; (107) Ilag Mohammed; (108) Elia Mohammed; (109) Elijah Muhammad Black; (110) Prophet Bogans; (111) Muhammad Elija; (112) Mohammed Allizah; (113) Allizah Mohammed; (114) Elijaa Muhammed; (115) Elijah Muhammud; (116) One Eli; (117) One Ely; (118) Muhammed Elias; (119) One Elizah; (120) Elijah Black; (121) Mohammed Bogans; (122) E. W. Mohammed; (123) Elijah Mukmah; (124) Mahammed Ah Fahnu Bey; (125) Charles Evans; (126) James Dodd; (127) J. Dodd.

II. Reported Aliases of Wallace D. Fard

(1) Wallace Don Ford; (2) Wallei Ford; (3) Wallie D. Ford; (4) Wally D. Ford; (5) W.D. Ford; (6) Wallace Farad; (7) W.D. Feraud; (8) Fred Dodd; (9) One Allah; (10) W.D. Fard; (11) Wallace Ford; (12) Wallie Ford; (13) Wallace D. Fard; (14) Wallace Don Fard; (15) Wallace Don Farad; (16) W.D. Farrad; (17) W.D. Mohammed; (18) W.D.F. Mohammed; (19) W.D. Fard Mohammed; (20) W.D. Farrow Mohammed; (21) W.D. Ferrad Muhammad; (22) Wallace Fard Muhammad; (23) W.F. Muhammad; (24) W.D. Farard; (25) W.D. Farrard; (26) W.D. Farrow; (27) W.D. Farard; (28) One Mahadiah; (29) One Mohammed; (30) Fard Muhammad; (31) W.D. F. Mukmuk; (32) Ali Mohammad; (33) Mohammad Ali; (34) Wali Farrad; (35) Mohammad Wali; (36) F. Mohammad Ali; (37) F. Ali Mohammad; (38) Farrad Mohammad; (39) Mohammad Farrad; (40) Allah; (41) Wally Ford; (42) Walker Ford; (43) W. Ford; (44) Moehamat Ali; (45) Mohamid Ali; (46) Mohamoud Ali; (47) Mohamed Alli; (48) Ali Mohammed; (49) Wali Mohammed; (50) Wallay Mohammed; (51) Walli Mohammed; (52) Mohammed Wali; (53) Wallace Muhammad; (54) Wallace D. Muhammad; (55) Fard Mohammed; (56) Mohammed Fard; (57) Muhammad Fard; (58) W.F. Muckmuck.

APPENDIX B

THE SCARLET LETTER

On January 5, 1973, Imam Hamaas Abdul Khaalis, leader of a Hanafi Muslim sect located in Washington, sent the second of two scathing letters to Elijah Muhammad, and also sent copies to the NOI's ministers and the mainstream media. The NOI's reaction to the letter led to the greatest mass murder in the history of the nation's capital.

Born Ernest Timothy McGee, Khaalis joined the NOI in the mid-1950s and became the first national secretary for the section in 1954. Three years later, he was replaced as national secretary by John Ali, a former member of the Philadelphia temple who was recommended for the post by Malcolm X. Shortly after the demotion, Khaalis parted ways with the NOI, citing Malcolm X as Elijah Muhammad's "Nemesis." Elijah Muhammad pleaded with him to return to the fold, but he declined. In the early 1960s, Khaalis moved to New York, where he studied orthodox Islam. In 1970, he opened a storefront mosque in Harlem, where he taught orthodox Islam. A few years later he relocated to Washington on the "Gold Coast," a reference to the upper-middle-class black neighborhood located near a northwestern border where Washington, D.C., meets Maryland. The home, which was purchased by basketball star Kareem Abdul-Jabbar (formerly known as Lew Alcindor) of the Los Angeles Lakers, was known as the Hanafi Madh-Hab Center.

The full text of the letter received by Muhammad, his ministers (including Louis Farrakhan), and the media is reprinted below.

446

Ministers:

You have received your first lesson in Allah Ta'Ala's Deenu-L-Islam; Not W.D. Fard's Islam: Holy Qur-an, Chapter 49, Verses 16 and 17. Elijah Mukammad* used to brag that W.D. Fard could speak 16 languages. Allah is over all languages. It is a pity that none of you ever took time to learn how to read the Arabic language of the Holy Qur-an Sharreef. Then you could have easily seen that Elijah Mukammad was a lying deceiver. If you had known that the term used by Elijah Mukammad—Lost-Found—had a sinister and diabolical meaning, many of you would have left the movement years ago. In the first chapter of the Holy Qur-an, which is titled "The Fatihah," in the last verse of this chapter: "Not the path of those who have gone astray."

The Arabic word "Maghubi" refers to the Lost (so-called Black Muslims of Elijah Mukammad's temples). Everyone of us were [sic] better off from a psychological point of view, before we heard or learned anything about Elijah Mukammad's temples with their lying masters of deceit; eaters of their brother's flesh. Elijah Mukammad (Al-Gharoor) should have studied his lesson much closer than he did. For he is the perpetrator of this Fard Man Myth Lie. We warn all of you of the nearness of the Day of Resurrection (Yawmu-L-Qiyamatun), and the penalty which will be put upon those who have set up an equal with Almighty Allah (Holy Qur-an, Chapter 6, Verse 19). Surely Allah Ta'Ala is sufficient to pay back the worst of the Mushreeks (those who have been set up as equals with Him, but only in their polluted minds) with the choices of the violent hot flame that will burn them forever. You all have been taught that there is no life after death. But in the Holy Qur-an, Allah Ta'Ala says that "He will bring you to life again, as he brought you to life before" (Holy Qur-an, Chapter 23 and Chapter 67). The Day of Resurrection or "Yawmu-L-Qiyamatun," is found in Chapter 75 of the Holy Qur-an.

Maghdubi people means: Those (people) who are lost in error, and found in error; and they cannot help but to continue to go astray (Dalleen).

This so-called god who spoke to Elijah Poole (incidentally Poole is the name of a very wicked king in the Bible; 1 Chronicles, Chapter 5, Verses 25 and 26.) In Strong's Exhaustive Concordance of the Bible, by James Strong, published by Abingdon Press (which you may purchase at any "Christian Science Reading Room"), on page 819, we find the world "pul" which refers to the name of this

---

*Mukammad means "sad, grieved and blackened; to be laden with sin; sorrow-bound because of evil committed through ignorance (error)."

king. In the back part of the Concordance there is a Hebrew and Chaldee dictionary. On page 94, opposite Number 6322, we see that the spelling of this word, is pronounced (Pool). We are not so naive to ignore the fact that Pool can also be spelled (Poole) with the silent (e). As ministers, you will also say that his name is Elijah. But you must remember this is an adopted given name, too. But you can also say that of Elijah Pitts [who] played football for the Green Bay Packers. Just because his given name is Elijah, that doesn't give him the right to lay claim to being the minor prophet Elijah, mentioned in the Bible. What madness is in your leader and teacher, what kind of minds do you have to be deaf, dumb and blind to everything?

Was this god the Pope of Rome? The Archbishop of Canterbury? The leader of the Parsees? The Brahmins? The Bahais? Mirza Ghulam, leader of the Ahmadiyya Movement? Or John Walker, a.k.a. W.D. Fard, the slightly cockeyed man who came from Greece. [He] was a Greek who came to this country at the age of 27 years of life, and who served 7 and 1/2 years in jail, in America, for stealing a truck load of junk in Gary, Indiana; and for raping a 17-year-old, so-called white girl. This man died in Chicago, Illinois, at the age of 78. Your Captain Raymond Sharrieff knows this. Do you? The question to you as ministers is: How did your leader and teacher meet this man—in jail? You will not find this information in your Problem Book. As W.D. Fard, god in Person, would not teach this. Remember your leader and teacher was sent to jail as a draft dodger in Chicago in the 1930s, after having taught your leader and teacher [for] 3 and 1/2 years. So what was your leader and teacher in jail for prior to the 1940s.

Also, many of the old followers of your leader and teacher used to call W.D. Fard, a.k.a. "John Walker" a Greek, as he looked like a Greek. But your leader and teacher teaches that his father was an original black man, and that his mother was a "Jewess" from the Caucasus Mountains region of what is now today called "Azerbaijan," or Southern Russia. Your leader and teacher, Elijah Mukammad, teaches that one of the reasons god married this woman from the Caucasus Mountains area was because god was so black that he was not about to mix among the other so-called fairer tribes of the world. So the new god had to be lighter, so this is your W.D. Fard. For references: Lost-Found Moslem Lesson No. 1; Also, Minister James [Anderson] Shabazz, who was one-time principal of your school; and also, His brother Lemuel, who was a minister. Refer to Supreme Captain Raymond Sharrieff, or any of Elijah Mukammad's children by his late wife. Make them tell you the truth; they know that their father is a deceiver.

Was this so-called god Father Divine, who was a god also? Or Prophet Jones, faggot, homosexual creep-freak? Or Sweet Daddy Grace, who called himself "Elijah Before the Fire"? Now, which one do you follow?

Hosea, the prophet, said that my people are destroyed for lack of knowledge. This statement certainly describes the bushy-heads in America and the West Indies. Out of fear of knowing that Allah will punish those of us who know the truth, and do not attempt to remove falsehood from among his creatures.

We do not want your money, your followers, or your false teachings, as you are.

Signed,

Hamaas Abdul Khaalis

P.S. When you cease to use the Holy Qur-an Shareef, the Revelations that were revealed to the Holy Prophet Muhammad (S.A.S.) who lived over fourteen hundred years ago, and cease using the divine attributes of Allah, then you will not hear from us. We do not care if you worship Ba'al (W.D. Fard); that is your business. But as long as you are deaf, dumb, and blind to Deenul-Islam, you will hear from us. We want you to use your invented books with your invented religion. Why didn't W.D. Fard (Ba'al) give you a book? Since he was God Almighty to you, why didn't he reveal through revelation to you a book?

APPENDIX C

Concise Genealogy of Elijah Muhammad

Irwin Pool (paternal grandfather)
Peggy [last name unknown] (paternal grandmother)
Willie Pool Sr. (father)
Mariah [aka Marie] Hall (mother)
  (Married: 1887)

Offspring:
  1. Sam Pool (1888)
  2. Annie Pool (1889)
  3. Willie Pool Jr. (1891)
  4. Tommie Pool (1892)
  5. Hattie (1894)
  6. Lula (1896)
  7. Elija Pool (1897)
  8. Charlie Pool (1900)
  9. Jarmin Pool (1904)
  10. Emma Pool (1906)
  11. Johnnie Pool (1907)
  12. James Pool (1909)
  13. John Pool (1912)

Elija Pool (Elijah Muhammad)
Clara Belle Evans—Quartus Evans (father), Mary Lue Thomas (mother)

(Married: March 7, 1919)

Offspring:
1. Emmanuel Muhammad (1921)
2. Ethel Muhammad (1922)
3. Lottie Muhammad (1925)
4. Nathaniel Muhammad (1926)
5. Herbert Muhammad (1929)
6. Elijah Muhammad Jr. (1931)
7. Wallace Muhammad (1933)
8. Akbar Muhammad (1939)

Elijah Muhammad's Concubines

Elijah Muhammad and Lucille (Rosary) Karriem Muhammad

Offspring:
1. Saudi (girl) (January 17, 1960)
2. Sumayyah, aka Lishah (girl) (October 13, 1961)
3. Bahiyyah (girl) (July 7, 1964)

Elijah Muhammad and June Muhammad

Offspring:
4. Abdullah Yasin Muhammad (boy) (December 30, 1960)
5. Ayesha Muhammad (girl) (September 4, 1962)

Elijah Muhammad and Evelyn Williams

Offspring:
6. Marie Muhammad (girl) (March 30, 1960)

Elijah Muhammad and Tynetta (Nelson) Deanar Muhammad

Offspring:
7. Madia Muhammad (girl) (1963)
8. Ishmael R. Muhammad (boy) (June 21, 1964)

9. Rasul H. Muhammad (boy) (September 5, 1965)
10. Ahmed Muhammad (boy) (August 28, 1967)

Elijah Muhammad and Ola (Hughes) Muhammad

Offspring:

11. Kamal Muhammad (boy) (April 24, 1960)

Elijah Muhammad and Lovetta Muhammad

Offspring:

12. Lovlita Claybourne Muhammad (girl) (July 15, 1964)

Elijah Muhammad and Bernique Cushmeer

Offspring:

13. Neemah Cushmeer Muhammad (girl) (January 6, 1965)

APPENDIX D

LOCATIONS AND INFRASTRUCTURE OF THE NATION OF ISLAM, 1958–1959

Source: Central Intelligence Agency: (According to List Shared by FBI/CIA in 1957–58)

LOCATION: Anniston, ALABAMA
Estimated Membership: 5
Minister: Chester X McNutt
Chairman: Tom X Thompson
Other Officials Unknown

LOCATION: Moundville, ALABAMA
Estimated Membership: 30
Officials Unknown

LOCATION: Los Angeles, CALIFORNIA
Estimated Membership: 72
Minister: Henry X Mims
Assistant Minister: Ray X Cook
Captain, FOI: Thomas X Huff
Secretary: Bertha X Cook
Treasurer: Leatha X Cotton

LOCATION: San Diego, CALIFORNIA
Estimated Membership: 28
Minister: Henry X Mims

Assistant Minister: Unknown
Captain, FOI: Joe X Barnes
Secretary: Frank X Livingston

LOCATION: *San Francisco, CALIFORNIA*
Estimated Membership: 40
Minister: Robert Thomas X Ashford
Assistant Minister: Verdell Scherstein X Prince
Captain, FOI: Verdell S. X Prince
Secretary: Jessie X Miller
Treasurer: Jessie X Miller

LOCATION: *Folsom Prison, CALIFORNIA*
Estimated Membership: 18
Officials Unknown

LOCATION: *San Quentin Prison, CALIFORNIA*
Estimated Membership: 22
Officials Unknown

LOCATION: *Hartford, CONNECTICUT*
Estimated Membership: 110
Minister: Thomas X Bridges
Assistant Minister: Edward L. X St. John
Secretaries: Alzena X St. John; Joseph A. X Link
Lieutenant, MGT: Grace X Brooks

LOCATION: *Jacksonville, FLORIDA*
Estimated Membership: 40
Minister: Ishmael X Knox
Assistant Minister: John Ali X Williams
Other Officials Unknown

LOCATION: *Pensacola, FLORIDA*
Estimated Membership: 5
Minister: George Roy X White
Assistant Minister: Joe X Allen
Other Officials Unknown

LOCATION: *Athens, GEORGIA*
 Estimated Membership: 12
 Minister: James Shabazz
 Assistant Minister: Thomas X Bennett
 Other Officials Unknown

LOCATION: *Atlanta, GEORGIA*
 Estimated Membership: 40
 Minister: Jeremiah X Pugh
 Assistant Ministers: Sidney X Walker; Thomas X Bennett
 Captain, FOI: Sidney X Walker
 Captain, MGT: Laura X Hardman

LOCATION: *Bainbridge, GEORGIA*
 Estimated Membership: 6
 Officials Unknown

LOCATION: *Savannah, GEORGIA*
 Estimated Membership: 2
 Minister: Thomas X Bennett
 Other Officials Unknown

LOCATION: *Chicago, ILLINOIS*
 Estimated Membership: 400–600
 Minister: James X Anderson
 Assistant Minister: Wallace Deen Muhammad*
 Captain, FOI: Raymond Sharrieff†
 Secretary: Ernest X McGhee‡
 Captain, MGT: Lottie Muhammad§

---

*Wallace Deen Muhammad (Chicago) is the son of Elijah Muhammad.
†Raymond Sharrieff (Chicago) is the son-in-law of Elijah Muhammad.
‡Ernest X McGhee (Chicago) left the NOI in 1960. He changed his name to Hamaas Abdul Khaalis and formed a Hanafi Muslim sect in Washington, D.C. He is currently serving a life sentence for his role in a hostage-taking incident in 1977 which resulted in the death of a reporter.
§Lottie Muhammad is the daughter of Elijah Muhammad.

LOCATION: *Joliet, ILLINOIS*
  Estimated Membership: 65
  Officials Unknown

LOCATION: *Gary, INDIANA*
  Estimated Membership: Unknown
  Minister: Not Yet Appointed

LOCATION: *South Bend, INDIANA*
  Estimated Membership: 18
  Minister: Not Yet Appointed

LOCATION: *Leavenworth, KANSAS*
  Estimated Membership: Unknown
  Prison Unit of NOI

LOCATION: *New Orleans, LOUISIANA*
  Estimated Membership: Unknown
  Temple in Organizational Stage

LOCATION: *Baltimore, MARYLAND*
  Estimated Membership: 45
  Minister: Isaiah X Edwards
  Captain, FOI: Carl X
  Secretary: Charles X

LOCATION: *Dorchester, MASSACHUSETTS*
  Estimated Membership: 85–100
  Minister: Malcolm X Little
  Assistant Minister: Louis X Walcott*
  Captain, FOI: Rodney X Smith
  Secretary: Carol X Harrell

---

*Louis X Walcott (Dorchester, Boston) is now known as Louis Farrakhan, and heads his own Islamic group, also called the Nation of Islam.

LOCATION: Springfield, MASSACHUSETTS
　　Estimated Membership: 20
　　Minister: Lloyd X Williams
　　Assistant Minister: James X Thaxton*
　　Secretary: Zelma X Williams
　　Treasurer: Osborne X Thaxton*

LOCATION: Worcester, MASSACHUSETTS
　　Estimated Membership: Unknown
　　Officials Unknown

LOCATION: Detroit, MICHIGAN
　　Estimated Membership: 100–175
　　Minister: Lemuel X Anderson
　　Assistant Minister: Wilfred X Little†
　　Captain, FOI: Harold X Goins
　　Captain, MGT: Gertrude X Bogans‡

LOCATION: Flint, MICHIGAN
　　Estimated Membership: 15–20
　　Minister: Norris X Storey
　　Other Officials Unknown

LOCATION: Inkster, MICHIGAN
　　Estimated Membership: 20–30
　　Minister: John Muhammad§
　　Assistant Minister: William X Good
　　Other Officials Unknown

*Osborne X Thaxton and James X Thaxton (Springfield, Massachusetts) were brothers who served time in prison with Malcolm X.
†Wilfred X Little (Detroit) was the oldest brother of Malcolm X. He died May 19, 1998 (coincidentally, on what would have been Malcolm's 73rd birthday).
‡Gertrude X Bogans is Elijah Muhammad's sister-in-law.
§John Muhammad (Inkster, Michigan) is the youngest brother of Elijah Muhammad.

LOCATION: *Jackson State Prison, MICHIGAN*
  Estimated Membership: 36
  Officials Unknown

LOCATION: *Lansing, MICHIGAN*
  Estimated Membership: 15–20
  Minister: Philbert X Little*
  Other Officials Unknown

LOCATION: *Pontiac, MICHIGAN*
  Estimated Membership: 5–8
  Officials Unknown

LOCATION: *Saginaw, MICHIGAN*
  Estimated Membership: 5–10
  Minister: Alphonso X Gadie
  Other Officials Unknown

LOCATION: *White Cloud, MICHIGAN*
  Estimated Membership: Unknown
  (Temple Farm Located Here)

LOCATION: *Minneapolis, MINNESOTA*
  Estimated Membership: 15
  Officials Unknown

LOCATION: *St. Louis, MISSOURI*
  Estimated Membership: 10–13
  Minister: Louis X Starks
  Assistant Minister: Clarence 2X Brown
  Other Officials Unknown

LOCATION: *Atlantic City, NEW JERSEY*
  Estimated Membership: 20–30

*Philbert X Little (Lansing, Michigan) was the brother of Malcolm X. He died in 1995.

Minister: Woodrow X Love
Captain, FOI: Joseph X Currey

LOCATION: *Camden, NEW JERSEY*
Estimated Membership: 28
Minister: John X Coffield
Captain, FOI: Henry X Jones
Captain, MGT: Marion X Sewell

LOCATION: *Jersey City, NEW JERSEY*
Estimated Membership: 30
Minister: Ulysses X Harrell
Assistant Minister: David X White
Captain, FOI: Fred X Austin
Secretary: Frances X White

LOCATION: *Albany, NEW YORK*
Estimated Membership: 8–10
Officials Unknown

LOCATION: *Buffalo, NEW YORK*
Estimated Membership: 30–35
Minister: Robert X Williams
Assistant Ministers: John X Strickland; Wayman X Diggs
Secretary: Ora Lee X Mims

LOCATION: *New York, NEW YORK*
Estimated Membership: 350
Minister: Malcolm X Little
Assistant Ministers: Hiawatha X Brown; Curtis X Johnson
Captain, FOI: Joseph X Gravitt Jr.
Secretaries: Susie X Kenner; Gloria X Harris

LOCATION: *Troy, NEW YORK*
Estimated Membership: 3
Minister: Frances X Jenkins Jr.
Other Officials Unknown

LOCATION: *Durham, NORTH CAROLINA*
  Estimated Membership: 7
  Officials Unknown

LOCATION: *Wilmington, NORTH CAROLINA*
  Estimated Membership: 2
  Officials Unknown

LOCATION: *Cincinnati, OHIO*
  Estimated Membership: 62
  Minister: Lemuel X Hassan Anderson
  Assistant Minister: Eddie X Davis
  Captain, FOI: William X Haynes
  Secretary: Howard X Montgomery
  Captain, MGT: Dorothy X Haynes

LOCATION: *Cleveland, OHIO*
  Estimated Membership: 25–40
  Minister: Theodore X Bost
  Captain, FOI: John 2X Underwood
  Secretary: Julius X Mahone

LOCATION: *Dayton, OHIO*
  Estimated Membership: 12
  Minister: Lemuel X Hassan Anderson
  Assistant Minister: Lucian X Carey
  Captain, FOI: James X Sloan

LOCATION: Youngstown, OHIO
  Estimated Membership: 30–45
  Minister: Louis X Powell
  Assistant Minister: King X Davenport
  Secretary: Joyce X Powell

LOCATION: *Beaver Falls, PENNSYLVANIA*
  Estimated Membership: Unknown
  Officials Unknown: Temple in Formation Stage

LOCATION: *Philadelphia, PENNSYLVANIA*
    Estimated Membership: 145
    Minister: Malcolm X Little
    Assistant Minister: George X Paden
    Captain, FOI: Clifford X Hyman
    Treasurer: Almeta X Paden

LOCATION: *Pittsburgh, PENNSYLVANIA*
    Estimated Membership: 75–100
    Minister: Robert X Davenport
    Secretary: Dorothy X Davenport

LOCATION: *Lancaster, SOUTH CAROLINA*
    Estimated Membership: 4
    Minister: Benjamin X Mitchell
    Other Officials Unknown

LOCATION: *Orangeburg, SOUTH CAROLINA*
    Estimated Membership: 30
    Minister: Lucius X Brown
    Assistant Minister: Leonard X Buskey

LOCATION: *Dallas, TEXAS*
    Estimated Membership: 6
    Minister: Clayborn X Johnson
    Assistant Minister: Willie Bert X Thomkins

LOCATION: *Fort Worth, TEXAS*
    Estimated Membership: 15
    Minister: Clayborn X Johnson
    Captain, FOI: Columbus X Martin
    Secretary: Earline X Martin

LOCATION: *Houston, TEXAS*
    Estimated Membership: 7
    Officials Unknown

LOCATION: WASHINGTON, D.C.
  Estimated Membership: 500
  Minister: Lucius X Brown
  Assistant Minister: Hilliard X Pryor
  Secretary: Willa Mae X Norris

LOCATION: *Milwaukee,* WISCONSIN
  Estimated Membership: 100
  Minister: Bernard X Donahue
  Assistant Minister: Walter X Perkins
  Captain, FOI: Henry X Allen
  Secretary: Joshua X Inge

LOCATION: *Alexandria,* VIRGINIA
  Estimated Membership: Unknown
  Officials Unknown

LOCATION: *Lynchburg,* VIRGINIA
  Estimated Membership: 9
  Minister: Richard X Wortham
  Treasurer: Gertrude X Mosby
  Secretary: Jean X Vaughn

LOCATION: *Richmond,* VIRGINIA
  Estimated Membership: 10
  Officials Unknown

APPENDIX E

Author's Note: In the early 1960s, Elijah Muhammad distilled the philosophy and goals of the NOI down to about two dozen simple principles and beliefs. These principles and beliefs appeared each week on the back page of Muhammad Speaks.

THE MUSLIM PROGRAM

I. What the Muslims Want

This is the question asked most frequently by both the whites and the Blacks. The answers to this question I shall state as simply as possible.

1. We want freedom. We want full and complete freedom.

2. We want justice. Equal justice under the law. We want justice applied equally to all, regardless of creed or class or color.

3. We want equality of opportunity. We want equal membership in society with the best in civilized society.

4. We want our people in America whose parents or grandparents were descended from slaves to be allowed to establish a separate state or territory of their own—either on this continent or elsewhere. We believe that our former slave masters are obligated to provide such land and that the area must be fertile and minerally rich. We believe that our former slave masters are obligated to maintain and supply our needs in this separate territory for the next 20 to 25 years—until we are able to produce and supply our own needs.

Since we cannot get along with them in peace and equality, after giving them 400 years of our sweat and blood and receiving in return some of the worst treatment human beings have ever experienced, we believe our contributions to this land and the suffering forced upon us by white America, justifies our demand for complete separation in a state of territory of our own.

5. We want freedom for all Believers of Islam now held in federal prisons. We want freedom for all Black men and women now under death sentence in innumerable prisons in the North as well as the South.

We want every Black man and woman to have the freedom to accept or reject being separated from the slave master's children and establish a land of their own.

We know that the above plan for the solution of the Black and white conflict is the best and only answer to the problem between two peoples.

6. We want an immediate end to the police brutality and mob attacks against the so-called Negro throughout the United States.

We believe that the federal government should intercede to see that Black men and women tried in white courts receive justice in accordance with the laws of the land—or allow us to build a new nation for ourselves, dedicated to justice, freedom and liberty.

7. As long as we are not allowed to establish a state or territory of our own, we demand not only equal justice under the laws of the United States, but equal employment opportunities—NOW!

We do not believe that after 400 years of free or nearly free labor, sweat and blood, which has helped America become rich and powerful, that so many thousands of Black people should have to subsist on relief, charity or live in poor houses.

8. We want the government of the United States to exempt our people from *all* taxation as long as we are deprived of equal justice under the laws of the land.

9. We want equal education—but separate schools up to 16 for boys and 18 for girls on the condition that the girls be sent to women's colleges and universities. We want all Black children educated and trained by their own teachers.

Under such a school system we believe we will make a better nation of people. The United States government should provide, free, all necessary text books and equipment, schools, and college buildings. The Muslim teachers shall be left free to teach and train their people in the way of righteousness, decency and self-respect.

10. We believe that intermarriage or race mixing should be prohibited. We want the religion of Islam taught without hindrance or suppression.

These are some of the things that we, the Muslims, want for our people in North America.

II. What the Muslims Believe

1. We believe in the One God Whose proper Name is Allah.

2. We believe in the Holy Quran and in the Scriptures of all the Prophets of God.

3. We believe in the truth of the Bible, but we believe that it has been tampered with and must be reinterpreted so that mankind will not be snared by the falsehoods that have been added to it.

4. We believe in Allah's Prophets and the Scriptures they brought to the people.

5. We believe in the resurrection of the dead—not in physical resurrection—but in mental resurrection. We believe the so-called Negroes are most in need of mental resurrection; therefore, they will be resurrected first. Furthermore, we believe we are the people of God's choice, as it has been written, that God would choose the rejected and the despised. We can find no other persons fitting the description in these last days more than the so-called Negroes in America. We believe in the resurrection of the righteous.

6. We believe in the judgment; we believe this first judgment will take place as God revealed, in America . . .

7. We believe this is the time in history for the separation of the so-called Negroes and the so-called white Americans. We believe the Black man should be freed from the names imposed upon him by his former slave masters. Names which identified him as being the slave master's slave. We believe that if we are free indeed, we should go in our own people's names—the Black people of the Earth.

8. We believe in justice for all, whether in God or not; we believe as others, that we are due equal justice as human beings. We believe in equality—as a nation—of equals. We do not believe that we are equal with our slave masters in the status of "freed slaves." We recognize and respect American citizens as independent peoples and we respect their laws which govern this nation.

9. We believe that the offer of integration is hypocritical and is made by those who are trying to deceive the Black peoples into believing that their 400-year-old open enemies of freedom, justice and equality are, all of a sudden, their "friends." Furthermore, we believe that such deception is intended to prevent

Black people from realizing that the time in history has arrived for the separation from the whites of this nation. If the white people are truthful about the professed friendship toward the so-called Negro, they can prove it by dividing up America with their slaves. We do not believe America will ever be able to furnish enough jobs for her own millions of unemployed, in addition to jobs for the 20,000,000 Black people as well.

10. We believe that we who declare ourselves to be righteous Muslims should not participate in wars which take the lives of humans. We do not believe this nation should force us to take part in such wars, for we have nothing to gain from it unless America agrees to give us the necessary territory wherein we may have something to fight for.

11. We believe our women should be respected and protected as the women of other nationalities are respected and protected.

12. We believe that Allah (God) appeared in the Person of Master W. Fard Muhammad, July 1930; the long-awaited "Messiah" of the Christians and the "Mahdi" of the Muslims.

We believe further and lastly that Allah is God and besides HIM there is no God and He will bring about a universal government of peace wherein we can all live in peace together.

APPENDIX F

SELECTED DECLASSIFIED GOVERNMENT DOCUMENTS ON ELIJAH
MUHAMMAD AND KEY FIGURES IN THE NATION OF ISLAM

I. FBI HQ File on Muslim Mosque Inc.
(Founded by Malcolm X in 1964)

Author's Note: Newly released documents leave little doubt that high-level government officials in the intelligence community used every weapon at their disposal to foment a violent conflict between Elijah Muhammad and Malcolm X. Some of the documents that shed light on the methods used are reprinted below.

(a)

Confidential

    1-Mr. Belmont
    1–Mr. Rosen
    1–Mr. Sullivan
    1–Liaison
    1–Mr. Baumgardner
    1–Mr. Rosack

(Internal Security) 25-220971
(Internal Security) 100-441765

Date: June 9, 1964
To: Chief, U.S. Secret Service
From: John Edgar Hoover, Director

Subject: Nation of Islam
        Internal Security–NOI
        Muslim Mosque, Incorporated
        Internal Security–MMI

This will confirm the following information orally furnished on June 6, 1964 by Special Agent [name redacted] of this Bureau to [name deleted], U.S. Secret Service; [name redacted], Office of Naval Intelligence; [name redacted], Assistant Chief of Staff for Intelligence, Department of the Army; and [name deleted], Office of Special Investigations, Air Force.

A confidential source [in this case, the source appears to be the wiretaps on Malcolm X's telephones] who has furnished reliable information in the past advised on June 6, 1964, that Malcolm X (Little), head of Muslim Mosque, Incorporated (MMI), was contacted on that date by his assistant James 67X Warden, also known as James Shabazz, who was in Phoenix, Arizona. Warden stated he had obtained a signed statement on June 5 from "the women" and had also taken photographs of the illegitimate children and the mothers. Warden stated he would attempt to get a bastardy warrant on June 6 against "him," presumably referring to Elijah Muhammad who is head of the Nation of Islam (NOI), and serve the warrant by noon (Phoenix time). Warden stated he would also attempt to arrange publicity for the serving of the warrant and the release of the bastardy story. Malcolm X advised Warden that if he could not get adequate publicity in Phoenix he should go to Los Angeles and see "Alexander" who would set up a press conference there.

It appears that Malcolm X is attempting to discredit Muhammad by making public information he is known to have of the illegitimate children of Muhammad and is apparently being assisted by one or more of the mothers who may be in Phoenix.

In addition to the above the following information has been received concerning this matter.

The "Alexander" referred to above apparently refers to Sanford Alexander, owner, *Los Angeles Herald Dispatch*, or his wife. The *Los Angeles Herald Dis-*

patch is a weekly newspaper published in Los Angeles, California, and was formerly the official organ of the NOI on the West Coast.

The confidential source mentioned above advised on June 6, 1964, that Warden contacted Malcolm X and advised him things in Phoenix were not going as swiftly as they had hoped. Warden stated he had the statement from the women revised and lengthened and hoped he could get it notarized which was about all he could get done on that date since it was too late for court action. On June 6, 1964, Warden was registered under his true name of James Warden in an unknown hotel in Phoenix with two women and an unknown number of children. One woman, name unknown, has three children and the second is "Sister Lucille," who is eight months pregnant, and also may have some children. Warden has mailed photographs he took of the children and their mothers to Malcolm X in New York City.

The source further advised if everything had gone according to plan "Sister Lucille" was to have driven Warden to Los Angeles on the evening of June 6 to contact Mrs. Alexander and set up a press conference there; however, due to delays the trip will probably be further delayed until everything in Phoenix is completed. Malcolm X warned Warden not to contact Mrs. Alexander in advance but to go to see her when he arrived in Los Angeles and show her the information he had gathered.

The Phoenix office has advised that William R. Johnson, a Mrs. Williams, a Miss Williams, a Mrs. Karriem and a Miss L. Karriem (age 4) left Phoenix on American Airlines Flight 929 for Los Angeles at 7:05 P.M., June 6. It appears the two women are probably Lucille Rosary (Karriem) and Evelyn Williams.

The above source advised on June 7, 1964 [the date, by the way, that Malcolm X received a death threat by telephone], that James Warden was then in Los Angles with "Sister Evelyn" and "Sister Lucille" and they apparently flew to Los Angeles from Phoenix on the night of June 6. Warden advised Malcolm X the only thing accomplished in Phoenix was the notarization of the statement. Malcolm X instructed Warden to contact Mrs. Alexander and tell her the complete story. The source advised that both women are extremely reluctant to tell their story publicly in spite of attempts by Malcolm X to persuade them to talk by claiming there will be "violence" between the NOI and the MMI if they do not talk.

The New York Office has advised the MMI held a public rally at Audubon

Ballroom, New York City, on the evening of June 7 with approximately 450 persons in attendance. The main speaker was Malcolm X who spoke of his recent African tour and the sympathy of the Africans for Negroes in America. In answer to a question Malcolm X indicated Elijah Muhammad of the NOI is the father of six illegitimate children which fact the NOI "covers up."

The NOI and the MMI are under investigation by this Bureau, the results of which are being furnished on a continuing basis to the agencies receiving instant communication. You will be advised of further pertinent information regarding this matter.

> 1–Mr. J. Walter Yeagley, Assistant Attorney General
> 1–Director of Naval Intelligence
> 1–Assistant Chief of Staff for Intelligence, Department of the Army
>   Attention: Chief, Security Division
> 1–Office of Special Investigations, Air Force
>   Attention: Chief, Counterintelligence Division

(b)

Federal Bureau of Investigation
Domestic Intelligence Division

Date: June 29, 1964

Informative Note

Muslim Mosque, Inc., (MMI) is a black nationalist group formed by Malcolm X. Little, former New York Nation of Islam (NOI) leader who has been attempting to discredit Elijah Muhammad, head of NOI.

Attached reports formation of group by Malcolm X. Little called "Organization of Afro-American Unity," which has announced purpose of sponsoring a reform program aimed at getting racial problems before United Nations. We have been following this development very closely.

Dissemination being made to [Justice] Department, State, CIA, Secret Service and Military agencies.

BCR: cwb

(c)

Federal Bureau of Investigation
U.S. Department of Justice
Communications Section

Teletype
FBI–New York
1:55 AM
Urgent
June 29, 1964
To: Director (100-441765)
From: New York SAC (100-152759)

Re: Muslim Mosque, Incorporated
    Internal Security–MMI

[Source's identity redacted] advised Six Twenty Nine Sixty Four [06/29/64] as follows . . .

MMI public rally held Audubon Ballroom, New York City, from Eight Fifteen to Ten Forty Five PM, Six Twenty Eight Sixty Four, with approximately five hundred persons in attendance. Speaker was Malcolm X who announced formation of new Non-White Civil Rights Action Group to be called "Organization of Afro-American Unity." New organization will sponsor educational, political, economic and social reform programs. It will be led by Malcolm X and the leading aim is to get U.S. Racial Problem before UN. Malcolm X claims support from many local organizations and from Afro-Asian nations, particularly Ghana. Leading supporters on stage with Malcolm X included William Worthy, Mrs. [Juanita] Sidney Poitier, Wilbur Tatum (Associated Artist for Freedom) and others. William Patterson is also a supporter according to Malcolm X but Patterson was not present. New organization will hold meeting next Sunday night at Audubon Ballroom and officers will be announced. Initial dues for group will be two dollars per person, and one dollar per week thereafter. Audience allowed to register for group following Six Twenty Eight meeting.

[Source redacted] has taped program which will be listened to in order to obtain full list of those supporting new group.

LHM [LetterHead Memorandum] follows.

II. FBI HQ file of W.D. Fard (alias Wallace Dodd Ford)

(a)

Confidential
Date: 02/19/63

To: Director, FBI (25-220971)
From: SAC, Chicago (100-35635–Sub B)

Nation of Islam
IS–NOI

Re Chicago letters to Bureau, dated 02/25/58 and 04/04/58; and Bureau letter to Chicago, dated 04/15/58, entitled "WALLACE DODD, FORD, SM–NOI."

In connection with efforts to disrupt and curb growth of the NOI, extensive research has been conducted into various files maintained by this office. Among the files reviewed was that of Wallace Dodd Ford.

In this review it was noted there was evidence indicating Ford, or ALLAH as he is known to the NOI, was last seen in September 1933 at which time he, or a person believed to be him, was arrested by the Chicago Police Department; that his former common-law wife stated she had seen him in either the summer of 1932 or 1933, at which time she said he told her he was going to return to New Zealand, adding he had always been factual in keeping her advised of his where-abouts since his release from San Quentin in 1929; that on the birth of Ford's son by this woman, Ford's birth was listed as New Zealand.

It is also noted Ford also claims to have been born on February 25, 1891 in Portland, Oregon, to Zared and Beatrice Ford who were born in Hawaii. Investigative efforts to verify this were negative.

[Last paragraph redacted]

3–Bureau (RM)
  1–105-63642 (WALLACE DODD FORD)

2–Chicago
   1–100-33683 (Wallace Dodd Ford)

Author's Note: The following memorandum is from the FBI's Detroit field office, and was not released until June 1995. It was a breakthrough of sorts, since it corroborates what scholars have argued for some time, namely that Elijah Muhammad and members of his family knew that Master Wallace D. Fard and Wallie D. Ford were one and the same.

(b)

Office Memorandum—United States Government

To: SAC (100-33683)
From: [Name Redacted], Correlation Clerk

   Subject: W. D. Fard, with aliases Wali Farrad, Wallace Farad, Wallie D. Ford, Wallace Don Fard, Wali Mohammed, Farrad Mohammed, F. Mohammed-Ali, Mohammed F. Ali
   Internal Security—Nation of Islam (NOI)
   Attention: SA [name deleted]
   (the majority of the first page is blackened out)

Miscellaneous

   Nation of Islam

   (Page 2)

   Willie Mohammed, 9536 Cameron, Detroit, Michigan

   25-5888-1

   Willie Mohammed, 9536 Cameron, Detroit advised SA's [name redacted] and SA [name redacted] on July 3, 1942 that he was born August 5, 1891 near Sandersville, Georgia.

It should be noted that the subject of this file is Willie Mohammed, with aliases Willie Poole, Wali Mohammed.

Willie Mohammed advised that he met Wallace D. Farad in Detroit in 1931. Wallace D. Farad at that time was the leader and organizer of the Islam religion in Detroit. In 1933 or 1934, according to Mohammed, Wallace D. Farad was arrested by the Detroit Police Department and a short time thereafter left the community. None of the members of the Nation of Islam Temple Number One at Detroit have heard from Wallace D. Farad (Allah) since he left Detroit and they have no idea where he is at the present time. Willie advised that he had been acting minister of the Temple of Islam in Detroit since 1937, and David Fard, the secretary, had been secretary since 1934.

A photograph of Wallace D. Fard taken by the Detroit Police Department in 1933 was exhibited to Willie Mohammed, who immediately identified the picture as being, "My Sweet Savior, My All Powerful Allah."

Willie admitted being a blood brother of Prophet Elijah who was under arrest in Washington, D.C. under the name of Gulam Bogans, charged with violation of the Selective Service for counseling, aiding and abetting evasion of registration for service as required under the act. Willie refused to sign a statement which was prepared by the agents.

III. FBI Memo Concerning COINTELPRO Measures in the Event of Elijah Muhammad's Death

Author's Note: On January 22, 1969, the FBI's Chicago field office sent a lengthy memorandum to J. Edgar Hoover outlining past and possible future counterintelligence (COINTELPRO) measures to be employed against Elijah Muhammad and the NOI. The memo, which is self-explanatory, is one of the first declassified documents in which the government admits its role in causing the schism between Malcolm and Elijah Muhammad, a dispute that led to the former's assassination. Prepared as a response to a query from FBI headquarters on January 7 ("reurlet" means "regarding your letter"), both memoranda are reprinted in full below.

(a)

United States Government
Date: January 7, 1969

From: SAC, Chicago (157-2209)
To: Director, FBI (100-448006)

Subject: Counterintelligence Program
        Black Nationalist—Hate Groups
        Racial Intelligence
        (Nation of Islam)

Although the Nation of Islam (NOI) does not presently advocate violence by its members, the group does preach hatred of the white race and racial separatism. The membership of the NOI is organized and poses a real racial threat. The NOI is responsible for the largest black nationalist newspaper, which has been used by other black extremists.

The NOI appears to be the personal freedom of Elijah Muhammad. When he dies a power struggle can be expected and the NOI could change direction. We should be prepared for this eventuality. We should plan how to change the philosophy of the NOI to one of strictly religious and self-improvement orientation, deleting the race hatred and separate nationhood aspects.

In this connection Chicago should consider what counterintelligence action might be needed now or at the time of Elijah Muhammad's death to bring about such a change in NOI philosophy. Important considerations should include the identity, strengths, and weaknesses, of any contenders for NOI leadership. What are the positions of our [high-level] informants in regard to leadership? How could potential leaders be turned or neutralized?

The alternative to changing the philosophy of the NOI is the destruction of the organization. This might be accomplished through generating factionalism among the contenders for Elijah Muhammad's leadership or through legal action in probate court on his death. Chicago should consider the question of how to generate the factionalism necessary to destroy the NOI by splitting into several groups. [Rest of line redacted].

Legal action against the NOI on the death of its leader depends on the answers to several questions:

1. Does Elijah Muhammad have a will?

2. Is the NOI incorporated?

3. In whose name and where are NOI bank accounts?

4. In whose name are other NOI assets, such as mosque buildings, Elijah Muhammad's homes, and NOI businesses?

Depending on the answers to these questions, probate law in Illinois, and whether Chicago might have a confidential source in probate administration, tying up the NOI in probate administration might be possible.

Chicago should examine the NOI from the above counterintelligence angle and advise the Bureau. Consider the possibility of drawing up specific counterintelligence recommendations, to be acted upon when necessary, with various contingencies covered.

(b)

United States Government
Date: January 22, 1969

To: Director, FBI (100-448006)
From: SAC, Chicago (157-2209) (P)

Subject: Counterintelligence Program
        Black Nationalist—Hate Groups
        Racial Intelligence
        (Nation of Islam)

Reurlet, January 7, 1969; Chicago letters December 24, 1968 and January 14, 1969.

ReBulet has been thoroughly studied and discussed by the SAC, the Supervisor, and Agents familiar with facets of the NOI which might indicate trends and possible future direction of the organization. The Bureau's concern is most understandable and suggestions appreciated.

Over the years considerable thought had been given, and action taken with Bureau approval, relating to methods through which the NOI could be discredited in the eyes of the general black populace or through which factionalism among the leadership could be created. Serious consideration has also been given towards developing ways and means of changing NOI philosophy to one whereby the members could be developed into useful citizens and the organization developed into one emphasizing religion—the brotherhood of mankind—and self-improvement.

Factional disputes have been developed—the most notable being Malcolm X Little. Prominent black personages have publicly and nationally spoken out against the group—U.S. District Court Judge James Benton Parsons being one example. The media of the press has played down the NOI. This appears to be a most effective tool as individuals such as Muhammad assuredly seek any and all publicity be it good or bad; however, if the press is utilized it would appear it should not concentrate on such aspects as the alleged strength of the NOI, immoral activities of the leadership, misuse of funds by these officials, etc.

It is the opinion of this office that such exposure is ineffective, possibly creating interest and maybe envy among the lesser educated black men, causing them out of curiosity to attend meetings and maybe join, and encourage the opportunist to seek personal gain—physical or monetary—through alignment with the group. At any rate it is felt such publicity in the case of the NOI is not overly effective.

As the Bureau is aware the NOI several years ago organized Progressive Land Developers, Inc., and more recently United Dynamic Corporation, both incorporated in the State of Illinois. Both have well known NOI officials as officers—Elijah Muhammad is not shown as involved in either. The professed purpose of these groups is economic in nature and gives no appearance of being religious in nature.

Activity by these groups was most limited until the past year to year and one half ago. Since that time the NOI has invested heavily in business properties in the Chicago area and in land in Michigan and Georgia. It was noted publicly regarding formation of these two corporations by the NOI was limited throughout the United States—only two articles have appeared and both dealt briefly with Progressive Land Developers, Inc. buying land in Michigan. Both articles were published in cities other than Chicago.

[First line of data redacted] contacted this office and volunteered data to the effect he had been surveying NOI business ventures and wanted to write an article about some but needed assistance. Bearing the above facts in mind re the two corporations, the Bureau was requested to give permission to furnish [name deleted] with pertinent public record material relating to ownership of these two nonreligious ventures with emphasis on the fact it appeared membership monies were possibly being misused. The Bureau granted permission and [name deleted] was given all possible assistance. At this time he is working on his articles and assures this office he will advise us of the article and its publication. Re Chicago letters set forth full details. It is hoped that publicity emphasizing NOI nonreligious ventures will cause factionalism among the leaders and discredit them among the black community and the organization's membership.

Elijah Muhammad is sole leader of the NOI, claiming to have been so appointed by Allah. He further claims to be the only divinely appointed leader of all black people in America. His "gimmick" in creating an aura of mysticism has been proclaiming the black man to be God and the future ruler of the Earth; branding the white man as the Devil whose future lies in his destruction by Allah through the forces of nature; and a call for a separate state or territory of their own or equal justice and equal opportunities in the United States if they cannot have separate territory. These "gimmicks" would be most attractive to many black people in the lower economic strata who would want to hear the white man condemned and castigated because of their own plight. Of course, the development of a seemingly large following would also attract the opportunist—a black man who would profess to believe Muhammad's teachings but is really out solely for personal gain. As is apparent, Muhammad has created through the above an almost fanatical devotion to him on the part of his following; however, this devotion and subservience is purely voluntary as members are specifically instructed to leave if they cannot follow all of the "Laws of Islam." The turnover is constant and while many have left because of the NOI's demands they still believe his teachings.

Elijah Muhammad, as far as is known, has not designated, or even shown a preference for, an heir apparent. With two exceptions the national leadership is composed of members of his family. All are dependent of Muhammad and the groups for their livelihood. Over the years various members of the "Royal Family" have been in the favor of Muhammad only to fall by the wayside because they dared question Muhammad's edicts. A prime example of this would be Wallace Muhammad who was until about 1964 considered the most likely to be the heir apparent and Muhammad himself indicated Allah might be communicating with Wallace. Of course, Wallace subsequently was suspended by his father because he refused to believe W.D. Fard was Allah. It is still believed Wallace Muhammad is the only member of the "Royal Family" who could give proper spiritual guidance to the organization. No one has emerged as a successor to Wallace insofar as this sphere of activity is concerned.

Recent indications are that Herbert Muhammad is closest to Muhammad. He is self-stated to be Muhammad's personal aide. He has illusions of running the NOI from "behind the scenes" when Muhammad passes on. There is no indication Herbert himself will be able to guide the flock spiritually nor is there any indication as to how he plans to accomplish same. He is interested only in such financial gain as the membership will make available to him.

In our opinion there is no one presently in the NOI who will be able to replace Muhammad and the mystical spell he is able to cast on some members of the black race. This must be done to ensure survival of the group. Further, there is no means at present to determine who will succeed Muhammad. Past experience has shown he does not particularly trust any of his sons or daughters and they could be in favor one day but completely in disfavor the next. Herbert Muhammad is as susceptible to this as any.

It appears the NOI is on a collision course for a factional split after the death of Muhammad. The power struggle could well develop among members of the "Royal Family" and could well involve some of the more prominent NOI ministers who could well align themselves with a certain member of the "Royal Family" or could entertain illusions of "ruling" a segment of the NOI. It is not beyond the realm of possibility that anyone of Muhammad's more prominent ministers could make a power play on Muhammad's death. At present, however, Muhammad seemingly had all of them totally subservient to him.

As mentioned earlier, the spiritual aspects of the NOI must be maintained to keep the group going. It is recalled that when Malcolm X Little defected and later was murdered, many dissenting NOI members sought out Wallace Muhammad for spiritual leadership. When Wallace Muhammad returned to his father on another occasion and was presented to NOI members gathered at the Annual Muslim Convention in Chicago he was wildly acclaimed. It is felt Wallace Muhammad is still warmly thought of by his father and he is the only son or daughter who is not monetarily motivated. It is known Muhammad still asks about Wallace.

It is further known Wallace is adamant in his belief W.D. Fard is not Allah. Wallace is acknowledged clandestinely by members of the "Royal Family" and is friendly with many of them. He is thought to be held in esteem by NOI members despite his suspension. It is not beyond expectations that he could be sought out for support in a power play by a member or members of the "Royal Family" or by various NOI ministers to be a figurehead or the leader. His beliefs are the brotherhood of mankind and self-improvement with no hate for other men. Wallace Muhammad is well aware of this and maintains his contacts.

The above is pure speculation but factual data can only be obtained as time passes and events occur. At this time proper courses of action can be planned and implemented.

ReBulet refers to legal action against the NOI on the death of its leader and asks such questions as:

(1) Does Muhammad have a will?

(2) Is the NOI incorporated?

(3) In whose name and where are NOI bank accounts?

(4) In whose name are NOI assets such as mosque buildings, Muhammad's home, etc.?

There is no information available as to whether or not Elijah Muhammad has a will. This would be information available only to Muhammad and, possibly, his attorney.

Muhammad's Temple No. 2 of the Holy Temples of Islam is shown as being an Illinois corporation at the Cook County Recorder's Office, Chicago; however, there is no evidence of same on file with the Secretary of State, Corporate Section, Springfield, Illinois.

Bank accounts maintained by Muhammad's Temple No. 2 in Chicago are in a state of complete flux at present. Accounts both savings and checking have been maintained for several years in the name of Muhammad's Temple No. 2 at the South East National Bank (all have balances of under $1,000.00); at Continental Illinois National Bank and Trust Company of Chicago (all now closed); at the American National Bank and Trust Company of Chicago (unavailable due to bank policy). Elijah Muhammad was not shown as being authorized to draw on any of the above accounts. Rather those authorized to draw included officers of the Temple—any two of four. Only one bank account was located for Elijah Muhammad. It was a savings account containing less than $5,000.00 and was in the name of Elijah and Clara (his wife) Muhammad.

NOI properties have been closely followed by this office insofar as title holder, evaluation, etc., are concerned. Muhammad's Temple No. 2, including the University of Islam No. 2, is in the name of Muhammad's Temple No. 2; various business ventures purchased by the NOI are in the name of Progressive Land Developers, Inc., or United Dynamics Corporation (both described above) as are land purchases in Michigan and Georgia. So far as can be determined NOI properties are in one of the above names. The exception to this are Muhammad's residence at 4847 South Woodlawn; his residence at 2118 East Violet Drive, Phoenix, Arizona; and a residence at 1122 Staples Street, N.E., Washington, D.C., which are in the name of Elijah and/or Clara Muhammad at present.

Chicago's experience insofar as Muhammad's legal advice is concerned dates back to 1959 at which time Elijah Muhammad on legal advice tempered his teachings against the white man and the government, both synonymous in NOI teachings, to avoid prosecution. At that time he de-emphasized religious aspects of the NOI and commenced emphasizing economic benefits to be derived by the black man who joined the organization. It appears, based on NOI land and business ventures in the past two years, Muhammad is implementing monies accrued from the membership and from appreciation from properties sold. His success or failure in those business and farming ventures remains to be determined as they have only been in effect for a year or so.

Over the years Muhammad's legal involvements have been closely followed. He has been represented by numerous attorneys and evidently seeks out advice on new endeavors. The Internal Revenue Service has reviewed the NOI and some of its officials but results were negative. Income tax returns filed by such individuals as Herbert Muhammad, who made substantial money as manager of Cassius Clay [Muhammad Ali], were reviewed and no discrepancies were noted. It was noted attorneys executed those returns. Perhaps the most significant factor is recognition of the NOI as a religion by [the United States District Court] and subsequent courts, both federal and state, approval for NOI services in Federal and State prisons.

Chicago has no source in Probate Court, Cook County, Chicago, and has not considered the development of same due to many scandalous allegations relating to political appointees and their associates in this area. It is not deemed advisable to approach such a person as the Bureau would be in an extremely embarrassing position if there were the slightest leak that the Bureau was involved in probate of any estate.

Chicago, as the Bureau is aware, has always been on the alert for methods by which the NOI could be directed or disrupted. As is evidenced by the present cooperation with [informant's name redacted], this policy continues. Chicago continues its contacts with its sources whose identities are known to the Bureau and feels these sources will be of possible extreme value at the time of the demise of Muhammad. At this time appropriate recommendations will be made.

(c)

Federal Bureau of Investigation
August 21, 1942

Memorandum for Mr. E.A. Tamm
Re: Allah Temple of Islam, 104 East 51st Street

Hyde Park Masonic Temple Building, Chicago
Internal Security—J, Selective Service, Sedition

While talking with SAC Johnson of Chicago regarding an investigation presently being conducted on the above group, he mentioned a matter which I thought might prove of interest.

Johnson stated that this particular meeting was in a colored district and it was extremely hard for the Agents to operate without being detected. He said, however, that when the meetings have been held, arrangements have been made to have the Agents made up by professional make-up artists so that by wearing dark glasses, the Agents could mingle unnoticed in a group of colored people. He advised, however, that under strong sunlight this make-up does not prove to be so effective.

Respectfully,

A. Rosen

(d)

Federal Bureau of Investigation
June 10, 1969
Route in Envelope

From: Mr. W.C. Sullivan
To: Mr. G.C. Moore

June [wiretaps, etc.] Mail

Martin Luther King, Jr.
Security Matter—Communist
Elijah Muhammad
Internal Security—Nation of Islam

The Director has asked who authorized the wiretaps on Martin Luther King, Jr. and Elijah Muhammad and has asked to see the original authorizations.

There was a wiretap on King's phone at his residence in Atlanta, Georgia, from November 8, 1963 to April 30, 1965, when he moved. Wiretaps of several days duration were also instituted at the Hyatt Motel in Los Angeles, California, the Claridge Hotel in Atlantic City, New Jersey, and at a temporary address at 125 East 72 Street, New York City. A wiretap was instituted at the headquarters of the Southern Christian leadership Conference (SCLC) in New York City on two occasions. All these wiretaps were on the authorization of Robert Kennedy, dated October 10, 1963, which is attached.

In addition, a wiretap on SCLC headquarters in Atlanta, Georgia, was instituted from November 8, 1963, to June 21, 1966, on Kennedy's authorization dated October 21, 1963, attached.

A wiretap on the residence of Elijah Muhammad in Chicago was authorized January 2, 1957, by Herbert Brownell, authorization attached. It was installed January 4, 1957. On this same authorization wiretaps were installed at additional residences of Elijah Muhammad in Chicago, Illinois, and Phoenix, Arizona. The wiretap installed on this authorization was discontinued June 23, 1966.

Ramsey Clark became Acting Attorney General on October 3, 1966.

Action: None. For Information.

100—106670; 105—24822

IV. The FBI and the Schism between
Elijah Muhammad and Malcolm X

Author's Note: In the mid-1980s, the FBI declassified a document dealing with the schism it helped create between Malcolm X, the national spokesman of the NOI, and Elijah Muhammad. Although all identification marks were redacted, it's known that the COINTELPRO was suggested several weeks before Elijah Muhammad decided to make Malcolm X's suspension permanent, and only weeks before the Messenger broached the idea of having Malcolm X murdered. The declassified memorandum appears in its entirety as it was released to the author.

(a)

[Information Redacted]

Elijah Muhammad
[line redacted]

Elijah Muhammad, the leader of the Black Muslim group, and his principal Lieutenant, Malcolm X Little, have been feuding since Muhammad silenced Little publicly and officially for making stupid and ill-timed remarks to the effect that the assassination of President Kennedy gave him (Little) pleasure.

Little is probably the most dynamic and forceful Nation of Islam (NOI) spokesman in the movement and the attached memorandum, which is worded in most general terms, could possibly widen the rift between Muhammad and Little and possibly result in Little's expulsion from the NOI.

The information set forth in the enclosed memorandum has been the subject of considerable discussion within the NOI and its disclosure will not prejudice our investigation or sources.

Recommendation: That the enclosed memorandum be routed to Assistant Director DeLoach for his consideration.

[Final lines and notations redacted]

(Page 2)

February 10, 1964

"The Rift Widens between Elijah Muhammad and His Principal Lieutenant Malcolm X Little"

The rift between Elijah Muhammad, self-proclaimed Messenger of Allah and the leader of the fanatical Black Muslim hate group, and his erstwhile Lieutenant Malcolm X Little appears to be widening. Little was silenced officially and publicly by Muhammad a short while after President Kennedy's assassination inasmuch as Little had made stupid and ill-timed remarks to the effect that President Kennedy's death gave him pleasure.

Little has not taken this disciplinary action gracefully and he has attempted to develop sympathy and backing for his position among other leaders of the Black Muslims in various sections of the country. He evidently feels that Elijah Muhammad is in his declining years and that he is slipping. It is no secret that Little would not hesitate one moment to take over the leadership of the Nation of Islam (NOI) and incidentally begin living in the regal style which Elijah

Muhammad enjoys. While Muhammad may be getting older, he is far from ready to hand over the reins of the NOI and all the affluent service benefits that go with it to Little. Muhammad is reportedly fuming at the temerity Little has exhibited in questioning the "Messenger's" judgment and it would not surprise anyone at all familiar with the works of the NOI to see Little summarily expelled from this organization if he continues to buck the orders and wishes of Elijah Muhammad.

[Final lines redacted]

V: The FBI's New York File on Malcolm X

Author's Note: Following Malcolm X's return from his second successful trip to Africa and mounting concerns by the FBI, the State Department, the Justice Department (notably Assistant Attorney General for Civil Rights Burke Marshall), and the CIA that his proposed United Nations petition was picking up support, the FBI beefed up its surveillance. Not only was there a wiretap on his office and home telephones, but physical surveillance was also reinforced, so much so that Malcolm X was watched by FBI agents from dawn to sundown. Below are two excerpts from the final days in the life of Malcolm X, as recorded by FBI agents who tracked him. Also included are excerpts from the wiretap on his home telephone.

(a)

Federal Bureau of Investigation

File No.: NY105-8999-A (January, 1965)

Physical Surveillance Log

Subject: Malcolm X Little
Date: January 20, 1965
Agents on Duty: [names deleted]
Code No.: [blank]
Shift: [blank]
Team: [blank]

Synopsis

Observed [checked]
Not Observed: [not checked]
Contact Made: [not checked]
Unusual Activity: [not checked]
Indexing Needed: No
Case Agent: [name deleted]

What follows are the handwritten notes of the agents following Malcolm X on January 20, 1965:

Observation of Malcolm X Little on January 20, 1965

9:07 A.M.: Surveillance instituted [in the] vicinity of 23-11 97th Street, East Elmhurst, Queens, New York [tiny redaction under FOIA Exception B7c suggest observing agent's initials were blotted out].

(Subject's car, 1963 midnight blue Oldsmobile, 4-door, NY license 1G-2220, parked around corner on 23rd Avenue, west of 97th Street).

1:00 p.m.: Subject's car with one unknown occupant observed crossing 97th Street traveling east on 23rd Avenue. Vehicle not observed thereafter [tiny redaction, again indicative of initials].

2:00 p.m.: Unknown Negro female, [half a line redacted], departed residence and entered [half a line redacted] driven by unknown Negro male. Drove north on 97th Street and turned west on 23rd Avenue [tiny redaction].

2:35 p.m.: Surveillance discontinued [indicating that agent's shift ended at 3:00 p.m].

3:02 p.m. Surveillance instituted [in the] vicinity of Hotel Theresa, 209 7th Avenue (at 125th Street, New York City). Subject's car parked on east side of 7th Avenue, one-fourth block north of 125th Street [tiny redaction].

4:00 p.m. Subject departed Hotel Theresa, walked to car, drove north on 7th Avenue to 135th Street, turned east on 135th Street and parked on north side of West 135th Street, opposite "22 West" restaurant, 22 West 135th Street, New York City [small redaction].

4:08 p.m.: Subject entered "22 West" restaurant [small redaction].

6:50 p.m. Surveillance discontinued. Subject's car still parked at above spot [small redaction].

(b)

Federal Bureau of Investigation

File No.: NY105-8999-A (January, 1965)

Physical Surveillance Log

Subject: Malcolm X Little
Date: January 21, 1965
Agents on Duty: [names deleted]
Code No.: [blank]
Shift: [blank]
Team: [blank]

Synopsis

Observed [check-marked]
Not Observed: [not checked]
Contact Made: [not checked]
Memo Prepared: [not checked]
Unusual Activity: [not checked]
Indexing Needed: No
Case Agent: [name deleted]

What follows are the handwritten notes of the agents following Malcolm X on January 21, 1965:

Observation of Malcolm X Little on January 21, 1965

9:11 A.M.: Surveillance instituted [in the] vicinity of 23-11 97th Street, East Elmhurst, Queens, New York [data, probably agent's initials, redacted].

9:25 A.M.: Subject departed residence, walked to corner of 97th Street and 23rd Avenue, and entered "Moe's Stationery" store, 90-02 23rd Avenue, East Elmhurst, Queens [same redaction].

9:30 A.M.: Departed store carrying newspaper and entered residence [same redaction].

1:15 P.M.: Subject [name redacted, but logically it was Betty Shabazz, Malcolm X's wife] departed residence with two children (girls) and walked south on 97th Street [same probable redaction].

1:22 P.M.: Subject departed residence and entered car [half a line of date blackened out], and drove to Harlem by proceeding west on 23rd Avenue to 94th Street, north on 94th Street to Grand Central Parkway [GCP], west on GCP over Tri-Borough Bridge to 125th Street, west on 125th Street in Harlem.

1:42 P.M.: Parked car in vicinity of 75 West 125th Street, New York City (possibly entered Carver Federal Savings Bank at that address).

1:47 P.M.: Returned to car and drove west on 125th to 7th Avenue [indecipherable] on 7th Avenue].

1:50 P.M.: Parked car on west side of 7th Avenue [word indecipherable] of 124th Street and entered Hotel Theresa, 209 7th Avenue, New York City [agent's initials probably redacted].

2:58 P.M.: Subject departed hotel, placed money in parking meter at his car and returned to hotel [initials blotted out].

3:03 P.M.: Surveillance discontinued [signaling end of this agent's shift, from 7 A.M. through 3 P.M.].

VI. Federal Bureau of Investigation/ELSUR

Author's Note: The FBI maintained a wiretap on Malcolm X's telephone for several years. Despite many requests for declassification of the electronic surveillance (ELSUR) logs and collateral material, the Bureau did not make the ELSUR logs generally available until 1996. One look at the files may expose why the FBI was hesitant to release the logs. They prove conclusively that the Bureau was aware as early as July 1964 that Malcolm X's life was in danger, and that the NOI was doing everything within its power to bring about his death. These excerpts provide a mere glimpse into information the FBI recorded during Malcolm X's final days.

File No.: NY105-8999-A (January, 1965)
Subject: Malcolm X Little

Electronic Surveillance (ELSUR) Log

(a)

Subject Malcolm X Little

File Number: 105-8999—Sub 1 (ELSUR Logs)

Time: 12:18 P.M.

Date: Friday, June 5, 1964

Special Agent [data deleted] R1382-14 & 08995-42

[Several lines redacted]

Malcolm says that he appeared on "The Joe Rainey (phonetic) Show" on radio last night (June 4, 1964). Malcolm said the radio show emanated from Philadelphia, Penn., and that during the course of the program a Muslim from Philadelphia telephoned the program and asked why he, Malcolm X, was thrown out of the NOI. Malcolm said he gave his explanation to this "without mentioning the Messenger's name." Malcolm said that he [about half a line of data redacted] discovered that six teenage sisters had become pregnant by the Messenger and that this same man (the Messenger) had these pregnant sisters thrown out of the Muslims because they were harlots and tramps. Malcolm continued that when the Messenger found out that he, Malcolm, was wise to the sexual degeneracies of the Messenger, the Messenger told the Fruit of Islam to kill him (Malcolm X), if possible, and to disrupt all meetings held by Malcolm. Malcolm says this policy of violence by the Messenger "can only lead to murder being committed by Muslim against Muslim." Malcolm says that if any [members] of the Messenger's Fruit of Islam try to break up any of his, Malcolm's meetings, there will be bloodshed [the majority of the rest of the page is blackened out].

(b)

Time: 1:08 P.M.

Date: Sunday, June 7, 1964

[Name redacted] called and wants Malcolm to call him at CV-2-66187.

Time: 1:50 P.M.
Sunday, June 7, 1964

Members of the Uruba Temple want Malcolm to call them at UN-4-5344.

Time: 3:25 P.M.
Date: Sunday, June 7, 1964

Malcolm X to Unwoman [unknown woman] asking her to tell [party's identity redacted] about the Messenger's escapades with his secretaries and how the Messenger made them all pregnant. Malcolm says that [party's identity blackened out] must be told that the Nation of Islam is factionalized and that both factions will commit murders on each other unless the truth is publicized about the Messenger's bad deeds. Malcolm says he is not fooling or speaking for effect when he says that bloodshed will take place as "it almost happened yesterday in New York when those who were in the Mosque came up to the corner where we had a meeting going on and absolutely tried to start some trouble." Malcolm continued: "The only thing that saved us and stopped trouble from starting was that one of [the] brothers went to the trunk of his car and got a shotgun out and chased away the Black Muslims." Malcolm says that if any violence takes place it will mean that innocent people will get killed. He continued that the Messenger and [identity redacted] are trying to "create a situation of bloodshed so that I (Malcolm X) will be caught up in it."

Unknown woman asks: "You mean the Messenger is that ruthless?"

Malcolm answers that "any man who will go to bed with his brother's daughter and then turn and make five other women pregnant and then accuse all these women of committing adultery is a ruthless man." Malcolm says that the only reason the Messenger wants him dead is that he, Malcolm, is the only one who can make the girls the Messenger has violated tell the truth about the Messenger. Malcolm tells unknown woman to tell all [two lines deleted] will be interested in knowing that the Messenger is now living in Phoenix, Arizona, with two teenage girls. . . .

Time: 4:02 P.M.
Date: Sunday, June 7, 1964
Special Agent: [identity deleted] R1874-37

Unknown woman to Malcolm X. Malcolm says the split in the Nation of Islam has brought about nothing by negative results. He says "every time I think of how those niggers threw me out of the Nation of Islam, I get mad." He continues that "it is dangerous to have the Muslims controlled by criminals of the ilk of [name redacted] and the like." He says there must be some way we can salvage the Black Muslim movement before it is too late. Unknown woman says she is sure Malcolm can save the Muslims from the clutches of the Messenger. He says he feels he can save the Muslims if he can lift the cloud of the Messenger's misdeeds from them by exposing the Messenger to the public. Malcolm says the FBI and the local police department do not want public exposure of the Messenger's sexual escapades as they (FBI and PD) would lose the whip they use to control the Black Muslims. Malcolm says that the Messenger's fear of exposure by law enforcement agencies keeps the Messenger from leading the Black Muslims to their full potential.

Unknown woman says that if Malcolm has faith in Allah, all will go well with his cause.

(c)

Time: 9:08 A.M.
Date: Monday, June 8, 1964
W-5392-24

Unknown man to unknown woman. Caller asks to speak to "Brother Malcolm." Woman answering asks who is calling. Man replies that he just wants to speak to Brother Malcolm. Then when woman again asks who is calling, the man says she can just give Malcolm the message: "Just tell him he's as good as dead." He then hangs up.

VII: Investigation of Malcolm X's Assassination

Author's Note: Within days of Malcolm X's assassination, the FBI's investigation focused on three mosques: Mosque No. 7 in Harlem, Mosque No. 11 in Boston, and Mosque No. 25 in Newark. The name of Minister Louis Farrakhan surfaced during the murder investigation as a leader with ties to all three mosques. Farrakhan was interrogated regarding the assassination, but the results were never made public. Moreover, the FBI's investigation indicated that Johnson and Butler probably were not involved, but at least two other individuals were; Linwood X and Edward Oliver, both of the Newark mosque, were identified by a number of witnesses to the murder.

Regarding the documents below, "NK" refers to Newark, while "NY" refers to New York. Similarly, "PH" in the second memo is an abbreviation for Phoenix, and "BS" refers to Boston. The excerpts are from a few key documents focusing on suspects who were never closely questioned by the FBI despite its suspicion of their complicity.

(a)

Date: April 9, 1965

To: Director, FBI
From, SAC, New York
Subject: Malcolm X Little

ReNKairtels, March 4, 1965 and March 8, 1965, and NYairtel, March 23, 1965 referring to a Linwood X.

The photo of [name deleted] enclosed with NK airtel March 4, 1965, was displayed to the [line redacted] with negative results.

(b)

Date: April 9, 1965

To: Director, FBI
From: SAC, Philadelphia

[Subject] Malcolm X Little

RePHairtel to Director, March 30, 1965, cc New York; NYairtel to Director, April 1, 1965, cc Philadelphia; Buairtel to New York and Philadelphia, April 2, 1965.

A photograph of Edward Oliver, furnished by the New York Office, was exhibited to [names redacted, along with other data] could identify Oliver. They stated that to their knowledge they had never seen him before.

In reNYairtel it is noted that [data redacted] resembled two individuals who sat in the middle of the audience at the Audubon Ballroom, New York City, on February 21, 1965 and jumped up at about the time Malcolm X appeared at the rostrum. One of these individuals shouted that someone "got into his pocket."

[Final paragraph redacted, along with next page]

(c)

Date: April 13, 1965

To: SAC, New York
From: Director, FBI
Subject: Malcolm X Little
  1—Mr. Horner
  1—Mr. Floyd
  1—Mr. Rosack

ReBSlet March 25, 1965 captioned [data blackened out], aka [data redacted], a copy of which is attached for the Newark Office which has not previously received copies.

New York should carefully review the information contained in referenced letter as furnished by the late [name redacted]. After this review, New York should determine whether [name redacted] had been interviewed by the [data deleted] during his visit there after the murder of Little. An attempt should be made to determine whether the information contained in referenced letter is already in the possession of the [organization's identification deleted], particularly the information alleging that the individual who fired the shotgun at Little was supposedly a lieutenant from the Newark Temple of the Nation of Islam (NOI). In the event this information is not already in the possession of the [organization's identification blackened out], such information should not be furnished to the NYCPD [New York City Police Department] without first receiving Bureau authority.

Newark should review its files for the purpose of identifying the lieutenant in the Newark Temple of the NOI. If Newark has not already done so, a photograph of this lieutenant should be furnished to the New York Office for the purpose of having [rest of line deleted]. This matter should be handled promptly.

Boston should in the future insure that copies of all communications are furnished to every interested office so that it will not be necessary for the FBI to furnish copies of such communications to additional interested offices.

2—Newark (enclosure)

1—Boston

VIII. FBI HQ File on Satohata Takahashi and the Society for the Development of Our Own

Author's Note: While it has long been rumored that Wallace D. Fard did not "disappear" in a puff of smoke as the NOI has suggested for more than half a century, the declassified documents on Satohata Takahashi, the Japanese expatriate who had a lasting influence on the NOI, were the first to corroborate charges first aired by Iman Hamaas Abdul Khaalis that Fard had never really left the United States after his arrest in September 1933. According to Khaalis, Fard maintained contact with Elijah Muhammad for decades after his alleged disappearance, and in fact was influential in shaping the movement behind the scenes. Malcolm X was unaware of his presence, but members of Muhammad's family were reportedly well aware of it, Khaalis maintains. The second letter written by Khaalis in early 1973 was the first significant document to link Fard with the SDOO, an organization which Fard allegedly took credit for organizing. Like the NOI, the SDOO had as many as 7,000 followers during Fard's affiliation. Note that the Articles of Incorporation for the SDOO were filed in Lansing, Michigan, less than two weeks after Fard's alleged disappearance (see memo, below).

The FBI never realized Fard's connection with the sect because he used yet another alias; according to Khaalis, Fard started using the alias of "John Walker" or "John M. Walker." There are, interestingly, references to "John Walker" in the Takahashi file. The pertinent portion of one memorandum appears below. Other prominent officers of the organization, notably, used the surname "Pharr," a name similar to the one Fard may have used while in San Francisco in the early 1920s.

(a)

U.S. Bureau of Investigation

From: D.M. Ladd, Special Agent in Charge
St. Louis, Mo.

To Director, U.S. Bureau of Investigation

File No. 62-709
Subject: Naka Nakane, aka Satahota Takahashi

    . . . One of the close friends of Mrs. Takahashi, when the organization, Development of Our Own was at its height in Nakane's absence, was Mrs. Dorothy Summers, 3624 Rivard Street. William A. Steen was also reported to be a particular friend of Mrs. Takahashi. It is also to be noted that Steen's name appears in the notebook found in Nakane's possession and it is noted further that he lives at 20185 Griggs Avenue, Detroit, Michigan.
    Others friends of Mrs. Takahashi, whose addresses Slatkin could not furnish were Evelyn Huddleston, Cora Mayo, Mary Moore and John M. Walker, who all testified in Mrs. Takahashi's case against Cash C. Bates et al. in October 1938 in her effort to regain control of the Development of Our Own. . . . [page 41]
    . . . The records of the Wayne County Circuit Court, Corporation Section, revealed that Michigan articles of incorporation (nonprofit) No. 32536 were filed on October 5, 1933, for the organization of the Development of Our Own with Frank D. Fitzgerald, Secretary of State, Lansing, Michigan. . . . There was also filed a certificate of amendment to the articles of incorporation No. 33529, under date of January 30, 1934, stating that the Development of Our Own, 2936 Monroe Street, Detroit, Michigan, at a meeting held November 23, 1933, had legally constituted the followings officers:

George C. Jones, President
2936 Monroe Street

William Pharr, Secretary
2149 Canfield Street

Isaiah TaBoard, Trustee Chairman
2685 Madison Street

Emanuel Pharr, Advisory Chairman
2149 Canfield Street   (page 49)

... Nakane stated that he resided with Kayama until proceeding to Detroit, Michigan, in 1930. He stated that during the war while England and Japan were allied, he helped the Japanese group in Vancouver, B.C., particularly among the young Japanese and he explained this by stating that the Japanese are considered citizens in Vancouver, especially if they serve in the British army. While living with Kayama in Tacoma, he alleges that he became aquainted with Reverend John White, a colored minister, who encouraged him to proceed to Detroit, Michigan, and work among the colored people.

On first coming to Detroit at the instance of Reverend White he communicated with Abdul Mohammed, and resided with Mohammed for approximately two weeks. It appears that Mohammed had written White and encouraged some Japanese in that territory to proceed to Detroit to work among the colored people. He [Nakane] stated that he left the residence of Mohammed because he considered him a fraud. Following this, he attended several colored churches and frequented the YMCA's in this city and at the instance of the colored people whom he met, was instrumental in organizing the Development of Our Own, which was incorporated in the State of Michigan. He alleges that this organization was started in 1930 although throughout the investigation no one could remember its existence before the latter part of 1932 or the early part of 1933.

(page 58)

(b)

Federal Bureau of Investigation

June 27, 1943

Memorandum for Mr. Tolson

I am attaching hereto memoranda which were furnished Elder Micheaux showing Japanese attempts to incite colored people in the past.

Attachment

(Page 3)

Mimo De Guzman

De Guzman, a Filipino, became affiliated with the Japanese movement to instigate racial grievances among the colored people through one Naka Nakane. Nakane was born in Tokyo and came to Tacoma, Washington, in 1922. He became a great organizer of colored groups favoring Japan and represented himself as Major Satakata Takahashi. Nakane obtained the assistance of De Guzman after a meeting of Negroes in Chicago in 1931. Thereafter Nakane introduced De Guzman as a Japanese under the name of Dr. Ashima Takis before Negro audiences throughout the country. De Guzman's duties were to organize colored people into groups that would follow Nakane's principles and accept speeches of a pro-Japanese tenor. The groups were to be part of a general movement known as the Pacific Movement of the Eastern World which has as its purpose the establishment of a government for Negroes in Africa. In reality, however, it was a propaganda organization designed to encourage racial prejudice.

De Guzman spoke at a number of meetings of the Universal Negro Improvement Association throughout the country and claimed to have been successful in securing a membership of 20,000 persons in Chicago among the Negroes after working there for two years. He had a disagreement with Nakane in the early 1930s and started out on his own to organize a similar movement in various cities throughout the United States.

In 1935, De Guzman and one Leonard Robert Jordan, a colored person, created the Ethiopian Pacific Movement Inc., in New York City. The movement, which held meetings at 113 Leonx Avenue, New York, for the colored people, fostered unrest and agitation as well as sympathy with Japan. De Guzman left the movement when Jordan at a meeting exposed him as a Filipino and not a Japanese.

De Guzman was indicted on June 20, 1942, for a violation of the postal laws arising out of a forged money order. He was sentenced subsequently to three years' imprisonment. Nakane was interned on April 2, 1942, as a dangerous enemy alien.

(c)

Federal Bureau of Investigation

Office of Origin: Detroit, Michigan
Report Made at: Indianapolis, Indiana
Date When Made: September 29, 1944
Period For Which Made: Sept. 13, 14, and 21, 1944
Report Made by: Edward E. Johnson

Title: Development of Our Own
Character of Case: Internal Security (J)

Synopsis of Facts: Ernest Bassett advised informant that although no meetings were held, members endeavor to contact each other each week. [Emmanuel] Pharr recently cautioned Bassett against meetings in Gary, Indiana. Bassett related that when proper time came the organization will have "ample things necessary to take charge."

Reference: Report of Special Agent Harry B. Behrmann, dated August 10, 1944, at Indianapolis, Indiana.

Details: At Gary, Indiana

The following investigation was conducted by Special Agent Hugh P. Steger:

The following information was received from [name deleted] on September 2, 1944:

Informant contacted Ernest Bassett who resides in the basement of 2129 Adams Street on August 23, 1944. He learned that he is working in the Wheel Mill, Gary Works, Carnegie Illinois Steel Corporation. Bassett told him that the organization, Development of Our Own, is not dead and that the members try to see each other individually once a week in order to keep the group alive. He pointed out, however, that there were no meetings being held at the present time as a result of the police pick-up of the members several years ago. He told the informant about having been picked up by the Gary Police Department at the time when all members of the organization were picked up in Gary and questioned [about registering for the draft].

Bassett insisted that he did not tell them anything about the organization in spite of the fact that the police drew a gun on him. He said he had not been bothered since. He told the informant that any new instructions or information concerning the organization were passed along from one member to another and that he would be kept posted. He also made the statement that they are not at the present time taking any new members into the organization because they are afraid.

Bassett stated he was in Detroit two or three weeks previously over the weekend to see Pharr, the leader. He said that Pharr again cautioned him not to have any meetings in Gary. Bassett commented that although the United States thinks it is winning the war, they will actually lose it. He said that when the proper time comes, the members of the organization will have "ample things necessary to take charge." Bassett claimed that members of the organization know the identify of the person who originally turned them in to the police and that they have dropped him completely and have had no further dealings with him.

On August 25, 1944, the informant saw Kallatt, who is also a member of the Development of Our Own, and works in the Wheel Mill of the Carnegie Illinois Steel Corporation, Gary, Indiana. Kallatt said that he has had no connection with the organization recently, but it was the informant's opinion that he is still connected with the group, although he is not as radical or active as Bassett.

The result of the mail cover placed against the residences of General Pope and Rebecca Brooks on July 17, 1944, are as follows. . . .

Author's Note: One of the aliases the FBI had the Messenger listed under was Eli Mohammed. Interestingly, the Bureau uncovered the alias incidental to surveillance of Takahashi's movement, and just a few months before the Messenger was arrested in Washington in May 1942. Also worth noting is that the report was made by Percy E. Foxworth, a powerful assistant director of the FBI in its formative years. As those who have studied the origins of Islam among African Americans will recognize, the FBI agents who made this report amalgamated information from four different sects: the NOI, the MSTA, the SDOO, and the OMA. The OMA was an offshoot of the SDOO.

(d)

Federal Bureau of Investigation

From: New York Field Division
To: Director
Date: June 2, 1942

Re: Development of Our Own, aka
     Onward Movement of America

Dear Sir:

Reference is made to Bureau letter dated March 12, 1942, to the Detroit Field Division concerning the above captioned matter of which this office received a copy. It is noted in the information furnished in the enclosure that it is reported that the above Movement numbers some five thousand members in New York City; further that Morra or Morrow (phonetic) is reported to be a well educated Japanese from Harlem, New York and to be a "Big Boy" of this organization.

To date, inquiries through sources in colored districts in and around New York have failed to disclose any organization under the above name or any information concerning Morra or Morrow.

In this connection, however, information has been received in this office from [identity redacted], New York City, which is as follows, the source of which is unknown:

A sect was organized some three years or four years ago by a Japanese whose name was not known and which sect consists of colored people with the exception of one individual; that this Japanese sneaked into the United States about a year ago after being deported three years ago and it was he who established this religious fanatic cult no doubt, and during his association with this outfit spent money leisurely. When this cult was formed, it was directed toward the extermination of the White Race and this motto still stands, as during the meetings and services a large sign is always displayed bearing the inscription "The Paleface has got to go." The meetings of this organization are being held regularly on Saturdays and Sundays of each week at 9316 Oakland Avenue, Detroit, Michigan, which is apparently their headquarters and place generally designated as the Moorish Science Temple of AM. When this organization was originally formed, it was designated as the Development of Our AM.

AM apparently has some reference to a mythological character. The attendance at their meetings runs between 300 and 350, and consists of ordinary negroes engaged in either skilled or semi-skilled occupations. One peculiar feature is that the majority of this outfit are employed in plants engaged in the production of airplanes. The leaders of this Movement are as follows:

W.R. Bey; Eli Lee Mohamet; El Walter Davis; Joseph Sanford of 1167 Wellington; Will Wright, 604 East Philadelphia.

Within the past six months an Italian joined this outfit who bears the name of Joseph Cooper, who is also an airplane worker and is employed by Ford Motor Company.

If the Detroit Office has any further information as to the activities of the above cult and their leaders, in or around New York City, it is requested that such be furnished this office.

Very truly yours,
P.E. Foxworth,
Assistant Director

IX. FBI HQ File on Clara Muhammad
(Including electronic surveillance [ELSUR] data)

Author's Note: The FBI used any number of counterintelligence measures to disrupt the activities of the black organizations, particularly during the 1960s and 1970s. One of the most effective devices it employed involved writing phony letters to black leaders. The letters, nearly all of which had bogus signatures, served various purposes—from something as benign as getting two black organizations into a time-consuming misunderstanding, to matters as grave as destroying marriages or organizational partnerships, to actually fomenting murderous rifts between competing groups. In the memorandum below, for instance, the FBI focused on ending the Messenger's marriage after discovering that his wife was contemplating divorcing him on grounds of adultery.

(a)

Date: July 31, 1962

To: SAC, Chicago (100-35635)
From: Director, FBI (25-3309710)

Subject: Nation of Islam
        Internal Security—NOI

Re Chicago airtel [of] July 25, 1962

Chicago is authorized to prepare and mail an anonymous letter to Clara Muhammad upon her return from Egypt. Chicago is also authorized to prepare and mail similar anonymous letters containing substantially the same information as the letter mailed to Clara Muhammad to selected individuals on page 3 of reAiretel. These letters should be mailed to the addresses of these individuals at which they would normally receive mail. The letters, which are to be hand-written on commercially purchased stationery without markings, should follow the sample letter proposed in reAirtel. Each letter, however, should contain minor variations so that each will not appear to be an exact copy of the original. These letters should be mailed at staggered intervals using care to prevent any possibility of tracing the mailing back to the FBI.

Chicago should remain alert to any results obtained from this action and keep the Bureau promptly advised.

1—Chicago (100-6989) (Elijah Muhammad)
1—Phoenix (105-93)
Note on Yellow: See memorandum Baumgardner to Sullivan dated July 20, 1962, same caption. RJR: cad.

X: The Plot to Kill Malcolm X

Author's Note: By cross-referencing documents obtained by the FBI on individuals and organizations, it's possible to ascertain what name, organization, or information has been redacted from some memoranda. In the July 7, 1964, memo below, for example, the name of Texas billionaire H.L. Hunt was black-

ened out. However, his name was not redacted from a similar memo in the recently released New York field office file (105-8999) on Malcolm X. When such details are obvious, I have included them as though they were not redacted. The most disturbing part of this document, obviously, is that as early as July 1964, the FBI knew about the plot to kill Malcolm X but fomented the war between him and Elijah Muhammad rather than intervening.

(a)

Date: July 7, 1964

To: Director, FBI (100-399321)
From: SAC, New York (105-8999)

Subject: Malcolm X. Little aka IS-MMI

On July 5, 1964 [source deleted] furnished the following information. If utilized in report form it should be paraphrased and classified "Confidential" to protect this source. The information is not being set forth in LHM at this time to protect the source since there is no corroborating information available.

    3—Bureau (RM)
    6—Chicago (RM)
       (1-100-35635) (Nation of Islam)
       (1-100-6989) (Elijah Muhammad)
       (1-100-32519) (Clara Muhammad)
[line redacted]

NY 105-8999

On July 5, 1964, subject was in contact with "Brother [name deleted]" in Chicago. [Name deleted] told him that orders to kill him (Malcolm) came from Chicago and he can furnish witnesses if Malcolm wants to take them to court. [Blank] also told Malcolm he should tell the FBI all about the threats against him.

They talked of recent stories revealing the illegitimate children of Elijah Muhammad and [blank] stated that [name of journalist deleted] of Chicago was writing articles exposing everything.

They then had a discussion regarding Elijah and Clara Muhammad sending money to foreign countries in order to save it. Switzerland and Beirut were mentioned.

On July 5, 1964, subject contacted [name deleted] of Chicago, Illinois. Malcolm informed [name deleted] that [blank] had filed suits against Elijah for illegitimacy and nonsupport, and he urged her to talk to one of the other mothers (not named) into filing suit against him. He also told her that Elijah had been putting money in Switzerland lately, and Clara had been putting hers in Beirut and Cairo. Malcolm also told her "that that fellow in Texas [named H.L. Hunt] has been giving Elijah money for several years."

The above is being furnished for information.

XI: The Issue of Malcolm X's Home

Author's Note: Months before Malcolm X's suspension, the FBI intercepted several phone calls in which the subject of Malcolm X and housing arose. It was patently clear that Elijah Muhammad had given his most valued servant the home on Elmhurst in New York to have and own, and not as a tenant (as Muslim lawyers would argue a year later).

May 29, 1963

To: SAC, Chicago (100-35635)
From: SAC, Phoenix (105-93)

Subject: Nation of Islam
          IS—NOI

[Source deleted], reliable, made available the following information on the dates designated . . .

May 22, 1963

[Blank] was in contact with Clara Muhammad at which time Clara stated Elijah was eating well and was about the same. Clara said that when she left Chicago [name deleted] was ill and had great pain in her legs. They wanted her to go see a doctor. Mention was made that Malcolm had not moved his family to Washington, D.C. Clara stated Elijah told Malcolm not to move them. She said that *Malcolm owns his own place in New York City* and it is a very beautiful home. (Emphasis provided)

XII: New York City Police Department
Bureau of Special Services (BOSSI)

Author's Note: In the early 1950s, the New York City Police Department opened an investigation into the NOI. The FBI aided the city by training a select group of policemen in intelligence gathering and counterintelligence techniques. The men assigned to this division, which was known as the Bureau of Special Services (BOSS or BOSSI), were trained in such small groups that often two men in the same precinct would not be aware of each other's association with BOSSI. The NOI was one of several large black nationalist groups targeted by BOSSI. The degree of success it had is perhaps indicated by the presence of Gene Roberts, a BOSSI agent, guarding Malcolm X when he was assassinated in the Audubon Ballroom on February 21, 1965. In addition to his duty as a security guard for Malcolm X, Roberts also served as the Recording Secretary for the Organization of Afro-American Unity.

The BOSSI surveillance was mainly confined to Malcolm X's activities in New York, but because of the NOI's ties to diplomats at the United Nations, the police department often found itself in the center of international intrigue, as the following documents from BOSSI's file on Malcolm X illustrate. They also prove that the FBI did have, as it would later boast, people it considered as top-level informants in the Messenger's inner circle. One of them was a Pakistani named Abdel B. Naeem, whom the Messenger depended upon for advice on foreign policy matters.

(a)

Date: May 6, 1959
From: Detective Anton Weidinger, Shield #2189
To: Commanding Officer B.S.S. [Bureau of Special Services]

Subject: Search of Files of B'nai B'rith,
        Re: Temples of Islam

1. Detectives 3rd Grade Anton Weidinger and Ernest Latty, [badge] #1373, assigned to this matter submit the following report.

2. Interviewed Mr. Milton Ellerin, Director of the National Fact Finding Board of the B'nai B'rith Anti-Defamation League, 515 Madison Avenue, New York City, who made the files of his organization on "The Temples of Islam" available to us. The data contained therein is of an historical and organizational nature, a synopsis of which appears below; the files contain nothing, however, of the events being investigated by the Civilian Complaint Review Board.

3. Origin of the Temples of Islam:

The founder of the Temples of Islam in 1930 was a Jamaican negro who called himself Ford (the Great) Mohammed. He claimed to be Allah the Almighty and to have come direct from Mecca. Little Ford, later Elijah, became one of his followers. In the middle 30s Ford disappeared, and Little Ford thereupon assumed leadership of the cult, calling himself Elijah Mohammed. Gradually he gave himself an aura of divinity. Aliases used by the subject are as follows: Elijah Poole, Elijah Muck Muck, Gulam Bogans, Little Ford.

There are 41 Temples of Islam categorized in their order of importance as follows:

Principal Temples: New York City, Chicago, Detroit.

Second String Temples: Washington, D.C., Philadelphia, Baltimore.

Third String Temples: Hartford, Boston, Lansing, Newark, San Diego, Cincinnati, Columbus. Other temples are located in Hawaii, Alaska, Jamaica, British West Indies, and three are located in U.S. jails. Membership is between 60,000 and 70,000 and an equal number of sympathizers raises the total to some 140,000. The first in authority among Elijah's clergy is Malcolm X, formerly Malcolm Little. Lucius Bey heads the Washington, D.C. temple. Lewis [Louis] X heads the Boston and New England temples. The University of Islam in Chicago adjoining the temple thereat has about 800 pupils.

The Chicago temple conducts eight business operations as follows: Temple #2 Bakery, Auto Repair and Paint Shop, Laundry and Dry Cleaning, Cleaning Plant, Grocery Store, Restaurant, Dress Shop, Fashion and Haberdashery.

4. There are negro nationalists who without being Temple members serve as connecting links between the Temples and Arab propagandists. Jim Lawson (known to this command), a rabble rouser of the Harlem riot days of the 30s.

Has been identified with a long string of nationalist causes. He is president of the United African Nationalist Movement.

Borai, the third secretary in the United Arab Republic Mission to the United Nations, is the most active and effective of Arab agents to the negroes. Basheer of the Mission also active and effective of Arab agents to the negroes. Basheer of the Mission also active among negroes. Both are listed in BOSS records as members.

5. Elijah Mohammed writes articles for the following newspapers: *Herald-Dispatch* of Los Angeles, the *Pittsburgh Courier,* and the [New York] *Amsterdam News.*

(b)

Date: July 23, 1959
Subject: Malcolm X as Nasser's Guest

About two months ago an invitation to visit Egypt came from the U.A.R. government to Elijah Muhammad. At first he wanted to go himself, but after discussing it with his associates, he selected Malcolm X to go in his place. Elijah chose him because Malcolm X goes all out in lauding Elijah and attributing divine power to him. Malcolm X would be the emissary who would pave the way for a subsequent visit by Elijah himself a few months from now (possibly in November.)

Travel arrangements for Malcolm X were made with Hilton Hill Inc., a Negro travel agency at #55 W 42nd Street. Mr. Hill told the writer that he arranged the plane trip but did not arrange for hotel accommodations in Cairo. [Abdel B.] Naeem, who went out to Chicago at Elijah's request and expense to discuss the trip with him tells the writer that Malcolm was invited to Egypt to be the guest of the government of Egypt. It is not known who paid the plane fare. Naeem showed the writer a letter received from Malcolm X that he received July 21, mailed from Saudi Arabia. In substance the letter said: "I spent nine days in Cairo and met very important people." (The names are not specified but Naeem said included positively from advance arrangements meeting Deputy Premier Anwar el-Sadat and probably Nasser.) "I was laid up two days with dysentery and now I am well again and have come on to Saudi Arabia. From here I will go to Khartoum then to Kano and then to Ghana and home. Owing to delay, I am cutting out a couple of places."

Malcolm X was dubious about the kind of reception he would receive from authentic Muslims, knowing that much of Elijah's ritual would be regarded as blasphemy by the devout. Malcolm X was assured by Borai, an Egyptian diplomat and others that he would receive a cordial reception from the U.A.R. government people.

These pseudo-Moslem sects are regarded askance by the Moslems. The devout are shocked by their illiteracy and cheap pageantry and the disregard for the dogma of the Koran. Nasser, however, has confirmed the importance he attaches to American Nationalist Negroes to serve as a minority pressure group. The Egyptian diplomatic people have been instructed to show courtesies to Negro Nationalists. Borai, who previously established close contacts with Elijah and with Malcolm X, has come back to New York City and is extending these contacts. Nasser's diplomatic people, who normally would not associate with Temple type low-class Negroes, now go out of their way to flatter them. They also are more politician than Moslem and close their eyes to the ridiculous dogma deviations in the Temple's sect.

Dawud, leader of a rival pseudo-Moslem sect in Philadelphia, has also just made a similar Cairo/Mecca pilgrimage, receiving much attention in Egypt.

Hill, a negro from Bermuda who ordinarily specializes in business to the Caribbean, has hired Naeem as an assistant to develop this Negro Nationalist type of business to the Middle East.

(c)

August 5, 1959

This is Abdel B. Naeem's account of Malcolm X's visit to Egypt. Naeem made all of the travel arrangements and has had several long talks with Malcolm X since his return. Early this year, Elijah Muhammad received an invitation from Borai and one or two other Egyptians to be the guest of the Egyptian government in Cairo. Elijah was first inclined to go but his disciples advised him to send one of them in his place and look over the ground, and if he liked it, prepare the way for Elijah's visit. Malcolm X was chosen. Elijah paid for Naeem's trip to Chicago to work out the travel details. Hilton G. Hill travel bureau, with which Naeem is associated, worked out the trip. Malcolm X paid for the trip, omitting to ask for hotel reservations in Cairo, where he was entertained. Naeem thinks the Temple paid the plane fare. Malcolm X took out his passport under the name of Malik el Shabazz. Borai, Naeem, and a delegation from the Temple saw him off at the airport. He was met by government people upon his arrival in Cairo. He was first to stay a couple of nights with a professor from the University of Cairo. Several prominent people put him up in turn. An architect offered to prepare plans gratis for any temple Elijah may choose to build in this country. Many Egyptians didn't identify him as negroid because of his color until they saw him closer. Malcolm X had a message of greeting as "a fellow African coming back to his real home and a Moslem, eager to pray at the seat of the one true religion."

The Egyptian government people had Malcolm X constantly in hand. He was given considerable time by Anwar el Sadat, who also plays on his color, and he met all of the top people in the Moslem congress. He was cordially received by the Ulemas of Al Azhar. They took the Temple [Nation of Islam] on its face value as a Moslem sect and had no idea that even the name Shabazz is part of Elijah's blasphemy.

Malcolm X said that he was given an opportunity to meet Nasser, but declined because he made it clear that he was just the forerunner and humble servant of Elijah Muhammad. From early morning until late at night, Malcolm was taken from one party to another. Tables were laden with food. As a result he developed acute indigestion, the usual dysentery coupled with excessive eating. He remained in Cairo about three days longer than he planned. Malcolm X was in bad shape when he went to Jidda en route to Mecca. He was given a friendly welcome by the Moslem travel director, a jet-black African who insisted this was the color of the authentic original Arab. Felled with dysentery in the 120-degree heat, Malcolm X had but one desire: to go home. He also had the responsibility of setting up a spectacular welcome for Elijah in New York. Lucius, his principal rival, had arranged a tremendous ovation for Elijah in Washington.

Naeem has been a consultant on Moslem ritual and etiquette to Elijah and his associates for several years now. Malcolm X, who claims that Arabic was their original language and has been conducting Temple ritual in a gibberish reportedly Arabic, confessed to Naeem that he was extremely embarrassed going through the prayers five times a day in Egypt. He did not know the Arabic and had only a sketchy notion of the ritual. He was observant and thinks he got by mumbling. On this point he advised Elijah that he should do some homework in Arabic before he goes to Egypt. Malcolm X also intends to do some studying with the idea of returning to Egypt in about six months. In Egypt, Malcolm X did a combined job of building up the importance of the Temple's movement and picturing his fellow blacks as oppressed by the arrogant American whites. The Egyptians loved it. He also took along pictures of their gatherings. Malcolm X is so delighted with his trip that he persuaded Elijah to go and is now promoting visits to Egypt among the Temples' congregations. Up until recently, Elijah discouraged his followers from reading the Koran and, above all, against visiting the Middle East.

[signed]
Detective Ernest B. Latty, Shield #1373

XIII: COINTELPRO and the Succession Issue

Author's Note: As the Bureau made plans in 1968 to discredit the NOI, it also pursued ways to control the group upon the Messenger's death. By early 1962, it had what it referred to as "high-level informants" among the ministers of the NOI; according to sources, two informants were actually part of the Messenger's inner circle. To control the NOI, in the same way that FBI agents controlled some branches or "klaverns" of the KKK, the Bureau made plans to remove any likely successors to the Messenger and supplant them with high-level informants. The plan to remove Herbert Muhammad, one of the Messenger's sons, is discussed in the following memoranda from the Black Nationalist—Hate Group file, under which a unique COINTELPRO was run against the NOI.

To: W.C. Sullivan
From: G. C. Moore

Subject: Herbert C. Mohammed
Racial Matters—Nation of Islam
Date: May 7, 1968

This is to request income tax forms for the past three years concerning Herbert C. Mohammed, Public Relations Director of the black nationalist extremist Nation of Islam (NOI).

Background:

Herbert C. Mohammed is the son of the national leader of the NOI, Elijah Muhammad. It is noted that father and son spell their last names differently. The NOI preaches hatred of the white race and advocates a separate nation for American Negroes. Herbert Mohammed is the logical successor to his father as leader of this extremist group.

Herbert Mohammed is involved in several businesses and is the manager of former heavyweight boxing champion Cassius Clay. Herbert Mohammed has been described as money crazy and one who will do anything for money. A review of his income tax returns might indicate he is vulnerable in this area.

If Herbert Mohammed could be removed as successor to the leadership of the NOI, it would place our top-level informants in a better position to neutralize this extremist cult. The Chicago Division, where the NOI is headquartered, recommended we develop long-range counterintelligence measures to neutralize Herbert Mohammed. A first step would be to review his tax returns.

Recommendations:

Attached are original and one copy of a blind memorandum for the Liaison Section to use in requesting Internal Revenue Service to furnish us copies of Herbert Mohammed's Federal income tax returns.

To: Director, FBI (100-448006)
From: SAC, Chicago (157-2209) (P)

Subject: Counterintelligence Program
Black Nationalist—Hate Groups
RM

Date: November 27, 1968

Re Chicago letter [of] 11/22/68 and Bureau airtel to Albany and all offices except Anchorage, Honolulu, and San Juan dated 05/16/68 captioned "Antiviolence Statements by Prominent Negroes, RM."

Attached to each copy of this letter are Xerox copies of the following:

(1) An article entitled, "Won't Clean Up Ghetto; Judge Parsons Rips Tax Aid for Gangs," which appeared on page 6 of the *Chicago American,* 3 Star Final, November 21, 1968.

(2) An article entitled, "Praises New Sprit of Negro Kids; Judge Looks at Ghetto and Is Awed," *Chicago American*, 3 Star Final, November 26, 1968, page 4.

The above set forth emphatic denunciations of black nationalists, youth gangs, and other militants by James Benton Parsons, Judge, Northern District of Illinois, along with concrete suggestions for combating evils connected therewith.

As the Bureau is aware, approval was given for [several words redacted] a high level counterintelligence program against the NOI by Bureau letter [dated] November 11, 1962, entitled "Nation of Islam, IS-NOI." This program was initiated by Chicago and resulted in a nationwide counterintelligence program which showed fallacies and weaknesses of the NOI to the public. It was conducted on an extremely high level and avoided name-calling, mud slinging, etc. This program continues [lines redacted]. . . .

Based on the above two articles, it appears [data redacted] have paid off and Judge Parsons is implementing his plans, which were direct results [data redacted to end of paragraph] . . . It is suggested the Bureau in this program may well desire to canvass various field offices in an effort to determine if they have some responsible Negro leaders, who could participate in a high level program designed to expose the disadvantages extremist black nationalist groups can have on their community and especially their children.

2—Bureau (RM)

2—Chicago

(1-100-35635, Sub. 2) [Nation of Islam—RM]

ACKNOWLEDGMENTS

This book, like most endeavors, is the product of the efforts of names too numerous to mention, faces too familiar to forget, and favors too great for one person to repay in a lifetime. Alas, my humble effort: I offer my sincere thanks to the readers of my earlier book about Malcolm, many of whom took the time to write or call me, and to offer information that they felt would be useful here. Among those whose assistance proved invaluable are documentary film producers Omar Shabazz and Jack Baxter of New York, both of whom provided me with rare interviews and outtakes from films they've produced or are in the process of producing.

The Honorable Rachel T. Lord of Washington County Probate Court was of enormous assistance, as were Toni Yasin and the staff of the FBI's Freedom of Information Division, Howard University student Danielle Anderson, and Washington paralegal Karen Stephenson. Professor Roger Axford, who knew Elijah Muhammad while in prison, offered a unique perspective, as did John Muhammad and other members of the family. Interviews with Wilfred Little, Malcolm X's brother, and his sister Ella Collins were of immeasurable value. Several Muslims close to Minister Farrakhan also provided information, and periodically relayed questions to the minister for me (Farrakhan declined all requests for interviews), and gave me replies that were represented as being from Farrakhan or based on their close association with him. A rare instance of timing and luck led me to Fard's prison record in the California State Archives; as it happens, Fard's record was one of the few saved from the early part of the century.

Owing to the nature of archiving in America, it is difficult to find repositories about controversial Americans, particularly controversial members of minority groups. Much of the information that appears in the book would not have been available without the assistance of dedicated news researchers at some of the nation's finest newspapers. Kudos to news research staffs at the following publications for their help: the *Chicago Tribune,* the *Chicago Defender,* the *New Chicago Crusader,* the *Detroit Free Press/News,* the *Washington Post* (especially Bobbye Pratt, Nancy Shiner, Madonna Lebling, Mary Lou White, and Jennifer Belton), the *Gary Post-Tribune,* the *Louisville Courier-Journal,* and *Muslim Journal* (formerly *Muhammad Speaks*).

A number of librarians took time to research matters that I could have done myself only at considerable expense. They include the staffs of various public libraries in Maryland and the District of Columbia, the Gary Public Library, the Cordele Public Library, the Sandersville Public Library, the Detroit Public Library, the Gwinnett County (Ga.) Public Library, the San Francisco Public Library, the Moorland-Spingarn Research Center at Howard University, and the incomparable staff at the Library of Congress. I am also grateful to Ms. Chawdri of the Embassy of Pakistan, Ahmed Nabal of the MIT/Harvard University Aga Khan Visual Archives, and Fareed H. Nu'man of the American Muslim Council.

Last but most importantly, my deep gratitude goes to my literary agent, Nina Graybill of Graybill and English LLC, to Altie Karper and the staff at Pantheon, and especially to my editor, Erroll McDonald.

PREFACE

1. The statement is from the preface to a review of David J. Armor, *Forced Justice: School Desegregation and the Law.* See Book Notes, *Harvard Law Review* 109, no. 5 (March 1996): 1144–49.

2. See, in general, Andres Tapia, "Soul Searching: How Is the Black Church Responding to the Urban Crisis?" *Christianity Today,* March 4, 1996, 26–30.

3. Mary H. Cooper, "Muslims in America," *The Congressional Quarterly Researcher,* April 30, 1993, 363–83.

4. J. Edgar Hoover's campaign to destroy Marcus Garvey, a West Indian who came to America in 1916, and who created one of the largest black nationalist organizations in the world within five years (the Universal Negro Improvement Association), is well-documented. At the end of Hoover's successful counterintelligence campaign, Garvey was convicted of mail-fraud charges and was deported "to avoid a possible exposé of what even Attorney General John Sargent considered prosecutorial misconduct." See O'Reilly, *Black Americans;* also see "Black Moses, Red Scare: The Clash of Marcus Garvey and J. Edgar Hoover," *Washington Post,* February 12, 1997, H01.

5. The celebration is formally called the Annual Saviour's Day Convention. Members of the Nation of Islam believe that God, or Allah, came to America "in human form" in 1930. The "living God" used several names, but is primarily called Master Wallace Fard Muhammad or Master Wallace Fard. See Muhammad, *Message to the Blackman in America;* also see Lincoln, *Black Muslims in America;* Essien-Udom, *Black Nationalism.*

6. The Nation of Islam's estimate of one million marchers conflicted with an estimate by the United States Park Police, which used aerial photographs to con-

clude that less than half a million people visited the Mall during the day-long event. Several weeks after the march, Farouk El-Baz, head of Boston University's Center for Remote Sensing, used a technique similar to that employed by the U.S. Park Police, but determined that between 670,00 and 1,004,000 people attended. See "Boston U. Sets March at 837,000; Estimates Hinge on Crowd Density," *Washington Post,* October 28, 1995, C03.

7. "Minister Louis Farrakhan Calls for One Million Man March." The article, which appeared before the Nation of Islam, had its own site on the World Wide Web, and so was picked up by another provider (http://www/afrinet . . . Fspeaks/marchcall.html).

8. The leading survey on the growth of Islam was conducted by the American Muslim Council in 1992. See *The Muslim Population in the United States* (pamphlet), American Muslim Council, 1992.

9. See "A Tribute to Malcolm X," Black Beat Superstar Special No. 8, Lexington Library, 1992. The hit recording by Public Enemy was titled "Party for Your Right to Fight," Def American Records, 1988.

10. His family, for the most part, were not convinced. See Barboza, *American Jihad,* 271; see also Muhammad, *Theology of Time,* book 1, 31.

11. Documentation establishing Islam as the religion of many Africans sold into slavery is voluminous. One of the most recent and fascinating accounts of slave rebellions, in fact, concerns how African Muslims taken to Brazil used pages in the Holy Quran to record details of an insurrection. See João José Reis, *Slave Rebellion in Brazil: The Muslim Uprising of 1835 in Bahia* (Baltimore: Johns Hopkins University Press, 1993). Also see Malcolm Cowley, *Adventures of an African Slaver* (New York: Albert & Charles Boni, 1928). Owing to the horrors of slavery, some slaves had trouble reconciling the slavemasters' behavior with the latter's professed religion. Thus, they rejected Christianity and talked about "that ol'–time religion." See, for example, the lyrics to the spiritual titled "Gimme Dat Ol'-Time Religion." Johnson and Johnson, *Books of American Negro Spirituals.* Wallace Muhammad currently spells his last name differently: Mohammed. For the sake of clarity, it is spelled herein consistently as Muhammad.

12. Muhammad, *How to Eat to Live*; book 1; Muhammad, *How to Eat to Live,* book 2.

13. See Forster and Epstein, *The New Anti-Semitism,* 175–220; Perlmutter, *The Real Anti-Semitism in America,* 182–203. The Nation of Islam offered a drug-abuse treatment program which was so effective that government offi-

cials sought the sect's help in the early 1960s in its fight to treat black drug addicts.

14. Correspondences between the student and FBI Director Kelley are included in the FBI's declassified main file on Wallace D. Fard.

15. The "headquarters" file on Wallace D. Fard has 372 pages; the Detroit field office file, 99 pages; and the Chicago field office file, 345 pages. Pages are duplicated for a charge of $0.10 a page, and the first 100 pages are duplicated free of charge. Thus, the total cost of the file (of 816 pages) is $71.60.

PROLOGUE: UNDERCOVER

1. *Minersville School District v. Gobitis*, 319 U.S. 624 (1940).

2. Marcus Tullius Cicero, *Pro Milone*, in Tryon Edwards et al, eds. *The New Dictionary of Thoughts* (New York: Standard Book Co. 1965). The Roman orator's statement "Silent enim leges inter arma" has also been translated as "The law is silent during war" or "Laws are dumb amidst the clash of arms." See Seldes, *The Great Quotations*, 158.

3. This account is based upon a very detailed FBI report of the arrest, interviews with members of Elijah Muhammad's family, a four-page confession Muhammad made at the time of his arrest, reports by other writers and scholars, and lectures by ministers of the Nation of Islam. This was the only portion of the book submitted to Elijah Muhammad's family for corroborative purposes. No one in the family disputed it. While members of the NOI have long argued that Elijah Muhammad was not hiding under the bed, no persuasive proof has been submitted to contradict the official record. Indeed, when Muhammad was interviewed in 1960, he did not dispute that he "was found in his mother's home rolled in a carpet under the bed." Wallace H. Terry, "Cult of Hate: Black Muslim Elijah's Lowly Start" (Part 2 of 6), *Washington Post*, December 12, 1960, A03; also see *Chicago Tribune*, September 22, 1942, A09.

4. The manhunt for Muhammad and his followers was so elaborate and time-consuming that the FBI compiled more than 80,000 pages of documents detailing it. Many of the documents indicate that Hoover was very angry about the Bureau's failure to apprehend Muhammad quickly.

5. A complete list of aliases used by Elijah Muhammad appears in Appendix A of this book. The Nation of Islam was originally called the "Lost-Found Nation of Islam in the Wilderness of North America." See Muhammad, *Message to the Blackman in America*; also see Lincoln, *Black Muslims in America*.

6. See "Moslem Leader Arrested," *Washington Star,* May 9, 1942, A07.

7. The Nation of Islam was first on a list of thirty-five organizations U.S. Assistant Attorney General Wendell Berge targeted for prosecution in the fall of 1942. The Justice Department was especially concerned about reports that Japanese radicals had been supplying arms to black nationalists. See, for example, Memorandum for the Director, Federal Bureau of Investigation. The document appears in the FBI HQ file on Elijah Muhammad, section 3, 1–3. Also see, in general, Hill, *The FBI's RACON.*

8. FBI Headquarters HQ file on Elijah Muhammad, memo dated September 22, 1942, 1–7.

9. Ibid. Also see Parole Progress Report on Gulam Bogans, aka Elijah Muhammad, Federal Correctional Institution at Milan, Michigan, dated April 23, 1945; Admission Summary, dated August 20, 1943; and Physical Examination and Correlated History, dated July 26, 1943. The reports are part of the FBI's HQ file on Elijah Muhammad; Associated Press interview and feature story titled "People in the News: Elijah Muhammad," Chicago, February 25, 1965.

1. BROTHER'S KEEPER

1. Joseph Conrad, *The Nigger of the Narcissus* (1897; reprint, Garden City, N.Y.: Doubleday, 1914), 32.

2. H. G. Wells, *The Invisible Man* (New York: Scholastic Book Services, 1963), 142.

3. Mellon, *Bullwhip Days: The Slaves Remember,* 441.

4. Interviews with Cordele Library staff members; interviews with the Honorable Rachel T. Lord, Washington County Probate Court; also see Clegg, *An Original Man,* 3–4.

5. "Middleton Pool," *Division of Estates,* book A: 1829–1871, Washington County Probate Court, 196–97; "Middleton Pool," *Wills,* book B: 1852–1903, Washington County Probate Court, 160. These documents are hereinafter jointly referred to as "Last Will and Testament of Middleton Pool."

6. John Pitman served as one of three witnesses to Pool's signing of his last will and testament. "Last Will and Testament of Middleton Pool," 3. Members of Elijah Muhammad's family of Pitman lineage still reside in Cordele, Sandersville, and Oconee, Georgia, according to Erskine Weaver, a friend of the family who is principal of Southwestern Elementary School in Cordele.

7. Ibid. Middleton Pool Jr. and his first wife lived in the village of Bold Springs for a few years before moving to Dekalb County. While some scholars have reported that Bold Springs was once part of Washington County and that Elijah was born there, they are in error. According to the sourcebook *Georgia Place Names,* Bold Springs has been in Walton County since it was established near the turn of the century. The name was changed to Williamsville in 1908, but reverted to Bold Springs a year later. The village of Bold Springs is approximately eighty miles northwest of Sandersville, and roughly at the thirty-five-mile mark between Atlanta and Athens. If Elija Pool had been born in Bold Springs, as several scholars have contended, it seems likely that he would have indicated his birthplace as being near Atlanta, not Sandersville. In fact, he told Malcolm X that he was born "in Sandersville." Haley, *Autobiography of Malcolm X,* 204.

8. "Last Will and Testament of Middleton Pool."

9. Ibid., 2.

10. Of name-changing, one scholar wrote: "A new name was both a symbol of personal liberation and an act of political defiance; it reversed the enslavement process and confirmed the free Negro's newly won liberty just as the loss of an African name had earlier symbolized enslavement." Berlin, *Slaves Without Masters,* 51–52.

11. "Last Will and Testament of Middleton Pool," 196–97.

12. The Black Codes were laws whose sole purpose was to negate the Emancipation Proclamation and other subsequent legislation aimed at ending slavery. It forced blacks under the age of eighteen to remain on their former master's plantation as wards if they were orphans or if their parents couldn't care for them properly. See Ploski and Kaiser, "The Black Codes of Mississippi," *The Negro Almanac,* 137–40; also see Bergman and Bergman, *Chronological History of the Negro,* 245–46.

13. Ferris, *The Presidents,* 156–63; also see Earl Schenck Miers, ed., *Lincoln Day by Day: A Chronology,* vol. 3, *1861–1865* (Washington: Lincoln Sesquicentennial Commission, 1960), 25.

14. Woodrow Wilson, "The Reconstruction of the Southern States," *Atlantic Monthly,* January 1901, 2–11, reprinted in Edwin C. Rozwenc, ed., *Problems in American Civilization: Reconstruction in the South* (Boston: D. C. Heath, 1952), 1–11.

15. Tucker, *The Dragon and the Cross,* 19–25. For a general history of the Ku Klux Klan, also see Chalmers, *Hooded Americanism*; Wade, *The Fiery Cross.*

16. Turner, *The Negro Question,* xi.

17. See *In Re Debs*, 158 U.S. 564 (1895); Colston E. Warne, *The Pullman Boycott of 1894: The Problem of Federal Intervention* (Boston: D. C. Heath, 1955); "Robert Todd Lincoln," *Funk & Wagnalls New Encyclopedia* (1983), vol. 16, 139.

18. *Plessy v. Ferguson*, 16 S. Ct. 1138, 1143, 163 U.S. 537 (1896).

19. Washington, *Up from Slavery*, 219–20.

20. Author's interviews with members of Elijah Muhammad's family; interviews of Pitman family via Erskine Bowles and others.

21. Henry McNeal Turner Papers: "The Writings of Henry McNeal Turner"; also see, in general, Douglas, *Black Christ*.

22. Meltzer, *The Black Americans*, 98–102.

23. "Negro Colonization Plan," *New York Times*, September 28, 1903, A01.

24. Meltzer, *The Black Americans*, 98–102.

25. Henry McNeal Turner Papers: "Autobiography."

26. Ibid.; also see "Religion's Changing Face: More Churches Depicting Christ as Black," *Washington Post*, March 28, 1994, A01.

27. Wallace Terry, "Cult of Hate: Black Muslim Elijah's Lowly Start" (part 2 of 6), *Washington Post*, December 12, 1960, A03; Muhammad, *History of the Nation of Islam*, 3–4, 46; also see, in general, Montgomery, *Under Their Own Vine and Fig Tree*.

28. Theodore P. Greene, ed., *American Imperialism in 1898* (Boston: D. C. Heath, 1955); "Headline," *New York Times*, October 27, 1897, A05.

29. "Negro Labor for Hawaii; A Report That Asiatics Will Gradually Make Way for the Overplus of the South," *New York Times*, August 5, 1897, A05.

30. See "Mourning Glory: The Ashanti King's Cloak of Symbols," *Washington Post*, February 9, 1997, G01.

31. Beller, *Herzl*, 26, 62–66; Herzl, *The Jewish State*, 25–41.

32. Ida B. Wells-Barnett, "Lynch Law in America." *Arena*, January 1900, 15–24; Scott, *Living Documents in American History*, vol. 2, 498–507.

33. Beller, *Herzl*, 81.

34. Elijah Muhammad knew he was born in October, but was never sure of the exact date. As he regarded 7 as a lucky number, he selected October 7 as his birthday. "Muhammad Meets the Press!" *Muhammad Speaks*, January 14, February 4, and February 11, 1972; booklet reprint, *Elijah Muhammad Meets the Press*, 19. Also see "Elijah Muhammad," *Current Biography 1971*, 293–95; Hakim, *True History of Elijah Muhammad*, 273.

35. Quoted in *Eyes on the Prize* (documentary); also see, in general, Bennett, *Before the Mayflower.*

36. See chart, "Lynchings by Race and Year: 1882–1962," in Ploski and Williams, *The Negro Almanac,* 368.

37. "Crime Grows in Georgia; Gov. Atkinson Calls the Attention of the Legislature to Its Increase," *New York Times,* October 28, 1906, A01.

38. "Lynch Law in the South; Georgia Legislators to Try and Find a Way for Its Suppression," *New York Times,* November 14, 1897, A09.

39. FBI HQ File on Elijah Muhammad, section 1.

40. Ibid.

41. FBI HQ File on Elijah Muhammad, Parole Progress Report on Ghulam Bogans, aka Elijah Muhammad (1943).

42. Author's interviews with Erskine Bowles.

43. Terry, "Cult of Hate" (part 2).

44. Haley, *Autobiography of Malcolm X,* 205–6.

45. "Say Negro Race Is Dying; Medical Expert Tells President Deaths Here Exceed the Births," *New York Times,* April 10, 1906, A01.

46. Muhammad, *Theology of Time,* part 1, 69–70; Hakim, *True History of Elijah Muhammad,* 37–38. One antilynching poster read "A Reign of Midnight Terror" across the top and "Ku Klux Devils Incarnate" at the bottom. See Harris, *The Black Book,* 59.

47. Hakim, *True History of Elijah Muhammad,* 37–38. For lyrics to "Steal Away to Jesus," see Johnson and Johnson, *Books of American Negro Spirituals,* 114–17.

48. Muhammad, *Theology of Time,* 227.

49. "Unknown Negro Is Lynched," *Atlanta Constitution,* October 17, 1903, A02.

50. FBI HQ file on Elijah Muhammad, Parole Progress Report on Ghulam Bogans; Haley, *Autobiography of Malcolm X,* 205–6; *Current Biography 1971,* 293–95.

51. *Slaughterhouse Cases,* 83 U.S. 36 (1873); *Peonage Cases,* 123 F. 671 (D.C.M.D. Ala. 1903). 42 United States Code 1581. The congressional statute was upheld in *Clyatt v. U.S.,* 197 U.S. 207 (1905).

52. "World's Fair Department of Anthropology: Portions of Ancient Cities Are to Be Represented and Unwritten History Revealed," *St. Louis Republic,* March 6, 1904, A01. Other articles about the treatment of Ota Benga are in the

appendix of a recent account of his life and death: see Bradford and Blume, *Ota Benga: The Pygmy in the Zoo.*

53. Ibid.

54. Ibid.

55. "Blacks and the Constitution: Justice Thurgood Marshall," *Washington Post,* July 5, 1987, D07.

56. *Berea College v. Commonwealth of Kentucky,* 211 U.S. 45 (1908).

57. "Negroes in the North; They Have Fewer Chances Here Than South, Washington Says," *New York Times,* September 20, 1906, A05.

58. Bergman and Bergman, *Chronological History of the Negro in America,* 347–48; "Paper Blamed for Riots; Grand Jury Accuses Atlanta News of Stirring Up Race Feeling," *New York Times,* September 28, 1906, A01.

59. "Atlanta Mobs Kill Ten Negroes; Maybe 23 or 30—Assaults on Women the Cause," *New York Times,* September 23, 1906, A01; "Rioting Goes On, Despite Troops; Exodus of Black Servants Troubles City," *New York Times,* September 24, 1906, A01.

60. "Whites and Negroes Killed in Atlanta; Mobs of Blacks Retaliate for Riots—Two Whites Killed," *New York Times,* September 25, 1906, A01.

61. "Will Be Riots Here—Dixon; Says New York Will Kill Negroes. B. T. Washington's Concern," *New York Times,* September 24, 1906, A01–2; also see Tucker, *The Dragon and the Cross,* 21. Dixon's book *The Clansman* later attracted the attention of D. W. Griffith, director of the controversial film *The Birth of a Nation.*

62. "Was It a 'Crime'?" *New York Times,* January 28, 1906, A06.

63. "Race War Is Coming, Says Senator Tillman; Predicts Killings in the South Far Worse Than Atlanta's," *New York Times,* October 8, A01.

64. "Plans a Negro Haven in West Africa; Bishop Smith Finds a Chance for Thousands in Liberia," *New York Times,* November 24, 1906, A11.

65. Cherry was founder of the Church of God, otherwise known as the "Black Jews." See Furtaw, *Black Americans Information Directory,* "Church of God" and "Church of God and Saints of Christ," 137–38; also see "Negro Prophet Elijah Awes Throng of Saints," *New York Times,* April 14, 1906, A11; "Blacks [Are] Israelites, Church Teaches," *Washington Evening Star,* August 28, 1971, A08; "Cicanci Referral Leads to Interesting Religious Excursion," *Providence Journal-Bulletin,* December 19, 1995, B01.

66. Ibid., *New York Times.*

2. ROOTS

1. Rolling Stones, "Paint It Black" (ABKO Music, 1966).

2. Thomas Pynchon, *Gravity's Rainbow* (New York: Bantam Books, 1974), 274.

3. Quoted in Watkins, *Anthology of American Negro Literature*, 211–13.

4. Bureau of National Literature, *Messages and Papers of the Presidents: William Howard Taft*, "Taft's Inaugural Address," 7375–77.

5. Ibid.

6. "Debt to the Negro; Taft Pledges His Support Toward Repayment," *Washington Post,* May 27, 1909, A01.

7. Bergman and Bergman, *Chronological History of the Negro in America,* 358.

8. Ibid., 365.

9. Cox, *White America,* 309–10. The book was a tardy rebuttal to *The Souls of Black Folk.*

10. Soper, *The Religions of Mankind,* 93.

11. "May Make Negroes White; Chicagoan Believes It Possible to Neutralize the Color Units," *New York Times,* January 3, 1910, A09.

12. Sklar, *The Nazis and the Occult,* 4–32.

13. Dorothy Mills, *The People of Ancient Israel* (New York: Scribner, 1932).

14. "Prof. Lyde on Original Color; London Scientist Says the First Color of Man was a Brownish-Yellow," *Savannah Tribune,* February 10, 1912, A02.

15. The author found only two published interviews where Elijah Muhammad revealed that Hamilton was the friend who was lynched. In 1960, he said that in the Cordele lynching a "young Negro man, charged with rape, was strung to a tree and shot to death." See Wallace Terry, "Cult of Hate: Black Muslim Elijah's Lowly Start," (part 2 of 6), *Washington Post,* December 12, 1960, A07. In the other, he referred to the victim as "Hamilton." Owing to Muhammad's reluctance to provide specifics about the lynching, four or five versions of the incident have been published. In Evanzz, *The Judas Factor,* a different version of the lynching was reported, which is the version I heard in the 1970s while visiting Mosque No. 28 in St. Louis. Like other earlier accounts, it was based on conflicting information from Muslim ministers. See, for example: Baldwin, *The Fire Next Time,* 71–105; Malu Halasa, *Elijah Muhammad* (New York: Chelsea House, 1990), 17–22; Cushmeer, *This Is the One,* 80–81.

16. "Hundreds Seeking Negro Assaulter; Crime Stirs Cordele; Prominent Young Woman Is Negro's Victim," *Savannah Morning News,* January 30, 1912, A01; "Cordele Jail Stormed; Crowds Lynch Negro," *The Atlanta Journal,* January 30, 1912, A01.

17. Ibid.

18. "Negro Assaults Cordele Woman; Lynching Will Probably Result if Black Is Caught," *Atlanta Constitution,* January 30, 1912, A01.

19. "Sheriff's Story of Lynching," *Savannah Morning News,* January 31, 1912, A09; "Storm Jail to Get Negro: Georgia Mob Siezes Girl's Assailant and Lynches Him," *New York Times,* January 31, 1912, A13.

20. "Cordele Men Kill Assailant Quickly; Hamilton Is Lynched," *Savannah Morning News,* January 31, 1912, A09.

21. Ibid.

22. "Shows Post Card Picture of Lynching," *Savannah Morning News,* January 31, 1912, A09.

23. Ibid.

24. Terry, "Cult of Hate" (part 2).

25. Based on Prison Intake Interview and Report for Gulam Bogans (aka Elija Poole).

26. Haley, *Autobiography of Malcolm X,* 206.

27. FBI HQ file on Clara Muhammad, document dated May 22, 1962 (relating to passport application).

28. Most accounts of their date of marriage indicate it occurred on March 7, but FBI files and some public records show March 17. Given Elijah's fondess for the number 7, and that several records indicate they were married on March 7, that's the date I have accepted. Since March 17 is Saint Patrick's Day, it is equally likely that he chose that as a "good luck" date for marriage; see Essien-Udom, *Black Nationalism* (March 7), 87, and Clegg, *An Original Man* (March 17), 12.

29. Ploski and Kaiser, *The Negro Almanac,* 830–44.

30. Muhammad, *Theology of Time,* 440.

31. Haley, *Autobiography of Malcolm X,* 206.

32. Tuttle, *Race Riot*; Platt, *Politics of Riot Commissions,* 93–158.

33. "The International Jew: The World's Problem," *Dearborn Independent,* May 22, 1920; Collier, *The Fords,* 101–6.

34. Salzman, *Bridges and Boundaries,* 177–78.

35. Powers, *Secrecy and Power,* 111. A number of authors have traced the origins of the *Protocols,* with varying results. See Baigent, *Holy Blood, Holy*

Grail, 163–69; Carmichael, *Satanizing of the Jews,* 152–59; Perlmutter, *Real Anti-Semitism in America,* 107.

36. Hoover, *Masters of Deceit,* vi.

37. Pfeffer, *A. Philip Randolph,* 9–16.

38. "K.K.K. Sends Human Hand; Negro Editor Gets Warning—With Mail Enclosure," *New York Times,* Sep. 6, 1922, A19.

39. Powers, *Secrecy and Power,* 104–5; Theoharis, *The Boss,* 72.

40. Flood, *Hitler,* 86–90; Toland, *Adolf Hitler,* 78–160; also see Pool, *Who Financed Hitler?*

41. "Seven Dead in Race Riots," *New York Times,* April 15, 1919, A24; "Lynching Kept Secret; Georgia Negro's Crime Was Defending Negroes Against White Man," *New York Times,* July 25, 1919, A15; "Kill Negro, Burn Church; Georgia Mob Shoots Colored Leader Down in the Edifice," *New York Times,* August 29, 1919, A03.

42. Platt, *Politics of Riot Commissions,* 93–158; Spear, *Black Chicago,* 189–222.

43. Tuttle, *Race Riot;* Salzman, *Bridges and Boundaries,* 187–89.

44. "Elijah Muhammad," *Current Biography 1971,* 293; "Muhammad Leaves Great Legacy of Pride and Respect," *Jet,* March 13, 1975, 6–14; Muhammad, *Message to the Blackman,* 178.

45. "Kill Sentenced Negro; Georgia Mob Takes Him from the Sheriff and Shoots Him," *New York Times,* October 8, 1919, A06.

46. "Kill Negro, Whip Two, Hold Five in Georgia," *New York Times,* October 6, 1919, A03; "Georgia Mob Burns Two Negroes Alive; Chain Victims to Stakes," *New York Times,* October 7, 1919, A02.

47. Supra, note 44; Clegg, *Original Man,* 11.

48. The entrance of African Americans into the general workforce led to what scholars termed the "flood time of racism." See Quarles, *The Negro American,* 403–33; "Denies Sectionalism in Anti-Lynch Bill," *Atlanta Constitution,* July 29, 1922, A12. Nonetheless, Macon and Atlanta both produced a thriving black middle class during the era.

49. FBI HQ file on Elijah Muhammad, section 12, Correlation Summary of April 9, 1969.

50. "4 Whites and Negro Shot in Atlanta Riot," *New York Times,* May 8, 1922, A18; "Did No Shooting, Declares Allen," *Atlanta Constitution,* July 29, 1922, A01; "Southern Railway Worker Bound Over," *Atlanta Constitution,* July 29, 1922, A01.

51. "Deputy Is Killed by Macon Negro; Colored Quarters Closed When General Firing Results—Two Negroes Wounded," *Atlanta Constitution,* July 30, 1922, A01; "Local Police Hunt Negro," *Atlanta Constitution,* July 30, 1922, A02.

52. "Negroes Shot Down in Riots at Macon," *New York Times,* July 30, 1922, A28; "2 Negroes Lynched by Mobs in South; Georgia Crowd of 300 Takes a Prisoner from Officers and Shoots Him to Death," *New York Times,* August 2, 1922, A19.

53. Ibid.

54. Ibid.

55. Supra, note 51.

56. Parole Progress Report on Gulam Bogans, aka Elijah Muhammad. Federal Correctional Institution at Milan, Michigan, dated April 23, 1945; Admission Summary, dated August 20, 1943; and Physical Examination and Correlated History, dated July 26, 1943. The reports are part of the FBI's HQ file on Elijah Muhammad; Associated Press interview and feature story titled "People in the News: Elijah Muhammad," Chicago, February 25, 1965. Also see "Elijah Muhammad," *Current Biography 1971,* 293; Haley, *Autobiography of Malcolm X,* 206.

57. Ibid.

3. PARADISE LOST

1. E. M. Forster, *A Passage to India* (1924; reprint, New York: Harcourt, Brace & World, 1952), 19.

2. Friedrich Nietzche, *Twilight of the Idols/The Anti-Christ* (1895; reprint, New York: Penguin Books, 1990), 195.

3. "President Says Negro Makes American Music; May Furnish the Foundation of the True National School," *New York Times,* February 15, 1906, A07. Dvořák's article ran in *Harper's* in 1895; also see "Indian and Negro Music: The President's Suggestions as to Their Value for American Composers," *New York Times,* February 25, 1906, section 4, 4.

4. Ibid.

5. Gilbert, *Harlem: The Making of a Ghetto,* 181.

6. Ploski and Kaiser, *The Negro Almanac,* 1159–60.

7. Confession of Elijah Muhammad to FBI on September 20, 1942; Wallace Terry, "Cult of Hate: Black Muslim Elijah's Lowly Start" (part 2 of 6), *Washington Post,* December 12, 1960, A07.

8. FBI HQ file on Elijah Muhammad, Parole Report.

9. Ibid.; also consult "Compton's Complete Street Guide" (CD-ROM), which vividly illustrates the proximity of Rockwood to railroad tracks; "Elijah Muhammad," *Current Biography 1971*, 293; Muhammad, *Message to the Blackman in America,* 178.

10. FBI HQ file on Elijah Muhammad, section 12, Correlation Summary, dated April 9, 1969.

11. Jackson, *Ku Klux Klan in the City,* 129; Woodward, *Strange Career of Jim Crow,* 113–18.

12. Ibid.

13. See, in general, Lemann, *The Promised Land.*

14. Hill, *The Marcus Garvey and Universal Negro Improvement Association Papers*; O'Reilly, *Black Americans,* 139–67; FBI HQ file on Marcus Garvey.

15. Though Elijah Muhammad admitted to the strong influence which Garvey had upon him, he denied having ever joined the UNIA. This is contradicted, however, by interviews conducted with Muslims and Garveyites by the Works Project Administration. See Bontemps and Conroy, *They Seek a City*; Fauset, *Black Gods of the Metropolis;* Eissen-Udom, *Black Nationalism*; Rashad, *History of Islam and Black Nationalism in the Americas,* 70–74.

16. Publisher unknown; Webb's book, however, is listed in the Library of Congress's card catalogue (go to http://www.loc.web on the Internet); Webb is also mentioned in the Marcus Garvey entry on Island Records Internet site for Bob Marley (http://www.bobmarley.com/life/rastafari/garvey).

17. Michael Ducille, "Black Moses, Red Scare," *Washington Post,* February 12, 1997, H01, H04; Ben F. Rogers, "W. E. B. DuBois, Marcus Garvey, and Pan-Africa," *Journal of Negro History,* April 1955, 154–59.

18. Ibid. The circulation of *Negro World* reportedly exceeded 800,000 copies per issue before Garvey's demise. See Muhammad, *Message to the Blackman,* xxiii.

19. Howard Carter, *The Tomb of Tut.Ankh.Amen,* 3 vols. (London: Cassel, 1923–33); Stewart, *The Pyramids and Sphinx,* 118–35.

20. See, in general, Van Loon, *Story of Mankind.*

21. Supra, note 17; also see FBI HQ file on Marcus Garvey; O'Reilly, *Black Americans,* 139–67.

22. Supra, note 17; "'African President' Held; Head of Black Star Line Accused of Illegally Using Mails," *New York Times,* January 13, 1922, A09.

23. Powers, *Secrecy and Power,* 128; O'Reilly, *Black Americans,* 140.

24. Bergman and Bergman, *Chronological History of the Negro,* 406–7.

25. Ibid.

26. FBI HQ file on Marcus Garvey.

27. "Lynching Bill Debated," *New York Times,* January 18, 1922, A19; also see *New York Times,* May 30, 1922, A08, and August 15, 1922, A10.

28. Muhammad mentioned his membership during numerous speeches, but never wrote anything substantive. In general, see Elijah Muhammad, *The Secrets of Freemasonry* (College Park; Ga., Secretarius M.E.M.P.S., 1994).

29. Confession of Elijah Muhammad to FBI on September 20, 1942; also see Muhammad, *Message to the Blackman,* 178.

30. Detroit Police Arrest Report of "Elija Pool," dated March 20, 1926.

31. W. Mohammad, *As the Light Shineth from the East,* 199; Barboza, *American Jihad,* 269.

32. Figures culled from FBI HQ files on Elijah and Clara Muhammad.

33. Elijah Muhammad, who denied any affiliation with Garvey's UNIA, also denied joining the MSTA. Members of the sect clearly recalled his involvement, and this is corroborated by information in his FBI files. The MSTA also claim to have photographs of Elijah Poole taken while he was a member. He never explained his close relationship, for example, with Sheik Joseph Gravitt-el, nor did he explain why there were so many striking similarities between the two sects. One of the reasons Fard was believed to have so many followers is because it was impossible to distinguish members of the MSTA from those of the NOI. This changed slightly in 1935 when Muhammad forbade members of the NOI to wear the maroon fez.

34. A photocopy of Noble Drew Ali's *Holy Koran* is contained in the FBI HQ file on the MSTA (also called the Noble Drew Ali file).

35. There is no evidence whatsoever of this event having transpired, but it is part of the interesting mythology of the sect. Eissen-Udom, *Black Nationalism,* 46, 371 (appendix C); Bontemps and Conroy, *They Seek a City,* 174–77.

36. Effendi, *Gleanings from the Writings of Baha'u'llah,* i–xii; *Masjid Baitur Rahman,* booklet published by the Ahmadiyya Movement in Islam on the history of the community.

37. FBI/CIA report on the origins of the Nation of Islam, contained in the CIA file on Elijah Muhammad.

38. Noble Drew Ali made no attempt to rewrite passages borrowed from Dowling's book, nor are there any discrepancies between the literature pub-

lished by the Ahmadiyya Movement and the sections plagiarized by Ali. See, for example, chapter 10 of Noble Drew Ali's *Holy Koran* and section 6 of chapter 28 of Dowling's *Aquarian Gospel.*

39. From the FBI's reproduction of Ali's *Holy Koran.*

40. FBI HQ file on Noble Drew Ali; literature also obtained from Sheila Seabreeze-Bey, archivist for the MSTA.

41. Parole Progress Report on Gulam Bogans, aka Elijah Muhammad, Physical Examination and Correlated History, 6, item no. 5. Report contained in FBI HQ file on Elijah Muhammad. Muhammad claimed that prison conditions caused his bronchial problems, but it seems more probable that the real damage to his lungs was caused while working in the foundry.

42. See Appendix A for a complete list of names as recorded during a forty-year intelligence gathering endeavor by the FBI. All names are from Enclosure 203 in the FBI HQ file on Elijah Muhammad.

43. Aaron Payne Papers, University of Chicago Library. According to Payne, Noble Drew Ali asked him to take the reins of the MSTA if anything should happen to him. See "Victim of Cult Gun Fight Dies; Twenty of Negro 'Moor' Order Are Held," *Chicago Tribune,* September 27, 1929, A01; "6 Held To Grand Jury for Cult Battle Murders," *Chicago Tribune,* September 28, 1929, A01; also see FBI HQ file on MSTA.

44. Ibid.; also see "Hold Moorish Temple 'Prophet' in Murder Plot; Blame Split in Cult for Brutal Crime," *Chicago Defender,* March 21, 1929, A01.

45. A photograph of DePriest and Noble Drew Ali is available in the Aaron Payne Papers at the University of Chicago. For general biography of DePriest, see Rather, *Chicago Negro Almanac and Reference Book*; Bergman and Bergman, *Chronological History of the Negro,* 441–42; Ploski and Kaiser, *The Negro Almanac,* 200.

46. Supra, note 44; also see FBI HQ file on MSTA.

47. Supra, note 43, Aaron Payne Papers; also see Gissen-Udom, *Black Nationalism,* 47; Bontemps, *Anyplace but Here,* 207–8.

48. "Death Bares Negro Cult in Temple Here," *Chicago Tribune,* May 14, 1929, A01; Bontemps, *Anyplace but Here,* 205–8.

49. Supra, note 44.

50. Ibid.; also see "Cult Leader Being Held in Murder Case," *Chicago Tribune,* May 18, 1929, A01.

51. FBI HQ file on Wallace D. Fard; also see Bontemps, *Anyplace but Here,* 217.

52. Author's interviews; Noble Drew Ali's death was reported in the *Chicago Defender* on July 24.

52. Author's interviews; CIA report on the NOI; also see Bontemps, *Anyplace but Here,* 222–23.

54. "To Disband Moors; Second Policeman Dead as Result of Cult Battle," *Chicago Defender,* October 5, 1929, A01; supra, note 47; *Chicago Tribune.*

55. "1,000 Police Guard District; Guns Captured; Negro 'Moor' Racket Bared by Killings," *Chicago Tribune,* September 26, 1929, A01.

56. Author's interviews with Anderson-el of the MSTA in Newark, and members of the MSTA in Baltimore and Philadelphia.

57. "Calls Negroes to Islam; Detroit Man Would Lead Exodus to Anatolia, Fleeing Color Prejudice," *New York Times,* May 25, 1930, A23. Lomax, a former chief assistant to Noble Drew Ali, had been on the run since a riot erupted in Paradise Valley on March 22. Moors who were loyal to Ali accused Lomax of conspiring with Greene. See "Detroit Followers Riot," *Chicago Defender,* March 23, 1929, A03.

58. "Urges Turk Negro Colony; Detroit Moslem Asks Permission of Kemal to Found Settlement," *New York Times,* June 30, 1930, A08.

59. Barboza, *American Jihad,* 269.

60. FBI HQ file on Elijah Muhammad, section 12, Correlation Summary dated April 9, 1969.

61. E. D. Beynon, "The Voodoo Cult Among American Negro Migrants in Detroit," *American Journal of Sociology* 43, no. 6 (May 1938): 895.

62. Era Bell Thompson, "America's Black Jews," *Ebony,* May 1975, 96–100; also see Drake and Clayton, *Black Metropolis,* and Fauset, *Black Gods of the Metropolis.*

63. Weisbrot, *Father Divine*; Watts, *God, Harlem U.S.A.*

64. Ibid.

65. Despite Muhammad's assertions to the contrary, his son and others swear that Clara was the first to meet Fard. She convinced her father-in-law, Willie, to go to a meeting. Clara subsequently invited Fard to dinner.

4. Lord of the Flies

1. Canot, *Adventures of an African Slaver,* 132.
2. George Orwell, *1984* (New York: New American Library, 1989), 5.
3. Barboza, *American Jihad,* 268.

4. E. D. Beynon, "The Voodoo Cult Among Negro Migrants in Detroit," *American Journal of Sociology* 43, no. 6 (May 1938): 894–907; Lincoln, *Black Muslims in America,* 10–14; FBI HQ file on Wallace D. Fard.

5. Parole Progress Report of Elijah Muhammad.

6. Bontemps, *Anyplace but Here,* 216–21; alse see Beynon, "Voodoo Cult."

7. Ibid.

8. Ibid.

9. Muhammad, *Message to the Blackman,* 112–22; Haley, *Autobiography of Malcolm X,* 164–68, 208.

10. Ibid.; also refer to "The Tricknology of the Enemy" (on audiocassette and in booklet form).

11. Ibid.; also see Guthrie, *Making of the Whiteman.*

12. Ibid.

13. Guthrie, *Making of the Whiteman,* 12 (Guthrie cites standard and arcane works to support Fard's thesis that Caucasians are innately evil); Muhammad, *Message to the Blackman,* 125–26.

14. Haley, *Autobiography of Malcolm X,* 156–66.; also see, generally, Muhammad, *How to Eat to Live.*

15. This allegation was a staple of sermons by Muslim ministers as late as 1980. Muhammad made reference to the myth in his Saviour's Day speech of 1972. See Chapter 17.

16. Ford was sued by Aaron Sapiro after the *Dearborn Independent* printed an article accusing him of exploiting farmers. In the settlement, Ford agreed to apologize publicly "to Sapiro individually and to the Jewish people as a whole." Collier, *The Fords,* 105–6; Lee, *Henry Ford and the Jews,* 67–85.

17. Regrettably, Elijah Muhammad's books are almost the sole source of much of Fard's philosophy. His statements regarding the same are recapitulated here for the lack of primary sources.

18. Fard had the good fortune to arrive in Detroit at a time when archaeologists were uncovering evidence that mankind began in Africa eons earlier than indicated in standard studies. The constant resetting of the age of man in Africa gave credence to his assertion that "there is no birth record of the black man." Muhammad, *Message to the Blackman,* 325; also see "Out of Africa 1.8 Million Years Ago; Java Man Fossils Older Than Thought," *Washington Post,* February 24, 1994, A04; "Prehistoric Tolls Deepen Evolutionary Mystery; Cache of Stone Implements Found in Ethiopia Predate Fossils of Ancestors of All People," *Washington Post,* January 23, 1997, A03.

19. See, generally, *The Age of God-Kings*.

20. McGinn, *Antichrist*, 70–71; see also *New Catholic Encyclopedia*; "Cyril of Alexandria, Saint," and "Cyril of Jerusalem, Saint," *Funk & Wagnalls New Encyclopedia* (1983), vol. 7, 418.

21. James I, King of England (1566–1625), *Daemonologie* (1597; reprint, New York: E. P. Dutton, 1924).

22. Guazzo's treatise has been reprinted by Dover (Montague Summers edition).

23. Sinistrari, *Demonality*, 21.

24. Ibid.

25. Volumes have been written on this subject. Most reputable studies report, for instance, that Native Americans believed illness accounted for the "pale face" of the Pilgrims. *Brewer's Dictionary of Phrase and Fable*, 678; Partridge, *Origins*, 465; also see Browder, *From The Browder File*, 8–9.

26. Generally, see Nolan, *Communism versus the Negro*, chap. 4, "The Slogan of Self-Determination in the Black Belt, 1928–45"; Bergman and Bergman *Chronological History of the Negro*, 457.

27. Hoover, *Masters of Deceit*, 243–44. That the NOI called for racial separation helps to explain Hoover's belief that the sect was Communist-inspired.

28. FBI HQ file on Langston Hughes; Crossman, *The God That Failed*, 103–46; Gayle, *Richard Wright*, 79–82.

29. FBI HQ file on Noble Drew Ali; Powers, *Secrecy and Power*, 163.

30. Muhammad, *Theology of Time*, book 1, 19.

31. Fard's etymology of "Eu" differs from that in most dictionaries.

32. Guthrie, *Making of the Whiteman*, 67.

33. Muhammad, *Our Savior Has Arrived*, 165; Hakim, *True History of Elijah Muhammad*, 220.

34. Hakim, *True History*, 222.

35. "The *Bible* is now being called the Poison Book by God Himself [i.e., Fard], and who can deny that it is not poison?" Muhammad, *Message to the Blackman*, 94; also see Haley, *Autobiography of Malcolm X*, 185.

36. "Elijah Muhammad," *Current Biography 1972*, 293–95.

37. Barboza, *American Jihad*, 269.

38. Hakim, *True History*, 37. According to Wallace Muhammad, his father told him that he could espouse a similar theology. Clegg, *Original Man*, 340, n. 10; Larry Muhammad, "The Muslims: Five Years Later," *Sepia*, March 1980, 32.

39. "Bigotry Detestable," letters to the editor, *Sunday Oklahoman*, May 21, 1995, A10; see, generally, Muhammad, *How to Eat to Live*.

40. Hakim, *True History*, 39.

41. Ibid., 37.

42. Muhammad, *Our Saviour Has Arrived*, 225; Muhammad, *Message to the Blackman*, 232–33; Muhammad, *The Supreme Wisdom*, vol. 2 (cover art).

43. FBI HQ file on Elijah Muhammad; J. Muhammad, *Journal of Truth*, 147.

44. Muhammad, *The Supreme Wisdom*, vol. 2, 53; Muhammad, *Our Saviour Has Arrived*, 32.

45. Muhammad, *Our Saviour Has Arrived*, 32–33.

46. Ibid.

47. FBI HQ file on Elijah Muhammad.

48. Marsh, *From Black Muslims to Muslims*, 109. According to one report, Fard chose the name Waris (which means "inheritor" in Arabic) instead of Wallace, "but Elijah's attempts to pronounce this would phonetically come out [as] Wallace. Fard wrote the spelling in chalk on a door." Larry Muhammad, "The Muslims," 32.

49. Reconstructed from police reports, news accounts, and FBI documents.

50. Detroit Police Department homicide report; "Head of Cult Admits Killing," *Detroit News*, November 21, 1932, A01; "Leader of Cult Admits Slaying at Home 'Altar'; Police Trying to Link Voodoo Chieftain to Evangelista Case," *Detroit Free Press*, November 21, 1932, A01.

51. "Voodoo Slayer Admits Plotting Death of Judges," *Detroit Free Press*, November 22, 1932, A01; "Leader of Cult Called Insane," *Detroit News*, November 22, 1932, A04.

52. Ibid.

53. Ibid.

54. Ibid.

55. "Negro Leaders Open Fight to Break Voodooism's Grip; Cult Conceived by Islamic Religious Fakir, Nurtured by Grafting Fanatics," *Detroit Free Press*, November 24, 1932, A01.

56. Detroit Police Department homicide report.

57. "Raided Temple Bares Grip of Voodoo in City; 'God of Asia Nation' Seized as Sequel to Altar Slaying," *Detroit Free Press*, November 23, 1932, A01.

58. Ibid.

59. Supra, note 55.

60. Supra, note 55.

61. "New Human Sacrifice with a Boy as Victim Is Averted by Inquiry," *Detroit Free Press,* November 26, 1932, A01.

62. "Cult Slayer Faces Hearing on Sanity," *Washington Evening Star,* November 25, 1932, A02; "Cult Slayer Pleads Guilty; Harris Argues With Judge Boyne at Arraignment on Murder Charge," *Detroit Free Press,* November 25, 1932, A01.

63. Ibid.

64. Ibid.

65. Supra, note 61.

66. Supra, note 55.

67. Supra, note 61.

68. Supra, note 57.

69. Supra, note 61.

70. Detroit Police Department file on Karriem.

71. Supra, note 61; "Voodoo's Reign Here Is Broken; Slayer Held Insane; Fard Quits City," *Detroit Free Press,* December 7, 1932, A07.

72. Hill, *The FBI's RACON,* 663.

73. Based on letters seized from the home of Elijah Muhammad on September 20, 1942; also see "Leader of Cult Called Insane," *Detroit News,* November 22, 1932, A04, where welfare workers discuss economic circumstances of Muslims.

74. J. Muhammad, *Journal of Truth,* 147; FBI HQ file on Elijah Muhammad; "Girl Recounts Lore of Islam; School's Mohammed Gets Probation," *Detroit Free Press,* April 26, 1934, A01.

75. Hakim, *True History,* 39, where Muhammad claimed during a transcribed speech that he received his final name in 1932; cf. Beynon, "Voodoo Cult," 907, where other Muslims contended that Fard never gave Elijah the last name of Muhammad.

5. BITTER FRUIT

1. Allport, *The Nature of Prejudice,* 309.

2. "Nepal's Shame; Girl-Trafficking Meets a Determined Roadblock," *Washington Post,* April 14, 1995, D01.

3. Woodson, *Mis-Education of the Negro,* 192.

4. Based on summaries of speeches in the FBI HQ file on Elijah Muhammad. The same analogy was made in 1969 by a leading African-American intel-

lectual. Helga Wild, "The Crisis in Black and White Is a Crisis in Social Theory," *SEHR* 4, no. 2 (on-line at http://www.shr.stanford.edu./shreview/4–2/text/wild.html).

5. A complete list of his aliases is in section 203 of the FBI HQ file on Elijah Muhammad; also see Hakim, *True History of Elijah Muhammad,* 39.

6. "Banished Leader of Cult Arrested; Fard Found in City Despite Promise to Leave," *Detroit Free Press,* May 26, 1933, A10; Detroit Police Deparment file on Wallace D. Fard, aka Wallace Dodd Ford; Muhammad, *The Supreme Wisdom, vol. 1, 15.*

7. Muhammad, *Our Saviour Has Arrived,* 36; Sahib, "The Nation of Islam," 71–77.

8. FBI's Chicago file on Wallace D. Fard.

9. Supra, note 4.

10. Muhammad, *The Supreme Wisdom,* 23–24, which Muhammad based on the Book of Revelation, 14:1.

11. "Voodooist Cult Revived in City; Negro Children Found in Islam School," *Detroit Free Press,* March 27, 1934, A01.

12. Ibid.

13. Ibid.

14. Ibid.

15. "'Islam' Faces Double Jeopardy; 'University' Believed to Be Cult's Home," *Detroit Free Press,* March 28, 1934, A07.

16. "Cult's University Raided by Police," *Detroit Free Press,* April 17, 1934, A01; "13 Policemen Hurt Battling Voodoo Band; Cult Backers March on Headquarters to Protest Arrests," *Detroit Free Press,* April 19, 1934, A01.

17. "U.S. May Fight Voodoo In City; Syndicalism Charges May Be Brought," *Detroit Free Press,* April 18, 1934, A23.

18. Supra, note 16.

19. Ibid.

20. Ibid.

21. Ibid.

22. Ibid.

23. Ibid.

24. FBI HQ file on Elijah Muhammad.

25. Interviews with John Muhammad. The FBI HQ file on Elijah Muhammad contains abstracts of several editions of *The Final Call to Islam.*

26. *The Final Call to Islam,* August 24, 1934. Muhammad and Muslim were initially spelled "Mohammed" and "Moslem" by the NOI. The later spellings are used here for clarity.

27. Ibid.

28. "I am Elijah of your Bible; I'm the Muhammad of your Holy Quran. . . . I am the one of [*sic*] whom the Holy Quran is referring." Hakim, *Theology of Time,* 3; also see Clark, *Malcolm X: The Final Speeches,* 250; Cushmeer, *This Is the One,* 140–41.

29. W. Muhammad, *As the Light Shineth from the East,* 11.

30. Barboza, *American Jihad,* 269; Muhammad, *Message to the Blackman,* 263–64.

31. FBI HQ file on the SDOO, vol. 2.

32. FBI HQ file on Naka Nakane, aka Satohata Takahashi.

33. CIA background report on the NOI; Boykins, *Handbook of the Detroit Negro.*

34. FBI HQ file on Takahashi.

35. "Amur River Society (Kokuryukai; literally, Black Dragon Society)," *Kodansha Encyclopedia of Japan,* vol. 1, 53; FBI HQ file on Naka Nakana, aka Satohata Takahashi.

36. FBI HQ file on Wallace Fard; FBI HQ file on the SDOO; FBI HQ file on Takahashi.

37. Ibid.

38. FBI HQ file on Elijah Muhammad.

39. Ibid.

40. FBI HQ file on Takahashi; FBI HQ file on SDOO.

41. Boykins, *Handbook of the Detroit Negro.*

42. FBI HQ file on SDOO, vol. 1.

43. Ibid.

44. Ibid., memo from St. Louis SAC to director, June 24, 1933.

45. Ibid., memo dated June 29, 1933.

46. Ibid.; also see "D.C. Filipino 'Ally' of Japs Held as Slacker," *Washington Post,* August 1, 1942, A01; "Filipino Agitator Seized Here by FBI; Spent Years in Stirring Up 'Dark Skinned Races' Against U.S., J. E. Hoover Says," *New York Times,* August 1, 1942, A01.

47. FBI HQ file on SDOO; also see "3 Years for Ashima Takis; Japanese Agitator Sentenced in St. Louis on Forgery Charges," *New York Times,* October 2, 1942, A06; Hill, *The FBI's RACON,* 517–22.

48. FBI file on SDOO; Hill, *The FBI's RACON*, 514–22; also see "Jew-Baiting Held Key Policy of Gerald Winrod's 'Defender,'" *Washington Post*, April 16, 1942, A08; "Financed Deal for Winrod, Jury Charges," *Washington Post*, December 15, 1942, A03; "Coughlin Accused of Using Official Nazi Propaganda," *Washington Post*, 1939, A05; "Five Who Urged Revolt in Harlem And Aid to Japanese Are Indicted," *New York Times*, September 15, 1942, A01.

49. FBI HQ file on Takahashi; FBI HQ file on Wallace D. Fard.

50. FBI HQ file on Wallace D. Fard.

51. "Little Filipino Goes 'Loco,' Kills 6 in Seattle," *Washington Daily News*, November 25, 1932, A04.

52. "Jap Arrested in Raid on Club; Alien Faces Questioning About Alleged Racial Plot Against Whites," *Detroit Free Press*, December 2, 1933, A01; FBI HQ file on Takahashi; Hill, *The FBI's RACON*, 665; "Jap Agent Seizure Sheds Light on Race Plot of the '30s," *Detroit Free Press*, August 3, 1942, A01.

53. FBI HQ file on SDOO.

54. Barboza, *American Jihad*, 268–69.

55. Muhammad, *Message to the Blackman*, 263–264; Hakim, *True History*, 66, 58.

6. ELIJAH THE PROPHET

1. "Kung Sees Threat to U.S. from Japan; Chinese Premier Believes That Dream of Domination Will Turn Across the Pacific," *New York Times*, October 17, 1939, A09.

2. Excerpts from speeches discovered in boxes at Elijah Muhammad's Chicago home are contained in the FBI HQ file on Elijah Muhammad.

3. Ibid.

4. Ibid.

5. Ibid.

6. "Cultists Riot in Court; One Death, 41 Hurt," *Chicago Tribune*, March 6, 1935, A01; Muhammad, *Message to the Blackman*, xxv–xxvi, 213–14 (Muhammad's account is inaccurate, as it fuses the April 1934 school incident with the Chicago courtroom riot). One newspaper erroneously reported that the Muslims were convicted. "Convict '40 Moors' in Courtroom Riot," *Chicago Defender*, March 16, 1935, A24.

7. Ibid.

8. Ibid.

9. Ibid.; "Capt. Palczynski a Chicago Policeman for Fifty Years," *Chicago Tribune,* March 6, 1935, A10.

10. *Chicago Tribune,* March 8, 1935, A04.

11. FBI HQ file on Elijah Muhammad.

12. Bontemps, *Anyplace but Here,* 224–25. FBI HQ file on Elijah Muhammad. Muhammad was so convinced of this that he and his wife reportedly never applied for a Social Security card. The FBI files report two different Social Security numbers for Elijah Muhammad, but neither matched his name when run through the Social Security Death Index (SSDI).

13. W. Muhammad, *As the Light Shineth from the East,* 19.

14. Ibid.; also see E. D. Beynon, "The Voodoo Cult Among," New Migrants in Detroit," *American Journal of Sociology* 43, no. 6 (May 1938): 900.

15. Although Muhammad said that he was unaware of even a ballpark figure on the size of the NOI's membership (though he ventured a guess periodically), the FBI intercepted several conversations in which he noted the high rate of attrition.

16. FBI HQ file on Elijah Muhammad; Muhammad, *Message to the Blackman,* 290–94.

17. Excerpts from lectures obtained by FBI in raid on Muhammad's home (contained in main file); Hakim, *Theology of Time,* 98–102; "Girl Recounts Lore of Islam," *Detroit Free Press,* April 26, 1934, A01.

18. Beynon, "Voodo Cult," 905.

19. By Muhammad's own estimate, more than 75 percent of the NOI's members turned against him during this period. Lee, *The Nation of Islam,* 25, citing Sahib, "The Nation of Islam," 80.

20. Benjamin Muhammad's story was frequently rerun in *Muhammad Speaks.* See "One Day the Messenger of Allah Knocked on My Door," *Muhammad Speaks,* March 1965; Barboza, *American Jihad,* 79–82.

21. "Moslem Goes on Trial Here," *Washington Times Herald,* November 25, 1942, A12; "Negro Moslem Cult Preaches Hate; Japs Believed Inciting 10,000 Weird Members," NEA News Service, August 20, 1942, included in Subsection A (newspaper articles) of the FBI HQ file on Elijah Muhammad (100–6582–A).

22. One of Malcolm X's brothers, for example, suffered a nervous breakdown after he was expelled. Similarly, Kallatt Muhammad suffered a nervous breakdown after he was refused readmittance to the NOI.

23. "Death Rituals Revived in City by Voodoo Cult; Woman Bares Threat of Impending Double Human Sacrifice," *Detroit Free Press,* January 19, 937, A01.

24. Ibid.

25. Ibid.; "Voodoo Probe in City Widens; Wife Says Husband Planned Sacrifice," *Detroit Free Press,* January 20, 1937, A04.

26. Ibid. "Jap Cult Head Seized by U.S.; Inter-Race Racket Is Under Inquiry," *Detroit Free Press,* June 28, 1939, A01.

27. Prison Intake Report on Elijah Muhammad. Aaron Bogans was married to Tommie Poole. See FBI HQ file on Elijah Muhammad, section 12, Biographical Data (in Correlation Summary of April 9, 1969).

28. Ibid.

29. FBI HQ file on Takahashi; FBI HQ file on SDOO, vol. 1.

30. "'Black Hitler' Jailed to Await Sentence," *New York Times,* January 16, 1935, A07; "Harlem's 'Hitler' Hoodwinks 'G' Men in Deportation," *The Afro-American,* June 29, 1935, A03; "Injuction Halts 'Black Hitlerites'; Justice Cotillo Forbids Sufi Abdul Hamid's Followers to Picket in Harlem," *New York Times,* July 16, 1935, A16; Hill, *The FBI's RACON,* 667; Watts, *God, Harlem U.S.A.,* 118; Weisbrot, *Father Divine,* 134–35.

31. Ibid., *New York Times.*

32. Ibid.; "Plane Crash Fatal to 'Harlem Hitler,'" *New York Times,* August 1, 1938, A01.

33. "Divine Is Deserted by His Head 'Angel,'" *New York Times,* April 22, 1937, A01; supra, note 30.

34. "Father Divine Routed out by Police From Hiding Place Behind Furnace," *New York Times,* April 23, 1937, A01.

35. Ibid.

36. Ibid.

37. Supra, note 30.

38. FBI HQ Racial Conditions in the United States (RACON) file; "Revenge All Planned by Harlem Fuehrer," *New York Times,* September 16, 1942, A16.

39. "Five Who Urged Revolt in Harlem and Aid to Japanese Are Indicted," *New York Times,* September 15, 1942, A01; "Four Face Court In Sedition Plot," *New York Times,* December 15, 1942, A16; "Filipino Accuses Jordan; Charges Negro on Trial for Sedition Said He Worked for Japanese Consulate," *New York Times,* December 18, 1942, A20; "Agent for Japan Turns on Jordan," *New York Times,* December 19, 1942, A06.

40. Ibid.; also see "4 Harlem Fascists Deny Sedition Talk; Jordan and Co-Defendants Call Transcripts of Voice Records Only Partly Correct," *New York Times,* December 29, 1942, A42.

41. FBI HQ file on Takahashi.

42. Ibid.

43. Ibid.

44. Ibid.; also see "Jap Cult Head Seized by U.S.; Inter-Race Racket Is Under Inquiry," *Detroit Free Press,* June 28, 1939, A01.

45. Ibid.; also see "Cult's Jap Leader Under $2,000 Bond," *Detroit Free Press,* June 30, 1939, A09; "U.S. Jury Convicts Jap in Bribe Offer; Propagandist Facing Incitement Count," *Detroit Free Press,* September 28, 1939, A03.

46. Ibid.; also see "Jap Agent's Seizure Shed Light on Race Plot of the '30s," *Detroit Free Press,* August 3, 1942, A01.

47. FBI HQ file on Takahashi.

48. Supra, note 1.

49. FBI HQ file on Takahashi.

50. Ibid.

51. Powers, *Secrecy and Power,* 238–39; Hoover, *Masters of Deceit,* 75; Hill, *The FBI's RACON,* 675.

52. Estimate based on FBI figures released to author.

53. Platt, *The Politics of Riot Commissions,* 211.

54. FBI HQ file on Elijah Muhammad.

55. Ibid.

56. FBI HQ file on Takahashi.

57. Ibid.

58. Ibid.; see, in general, Hill, *The FBI's RACON.*

59. Prange, *At Dawn We Slept,* 4.

60. Castleden, *World History,* 546.

61. *American Military History* (ROTC Manual), 378–79.

62. FBI HQ file on Takahashi.

63. Powers, *Secrecy and Power,* 247–49.

64. FBI HQ file on Elijah Muhammad, memo from Berge to director dated April 21, 1942, 1; Hill, *The FBI's RACON,* 17–35.

65. Ibid., Berge memo.

7: MOLES IN THE MOSQUE

1. Niccolò Machiavelli, *The Prince,* trans. Luigi Ricci (New York: New American Library, 1980), 50.

2. William Shakespeare, *The Life of Henry V,* ed. Louis B. Wright and Virginia A. Lamar (New York: Washington Square Press 1960), act II, scene ii.

3. FBI HQ file on Elijah Muhammad, section 2, 40–41. This letter, along with dozens more, was transcribed after the Bureau arrested Elijah Muhammad on September 20, 1942.

4. Ibid.

5. Ibid.

6. Lochner, *The Goebbels Diaries,* 209.

7. FBI HQ file on Elijah Muhammad, section 2.

8. Muhammad, *Message to the Blackman,* 264; Barboza, *American Jihad,* 79–82.

9. "Mohammed of U Street Faces Court on Draft Evasion Charges," *Washington Star,* May 9, 1942, A01; "Moslem Goes on Trial Here; Disciples Hear Bogans Testify in Draft Case," *Washington Times-Herald,* November 25, 1942, A07.

10. "Paul Robeson Sings Here Tomorrow," *Washington Post,* May 9, 1942, A18; "Robeson to Sing Spirituals and Arias in Benefit Sunday," *Washington Times,* May 8, 1942, A-BB.

11. FBI HQ file on Elijah Muhammad, memo from Ladd to Tamm dated May 5, 1942.

12. "Bond of $5,000 Is Set for Moslem Leader," *Washington Star,* May 21, 1942, B01.

13. FBI HQ file on Elijah Muhammad.

14. Ibid.

15. Ibid.

16. Ibid.

17. "Moslems Demand Jail to Be with Leader," *Washington News,* June 4, 1942, A41.

18. FBI HQ file on Elijah Muhammad; "$5,000 in Cash Donated to Free 'Mohammed,'" *Washington Star,* July 24, 1942, A04.

19. FBI HQ file on SDOO, vol. 2, memo dated June 2, 1942.

20. Ibid., memo from Indianapolis to FBI HQ dated September 9, 1944.

21. "Cult Leader Out on Bond in Draft Case," *Washington Post*, July 24, 1942, A04.

22. "Moslem Bailed on Draft Charge; Wears Desert Robes Into District Court," *Washington Times-Herald*, July 24, 1942, A03.

23. FBI HQ file on Elijah Muhammad, memo from Rosen to Tamm dated August 21, 1942.

24. FBI HQ file on Elijah Muhammad, letter from from Dorothy X to Elijah Muhammad dated Sep. 7, 1942.

25. "'Moslem' Sect's Membership Declining Under Prosecution; Two More Followers Get Jail for Failure to Register for Draft," *Washington Star*, December 19, 1942, A19.

26. FBI HQ file on Takahashi; "FBI to Bring Guzman Here; Linked to Japs," *Washington Post*, August 2, 1942, A09; "Draft Evasion Charges Face DeGuzman," *Washington Post*, August 14, 1942, A08; "Two Cities to Try DeGuzman," *Washington Post*, August 21, 1942, A15.

27. FBI HQ file on Elijah Muhammad.

28. Ibid.

29. "FBI Seizes Key Woman in Cults, Seeks to Trace Japanese Funds," *New York Times*, September 23, 1942, A27.

30. Ibid.

31. Ibid.

32. Muhammad, *Our Saviour Has Arrived*, 162–63.

33. FBI HQ file on Elijah Muhammad, memo from Washington field office to HQ dated June 19, 1943, 10.

34. Muhammad was carrying a clipping from the *Detroit Free Press* regarding Takahashi's arrest.

35. Hill, *The FBI's RACON*, 705.

36. FBI HQ file on Elijah Muhammad; Hill, *The FBI's RACON*, "Chronology of Events," 683–719. Linn Karriem's given name was Henry Freeman. He was given the new name by Wallace D. Fard, according to an FBI interview with Karriem following his arrest on September 20, 1942. Freeman's relationship with the Messenger began when their fathers met in Havanah, Arkansas. See Chapter 1 of this book.

37. Ibid.

38. Ibid.

39. FBI Chicago field office file on Elijah Muhammad; FBI HQ file on Elijah Muhammad.

40. Ibid.

41. Ibid. Similar damaging statements were used against other black nationalists. For example, during Leonard R. Jordan's trial on September 15, 1942, an informant attributed the following statement to Jordan: "No one should be afraid to join this movement [PME]. We are protected by big people. This is an international setup. I was sent here to organize you people. Our present main office is in Hawaii. We are connected with the Black Dragon organization in Japan." See "Revenge All Planned by Harlem Fuehrer," *New York Times*, September 16, 1942, A16.

42. Ibid.

43. "Four Face Court in Sedition Plot," *New York Times*, December 15, 1942, A03; "Filipino Witness Accuses Jordan," *New York Times*, December 18, 1942, A07; Hill, *The FBI's RACON*.

44. Hill, *The FBI's RACON*.

45. FBI HQ file on the MSTA, memo dated February 17, 1943.

46. FBI HQ file on Wallace D. Fard; FBI Chicago field office file on Wallace D. Fard.

47. Platt, *Politics of Riot Commissions*, 202.

48. Ibid., 206.

49. Ibid., "Detroit 1943"; also see FBI HQ file on SDOO, memo from Detroit to HQ dated December 19, 1933 (meeting places).

50. Platt, *Politics of Riot Commissions*, 202.

51. Ibid.; also see Pfeffer, *A. Philip Randolph*, 87.

52. Platt, *Politics of Riot Commissions*, 211

53. Ibid., 199–200; Thurgood Marshall, "The Gestapo in Detroit," *Crisis* 50 (1943): 232–33.

54. Hill, *The FBI's RACON*, 209.

55. "6 Cult Members Jailed for Draft Evasion," *Washington Evening Star*, April 7, 1943, A06.

56. Barboza, *American Jihad*, 268–71; Hakim, *True History of Elijah Muhammad*, 66–67.

57. Parole Report on Elijah Muhammad.

58. Ibid., report dated September 19, 1943.

59. Ibid.

60. Ibid.

61. Ibid.

62. Muhammad, *How to Eat to Live*, book 1, 54–55.

63. Author's interviews.

64. Author's interviews with Axford.

65. Ibid.

66. Ibid.; FBI HQ file on Elijah Muhammad; Hakim, *Theology of Time*, 26; cf. Jabril Muhammad, *This Is the One*, 168–69.

67. Terkel, *Coming of Age*, 240–47.

68. Ibid.

69. FBI HQ file on Elijah Muhammad; Barboza, *American Jihad*, 268–71.

70. Marsh, *From Black Muslims to Muslims*, 117.

71. FBI HQ file on Elijah Muhammad, Parole Report.

72. Ibid.

73. Muhammad attributed his brother's death to the chastisement of God over a decade-old disagreement. See Muhammad, *Message to the Blackman*, 264.

74. Ibid., 212.

8. KAABALLAH

1. Lewis, *W. E. B. DuBois*, 568.

2. Griffin, *Black Like Me*, 127.

3. Ralph Ellison, *Invisible Man* (New York: Vintage Books, 1981), 502.

4. Muhammad, *The Supreme Wisdom*, vol. 2, 20.

5. Ibid., 42–43; Muhammad, *Our Saviour Has Arrived*, 92, 190.

6. Cushmeer, *This Is the One*, 126. As for the contention by the Black Hebrews that the "original Jews" were dark-skinned Africans, see Greenberg, *The Moses Mystery*; Osman, *The House of the Messiah*; Bierlein, *Parallel Myths*; and Ben-Jochannan, *We the Black Jews*.

7. "Negroes to Bring Cause Before U.N.," *New York Times*, October 12, 1947, A52; "Negro Plea Up Thursday," *New York Times*, October 19, 1947, A48; "U.N. Gets Charges of Wide Bias in U.S.," *New York Times*, October 24, 1947, A09.

8. Ibid.

9. Ibid.

10. Ibid.

11. As a former Garveyite, Muhammad surely must have had knowledge of the origins of Liberia. Garvey spoke of it repeatedly. "The only thing for the

Negro to do is get a country of his own—Liberia—where the red, black, and green can practice socialism itself." FBI HQ file on Marcus Garvey, memo dated February 28, 1923; O'Reilly, *Black Americans*, 161.

12. FBI HQ file on Elijah Muhammad. Other mosques had paltry memberships as well. When Malcolm X arrived in Harlem in 1954, he observed that "one bus couldn't have been filled with the Muslims in New York City!" Haley, *Autobiography of Malcolm X*, 217.

13. Hakim, *True History of Elijah Muhammad*, 223–28; Muhammad, *Theology of Time*, vol. 1, 31–32.

14. Author's interviews with Wilfred Little; Strickland, *Malcolm X: Make It Plain*, 60.

15. Ibid.

16. Haley, *Autobiography of Malcolm X*, 169, 186, 196. Copies of some of Malcolm's replies to Muhammad's letters are contained in the FBI's HQ file on Malcolm X.

17. Ibid., 155–57.

18. Lee, *By Any Means Necessary*, 48–49; Haley, *Autobiography of Malcolm X*, 1–22; Vincent, "The Garveyite Parents of Malcolm X," *The Black Scholar*, March/April, 1989, 10–13.

19. Lee, *By Any Means Necessary*; Haley, *Autobiography of Malcolm X*, 393–94.

20. FBI New York file on Malcolm X. Haley, *Autobiography of Malcolm X*, 393–94.

21. *Springfield Union*, April 21, 1951, A01.

22. Haley, *Autobiography of Malcolm X*, 198–201.

23. Ibid., 212–15.

24. Ibid.

25. FBI NYC file on Malcolm X.

26. FBI HQ file on Joseph Gravitt Jr., vol. 1.

27. Ibid., memo from New York field office dated February 26, 1959.

28. Ibid.

29. FBI HQ file on the MSTA.

30. Lee, *By Any Means Necessary*, 65.

31. FBI HQ on Joseph Gravitt Jr.

32. Ibid.

33. FBI HQ file on Elijah Muhammad.

34. Based on court records; also see FBI HQ file on Elijah Muhammad; "Rival Leader Tells of Efforts to Convert Black Muslims," *New York Times,* January 21, 1973, A10.

35. FBI HQ file on Elijah Muhammad.

36. Ibid.

37. Ibid.

38. Ibid.

39. Hill, *The FBI's RACON,* 17–24; Evanzz, *The Judas Factor,* 36.

40. FBI HQ file on Elijah Muhammad; U.S. Army's file on Elijah Muhammad.

41. Supra, note 39.

42. FBI NYC file on Malcolm X.

43. Ibid.

44. Ibid.

45. New York Police Department BOSSI file on Malcolm X.

46. The practice extends as far back as the late 1930s. By the late 1960s, the CIA was equally involved, and also launched its own domestic counterintelligence programs, among them Operation MERRIMAC, Operation RESISTANCE, and Operation CHAOS. See the *Church Committee Report,* book 3, 220–23, 252–55 (Ghetto Informants Program), 681–92 (CIA domestic operations); also see David Stafford, *Camp X* (New York: Dodd, Mead 1986).

47. While Marshall's name is inextricably linked to the success of *Brown,* the legal team also included Robert L. Carter, George Hayes, Jack Greenberg, Spottswood Robinson III, and Dr. Kenneth Clark.

48. See, generally, Patterson, *We Charge Genocide.*

49. *New York Times,* February 2, 1952, A10.

50. *New York Times,* January 14, 1954, A17.

51. *New York Times,* April 11, 1954, A56.

52. Muhammad viewed any effort to integrate society as evidence of "tricknology."

53. Bergman and Bergman, *Chronological History of the Negro in America,* 536.

54. Ibid., 538.

55. Magida, *Prophet of Rage,* 31–32.

56. Ibid.

57. Author's interviews with former members of Harlem mosque. Alvan, who later changed his name to Shuib Farrakhan, died on October 15, 1994. The

Million Man March, held on October 16, 1995, was rumored to be Farrakhan's tribute to his brother.

58. Magida, *Prophet of Rage*, 31–32.

59. FBI HQ file on Elijah Muhammad.

60. See, in general, Hoover, *Masters of Deceit*; Garrow, *Bearing the Cross*; and Nolan, *Communism versus the Negro*.

61. "The Lord God of Islam taught me that in 1555 a devil by the name of John Hawkins . . . brought the first of our parents here for slave purposes." Muhammad, *Message to the Blackman*, 230. "Their [Caucasian] being loose [free] to deceive the nations of the earth would refer to the time A.D. 1555 to 1955, during which they were loose to travel over the earth and deceive the people." Muhammad, *The Supreme Wisdom*, vol. 1, 43; Muhammad, *Our Saviour Has Arrived*, 92–94.

62. FBI NYC file on Malcolm X.

63. Ibid.

64. FBI's JUNE (wiretap) Mail file on Elijah Muhammad.

65. Ibid.

66. "Army Feared King, Secretly Watched Him; Spying on Blacks Started 75 Years Ago," *Commercial Appeal* (Memphis), March 21, 1993, A01.

67. Ibid., A08.

68. "Six Charged in Midnight Melee Aboard Train Here; Held Without Bond; 3 Policemen Injured During Silver Spring Fight With Cultists," *Washington Post*, February 25, 1951, A13.

69. FBI HQ file on Elijah Muhammad.

70. Ibid.; FBI NY file on Malcolm X; also see Goldman, *Death and Life of Malcolm X*, 56–59.

71. BOSSI file on Malcolm X; Strickland, *Malcolm X: Make It Plain*, 77.

72. FBI NYC file on Malcolm X.

73. See, in general, Garrow, *Bearing the Cross*.

74. Ibid.

75. Bergman and Bergman, *Chronological History of the Negro*, 545.

76. FBI NYC file on Haley, *Autobiography of Malcolm X*, 222–25.

77. FBI HQ file on Elijah Muhammad.

78. Ibid. Copies of Muhammad's column are included in the main file.

79. *Pittsburgh Courier*, November 16, 1957, 10.

80. FBI HQ file on Malcolm X. Copies of Malcolm X's column are included in the main file.

81. The newspaper was more adversely affected than the NOI. Its circulation plunged after Muhammad's column was dropped.

82. FBI HQ file on Elijah Muhammad.

83. FBI HQ file on Wallace D. Muhammad.

84. Ibid.

85. Ibid.

86. FBI HQ file on Elijah Muhammad.

87. Ibid.; FBI HQ file on Wallace Muhammad.

88. FBI NYC file on Malcolm X.

89. FBI HQ file on Malcolm X.

90. Ibid.

91. Ibid.

92. FBI HQ file on Joseph Gravitt Jr.; FBI HQ file on the MSTA.

93. Captain Joseph was appointed East Coast director of the NOI in early 1960, making him one of the top ten leaders of the sect.

9: Arabesque

1. Hitler, *Mein Kampf,* 313.

2. Lincoln, *Black Muslims in America,* 166.

3. Statement made in Harlem on September 2, 1998, on the eve of the Million Youth March. The march was one of two so-called Million Youth marches; the other was sponsored by a coalition of civil rights leaders and took place in Atlanta. See "March Head Blasts Jews," *New York Daily News,* September 3, 1998, A04; also see "Baltimore College Will Allow Controversial Muslim to Speak," *Washington Post,* February 3, 1994, A17.

4. FBI HQ file on Elijah Muhammad (newspaper clippings).

5. Oddly, statements regarding the mail cover are redacted in the FBI files on Elijah Muhammad, but were uncensored in the FBI HQ file on Joseph Gravitt Jr.

6. FBI HQ file on Elijah Muhammad, memo from Baltimore SAC to Chicago SAC dated March 15, 1959; FBI NY file on Malcolm X, section 14, serial 1100–70, Baltimore SAC to Chicago SAC, March 15, 1959, 20.

7. Saviour's Day address (audiocassette); FBI HQ file on Elijah Muhammad.

8. Ibid.; also see Lomax, *Negro Revolt,* 178–81.

9. Ibid.; also see Lincoln, *The Black Muslims,* 224–26.

10. "Nasser Says UAR Will End 'Imperialism,'" *Washington Post*, September 5, 1958.

11. "Seven Nations Recognize New Arab Republic," *Washington Post*, February 24, 1958; "Nasser Hailed on Syria Visit," *Washington Post*, February 25, 1958.

12. "Syria Charges Saud Plotted to Kill Nasser," *Washington Post*, March 6, 1958; Andrew, *For the President's Eyes Only*, 223–27.

13. Ibid.; also see "Cairo Talks of Moslem 'World Court' to Try Saud," *Washington Post, March 9*, 1958; "Nasser Assails Ike's 'Doctrine,'" *Washington Post*, March 21, 1958.

14. FBI NY file on Malcolm X.

15. Ibid.; FBI HQ file on Elijah Muhammad; also see *New York Courier*, March 8, 1958, A07.

16. Ibid.

17. Ibid.

18. "Fisur" file on Malcolm X; FBI HQ file on Elijah Muhammad; FBI NY file on Malcolm X.

19. New York Police Department BOSSI file on Malcolm X.

20. FBI HQ file on Adam Clayton Powell Jr.; FBI HQ file on Malcolm X; also see *Pittsburgh Courier*, July 20, 1957.

21. BOSSI file on Malcolm X.

22. "Moslems Feast Two Days in New York," *Pittsburgh Courier*, July 27, 1957, A05; FBI JUNE (wiretape) Mail file on Elijah Muhammad.

23. Ibid.

24. *Los Angeles Herald Tribune*, February 27, 1958.

25. "Syrians Protest to U.N. on Israel," *New York Times*, May 14, 1957; "Israel Bridge Debated in U.N.; Syria Charges Border Span Could Transport Troops to Demilitarized Zone," *New York Times*, May 24, 1957.

26. BOSSI file on MX, memo dated July 23, 1959.

27. "Mr. Muhammad Speaks," *Pittsburgh Courier*, February 18, 1958, A05.

28. FBI file on Wallace D. Fard; also see *Los Angeles Herald Dispatch*, April 10, 1958.

29. Ibid.

30. Ibid.

31. *Sepia*, October 1957.

32. FBI HQ file on Elijah Muhammad; FBI NY file on Malcolm X.

33. Ibid.

34. FBI HQ file on Elijah Muhammad. Muhammad also spoke lightheartedly about himself as "Papa" when addressing Malcolm as his son. See JUNE mail file on Elijah Muhammad; also see Collins, *Seventh Child*, 135–36.

35. "New York Cops Rip Moslem Leader's Home, Land in Hospital," *Los Angeles Herald Tribune*, May 22, 1958, 1, 40. "New York Muslims Repulse Fascist Attack," *Los Angeles Herald Dispatch*, May 29, 1958, 1.

36. Ibid.

37. Ibid., June 26, 1958; also see FBI Chicago file on Wallace D. Fard; FBI NY file on Malcolm X.

38. FBI HQ file on Elijah Muhammad; also see, Haley, *Autobiography of Macolm X,* 206.

39. Supra, note 35; FBI NY file on Malcolm X.

40. "Hanafi Massacre," *Washingtonian,* February 1980, 87–88; Hakim, *True History,* 226–30; "Rival Leader Tells of Efforts to Convert Black Muslims," *New York Times,* January 31, 1973; "Hanafi Muslim Chief Quit Key Muslim Post," *Washington Post,* February 2, 1973, A01.

41. Ibid.; FBI HQ file on Elijah Muhammad.

42. Evanzz, *The Judas Factor,* 88–92; also see "Text of Talks by Lodge, Wagner, and Khrushchev at Luncheon Given by City," *New York Times,* September 18, 1959, A16.

43. Ibid.

44. "Nasser Donates to U.S. Moslems; Two Midwesterners Fulfill Mission in Cairo—Imams Will Be Sent to Teach," *New York Times,* September 20, 1959, A21; "Despite Worldwide Growth, Muslims Are Still Scarce in the U.S.," *Baltimore Sun,* April 9, 1979, A14.

45. FBI HQ file on Elijah Muhammad; FBI HQ file on Malcolm X; also see "Notables," *New York Courier,* July 19, 1958.

46. Ibid.; also see "The Black Supremacists," *Time,* August 10, 1959, 24–25.

47. *Pittsburgh Courier,* August 2, 1958, 14.

48. FBI HQ file on Malcolm X; also see *Los Angeles Herald Dispatch,* August 7, 1958.

49. FBI HQ file on Elijah Muhammad, section 3; JUNE Mail file on Elijah Muhammad.

50. Ibid.

51. Ibid.

52. *Los Angeles Herald Tribune,* April 16, 1959, 1.

53. FBI HQ file on Betty Shabazz; FBI NY file on Malcolm X; Public Source Material file on the NOI.

54. FBI HQ file on Malcolm X.

55. FBI NY file on Malcolm X.

56. BOSSI file on Malcolm X, memo dated May 6, 1959.

57. BOSSI file on Malcolm X.

58. Ibid.

59. CIA file on Elijah Muhammad.

60. FBI HQ file on Elijah Muhammad, section 3, memo dated May 26, 1959.

61. Ibid.

62. FBI NY file on Malcolm X; FBI HQ file on Elijah Muhammad.

63. Ibid.

64. CIA file on Elijah Muhammad, memo dated February 10, 1960, quoting from the FBI's memo of June 5, 1959.

65. "UAR Envoy Here Reported Named," *Washington Post,* March 27, 1958.

66. FBI HQ file on Elijah Muhammad.

67. Ibid.

68. "The Hate that Hate Produced," excerpts of which appear in transcript form in the FBI HQ file on Elijah Muhammad; also see "Wallace's Guide to the 'Black Supremacy' Movement Challenged by Experts," *New York Times,* July 22, 1959, A53.

69. Ibid.

70. "Egypt's Nasser Dares Israel to Attack," *U.S. News & World Report,* August 10, 1959, 20.

71. "Dr. King, Keating Blast Muslims Group," *Pittsburgh Courier,* August 29, 1959, 6.

72. "The Rev. Abernathy Says: 'Working for Brotherhood . . . Not Black Supremacy,'" *Pittsburgh Courier,* May 30, 1959, section 2, 1.

73. "The Hate That Hate Produced"; FBI NY file on Malcolm X.

74. Supra, note 71.

75. Lincoln, *Black Muslims,* 129; "S. B. Fuller New Courier Board Member," *Pittsburgh Courier,* July 18, 1959, 2; also see "Banquet Ends Fuller Confab," *Pittsburgh Courier,* August 22, 1959, 4–5.

76. BOSSI file on Malcolm X.

77. Ibid.

78. Ibid.

79. "Arabs Send Warm Greetings to 'Our Brother' of Color in U.S.A.; Malcolm X Finds Africans, Arabs Fret More About Us Than Selves," *Pittsburgh Courier,* August 15, 1959, magazine section, 1

80. FBI HQ file on Elijah Muhammad.

81. Also see "Muslim Leader Calls Moslem Leader 'Phony,'" *New York Amsterdam News,* October 30, 1959, 11; "Singer Lashes Mike Wallace; Dakota Says There's No Connection 'Tween Her Faith, Muhammad," *Pittsburgh Courier,* August 1, 1959, 10.

82. "Is New York Sitting on a 'Powder Keg'?" *U.S. News & World Report,* August 3, 1959, 48–51.

83. Supra, note 46.

84. Muhammad steadfastedly denied that he was hiding under the bed. See Cushmeer, *This Is the One,* 68.

85. BOSSI file on Malcolm X.

86. Ibid.

10: Compromised

1. Theodore Dreiser, *An American Tragedy* (New York: Signet, 1964), 85.

2. "Lip-Profession," Holy Quran; trans. Maulana Muhammad Ali, 10.

3. "Baltimore College Will Allow Controversial Muslim to Speak," *Washington Post,* February 3, 1994, a17.

4. "Negro Cult School in Detroit Closed," *New York Times,* A08.

5. FBI HQ file on Elijah Muhammad.

6. FBI JUNE (wiretap) mail file on Elijah Muhammad; FBI NY file on Malcolm X.

7. Ibid.

8. Ibid.

9. "White Man Is God for Cult of Islam," *Chicago New Crusader,* August 15, 1959, 1.

10. FBI NY file on Malcolm X; FBI HQ file on Elijah Muhammad.

11. Ibid.

12. FBI HQ file on Elijah Muhammad; also see Collins, *Seventh Child,* 213–18.

13. "Stoner Accuses Blacks, Jews of Plotting against Whites," United Press International, May 30, 1990; "Racist Group Claims Bombs Avenge Rape, Pledges More Killings," *Washington Times,* December 29, 1989, A01.

14. Supra, note 12.

15. FBI HQ file on Elijah Muhammad.

16. Ibid.

17. Ibid.

18. Ibid.

19. Ibid.

20. "Marshall Calls 'Moslem' Leaders 'Lawless' Thugs," *Chicago Defender,* October 24, 1959, 1.

21. FBI NY file on Malcolm X, summary of statements dated May 15, 1960, 17.

22. Ibid.; also see FBI HQ file on Elijah Muhammad.

23. FBI HQ file on Elijah Muhammad.

24. Author's interviews with Ella Collins and her son, Rodnell P. Collins; also see FBI NY file on Malcolm X.

25. JUNE Mail file on Elijah Muhammad.

26. Ibid.

27. Supra, note 24.

28. FBI NYC file on Malcolm X, memo dated October 15, 1959; FBI HQ file on Elijah Muhammad.

29. Supra, note 24; also see Collins, *Seventh Child,* 134–35.

30. Ibid.

31. FBI JUNE Mail file on Elijah Muhammad; FBI HQ file on Evelyn Lorene Williams.

32. Ibid.

33. FBI HQ file on Elijah Muhammad, section 5, summary report dated March 30, 1960.

34. Ibid.

35. Ibid.

36. Ibid.

37. The "U" was a code to indicate that the document was "unclassified."

38. CIA and U.S. Army intelligence files on Elijah Muhammad, Akbar Muhammad, and Herbert Muhammad.

39. Hirst and Beeson, *Sadat,* 87–88; "Anwar Sadat," *Current Biography 1971,* 358–61.

40. Ibid.; also see Lincoln, *Black Muslims,* 148–149, and Muhammad, *Our Saviour Has Arrived,* 8, 71, 76, 160–67.

41. Hakim, *Theology of Time,* 339.

42. Army Intelligence file on Elijah Muhammad, memo from U.S. Army Staff Communications Office to Washington, January 7, 1960, 1; FBI HQ file on Elijah Muhammad, section 4, memo from Chicago SAC to HQ, dated January 13–14, 1960.

43. "Muhammad Speaks," *Los Angeles Herald Dispatch,* January 14, 1960, A01.

44. Supra, note 42.

45. "Muhammad Speaks," *Los Angeles Herald Tribune,* January 14, 1960.

46. FBI JUNE Mail file on Elijah Muhammad.

47. Ibid.; FBI JUNE Mail file on Clara Muhammad.

48. Ibid.

49. FBI HQ file on Clara Muhammad; FBI NY file on Malcolm X.

50. Ibid.

51. FBI HQ and JUNE Mail file on Clara Muhammad.

52. FBI HQ file on Elijah Muhammad; FBI HQ file on Ola Hughes.

53. Ibid.

54. FBI HQ file on Clara Muhammad.

55. FBI JUNE Mail file on Clara Muhammad.

56. Author's interviews. Also see JUNE Mail file on Malcolm X. The brother's name has been omitted to protect the privacy of his daughter.

57. FBI NY file on Malcolm X.

58. FBI HQ file on Elijah Muhammad.

59. Ibid.

60. Hauser, *Muhammad Ali,* 91.

61. Author's interviews; also see William Raspberry, "Local Muslim Has Little Patience with the New Black Nationalism," *Washington Post,* June 15, 1966.

62. FBI HQ file on Elijah Muhammad, section 5, memo from Chicago SAC to director dated April 4, 1960.

63 Ibid., section 5, memo dated May 20, 1960.

64. Ibid.

65. FBI June Mail file on Elijah Muhammad, memo dated May 27, 1960.

66. "Stinking to High Heaven," *Time,* March 4, 1996, 30.

67. FBI HQ file on Elijah Muhammad, section 5, summary.

68. A list of Fard's aliases are in Appendix A of this book.

69. FBI HQ file on Elijah Muhammad.

70. FBI HQ file of Malcolm X; Haley, *Autobiography of Malcolm X*, 264.

71. FBI HQ file on Malcolm X.

72. The color selection was also odd because Muhammad taught that the color blue represented "falsehood" and "illusion." Ministers teach that the blue section of the flag represents the sky, which, they say, is an illusion.

73. Eissen-Udom, *Black Nationalism*, 417, n. 76.

74. FBI HQ file on Tynetta Nelson; FBI HQ file on Elijah Muhammad.

75. Ibid.

76. Ibid.

77. Wallace Terry, "Cult of Hate" (part 2 of 6), *Washington Post*, December 12, 1960.

78. Supra, note 74.

79. FBI HQ file on Elijah Muhammad.

80. Hoover, *Masters of Deceit*, 246.

81. FBI HQ file on Nat King Cole.

82. Ibid.

83. FBI HQ file on Lorraine Hansbery, memo dated March 30, 1959.

84. FBI HQ file on Edward Kennedy Ellington.

85. Ibid.

86. FBI HQ file on Mahalia Jackson (cross-reference file).

87. All of the celebrities were direct or indirect subjects of FBI's elaborate filing system. Thus, even though the Bureau claimed that it did not have a direct file on Ellington, Jackson, and others, the fact that it produced "cross-referenced material" with the names of the subjects highlighted suggests that its interest in monitoring their activities was more than merely casual.

88. Lucy, Einstein, and others were suspected members of the Communist Party, but Einstein's efforts on behalf of Israel also played a role in the Bureau's monitoring of his activities.

89. FBI HQ file on Elijah Muhammad.

90. Ibid.

91. Ibid.; FBI NY file on Malcolm X.

92. Haley, *Autobiography of Malcolm X*, 9–10.

93. Carson, *Malcolm X: The FBI File*, 65, 203–4; Perry, *Malcolm X: The Last Speeches*, 135–36.

11: BLACK MACBETH

1. *Macbeth* (New York: Washington Square Press, 1964), act IV, scene iii.

2. Abraham Lincoln to Joshua F. Speed, August 24, 1855, cited in Seldes, *The Great Quotations,* 422. Italics in original.

3. This tenet was central to Fard's so-called "Five-Percent" theory. See FBI HQ file on the Five-Percenters; Lee, *By Any Means Necessary,* 58–59.

4. FBI HQ file on Raymond Sharrieff; FBI HQ file on Elijah Muhammad.

5. Ibid.

6. FBI HQ file on Elijah Muhammad.

7. Ibid.; also see FBI HQ file on Raymond Sharrieff.

8. FBI HQ file on Elijah Muhammad; FBI HQ file on Elijah Muhammad Jr.

9. FBI HQ file on Ethel Muhammad; FBI HQ file on Raymond Sharrieff; FBI HQ file on Elijah Muhammad.

10. Ibid.; also see FBI HQ file on Malcolm X.

11. FBI NY file on Malcolm X.

12. Ibid.; also see Betty Shabazz, "Loving and Losing Malcolm," *Essence,* February 1992.

13. Ibid.

14. FBI HQ file on Elijah Muhammad; FBI NY file on Malcolm X.

15. FBI HQ file on Elijah Muhammad.

16. Ibid.

17. Author's interviews.

18. FBI HQ file on Alex Haley.

19. *Chicago American,* July 29, 1959, 12.

20. *Chicago Daily News,* July 29, 1959.

21. FBI NY file on Malcolm X.

22. FBI HQ file on Malcolm X.

23. Muhammad constantly changed the date of the demise of European nations. Initially, it was 1914, then 1935, then 1955, 1970, and later 1975. Muhammad, "The Time and the Judgement" (albums 1–3); Wallace Terry, "Cult of Hate" (part 3 of 6), *Washington Post,* December 13, 1960, B03.

24. Public Source Information file on Elijah Muhammad.

25. FBI HQ file on Elijah Muhammad.

26. Ibid.; FBI HQ file on Martin Luther King Jr.; *Church Committee Report,* book 3, 220; Garrow, *Bearing the Cross,* 129–32.

27. See, in general, David Halberstam, *The Best and the Brightest* (New York: Random House, 1969); John Kenneth Galbraith, *Ambassador's Journal: A Personal Account of the Kennedy Years* (Boston: Houghton Mifflin, 1969).

28. "Muslims Give JFK a Fit," *New Jersey Herald Tribune*, February 4, 1961.

29. Ibid.

30. FBI NY file on Muslim Mosque Inc.

31. "Howard Students' Bid to Muslim Canceled," *Washington Post*, February 24, 1961.

32. FBI NY file on Malcolm X, memo from Boston SAC to director.

33. FBI NY file on Malcolm X, section 32.

34. FBI JUNE (wiretap) Mail file on Elijah Muhammad.

35. FBI HQ file on Elijah Muhammad.

36. Ibid.

37. Ibid.

38. Ibid.

39. For reasons which may have had to do with immigration, Naeem was extremely cooperative with the FBI and BOSSI. He is repeatedly identified by name in the BOSSI file on Malcolm as a highly reliable source.

40. Haley, *Autobiography of Malcolm X*, 288.

41. FBI HQ file on Elijah Muhammad, section 6, memo dated October 6, 1961.

42. FBI HQ file on Elijah Muhammad.

43. Ibid.

44. Ibid.; FBI HQ file on Tynetta Nelson.

45. FBI HQ file on Wallace Muhammad.

46. Ibid.

47. Ibid.

48. FBI JUNE Mail file on Clara Muhammad.

49. Ibid.; FBI HQ file on Elijah Muhammad.

50. Ibid.

51. FBI HQ file on Elijah Muhammad.

52. Public Source Material file on Elijah Muhammad.

53. Ibid.

54. FBI HQ file on Elijah Muhammad.

55. Ibid.

56. Ibid.

57. Ibid.; also see Public Source Material file on Elijah Muhammad.

58. FBI Public Source Material file on John Ali, aka John Simmons Jr. Conrad Lynn, an attorney who represented hundreds of Muslims during this period, said that he was appalled when he discovered that the NOI had accepted a donation from Rockwell. "I could not understand, for example, how . . . Elijah could accept twenty-five dollars from George Lincoln Rockwell, leader of the American Nazi Party. It reminded me of Marcus Garvey's acceptance of support from Bilbo in the 1920s." Lynn, *There Is a Fountain,* 187–89.

59. Ibid.

60. Despite Muhammad's assertion that the owners of the *Los Angeles Herald Tribune* disliked Malcolm X and therefore would not lend coverage to the suit, the newspaper was the first to carry a full-length story on the scandal. In a story that ran in the July 10 edition, the paper ran a large photograph of attorney Gladys Root with the two secretaries and their children. "Elijah's Two Paternity Suits—'The Will of Allah,' He Claims," *Los Angeles Herald Tribune,* July 10, 1964, D01. Lucille Rosary was quoted thus: "He told us that under the teaching of the Holy Quran we were not committing adultery and that we were his wives." Author's interviews with members of Muhammad's family; also see Haley, *Autobiography of Malcolm X,* 298–99.

61. FBI HQ file on Clara Muhammad.

62. Ibid.

63. Ibid.; also see FBI HQ file on Herbert Muhammad.

64. FBI HQ file on Elijah Muhammad, section 8.

65. Evanzz, *The Judas Factor,* 117–26; Bontemps, *Anyplace but Here,* 237.

66. Ibid.

67. FBI HQ file on Elijah Muhammad.

68. Ibid. John Shabass is not to be confused with John Shabazz.

69. FBI JUNE Mail file on Elijah Muhammad; also see Karim, *Remembering Malcolm,* 133–38.

70. FBI HQ file on Elijah Muhammad; FBI HQ file on Malcolm X.

71. Public Source Material file on Elijah Muhammad.

72. Supra, note 69.

73. FBI HQ file on Elijah Muhammad.

74. Ibid.

75. Ibid.; FBI HQ file on Tynetta Nelson.

76. FBI HQ file on Clara Muhammad.

77. FBI JUNE Mail file on Elijah Muhammad.

78. FBI HQ file on Elijah Muhammad; also see Shabazz, "Loving and Losing Malcolm."

79. FBI HQ file on Raymond Sharrieff; FBI HQ file on Elijah Muhammad.

80. FBI JUNE Mail file on Elijah Muhammad.

81. Ibid.

82. FBI HQ file on Elijah Muhammad.

83. Ibid.

84. FBI NY file on Malcolm X.

85. Ibid.

86. See Davis, *Malcolm X: The Great Photographs*, 78–85.

87. Public Source Material file on Elijah Muhammad.

88. Ibid.; "Black Muslim Inquiry Tentatively Approved," *Washington Post*, August 15, 1962, A03.

89. Ibid.

90. FBI HQ file on Elijah Muhammad.

91. FBI HQ file on Malcolm X; also see Haley, *Autobiography of Malcolm X*, 284–85.

92. FBI NY file on Malcolm X, memo from New Haven SAC to NYC SAC dated September 21, 1962.

93. FBI HQ file on Elijah Muhammad.

94. *Muhammad Speaks*, December 30, 1962, 4.

95. "Woman Beaten, Nab Son of Muhammad; Says She Was Once Lover of Leader's Son, *Chicago Defender*, October 13–19, 1962, A01.

96. "Muslims Blast 'False Charges,'" *Chicago Defender*, October 20–26, A01.

97. "LA Grand Jury Scores U.S.; Indicts Muslim," *Chicago Defender*, June 3–9, 1961; also see Joint Legislative Committee on Un-American Activities (State of Louisiana), report no. 3, January 9, 1963.

98. FBI JUNE Mail file on Elijah Muhammad.

99. FBI HQ file on Elijah Muhammad, section 4, summary memo dated October 24, 1962.

100. "Black Muslims in Prison: Of Muslim Rites and Constitutional Rights," *Columbia Law Review* 62 (December 1962): 1488.

12: Sons and Lovers

1. Richard Lovelace, "To Althea: From Prison," cited in *Bartlett's Familiar Quotations*, 11th ed. (Boston: Little, Brown, 1968), 358.

2. D. H. Lawrence, *Sons and Lovers* (New York: Viking, 1913; reissued 1972), 388.

3. FBI HQ file on Elijah Muhammad, Search Slip Summary, dated April 9, 1969, 40. In a wiretapped call, Clara said Wallace was released on January 10. FBI main file on Clara Muhammad, memo from Phoenix SAC to Miami SAC dated January 21, 1963, 1–2.

4. FBI HQ file on Elijah Muhammad; FBI HQ file on Clara Muhammad.

5. FBI JUNE (wiretap) Mail file on Elijah Muhammad.

6. Ibid.

7. Ibid.

8. FBI HQ file on Wallace Muhammad; FBI NY file on Malcolm X.

9. Ibid.

10. FBI JUNE Mail file on Elijah Muhammad.

11. FBI HQ file on Wallace Muhammad; Bruce M. Gans, "The Islam Connection," *Playboy*, April 1980, 200.

12. FBI HQ file on Elijah Muhammad; Haley, *Autobiography of Malcolm X*, 265, 290.

13. FBI HQ file on Elijah Muhammad, section 8, summary from Chicago SAC to HQ dated April 5, 1963.

14. FBI HQ file on Malcolm X, memo from Rosen dated February 28, 1963.

15. Ibid.

16. FBI NY file on Malcolm X; Haley, *Autobiography of Malcolm X*, 296–98.

17. FBI HQ file on Elijah Muhammad; FBI NY file on Malcolm X.

18. "Muslim Message," *Washington Post*, February 28, 1963, A07.

19. Author's interviews with members of Malcolm X's family. See, generally, Collins, *Seventh Child*.

20. FBI HQ file on Malcolm X.

21. Haley, *Autobiography of Malcolm X*, 297; Karim, *Remembering Malcolm*, 153.

22. Author's interviews.

23. FBI NY file on Malcolm X; FBI JUNE Mail file on Malcolm X.

24. Haley, *Autobiography of Malcolm X*, 298–99.

25. Ibid., 297.

26. FBI JUNE Mail file on Elijah Muhammad.

27. Ibid.

28. Ibid.

29. FBI HQ file on Akbar Muhammad.

30. A copy of the story appears in the FBI HQ file on Wallace D. Fard (go to http://www.fbi.gov/foipa/fard.htm). Cross was then head of the mathematics department. See William Raspberry, "Local Muslim Has Little Patience with New Black Nationalism," *Washington Post*, June 15, 1966.

31. FBI HQ file on Elijah Muhammad.

32. The letter was also printed on the front page of *Muhammad Speaks* on August 16, 1963; also see "Reports Anger Black Muslims; Did Muhammad Come from Mecca or from Jail?" *Washington Daily News*, August 20, 1963, A05.

33. Cushmeer, *This Is the One*, 70.

34. Supra, note 30.

35. Supra, note 32.

36. FBI HQ file on Elijah Muhammad; FBI HQ file on Malcolm X.

37. "Message to the Grass Roots" (Douglas Recording album, 1963); Breitman, *Malcolm X Speaks*, 3–17; Carson, *Malcolm X: The FBI File*, 229–30; FBI HQ file on Malcolm X.

38. Ibid.

39. FBI NY file on Malcolm X.

40. FBI HQ file on Elijah Muhammad, section 12.

41. Ibid.

42. Ibid.

43. FBI NY file on Malcolm X.

44. "25 Years Later: The Assassination of Malcolm X," videotape produced by Louis Farrkhan during speech at Malcolm X Community College on February 20, 1990.

45. Karim, *Remembering Malcolm*, 159–60; Haley, *Autobiography of Malcolm X*, 308–9.

46. According to speech by Minister Farrakhan.

47. FBI HQ file on Elijah Muhammad.

48. Ibid.; FBI HQ file on Clara Muhammad.

49. FBI JUNE Mail file on Elijah Muhammad, memo from Chicago SAC to director.

50. See *United States v. Clay,* 430 F. 2d. 165 (1970), where the court ruled that "wiretaps of telephone conversations" made in connection with someone else (Muhammad) did not prejudice Muhammad Ali's draft evasion case.

51. *Make It Plain* (documentary), Blackside, 1993, interview with Sharon 10X (aka Amina Rahman), former member of the Harlem mosque.

52. FBI HQ file on Elijah Muhammad.

53. Author's interviews.

54. FBI JUNE Mail file on Elijah Muhammad.

55. FBI NY file on Malcolm X; Strickland, *Malcolm X: Make It Plain,* 145.

56. Ibid.

57. Ibid.

58. Wilfred Little described the expression as a popular West Indian aphorism that Malcolm had used since childhood. But the expression's origins lay in many places: "Curse away! And let me tell thee, Beauseant, a wise proverb the Arabs have,—Curses are like young chickens, and still come home to roost." Edward Bulwer-Lytton, *The Lady of Lyons,* act V, scene ii, cited in *Bartlett's Familiar Quotations,* 425; also see *Brewer's Dictionary of Phrase and Fable,* 261.

59. FBI HQ file on Elijah Muhammad; FBI JUNE Mail file on Elijah Muhammad.

60. There are any number of thorough books on the subject: Bledowska and Bloch, *KGB/CIA*; Hersh, *The Old Boys*; Wise, *The Invisible Government*; Ranelagh, *The Agency*; Phillips, *The Night Watch*.

61. Demaris, *The Director,* 205.

62. FBI JUNE Mail file on Elijah Muhammad.

63. *Make It Plain* (documentary); "Malcolm X Censured for View on JFK," *Washington Post,* December 5, 1963.

64. FBI NY file on Malcolm X; also see Ron Manlana Karenga, "Malcolm and the Messenger: Beyond Psychological Assumptions to Political Analysis," *Black News* 4, no. 21 (1983): 4–11.

65. FBI HQ file on Elijah Muhammad.

66. Ibid., memo from Phoenix SAC to director dated December 6, 1963.

67. FBI JUNE Mail file on Elijah Muhammad.

68. Ibid.

69. Ibid.

70. Ibid.

71. FBI NY file on Malcolm X; FBI HQ file on Wallace Muhammad.

72. Ibid.

73. Karim, *Remembering Malcolm,* 156.

74. FBI JUNE Mail file on Clara Muhammad.

75. Ibid.

76. FBI JUNE Mail file on Elijah Muhammad.

77. Ibid.

78. Supra, note 44; Magida, *Prophet of Rage,* 76–78.

79. FBI NY file on Malcolm X; Clarke, *Malcolm X: The Man and His Times,* 182–205.

80. FBI HQ file on Malcolm X.

81. FBI HQ file on Elijah Muhammad, memo from Black to Sullivan dated February 7, 1964.

82. FBI NY file on Muslim Mosque Inc., section 57.

13: Devil's Disciples

1. "Envy: The Mother of Murder," *The Final Call,* January 25, 1995 (Farrakhan's column). Reprint, August 20, 1996, 20–21.

2. Nikolai Gogol, *Dead Souls,* trans. Bernard Guilbert Guerney (New York: Modern Library, 1965), 332.

3. FBI HQ file on Malcolm X; Haley, *Autobiography of Malcolm X,* 304.

4. Interviews with former members of the Harlem mosque, including Thomas 15X Johnson; outtakes from "Brother Minister" of interviews with prominent members of Mosque No. 7.

5. Lee, *By Any Means Necessary,* 51.

6. "Father Says Clay Joined Muslims at 18," *Washington Post,* February 7, 1964; Hauser, *Muhammad Ali,* 100.

7. Ibid.

8. See, in general, Ali, *The Greatest*; Hauser, *Muhammad Ali,* 57–67; Barry Golson, ed., *The Playboy Interviews* (New York: Playboy Press, 1981), 76–111.

9. Lomax, *To Kill a Black Man,* 129.

10. Ibid., 128–29.

11. FBI HQ file on Charles "Sonny" Liston; "The Outlaw Champ," *Vanity Fair,* February 1998, 146–66.

12. Saviour's Day audiocassette; FBI Public Source Material file on Elijah Muhammad.

13. Cosell, *Cosell,* 77.

14. FBI HQ file on Malcolm X.

15. FBI HQ file on Elijah Muhammad.

16. Ibid.

17. Ibid.

18. Ibid.

19. Comments of Captain Joseph X Gravitt (aka Yusuf Shah) in *Make It Plain* (documentary), Blackside, 1993.

20. FBI HQ file on Elijah Muhammad.

21. Ibid.

22. Ibid., memo from Phoenix SAC to HQ dated March 23, 1964; FBI JUNE (wiretap) Mail file on Elijah Muhammad; Kondo, *Conspiracy,* 170–71.

23. Karim, *Remembering Malcolm,* 156; *Brother Minister* (documentary), X-Ceptional Productions, 1997.

24. FBI NY file on Muslim Mosque Inc., section 57.

25. FBI HQ file on Elijah Muhammad.

26. FBI NY file on Muslim Mosque Inc., section 57.

27. FBI HQ file on Elijah Muhammad.

28. FBI JUNE Mail file on Elijah Muhammad.

29. FBI NY file on Malcolm X.

30. FBI HQ file on Muslim Mosque Inc.

31. See Haley's Epilogue in the *Autobiography of Malcolm X.*

32. Author's interviews with Wilfred Little.

33. FBI HQ file on Malcolm X.

34. FBI HQ file on Elijah Muhammad.

35. "Black Muslim Brothers Wage War of Words," *Washington Evening Star,* March 28, 1964, A02.

36. "The X Brothers," *New York Herald Tribune,* March 28, 1964, A05; Strickland, *Malcolm X: Make It Plain,* 174; also see interview with Philbert X Little in *Make It Plain* (documentary).

37. FBI HQ file on Elijah Muhammad, memo dated April 12, 1964.

38. Ibid.

39. FBI NY file on Muslim Mosque Inc., memo dated May 11, 1964, 2.

40. FBI HQ file on the Organization of Afro-American Unity.

41. Interviews of Benjamin Karim by Jack Baxter (in outtakes of *Brother Minister*).

42. "Malcolm Says He Is Backed Abroad; Asserts U.N. Will Get Case on U.S. Negro This Year," *New York Times,* May 22, 1964, A22; also see press state-

ment issued by Malcolm X (available via AFRAM Associates in New York); CIA file on Malcolm X; FBI HQ file on Malcolm X.

43. Affidavit of Talmadge Hayer, obtained from the Center for Constitutional Rights.

44. FBI HQ file on Elijah Muhammad; FBI HQ file on Wallace Muhammad.

45. FBI HQ file on Wallace Muhammad, airtel from Chicago SAC to director dated June 2, 1964; also see "Black Muslim Fights Cops, Is Held," *Chicago Sun-Times,* June 2, 1964, 26.

46. Interviews with participants in harrassment campaign; FBI HQ file on Malcolm X.

47. FBI HQ file on Muslim Mosque Inc.

48. Ibid., memo from Chicago SAC to director dated June 16, 1964; FBI JUNE mail file on Clara Muhammad.

49. FBI HQ file on Muslim Mosque Inc., section 3.

50. FBI JUNE Mail file on Elijah Muhammad; FBI NY file on Malcolm X, memo from Chicago SAC dated July 10, 1964.

51. Ibid.

52. Karim, *Remembering Malcolm,* 183–84.

53. FBI HQ file on Malcolm X; FBI HQ file on Leon 4X Ameer, aka Leon Phillips.

54. "Boston Honors Abdul Jabbar Muhammad (formerly Clarence Gill)," *The Final Call,* June 4, 1994, 4.

55. FBI HQ file on Leon 4X Ameer; "The Black Muslims Are a Fraud," *Saturday Evening Post,* February 27, 1964.

56. Ibid.

57. Ibid.

58. Ibid.

59. FBI NY file on Muslim Mosque Inc.; FBI NY file on Malcolm X.

60. Ibid.; also see Karim, *Remembering Malcolm,* 182–84; Collins, *Seventh Child,* 177–78.

61. Supra, note 59.

62. Ibid.

63. Ibid.

64. FBI HQ file on Raymond Sharrieff; FBI HQ file on Malcolm X.

65. Ibid.; also see FBI HQ file on Elijah Muhammad and the main file on Wallace Muhammad.

66. FBI HQ file on Elijah Muhammad; FBI NY file on Malcolm X.

67. FBI HQ file on Muslim Mosque Inc.

68. Ibid.

69. Perry, *Malcolm X: The Last Speeches*, 136–37; Goldman, *Death and Life of Malcolm X*, 414; Norman 3X Butler Interview, *Black News*, February and March/April 1979 issues.

70. FBI HQ file On Muslim Mosque Inc.; also see "Malcolm X to Start Own Muslim Group," *Washington Post*, March 8, 1964.

71. Haley, *Autobiography of Malcolm X*, 295; "Muslim Leader Named in Two Paternity Suits," *Washington Post* (via Associated Press), July 4, 1964.

72. Interviews with author.

73. FBI HQ file on Muslim Mosque Inc.

74. "False Charges Made Against Muhammad," *Chicago New Crusader*, July 7, 1964, A05.

75. Evanzz, *The Judas Factor*, 246.

76. FBI HQ file on Wallace Muhammad.

77. FBI HQ file on Malcolm X.

78. FBI HQ file on Wallace Muhammad.

79. Ibid.

80. FBI JUNE Mail file on Elijah Muhammad.

81. Ibid.

82. Ibid.

83. FBI HQ file on Leon 4X Ameer.

84. Ibid.

85. Ibid.

86. Ibid.

87. FBI HQ file on Leon 4X Ameer, memo dated March 17, 1965.

88. FBI HQ file on Clara Muhammad.

89. Ibid.

90. *Muhammad Speaks*, November 20, 1964.

91. Ibid.

92. FBI HQ file on Akbar Muhammad; "Muhammad's Son Favors Malcolm X," *New York Courier*, December 26, 1964; "Muhammad Denies Break with His Son," *New York Times*, August 18, 1964.

93. Cuthbert Ormond Simpkins, *Coltrane: A Biography* (New York: Herndon House, 1975), 175.

94. FBI NY file on Malcolm X.

95. Ibid.

96. Ibid.

97. FBI New York file on Muslim Mosque Inc., section 3.

98. *Muhammad Speaks,* January 1, 1965.; FBI HQ file on Elijah Muhammad.

14: THE PEN AND THE SWORD

1. Joel Whitburn, *The Billboard Book of Top 40 Hits* (New York: Billboard Publications, 1985), 470–75.

2. "The Sounds of Silence," Simon and Garfunkel (CBS Records: 1966).

3. Spoken by George Hanson (Jack Nicholson); see "Easy Rider," *All-Movie Guide On-Line* (www.allmovie.com).

4. "Minister Who Knew Him Best (Part 1); Rips Malcolm's Treachery, Defection," *Muhammad Speaks,* December 4, 1964.

5. Friedly, *Malcolm X: The Assassination,* 231–32.

6. FBI HQ file on Leon 4X Ameer.

7. Ibid.

8. Strickland, *Malcolm X: Make It Plain,* 174; *Make It Plain* (documentary), interview with Wallace Muhammad.

9. FBI HQ file on Muslim Mosque Inc., memo dated September 21, 1964, 2.

10. Ibid., memo from Philadelphia SAC to Director dated December 30, 1964.

11. "Malcolm X Woos 2 Rights Leaders," *New York Times,* May 19, 1964; FBI JUNE (wiretap) Mail file on Elijah Muhammad; FBI HQ file on Muhammad, section 9.

12. Evanzz, *The Judas Factor,* 223–42.

13. FBI HQ file on Chauncey Eskridge; FBI JUNE Mail files on Elijah Muhammad, Malcolm X, and Martin Luther King Jr.

14. FBI JUNE Mail files on Elijah Muhammad.

15. FBI HQ file on Elijah Muhammad, memo dated February 18, 1965.

16. FBI NY file on Malcolm X, memo from NY SAC dated July 7, 1964, and another memo dated July 1, 1964, which states: "Jones mentioned that Malcolm X is to go to Africa in ten days. Jones and the man, whom the source could not identify, planned to meet with Martin Luther King and Malcolm X before Malcolm X goes to Africa"; also see Garrow, *Bearing the Cross,* 392; Lynn, *There Is a Fountain,* 188–89; "Slater Hunter King" interview, Civil Rights Documentation Project papers, Moorland-Spingarn Research Center, Howard University.

17. FBI HQ file on Leon 4X Ameer.

18. Author's interviews with former members of Harlem mosque.

19. FBI HQ file on Leon 4X Ameer.

20. Ibid.

21. Author's interviews with former members of Harlem mosque.

22. "Muslim Overlords Here Named," *New York Journal American,* February 26, 1965, A01; FBI HQ file on Leon 4X Ameer; also trial transcript in *People v. Hayer,* et al.

23. See ad in *Muhammad Speaks.*

24. *Lucille Rosary v. Elijah Muhammad,* Superior Court of Los Angeles, #D652479 (1964).

25. Author's interviews with Gladys Towles Root; FBI Public Source Material file on Malcolm X.

26. The petition was of such concern to the CIA that President Johnson was briefed about it. See the CIA file on Malcolm X; FBI HQ file on Malcolm X, but see Atwood, *The Reds and the Blacks,* 156–57, 188–95, 289; Council on Foreign Relations, *Documents on American Foreign Relations* (New York: Simon & Schuster, 1939–1970), vols. 1960–1966; Rusk, *Waging Peace and War;* Johnson, *The Vantage Point,* 154–79.

27. "Malcolm X Seeks U.N. Negro Debate; He Asks African States to Cite U.S. Over Rights," *New York Times,* August 13, 1964, A22. One intellectual and activist who saw the significance of the petition was author Langston Hughes. "Malcolm in Cairo," *New York Post,* July 17, 1964, A32.

28. Leeming, *James Baldwin,* 210; FBI HQ file on the Organization of Afro-American Unity, memo from NY SAC dated April 1, 1965.

29. Ibid.; also see *Yearbook of the United Nations: 1964,* 33, 599–604, *Yearbook of the United Nations: 1965,* 617–19; *Yearbook of the United Nations: 1963,* 498, 706, 711 (when Quaison-Sackey served as head of the U.N. Security Council for the month of June); also see FBI HQ file on Malcolm X; FBI HQ file on the Organization of Afro-American Unity.

30. Haley, *Autobiography of Malcolm X,* 426.

31. Lomax, *To Kill a Black Man,* 103–5, 128–30, 184, 198, 250–52; Evanzz, *The Judas Factor,* 246–47.

32. Ibid.; "Driver Tells How Malcolm X Escaped Death in Chase," *Washington Star,* February 24, 1965; also see Jamal, *From the Dead Level.*

33. Though their names are redacted in the FBI HQ file on Malcolm X, a comparison between pages there and in the FBI documents on Wallace and Has-

san reveals that Chicago agents were describing the two as "highly reliable sources" and as sources "close to Muhammad."

34. FBI NY file on Malcolm X, memo from Phoenix SAC to Los Angeles SAC dated March 13, 1965.

35. Ibid.

36. Ibid.

37. FBI NYC file on Muslim Mosque Inc., memo dated March 13, 1965, 1–2.

38. Ibid.

39. Interviews with former members of the Harlem mosque.

40. Clark, *Malcolm X: The Final Speeches*, 133–35.

41. New York Police Department BOSSI file on Malcolm X.

42. FBI HQ file on the Organization of Afro-American Unity, memo from NY SAC to HQ dated February 16, 1965 and similar memo from Philadelphia SAC to HQ on same date; Haley, *Autobiography of Malcolm X*, 428.

43. Ibid., 430–33; Clark, *Malcolm X: The Final Speeches*, 34–38.

44. "4G for Malcolm's Widow," *New York Post*, March 2, 1965, A03; FBI HQ file on Sammy Davis Jr.; FBI NY file on Malcolm X.

45. Collins, *Seventh Child*, 184–86;

46. Haley, *Autobiography of Malcolm X*, 429; Gordon Parks, "The Violent End of a Man Called Malcolm X," *Life*, March 5, 1965, 28–30.

47. Herb Boyd, "Hero or 'Charlie Bad Guy?' Gene Roberts, Muslim/Panther Infiltrator, Says He's Neither," *Class*, December/January 1992, 54–57; FBI NY file on Malcolm X. Roberts, who was described by police as an "informant," told his superiors at least six days before the assassination that a rehearsal had taken place on February 16 at the Audubon. "Hint Muslim 'Rehearsal' to Kill Malcolm," *Chicago American*, March 4, 1965, A06; "How Malcolm X Assassins Held Dress Rehearsal," *New York Journal American*, March 4, 1965, A01.

48. *New York Times*, February 22, 1965, A01.

49. FBI HQ file on Elijah Muhammad (transcript of program).

50. Ibid.

51. Ali, *The Greatest*, 191–92.

52. "Saviour's Day 1965" (audiocassette); FBI HQ file on Elijah Muhammad.

53. Author's interviews with Wilfred Little.

54. *Washington Post*, February 27, 1965.

55. Lee, *By Any Means Necessary*, 51.

56. *Chicago American*, February 25, 1965.

57. *Washington Post*, March 1, 1965.

58. "Wanted," *Muhammad Speaks*, March 4, 1965. The New York Police Department later demanded that the newspaper run a retraction regarding the misleading article; "Malcolm X Aide Charges Muslim Plot to Kill Him," *New York Journal American*, March 11, 1965.

59. *Washington Post*, March 6, 1965.

60. Affidavit of Talmadge Hayer, obtained by the author from the Center for Constitutional Rights.

61. *People v. Hayer* (trial transcript); "An Order to Kill Malcolm Hinted; Prosecutor Tells of Muslim Official's Presence Here," *New York Times*, March 3, 1966, A24; FBI NY file on Malcolm X; FBI HQ file on Malcolm X.

62. FBI HQ file on Malcolm X; FBI NY file on Malcolm X.

63. One of the last interviews Malcolm X did before his assassination included Barnette as a copanelist. A copy of the WINS-AM radio transcript appears in Clark's *Malcolm X: The Final Speeches*, 184–211. The transcript is also included in the FBI NY file on Malcolm X.

64. "Police Accuse Muslim in Malcolm X Killing," *Washington Post*, February 27, 1965, A02.

65. FBI Public Source Material file on Malcolm X.

66. Ibid.

67. Garrow, *Bearing the Cross*, 392; *New York Times*, February 27, 1965.

68. Author's interviews with Rodnell Collins; interviews with Ella Collins.

69. "From 7 May to 18 June, the Parties presented their oral reply and rejoinder on questions of law. At the end of their oral reply, Ethiopia and Liberia filed final submissions on May 19, when they announced that they had concluded their case. . . ." *Yearbook of the United Nations 1965*, 618.

70. The case against South Africa was closed in 1966.

71. Supra, note 58.

72. FBI HQ file on Leon 4X Ameer.

73. Author's interviews with former OAAU member A. Peter Bailey. The FBI HQ file on the organization clearly shows that the OAAU and Muslim Mosque Inc. were saturated with informants. According to one document, a young man from Philadelphia who was awarded one of the scholarships that Malcolm X received from Nasser was an informant for the FBI.

74. Interviews with Rodnell Collins. The Bureau was well aware of the hostilities between Betty Shabazz and Malcolm X's family, and made notes of it in the HQ file on the OAAU. Also see Lee, *By Any Means Necessary*, 49 (where

Wilfred Little confessed that Betty had refused to permit the Shabazz children to have contact with their father's family).

75. FBI HQ file on Elijah Muhammad.

76. FBI HQ file on Clara Muhammad.

77. See Appendix C in this book.

78. FBI HQ file on Muhammad.

79. Ibid.; also see *Washington Post*, February 25, 1966.

80. *Muhammad Speaks*, February 25, 1966, 3.

81. *Washington Post*, February 28, 1966.

82. Ibid. June 21, 1966.

83. Ibid.

84. *Washington Post*, August 29, 1966.

85. FBI HQ file on Muhammad.

86. Ibid., memo dated July 30, 1967.

87. *Washington Post*, September 9, 1965.

88. *Los Angeles Times*, October 13, 1967.

89. *Washington Post*, October 13, 1967; *Washington Post*, October 23, 1967.

90. FBI HQ COINTELPRO file on Black Extremists.

91. Ibid.

92. FBI HQ file on Muhammad.

93. O'Reilly, *Black Americans*, 257–58.

94. "Army Feared King, Secretly Watched Him," *Commercial Appeal*, March 21, 1993.

15: Apollo Fires

1. Theodore Roszak, *The Making of a Counter Culture* (Garden City, N.Y.: Doubleday/Anchor Books, 1969), 47.

2. "Army Feared King, Secretly Watch Him; Spying on Blacks Started 75 Years Ago," *Commercial Appeal* (Memphis), March 21, 1993, A01; see also "Ex-Army Agents Discuss 1968 Monitoring of King," *Washington Post*, December 1, 1997, A14.

3. Ibid., *Commercial Appeal*, A09.

4. FBI HQ file on Elijah Muhammad.

5. Garrow, *Bearing the Cross*, 607.

6. King refused President Johnson's personal plea to abandon the march. "King Says 'No' to LBJ on March," *Washington Post*, February 6, 1968. At that

point, Johnson ordered the Pentagon to prepare for a revolution in the streets of Washington. Government preparations were uncovered by *Washington Post* reporters Robert G. Kaiser and Carl Bernstein. "U.S. to Aid City If Riots Occur Here; Troops Proposed to Help Police in Curbing Violence," *Washington Post,* February 14, 1968. Rowland Evans and Robert Novak, who had sources inside the Johnson administration, relayed the president's fears to the public. "Official Fears Grow That Carmichael Will Seize Dr. King's 'March of Poor,'" *Washington Post,* February 19, 1968.

7. FBI HQ file on Martin Luther King Jr., memo dated March 29, 1968; *Church Committee Report,* book 3, 181–83.

8. Ibid. The Church Committee found "no evidence that the FBI was responsible for Dr. King's move to the Lorraine Hotel"; but see, generally, Pepper, *Orders to Kill*; Gregory and Lane, *Code Name "Zorro."*

9. "Dr. Martin Luther King Jr. 1929–1968" (Brotherhood Records: 1980). The speech is also known as the "Drum Major" speech. A copy appears in the FBI HQ file on King and also is available on audiocassette; also see "Catching Up with a Dream: Evangelicals and Race 30 Years After the Death of Martin Luther King Jr.," *Christianity Today,* March 2, 1998 (cover story).

10. "Gospel Singer Searches for 'God's Will,'" *Washington Post,* April 9, 1968, D01.

11. Campbell, *Talking at the Gates,* 207 (Malcolm X) and 223 (Dr. King).

12. Ploski and Kaiser, *The Negro Almanac,* 245; Platt, *The Politics of Riot Commissions,* 341–527 (a chronicle of rioting in the three years after the assassination of Dr. King).

13. Hilliard, *This Side of Glory,* 182–93; Moore, *Rage,* 73–78; and see, generally, Charles E. Jones, ed. *The Black Panther Party Reconsidered* (Baltimore: Black Classic Press, 1998).

14. FBI HQ file on Elijah Muhammad.

15. *Washington Post,* February 27, 1968.

16. FBI HQ file on COINTELPRO: Black Extremists.

17. Ibid. A reproduction of the comic book is in the file.

18. Ibid.

19. Author's interviews with former members of Harlem mosque.

20. Lee, *By Any Means Necesssary,* 65.

21. FBI HQ file on Herbert C. Muhammad; FBI HQ file on Black Extremists

22. "Ali Captivates AU Students, Advises Against Violence," *Washington Post,* May 4, 1968, B03; also see "Ali Warns Violence Won't Win," *Washington*

Post, May 2, 1968, B03 (friendly encounter between Ali and Rev. Ralph D. Abernathy of the SCLC several weeks after King was assassinated).

23. FBI HQ file on COINTELPRO: Black Extremists, memo dated November 27, 1968, 1–3.

24. A complete list of radio stations that carried the program is included in the FBI HQ file on Elijah Muhammad, and was also printed in each edition of *Muhammad Speaks.* The ranking of the ministers listed is based upon interviews with members of the NOI.

25. The programs were not dropped, but were rearranged to make room during prime time for the more popular Muslim program.

26. See, generally, Berry Gordy, *To Be Loved: The Music, the Magic, the Memories of Motown* (New York: Warner Books, 1994).

27. "The Last Poets," by The Last Poets (Metrotone: 1970); "This Is Madness" (Celluloid: 1971); see also "The Last Poets," All-Music Guide On-Line (www.all-music.com).

28. FBI HQ file on Elijah Muhammad, memo dated August 7, 1968, section 12.

29. Muhammad, *How to Eat to Live.*

30. FBI HQ file on COINTELPRO: Black Extremists.

31. Ibid.

32. Ibid.

33. "Bandits Tie, Rob Black Muslims," *Chicago Daily News,* February 4, 1969, A01; "Black Muslim Goal: A Strong Economic Base," *Chicago Daily News,* February 5, 1969, A06; also see William Brashler, "Black on Black: The Deadly Struggle for Power," *New York,* June 9, 1975, 55.

34. FBI HQ file on Raymond Sharrieff; FBI public source file on Raymond Sharrieff.

35. "Malcolm X Aide Is Shot in Bronx; Kenyatta 37X Reported in Critical Condition—He Helped City in Slums," *New York Times,* June 8, 1969, A01.

36. Ibid.

37. FBI HQ file on Raymond Sharrieff; FBI HQ file on Elijah Muhammad.

38. Muhammad, *Our Saviour Has Arrived,* 33 (partial transcript of the Saviour's Day speech).

39. FBI HQ file on the Five Percenters.

40. "Black Militant Slain in Harlem; Former 'Five Percenter' Ran a School for Dropouts," *New York Times,* June 14, 1969.

41. *New York Times,* June 15, 1969.

42. Supra, note 35.

43. *New York Times,* June 15, 1969.

44. FBI HQ file on Five Percenters.

45. Hauser, *Muhammad Ali,* 193–95.

46. Ibid. Also see "Ali Repents, Will Forget Comeback," *Washington Post.* April 1, 1969.

47. FBI HQ file on Elijah Muhammad.

48. Ibid.; also see Hauser, *Muhammad Ali*; Muhammad, *Theology of Time,* Introduction.

49. *Washington Post,* June 8, 1969.

50. Ibid., June 6, 1969.

51. Ibid.

52. FBI HQ file on Elijah Muhammad.

53. *Washington Post,* June 8, 1969.

54. FBI HQ file on Elijah Muhammad.

55. Ibid.

56. *Muhammad Speaks,* October 3, 1969, 20.

57. *Washington Post,* December 11, 1969.

58. Ibid.

59. Ibid. Three months later a federal court in Alabama agreed with attorneys for the NOI that the "Muslim Registration Law" was unconstitutional. *Washington Post,* June 1, 1970. By then, Muhammad had decided that the cost of growing food there was too high. With the help of bright young lawyers, accountants, and business school graduates, he purchased a bank, and over government opposition, signed an international trade agreement with the government of Peru for fish. Within a few years, the operation was grossing an estimated $25,000,000 a year.

60. *Washington Post,* March 19, 1970.

61. "Era's Songs Endure," *Orange County Register,* January 29, 1995, F16.

62. Castleden, *World History,* 587.

63. Haley, *Autobiography of Malcolm X,* 296; also see Davis, *Malcolm X: The Great Photographs,* 74–75; Strickland, *Malcolm X: Make It Plain,* 141.

64. "Dick Gregory: Caught in the Act" (Poppy Records/United Artists Records Inc., 1973).

65. *Church Committee Report,* vol. 2, 303–10 (Appendixes).

66. Ibid.

67. Ibid.

68. Ibid., 309.

69. *Mobfathers* (PBS documentary); "Now the Black Mafia Bilks Banks," *Philadelphia Inquirer*, August 24, 1975; "Secrecy Key to Successful Prison Raid," *Morning Call* (Allentown, Pa.), October 30, 1995, B01.

70. Ibid.

71. Ibid.

72. Ibid.; also see "Dubrow Witness, Wife Found 'Executed' in Home," *Philadelphia Inquirer*, January 26, 1976; "Convict Surprised by Witness' Death," *Philadelphia Inquirer*, January 28, 1976; "Tip Links 2 to Witness' Killing," *Philadelphia Inquirer*, January 29, 1976.

73. *Mobfathers* (PBS documentary).

74. Supra, note 69, *Philadelphia Inquirer*.

75. FBI HQ file on COINTELPRO: Black Extremists.

76. Ibid.

77. *New York Times*, February 16, 1971, A37.

78. Brown, *A Taste of Power*, 286–90.

79. Ibid.

80. Ibid.

16: And Mercury Falls

1. Cited in Seldes, *The Great Thoughts*, 159.

2. More than 100,000 pages of documents have been declassified by the FBI.

3. *Church Committee Report*, book 3, 332, memo dated November 3, 1970.

4. Ibid.

5. FBI Public Source Material file on John Ali; FBI HQ file on Elijah Muhammad.

6. See, generally, Lomax, *When the Word Is Given*; and Lomax, *To Kill a Black Man*.

7. Author's interviews with Larry 4X Prescott (aka Abdul Aziz and Abdul Karriem). Karriem presently heads NOI's (Farrakhan's sect) branch in Ghana.

8. *Chicago Defender*, May 9–15, 1970, 1.

9. FBI Public Source Material on John Ali.

10. *Elijah Muhammad Meets the Press*, booklet reprint of interview Elijah Muhammad held at his home on January 14, 1972; William Brashler, "Black on Black: The Deadly Struggle for Power," *New York*, June 9, 1975, 55. Also see

Washington Post, February 3, 1972; *Chicago Sun Times,* December 4, 1973, A57.

11. Ibid.

12. FBI HQ file on Elijah Muhammad.

13. Hakim, *Theology of Time,* 215–16; FBI HQ file on Elijah Muhammad.

14. FBI HQ file on Elijah Muhammad.

15. *Muhammad Speaks,* February 20, 1970, 16.

16. FBI HQ file on COINTELPRO: Black Extremists.

17. Supra, note 10, *Washington Post.*

18. *Washington Post,* January 12, 1972, A06.

19. "Leader Asks Self-Haters to Stop Muslim Infighting," *Washington Post,* January 15, 1972, A03.

20. Supra, note 10, 2–7.

21. "Saviour's Day 1972" (audiocassette); "Black Muslims to Focus Development on Economics," *Washington Post,* February 27, 1972 A24.

22. Ibid.

23. Hakim, *Theology of Time,* 103.

24. "Bio of Murder Victim Is Part of Author's Healing Process," *Boston Herald,* April 4, 1994, A25; Richards, *Played Out,* 288; "The Other Brother X: Michael X, Britain's Answer to Malcolm X," *The Guardian,* March 2, 1993, 2.

25. *Los Angeles Sentinel,* March 21, 1968.

26. The best source on the genealogy of Jacqueline Bouvier Kennedy is a recent book penned by her first cousin: John H. Davis, *Jacqueline Bouvier: An Intimate Memoir* (New York: Wiley, 1998).

27. FBI HQ file on Hakim A. Jamal; Richards, *Played Out,* 218.

28. FBI HQ file on Jean Seberg; FBI HQ file on Hakim A. Jamal. The LAPD squad also kept surveillance files on Michael Jackson, Sugar Ray Leonard, Connie Chung, Robert Redford, Pat Buchanan, and scores of others. See Rothmiller, *L.A. Secret Police,* 21, 51 (baseball great Joe Morgan and basketball star Jamaal Wilkes).

29. Supra, note 24.

30. See, generally, Athill, *Make Believe;* also see "Total Paranoia Takes Over," *Daily Telegraph,* January 30, 1993, 19.

31. Supra, note 24.

32. Davis, *Jacqueline Bouvie;* Richards, *Played Out,* 287–89.

33. Ibid.

34. Ibid.

35. Richards, *Played Out*, 288–89; also see V. S. Naipaul, *The Return of Eva Peron, with The Killings in Trinidad* (New York: Knopf, 1980).

36. Jamal's book, *From the Dead Level*, reiterated many of the allegations that Malcolm X made against Muhammad in late 1964.

37. "Black Leader Slain by Boston Gunmen; Muslim Feud Hinted," *New York Times*, May 3, 1972, A26.

38. "8 Blacks Accused of Killing Whites; Slaying of 9, Including 7 in 2 Families, Laid to Gang of Vietnam Veterans," *New York Times*, October 16, 1972, 1; "Mau Mau Link Sought to Nationwide Killings," *Washington Post*, October 17, 1972, A03.

39. "7 Arrested Men Tied to Muslims; Minister to Hire Lawyers for Suspects in Zebra Case," *New York Times*, May 3, 1974; "Pair Convicted in Zebra Killings Denied Parole," *San Diego Union-Tribune*, August 1, 1985, A10; also see *New York Times*, October 16, 1972, A01; *New York Times*, November 30, 1975, A49. See, generally, Howard, *Zebra*.

40. *Washington Post*, March 4, 1976.

41. "5 Policemen Hurt in Harlem Melee; Clash as 2 Patrolmen Enter a Muslim Mosque Erupts Into General Disorder," *New York Times*, April 15, 1972, A01.

42. Ibid.

43. *New York Times*, April 16, 1972, A65.

44. "Soul Singer Quits to Be a Preacher," *Washington Post*, July 10, 1972.

45. Ibid.

46. "Joe Tex" (http://www.allmusic.com).

47. See, generally, Ali, *The Greatest*, and Tremlett, *Gadaffi*.

48. *Washington Post*, June 15, 1972. "I personally picked up a cashier's check for $2.3 million from the Libyan Embassy in Washington for the Nation of Islam," Abbass Rassoull said. Muhammad, *Theology of Time*, xxxviii.

49. *Chicago Sun Times*, May 8, 1972, A03.

50. FBI HQ file on EM, section 12, memo dated October 7, 1971.

51. FBI HQ file on Nation of Islam; also see "Church Sale to Muslims Is Approved," *Washington Post*, July 31, 1971, B09.

52. FBI HQ file on Elijah Muhammad, section 14, memo, 18.

53. Ibid., 10

54. *Washington Post*, February 2, 1973.

55. FBI HQ file on Elijah Muhammad.

56. Ibid.

57. Letter from FBI HQ to author.

58. FBI HQ file on Elijah Muhammad, memo from Chicago SAC to director dated June 15, 1973.

59. FBI HQ file on Clara Muhammad.

60. Ibid.

61. FBI Public Source Material file on Elijah Muhammad.

62. Supra, note 10, *Elijah Muhammad Meets the Press.*

63. Brashler, "Black on Black," 48; Gardell, *In the Name of Elijah Muhammad,* 410, n. 188.

64. *Chicago Sun Times,* March 26, 1972, section 2, 3.

65. *New York Times,* January 21, 1972.

66. "Black Professionals Hear Muslim Plea for Unity," *New York Times,* October 2, 1972.

67. Ibid.

68. "Muslims Purge Police Members; Order Is Said to Fear They Were Undercover Agents," *New York Times,* October 29, 1972.

69. "Now the Black Mafia Bilks Banks," *Philadelphia Inquirer,* August 24, 1975.

70. Ibid.

71. Ibid.

72. Ibid.

73. Ibid.; also see *Mobfathers* (PBS documentary).

74. "Black Muslim Leader in Newark Shot to Death; Two Men Sought," *New York Times,* September 5, 1973, A50.

75. Ibid., October 27, 1973.

76. "Decapitated Bodies of 2 Found in a Newark Park," *New York Times,* October 19, 1973, A47. Just as Malcolm X had been killed only weeks after Farrakhan wrote that he was worthy of death, the decapitated Muslims were discovered less than three weeks after Farrakhan implied during a radio address that McGregor's murderers deserved decapitation. Claiming to quote the Holy Quran, Farrakhan said: "Cut off their heads, roll it [*sic*] down the street and make the world know that the murderer of a Muslim must be murdered. . . ." See Magida, *Prophet of Rage,* 99–102.

77. Ibid. September 8, 1973 (New Jersey edition).

78. *Make It Plain* (documentary). Interview with Ella Collins.

17: IN THE NAME OF ALLAH

1. Holy Bible, King James version. The commandments aren't numbered per se, but this one is considered the sixth in Christianity and the seventh in Judaism. "There Are 10, but Their Order Isn't Carved in Stone," *Washington Post,* February 21, 1998, D08.

2. Farrakhan's speech, which is sold on videotape and audiocassettes at Muslim-owned stores, was recorded on February 20, 1993. He was referring, in general, to the assassination of Malcolm X by members of the NOI twenty-five years earlier.

3. Holy Quran, trans. Maulana Muhammad Ali, "The Cow," section 2, 10.

4. "Muhammad Meets the Press!" *Muhammad Speaks,* January 14, February 4, and February 11, 1972; reprinted in booklet form as *Elijah Muhammad Meets the Press.*

5. Ibid., January 14, 1972.

6. "Hanafi Muslim Chief Quit Key Muslim Post," *Washington Post,* February 2, 1973, A01

7. See, generally, Nanji, *The Muslim Almanac.*

8. Supra, note 6.

9. Based on data in author's files.

10. See, in general, Abdul-Jabbar, *Giant Steps.*

11. Ibid., 222–35.

12. Ibid.

13. Ibid., 226.

14. See Appendix B in this book for full text of letter.

15. Ibid.

16. FBI HQ file on Elijah Muhammad.

17. See *William Christian v. United States,* 394 A. 2nd 1 (1978); also see John Sansing, "Hanafi Massacre, Hanafi Siege," *Washingtonian* magazine, February 1980, 87–96.

18. Ibid.

19. Ibid.

20. Ibid.

21. This reconstruction of the crime is based on news accounts, firsthand interviews, trial transcripts in *United States v. Christian, et al.,* and appellate actions.

22. "Seven 'Executed' in District's Biggest Mass Murder," *Washington Post,* January 19, 1973, A01.

23. "Jury Probes Massacre of 7 Moslems," January 27, 1973.

24. Ibid.

25. Ibid.

26. "Muslims Linked to Pa. Rapes," *Washington Post,* January 30, 1973, A01; also see *United States v. William Christian et al.,* D.C. Sup. Ct., Criminal No. 47900–73 through 47906–73 (1973).

27. Ibid., *United States v. Christian et al.*

28. Sansing, "Hanafi Massacre, Manafi Siege."

29. Farrakhan's warning was issued in the middle of the murder trial, and just five days after James Price was contacted by a Muslim minister posing as an attorney. The minister was identified as David Pasha of Cincinnati. "Witness Balks at Testifying," *Washington Post,* March 30, 1974, B01; "Black Muslim Traitors Warned of Vengeance," *Washington Post,* April 5, 1974, B01; also see *Washington Post,* January 29, 1973, A01; *New York Times,* January 29, 1973, A57.

30. Ibid.

31. Supra, note 17. All of the defendants were career criminals. "7 Slaying Suspects Have Long Records," *Washington Post,* August 20, 1973, A01.

32. "Black Muslim Informer Slain in Philadelphia Prison Cell," *Washington Post,* December 31, 1974, A01.

33. "Saviour's Day 1973" (videotape and audiotape).

34. Ibid.

35. Ibid.

36. See Appendix B.

37. "Saviour's Day 1973" (videotape and audiotape).

38. Ibid.

39. Ibid.; also see Muhammad, *Message to the Blackman,* 103–22.

18: KEYS TO THE KINGDOM

1. Bloom, *The American Religion,* 248.

2. George Santayana, *The Life of Reason* (1905–1906).

3. "Spirits Known and Unknown" by Leon Thomas (Flying Dutchman Records, 1969).

4. "Saviour's Day 1973" (videotape and audiotape).

5. Shoemaker, *Russia, Eurasian States, and Eastern Europe 1995,* "The Repubic of Azerbaijan," 140–45.

6. W. Muhammed, *As the Light Shineth from the East,* 29.

7. This is a flagrant falsehood. Non-Muslims were barred from Mecca, but not whites. White-skinned Muslims are as welcome as black-skinned Muslims. See Wolfe, *One Thousand Roads to Mecca.*

8. E. D. Beynon, "The Voodoo Cult Among American Negro Migrants in Detroit," *American Journal of Sociology* 43, no. 6 (May 1938): 894.

9. The following statement appeared on the NOI's Web site on March 28, 1996: "When America entered the era of the Great Depression, beginning in 1929 and the early 1930s, during the administration of President Herbert Hoover, a Wise Master came to America from the East and met with the former President. He revealed Himself publicly for the first time in 1930" (htt://www. noi.org/history.html). The article, entitled "Brief History on the Origin of the Nation of Islam in America," has been corrected.

10. Hakim, *True History of Elijah Muhammad,* 41.

11. Query by author of admissions office officials at the University of Southern California at Los Angeles.

12. FBI HQ file on Wallace D. Fard.

13. Ibid., memo to Chicago from director dated March 12, 1963, 1; also see Marriage Indices for Multnomah County, p. 224 of Marriage Index for Period July 1910 to October 1915. Marriage Certificate #28247 was issued to Fred Dodd and Pearl Allen on May 9 in Marion County, Oregon. The license was requested on April 14, 1914.

14. FBI interview with Hazel Barton Ford, as reflected in FBI HQ file on Wallace D. Fard.

15. FBI HQ file on Wallace D. Fard.

16. Ibid.

17. Ibid.

18. FBI Public Source Material file on Wallace D. Fard; also see "White's Black Record; 'Prophet' of Muslims Afoul of Law in L.A.," *Los Angeles Herald Examiner,* July 28, 1963, A01.

19. Ibid.

20. 14th Census Report of the United States (1920), Los Angeles County; also see Census Card for Wallace Dodd Ford.

21. FBI HQ file on Wallace D. Fard.

22. Donaldson denied ever living outside of Los Angeles, but this is contradicted by his criminal record, a microfilmed copy of which is maintained as part of the California State Archives.

23. Office of Naval Intelligence report on Chatterjee. Also see Washington, *Madame Blavatsky's Baboon,* 88–89. The interesting thing about Farr's connection to Chatterjee is that W. B. Yeats, who fell under Blavatsky's spell in the early 1900s, was very fond of a woman named Florence Farr, an ardent admirer and associate of Chatterjee. That Florence Farr and George Farr were both linked to Chatterjee concurrently may be entirely coincidental. Other than the Chatterjee connection and the fact that Florence Farr lived in London (where Fard claimed to have spent part of his youth), no leads were uncovered. I should note, however, that my research was only cursory. See Jeffares, *W. B. Yeats: A New Biography* (including photo of Florence Farr).

24. Hill, *Marcus Garvey Papers,* vol. 2, 233–39, 311–12, 338–39, 477–79, 678.

25. Ibid., 234.

26. Ibid.

27. Ibid., 235.

28. Ibid.

29. Ibid.

30. Criminal record of Edward Donaldson, obtained from California State Archives division.

31. Fard is listed as "restaurant keeper" on some documents, and "owner" on others. The restaurant's name obviously suggests ownership. FBI HQ file on Wallace D. Fard.

32. Ibid.

33. Ibid.

34. Ibid.

35. FBI main file on Wallace D. Fard, memo from Los Angeles SAC to director dated August 29, 1963, 1–6; also see FBI Chicago file on Wallace D. Fard, and FBI Detroit file on same.

36. Chicago police department. FBI Chicago file on Wallace D. Fard, memo from Chicago SAC dated August 28, 1957, 1.

37. Ahmad, "The Ahmadiyya Movement in Islam" (brochure); also see Braden, *They Also Believe,* 461–62.

38. Agents queried by the author about the evidence explained that it was misplaced or possibly discarded. Given the vast number of items seized as evidence, the misplacement of a sixty-year-old item is certainly understandable.

39. A copy of the birth certificate appears in the FBI HQ file on Wallace D. Fard.

40. FBI HQ file on Wallace D. Fard. Agents pursued this angle in 1957, but by then all the leads were cold.

41. According to several accounts, Wallace asserted: "Master Fard Muhammad is not dead, brothers and sisters. He is physically alive and I talk to him whenever I get ready. I don't talk to him in any spooky way. I go to the telephone and dial his number." Bloom, *The American Religion*, 248–49; also see Magida, *Prophet of Rage*, 56–57.

42. This, according to an on-line English-Urdu dictionary.

43. Author's search of *Washington Post* database on July 22, 1997, and May 19, 1998.

44. Ibid.

45. Nanji, *The Muslim Almanac*, 55; also see note 42, supra.

46. Nyrop, *Pakistan: A Country Study*, 24.

47. Sorrenson, *Maori Origins and Migrations*, 59.

48. Ibid.

49. Nyrop, *Pakistan: A Country Study*, 10.

50. Ibid., 128; literature obtained by author from the Embassy of Pakistan in Washington, D.C.

51. Ibid.

52. Ibid.; also see Khaalis's letter in Appendix B in this book.

53. Hakim, *History of the Nation of Islam*, 5–6; Muhammad, *History of Jesus' Birth, Death, and What It Means* (a reprint of his *Pittsburgh Courier* newspaper column of July 27, 1957), 2–3.

54. Lending further credence to arguments that Fard was of Pakistani origin was his insistence that the Holy Quran of Maulana Muhammad Ali was the most accurate. See Muhammad, *History of Jesus' Birth*, 4; also see Hakim, *True History of Elijah Muhammad*, 51; This statement appears in the preface of the Holy Quran used by Elijah Muhammad: "And lastly, the greatest religious leader of the present time, Mirza Ghulam Ahmad of Qadian, has inspired me with all that is best in this work" (iii). And this excerpt from a book review

appears on the same page: "A careful comparison of Mr. Pickthall's translation with that of the Ahmadiyya translator, Maulana Muhammad Ali, shows conclusively that Mr. Pickthall's work is not very much more than a revision of the Ahmadiyya version." Also see Magida, *Prophet of Rage*, 231, n. 24.

55. Barboza, *American Jihad*, 106.

56. Author's interviews.

57. Author's interviews.

58. Muhammad, *The Supreme Wisdom*, vol. 1, 53.

59. Muhammad, *History of the Nation of Islam*, 4–5.

60. Exhibit 176 was among the items that the FBI says have been misplaced or otherwise lost. It was described in detail in the Bureau's Chicago file on Wallace D. Fard, Correlation Summary dated November 15, 1957, 32; also see FBI HQ file on Elijah Muhammad.

61. Her description accurately depicts Fard as he appeared in a mugshot taken on May 26, 1933. FBI's Detroit file on Wallace D. Fard, memo from Los Angeles SAC to director dated October 18, 1957, 1–5.

62. FBI HQ file on Wallace D. Fard.

63. Fard's name appears as "Farr" in a few FBI records, but these instances apparently were overlooked during the investigations.

64. FBI HQ file on the SDOO.

65. FBI HQ file on Wallace D. Fard.

66. FBI NY file on Malcolm X.

67. Muhammad, *The Supreme Wisdom*, vol. 1, 15; Elijah Muhammad, "Christianity vs. Islam" (audiocassette).

68. FBI Chicago file on Wallace D. Fard.

69. This contradiction was a major bone of contention between Wallace and his father. "You talk black, black, black, but you still can't see anything but white, white, white. You'd rather have a white Dr. Fard and go back in the jungles of primitive understanding than to stay in the light and get into the mainstream of America with a Bilalian-looking Wallace Deen Muhammad." W. Muhammad, *As the Light Shineth from the East*, 147.

19: A Con for a Con

1. "Ball of Confusion," by the Temptations (Gordy, 1969).

2. "Saviour's Day 1974" (audiocassette); Barboza, *American Jihad,* 271; FBI HQ file on Elijah Muhammad, summary memo from Chicago SAC to U.S. Secret Service dated May 24, 1974, 4–9.

3. FBI HQ file on Elijah Muhammad.

4. Scott's family owned more than thirty black-oriented newspapers in the South, including the *Atlanta Daily World.* See Obituaries: Stanley S. Scott, 59, Nixon and Ford Aide, *New York Times,* April 7, 1992, B08.; Ploski and Kaiser, *The Negro Almanac,* 1415–16.

5. FBI HQ file on Elijah Muhammad.

6. Ibid.

7. Ibid.

8. Ibid.; FBI Public Source Material file on Elijah Muhammad.

9. FBI HQ file on Elijah Muhammad.

10. Ibid.

11. Ibid.

12. Ibid.

13. Muhammad, *The Fall of America,* 125–45.

14. William Brashler, "Black on Black: The Deadly Struggle for Power," *New York,* June 9, 1975, 44–57; also see Barboza, *American Jihad,* 271.

15. FBI HQ file on Elijah Muhammad.

16. Ibid.

17. Ibid.

18. Ibid.; FBI Public Source Material on Elijah Muhammad.

19. "Nation Mourns Muslim Leader" (cover story), *Jet,* March 13, 1975, 20–22.

20. *Elijah Muhammad Meets the Press,* 13–15.

21. "Saviour's Day 1975" (audiocassette and videocassette); FBI HQ file on Elijah Muhammad.

22. "Nation Mourns Muslim Leader," *Jet,* March 13, 1975, 16; FBI Public Source Material file on Elijah Muhammad; *Chicago Defender,* February 27, 1975.

23. Clegg, *An Original Man,* 340.

24. *Chicago Tribune,* March 1, 1975, A04.

25. *Chicago Daily News*, March 7, 1975, A42; *Chicago Tribune*, March 11, 1975, A05.

26. Author's interview with Farrakhan's aides, September 19, 1979.

27. *New York Amsterdam News*, cited on-line at http://www.muhammad-speaks.com.

28. Ibid.

29. *Washington Post*, March 8, 1975.

30. Ibid., July 1, 1975.

31. *Church Committee Report*, book 3, 33.

32. Ibid., book 6, 37.

33. "Saviour's Day 1995" address of Farrakhan; Larry Muhammad, "Louis Farrakhan: Muslim Leader or Hypocrite?" *Sepia*, April 1980, 30–33. More than 200 movies with black themes were released between 1970 and 1980. The majority were low budget, and some raked in astronomical profits. One film, *Uptight!*, starred a controversial black activist (Julian Mayfield) and theme (that bad things happen to government informants), and the FBI tried to prevent its release. See, in general, Gerald Martinez, et al., *What It Is . . . What It Was! The Black Film Explosion of the 70s in Words and Pictures* (New York: Hyperion, 1998); FBI HQ on COINTELPRO: Black Extremists.

34. Bloom, *The American Religion*, 249; Magida, *Prophet of Rage*, 56–57.

35. "The Muslims: Five Years After Elijah, *Sepia*, March 1980, 31–37.

36. *United States v. Nathaniel Muhammad et al.*, U.S. Dist. Ct., Western Div. (Mo.), Criminal No. 75 CR 220-W-4 (1975); *Washington Post*, September 26, 1975.

37. *Washington Post*, February 3, 1976.

38. Author's interviews with eyewitness.

39. Lee, *By Any Means Necessary*, 62.

40. *In the Matter of the Estate of Elijah Muhammad, Deceased*, October 13, 1978, testimony of Emmanuel Muhammad, 2–26.

41. *Lucille Rosary v. Elijah Muhammad*, Superior Court of Los Angeles, #D652479 (1964), "Order to Show Cause," dated July 6, 1964, 3.

42. Supra, note 40, 8.

43. *Washington Post*, March 1, 1976.

44. "Chief Executive Officer, The Lost-Found Nation of Islam," at http://members.aol.com/akankem/Ceo.htm, 1–3.

45. Ibid.

46. Peter Noel, "One Nation?" *Vibe,* February 1996, 70; also see www.vibe.com/vibe/archive/feb96/docs/noi.html.

47. Muhammad, *Theology of Time,* Introduction.

48. Ibid.

49. Ibid.

50. From advertisment published in *Your Black Books Guide,* February 1997; Fardan, *Yakub and the Origin of White Supremacy.*

Epilogue: Virtual Religion

1. Philo Judaeus, Alexandrian philosopher (20 B.C.–45 A.D.?), cited by Seldes in *The Great Thoughts,* 329.

2. From the World Wide Web site of the United Nation of Islam on October 1997 (http://www.unoi).

3. Ibid.

4. Ibid.

5. "A Brief History on the Origin of the Nation of Islam," from the World Wide Web site of the NOI (faction directed by Farrakhan) on March 8, 1998 (http://www.noi.org).

6. Ibid.

7. See, in general, T. Muhammad, *The Comer by Night.*

8. The Web site is run by a faction of the NOI that appears to be close to or controlled by John Muhammad (http//:www.muhammadspeaks.com). As of this writing in March 1998, a copy of Elijah Muhammad's death certificate is posted on the Web site run by Elijah Muhammad's brother John. A copy of his headstone also appears in the article.

9. Ibid.

10. Ibid.

11. J. Muhammad, *Journal of Truth,* 70–73.

12. Interviews with Wali Muhammad, Elijah Muhammad's nephew.

13. "A Waste of Time," *Washington Post,* March 9, 1998, B02.

14. The photograph of the Mandela-Farrakhan kiss was taken on January 5, 1998, by AP photographer Denis Farrell, at a news conference in Soweto, South Africa, during which "Farrakhan criticized South Africa's Truth and Reconciliation Commission while praising Winnie Madikizela-Mandela, the focus of a commission probe on human rights abuses."

15. At the time of the kiss, Mandela was under investigation for her alleged role in the murder of several young South African activists. Farrakhan's name has surfaced on many occasions for his alleged role in the plot to kill Malcolm X.

16. Peter Noel, "One Nation?" *Vibe,* February 1996, 70–73.

17. Larry Muhammad, "Louis Farrakhan: Muslim Leader or Hypocrite?" *Sepia,* April 1980, 30–32; Magida, *Prophet of Rage,* 123.

18. "Omar Muhammad: Former Muslim Turns to Jesus Christ," Christian Broadcasting Network, "700 Club." The story was placed on the World Wide Web in November 1998 at http://www.the700club.org/amazing/omarmuhammad.asp.

19. Ibid.

20. Thomas Jefferson, *Notes on the State of Virginia,* Query 17, reprinted in *Thomas Jefferson: Monticello, Virginia, USA* (New York: Westvaco Corp., 1975).

BIBLIOGRAPHY

FREEDOM OF INFORMATION ACT (FOIA) RELEASES

I. Central Intelligence Agency (CIA)

(*Key names and organizations cited in files released on Elijah Muhammad and Malcolm X*)

Alex Haley
Hakim Abdullah Jamal
Martin Luther King Jr.
Louis E. Lomax
Akbar Muhammad
Clara Muhammad
Elijah Muhammad
Herbert Muhammad
Malcolm X
Nation of Islam

II. Federal Bureau of Investigation (FBI)

(*Listed by FBI numerical file number*)

44-HQ-47984	George Jackson
44-HQ-50522	George Jackson—victim
61-7099	Albert Einstein
62-293	Noble Drew Ali

62-95834	Josephine Baker
62-25889	Noble Drew Ali
62-102926	Louis E. Lomax
65-562	Satahota Takahashi, aka Naka Nakane
65-562	Society for the Development of Our Own
72-1495	Slater Hunter King
92-7389	Charles Liston, aka Sonny Liston
100-3-116	Communist Party USA, Negro Question
100-4087	Development of Our Own Society
100-5549	Allah Temple of Islam
100-5631	Malcolm X (Phoenix file)
100-8420	Moorish Science Temple of America
100-12304	Paul Robeson
100-15139	Langston Hughes
100-25356	Wallace D. Fard
100-32805	Malcolm X (D.C. file)
100-33593	Malcolm X (Chicago file)
100-35635	Nation of Islam: Internal Security
100-36506	Clara Muhammad
100-51230	Adam Clayton Powell Jr.
100-88143	Universal Negro Improvement Association
100-106670	Martin Luther King Jr.
100-146553	James Baldwin
100-150520	Clarence 13X Smith
100-161140	Nation of Islam (New York file)
100-393031	Lorraine Hansberry
100-399321	Malcolm X
100-430081	Leon 4X Ameer
100-434443	Edward Kennedy "Duke" Ellington
100-438995	Louis "Satchmo" Armstrong
100-442529	Communist Influence in Racial Matters
100-441765	Muslim Mosque Inc.
100-442735	Organization of Afro-American Unity
100-444622	Hakim Abdullah Jamal
100-448006	COINTELPRO: Black Nationalist-Hate Groups
100-450712	Sammy Davis Jr.
100-469601	Elijah Muhammad (consolidated file)

105-8999	Malcolm X (New York file)
105-24822	Elijah Poole, aka EM-NOI
105-32140	Leon 4X Ameer
105-32655	Joseph Gravitt Jr.
157-515	Chauncey Eskridge
157-1489	Five Percenters
157-2209	Nation of Islam (Chicago file)
157-13876	Jean Seberg
160-15464-1	Richard Wright

A. *Cross-Referenced File Material Releases*

- A. Peter Bailey*
- Aubrey Barnett
- Communist Infiltration of NAACP
- Ella Little Collins
- Rodnell Collins
- John Coltrane
- Ossie Davis
- Louis Farrakhan, aka Louis X Walcott
- Rev. Clarence "C.L." Franklin
- Joseph Gravitt Sr.
- Dick Gregory
- Mahalia Jackson
- Betty Sanders, aka Betty Shabazz
- Juanita Poitier
- Larry 4X Prescott
- Ruby Wallace, aka Ruby Dee
- Thomas Wallace
- James 67X Warden
- Dinah Washington

25-66890	Miles Dewey Davis
25-90417	Willie Muhammad
25-117905	Emmanuel Muhammad
25-330971	Nation of Islam
100-145486	James 67X Warden

* No file number listed.

100-27167	Raymond Sharrieff
100-31166	Herbert C. Muhammad
100-32090	Wallace Delaney Muhammad
100-32814	Lottie Mae (Poole) Muhammad
100-33335	Akbar Muhammad
100-33544	Lucille Rosary (Main file)
100-37182	Tynetta (Nelson) Deanar (Main file)
100-133629	Amiri Baraka, aka Leroi Jones
100-436766	Ethel (Poole) Sharrieff
100-430085	Akbar Muhammad
100-438731	Hassan Sharrieff
100-442684	Revolutionary Action Movement (RAM)
100-446080	Stokely Carmichael
105-28755	Arab Activities in the U.S.
105-24951	Raymond Sharrieff (Chicago file)
105-25519	John Muhammad
105-33561	John W. Simmons Jr., aka John Ali
105-37357	Lucille Viola Rosary (Chicago file)
105-38394	Evelyn Lorene Williams (Chicago file)
105-436351	Cassius Clay, aka Muhammad Ali
105-44912	Elijah Muhammad Jr.
105-54773	Herbert C. Muhammad
105-58692	Wallace Delaney Muhammad
105-60406	William M. Fagin, aka Wali Muhammad
105-69067	Lottie Muhammad (Chicago file)
105-69747	James (Jam) Muhammad
105-72080	Nathaniel Muhammad
157-2668	Hanafi American Mussulman
157-5384	Abass Rassoull
157-18253	Soledad Brothers

B. FBI: *Public Source Material Releases (Data obtained from media, vital
   records, etc.)*
John Ali
Muhammad Ali
Abdul Aziz
Norman 3X Butler

Rev. Albert Cleage
Ella Collins
Chauncey Eskridge
Wallace D. Fard
Louis Farrakhan
Rev. C.L. Franklin
Talmadge X Hayer
Jesse L. Jackson
Hakim Abdullah Jamal
Thomas 15X Johnson
Hamaas Abdul Khaalis
Martin Luther King Jr.
Slater Hunter King
Balm Leavell
William R. Ming Jr.
Akbar Muhammad
Clara Muhammad
Elijah Muhammad
Herbert Muhammad
Wallace D. Muhammad
Abbass Rassoull
Jean Seberg
Betty Shabazz
Raymond Sharrieff
Satahota Takahashi
Robert Williams
Malcolm X

III. New York Police Department FOIA Releases
(Bureau of Special Services)

Malcolm X

IV. Detroit Police Department FOIA Releases

Wallace Dodd Ford, with aliases
Elijah Poole, with aliases

V. U.S. Air Force
Office of Special Investigations (OSI)

10D24C-907   Hakim Abdullah Jamal

VI. U.S. Navy
Office of Naval Intelligence (ONI)

America First Party
Father Charles E. Coughlin
James Farr
Marcus Garvey
Langston Hughes
Elijah Muhammad
Gerald L. K. Smith
Gerald B. Winrod

VII. U.S. Army

Langston Hughes
William R. Ming Jr.
Elijah Muhammad

VIII. U.S. Department of State

Edward Kennedy "Duke" Ellington
Langston Hughes
Hakim Abdullah Jamal
Akbar Muhammad
Clara Muhammad
Elijah Muhammad
Herbert Muhammad
Wallace Muhammad
Malcolm X
Nation of Islam

IX. The Foreign Service of the United States

Akbar Muhammad
Clara Muhammad
Elijah Muhammad
Herbert Muhammad
Malcolm X

X. U.S. Treasury Department
(Bureau of Customs)

Hakim Abdullah Jamal

COURT CITATIONS AND LAW JOURNALS

Dred Scott v. Sanford, 19 Howard U.S. 393 (1857).

Plessy v. Ferguson, 163 U.S. 537 (1896).

Berea College v. Kentucky, 211 U.S. 45 (1908).

Ancient Egyptian Arabic Order of Nobles of the Mystic Shrine, et al. v. Micheaux et al., 279 U.S. 737 (1929).

Yates v. United States, 354 U.S. 298, 1 L. Ed. 2d 1356 (1957).

Evelyn Williams v. Elijah Muhammad, Superior Court of Los Angeles, #D652475 (1964).

Lucille Rosary v. Elijah Muhammad, Superior Court of Los Angeles, #D652479 (1964).

Muhammad's Temple of Islam, Inc. v. Malcolm X Little, Queens County Cir. Ct., Landlord and Tenant Division, No. 4845/64 (1964).

People of the State of New York v. Muhammad Abdul Aziz et al., New York Sup. Ct., Ind. #871/65 (1965).

People of the State of New York v. Afeni Shakur et al., New York Sup. Ct., Ind. #1848-1/2/69 (1969).

Cassius M. Clay v. United States, 403 U.S. 698 (1970).

United States v. Cassius M. Clay, 430 F. 2nd 165 (1970).

United States v. William Christian et al., D.C. Sup. Ct., Criminal No. 47900-73 through 47906-73 (1973).

In the Matter of the Estate of Elijah Muhammad, Deceased, Cook County Cir. Ct., #75-P-4128-806-541 (1975).

United States v. Nathaniel Muhammad et al., U.S. Dist. Ct., Western Div. (Mo.), Criminal No. 75CR220-W-4 (1975).

William Christian et al. v. United States, 394 A. 2nd 1 (1978).

Hamaas Abdul Khaalis, et al. v. United States, 408 A. 2d 313 (1979).

United States v. William Hohri et al., 482 U.S. 64, 96 L. Ed. 2d 51 (1987).

"Black Muslims in Prison: Of Muslim Rites and Constitutional Rights." *Columbia Law Review* 62: 1488, December 1962.

FEDERAL AND STATE GOVERNMENT HEARINGS

California State Senate Fact-Finding Subcommittee on Un-American Activities, Eleventh Report (1961), pp. 131–38.

House Un-American Activities Committee, 31 October and 1 November 1967, p. 935 (aka HUAC Committee).

Senate Permanent Subcommittee on Investigations, 1, 2, 3, and 6 November 1967, p. 322.

Senate Permanent Subcommittee on Investigations, 5, 6, and 7 December 1967, p. 1119.

House Committee on Internal Security, 9 and 10 May, 1 and 20 June 1972, p. 7410.

Select Committee to Study Governmental Operations with Respect to Intelligence Activities, vols. 1–6, November 1975 (aka the Church Committee Report).

GOVERNMENT AND QUASI-GOVERNMENT SOURCES

Report to the President by the Commission on CIA Activities Within the United States, June 1975 (aka the Rockefeller Commission Report).

Biographic Register, U.S. State Department, vols. 1959–75.

SELECT NEWSPAPERS AND JOURNALS (ABBREVIATED LIST)

AIM Report; Al-Qalam; American Lawyer; Amnesty International; Arizona Republic; Big Red News; BBB Interviews; Bilalian News; Black Film Review; Black News; Boston Real Paper; Caribbean Voice-American; Chicago Lawyer; Chicago Tribune; Class; Commercial Appeal (Memphis); *Contrast* (Canadian publication); *Detroit Free Press; Detroit News;*

Ebony; Emerge; Encore; Egyptian Gazette (Cairo, Egypt); *Essence; Esquire; Front Page; Freedom Journal* (Church of Scientology); *Houston Post; Insight; JET; Los Angeles Herald Tribune; Los Angeles Times; Magnet News; Memories; Mother Jones; Muhammad Speaks; Muslim Journal; National Geographic; Newsday; Newsweek; New York Amsterdam News; New York Post; New York Times; Parade; Penthouse; People; People's Voice; Playboy; Post-Tribune* (Gary, Indiana); *Ramparts; Regardie's; Readers' Digest; Saint Louis Argus; San Francisco Chronicle; Saturday Evening Post; Sepia; Texas Monthly; Tikkun; Time; Village Voice; Washington Herald-Tribune; Washington Jewish Week; Washington Post; Washington Star; Washington Times; Watchtower; Washingtonian; The Black American; The Black Collegian; The Black Scholar; The Chicago Crusader; The Chicago Defender; The Final Call of Islam* (1934 publication); *The Final Call* (Farrakhan); *The Militant; The National; The National Law Journal; The New Day* (Father Divine); *The Sunday Trentonian.*

Videotape Sources, Television Transcripts, and Radio Transcripts

- "Brother Minister: The Assassination of El Hajj Malik El Shabazz." X-Ceptional Productions, 1997.
- "Brother Minister: The Assassination of El Hajj Malik El Shabazz" (outtakes). X-Ceptional Productions, 1997.
- "The CIA: Assassinations." WETA-TV Channel 26 (Washington, D.C.), 1992.
- "Covert Action Against Malcolm." *Like It Is.* WNBC-TV (New York), February 20, 1983.
- "Eartha Kitt." *60 Minutes.* CBS-TV, July 22, 1990.
- "El Hajj Malik El Shabazz (Malcolm X)." WNBC-TV (New York), 1979.
- "Elijah Muhammad: The Messenger from Violet Drive." KOED-TV (Indiana University), 1964.
- "Elijah Muhammad: Historical Documentary." Secretarius Memps Publications, 1992.
- "Eyes on the Prize." PBS-TV, Blackside Inc., January 14–18, 1990.
- "Farrakhan and the Milton Coleman Controversy." *Nightline.* ABC-TV, April 5, 1984.

- "The FBI's War on Black America." Maljack Productions, 1989.
- "Geronimo Pratt." *60 Minutes.* CBS-TV, July 21, 1991.
- "The Hate That Hate Produced" (Mike Wallace/Louis E. Lomax documentary). WNTA-TV Channel 13 (New York), June 13, 1959.
- "An Interview with Wallace D. Muhammad." Positive Images/Communicator Productions, 1992.
- "An Interview with Imam Warith D. Muhammad." *Like It Is.* WNBC-TV (New York), May 18, 1986.
- "An Interview with Louis Farrakhan." *Nightline.* ABC-TV, 1986.
- "An Interview with Louis Farrakhan" by Sam Donaldson. *Nightwatch.* ABC-TV, March 7, 1990.
- "The Laughing Lieutenant: The Execution of Malcolm X." Omar Shabazz Productions, New York, 1997.
- "Lie Detector: F. Lee Bailey interviews Khalil Islam (aka Thomas 15X Johnson)," ca. 1990.
- "Louis Farrakhan." *60 Minutes.* CBS-TV, April 14, 1996.
- "Louis Farrakhan." *20/20.* ABC-TV, April 22, 1994.
- "Malcolm X." *60 Minutes.* CBS-TV, February 23, 1992.
- "Malcolm X." A documentary. Marvin Worth. Warner Bros., May, 1972 (theatrical release).
- "Malcolm X." A documentary. Mntex Entertainment (Prior Lake, Minnesota), 1993.
- "Malcolm X: Make It Plain." PBS-TV. Blackside Inc., January 26, 1994.
- "Malcolm X Remembered." *Evening Exchange.* WHUR-TV (Washington, D.C.), February 21, 1992.
- "Malcolm X: The Real Story." CBS News Home Video, 1992.
- "Malcolm X's Death: Other Voices." *Tony Brown's Journal.* PBS-TV, February 1993.
- "Minister Farrakhan Speaks on the Murder of Malcolm X." Final Call Productions, February 21, 1990.
- "The Mormons." *60 Minutes.* CBS-TV, April 17, 1996.
- "The Nation of Islam." NBC-TV Channel 4 (Washington, D.C.), November 27, 1995.
- "Our Voices: A Look at Spike Lee's 'X'." Black Entertainment Television (Washington, D.C.), November 17, 1992.
- "Saviour's Day, 1973." Secretarius Memps Publications, Atlanta, Georgia.
- "Saviour's Day, 1974." Secretarius Memps Publications, Atlanta, Georgia.

- "Saviour's Day, 1975." Secretarius Memps Publications, Atlanta, Georgia.
- "Saviour's Day, 1995." Final Call Productions, Chicago, Illinois.
- "The Secret Files of J. Edgar Hoover." WTTG-TV Channel 5 (Washington, D.C.), December 4, 1989.
- "Talmadge Hayer." *Tony Brown's Journal.* PBS-TV, March 23, 1980.
- "Who Killed JFK?" WTTG-TV Channel 5 (Washington, D.C.), November 24, 1988.
- "Who Killed Malcolm X?" *60 Minutes.* CBS-TV, January 17, 1982.

SPEECHES, RADIO ADDRESSES, AND OTHER RECORDINGS
(FEATURING MUHAMMAD OR KEY NOI OFFICIALS)

1. "Accept Your Own and Be Yourself" (undated).
2. "Assassination of Rulers" (undated).
3. "Be Yourself" (July 12, 1970).
4. "The Beast of Revelations" (undated).
5. "Betty Shabazz: Howard University Speech" (February 28, 1979).
6. "The Black Man's Necessary Qualifications to Be Accepted" (April 11, 1965).
7. "Buzz Anderson Interview of Elijah Muhammad" (1964).
8. "Christianity Deceived the Black Nation" (undated).
9. "Defense Against Orthodox Muslims" (undated).
10. "Defense of Messengership" (undated).
11. "The Dragon" (undated).
12. "Elijah Muhammad: Response to Allegation of Fard Hoax Charges" (July 1963).
13. "The Future of the American So-Called Negro" (undated).
14. "Give Up That Old Slavery Idea" (undated).
15. "Knowledge of the Time" (undated).
16. "Lost for 400 Years: God Is Man" (undated).
17. "Louis Farrakhan: An Interview" (transcript of interview with publisher, editors and reporters at the *Washington Post*) (March 1, 1990).
18. "Louis Farrakhan: Speech at Ujamaa House," Washington, D.C. (1979).
19. "Malcolm X: Crisis of Racism" (May 1962).
20. "Malcolm X: A Final Message" (Detroit) (February 14, 1965).
21. "Malcolm X: Harvard Law School Forum" (December 16, 1964).
22. "Malcolm X: His Wit and Wisdom," Douglas Recording (1969).

23. "Malcolm X: An Interview at University of California at Berkeley (October 1963).

24. "Malcolm X: Lecture at Michigan State University" (January 1962).

25. "Malcolm X: The Mississippi Freedom Democratic Party" (December 1964).

26. "Malcolm X: Prospects for Freedom in 1965 (1965).

27. "Malcolm X Speaks to Harlem" (January 7, 1965).

28. "Malcolm X Speaks to the People of Harlem" (August 1963).

29. "The Man of Sin (undated).

30. "Master Fard Muhammad—Not a Peddler" (undated).

31. "Natural Religion" (undated).

32. "Negro Preacher Worst Enemy to His People" (undated).

33. "No Justice for Black People under Rule of White People" (undated).

34. "One Apostle at a Time" (undated).

35. "Open Mind" (news program transcript) (April 1961).

36. "Opposition Against Truth Is Punished" (March 14, 1964).

37. "Original and the Non-Original" (August 21, 1961).

38. "Our Enemies Seek to Destroy Us" (undated).

39. "The Pope and the Catholic Church" (undated).

40. "Saviour's Day: 1964."

41. "Self-Preservation" (undated).

42. "Separation" (August 25, 1963).

43. "The Shame of Intermixing of Races" (August 31, 1963).

44. "That Which You Should Know (Interpretation of Signs)" (undated).

45. "That Which You Should Know: Separation or Death" (undated).

46. "The Time and What Must Be Done" (undated).

47. "True Religion" (undated).

48. "Truth Upsets Christian World" (undated).

49. "The War of Armageddon" (undated).

50. "We Can Preserve Our Black Nation" (undated).

51. "What the So-Called Negro Should Know: The Time" (May 3, 1964).

52. "The White Man Losing Power" (undated).

53. "Who Are the Muslims?" (undated).

COMPUTER SOFTWARE RESOURCES

CIA Base/NAME Base. Public Information Research. P.O. Box 680635, San Antonio, Texas, 78268.

A database containing the names of thousands of CIA and KGB officers and other government officials, this software permits a researcher to determine which country an individual officer was stationed in for any given year. It also provides a list of books and articles in which an individual is mentioned.

Lexis-Nexis. Lexis is a database used by attorneys and paralegals for legal research. It contains the judicial opinions (verdicts) of millions of official court cases. Nexis is a database containing the complete text of articles appearing in major newspapers and magazines.

Compton's Complete Street Guide. Compton's New Media, 1995.

INTERNET AND WORLD WIDE WEB SITES

■ **Afrinet:** An informational guide to resources on African and African-American culture. (http://www.afrinet.com)

■ **Afro-American Newspaper:** A limited on-line version of a black-oriented paper founded in 1892. (http://www.afroam.org)

■ **Afrocentric Resources On-Line:** A host of Web pages devoted to Afrocentrism, Black Nationalism, and related philosophies. (http://melanet.com)

■ **Aga Khan Visual Archive:** One of several sites located in the Rotch Library Visual Collections at the Massachusetts Institute of Technology, this archive contains striking photographs and textual materials related to mosques in the United States and around the world. It is the only source (to my knowledge) at present with photographs of the Shahbaz Qalandar Shrine. (http://libraries.mit.edu/rvc/)

■ **Ancestry Home Town:** A database designed for genealogical research, it also contains the birth dates and dates of death for millions of Americans, provided they had a Social Security number. (http://www.ancestry.com)

■ **Diversity Page:** A guide to resources on ethnic diversity on the Internet. (http://latino.sscnet.ucla.edu/diversity1.html)

■ **FBI On-Line:** Due to growing interest in declassified documents on famous and infamous individuals, the FBI has placed a number of files at its Web site. Among those available at the site are the files on Paul Robeson, Wallace D. Fard, "Baby Face" Nelson, and Leon Trotsky. (http://www.fbi.gov)

■ **John Henrik Clarke Africana Library:** Devoted to Clarke's collections available at Cornell University. (http://132.236.31.11/Afr.html)

■ **Library of Congress On-Line:** A digital archive of many materials available only at the nation's largest library. (http://lcweb.loc.gov/)

- **Muhammad Speaks On-Line:** This group is another offshoot of the Nation of Islam. It's an excellent source for alternative views to the teachings of Elijah Muhammad as interpreted by Farrakhan. (http://www.muhammad-speaks.com)

- **NOI On-Line:** (Farrakhan/Chicago): The informational database maintained by the branch of the NOI by Minister Louis Farrakhan. (http://www.noi.org)

- **The Drum Homepage:** Like the Diversity Page, this site is an excellent guide to resources on the Internet concerning the African and African-American community. (http://drum.ncsc.org)

- **United Nation of Islam On-Line:** The Web site features articles about another offshoot of the NOI. The UNOI claims that its leader, Solomon, is God in human form, and that one of its members is the reincarnation of Elijah Muhammad. (http://www.qni.com/~unoi/)

- **Urdu Language Web Site:** A "small-sized Urdu dictionary," placed on-line in 1992. Urdu is the official language of Pakistan. (Gopher/Library/Article/Language/Urdu.dic)

MAGAZINES, PAMPHLETS, AND SELECTED ARTICLES

Abdul-Rauf, Muhammad. "Pilgrimage to Mecca." *National Geographic* 154, no. 5 (November 1978): 581–607.

Abercrombie, Thomas J. "When the Moors Ruled Spain." *National Geographic* 174, no. 1 (July 1988): 86–119.

Accuracy in Media (AIM) Report. "The FBI Did Not Kill Jean Seberg," September 1, 1980, 1.

"Afrocentrism: Was Cleopatra Black?" *Newsweek,* September 23, 1991, 42–50.

Agnes, Ted, Jerry Seper, and Glenn Emery. "We Are Going to Shake the World: Louis Farrakhan and the Nation of Islam." *Washington Times, Insight,* November 11, 1985, 7–19.

Ahmad, Mubasher, ed. "The Ahmadiyya Movement in Islam" (brochure), The Ahmaidyya Movement in Islam, Inc., U.S.A., 1994.

Alter, Jonathan, et al. "The Long Shadow of Slavery." *Newsweek,* December 8, 1997, 58–68.

Ammeson, Jane. "Rich Heritage Provides Ample Literary Fodder for Alex Haley." *Compass Readings Magazine* (Northwest Airlines), January 1992, 70–74.

Amnesty International. *Proposal for a Commission of Inquiry Into the Effect of Domestic Intelligence Activities on Criminal Trials in the United States of America*. London: Amnesty International, 1981.

————. "FBI Misconduct in Trials of Militants." *Encore,* January 1982, 8–10.

Arden, Harvey. "In Search of Moses. *National Geographic* 149, no. 1 (January 1976): 2–37.

————. "Chicago!" *National Geographic* 153, no. 4 (April 1978): 463–92.

"Assassin Squeals After 43 Years." *Korea Newsreview,* April 18, 1992, 23.

Bailey, A. Peter. "Remembering Malcolm X: He Was a Master Teacher." *Emerge,* February 1990, 27–28.

————. "Remembering Malcolm X." *YSB Magazine,* May 1992, 51–53.

Baldwin, James. "There's a Bill Due That Has to Be Paid." *Life,* May 24, 1963, 81–90.

Balk, A., and Alex Haley. "Black Merchants of Hate." *Saturday Evening Post,* January 26, 1963, 68–72.

Barboza, Steven. "A Divided Legacy." *Emerge,* April 1992, 26–32.

Barnes, Fred. "The Farrakhan Factor: Farrakhan Frenzy." *New Republic,* October 28, 1985, 13–15.

Barnette, Aubrey, with Edwin Linn. "The Black Muslims Are a Fraud." *Saturday Evening Post,* February 27, 1965, 23–29.

BBB Interviews. "C. Eric Lincoln." November 1979, 37–39.

BBB Interviews. "Louis Farrakhan." December 1977, 42–44.

Benjamin, Playthell. "Who Is Listening to Louis Farrakhan? . . . And How Did He Become Big Man on Campus? *Village Voice,* August 15, 1989, 23–31.

————. "Would Malcolm Now Be Farrakhan?" *Emerge,* February 1990, 24–25.

————. "Spike Lee: Bearing the Cross." *Emerge,* November 1991, 26–32.

Benyon, E. D. "The Voodoo Cult Among Negro Migrants in Detroit. *American Journal of Sociology* 43, no. 6 (May 1938): 894–907.

Berger, Alan. "Who Killed Malcolm X?" *Seven Days* (part 1 of 2), March 24, 1978.

————. "Who Killed Malcolm X?" *Seven Days* (part 2 of 2), April 7, 1978.

Berger, Monroe. "Black Muslims." *Horizon,* Winter 1964, 48.

Bernal, Martin. "The Case for Massive Egyptian Influence in the Aegean." *Archaeology,* September/October 1992, 53–55, 82–86.

Berry, Mary Frances. "Plessy v. Ferguson." *Emerge,* May 1996, 54–58.

"Black Muslims in Prison: Of Muslim Rites and Constitutional Rights." *Columbia Law Review* 62, no. 148 (December 1962): 1488.

Blum, Andrew. "JFK Conundrum." *The National Law Journal,* December 23, 1991, 34–36.

"Book Notes: The Desegregation Dilemma." *Harvard Law Review* 109, no. 5 (March 1996): 1144.

Boyd, Herb. "Hero or 'Charlie Bad Guy?' Gene Roberts, Muslims/Panther Infiltrator, Says He's Neither." *Class,* December/January 1992, 54–57.

———. "Malcolm X: Son of the Caribbean." *Class,* April 1992 (cover story).

"Boxer Rebellion." *Newsweek,* February 28, 1966, 54.

Braden, Charles S. "Moslem Missions in America." *Religion in Life,* Summer 1959, 331.

———. "Islam in America." *International Review of Missions,* July 1959, 309.

Bradley, Edward, as told to Louis E. Lomax. "Driver Tells How Malcolm X Escaped Death in Chase." *North American Newspaper Alliance* (NANA), February 24, 1965.

Brashler, William. "Black on Black: The Deadly Struggle for Power." *New York,* June 9, 1975, 44–57.

Burns, W. Haywood. "The Black Muslims in America: A Reinterpretation." *Race,* July 1963, 26.

Chomsky, Noam. "COINTELPRO: What the (deleted) Was It? Engineering of Consent." *The Public Eye,* Spring 1978, 14–38.

Coleman, John E. "Did Egypt Shape the Glory That Was Greece? The Case Against Martin Bernal's *Black Athena.*" *Archaeology,* September/October 1942, 48–52, 77–81.

Cooper, Mary H. "Muslims in America." *Congressional Quarterly Researcher* (CQR), April 30, 1993, 363–83.

Cottman, Michael H. "Million Man Moves: Beyond the March." *B.E.T. Weekend Magazine,* September 1996, 12–16.

Coughlin, Ellen K. "Politics and Commerce in the Rebirth of Malcolm X." *Chronicle of Higher Education,* October 7, 1992, 8, 14.

Curry, George E. "Farrakhan: Some Straight Talk and a Few Tears for Malcolm from the Minister." *Emerge,* August 1990, 28–41.

———. "Malcolm X in Transition." *Emerge,* February 1995, 34–47.

Curtis, Tom. "The Origins of AIDS." *Rolling Stone,* March 19, 1992, 54–61, 106–8.

Davis, Angela. "Malcolm X." *Emerge,* December 1992, 35–37.

Dille, John. "We Who Tried: The Untold Battle Story of the Men on the Beach at the Bay of Pigs." *Life,* May 10, 1963, 20–34, 69–83.

Dreifus, Claudia. "Andrew Young: On Life, Sin, and the Murder of Friends." *Modern Maturity,* March/April 1997, 52–59, 73–76.

"Egypt: Ancient Land of Nubia, Below the Waters." *The Middle East,* July/August 1994, 35–37.

Ernest E. "Gil Noble: Media's Warrior." *Encore,* October 1981, 20–23.

Evanzz, Karl. "Black Hollywood and the FBI." *Black Film Review,* Winter 1987/88, 16–19.

———. "The State Department, the CIA and Malcolm X's Death." *Big Red News,* July 28, 1990, 1.

Farrakhan, Louis. "Farrakhan on Jesse Jackson: A Warning to Black Americans." *Essence,* February 1984, 90–92.

"FBI Sought to Disrupt Black Panthers, Tried to Use Black Reporters." *JET,* November 6, 1980, 25.

Fields-Meyers, Thomas, et al. "The Flames of Hate." *People Weekly,* April 8, 1996, 96–102.

"FOCUS: Stanley Robinson Raises Issues That Cannot Lightly Be Dismissed" [FBI informant issue]. *Chicago Lawyer,* January 1982.

Frederickson, George M. "African Americans and African Africans." *New York Review of Books,* September 26, 1991.

"Freedom March Ends in a Murder [Viola Liuzzo]." *Life,* April 2, 1965, 45.

Gaber, Hosny M. "Outline of Islam." *Islamic Center Publications,* 1975.

Galloway, Joseph L., et al. "Debt of Honor: A Half-Century Later, Seven Black Heroes Have Been Nominated for the Medal of Honor." *U.S. News & World Report,* May 6, 1996, 28–46.

Gans, Bruce Michael, and Walter L. Lowe. "The Islam Connection." *Playboy,* April 1980, 119–20, 130, 180, 200–4.

Gillespie, Marcia Ann. "25 Years Later: Malcolm's Journey from Troubling Prophet to Icon." *Emerge,* February 1990, 22–23.

Goldman, Peter. "Who Killed Malcolm?" *Newsweek,* May 7, 1979, 39.

Gore, Rick. "Ramses the Great." *National Geographic* 179, no. 4 (April 1991): 2–32.

Greenfield, Jeff. "The Yale Plot to Run America." *M Magazine,* May 1992, 76–79.

Halberstam, David. "Taking Issue: Missing a Beat." *Memories,* February/March, 1990, 101.

Hall, Alice J. "Dazzling Legacy of an Ancient Quest." *National Geographic* 151, no. 3, (March 1977): 293–311.

Hercules, Frank. "To Live in Harlem . . ." *National Geographic* 151, no. 2 (February 1977): 178–207.

"Honoring Our Black Prince." *YSB* Magazine (cover story), May 1992.

"Hoover Offered $500 Bonus to Have Panther Leader Hampton Killed." *JET,* November 6, 1980, 25.

"Indonesia: Change at the Top." *Newsweek,* March 21, 1966, 42.

"Interview with Minster Farrakhan." *First World,* Spring 1978, 11.

Karenga, Ron Maulana. "Malcolm and the Messenger: Beyond Psychological Assumptions to Political Analysis." *Black News* 4, no. 21 (1983): 4–11.

Keating, Bern. "Pakistan: Problems of a Two-Part Land." *National Geographic* 131, no. 1 (January 1967): 1–48.

Kelly, Brian, and Harry Jaffe. "The Farrakhan Fiasco." *Regardie's,* January 1990, 47–55.

Kelly, Orr, with Ted Gest and Joseph Shapiro. "The Secret Files of J. Edgar Hoover." *U.S. News & World Report,* December 19, 1983, 45–50.

Kempner, Aviva. "Marvin Worth's 25 Years on 'Malcolm X': Jewish Filmmaker Slogged His Way to Drama." *Washington Jewish Week,* December 24, 1992, 17–18.

Kennedy, John F. Jr. "One In a Million (An Interview with Louis Farrakhan)." *George,* October 1996, 106–10, 143–44.

La Fay, Howard." Where Jesus Walked." *National Geographic* 132, no. 6 (December 1967): 739–81.

Lanouette, William. "50 Years Later: Why We Dropped the Bomb." *Civilization,* January/February 1995, 28–39.

Lehner, Mark. "Computer Rebuilds the Ancient Sphinx." *National Geographic* 179, no. 4 (April 1991): 32–39.

Lemonick, Michael D. "Are the Bible's Stories True?" *Time,* December 18, 1995, 62–70.

Lester, Julius. "The Farrakhan Factor: The Time Has Come." *New Republic,* October 28, 1985, 11–12.

Lewis, Ida. "Black Mask of Angry Africa." *Life,* April 2, 1965, 111–23.

Linden, Eugene. "Lost Tribes, Lost Knowledge." *Time,* September 23, 1991, 46–55.

Love, Iris. "The Strange Journey of Hitler's Watercolors." *Parade,* January 19, 1989, 4–6 .

"The Madison Bomb Story: The Death the FBI Saw, Heard and Won't Talk About." *Mother Jones,* February/March 1979, 56–63.

Major, Reginald W., and Marcia D. Davis. "Prisoner of War [Geronimo Pratt]." *Emerge,* June 1994, 30–35.

Makdisi, Nadin. "The Moslems in America." *Christian Century,* August 26, 1959, 969.

"Malcolm X: Menace or Messiah?" *Memories,* February/March 1990, 80–88.

Marable, Manning. "Manning Marable on Malcolm X: His Message and Meaning." *Open Media,* November 1992, pamphlet no. 22.

McCarthy Todd. "Reviews: X." *Variety,* November 16, 1992, 64–65.

McKinley, James. "Playboy's History of Assassination in America. Part VI: Death Crosses the Color Line." *Playboy,* June 1976, 127–30, 210–27.

McLeish, Kenneth. "Abraham, the Friend of God." *National Geographic* 130, no. 6 (December 1966): 739–89.

Meier, A. "Negro Protest Movements and Organizations." *Journal of Negro Education* 32 (Fall 1963): 437.

Michio, Fujimura. "Amur River Society (Black Dragon Society)." *Kodansha Encyclopedia of Japan* 1: 53.

"Mohammad, Messenger of God: A Movie to Be Seen, Discussed, Understood." *Al-Islam,* April/May 1977, 7–8.

Moldea, Dan E. "Who Really Killed Bobby Kennedy?" *Regardie's,* June 1987.

Morrison, Allan. "Who Killed Malcolm X?" *Ebony,* October 1965, 135–36.

"Muhammad Leaves Great Legacy of Pride and Respect." *JET,* March 13, 1975, 6–14.

Muhammad, Abdullah Yasin. "It's Still Nation Time." *Emerge,* April 1992, 33–34.

Muhammad, Elijah. "Now Hear the Message to the Black Muslims From Their Leader." *Esquire,* April 1963, 97.

———. "What the Black Muslims Believe." *Negro Digest,* November 1963, 3.

Muhammad, Larry. "The Muslims: Five Years After Elijah." *Sepia,* March 1980, 31–37.

———. "Louis Farrakhan: Muslim Leader or Hypocrite?" *Sepia,* April 1980, 30–32.

Murphy, W. E. "Some Strange New Coverts to the Cause of Civil Rights." *Reporter* 16 (June 27, 1957): 13.

"Muslim Message: All White Men Devils, All Negroes Divine." *Newsweek,* August 27, 1962, 26.

"A Myth Is Broken." *Newsweek,* March 6, 1966, 43–44.

Nader, George A. "The View from Tripoli: An Interview with Muammar Qadhafi of Libya." *Middle East Insight,* September/October, 1993, 35–39.

"The Nation Surges to Join the Negro on His March." *Life,* March 26, 1965, 30–37.

Neff, James. "Is Justice Blind?" *George,* October 1996, 126–29, 153–55.

"Negro Jihad: The Nation of Islam, a Movement Among American Negroes." *Economist,* February 25, 1961, 31.

Newfield, Jack. "'I Want Kennedy Killed!' Hoffa Shouted . . . An Eyewitness Account." *Penthouse,* May 1992, 30–36, 102–6.

Newsweek. "Special Report: The Two Faces of Farrakhan." October 30, 1995, 27–48.

"1965: February and March 5 Years Ago; Bomb Plot." *Memories,* February/March 1990, 75.

Noble, Gil. "Rewriting the Bible: An Interview with Yosef ben-Jochannan." *Encore,* October 1981, 24–25.

Noel, Peter. "One Nation?" *Vibe,* February 1996, 70–73.

Norden, Eric. "Who Killed Malcolm X?" *Realist,* February 1967, 26.

"Notes Toward a Definition of National Security." *Washington Monthly,* December 1975.

Nu'man, Fareed H., ed. "The Muslim Population in the United States." *The American Muslim Council Report,* December, 1992.

Opala, Joseph A. "The Gullah: Rice, Slavery and the Sierra Leone-American Connection" (pamphlet). *United States Information Service Report.* Freetown, Sierra Leone, 1987.

"Othello." *Penthouse,* April 1980, 135.

Palmer, Colin. "African Slave Trade: The Cruelest Commerce." *National Geographic* 182, no. 3 (September 1992): 65–91.

Parks, Gordon. "White Devils' Day Is Almost Over." *Life,* May 31, 1963, 22–33, 78–79.

———. "The Violent End of the Man Called Malcolm X." *Life,* March 5, 1965, 26–31.

Perry, Mark, and Jeff Goldberg. "The Secret Plot to Oust Saddam Hussein." *Regardie's,* November 1990, 42–56.

"The Prophet: Joseph Smith's Testimony." The Church of Jesus Christ of Latter-Day Saints, 1991 (pamphlet).

"The Quakers Warn that Police Spying on Political Activists Did Not End with Vietnam." *People Weekly,* June 11, 1979, 89–92.

"Remembering Malcolm X, 25 Years Later." *Emerge* (cover story), February 1990.

Rogers, Ben F. "W. E. B. DuBois, Marcus Garvey and Pan-Africa." *Journal of Negro History,* April 1955, 154–59.

Rogers, J. A. *The Five Negro Presidents.* St. Petersburg, Fla.: Helga M. Rogers, 1965 (pamphlet).

Roy, Sara. "Separation or Integration: Closure and the Economic Future of the Gaza Strip Revisited." *Middle East Journal* 48, no. 1 (Winter 1994): 1130.

Scott, Peter Dale, et al. "JFK: The Assassination, the Movie, and the Coverup." *Tikkun,* March/April 1992, 37–55.

Shabazz, Betty. "The Legacy of My Husband, Malcolm X." *Ebony,* June 1969, 172–82.

Shabazz, Betty, Susan Taylor, and Audrey Edwards. "Loving and Losing Malcolm." *Essence,* February 1992, 50–52, 54, 104–9, 110, 112.

Shearer, Lloyd. "FBI Making Progress, Except . . ." *Parade,* April 23, 1989, 2.

Sheler, Jeffrey L. "The First Christians." *U.S. News & World Report,* April 20, 1992, 58–71.

Sheler, Jeffrey L., with Mike Tharp and Jill Jordan Seider. "In Search of Jesus." *U.S. News & World Report,* April 8, 1996, 47–53.

Shreeve, James. "Homo Erectus Rises Again! Now He's In Asia, and He's Shaking Our Family Tree." *Discover,* December 1994, 80–89.

Simms, Gregory. "Nation Mourns Muslim Leader." *JET,* March 13, 1975, 14–22, 52–57.

Solomon, Alisa et al. "Why Are We Still Listening to Louis Farrakhan?" *Village Voice,* February 15, 1994, 22–30, 94 (special feature).

"Special Report: The World of Islam." *Time,* April 16, 1979, 40–54.

Specter, Michael. "Rabbi Menachem Schneerson: The Oracle of Crown Heights." *New York Times Magazine,* March 15, 1992, 35.

Stuart, Reginald. "Time Marches On: From 1963 to 1993." *Emerge,* August 1993, 26–34.

"Suit Charges Late Muslim Leader's Estate Misused." *JET,* March 26, 1981, 6.

Tapia, Andres. "Soul Searching: How Is the Black Church Responding to the Urban Crisis?" *Christianity Today,* March 4, 1996, 26–30.

Thompson, Anne. "Malcolm, Let's Do Lunch." *Mother Jones,* July/August 1991, 24–29, 57.

Tosches, Nick. "The Outlaw Champ." *Vanity Fair,* February 1998, 146–66.

Van Biema, David, et al. "The Gospel Truth?" *Time,* April 8, 1996, 52–60.

Van Dyk, Jere. "Growing Up in East Harlem." *National Geographic* 177, no. 5 (May 1990): 52–75.

Vincent, Ted. "The Garveyite Parents of Malcolm X." *The Black Scholar.* March/April 1989, 10–13.

Wallace, A. F. C. "Revitalization Movements." *American Anthropologist,* April 1956, 264.

"The War of the Moles." *New York Magazine* (cover story), February 1978.

Warren, R. P. "Malcolm X: Mission and Meaning." *Yale Review,* December 1966, 161–71.

Washington, Iris. "The FBI Plot Against Black Leaders." *Essence,* October 1979, 70–73, 97–105, 146.

Whitaker, Charles. "Who Killed King and JFK? An Interview with Rep. Louis Stokes." *Ebony,* April 1992, 24–28.

"Who Issued the Orders?" *Newsweek,* March 21, 1966.

"Who Killed Malcolm X?" (part 1: An Interview with Norman 3X Butler). *Black News,* February 1979, 6–9, 35.

"Who Killed Malcolm X?" (part 2: An Interview with Norman 3X Butler). *Black News,* March/April 1979, 12–15, 19.

"Why Sing Now?" *Korea Newsreview,* April 25, 1992, 27.

Williams, Juan. "They Wanted to Be Heroes: Pictures from a Revolution." *Washington Post Magazine,* February 6, 1994, 8–15.

Wood, Joe. "X Appeal in the Nineties: Talking Back to Malcolm." *Elle,* November 1992, 126–130.

Woodward, Kenneth L. "Rethinking the Resurrection." *Newsweek,* April 8, 1996, 60–69.

Zoba, Wendy Murray. "Separate and Equal." *Christianity Today,* February 5, 1996, 14–24.

MANUSCRIPT AND ORAL HISTORIES COLLECTIONS

▪ Civil Rights Documentation Project Papers. Moorland-Springarn Library, Howard University, Washington, D.C.

▪ Slater Hunter King Papers. Fisk University Library, Nashville, Tennessee.

■ Henry McNeal Turner Papers. Moorland-Springarn Library, Howard University, Washington, D.C.

■ Edwin Anderson Williams Papers. Maryland Historical Society, Baltimore, Maryland.

REFERENCE BOOKS AND MATERIALS

Ali, Noble Drew. *The Holy Koran of the Moorish Science Temple of America.* 1929. Photocopy. FBI File on Noble Drew Ali.

Ali, Maulana Muhammad, trans. *The Holy Quran.* 1917. Reprint. Columbus, Ohio: Ahmadiyyah Anjuman Isah'at Islam, 1995.

Ali, Yusuf Abdullah, trans. *The Holy Koran.* New York: McGregor & Werner, 1946.

Alleged Assassination Plots Involving Foreign Leaders. New York: Norton, 1976.

Amory, Cleveland, et al. *International Celebrity Register* (U.S. Edition). New York: Celebrity Register Ltd., 1959.

Bergman, Peter M., and Mort N. Bergman. *The Chronological History of the Negro in America.* New York: Mentor Books, 1969.

The Book of Mormon: Another Testament of Jesus Christ. Translated by Joseph Smith Jr. 1830. Reprint. Salt Lake City: Church of Jesus Christ of Latter-Day Saints, 1991.

Brewer's Dictionary of Phrase and Fable. New York: Harper & Brothers, 1956.

Burke, Joan Martin. *Civil Rights: A CBS News Reference Book.* 2nd ed. New York: R. R. Bowker, 1974.

Castleden, Rodney. *World History: A Chronological Dictionary of Dates.* New York: Shooting Star Press, 1994.

Cirot, J. E. *A Dictionary of Symbols.* New York: Philosophical Library, 1962.

Comay, Joan, and Ronald Brownrigg. *Who's Who in the Bible.* New York: Bonanza Books, 1980.

The Constitution of the United States of America: Analysis and Interpretation. Congressional Research Service, 1973.

Cooper, J. C. *An Illustrated Encyclopedia of Traditional Symbols.* London: Thames & Hudson, 1978.

Current Biography. Vols. 1953–1992.

Dawood, N. J., ed. *The Koran* (English translation). New York: Penguin Books, 1974.

Department of the Army. *American Military History 1607–1953*. Washington, D.C., 1956.

Dowling, Levi M. *The Aquarian Gospel of Jesus the Christ*. Kempton, Ill.: Adventures Unlimited, 1997.

Encyclopedia Judaica. Jerusalem: Keter Publishing, 1972.

Ferris, Robert G., ed. *The Presidents*. Washington, D.C.: U.S. Department of the Interior, 1977.

Fishel, Leslie H. Jr., and Benjamin Quarles. *The Negro American: A Documentary History*. Glenview, Ill.: Scott, Foresman, 1967.

Furtaw, Julia C., ed. *Black Americans Information Directory, 1992–1993*. Detroit: Gale Research, 1992.

Gertner, Richard, ed. *1973 International Motion Picture Almanac*. New York: Quigley Publications, 1973.

Good News Bible: The Bible in Today's English Version. New York: American Bible Society, 1978.

Grant, Joanne. *Black Protest: History, Documents and Analyses*. Greenwich, Conn.: Fawcett Publications, 1968.

Graves, Robert. *New Larousse Encyclopedia of Mythology*. New York: Crescent Books, 1968.

Hanson, H. W., with Dora Jane Hanson. *History of Art*. 2nd ed. Englewood Cliffs, N.J.: Prentice-Hall, 1977.

Hardesty, Von, and Dominick Pisano. *Black Wings: The American Black in Aviation*. Washington, D.C.: Smithsonian Press, 1984.

Harris, Middleton A., ed. *The Black Book*. New York: Random House, 1974.

The Holy Bible. New York: American Bible Society, 1846.

The Holy Bible (Authorized King James Version). New York: World Publishing, 1964.

Hone, William, William Wake, and Jeremiah Jones. *The Lost Books of the Bible*. 1820. Reprint. New York: Crown Publishers, 1979.

Hornsby, Alton Jr. *Chronology of African American History*. 2nd ed. Detroit: Gale Research, 1997.

Jacobus, Melancthon W., et al. *A New Standard Bible Dictionary*. New York: Funk & Wagnalls, 1926.

Joel Whitburn's Top Pop Singles 1955–1996. Menomonee Falls, Wis.: Record Research, 1997.

Johnson, James Weldon, and J. Rosamond Johnson. *The Books of American Negro Spirituals*. 1926. Reprint. New York: Da Capo Press, 1991.

Kane, Joseph Nathan. *Facts About Presidents: A Compilation of Biographical and Historical Information*. 5th ed. New York: H. W. Wilson, 1989.

Kodansha Encyclopedia of Japan. New York: Harper & Row, 1983.

Kolatch, Alfred J. *Complete Dictionary of English and Hebrew First Names*. Middle Village, N.Y.: Jonathan David Publishers, 1984.

May, Herbert G., and Bruce M. Metzger, eds. *The New Oxford Annotated Bible: The Holy Bible*. New York: Oxford University Press, 1971.

Nanji, Azim A., ed. *The Muslim Almanac*. Detroit: Gale Research, 1996.

New Catholic Encyclopedia. Washington, D.C.: Catholic University of America, 1967.

New York Times. *Report of the National Advisory Commission on Civil Disorders*. New York: Bantam Books, 1968.

Nyrop, Richard F., et al. *Pakistan: A Country Study*. 4th ed. Washington, D.C.: U.S. Department of the Army, 1983.

O'Neil, Thomas. *The Grammys: For the Record*. New York: Penguin Books, 1993.

Partridge, Eric. *Origins: A Short Etymological Dictionary of Modern English*. New York: Greenwich House, 1983.

Pfeiffer, Charles F., and Everett F. Harrison, eds. *The Wycliffe Bible Commentary*. 1962. Reprint. Chicago: Moody Press, 1969.

Ploski, Harry A., and Ernest Kaiser, eds. *The Negro Almanac*. New York: Bellwether, 1971.

Ploski, Harry A., and James Williams, eds. *The Negro Almanac: A Reference Work on the African American*. 5th ed. Detroit: Gale Research, 1989.

Riedel, Eunice, et al. *The Book of the Bible*. New York: Morrow, 1979.

Sadler, Henry. *Masonic Facts and Fictions*. Northamptonshire, U.K.: Aquarian Press, 1985.

Sahib, Hatim A. "The Nation of Islam." Master's thesis, University of Chicago, 1951.

Schulberg, Lucille, et al., eds. *Great Ages of Man: Historic India*. New York: Time-Life Books, 1968.

Scott, John Anthony. *Living Documents in American History*. Vol. 2, *From Reconstruction to the Outbreak of World War I*. New York: Washington Square Press, 1968.

Seldes, George. *The Great Quotations*. New York: Caesar-Stuart, 1960.

———. *The Great Thoughts*. New York: Ballantine Books, 1996.

Shoemaker, M. Wesley. *The World Today Series: Russia, Eurasian States, and Eastern Europe 1995.* Harpers Ferry, W. Va.: Stryker-Post Publications, 1995.

Sicherman, Barbara, et al. *Notable American Women: The Modern Period.* Cambridge, Mass.: Belknap Press, 1980.

Smythe, Mabel M., ed. *The Black American Reference Book.* Englewood Cliffs, N.J.: Prentice-Hall, 1976.

Stebbens, Richard P., ed. *Documents on American Foreign Relations, 1960.* New York: Harper & Brothers, 1961.

United Nations. *Yearbook of the United Nations.* Vols. 1964–1969. New York: Columbia University Press, 1964–1969.

U.S. Department of State. *The Biographic Register,* 1959, 1963, and 1977.

Watkins, Sylvestre C., ed. *Anthology of American Negro Literature.* New York: Modern Library, 1944.

BOOKS

Abdul-Jabbar, Kareem, and Peter Knobler. *Giant Steps: The Autobiography of Kareem Abdul-Jabbar.* New York: Bantam Books, 1983.

Adams, James. *Secret Armies: Inside the American, Soviet and European Special Forces.* New York: Atlantic Monthly Press, 1988.

The Age of God-Kings: TimeFrame 3000–1500 B.C. Alexandria, Va.: Time-Life Books, 1987.

Agee, Philip. *Inside the Company: CIA Diary.* New York: Bantam Books, 1975.

———. *On The Run.* New Jersey: Lyle Stuart, 1987.

Agee, Philip, and Louis Wolf. *Dirty Work: The CIA in Western Europe.* New York: Dorset Press, 1978.

Ali, Muhammad. *The Greatest.* New York: Random House, 1975.

Allport, Gordon W. *The Nature of Prejudice.* Cambridge, Mass.: Addison-Wesley, 1954.

Anastasia, George. *The Goodfella Tapes.* New York: Avon Books, 1998.

Andrew, Christopher. *For the President's Eyes Only: Secret Intelligence and the American Presidency from Washington to Bush.* New York: Harper-Collins, 1995.

Angelou, Maya. *I Know Why the Caged Bird Sings.* New York: Random House, 1970.

———. *The Heart of a Woman.* New York: Random House, 1981.

Archer, N. P., ed. *The Sufi Mystery.* London: Octagon Press, 1980.

Athill, Diana. *Make Believe*. London: Sinclair-Stevenson Books, 1992.

Attwood, William. *The Reds and the Blacks*. New York: Harper & Row, 1967.

Bagdikian, Ben H. *The Media Monopoly*. Boston: Beacon Press, 1984.

Baigent, Michael, Richard Leigh, and Henry Lincoln. *Holy Blood, Holy Grail*. New York: Delacourt Press, 1982.

——. *The Dead Sea Scrolls Deception*. New York: Summit Books, 1991.

Baigent, Michael, et al. *The Messianic Legacy*. New York: Dell, 1986.

Baldwin, James. *The Fire Next Time*. New York: Dell, 1963.

——. *No Name in the Street*. New York: Doubleday, 1972.

——. *One Day When I Was Lost*. New York: Dell, 1972.

——. *The Price of the Ticket: Collected Nonfiction, 1948–1985*. New York: St. Martin's Press, 1985.

Bamford, James. *The Puzzle Palace: Inside the National Security Agency, America's Most Secret Intelligence Organization*. New York: Houghton Mifflin, 1982.

Barboza, Steven. *American Jihad: Islam in America After Malcolm X*. New York: Doubleday, 1994.

Bauval, Robert and Adrian Gilbert. *The Orion Mystery: Unlocking the Secret of the Great Pyramids*. New York: Crown Publishers, 1994.

Beit-Hallahmi, Benjamin. *Original Sins: Reflections on the History of Zionism and Israel*. London: Pluto Press, 1992.

Beller, Steven. *Herzl*. New York: Grove Weidenfeld, 1991.

Ben-Jochannan, Yosef A. A. *We the Black Jews*. Vols. 1 and 2. 1983. Reprint. Baltimore: Black Classic Press, 1993.

Bennett, Lerone Jr. *Before the Mayflower: A History of Black Americans*. 4th ed. Chicago: Johnson, 1969.

Berlin, Ira. *Slaves Without Masters: The Free Negro in the Antebellum South*. 1974. Reprint. New York: New Press, 1992.

Bierlein, J. F. *Parallel Myths*. New York: Ballantine Books, 1994.

Bishop, Jim. *The Days of Martin Luther King Jr.: A Biography*. New York: Putnam, 1971.

Blackstock, Nelson. *COINTELPRO: The FBI's Secret War on Political Freedom*. New York: Vintage Books, 1976.

Blavatsky, H. P. *The Secret Doctrine*. Vol. 2. Pasadena, Cal.: Theosophical University Press, 1974.

Bledowska, Celina, and Jonathan Bloch. *KGB/CIA: Intelligence and Counter-Intelligence Operations*. Greenwich, Conn.: Brompton Books, 1987.

Bloom, Harold. *The American Religion: The Emergence of the Post-Christian Nation.* New York: Simon & Schuster, 1988.

Bontemps, Arna, and Jack Conroy. *They Seek a City.* Garden City, N.Y.: Doubleday, Doran, 1945.

———. *Anyplace but Here.* New York: Hill & Wang, 1966.

Booker, Simeon. *Black Man's America.* Englewood Cliffs, N.J.: Prentice-Hall, 1964.

Bouscaren, Anthony T. *Tshombe.* New York: Twin Circle, 1967.

Boykin, Ulysses W. *A Handbook on the Detroit Negro.* Detroit: Minority Study Associates, 1943.

Braden, Charles Samuel. *They Also Believe: A Study of Modern American Cults and Minority Religious Movements.* New York: Macmillan, 1949.

Bradford, Phillips Verner, and Harvey Blume. *Ota Benga: The Pygmy in the Zoo.* New York: St. Martin's Press, 1992.

Breasted, James Henry. *The Conquest of Civilization.* New York: Harper & Brothers, 1926.

———. *Egypt: A Journey Through the Land of the Pharaohs 1905.* Reprint. New York: Camera/Graphic Press, 1978.

Breitman, George. *The Last Year of Malcolm X.* New York: Schocken Books, 1967.

———. *Malcolm X: By Any Means Necessary.* New York: Pathfinder Press, 1970.

Breitman, George, ed. *Leon Trotsky on Black Nationalism and Self-Determination.* New York: Pathfinder Press, 1978.

———. *Malcolm X Speaks: Selected Speeches and Statements.* New York: Grove-Atlantic, 1990.

Breitman, George, et al. *The Assassination of Malcolm X.* New York: Pathfinder, 1968.

Broussard, Albert S. *Black San Francisco: The Struggle for Racial Equality in the West, 1900–1954.* Lawrence: University Press of Kansas, 1993.

Browder, Anthony T. *From the Browder File.* Washington, D.C.: Institute of Karmic Guidance, 1989.

Brown, Jim. *Out of Bounds.* New York: Zebra Books, 1989.

Budge, E.A. Wallis, ed. *The Book of the Dead.* New York: Bell Publishing, 1960.

Buitrago, Ann M., and Leon A. Immerman. *Are You Now Or Have You Ever Been in the FBI Files?: How to Secure and Interpret Your FBI Files.* New York: Grove Press, 1981.

Butcher, Margaret Just. *The Negro in American Culture*. New York: Mentor Books, 1956.

Campbell, James. *Talking at the Gates: A Life of James Baldwin*. New York: Viking, 1991.

Canot, Theodore. *Adventures of an African Slaver*. New York: Albert & Charles Bondi, 1928.

Carmichael, Joel. *The Satanizing of the Jews: Origin and Development of Mystical Anti-semitism*. New York: Fromm International Publishing, 1992.

Carson, Clayborne, ed. *The Eyes on the Prize Civil Rights Reader*. New York: Penguin Books, 1991.

————. *Malcolm X: The FBI File*. New York: Carroll & Graf, 1991.

Chalmers, David M. *Hooded Americanism: The History of the Ku Klux Klan*. Durham, N.C.: Duke University Press, 1987.

Chaney, Lindsay, and Michael Cieply. *The Hearsts: Family and Empire—The Later Years*. New York: Simon & Schuster, 1981.

Chapman, Abraham. *Black Voices*. New York: New American Library, 1968.

Chapman, Gil, and Ann Chapman. *Who's Listening Now? An Expose of the Wiretapping and Bugging Scandals Sweeping the Country*. San Diego: Publishers Export, 1967.

Clark, Steve, ed. *Malcolm X: The Final Speeches*. New York: Pathfinder Press, 1992.

Clarke, John Henrik, ed. *Malcolm X: The Man and His Times*. 1969. Reprint. Trenton, N.J.: Africa World Press, 1990.

Cleaver, Eldrige. *Soul on Ice*. New York: Dell, 1968.

Clegg, Claude A. III. *An Original Man: The Life and Times of Elijah Muhammad*. New York: St. Martin's Press, 1997.

Clifford, Clark, with Richard Holbrook. *Counsel to the President: A Memoir*. New York: Random House, 1991.

Collier, Peter, and David Horowitz. *The Fords: An American Epic*. New York: Summit Books, 1987.

Collins, Rodnell, P. with A. Peter Bailey. *Seventh Child: A Family Memoir of Malcolm X*. New York: Birch Lane Press, 1998.

Colvin, Ian. *The Rise and Fall of Moise Tshombe*. London: Leslie Frewin Publishers, 1968.

Cone, James H. *Malcolm and Martin and America: A Dream or a Nightmare*. Maryknoll, N.Y.: Orbis, 1991.

Cookridge, E. H. *Gehlen: Spy of the Century*. New York: Pyramid Books, 1971.

Copeland, Miles. *Beyond Cloak and Dagger: Inside the CIA.* New York: Pinnacle Books, 1974.

Corson, William R. *The Armies of Ignorance: The Rise of the American Intelligence Empire.* New York: Dial Press/James Wade Books, 1977.

Cosell, Howard. *Cosell.* New York: Playboy Press, 1973.

Cosell, Howard, with Peter Bonventre. *I Never Played the Game.* New York: Morrow, 1985.

Cox, Earnest Seivier. *White America.* Richmond, Va.: White America Society, 1923.

Cranston, Sylvia. *HPB: The Extraordinary Life and Influence of Helena Blavatsky, Founder of the Modern Theosophical Movement.* New York: Putnam, 1993.

Crossman, Richard, ed. *The God That Failed.* New York: Harper & Row, 1950.

Cushmeer, Bernard. *This Is the One: Messenger Elijah Muhammad.* Phoenix, Ariz.: Truth, 1970.

Danielou, Jean. *The Dead Sea Scrolls and Primitive Christianity.* New York: Mentor Omega Books, 1958.

David, James Kirkpatrick. *Spying on America: The FBI's Domestic Counterintelligence Program.* New York: Praeger, 1992.

David, Lester, and Irene David. *Bobby Kennedy: The Making of a Folk Hero.* New York: Dodd, Mead, 1986.

Davis, Angela. *If They Come in the Morning.* New York: Third Press, 1971.

Davis, John H. *Mafia Kingfish: Carlos Marcello and the Assassination of John F. Kennedy.* New York: Signet, 1989.

Davis, Miles, with Quincy Troupe. *Miles.* New York: Touchstone, 1990.

Davis, Thulani. *Malcolm X: The Great Photographs.* New York: Stewart, Taburi & Chang, 1993.

De Caro, Louis A. Jr. *Malcolm and the Cross.* New York: New York University Press, 1998.

De Gramont, Sanche. *The Secret War: The Story of International Espionage Since World War II.* New York: Putnam, 1962.

Demaris, Ovid. *The Director: An Oral Biography of J. Edgar Hoover.* New York: Harper's Magazine Press, 1975.

DeToledano, Ralph. *R.F.K.: The Man Who Would Be President.* New York: Putnam, 1967.

Dimont, Max I. *Jews, God and History.* New York: New American Library, 1962.

Dixon, Thomas. *The Clansman: A Historical Romance of the Ku Klux Klan.* New York: n.p., 1905.

Donner, Frank J. *The Age of Surveillance: The Aims and Methods of America's Political Intelligence System.* New York: Vintage Books, 1980.

Douglas, Kelly Brown. *The Black Christ: The Bishop Henry McNeal Turner Studies in North American Black Religion,* Vol. 9. Maryknoll, N.Y.: Orbis Books, 1994.

Drake, St. Claire and Horace R. Cayton. *Black Metropolis: A Study of Negro Life in a Northern City.* New York: Harcourt, Brace, 1945.

Draper, Theodore. *The Rediscovery of Black Nationalism.* New York: Viking, 1970.

Drosnin, Michael. *The Bible Code.* New York: Simon & Schuster, 1997.

Duberman, Martin Bauml. *Paul Robeson: A Biography.* New York: Knopf, 1989.

Dulles, Allen. *The Craft of Intelligence.* New York: Harper & Row, 1963.

Eakin, Sue, and Joseph Logsdon. *Solomon Northrup: Twelve Years as a Slave.* 1853. Reprint. Baton Rouge: Louisiana State University Press, 1968.

Effendi, Shoghi, trans. *Gleanings from the Writings of Baha'u'llah.* Wilmette, Ill.: Baha'i Publishing Trust, 1939.

Eisenhower, Dwight D. *The White House Years: Waging Peace 1956–1961.* New York: Doubleday, 1965.

Eissen-Udom, E. U. *Black Nationalism: A Search for Identity.* Chicago: University of Chicago Press, 1962.

Epps, Archie, ed. *Malcolm X: Speeches of Malcolm X at Harvard.* New York: Morrow, 1968.

Epstein, Edward J. *Legend: The Secret World of Lee Harvey Oswald.* New York: Bantam Books, 1978.

Evanzz, Karl. *The Judas Factor: The Plot to Kill Malcolm X.* New York: Thunder's Mouth Press, 1992.

Fanon, Frantz. *Black Skin, White Masks.* New York: Grove Press, 1967.

———. *The Wretched of the Earth.* New York: Grove Press, 1968.

Fardan, Dorothy B. *Takub and the Origin of White Supremacy.* 3rd ed. Newport News, Va.: United Brothers and United Sisters Communications Systems, 1997.

Farmer, James. *Lay Bare the Heart: An Autobiography of the Civil Rights Movement.* New York: New American Library, 1985.

Fauset, Arthur F. *Black Gods of the Metropolis: Negro Religious Cults of the Urban North*. 1944. Reprint. New York: Octagon Books, 1970.

Fensterwald, Bernard Jr. *Coincidence or Conspiracy?* New York: Zebra Books, 1977.

FitzGerald, Frances. *Fire in the Lake*. New York: Atlantic Monthly Press, 1972.

Flood, Charles Bracelen. *Hitler: The Path to Power*. Boston: Houghton Mifflin, 1989.

Ford, Henry Sr. *The International Jew: The World's Foremost Problem*. Detroit: The Dearborn Independent, 1922.

Forster, Arnold, and Benjamin R. Epstein. *The New Anti-Semitism*. New York: McGraw-Hill, 1974.

Fox, Stephen. *Blood and Power: Organized Crime in Twentieth-Century America*. New York: Morrow, 1989.

Frank, Gerald. *An American Death*: Garden City, N.Y.: Doubleday, 1972.

Frasier, Howard. *Uncloaking the CIA*. New York: Free Press, 1978.

Frazier, E. Franklin. *Black Bourgeoisie: The Rise of a New Middle Class in the United States*. New York: Free Press, 1962.

Freidel, David, Linda Schele, and Joy Parker. *Maya Cosmos: Three Thousand Years of the Shaman's Path*. New York: Morrow, 1993.

Friedly, Michael. *Malcolm X: The Assassination*. New York: Carroll & Graf, 1992.

Gallen, David, ed. *Malcolm X: As They Knew Him*. New York: Carroll & Graf, 1992.

Gardell, Mattias. *In the Name of Elijah Muhammad: Louis Farrakhan and the Nation of Islam*. Durham, N.C.: Duke University Press, 1996.

Garrison, Jim. *On the Trail of the Assassins*. New York: Warner Books, 1988.

Garrow, David J. *The FBI and Martin Luther King Jr.: From Solo to Memphis*. New York: Norton, 1981.

———. *Bearing the Cross: Martin Luther King, Jr., and the Southern Christian Leadership Conference*. New York: Morrow, 1986.

Garwood, Darrell. *Undercover: Thirty-Five Years of CIA Deception*. New York: Grove Press, 1985.

Gayle, Addison. *Richard Wright: Ordeal of a Native Son*. New York: Doubleday Anchor Books, 1980.

Gentry, Curt. *J. Edgar Hoover: The Man and His Secrets*. New York: Norton, 1991.

Giancana, Sam, and Chuck Giancana. *Double Cross: The Explosive Inside Story of the Mobster Who Controlled America.* New York: Warner Books, 1992.

Goldman, Peter. *The Death and Life of Malcolm X.* New York: Harper & Row, 1973. Reprint. Urbana: University of Illinois Press, 1979.

Graham, Lloyd M. *Deceptions and Myths of the Bible.* New York: Citadel Press, 1975.

Greenberg, Gary. *The Moses Mystery: The African Origins of the Jewish People.* Secaucus, N.J.: Birch Lane Press, 1996.

Grier, William H., and Price M. Cobbs. *Black Rage.* New York: Basic Books, 1968.

Griffin, John Howard. *Black Like Me.* New York: Houghton Mifflin, 1960.

Groden, Robert J., and Harrison E. Livingston. *High Treason: The Assassination of President Kennedy and the New Evidence of Conspiracy.* New York: Conservatory Press, 1989.

Grosh, Aaron B. *The Odd-Fellows Manual.* Philadelphia: H. C. Peck and Theo. Bliss, 1858.

Gruber, Ruth. *Rescue: The Exodus of the Ethiopian Jews.* New York: Atheneum, 1987.

Guazzo, Francesco Maria. *Compendium Maleficarum: The Montague Summers Edition.* 1929. Reprint. New York: Dover, 1988.

Guthrie, Paul Lawrence. *Making of the Whiteman: History, Tradition and the Teachings of Elijah Muhammad.* San Diego: Beacon Communications, 1992.

Hakim, Nasir Makr, ed. *The Theology of Time.* Atlanta: Secretarius M.E.M.P.S. Publications, 1997.

———. *The True History of Elijah Muhammad, Messenger of Allah.* Atlanta: Secretarius M.E.M.P.S. Publications, 1997.

Haley, Alex, with Malcolm X. *The Autobiography of Malcolm X.* New York: Grove Press, 1965.

Halperin, Morton H., et al. *The Lawless State: The Crimes of the U.S. Intelligence Agencies.* New York: Penguin Books, 1976.

Hamilton, Charles. *Adam Clayton Powell Jr.: The Political Biography of an American Dilemma.* New York: Atheneum, 1991.

Hammer, Richard. *The Vatican Connection.* New York: Holt, Rinehart & Winston, 1982.

Hancock, Graham. *The Sign and the Seal: The Quest for the Lost Ark of the Covenant.* New York: Crown Publishers, 1992.

Hankins, F. H. *The Racial Basis of Civilization.* New York: Knopf, 1926.

Hauser, Thomas. *Muhammad Ali: His Life and Times.* New York: Simon & Schuster, 1991.

Haykal, Muhammad Husayn. *The Life of Muhammad.* New York: North American Trust Publications, 1976.

Hempstone, Smith. *Africa: Angry Young Giant.* New York: Praeger, 1961.

———. *Rebels, Mercenaries, and Dividends: The Katanga Story.* New York: Praeger, 1962.

Herman, Edgar S., and Noam Chomsky. *Manufacturing Consent: The Political Economy of the Mass Media.* New York: Pantheon Books, 1988.

Herndon, Booton. *Ford: An Unconventional Biography of the Men and Their Times.* New York: Weybright & Talley, 1969.

Hersh, Burton. *The Old Boys: The American Elite and the Origins of the CIA.* New York: Scribner, 1992.

Herzl, Theodor. *The Jewish State.* 1896. Reprint. New York: Dover, 1988.

Hill, Robert, A., ed. *The Marcus Garvey and Universal Negro Improvement Association Papers.* Vols. 1–3. Berkeley: University of California Press, 1983.

———. *The FBI's RACON: Racial Conditions in the United States During World War II.* Boston: Northeastern University Press, 1995.

Hilliard, David, and Lewis Cole. *This Side of Glory: The Autobiography of David Hilliard and the Story of the Black Panther Party.* New York: Little, Brown, 1993.

Hirschfeld, Fritz. *George Washington and Slavery: A Documentary Portrayal.* Columbia: University of Missouri Press, 1997.

Hirst, David, and Irene Beeson. *Sadat.* London: Faber & Faber, 1981.

Hitler, Adolf. *Mein Kampf.* 1925. Reprint. Boston: Houghton Mifflin, 1971.

Hodgin, Thomas. *Nationalism in Colonial Africa.* New York: New York University Press, 1957.

Hoffman, Banesh, with Helen Dukas. *Albert Einstein, Creator and Rebel.* New York: Viking, 1972.

Hoffman, William, and Lake Headley, *Contract Killer.* New York: Thunder's Mouth, 1992.

Hoopes, Townsend. *The Devil and John Foster Dulles.* New York: Atlantic Monthly Press, 1973.

Hoover, J. Edgar. *Masters of Deceit.* New York: Henry Holt, 1958.

————. *A Study of Communism.* New York: Holt, Rinehart & Winston, 1962.

Horton, Richard. *The Image of the Beast, A Secret Empire.* Philadelphia: n.p., 1866.

Hougan, Jim. *Spooks.* New York: Bantam Books, 1978.

————. *Secret Agenda: Watergate, Deep Throat and the CIA.* New York: Random House, 1984.

Howard, Clark. *Zebra.* New York: Richard Marek Publishers, 1979.

Hunt, E. Howard. *Undercover: Memoirs of an American Secret Agent.* New York: Putnam, 1974.

Hunt, Linda. *Secret Agenda: The United States Government, Nazi Scientists, and Project Paperclip, 1945–1990.* New York: St. Martin's, 1991.

Jackson, George. *Soledad Brother: The Prison Letters of George Jackson.* New York: Bantam Books, 1970.

Jackson, Kenneth T. *The Ku Klux Klan in the City, 1915–1930.* New York: Oxford University Press, 1967.

Jamal, Hakim A. *From the Dead Level.* New York: Random House, 1971.

James, George G. M. *Stolen Legacy.* 1954. Reprint. Trenton, N.J.: Africa World Press, 1992.

Jeffares, A. Norman. *W. B. Yeats: A New Biography.* New York: Farrar Straus & Giroux, 1988.

Johnson, Loch K. *America's Secret Power: The CIA in a Democratic Society.* New York: Oxford University Press, 1989.

Johnson, Lyndon Baines. *The Vantage Point: Perspectives on the Presidency 1963–1969.* New York: Holt, Rinehart & Winston, 1971.

Johnson, Walter, ed. *The Papers of Adlai E. Stevenson.* Vol. 7. Boston: Little, Brown, 1977.

Jones, Max, and John Chilton. *Louis: The Louis Armstrong Story 1900–1971.* London: Da Capo Press, 1988.

Jordan, Winthrop D. *White Over Black: American Attitudes Toward the Negro, 1550–1812.* New York: Norton, 1968.

Karim, Benjamin, with Peter Skutches and David Gallen. *Remembering Malcolm.* New York: Carroll & Graf, 1992.

Khalifa, Hakim K. *Essays on the Life and Teachings of Master W. Fard Muhammad.* Newport News, Va.: U.B. & U.S. Communications Systems, 1995.

Khan, Muhammad Zafrulla. *Deliverance From the Cross.* London: Alden Press, 1978.

King, Coretta Scott. *My Life with Martin Luther King Jr.* New York: Holt, Rinehart & Winston, 1969.

Klingaman, William K. *1941: Our Lives in a World on the Edge.* New York: Harper & Row, 1988.

Knight, Stephen. *The Brotherhood: The Secret World of the Freemasons.* New York: Dorset Press, 1986.

Kondo, Zak A. *Conspiracy: Unraveling the Assassination of Malcolm X.* Washington, D.C.: Nubia Press, 1993.

Krakow, Kenneth K. *Georgia Place-Names.* Macon, Ga.: Winship Press, 1975.

Kunnes, Richard. *The American Heroin Empire: Power, Profits and Politics.* New York: Dodd, Mead, 1972.

Lacouture, Jean. *Nasser: A Biography.* New York: Knopf, 1973.

Lacy, Leslie Alexander. *The Rise and Fall of a Proper Negro: An Autobiography.* New York: Macmillan, 1970.

Lamb, Harold. *The March of the Barbarians.* New York: Literary Guild, 1940.

Landess, Thomas H., and Richard M. Quinn. *Jesse Jackson and The Politics of Race.* Ottawa, Ill.: Jameson Books, 1985.

Lane, Mark. *Rush to Judgment.* New York: Holt, Rinehart & Winston, 1966.

———. *Plausible Denial: Was the CIA Involved in the Assassination of JFK?* New York: Thunder's Mouth Press, 1991.

Lane, Mark, and Dick Gregory. *Code Name "Zorro": The Murder of Martin Luther King, Jr.* Englewood Cliffs, N.J.: Prentice-Hall, 1977.

Lasky, Victor. *The Ugly Russian.* New York: Trident Press, 1965.

Lederer, William J., and Eugene Burdick. *The Ugly American.* New York: Norton, 1958.

Lee, Albert. *Henry Ford and the Jews.* New York: Stein & Day, 1980.

Lee, Martha F. *The Nation of Islam: An American Millenarian Movement.* New York: Edwin Mellen Press, 1988.

Lee, Spike, with Ralph Wiley. *By Any Means Necessary: The Trials and Tribulations of the Making of Malcolm X.* New York: Hyperion, 1992.

Leeming, David. *James Baldwin: A Biography.* New York: Knopf, 1994.

Lemann, Nicholas. *The Promised Land.* New York: Knopf, 1991.

Lemesurier, Peter. *The Great Pyramid Decoded.* Rockport, Mass.: Element, 1993.

Lewis, Bernard. *Race and Slavery in the Middle East: An Historical Enquiry.* New York: Oxford University Press, 1990.

Lewis, David Levering. *W. E. B. DuBois: A Reader.* New York: Henry Holt, 1995.

Liberatore, Paul. *The Road to Hell: The True Store of George Jackson, Stephen Bingham and the San Quentin Massacre.* New York: Atlantic Monthly Press, 1996.

Lifton, David S. *The Best Evidence: Disguise and Deception in the Assassination of John F. Kennedy.* New York: Carroll & Graf, 1988.

Lincoln, Eric C. *The Black Muslims in America.* Boston: Beacon Press, 1961.

Logan, John A. *The Great Conspiracy.* New York: A. R. Hart, 1886.

Lomax, Louis E. *The Negro Revolt.* New York: Harper & Row, 1962.

———. *When the Word Is Given.* Cleveland: World Publishing, 1963.

———. *To Kill a Black Man.* Los Angeles: Holloway House, 1968.

Ludlum, Robert. *The Chancellor Manuscript.* New York: Dial, Press, 1977.

Ludwig, Emil. *The Nile: The Life-Story of a River.* New York: Viking, 1937.

Lynn, Conrad. *There Is a Fountain: The Autobiography of a Civil Rights Lawyer.* Westport, Conn.: Lawrence Hill, 1979.

Machiavelli, Niccolò. *The Prince.* Translated by Luigi Ricci. 1903. Reprint. New York: New American Library, 1952.

Magida, Arthur J. *Prophet of Rage: A Life of Louis Farrakhan and His Nation.* New York: Basic Books, 1996.

Marchetti, Victor, and John D. Marks. *The CIA and the Cult of Intelligence.* New York: Dell, 1974.

Marcus, Sheldon. *Father Coughlin: The Tumultuous Life of the Priest of the Little Flower.* Boston: Little, Brown, 1973.

Marks, John. *The Search for the "Manchurian Candidate."* New York: McGraw-Hill, 1980.

Marsden, Victor E., ed. *The Protocols of the Elders of Zion.* Russia: n.p., 1934.

Marsh, Clifton E. *From Black Muslims to Muslims: The Transition from Separatism to Islam, 1930–1980.* Metuchen, N.J.: Scarecrow Press, 1984.

Martin, Ernest L. *Secrets of Golgotha: The Forgotten History of Christ's Crucifixion.* Alhambra, Calif.: ASK Publications, 1988.

———. *The Star That Astonished the World.* Alhambra, Calif.: ASK Publications, 1991.

Mboya, Tom. *The Challenges of Nationhood.* New York: Praeger, 1970.

McDonald, Forrest. *Novus Ordo Seclorum: The Intellectual Origins of the Constitution.* Lawrence: Kansas University Press, 1985.

McGinn, Bernard. *Antichrist: Two Thousand Years of Human Fascination with Evil.* New York: HarperCollins, 1994.

Mellon, James, ed. *Bullwhip Days: The Slaves Remember; An Oral History.* New York: Widenfeld & Nicholson, 1988.

Meltzer, Milton. *The Black Americans: A History in Their Own Words 1619–1983.* Reprint. New York: Harper & Row, 1984.

Messadie, Gerald. *A History of the Devil.* New York: Kodansha International, 1996.

Miller, Nathan. *Spying for America: The Hidden History of U.S. Intelligence.* New York: Paragon House, 1989.

Mitgang, Herbert. *Dangerous Dossiers: Exposing the Secret War Against America's Greatest Authors.* New York: Donald I. Fine, 1988.

Moldea, Dan E. *The Hoffa Wars: Teamsters, Rebels, Politicians and the Mob.* New York: Paddington Press, 1978.

———. *Dark Victory: Ronald Reagan, MCA, and the Mob.* New York: Viking, 1986.

———. *The Killing of Robert F. Kennedy: An Investigation of the Motive, Means, and Opportunity.* New York: Norton, 1995.

Montague, W. Ashley. *Man's Most Dangerous Myth: The Fallacy of Race.* New York: Columbia University Press, 1945.

Montgomery, William E. *Under Their Own Vine and Fig Tree: The African-American Church in the South 1865–1900.* Baton Rouge: Louisiana State University Press, 1993.

Moore, Gilbert. *Rage.* New York: Carroll & Graf, 1993.

Morton, Frederic. *The Rothschilds: A Family Portrait.* New York: Atheneum, 1962.

Mosley, Leonard. *Dulles: A Biography of Eleanor, Allen and John Foster Dulles and Their Family Network.* New York: Dial Press/James Wade, 1978.

Muhammad, Elijah. *The Supreme Wisdom: Solution to the So-Called Negroes' Problem.* Vols. 1 and 2. Chicago: University of Islam, 1957.

———. *Message to the Blackman in America.* Chicago: Muhammad's Temple of Islam No. 2, 1965.

———. *How to Eat To Live.* Book 1. Chicago: Muhammad's Temple of Islam No. 2, 1967.

———. *How to Eat To Live.* Book 2. Chicago: Muhammad's Temple of Islam No. 2, 1972.

———. *The Fall of America*. Chicago: Muhammad's Temple of Islam No. 2, 1973.

———. *Our Saviour Has Arrived*. Chicago: Muhammad's Temple of Islam No. 2, 1974.

———. *The Theology of Time*. Book 1. Hampton, Va.: United Brothers & United Sister Communications Systems, 1992.

———. *The History of Jesus' Birth, Death, and What It Means to You and Me*. Atlanta, Ga.: Secretarius M.E.M.P.S., 1993.

———. *History of the Nation of Islam*. Atlanta, Ga.: Secretarius M.E.M.P.S., 1995.

Muhammad, Jabril. *This Is The One*. Vol. 1, *The Most Honorable Elijah Muhammad*. Phoenix, Ariz.: Book Company, 1996.

Muhammad, John. *The Journal of Truth*. Hampton, Va.: U.B. and U.S. Communications Systems, 1996.

Muhammad, Tynetta Deanar. *The Comer by Night, 1986*. Chicago: Hon. Elijah Muhammad Educational Foundation, 1986.

Muhammad, Wallace D. *As the Light Shineth from the East*. Chicago: WDM Publishing, 1980.

Muhammad, Wallace D. Fard. *Secret Ritual of the Nation of Islam*. Detroit: Wallace D. Fard Muhammad, 1931.

Mustafaa, Ayesha K. *Wallace Muhammad*. Chicago: Zakat Publications, 1988.

Nevins, Allan, and Frank Ernest Hill. *Ford: Expansion and Challenge, 1915–1933*. New York: Scribner, 1957.

Nietzsche, Friedrich. *Twilight of the Idols/The Anti-Christ*. 1895. Reprint. New York: Penguin Books, 1990.

Nkrumah, Kwame. *Africa Must Unite*. New York: New World Paperbacks, 1963.

———. *The Struggle Continues*. London: Panaf Books, 1973.

Nolan, William A. *Communism versus the Negro*. Chicago: Henry Regnery, 1951.

Nutting, Anthony. *Nasser*. New York: E.P. Dutton, 1972.

Offiong, Daniel A. *Imperialism and Dependency: Obstacles to African Development*. Washington, D.C.: Howard University Press, 1982.

Oliver, George. *The Pythagorean Triangle: Or, The Science of Numbers*. 1866. Reprint. Minneapolis: Wizards Book Shelf, 1975.

Ollestad, Norman. *Inside the FBI.* New York: Lyle Stuart, 1967.

O'Reilly, Kenneth. *"Racial Matters"; The FBI's Secret File on Black America, 1960–1972.* New York: Free Press, 1989.

———. *Black Americans: The FBI Files.* New York: Carroll & Graf, 1994.

Osman, Ahmed. *The House of the Messiah: Controversial Revelations on the Historical Jesus.* New York: HarperCollins, 1994.

Osofsky, Gilbert. *Harlem: The Making of a Ghetto; Negro New York, 1890–1930.* 2nd ed. New York: Harper Torchbooks, 1971.

O'Toole, G. J. A. *Honorable Treachery: A History of U.S. Intelligence, Espionage, and Covert Action From the American Revolution to the CIA.* New York: Morgan Entrekin Books, 1991.

Oudes, Bruce. *From: The President: Richard Nixon's Secret Files.* New York: Harper & Row, 1989.

Panati, Charles. *Sacred Origins of Profound Things.* New York: Penguin/Arkana Books, 1996.

Parks, Gordon. *Voices in the Mirror: An Autobiography.* New York: Doubleday, 1990.

Parsons, Talcott and Kenneth B. Clark, eds. *The Negro American.* Boston: Beacon Press, 1965.

Patrice Lumumba. London: Panaf Books, 1978.

Patterson, William L., ed. *We Charge Genocide.* New York: International Publishers, 1971.

Pepper, William F. *Orders to Kill: The Truth Behind the Murder of Martin Luther King.* New York: Carroll & Graf, 1995.

Perlmutter, Nathan, and Ruth Ann Perlmutter. *The Real Anti-Semitism in America.* New York: Arbor House, 1982.

Perry, Bruce. *Malcolm: The Life of a Man Who Changed Black America.* New York: Station Hill, 1991.

Perry, Bruce, ed. *Malcolm X: The Last Speeches.* 1989. Reprint. New York: Pathfinder Press, 1992.

Persico, Joseph E. *Casey: From the OSS to the CIA.* New York: Viking, 1990.

Peters, Rudolph. *Jihad in Classical and Modern Islam.* Princeton: Markus Wiener Publishers, 1996.

Pfeffer, Paul F. *A. Philip Randolph, Pioneer of the Civil Rights Movement.* Baton Rouge: Louisiana State University Press, 1990.

Phillips, David Atlee. *The Night Watch*. New York: Ballantine Books, 1977.

Platt, Anthony M. *The Politics of Riot Commissions, 1917–1970*. New York: Macmillan, 1971.

Pool, Suzanne and James. *Who Financed Hitler? The Secret Funding of Hitler's Rise to Power 1919–1933*. New York: Dial, Press, 1978.

Powers, Richard Gid. *Secrecy and Power: The Life of J. Edgar Hoover*. New York: Free Press, 1987.

Powers, Thomas. *The Man Who Kept the Secrets: Richard Helms and the CIA*. New York: Knopf, 1979.

Prados, John. *Presidents' Secret Wars: CIA and Pentagon Covert Operations from World War II Through Abscam*. New York: Morrow, 1986.

Prange, Gordon W. *At Dawn We Slept: The Untold Story of Pearl Harbor*. New York: McGraw-Hill, 1981.

Quarles, Benjamin. *The Negro in the Civil War*. New York: Little, Brown, 1953.

Rabinowitz, Howard N. *Southern Black Leaders of the Reconstruction Era*. Chicago: University of Illinois Press, 1982.

Raddatz, Fritz J. *Karl Marx: A Political Biography*. Boston: Little, Brown, 1978.

Rahman, Fazlur. *Islam*. New York: Holt, Rinehart & Winston, 1966.

Ranelagh, John. *The Agency: The Rise and Decline of the CIA*. New York: Simon & Schuster, 1986.

Rashad, Adib. *The History of Islam and Black Nationalism in the Americas*. Beltsville, Md.: Writers, Inc., 1991.

Redkey, Edwin S., ed. *Respect Black: The Writings and Speeches of Henry McNeal Turner*. New York: Arno Press, 1971.

Reeves, Thomas C. *The Life and Times of Joe McCarthy: A Biography*. New York: Stein & Day, 1982.

Richards, David. *Played Out: The Jean Seberg Story*. New York: Random House, 1981.

Robertson, Pat. *The New World Order*. Dallas: Word Publishing, 1991.

Robinson, John J. *Born in Blood: The Lost Secrets of Freemasonry*. New York: M. Evans, 1989.

Rodriguez, Felix I., and John Weisman. *Shadow Warrior: The CIA Hero of a Hundred Unknown Battles*. New York: Simon & Schuster, 1989.

Rogers, J. A. *World's Great Men of Color*. Vol. 1. 1946. Reprint. New York: Touchstone, 1996.

————. *World's Great Men of Color.* Vol. 2. 1947. Reprint. New York: Touchstone, 1996.

Rooney, David. *Kwame Nkrumah: The Political Kingdom in the Third World.* New York: St. Martin's Press, 1988.

Rowan, Carl T. *Breaking Barriers: A Memoir.* New York: Little, Brown, 1991.

Russell, Dick. *The Man Who Knew Too Much.* New York: Carroll & Graf, 1992.

Russell, Francis. *The Shadows of Blooming Grove: Warren G. Harding In His Times.* New York: McGraw-Hill, 1968.

Rustin, Bayard. *Strategies for Freedom: The Changing Patterns of Black Protest.* New York: Columbia University Press, 1976.

Rutherford, Joseph F. *The Final War.* New York: Watch Tower Publications, 1932.

————. *Who Is God?* New York: Watch Tower Publications, 1932.

————. *Universal War Near; A Bible Treatise.* New York: Watch Tower Publications, 1935.

Salzman, Jack, ed. *Bridges and Boundaries: African Americans and American Jews.* New York: George Braziller, 1992.

Scheim, David E. *Contract on America.* New York: Zebra Books, 1988.

Schlesinger, Arthur M. Jr. *Robert Kennedy And His Times.* Boston: Houghton Mifflin, 1978.

Schoenbaum, Thomas J. *Waging Peace and War: Dean Rusk in the Truman, Kennedy and Johnson Years.* New York: Simon & Schuster, 1988.

Scholem, Gershom. *Kabbalah.* New York: Dorset Press, 1974.

Shaw, Isobel. *Pakistan: At the Crossroads of Asia.* Lincolnwood, Ill.: Passport Books, 1996.

Sinistrari, Lodovico Maria. *Demonality: The Montague Summers Edition.* 1927: Reprint. New York: Dover, 1989.

Sklar, Dusty. *The Nazis and the Occult.* New York: Dorset Press, 1989.

Smith, Hudson. *The Religions of Man.* New York: Harper & Row, 1958.

Smith, R. Harris. *OSS: The Secret History of America's First Central Intelligence Agency.* Berkeley: University of California Press, 1972.

Smith, William Gardner. *Return to Black America.* Englewood Cliffs, N.J.: Prentice-Hall, 1970.

Smyth, Piazzi. *The Great Pyramid: Its Secrets and Mysteries Revealed.* 1864. Reprint. New York: Crown Publishers, 1978.

Soper, Edmund Davison. *The Religions of Mankind.* New York: Abingdon-Cokesbury Press, 1938.

Sorrenson, M. P. K. *Maori Origins and Migrations.* Auckland, N.Z.: Auckland University Press, 1990.

Spear, Allan H. *Black Chicago: The Making of a Negro Ghetto, 1890–1920.* Chicago: University of Chicago Press, 1967.

Stampp, Kenneth M. *The Peculiar Institution: Slavery in the Ante-Bellum South.* New York: Vintage Books, 1956.

Stewart, Desmond, et al. *The Pyramids and Sphinx.* New York: Newsweek Books, 1976.

Stone, Chuck. *Black Political Power in America.* New York: Delta Books, 1970.

Strickland, William. *Malcolm X: Make It Plain.* New York: Viking Penguin, 1994.

Sullivan, William, with Bill Brown. *The Bureau: My Thirty Years in Hoover's FBI.* New York: Norton, 1979.

Summers, Anthony. *Conspiracy.* New York: McGraw-Hill, 1980.

———. *Goddess: The Secret Lives of Marilyn Monroe.* New York: New American Library, 1985.

———. *Official and Confidential: The Secret Life of J. Edgar Hoover.* New York: Putnam, 1993.

Swanson, Earl H., et al. *The Ancient Americas.* New York: Peter Bedrick Books, 1989.

Szulc, Tad. *Fidel: A Critical Portrait.* New York: Morrow, 1986.

Taylor, Edmond. *The Fall of Dynasties: The Collapse of the Old Order, 1905–1922.* New York: Doubleday, 1963.

Teresa, Vincent, with Thomas C. Renner. *My Life in the Mafia.* New York: Doubleday, 1973.

Terkel, Studs. *Coming of Age: The Story of Our Century by Those Who Lived It.* New York: New Press, 1995.

Theoharis, Athan G., and John S. Cox. *The Boss: J. Edgar Hoover and the Great American Inquisition.* Philadelphia: Temple University Press, 1988.

Thomas, Lowell. *Seven Wonders of the World.* Garden City, N.Y.: Hanover House, 1956.

Thompson, Elizabeth Bartlett. *Africa Past and Present.* Boston: Houghton Mifflin, 1966.

Thompson, J. A. *The Bible and Archaeology.* Grand Rapids, Mich.: Wm. B. Erdmans Publishing, 1962.

Toland, John. *Adolf Hitler.* New York: Doubleday, 1976.

Tompkins, Peter. *The Magic of Obelisks.* New York: Harper & Row, 1981.

Tremlett, George. *Gadaffi: The Desert Mystic.* New York: Carroll & Graf, 1993.

Tuccille, Jerome. *Kingdom: The Story of the Hunt Family of Texas.* Ottawa, Ill.: Jameson Books, 1984.

Tucker, Richard K. *The Dragon and the Cross: The Rise and Fall of the Ku Klux Klan in Middle America.* New York: Archon Books, 1991.

Tully, Andrew. *The Super Spies.* New York: Morrow, 1969.

———. *Inside the FBI.* New York: McGraw-Hill, 1980.

Turner, Arlin, ed. *The Negro Question: A Selection of Writings on Civil Rights in the South by George W. Cable.* New York: Doubleday/Anchor Books, 1958.

Turner, William W., and John G. Christian. *The Assassination of Robert F. Kennedy.* New York: Random House, 1978.

Tuttle, William M. Jr. *Race Riot: Chicago in the Red Summer of 1919.* New York: Atheneum, 1970.

Ullendorff, Edward. *The Two Zions: Reminiscences of Jerusalem and Ethiopia.* New York: Oxford University Press, 1988.

Ungar, Sanford J. *FBI.* Boston: Little, Brown, 1975.

Van Loon, Hendrik. *The Story of Mankind.* London: Boni & Liveright, 1921.

Volkman, Ernest, and Blaine Baggett. *Secret Intelligence: The Inside Story of America's Espionage Empire.* New York: Berkley, 1991.

Wade, Wyn Craig. *The Fiery Cross: The Ku Klux Klan in America.* New York: Simon & Schuster, 1987.

Walker, Samuel. *Hate Speech: The History of an American Controversy.* Omaha: University of Nebraska Press, 1994.

Wallace, Mike, and Gary Gates. *Close Encounters: Mike Wallace's Own Story.* New York: Morrow, 1984.

Walvin, James. *Black Ivory: A History of British Slavery.* Washington, D.C.: Howard University Press, 1994.

Washington, Booker T. *Up From Slavery.* 1901. Reprint. New York: Penguin Books, 1986.

Washington, Peter. *Madame Blavatsky's Baboon: A History of the Mystics, Mediums, and Misfits Who Brought Spiritualism to America.* New York: Schocken Books, 1993.

Waterfield, Gordon. *Egypt.* New York: Walker, 1967.

Watters, Pat, and Stephen Gillers, eds. *Investigating the FBI.* New York: Doubleday, 1973.

Watts, Jill. *God, Harlem U.S.A.: The Father Divine Story.* Berkeley: University of California Press, 1995.

Webb, James Morris. *The Black Man, the Father of Civilization.* Seattle: Acme Press, 1910.

———. *A Black Man Will Be the Coming Universal King.* Chicago: n.p., 1919.

Weisbrot, Robert. *Father Divine.* New York: Beacon Press, 1984.

———. *Freedom Bound: A History of America's Civil Rights Movement.* New York: Norton, 1990.

Weiss, Nancy J. *Whitney M. Young Jr. and the Struggle for Civil Rights.* Princeton: Princeton University Press, 1989.

Welch, Galbraith. *Africa, Before They Came: The Continent, North, South, East and West, Preceding the Colonial Powers.* New York: Morrow, 1965.

Welch, Neil J., and David W. Marston. *Inside Hoover's FBI: The Top Field Chief Reports.* New York: Doubleday, 1984.

Whitehead, Don. *The FBI Story.* New York: Random House, 1956.

Williams, Chancellor. *The Destruction of Black Civilization.* Chicago: Third World Press, 1974.

Winrod, Gerald B. *Adam Weishaupt, A Human Devil.* Kansas: Defender Publications, 1935. Reprint. Hollywood: Sons of Liberty, 1969.

Wise, David. *The American Police State: The Government Against the People.* New York: Vintage Books, 1976.

Wise, David, and Thomas B. Ross. *The Invisible Government.* New York: Random House, 1964.

———. *The Espionage Establishment.* New York: Random House, 1967.

Wolf, Michael, ed. *One Thousand Roads to Mecca: Ten Centuries of Travelers Writing About the Muslim Pilgrimage.* New York: Grove Press, 1997.

Wolfenstein, Victor. *The Victims of Democracy: Malcolm X and the Black Revolution.* Los Angeles: University of California Press, 1981.

Wolff, Daniel, with S.R. Crain, et al. *You Send Me: The Life and Times of Sam Cooke.* New York: Morrow, 1995.

Wolpert, Stanley. *India.* Berkeley: University of California Press, 1991.

Wood, Joe, ed. *Malcolm X: In Our Image.* New York: St. Martin's Press, 1992.

Woodson, Carter G. *The Mis-Education of the Negro.* 1933. Reprint. Trenton, N.J.: Africa World Press, 1993.

Woodward, C. Vann. *The Strange Career of Jim Crow.* 1954. Reprint. New York: Oxford University Press, 1974.

Wright, Richard. *Native Son.* New York: Harper & Brothers, 1940.

INDEX